YOU CAN
DO IT!

Whatever you can do, or
dream you can, begin it.
Boldness has genius,
power, and magic in it.
Begin it now.

—J.W. Goethe

YOU CAN DO IT!

THE MERIT BADGE HANDBOOK FOR GROWN-UP GIRLS

LAUREN CATUZZI GRANDCOLAS

WITH

YVETTE BOZZINI

ILLUSTRATIONS BY

JULIA BRECKENREID

CHRONICLE BOOKS

SAN FRANCISCO

produced in association with
Herter Studio LLC
432 Elizabeth Street
San Francisco, CA 94114
www.herterstudio.com

Caroline Herter/Producer and Creative Director ★ **Vaughn Lohec and Dara Near**/Editorial Advisors ★ **Yvette Bozzini**/Writer
Julia Breckenreid/Illustrator ★ **Debbie Berne**/Project Manager and Designer ★ **Alison Bing**/Contributing Editor
Nicole Solis and Carolyn Keating/Proofreaders ★ **Amanda Scotese and Bessie Weiss**/Fact Checkers ★ **Nara Wood**/Indexer

We'd love to hear from you!
If you would like to share your own badge adventures, or have ideas for new badges, please email us at youcandoit@herterstudio.com.

Library of Congress Cataloging-in-Publication Data available.

ISBN 0-8118-4635-0

Manufactured in China

Distributed in Canada
by Raincoast Books
9050 Shaughnessy Street
Vancouver, BC V6P 6E5

10 9 8 7 6 5 4 3

Chronicle Books LLC
85 Second Street
San Francisco, CA 94105

www.chroniclebooks.com

For women who
dare to dream—
and do.

table of contents

You Can Do It!

was our sister's vision.

Her name was Lauren Catuzzi Grandcolas. Lauren imagined a book that would boost women's self-esteem by helping them achieve their goals, realize their dreams, and embrace life's joys and challenges to the fullest.

Lauren's exuberance—like her smile—was infectious. She pursued a career in marketing and advertising; Joe Boxer founder Nick Graham referred to her as "a sparkle in a gray suit world." She lavished love and attention on her husband, Jack, and on her friends and family around the country. And she dedicated herself to tackling and mastering new skills, subjects, and activities. Our mother calls Lauren's a "can-do spirit," and we sometimes think the Nike people had her in mind when they came up with their "Just do it!" slogan.

Lauren tooled around her Northern California neighborhood on inline skates. Daring and fit, she loved the outdoors and regularly hiked, jogged, and kayaked. Ever interested in learning something new, she took cooking, gardening, scuba diving, and wine appreciation classes. Not content with "wouldn't it be nice" day-dreams, she made things happen. On her thirtieth birthday, she surprised Jack with plans to go skydiving. (You should see the grin lighting up her face in a video made of the jump!)

More than anyone we know, Lauren treasured her female friends and made a point of nurturing those relationships that so often fall by the wayside after marriage. Perhaps because she was a grown-up Girl Scout (whose sash of badges hung in her office), her "do it yourself" attitude often turned into "C'mon, let's do it together." She truly relished the camaraderie, support, and sheer fun of pursuing new experiences with friends.

Tragically, on September 11, 2001, Lauren was flying home from our grandmother's funeral on United Airlines Flight 93. Already a hero to all who knew her, she became another kind of hero on that horrible day. As the National Commission on Terrorist Attacks Upon the United States reported, "The nation owes a debt to the passengers of United 93. Their actions saved the lives of countless others and may have saved either the U.S. Capitol or the White House from destruction." Lauren was a certified emergency medical technician and knew how to handle herself and help others in emergency situations. We take comfort in the knowledge that she left us the way she lived—strong, determined, generous, and courageous.

Lauren's family—our mother and father, Barbara and Lawrence Catuzzi, our brother-in-law, Jack Grandcolas, and both of us—knew how much this book meant to her. It has been an honor to make it a reality. We felt her smiling on us as we worked on it and can already hear her cheering you on as you use it to help you do and be your best.

Lauren loved a quote from the 1994 movie *The Shawshank Redemption* so much that she wrote it down and attached it to her refrigerator. It reads, "Get busy living, or get busy dying." Your accomplishments as you earn the badges in this book she envisioned are the perfect legacy of Lauren's extraordinary life. She always knew you could do it!

Vaughn Catuzzi Lohec and Dara Catuzzi Near

Proceeds from You Can Do It! *go to the Lauren Catuzzi Grandcolas Foundation, which was established by Lauren's family and friends to support charitable causes of interest to Lauren. The foundation has provided college scholarships to outstanding high school senior women, a birthing room for Marin General Hospital (Marin County, California), neonatal units for Texas Children's Hospital (Houston, Texas), and support for the Houston Area Women's Center, which is dedicated to helping abused women and their children. The Foundation is helping to build a garden in Houston in memory of the victims of September 11, 2001, which will be called Lauren's Garden. Donations and information: Lauren Catuzzi Grandcolas Foundation, c/o Andrews & Kurth LLP, 600 Travis, Suite 4200, Houston, Texas 72002.*

getting started

why you can do it

- ★ **Because it's high time your want-to-do list got as much attention as your to-do list**
- ★ **Because even though you *can* do anything, sometimes you need a little help figuring out how**
- ★ **Because wherever you are is the perfect place to begin**

When was the last time you played like a kid, learned something new, or did something just for you? Do you remember your dreams? Not the ones you have while you sleep, but the ones you keep in the back of your mind—or maybe on a list at the bottom of a drawer. They're the things you thought you'd do when you grew up or got settled, the things you feel envious of other people for doing, or the things you resolve to do, learn, or try every darn New Year's. Whether it's speak Italian, surf, trek in Nepal, learn Quark, or run for office, every now and then you look up from your bills or laundry and think, "One of these days . . . "

Today is that day.

What's that you say? Get real, I don't have time. No way, I'm too tired. That's silly, I'm too old. (Or maybe all of the above!) Understood. As is the fact that you already multitask your way through days that would make a juggler dizzy. But if you look at the feats of daring, determination, creativity, caring, and know-how you pull off every jam-packed day, you'll realize that you're plenty capable. **You just need a little practical help, real-world inspiration, and savvy support.**

Some of us got just that in Girl Scouts. By awarding real badges for achieving real goals, that organization has given millions of young girls a surefire way to feel good about themselves and a fearlessness about facing the unknown. They do it by breaking any challenge down into small, doable steps; building in lots of guidance and support; and then celebrating the achievement with a tangible ta-da: a badge.

Though we're all grown up, Girl Scout logic still applies. *You Can Do It!*'s buffet of badge activities takes you from "Wouldn't it be nice . . . " to "I did it!" in simple, straightforward, one-foot-in-front-of-the-other steps. The guidance, support, and celebration—in the form of bold, beautiful badges—are built in. Best of all, *You Can Do It!* doesn't just add items to your list of what you could, should, or would like to do, it gets you doing, not just dreaming. And each time you do "it," you boost your confidence, build your repertoire, and get more of the goods you need to tackle your next deep-down dream.

That last point is worth emphasizing. **You'll never know how far you can go until you get going.** The domino effect applies to dreams: When we try something new or tackle something long put off, one thing leads to another. Our accomplishment fuels future accomplishments because we've got proof positive that it's possible.

Ready to rev up the engine on your dream machine? Cool. Let's pop the hood and see how it works.

how to do it

For many of us, thinking about what we really want to do (as opposed to all the things we have to do) is the hardest and maybe even the scariest part. If that's true for you, Dare to Dream, page 2, will help clarify and catalyze your dreams.

Remember that no dream is too big, too small, or too silly. "Ride my bike three times a week" and "ride the Trans-Siberian Railway" are both great. "Change jobs—and hair color." Fine! "Get a clue about art and get control of my credit card debt." Okay. "Hang ten in Hawaii, and hang out with kids more." Excellent! *You Can Do It!* has got these covered (and then some!).

So, what's next?

Find your dreams. **Chances are that you'll find the very thing you've been dying to do in the Table of Contents,** but you can also use the badge activity template and blank stickers at the back of the book to make up your own. There are sixty badges in all—from singing to scuba diving, beading to being your own boss, growing money to growing a garden—organized into seven sections that help you Dare, Create, Learn, Play, Deal, Connect, and Dream.

Meet your dream mentor. **You're never alone in *You Can Do It!* because you are guided through each badge activity by an expert in the field**—a real woman who knows how to get started, can help you avoid pitfalls, anticipates your questions, and provides insider tips, trivia, and favorite resources. What do we mean by "expert"? The executive editor of Kiplinger's *Personal Finance* magazine, the leader of the first American climb of the highest peak in the Himalayas, and the chairperson of the Fashion Design Department at the Fashion Institute of Technology are just three of the award-winning, go-getting, dream-weaving women who cheer you on in *You Can Do It!* In addition, you hear from other newbies whose triumphs keep you motivated and whose missteps keep you from learning the hard way.

Follow your dreams. **Because beginning is often half the battle, each badge reminds you of the rewards of each activity, helps you gear up, and gives you clear "start here" instructions.** The activity is then broken down into straightforward, concise, doable steps complete with the facts you need to keep going and tips that make it fun along the way. You'll also get plenty of ideas about how to dream on and go "beyond the badge," delving deeper into your newfound skills and experience.

Celebrate your dream come true. **When you've earned your badge, please don't skip the patting yourself on the back part** (something we do for others all the time!). Mark your accomplishment by finding the full-color badge sticker that corresponds to your activity at the back of the book. This may sound silly, but it's key. You did it and you deserve it! Paste the badge anywhere you like: over the drawing on the first page of your activity, on your fridge, your bumper, your backpack, your briefcase, your bathroom mirror, in a special journal or small frame—anywhere you can see it and savor it with pride. Sign your name and record the date. But why stop there? Show off your skills, savor the kudos, and get used to—even revel in—the feeling that ***you can do it!***

you can do it . . . right now!

We know you're itching to hit the road, but to ensure your success—and nip any lingering procrastination in the bud—add these last few tips to your "I Can Do It" toolkit:

Write it down. **Buy yourself a blank journal to use as a companion to this book.** Use it to note your progress, rant and rave, record contacts and resources, reflect on questions, complete exercises, plan your next adventure, and make your own badge!

Make it real. **Think about why you want to achieve your goal, and picture yourself doing it.** Anticipate how good it will feel. Then write a date to make it happen on your calendar—in ink! As soon as you put that pen down, take your first small step toward that goal. What's the one bit of preliminary research you could do now, the one supply you could buy, the one phone call you could make? Do it! And to keep your momentum going, gather your supplies and keep them where you'll see—or trip over—them often.

Get to know your local resources. **Help is right around the corner.** The gal wearing the stunning necklace says she made it herself, and that woman at the museum doesn't seem the least bit flummoxed by modern art. If someone has a skill you admire and you ask nicely, they might very well enjoy helping you get started. Specialty shop owners, reference librarians, and teachers of every kind live for such inquiries. Look also for class listings on bulletin boards around town, browse bookstores and libraries for helpful texts, and seek out expert advice on the Internet using www.google.com, www.ask.com, or www.ixquick.com.

Make badge buddies. **The encouragement of friends may make the difference between persevering and giving up.** There's power, camaraderie, and fun in numbers. Tell someone else what you're going to do, and/or make a date to do it together—most of us are less likely to stand up another person than we are to stand up ourselves. You can learn from each other, find the humor in every predicament, and will have someone to high-five at the finish line.

Go your own way. **Only you can do it your way.** And while *You Can Do It!* provides you with more than sixty beginnings, middles, and ends, it's not your mother and you aren't in Girl Scouts anymore. Pick an activity and have *fun* with it. Innovate, talk back, and make it work for *you*.

And last, but not least . . .

Share your dreams. **This is one of the things we do best as women, and passing it along is one of the great rewards of learning.** Helping other women realize their dreams was Lauren's greatest gift, and it can be yours as well. Maybe you'll become the mentor to a younger woman or do crafts with an older person, run a workshop or run a race for charity. Whatever it is and however you do it, reward yourself and help others by sharing your experience, strength, and hope whenever and wherever you can.

But enough talk. It's time to do! Start your engines, feel your power, and . . .

Begin it now!

dare

All serious daring starts
from *within.*

—Eudora Welty

1 DARE TO DREAM

★ the first step ★

It is not because things are difficult that we do not dare; it is because we do not dare that they are difficult.

—Seneca

Imagine This . . . Anytime you want you can leave behind the world as you know it and enter the world as you dream it. Follow your imagination all the way up to the podium to accept your Nobel Peace Prize, or onstage to take a bow with Baryshnikov. You allow yourself to think bigger than life, because even the most fantastic dreams have something to tell us about who we are—and who we may yet become. When you finally let those deep-down dreams bubble up, your spirit soars, and everyone around you is uplifted by your example. Deny your dreams? Now that's one thing you'd never dream of doing. Will they come true? There's only one way to find out . . . name them, and you begin to claim them. *You can do it!*

The Payoffs

- **Liberation.** Owning what you want to do can be scary, but when you allow your secret desires to surface for more than a fleeting second and if you stay with them long enough to play them out and commit them to paper, you will have—in that very act—freed yourself from the fear of becoming who you are, as opposed to who you (and others) think you should be.
- **Power.** Yours.
- **Bliss.** As Goethe and Joseph Campbell both note, the universe moves in mysterious ways when you truly commit to finding and following your bliss.
- **Passion.** Dreaming fuels passion, and passion is itself a potent fuel. It will provide you with the drive, determination, and joy to pursue your dreams. And because passion is a renewable resource, its energy will spill over into other areas of your life, and the lives of the people around you.

BADGE STEPS

1. Invite your dreams to come out and play.

You really can divine (and define) your goals and dreams—but they're not always instantly clear. Insecurities, atrophied dream muscles, and daily drudgery can blur our vision and stunt our imaginations. The truth is, few of us take the time to dream (it's not something you can do absentmindedly while calling your sister and doing the laundry at the same time), and there's just no way around it: You have to create space for your dreams to come to you.

So don't wait for inspiration to strike—over the next two weeks, schedule three one-hour "play dates" with yourself in your calendar. Use this time to capture your dreams on paper as you work through the exercises below. Notes and doodles are fine, so long as they mean something to you. The point here is not to fill up page after page with perfectly crafted text; it's simply to accord your dreams the same consideration you do your grocery list! How to find the time:

Make it a wake-up or bedtime ritual. Many people find the first thing in the morning or last thing at night to be the ideal dreamtime. Buy yourself a pretty blank book and a pen that feels good to keep by your bed, so you'll see them morning and evening and put them to good use.

Find gaps in your schedule. Stash a small notebook in your purse and stick a pad of paper onto your dashboard, so that you make use of those precious moments when you're between engagements. Schedule more time than you think you'll need to do daily tasks, and when you finish early, dream on!

Free up your free time. They call it a lunch break for a reason . . . don't waste it running errands when you could be dreaming! Take a seat at the lunch place or café where you usually just run in and dash out, and bring your blank book and pen with you.

Go on a mini-retreat. Unplug the phone at home one afternoon, or go sit on a park bench away from the distractions of home and work. Then write in your book until you're good and ready to return to reality.

Make three play dates with your imagination.

2. Jumpstart your dream machine.

To get your creative juices flowing, answer these questions:

- What have been the proudest moments in your life?

To accomplish great things,
one must not only act,
but DREAM.

—Unknown

I DID IT!

"When I was a kid I had a pony named Dolly. When I was fourteen, my parents found out I'd been cutting school, and to punish me, they gave Dolly away—to my sister, no less! Twenty years later, I was no longer cutting school. In fact, I was going to law school at night while working full-time days. My therapist pointed out that while I was good at achieving my career goals, I'd lost touch with my dream pursuits. When I told her the Dolly story, she said I needed to 'take back my pony!' So I found some nearby stables, started riding again, and even took a riding trip in France. But even better than riding again was realizing that I could and should do the things I love. That lesson has helped me try new things—like online dating—and realize goals—like buying a home."
—Julie

SAY YES

"I rarely regret things I've done, but often regret things I haven't—whether it's a dinner invitation I turned down, a class I didn't take, or a trip I thought I was too busy for. Why is it so much easier to talk yourself out of things than into things?! I suppose 'just say no' has its place, but to really live, I'm learning it's also important to say 'yes!'"
—Maria

- What would you do if you won the lottery, and money were no object?
- What are the roads you didn't take because at the time they seemed wrong to you, unfamiliar, too rocky, or just less traveled?
- What did you daydream about as a kid?
- What childhood pursuits or pastimes would you like to pick up again?
- What makes you feel free, serene, or full of nervous excitement? (Sometimes the adrenaline of eager anticipation can register as anxiety.)
- What would your perfect day contain from sunup to sundown?
- List the women you most admire. What traits and achievements make them admirable?
- Are there dreams you are a bit embarrassed to admit you have? Why?

Commit your dreams to paper.

3. Imagine, if you will . . .

To coax a dream out of hiding:

- Get physically comfortable, sitting or lying down.
- Take a few slow, deep breaths. (Try counting as you breathe, inhaling for four counts and exhaling to the count of eight.)
- Move up or down your body, tensing and relaxing as you go.
- Once you're relaxed, complete the sentence, "I would like to be . . ."
- Restate this goal in the present tense, "I am . . ."
- Picture yourself living up to that I-am sentence, and imagine a scenario that would allow you to get that much closer to your ideal.
- Complete the sentence, "I see myself . . ."

Entertain the possibilities.

4. Envision it.

Write down the results of your Step 3 visualization. Note every detail of your "I see myself . . ." scene. If you're singing, are you fronting a rock band? Getting a standing ovation at the Met? Cutting an album? See yourself hitting the high note, and feel the weight of the microphone (or maybe a Grammy!) in your hand. As you do this, you're creating a mental video of the scenario that is yours to replay whenever you wish.
Picture yourself living the dream.

5. Make it real.

The more you see and talk about your dream, the more real it becomes. Surround yourself with people who pursue, rather than pooh-pooh, their own dreams—and yours. Gather inspiring quotes, photos, notes from friends, articles, and other encouraging ephemera to light your path. Put these pieces of your dream in a beautiful box or accordion file, and from time to time pull a new item out of this file to tack up at your office, stick on your fridge, or write in your dream book to contemplate during your lunch hour or before you go to bed. ***Let your dream take shape.***

6. Take the first step.

Not sure where to begin? Not to worry! *You Can Do It!* is all about making dreams doable, and building up the expertise you need to get you to your goal. So as you dream on, read on! Turn back to the Table of Contents to find the badges that correspond to your newly discovered or dusted-off dreams, or turn to Dream On, page 485, to create one of your own. ***Dream on!***

CONGRATULATIONS!

You've dared to dream—and opened up a world of possibilities to pursue. You did it!

I DID IT!

Name: ______________________

Date: ______________________

The future belongs to those who believe in the BEAUTY of their dreams.

—Eleanor Roosevelt

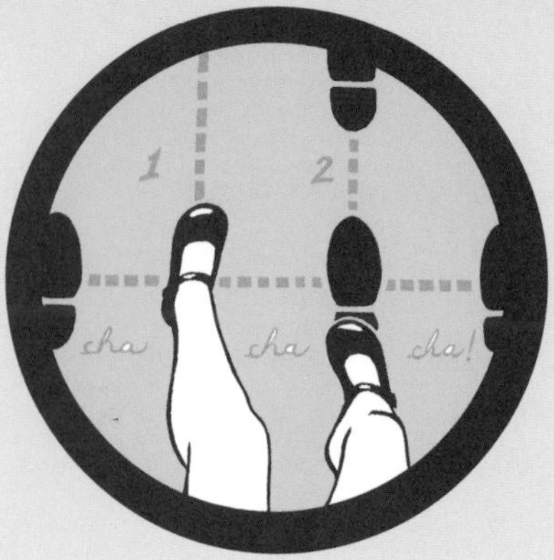

2
BUST A MOVE
★ dancing ★

To live is to dance.
I would like to die,
breathless, spent,
at the end of a dance.
—Josephine Baker

So, what's your motivation?
Take a moment.
Dream a little, think big,
and then complete this sentence:
I see myself . . .

Imagine This . . . Sit this one out? Not you! You stride confidently to the center of the dance floor and salsa, swing, or hustle with such panache that soon the other dancers gather round to watch. Maybe you own a copy of *The Turning Point* and treat your kitchen counter as a makeshift ballet bar while your bread toasts. Or perhaps you wish you could do more than tap your foot politely to a funky beat or bang your head at Metallica shows . . . if only you didn't have two left feet. When you take the steps in this badge, your wallflower days will be over. Whether you want to dip, do-si-do, tap, twirl, leap, or lindy, once you free your mind, your feet will follow. *You can do it!*

The Payoffs

- **Fun.** Wouldn't it be fun not to panic when that handsome stranger at your friend's wedding walks your way and asks, "May I have this dance?"
- **Freedom.** From the dramatic interpretive dancer in Jules Feiffer cartoons to Snoopy's delirious nose-in-the-air moves, dance expresses feelings and ideas. The discipline of dance is liberating, freeing us to communicate in a new language.
- **Fitness.** We're so used to critiquing the way our bodies look. Dance gives you a way to appreciate yours for what it can do. (And yes, you will burn calories and improve your posture, balance, and agility.)
- **Human contact.** There are few better ways to meet people—and few more legitimate ways to reach out and touch someone!

Meet Your Mentor

ROZANN KRAUS

What She Does: Founder and president of the Dance Complex, an artist-run studio in Cambridge, Massachusetts, Rozann has taught at the Yale School of Drama, Boston University, and the New England Conservatory of Music, and has won numerous awards and commissions for her choreography.

Why She Does It: "I taught myself how to dance by watching it on television and imitating what I saw. I figured if they could do it, I could do it! I was ten, living in Cleveland, Ohio, and one of my aunts had a friend who produced a local children's TV series. I told him I was a dancer, and asked if I could dance on his program. He said yes, so I choreographed a duet for myself and a friend, and we did it on the show. As a teenager, I talked my way into my first job, teaching dance at a summer camp, by pretending to have had teaching experience. I didn't take my first real dance class until I was eighteen and a newlywed. I was in Nice, France, with my husband, a flutist who was there to study with Jean-Pierre Rampal. I found a dance class for myself, not realizing it was with the ballet mistress of the Paris Opera Ballet, who was in Nice with her dance company for the summer. Jean-Pierre would come and watch me in class from the doorway. I'm sure the teacher would have ignored me—or just said, 'Sure you can dance, but please stay out of our way'—except that this world-famous musician was taking an interest in me. So the teacher did, too. She worked with me every day after class, giving me a basic ballet vocabulary—but making me promise that I would never try to be a ballerina!"

© Peter Schweitzer

We're most honest when we communicate with our bodies, and dance is its own language.

—Rozann Kraus

Word from the Wise: "Your mind can help or prevent your body from accomplishing things. Kids can often do things that confound adults, because grown-ups think too much about doing it. Students need to learn when to engage and when to disengage their minds."

BADGE STEPS

FANCY FOOTWORK

Explore the dance around the world

African dance. The style taught and performed in the U.S. is often of West African origin and incorporates drumming and Caribbean influences.

Belly dance. This has roots in the Middle East, and is something of a misnomer—dancers use their torso and hips more than their belly.

Capoeira. This was originally a martial art in Brazil, but was made into a dance form by the slaves who were forbidden to practice it.

Flamenco. This originated with the Gypsies in Andalusia, Spain.

Hora. A circle dance from the Balkans, where it is a metaphor for community.

Hula. A Polynesian dance called "the heartbeat of the Hawaiian people."

Mambo. A forerunner of salsa, this is danced to a fusion of traditional music from Cuba and Haiti and American jazz swing.

Mazurka. Poland's national dance.

Polka. A couple dance originating in Eastern Bohemia (now the Czech Republic).

Tango. Argentina's national dance.

Tarantella. An Italian folk dance named after a spider.

1. Know what moves you.

What kind of dance do you yearn to do? Are you motivated to look great dancing at your wedding or explore the ancient art of belly dancing? Do you have season tickets to the ballet, a crush on those dancers from Stomp, or a habit of doing the tango while vacuuming? Does *Saturday Night Fever* or *Strictly Ballroom* or *Singin' in the Rain* get your feet moving every time? Is there an ethnic dance that your relatives do on special occasions that you've always been too timid to try?

Your goals and musical likes and dislikes can direct you. A few ballroom dance classes can set you up for a special occasion. If you want to meet people and socialize, folk, square, salsa, or swing dancing might be best. For burning calories, a hip-hop class might be just the thing. And if you love Hawaiian music or Astor Piazzolla, can the hula or tango be far behind? ***Go with your flow.***

2. Find the movers and shakers in your community.

Look in your phone book for dance studios and teachers, request catalogs from community colleges and recreation centers, and call your local arts council. Some nightclubs that feature dance nights also host regular lessons, too. If you see someone who looks great on the dance floor, ask them where they study.

Go and observe at least three different classes. Do people look like they are having fun? Do you like the music being played? Does the teacher welcome questions? Does the level of instruction feel like a match with your level of expertise?

After class, stick around and socialize. Talk to the students and find out how long they've been coming, what they like most about the class, and whether they've ever had an injury. Find out if you'll need to buy footwear and what kinds of clothes are recommended.

Also chat with the teacher about your goals. A teacher should realize that students dance for a variety of different reasons and have their own goals. Rozann had an epiphany while teaching skilled intermediate-level dancers at Trinity College. She was frustrated at not being able to motivate them to aspire to another level. One day she was swimming laps, and when she was done, a fellow who'd been watching her asked if he could give her some pointers on her stroke. She wasn't at all interested, because she didn't really care to know how to swim faster or "better." She just enjoyed moving through the water. Rozann realized that her dance students probably felt the same way—and she became a better teacher. A good teacher should be adaptable to your goals. ***Check out a dance class.***

3. Get a move on.

Sign up for a series of classes with one of the teachers you observed, and plan to stick with it for at least three months. You'll feel great from the get-go, but should give yourself enough time to transform what you are learning into instinctive body movements. Keep your goal in mind, whether that's ease with social dancing, a perfect pirouette, or incorporating the splits into your breakdancing.

Rozann claims never to have needed to be encouraged to get to class. "Why wouldn't I want to be in a nice room filled with people who have common interests, doing things that make my body feel wonderful?" But if you need incentive when your day was exhausting or your bed feels too good to leave, remind yourself of how good you'll feel when you get there. Rozann's tip is to always look at class as a gift you give to yourself—not work or something you have to do. "If your mind can't embrace it, your body will. No matter how tired or stressed you are, there will be a release. In class you can leave it all behind and be guided by the teacher." ***Get into the groove at class.***

4. Stay inspired.

Look for ways to make dance part of your everyday life. Rent musicals, watch performances on television and music videos, and most importantly, go see live productions whenever you can. Touring companies often give lectures and demonstrations and have open rehearsals that the public can watch.

Purchase CDs of the music you dance to in class so you can practice at home. And if you're studying ballroom, Latin, hip-hop, or swing, go to clubs where you can show off your new moves or see what you have to aspire to.

Don't go it alone. If you can't get your mate interested in learning to dance with you, gather up some girlfriends. Pals make it easier to go to class and less intimidating to boogie down in public. Of course, you're also likely to make some new friends in class.

GO-GO GEAR

Pack your dance bag

Shoes. Flamenco, tap, and ballet require specific kinds of shoes—however, the Dance Complex is not a hair-pulled-back-in-a-bun kind of place, so they do not require ballet slippers in any class other than pointe class.

Clothing. Anything you wear should accommodate movement. In ballet or modern dance, leotards—which are formfitting but not constraining—help you and your teacher check your moves. Really loose clothing that you can trip on or get tangled up in is not a good idea (though it may be trendy in hip-hop class). The Dance Complex has no dress code, but your teacher or studio may.

Water and Band-Aids. That's all the first aid you should need. You really shouldn't need an ice pack, Tiger Balm, or Bengay, since a good teacher will warm you up, work you hard, and stretch you out at the end. "Dancing should not hurt, and it's a teacher's responsibility to make sure it doesn't," says Rozann.

I DID IT!

"I loved going to the ballet and idolized ballerinas when I was growing up. But even when I took ballet class religiously, I never got much encouragement to take it seriously. At thirty-two, after having my first baby, I decided to take a class to firm up after many years away from it. It was hard to make the time, but I stuck with it. At the end of the year, we had a recital in a beautiful local theater. I invited my friends and family and danced to Chopin and Erik Satie. My husband videotaped it, and at the end, my brother walked to the lip of the stage and presented me with a bouquet of flowers. I was (finally!) a ballerina."
—Molly

OFF POINT

"Because I'd never gone en pointe as a kid, I always wondered if I could. So when I was taking ballet as an adult, I got my teacher, Miss Jacqueline, to help me try it. I finally owned the beautiful shoes of my dreams, but one morning, as I was sitting in the kitchen eating breakfast barefoot, my husband came in and exclaimed, 'What's wrong with your feet?!' I knew he wasn't talking about my hot pink pedicure. He was talking about my hot pink bunions. I knew I had to stop the madness then and there. I hung up the pointe shoes—but not my dancing shoes!"
—Molly

ROZANN'S EXPERT TIPS

KEEPING ON YOUR TOES

DO go to class. If you're grumpy, tired, and feel like anything but dancing, remember how much better you'll feel after class.

DO bring a pal who will keep you going—and laughing.

DON'T set yourself up to feel like a failure. (Getting to class is a victory.) And set your own goals—ones that don't revolve around what you used to be able to do or what the class star can do.

DON'T let the mirror bring you down. Use it to check your form, or better yet, ignore it. (When asked what students should look for in the mirror, Rozann says, "a beautiful person having a wonderful time!")

DON'T let more accomplished classmates bum you out. If you can't ignore them, learn from them—or follow their lead if you get lost.

You can also look for a mentor. Rozann believes that "most of the time, when people are moved to embrace something new, it's because there was a remarkable person who they really clicked with." Your role model can be a public figure (how does Madonna do it at her age after having two kids?!), your teacher, or an accomplished fellow student. Ask for pointers and feedback (though Madonna might be hard to reach!). ***Keep your toes tapping outside of class.***

5. Earn extra credit.

While dance is Rozann's first love, she has always engaged in what has come to be called cross-training, i.e., she runs, swims, and rides a bike. Good general physical conditioning (see Exercise Your Options, page 250) will enhance your dance experience. So will time spent relaxing your body (see Stretch Yourself, page 258). Your body needs time to get centered and recover as much as it craves movement. Strive to give your body what Rozann calls a well-rounded diet—different types of movement and exertion plus downtime. ***Cross-train.***

6. Strut your stuff.

At Rozann's Dance Complex, anyone who wants to be involved in a performance can be. Mentors help new performers, producers, and choreographers stage productions. Recognizing that not everyone wants to perform, the Complex is more process- than goal-oriented, knowing that success lies in doing one's best and having a good time. This is more than okay for you, too. The point is to find your venue and shake, swing, twirl, or tap—even if that means moving the furniture and dancing around in your living room.

If you're not shy about showing off a little for family and friends, many dance teachers and studios feature recitals at the end of a class series. You can also step into the limelight at dance venues and nightclubs, in dance contests, and at festivals that celebrate the food, music, and dance of various cultures (Greek festival, St. Patrick's Day, Kwanzaa). ***Let yourself be moved, and you just might move others, too!***

CONGRATULATIONS!

Your dance card is full. How does it feel to be the belle of the ball? You did it!

I DID IT!

Name: ______________________________

Date: ______________________________

TWINKLE TOES

Women who gotta dance

Paula Abdul

Alicia Alonso

Josephine Baker

Isadora Duncan

Suzanne Farrell

Margot Fonteyn

Martha Graham

Natalia Makarova

Liza Minnelli

Anna Pavlova

Ann Reinking

Ginger Rogers

Ruth St. Denis

Twyla Tharp

Mary Wigman

BEYOND THE BADGE

If you love it as much as you thought you would, dream on . . .

- **Pick up some moves abroad.** Travel affords numerous opportunities to expand your dance repertoire. You can make Senegal your destination purely to deepen your appreciation of African dance, or venture off the tourist path wherever you happen to be traveling by taking a class in an indigenous style. There are also travel services that specialize in creating dance-based itineraries, including study abroad, dance camps, dance cruises, and international dance competitions. (See the Troupe around the World sidebar.)
- **Dance in the streets.** Rozann founded DanceMonth with the mayor of Cambridge in 1993. The first of these citywide celebrations kicked off on the steps of City Hall with a proclamation from the mayor, and a key to the city presentation to visiting superstar Mark Morris. Massachusetts Avenue was closed to traffic so people could dance in the streets. Throughout the month of May, there are workshops in the schools, performances, awards, and dance parties. "Dance Distractions" take place just about anywhere people are gathered, enlivening bank lobbies, city council meetings, etc. Why not approach the dance teachers, performance spaces, and city power brokers in your town to organize a day or weekend of the same? Or, at the very least, spice up your next block party barbecue with some samba—blame it on Rio and start a conga line that won't quit!
- **Make up your own.** See if you can audit a choreography class at a local college (in the music, theater, or fine arts departments), or observe a local production's choreographer at work. And remember that choreographers direct dancers in many different places—amusement parks, television, and dinner theaters, as well as dance studios and companies. If you're inspired to choreograph, Rozann says the important thing is to "make a dance and make people watch it! Tell the people you love that if they'd come to your funeral, they should come to see your work, too!" Volunteer to stage an informal charity or school-based production and learn to work as part of a team—with dancers, producers, and those interested in stagecraft. Rozann considers performing her own dances well among the high points of her dance life.

TROUPE AROUND THE WORLD

. . . with these dance-focused travel companies

Dance Holidays. Incorporate dance lessons, performances, and parties into your sightseeing. www.danceholidays.com.

Let's Dance Cruises. Lets you explore travel destinations when you dock and dance the days and nights away en route. www.letsdancecruises.com or 800-591-1868.

Dance! A country-western and swing dancer's online travel guide. Lets you click on a region—Europe, Japan, Mexico, etc.—to find international dance opportunities. www.home.earthlink.net/~travelguide.

A DANCER'S PICKS

BOOKS

Dancing Many Drums: Excavations in African American Dance by Thomas F. Defrantz (editor)
Histories of African-American dance traditions, from early vaudeville to Hollywood extravaganzas.

Dancing Revelations: Alvin Ailey's Embodiment of African American Culture by Thomas F. Defrantz
Chronicles the famous dancer-choreographer's contributions to culture and dance.

Latin Dancing: Get in Touch with Your Passionate Side with Three Scorching Latin Classics by Orod Ohanians and Dessi Ohanians
Illustrated manual to remind you of the basic steps to salsa when you're not in class.

Native American Dance: Ceremonies and Social Traditions by Charlotte Heth (editor) and the National Museum of the American Indian
Essays about Native American dance forms and expression from the Smithsonian.

Play of a Fiddle: Traditional Music, Dance, and Folklore in West Virginia by Gerald Milnes
Hear the call of the fiddle in this book about Appalachian music and square dancing.

The Story of Irish Dance by Helen Brennan
Tells stories of dance from different parts of Ireland and from eminent dancers.

Tango Argentino by Paul Bottomer
World champion in tango guides you through tango figures to help you practice at home.

Yes Yes Y'all: The Experience Music Project Oral History of Hip-Hop's First Decade by Jim Fricke and Charlie Ahearn (editors)
Stories of hip-hop dance and culture from some of its early innovators.

MAGAZINES

5678 Dance
www.5-6-7-8.com
Covers social dance—including swing, lindy, and country—with interviews, news, dance technique, and step descriptions.

Dance
www.dancemagazine.com
A standard for more than seventy-five years: news, worldwide dance event listings, reviews.

Dancing USA
www.dancingusa.com
Tips on practice, gear, and venues for ballroom, swing, and Latin dance.

ORGANIZATIONS

The Dance Complex
www.dancecomplex.org
Rozann's dance studio.

Dosado
www.dosado.com
Community site for western square dancers.

Folk Dance Association
www.folkdancing.org
Helpful articles plus directories of events, groups, and classes throughout North America.

International Association of Blacks in Dance at Howard University
www.howard.edu/collegefinearts/2003iabdconference
Hosts annual conference and promotes scholarship about dance with African roots.

Middle Eastern Culture and Dance Association
www.mecda.org
Lists teachers, events, and retreats for Middle Eastern dance in the U.S.

U.S. Amateur Ballroom Dancers Association
www.usabda.org
Ballroom dance articles, events, and competitions.

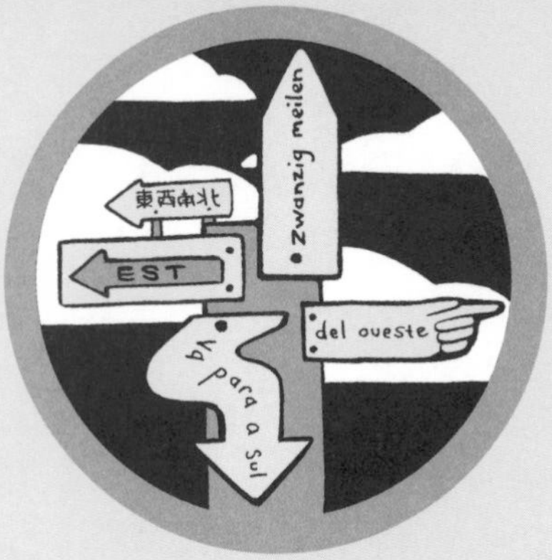

3

ROAM WHERE YOU WANT TO

★ travel ★

The world is the traveler's inn.

—Afghan proverb

Imagine This . . . Paris, Machu Picchu, the Lower East Side—the world is your oyster and you know how to see and savor it all! Eating your way through Italy, tracing your Asian roots, sunbathing on a Greek isle—whatever your fantasy, it's time to make it real. No time, you say? Not enough money? Fear of flying? Details, details, details. This badge deals with those. You'll define your dream trip, prepare for takeoff, and wind up with a departure date, itinerary, and perfectly packed bag. Consider St. Augustine's words: "The world is a book; those who stay home read only one page." So go ahead, read the next few pages, and get ready to say *bon voyage*. *You can do it!*

The Payoffs

- **Wisdom.** The best way to get wise to the ways of the world is to get out in it, and experience it firsthand!
- **Adventure.** Even in this age of globalization, you'll find the different and the new when you hit the road. Variety is the spice of life—especially if you don't eat at every fast food joint you find.
- **Challenge.** Venturing off your lily pad and leaping into the unknown is an adventure that stretches you. You'll be surprised how resourceful, creative, and courageous you can be.
- **Appreciation.** If you love Jane Austen, skiing, Thai food, or reggae music, think how much more you'd have to love if you visited their birthplace or world headquarters.

So, what's your motivation?
Take a moment.
Dream a little, think big,
and then complete this sentence:
I see myself . . .

Meet Your Mentor

CONNER GORRY

What She Does: A freelance writer, Conner has been researching and writing guidebooks for Lonely Planet since 1998. Her titles include: *South America on a Shoestring, Read This First: Central and South America, Guatemala, Out to Eat San Francisco, Hawaii: The Big Island, New York City,* and *Cuba.*

Why She Does It: "My mom loves to travel, so I had a great early role model. She took the family to Vieques, Puerto Rico, when I was eight and right after that to the Dominican Republic. I was enchanted, and have been traveling ever since. My first published piece was my master's thesis on the Cuban embargo, and when it came out I thought, 'Gee, you mean people actually want to read what I've written?' That gave me the confidence boost to give a writing career a shot. I went to Peru and lived out an old dream to see Machu Picchu. After I returned from my next trip (to Morocco), I heard about an editor's job at Lonely Planet. They wound up asking if I'd be interested in writing for them. Of course I said yes! Traveling is about discovery: not only discovering things about the world, but about yourself as well. Meeting new faces, seeing new places, and learning different ways of living recaptures an essence of childhood we tend to lose as we grow up. I'm talking about travel in general—to the next state or a neighboring island. It's a challenge, demanding you do and try things outside of your experience or skill set. You pull through situations and develop new strengths and talents. Travel helps you grow."

> Life can grab you when you venture out: One small move can lead to a big break or revelation, and your horizons completely change.
>
> —Conner Gorry

Word from the Wise: "You don't have to be rich or multilingual or brave. You just have to save a little money and go. All different kinds of people travel—teenagers, grannies, solo women, disabled folks, families, survivors. Every type of person you can imagine is out there making their memories!"

BADGE STEPS

THE CALL OF THE WILD

Adventures for women with a wild streak

Adventure Divas. This "girl-driven media empire" has a public television series that "explores cultures with divavision" and a Web site to exchange information, plan a pilgrimage, or get "avant-garde travel advice from columnist Inga La Gringa." www.adventuredivas.com.

Call of the Wild. Try snowshoeing in Lake Tahoe, hiking in Kauai, backpacking in Big Sur. www.callwild.com or 888-378-1978.

Chicks with Picks. Sets up ice-climbing excursions in Colorado and New Hampshire. www.chickswithpicks.net or 970-626-4424.

Luna Tours. Road biking in Montana, northern California, and the Canadian Rockies. www.lunatours.com or 877-404-6476.

Mariah Wilderness Expeditions. Rafting, sea kayaking, and hiking packages in the American west and Costa Rica. www.mariahwomen.com or 800-462-7424.

1. Find your dream destination.

Do you already have a dream trip in mind? Is it touring a country, seeing a city or hanging out in a world-renowned café? Be specific: Do you want to go to France, take a boat ride through Paris, or spend a week reading at Paris's Deux Magots café? Do you picture yourself there alone or do you have company? Is it summer, spring, fall, or winter?

If you don't have a dream trip in mind, consider your interests and needs. Do you want room service and good shopping or a kayak and a knapsack? Are you interested in world history? Art and music? Do you want to get physical or be pampered? Would you like someone to show you around town and plan out every meal, or do you need to be free to improvise?

Think seriously about whether your destination meshes with your personality. If you don't like crowds, for instance, Beijing may not be your best bet. If you want to climb a mountain, pick an attainable peak—challenging but doable. It's important not to set yourself up for disappointment. One trip will likely lead to others, so don't feel like you have to do it all on the first go. If you really want to just chase down truffles in Italy, don't force yourself to visit every church and museum as well. Follow your heart. Conner has a friend who is a "fanatic (and fantastic) knitter." She made a trip to the Andes to learn about alpaca wool and ancient weaving and knitting practices there.

Decide where you want to go. Turn a picture of this place into your computer's screensaver, attach an image of it to your fridge or bathroom mirror. Think of how much fun you'll have there every time you look at it. ***Match your dreams to your destination.***

2. Decide if you're taking someone along or going solo.

If you want company, family members can be good candidates because you already share a common history, ways of communicating, and points of reference. Friends can be great—but discuss your priorities and independence level up front. If you decide to bring your kids or a lucky niece or nephew, you may have to modify your travel agenda. Chances are, most kids won't be itching to watch Wagner's entire nine-hour Ring cycle at the opera with you—but you might get to see a child's face light up at the circus instead.

If your schedule and agenda aren't a match with friends or family members, sign up for an organized trip that provides structure and built-in travel partners. You could go as part of a tour or meet up with a traveler or two with similar interests. Classified ads in travel magazines and bulletin boards on travel Web sites often have a section for people looking for travel partners. Proceed cautiously, meeting with the person beforehand if possible. In any case, you should try a small trip first with a new travel partner to test the waters.

Don't put off a trip because you don't have someone to do it with. Traveling solo can be wonderful, and though you may fear loneliness, Conner says, "You're never really alone unless you want to be. Before I traveled solo, I never knew how many friends you make on the road." ***Find good company or decide to go it alone.***

3. Get in the know about where you want to go.

Planning and research can save you time, money, and disappointment. You don't want to get home and realize your Paris hotel was a block from Picasso's house—which you didn't know about and didn't visit. So visit the travel aisle of your nearest bookstore, library, or travel shop stocked with guidebooks. But don't stop there:

- Do some Web research as well, and check out traveler's bulletin boards (see Conner's Picks, page 23, for suggestions).
- Rent documentaries and feature films that give you a real feel for the place.
- Talk to people about your trip, especially people who have been there or know someone who has. Get personal recommendations about everything you can think of—hotels, restaurants, shops, places to avoid, and places not to be missed.
- Read up on the current events of where you're thinking of going in the newspaper. This will help you connect with locals once you arrive and will also alert you to any troubles that may be brewing in the region.

Start a list of all the places you'll go and things you'll see. Without even trying, you're creating your itinerary. But leave room for some spontaneity as well. Unless you're in imminent danger, detours, delays, and even getting lost can lead to pleasant surprises. ***Invent an itinerary.***

GREAT PLACES TO PARTY

Festive occasions in great locales

Carnival, Port of Spain, Trinidad. February or March. The biggest Carnival in the region.

Carnival, Rio de Janeiro. February or March. This famous festival lasts four nights, beginning the Friday night before Ash Wednesday.

The Gay and Lesbian Mardi Gras, Sydney. February or March. Australia's biggest regular tourist event.

Mardi Gras, New Orleans. February or March. Floats, beads, costumes, parades, dancing, and general revelry.

Notting Hill Carnival, London. Last weekend in August. The biggest arts festival in Europe, the Notting Hill Carnival was begun by Caribbean immigrants in 1964 and retains a strong island influence.

The Venice Carnevale, Venice, Italy. February or March. Music, dance, theater, parades, and centuries-old traditions.

I DID IT!

"On Christmas Eve in 2001, I was living on the Big Island of Hawaii writing a guide. I was alone for the holidays and it was just three months after September 11. (I'm from New York and my family still lives there.) I planned a long, hot solo hike, close to twenty miles across lots of hardened, black lava to the Pu'u O'o volcanic vent. But every step felt cathartic, and when I finally caught sight of the vent and made my offering to Madame Pele, I knew, somehow, that everything was going to be all right. I cried eating my smooshed sandwich on a small rise overlooking the vent and realized life was about moments like this. I felt very blessed—even though my feet hurt like hell!"

—Conner

SURVIVAL OF THE FITTEST?

"We were on the cheapest Galápagos tour available, in a small, rickety tug. We set off at night and the seas were super rough. My then-boyfriend started vomiting immediately. The waves got bigger and the boat was rising up and slamming down. Even the crew was getting sick. After a few hours of this, when he was curled up on the deck in the fetal position, shivering and gagging, he croaked 'I don't want to die in Ecuador!' I had to insist, in my bad Spanish, that we head the eight hours back to shore. Don't go with the cheapest option when realizing a travel dream."

—Conner

4. Make time.

Set a departure date about six months from now, to give yourself plenty of time to build your trip around your work schedule and other responsibilities. If you're budget-minded, you may want to travel during low season for optimal airfares and hotel rates at your destination—just check guidebooks and the Web to be sure that your visit isn't smack in the middle of hurricane or blizzard season. You may also want to plan your arrival to coincide with major local holidays—or avoid them if you're pressed for time.

If you don't think you have time to travel, here's how you might be able to find some:

- If you have sabbatical or leave of absence options, consider yourself very lucky.
- Save up comp time, personal days, and vacation leave.
- Plan a trip around a national holiday, which can build in a couple of extra days.
- Will staying connected via Internet, cell phone, and fax allow you more time away from the office? It's not ideal working on the road, but if that's the only way you can do it . . .
- Are there slow times of the year in your industry? That might be a good time to take a trip.
- Can you double up on shifts for a few weeks and make up the time that way?
- If you're up for a review and your employer can't give you additional salary, perhaps you can negotiate additional time off instead.

Whether your trip is six months traveling around the world or two weeks in Tahiti, secure the time you'll need. ***Set aside some quality travel time.***

5. Start a travel fund.

Conner says that one of the biggest misconceptions about travel is that you need a lot of money. "There are ways to make an expensive destination more affordable: traveling off-season, apartment swaps instead of hotels, eating as the locals do."

The key to finding the money for travel is saving. When Conner was growing up with that travel-loving mom of hers, her mother would make one meatless meal a week for a year to save money for their travels. "Little did we know that when there was meat, it was 'reduced for quick sale' as well!" says Conner. "When we went away during Christmas, we knew that the trip was our gift. Our present was seeing a sea turtle swim by a reef or eating a conch sandwich on a fishing pier poking into the Caribbean Sea."

Small steps can add up to a sizable travel fund. For example:

- If you eat out a lot, cook at home for a while and take lunch to work.
- Go to bargain matinees instead of the eight o'clock movie.
- Behavior modification and delayed gratification can help you get the money together. Put a postcard of your destination in your purse, and look at it whenever you're tempted to make a major purchase.
- Buying your plane ticket early (at least thirty days in advance) can help. (See Step 7.)

Make your trip a priority, and get some funds together.

6. Learn the lingo.

Taking a language class and listening to instructional tapes in your car can be fun ways to prepare for your trip. But don't let a lack of fluency postpone your departure date! The people you meet in your travels are more apt to have conversational English skills than you are to be multilingual. It's okay. Smile, make an effort, and be patient. As Conner points out, "Once you struggle with a language you don't speak well or at all, you gain appreciation for people back home who struggle with English."

Sometimes you just have to laugh at yourself. As a cigar lover, Conner was excited to see a sign on a house in Baracoa, Cuba, that read: "Se vende Coronas (We sell Coronas)." She knocked on the door and after mystifying a young boy and his mother, realized that they sold *coronas* as in funeral wreaths, not Coronas as in cigars. "I think I'm famous in Baracoa now as the wacky *turista* who wanted to buy a funeral wreath! These are experiences we carry back with us; they put new tools in our life kit." ***Brush up your language skills.***

7. Get your ticket.

Will you travel by plane, train, auto, ship, or a combination of these? Are you staying in hotels, campsites, or a swapped apartment? Your research, reading, and networking have probably given you a good sense of all of the details involved—and now's the time to nail it all down.

RELAX, ALREADY!

Put your mind at ease with a little preparation

- **Familiarize yourself with the local customs at your destination. Read up on dos and don'ts for dress (important for women in many cultures), male and female socializing, and women going out alone.**
- **Stay on top of the current events in your destination. Check out the U.S. State Department for any travel advisories, and the U.K. Foreign and Commonwealth Office online for e-mail news alerts on countries that interest you (see Conner's Picks, page 23, for more).**
- **If it would make you feel more confident, take a self-defense class. Before her first big solo trip, Conner took such a course. "It changed my life, and that's not overstating matters! I encourage all women to take this sort of course, whether or not they plan to travel; the skills you learn are invaluable."**
- **If you fear flying, work with a therapist who specializes in this phobia, educate yourself about the risks (flying is safer than driving, bathing, or crossing the street), check out your carrier's safety record before buying your ticket, and bring a relaxing CD and player on board. (See Conner's Picks, page 23, for safety record resources.)**

CONNER'S EXPERT TIPS

MAKE A LIST, CHECK IT TWICE

- At home, have the post office hold your mail and cancel newspaper delivery. Put jewelry and other valuables in a safe place. Secure all doors and windows, park your car in the driveway so it looks like someone is home, and set lights on timers. Is the kid next door feeding Fido or Fifi? If you're traveling for more than a few weeks, set up automatic bill payment.
- If you are venturing out of the U.S. or Canada, call the toll-free numbers on the credit cards you are taking with you and obtain numbers that you can call collect from overseas should you lose the cards.
- Make a passport plan. Are you packing clothing with a zippered pocket where you can stash it, or should you consider a neck pouch? Is there a place you can lock it in your luggage? Make a photocopy of it, your credit and phone cards, and any other documents you are carrying.
- Leave a copy of your travel itinerary with a friend or family member.
- Bring a short-wave radio. "I find radio becomes important on longer trips for news, music, weather, and breaking stories, especially if you're traveling alone," says Conner. "It's something to listen to besides your own brain."

GOOD TO GO

Get ready and raring to go

- Make sure your passport is good for at least six months past the time of your departure.
- Check out the visa requirements at the consular office of the country you are visiting.
- Review immunization requirements at the U.S. Center for Disease Control and Prevention Web site: www.cdc.gov/travel.
- Check with AAA or the National Auto Club about how to obtain an international driver's license.
- If you're taking a walking, biking, snorkeling, or otherwise physically strenuous excursion, up the ante on your fitness regimen to prepare.

Let's assume you're flying and looking for hotel accommodations. Grab a cup of coffee, log on, and do a little online sleuthing. Here's what you might find on the Web:

- Some Web sites are virtual versions of the old-fashioned, all-purpose travel agency down the block, offering packages that include hotel reservations and car rentals. To be sure the deal is as good as it sounds, check out the hotels offered in any packages you find in a travel guidebook, such as *Lonely Planet* or *Fodor's*.
- Many Web sites let you search by lowest available fare, and some let you name the price you're willing to pay.
- Be sure to try the Web sites of various airlines, too. Some low-cost carriers don't offer their flights through travel consolidators, and you can redeem frequent-flier miles for tickets on airline sites.

Next, visit a travel agent or two with these thoughts in mind:

- See if they can beat the prices and convenience of the travel plan you've mapped out online.
- Get agent recommendations from friends who travel a lot.

- If your trip covers multiple destinations, you might want to use an agent upfront.
- If money is no object, you might want to employ a custom travel planner. They will tailor just about everything to fit the needs and preferences you describe, and can offer you insider access.

Once you've got the details settled and the tickets paid for, print out your itinerary and count down the days to departure. ***Check you out—you're going places!***

CONGRATULATIONS!

You're ready to write, "Having a great time, wish you were here!" You did it!

I DID IT!

Name: ______________________

Date: ______________________

TRAVEL SMARTER

While you're out there . . .

- Always listen to your instincts—don't second-guess yourself.
- Keep a spare twenty dollars on you in a safe place, separate from the rest of your cash.
- Some single women wear wedding bands when traveling to fend off advances.
- Take advantage of safety deposit boxes in hotels and only take "walking around money" out with you. And don't travel with anything you're not willing to lose.
- If arriving at your destination at night, and especially if traveling solo, arrange that first night's accommodation in advance. Also, take reliable transportation from the airport to the hotel.
- Bring a relevant book for quality downtime. Says Conner: "I like to travel through a place reading a book by a native author or a book set in that country: Paul Bowles's *The Sheltering Sky* in Morocco, the Cairo trilogy by Nobel prize–winner Naguib Mahfouz in Egypt, or Hemingway's *The Old Man and the Sea* in Cuba."

BEYOND THE BADGE

If you love it as much as you thought you would, dream on . . .

- **Make a pilgrimage.** You might make a journey of faith to Lourdes, the Ganges, Mount Sinai, or Lhasa (or all of the above). Then again, tennis fans may feel positively reverential at Wimbledon, literature lovers flock to the Brontë sisters' moors, and many a cook has felt called to the Cordon Bleu.
- **Circumnavigate the globe.** Buy a round the world (RTW) ticket, which allows you a certain number of stops in several continents. Because this type of plane ticket will cost $2,500 and up, you'll want to plan carefully to make the most of it. For instance, on any RTW ticket, it's hard to get to South or Central America. You also can't backtrack on RTW tickets. With a healthy combination of saving, planning, and time, you'll have the trip of a lifetime.
- **Work around the world.** You can teach English, educate kids at international schools and U.S. military bases, or hook up with an American business seeking to teach their overseas employees a thing or two. You can also work as a tour guide or for an airline or cruise ship. Volunteering is another rewarding way to travel. There's the Peace Corps, of course, but there's also Doctors Without Borders, American Friends Service Committee, Witness for Peace, and many other organizations doing good work. Last but not least, take a tip from Conner and write about the corners of the world you know well. Check out who publishes the guidebooks you love, and peruse their Web sites to learn about how they choose and assign writers.

OPPORTUNITIES ABROAD

Subsidize your travels

Department of Defense Education Activity. Land a teaching post on a military base. www.odedodea.edu.

Global ESL Network. Find ESL teaching positions abroad. www.eltweb.com.

Teach Abroad. Find out where the demand is and what skills are in need. www.teachabroad.com.

Transitions Abroad. Magazine chock full of information for people who want to live, work, or volunteer abroad. www.transitionsabroad.com.

Witness for Peace. Work or travel in Latin America with this grassroots organization. www.witnessforpeace.org.

CONNER'S PICKS

BOOKS

Culture Shock! guidebook series
Written for people who are planning to live abroad, these books offer insight into table manners, dress, punctuality, and humor in scores of countries.

The Gift of Fear and Other Survival Signals That Protect Us from Violence by Gavin DeBecker
Lots of self-defense tips travelers can use.

Lonely Planet's Journeys series
This well-written, captivating travel literature primes you to hit the road.

Lonely Planet's Read This First series
With titles like *Europe, Central and South America, Africa,* and *Asia and India,* these books are a snappy orientation to regional travel.

Travelers' Tales guidebook series
These great travelogue titles are organized by country or theme. Check out their tales written by women.

GEAR

Grundig
www.grundig.de
This is the way to go for a lightweight, affordable short-wave radio.

Macpac
www.macpac.co.nz
Fantastic backpacks from cutting-edge convertible models to classic workhorses.

REI
www.rei.com
An all-purpose outdoor outfitter.

Sierra Designs
www.sierra-designs.com
A terrific outdoor gear company—you can get at least ten years out of their tents.

WEB SITES

www.aircourier.org
Super-cheap flights; lots of flexibility required.

www.airsafe.com
Lets you check the safety records of individual airlines.

www.cheaptickets.com
Cheap flights to anywhere you might want to go—except Cuba!

www.ecotour.org/ecotour.htm
Conservation International's eco-tourism guidelines for conscientious travelers.

www.expedia.com
Another searchable flight site.

www.expressvisa.com
Handles visa and passport needs for a fee.

www.fco.gov.uk
Sign up with the U.K. Foreign and Commonwealth Office for e-mail alerts on your destination.

www.itmb.com
Maps from around the world.

www.lanic.utexas.edu/subject/countries.html
The best clearinghouse for Latin American links organized by country.

www.naturaltraveler.com
Top-quality travel writing to get you moving, laughing, thinking, and dreaming.

www.oanda.com
Worldwide currency exchange rates.

www.state.gov
Check this U.S. State Departement site for travel advisories.

www.thebathroomdiaries.com
For clean bathrooms and funny stories around the world.

thorntree.lonelyplanet.com
Network with other travelers for tips, warnings, and travel partners.

www.travel.epicurious.com
Search for festivals and events worldwide by country, theme, or date.

www.travelocity.com
Info-packed site that allows you to search for flights, hotel, packages, etc.

www.visa.com and www.mastercard.com
Handy ATM locators and PIN code requirements for various countries (some require at least six digits).

4

TAKE THE STAGE

★ acting ★

If you always do what interests you, at least one person is pleased.

—Katherine Hepburn

Imagine This . . . There's something about immersing yourself in a character. Thinking her thoughts, sensing her feelings, and speaking her words makes you feel electric, alive. And convincing an audience that you are that character—what a rush! Remember when you were a kid and the living room rug was your stage, where you starred and directed your siblings in plays that always won standing ovations (at least from your parents)? Or when you landed a role in your high school's production of *Our Town,* and you strutted down your street like it was Broadway? Well, you're due for a comeback! You'll need to find a theater, pay your dues, and hone your craft until you can hit your mark and nail every line at an audition. Break a leg, kid . . . *You can do it!*

So, what's your motivation?
Take a moment.
Dream a little, think big,
and then complete this sentence:
I see myself . . .

The Payoffs

- **Community.** The show must go on, and the director, your fellow actors, stage hands, makeup artists, and everyone else behind the scenes will make sure it does. Add the audience, and you've got a complete circle of communication—and community.
- **Magic.** You're a wizard when you transform some words, a few props, and yourself into something new: a world of make-believe that makes believers of us all.
- **Adulation.** Sally Field knew we liked her, we really liked her, when she won an Academy Award. Audiences applaud performers who make them laugh, cry, and think about our human condition.
- **Power.** Once you've had an audience eating out of the palm of your hand, you'll feel the power of the stage.

Meet Your Mentor
LISA LEWIS

What She Does: A versatile actor, respected improviser, and in-demand voice-over talent, Lisa has also served as president of the Screen Actors Guild in Chicago.

Why She Does It: "I was born and raised in Davenport, Iowa, where acting is not on the short list of life options! My love of acting began with a love of reading. That morphed into performance, because theater and English departments are often enmeshed in high school. When I was fifteen, I auditioned for my high school play: Molière's *The Miser*. I got in, had three lines, and the rest is history! I was bitten by the bug. As I got older, I tried to figure out how to incorporate this love of acting into something more practical, like law school (good litigators are great actors) or broadcasting, which is funny because one of my current clients is *NBC Nightly News*—I do the promos for upcoming news features. All the while I kept doing what I really loved: plays. And after a while, people started to pay me to do plays, and then for voice-over work and commercials. Before I knew it, what I loved seemed viable. I followed my love of the work, and the rest took care of itself. I firmly believe that making a living in acting is not something you choose; it chooses you. It's not fair—lots of talented people don't get to do it—and I actually think that if you pursue it for the money or the fame, it probably won't happen. Follow your interest in performing instead; focus on the joy and excitement."

No one ever died from forgetting a line. Take a chance!

—Lisa Lewis

Word from the Wise: "At least once a year, if not once a month, I try to do something that scares the $#!& out of me! I don't ever want to be the person who won't get on the roller coaster!"

BADGE STEPS

1. Find your voice.

Whether your ultimate goal is to do community theater, perform Shakespeare in a park, or act in commercials or movies, there are ways to warm up your public performance muscles. Lisa suggests that you:

- Volunteer to do readings in church, lead a discussion at a club meeting, or make a presentation at work—anything that will get you comfortable speaking in front of people.
- Read to kids, and do it with gusto. "That's what actors are always trying to recapture—the spirit of play, the magic land of 'as if.'"
- Choose a scene from a favorite movie and transcribe a one-minute section of a monologue by a character you feel somehow connected to. Work on committing it to memory and find a way to make the words your own.

If the mere thought of speaking in front of others fills your stomach with frantic butterflies, see Speak Up, page 38, for good advice on dealing with speaking and performance anxiety. ***Get comfortable in the spotlight.***

2. Get involved in the theater.

While you're warming up, give some attention to the performers around you:

- Find local theater companies by looking through the entertainment listings in your local newspaper or the Yellow Pages. Go to their performances and to any professional touring productions that might be coming to your town or one nearby.
- Watch as a peer rather than as an audience member. Think about the ages and physical characteristics of the actors. Has the director made an unusual casting choice? Read the program for information on the cast members' training and previous credits. Do any of their career paths sound like a route you could follow? Read the plays in advance if you can, and think about whether the material is being done the way you imagined it. What were the most interesting choices, and how would you do it differently?
- Volunteer to work backstage during an upcoming production at a local theater. "You'll get a bird's-eye view of what people do, a realistic sense of the time commitments involved, and best of all, you'll get to

MEMORIZATION MADE EASY (OR EASIER!)

Tips on remembering your lines

- Highlight your lines in a script and use another color to highlight your cues.
- Make a tape with your lines on it that you can listen to while driving, jogging, or doing housework. You might also make a tape with your cue lines on it and pause it while you talk back with your lines.
- Read with a partner who reads your cues.
- If memorization is really tough for you, shoot for small roles at first, and build your confidence from there.
- The rehearsal process is all about putting the material on its feet, so be patient and trust that once you've associated the words with something you are doing on stage, memorization will become a much easier task.
- Outside of acting, look for ways to improve your memory overall. Work crossword puzzles, play Scrabble or other word games, and challenge your brain to become more agile.

know people," says Lisa. At every level of "the business," knowing people helps open doors.

Volunteer to work backstage at one production.

3. Learn your craft.

You may be a natural, but acting is a craft that takes real skill—even if you don't swear by "the Method." Read the Con Artistes sidebar carefully to avoid fly-by-night teachers and classes, and use the tips below to choose a more proven path of study:

- If you live in a city with a resident professional theater company, inquire about any classes they offer.
- Look for a theater or acting class through a local college extension program.
- If you are intimidated by all those lines you'll have to memorize, start with an improv class instead. Improvisation is an unscripted method of rehearsal, training, and performance, so you won't have to learn any lines.
- Visit the Screen Actors Guild (SAG), American Federation of Television and Radio Artists (AFTRA), and Actors Equity Association (AEA) Web sites for reliable information about acting as a profession (see Lisa's Picks, page 31).

Show your class at acting class.

4. Give it your best shot.

As you go to theater productions, work backstage, and go to acting class, you'll begin to hear about upcoming community theater productions that are being cast. This could be your big break—so find a role to audition for, and prepare to rise and shine!

Before you audition:

- Learn what you are expected to prepare. You may be asked to bring in your own material or a monologue you've perfected. But sometimes you'll be given a scene to prepare from the production being cast, and other times you'll be asked to come in "cold," and be given a scene to read at the audition.
- Try to get a copy of the script in advance from the casting director (or the library) even if you are coming at the material cold, so that you

CON ARTISTES

Don't get taken in by scams!

- **If you have any doubts about the legitimacy of an acting class, agent, etc., call your local Better Business Bureau and check them out.**
- **Never pay someone to represent you—reputable agents are paid when you are, not before.**
- **Never allow someone to sell you something you don't need. For example, you usually do not need head shots or a modeling portfolio if you are only planning to audition for local plays.**
- **To avoid scams, take classes at established schools and professional theater companies, or through a reputable adult education program.**

don't freeze up completely! And if you know the piece you will be presenting, read it out loud in the mirror and try different interpretations, then ask for feedback from a frank friend or colleague. But beware of overrehearsing—you might become rigid or stale and have trouble letting go of your original choice if the director asks you to try something different with the material.

At the audition:

- Listen and learn from what the director says. Sometimes she will say a few words about how she sees the characters and the show before the auditions begin. As other actors try out, pay attention to what the director says to them, and use this to hone your own interpretation.
- Don't be afraid to ask the director how she sees your character. She may not say much—preferring to see what you think—but she may also offer you important tips.
- Take direction. If the director asks you to try something different or offers advice, it usually means you've gotten her attention, and now she wants to see how well you will take direction if cast.
- Think ahead. No matter how much you want the part, give it your all, learn from the experience, and then put it behind you and start planning for the next audition. That way whether you get the call or not, you'll be looking forward to what's next. Remember Lisa's wise words: "Acting is an art form that requires you to keep all of your emotions close to the surface, so you can call upon them and use them. But at the same time, you are seeking to work in a competitive arena in which you face rejection. So you have to wear your heart on your sleeve and have a very thick skin."

Audition!

CONGRATULATIONS!

You've got the audience on their feet! Encore! You did it!

I DID IT!

Name: ______________________________

Date: ______________________________

I DID IT!

"One day at the bookstore, a woman working on the casting of extras for a movie that was shooting in town came up to me, gave me her card, and said I had the perfect look for a scene they were doing. I said yeah, right, but she told me to look at the ad they were running in the paper and to come to the call if I was at all interested. I looked at the ad, saw that I needed to bring a photo to the call, and went. I wound up spending a long but very fun day walking up and down a sidewalk in a crowd scene. I was even visible in the movie for a few seconds—walking by the pay phone Al Pacino (!!!) was using."
—Jolie

CUT!

"I loved doing plays and musicals when I was in high school and college. I never thought of it as a career option—but when I became a high school English teacher, I found many opportunities to use performance, especially in Shakespeare class where I read aloud a lot and had students do scenes. When I took an evening acting class, I told myself it was to help with my teaching, but one thing led to another, and I was encouraged by my teacher to audition for the *Romeo and Juliet* production a local company was doing. This was a good theater group, and I was scared to death. But I made it through two rounds of auditions. While I didn't get the part, I did get the courage to apply for (and get!) a Folger Fellowship to study the Bard at the Folger Shakespeare Library in Washington, D.C., the following summer."
—Candace

BEYOND THE BADGE

If you love it as much as you thought you would, dream on . . .

- **Put on a play.** If, like all those Hollywood actors, you've "always wanted to direct," or you're just frustrated by the lack of live theater in your community, why not spearhead a production of your own? Visit www.communitytheater.org—this "Home of Professional Amateurs" offers a vast and practical array of resources, including a searchable discussion board organized by topics; expert articles and how-tos; scripts; links; and a store featuring tools like *The Play Director's Survival Kit* by James W. Rodgers and Wanda C. Rogers, *The PR Bible for Community Theatres* by Chris Mackowski, and *The Community Theater Handbook* by Gary P. Cohen.
- **Get an agent.** Yes, you'll owe them 10 to 15 percent of your paychecks—but since they'll help you get paychecks, it's not a bad deal. Remember that the major markets for major acting gigs are in Los Angeles and New York City, with secondary markets in theater towns like Chicago and San Francisco. See Lisa's Picks, page 31, and Who's Your Agent? sidebar for more information.
- **Write your own script.** See Be an Author, page 96 for tons of tips on cuddling up to your muse and getting the greatness in your head down on the printed page. If you want to write:

  Plays. See tons of plays, and as noted above, volunteer to work on productions so that you can get a realistic sense of what can and can't readily be done on the stage. You never know: The company you volunteer with may just want to stage that play of yours! Get to know actors so that they can help you hear your dialogue. Check out the current year's *Writer's Handbook* (buy a copy or check your library's reference section) for how-to articles, play publishers, and regional and university theaters.

  TV shows. Get scripts and study their formats (www.script-o-rama.com or www.scriptcity.net) and use a software program like Final Draft or Scriptware to get the format just right. You'll want to register your perfected scripts with the Writers Guild of America and then send query letters to literary agents who specialize in the field. You'll find names at the Guild Web site (www.wga.org).

  Movies. See Beyond the Badge in Roll 'Em, page 112.

WHO'S YOUR AGENT?

It's not just what you know but who you know

- In the major markets, most reputable agents are franchised by SAG, AFTRA, and/or AEA. Many nonfranchised agents are trustworthy, but the union franchise is an important added layer of protection for actors.
- You can get lists of such agents in your area from these unions. Visit them online (see Lisa's Picks, page 31) or at the offices they maintain in major cities.
- You'll need a photo and a resume (check reference books for industry standards) to land an agent—and since these are rarely enough to get you a contract, you'll also want to seek personal referrals and references (from your acting coach, for instance) and participate in industry showcases where you can strut your stuff.

extra credit

STAND-UP COMEDY

MEET YOUR STAND-UP MENTOR

By day, you'll find Janet Rosen surrounded by books and manuscripts. (She's a literary agent at Sheree Bykofsky Associates in New York.) But many a night, Janet is surrounded by laughter and applause as she performs stand-up comedy in clubs and night spots around town. Why does she do it? "There really is no rational reason to do this. The chances of getting a ton of money or recognition are slim. But getting laughs is addictive. I am compelled—like a salmon swimming upstream!"

JANET'S PICKS

Sandra Bernhard: Without You I'm Nothing (film)

The Last Laugh by Phil Berger

Laughing in the Dark by Laurie Stone

Mel Brooks' **The Producers** (film)

She's So Funny: 1,768 of the Best Jokes from Women Comedians by Judy Brown (editor)

If you know you're funny and want to show the world:

Study the funny. As you go to comedy clubs or watch comics on TV, analyze what makes a schtick click. How do they set up their jokes? Do they use props or body language? How do they make use of silence? Pauses can be funny, too.

Figure out what makes you funny. Boil your wit down to its essence, then tighten it and work on making it universal. Funny at the copier is different from funny on stage. And don't copy others' style or use their material. Be original!

Write your material. Carry a notebook or tape recorder to capture all the situations you find funny—but when drawing on your life, be considerate. Janet Rosen jokes about friends but changes their names, and they often don't know they are the subject of the routine that has them rolling in the aisles laughing. While you'll probably get only five to ten minutes of stage time to start, work up more for fallback.

Jokes usually begin with a line or two of set-up followed by a punch line: "You have to stay in shape. My grandmother started walking five miles a day when she was sixty. She's ninety-seven now, and we don't know where the hell she is." (Ellen DeGeneres) Others make a witty observation: "I don't know if I'm submissive because it turns me on, or if it's just because I'm lazy." (Margaret Cho) (Don't steal these or any other jokes. Comics who do get less respect than Rodney Dangerfield!) Make your set-ups as short and sharp as you can—audiences prefer laughing to listening. Also think about the order you'll tell your jokes. Yes, all your jokes are funny, but you want to make sure that you come out swinging and leave them laughing.

Perform your material. Select an open mike or amateur night venue that feels friendly and fun, and find out about the performance procedure. As you watch other comics perform, be supportive. Everyone is probably battling their own version of stage fright. Most novices report being surprised by how good they feel when they take the stage. (The waiting is the hard part!) The sound of your own voice gives you energy, and that first laugh propels you on. Chances are you won't want to get off the stage! And when you do, you'll be plotting your return. What about hecklers? "At least they're paying attention," quips Janet. Make them work for you—your response to one can totally bring the audience around to you.

LISA'S PICKS

BOOKS

Audition: Everything an Actor Needs to Know to Get the Part by Michael Shurtleff
Eliminate the mystery surrounding audition with Shurtleff's Twelve Guideposts, plus how to deal with the nitty-gritty of auditioning (what to wear, how to present your past experience, etc.).

Casting Qs: A Collection of Casting Director Interviews by Bonnie Gillespie
A compilation of over 120 interviews with casting directors in Los Angeles and New York from her weekly column in the actors' trade weekly, *Back Stage West*.

How to Audition: For TV, Movies, Commercials, Plays, and Musicals by Gordon Hunt
Written by actress Helen Hunt's father, the book includes informative interviews with Richard Dreyfuss, Hal Prince, Gordon Davidson, and others, as well as specific advice for auditioning.

How to Be a Working Actor: The Insider's Guide to Finding Jobs in Theater, Film, and Television by Mari Lyn Henry and Lynne Rogers
This celebrated survival guide for actors offers an insider's view of how casting decisions are made, as well as advice on financial survival, networking, meeting agents and casting directors, the performing unions, selecting a wardrobe, and studying a role.

I, An Actor by Nicholas Craig
Reading the hilarious "memoirs" of this fictional British actor will prevent you from ever taking yourself too seriously.

WEB SITES

www.backstage.com
East (NY) and West (LA) versions of the paper are published.

www.broadway.com
If you're heading to New York or London, check out this site for theater tickets to the big shows.

www.communitytheater.org
Contains lists of community theater groups, a discussion board, and a bookstore.

www.performink.com
Professional trade paper for actors in the Midwest/Chicago.

ACTOR'S UNIONS

Actors Equity
www.actorsequity.org
A labor union representing over 45,000 American actors and stage managers working in the professional theater.

American Federation of Television and Radio Artists
www.aftra.com
A national labor union representing nearly 80,000 performers, journalists, and other artists working in the entertainment and news media.

Screen Actors Guild
www.sag.org
Screen actor's union. See their Web site for eligibility requirements and benefits of becoming a member.

FILMS

Some of Lisa's favorite performances by women:

All About Eve
"Every single female performance in this film is a gem: Bette Davis, Anne Baxter, Celeste Holm, the fabulous Thelma Ritter, and a very young Marilyn Monroe," says Lisa.

Kathy Bates in anything!
"Although everyone loves her performance in *Misery* (and it's what garnered her the Oscar), I think she was absolutely shattering in both *Dolores Claiborne* and *Primary Colors*."

Ellen Burstyn in **Requiem for a Dream**
"Unbelievable!"

Judy Holliday in **Born Yesterday**
"I saw this film for the first time when I was twelve, and it's what made me want to be a comedic actress. She was—and remains—an absolute inspiration to me," says Lisa.

Angela Lansbury in The Manchurian Candidate
"An amazing performance with Lansbury as a "middle-aged mother"—a role her advisors cautioned her not to accept because she was too young to be playing a mother. Ha ha! She showed them all!"

5

WALK ON FIRE

★ firewalking ★

The weakest of all weak things is a virtue which has not been tested in the fire.

—Mark Twain

Imagine This . . . In the middle of the night, you channel-surf into a Tony Robbins infomercial and learn he's a firewalker. A few days later you have lunch with your spiritual seeker of a little sister, and all she can talk about is the firewalk workshop she attended the previous weekend. Has the world gone mad? What's it all about? Why aren't these people in a burn ward? So you did a little research and got really intrigued: Can firewalking really boost corporate sales or transform our perceptions of mind and matter, as many Web sites devoted to the subject claim? There's only one way to find out: Witness the event yourself, and take a workshop that teaches you how to hot-foot it. Ready to jump into the fire? *You can do it!*

So, what's your motivation?
Take a moment.
Dream a little, think big,
and then complete this sentence:
I see myself . . .

The Payoffs

- **Sheer amazement.** Whether you're the one walking or just a casual observer, participating in a firewalk is mind-blowing! Why doesn't it burn?!
- **Fuel for change.** Some firewalkers say they feel the fear and do it anyway. Aren't there a zillion times in life when the ability to walk right through our fears might come in handy?
- **New possibilities.** If we can do something everyone says is impossible, what can't we do?
- **A mind-body connection.** Many firewalkers believe that getting through it unscathed is a testament to "mind over matter"—but they also learn to listen carefully to their bodies, which sometimes lead them to sit out a walk.

Meet Your Mentor
HEATHER ASH AMARA

What She Does: The author of *The Four Elements of Change* and the founder of the Toltec Center of Creative Intent and the SpiritWeavers programs, Heather travels the world sharing practical tools and wisdom from a variety of shamanic traditions to support individual growth and spirit-based community.

© Willie Peck

Why She Does It: "I grew up traveling, living in Asia for long stretches and journeying around the world with my family. In Asia, I found a deep sense of spirituality and community embedded in the culture. When I first moved to the States, it was to go to the University of California at Davis, where I got a degree in International Community Relations. I had a hard time adjusting; I knew something was missing but didn't know what. I suspected that part of it was the lack of a sense of spiritual connection and community, so I went to the library and checked out every book I could find on spirituality. I was especially drawn to European shamanism, because that's my heritage. It instantly felt like what I'd been missing. A friend and I decided to offer a campus class on what we were reading in this area. Sixty people showed up, and that was the beginning of my teaching. Then and now, I share what I learn, and this sharing has become my life—and my passion!"

The fire has taught me to honor the flames within myself and to walk through ALL the firewalks in my life.

—Heather Ash Amara

Word from the Wise: "A firewalk can change your life, because you learn that what you thought was true about the world—fire always burns—and what you thought about yourself—I can't touch fire without getting burned—isn't always so. People have told me that they've gone on job interviews the day after a walk and felt their usual nervousness but then thought: 'I just walked on fire, so heck, this is certainly possible!' Your belief systems and the ways you've limited yourself are challenged and broken wide open."

BADGE STEPS

1. Examine your goals.

People firewalk for a number of reasons: A firefighter wants to learn "the trick," a woman badly burned in a house fire as a child wants to face and overcome her fear of fire, a woman undergoing cancer treatment wants to get in touch with her courage and strength, a spiritual seeker wants to experience the walk as part of her exploration of ancient arts and rituals. And as Peggy Dylan, who is often called the mother of the modern firewalking movement, writes, "during the booming economy of the early 1990s, the firewalk caught the attention of managers and corporations as a way to inspire creativity and empower visions of higher horizons in their employees." In addition to working with organizations like Microsoft and American Express to further these goals, Dylan walks with spiritual groups who use the firewalk as a tool for personal empowerment and as a ritual for spiritual communion.

Heather is supportive of all the varied goals that bring walkers to the fire. But some motivations are less valid—and more dangerous—than others. "I was once burned while demonstrating firewalking to a large crowd," she explains. "I never recommend that anyone walk to demonstrate to anyone else that it's possible. Showing off or proving something are not good reasons to walk." As with every badge in this book, you're assuming a certain amount of risk here, and only you can tell whether the potential personal rewards outweigh the obvious dangers. ***Define why you'd like to participate in a firewalk.***

2. Find a friendly fire.

Would-be firewalkers should seek out a walk led by a certified instructor. "I would never walk with someone who was not certified," says Heather. Sundoor International Firewalking School certifies walkers and lists upcoming workshops and seminars (see www.sundoor.com).

When you investigate a firewalking event, be sure the focus of that walk is a good match (no pun intended) for your own goals. Some walks are very business- and career-oriented, while others are more spiritually focused. ***Locate a firewalking course or workshop that meets your needs.***

FIRE FACTS

Then and now

Firewalking has existed in cultures around the world throughout the ages. It has usually served two purposes: Warriors firewalked in preparation for battle in order to gain focus and energy for the arduous task ahead, while shamans, priests, or healers of a culture often walked before doing hands-on healing in their community. They walked to absorb energy from the fire that they could then use to help other people.

In most modern firewalks, a bonfire is lit and allowed to burn down to a heap of coals. The coals are then raked and formed into a path, often about twelve feet long and approximately 1200° Fahrenheit. Walkers then proceed barefoot across the coals, walking at a normal speed.

3. Contemplate the fire.

It's helpful to do some mental preparation before showing up for your firewalk, so that you come prepared to confront your fears. To prepare for your walk, let's look at the structure of Heather's firewalking workshops.

At the outset, Heather asks participants to think about what they would do if they had more energy in their life. What would they hope to accomplish? The group then builds a big bonfire outside, under the stars. "As we stack the wood, we think about our personal intentions, and ask the fire to help us manifest them."

As the fire burns down, participants spend a couple of hours discussing their self-imposed limitations and fears, how they are stopped by them, and how they can work with them. "I invite people to share their specific fears and to release them into the group—which can really zap those fears of their power," our expert says. "We also explore the ways we use our energy. If you want to make changes in your life, you need energy, so we look at unproductive energy expenditures. When we hit a roadblock, do we blame other people? Curse fate? Indulge in denial, and pretend the block doesn't even exist?"

Heather then addresses ways to listen to our bodies. At the fire, some people experience a pure sense of knowing that they can walk. Others heed the direction to observe but not walk. "The evening of a firewalk is not about walking on fire; it's about learning to listen to your body," says Heather. "We ask people to try to be free of the belief that they certainly will or absolutely won't walk. We want them to listen to their bodies and then act accordingly."

Whether you walk or observe, "Your fundamental belief dating from early childhood that to touch fire equals getting burned will be shattered. This leads to a reexamination of virtually everything else we think is true or inevitable." Heather goes on to describe "a participant at a walk who had walked on fire many times before decided not to walk this evening. Not walking was a profound experience for her, because she realized she was always pushing herself to do, do, do in many areas in her life."

Many people participating in a firewalk realize that the mind and body are not always in alignment. While the mind says, "This is impossible," the body knows how to do it. "Your body is incredibly perceptive," says

WHY THEY DON'T FEEL THE BURN

Some theories

- The Leidenfrost Effect suggests that moisture on the bottoms of walkers' feet creates a vapor barrier between the foot and the coals.
- The Conductivity Theory hypothesizes that coals are poor conductors of heat, so that no matter how high the temperature of the coals, they won't burn a walker's feet.
- Many instructors, including Heather, don't subscribe to the above theories, in part because they have seen or experienced firewalking burns on occasion. Many walkers think it's possible because the energy of those assembled matches the energy of the fire. Others believe the body is able to cool and protect itself. Most believe that the walker's mental state is key and that firewalking shows how our thoughts can affect our surroundings.

Heather. "If you tell it, 'Here's fire and I want to walk through it without getting burned,' your body knows what to do. It sounds crazy, but I've seen it over and over again." ***Prepare for the big event.***

4. All fired up.

What can you expect while you walk? "The first time I walked, I felt no discomfort," recalls Heather. "The coals actually felt soft. The second time I walked, I got halfway across and my mind screamed, 'This is fire!' In that moment, I felt a wave of heat come up my body. We tell people that if they feel heat, it doesn't necessarily mean they are burned; it means they have energy at their feet. We tell people to keep breathing the energy up."

After everyone has had a chance to walk across, an "open fire" period may follow. At this time, people can walk with a partner, dance, do cartwheels—whatever. Heather says this is incredibly joyful, and that it shows people that change and transformation don't have to always be serious or somber. "It can be fun to walk through your fears!"

After the walk, Heather suggests you take some time to absorb what you've seen, felt, and learned. "Whenever we do something that brings a lot of new information or energy into our lives, it's very important that we integrate it. Stay in touch with other walkers, and journal about your experience to observe the ways you embrace or resist any changes it has wrought in you." ***Walk or watch, and then reflect on the experience.***

CONGRATULATIONS!

You can take the heat, and keep your cool, too! You did it!

I DID IT!

Name: ____________________

Date: ____________________

I DID IT!

"I wasn't sure why I signed up for the walk, so when, in preparation, we were asked to share our reasons for being there, I kind of stammered. I felt stuck in my life. I was afraid and had no sense that I could make the changes I was yearning to make. Finally I blurted out that I guessed I needed to 'light a fire under my butt.' I laughed but knew I was actually quite serious. The walk was not a miracle cure but I did end the evening with a feeling of personal power—and you know what? Within a few months I had made significant changes in my life. Now, when fear and self-doubt creep up, I see them as cold water trying to put out the fire of my dreams and passions. I remember the walk and know that I don't have to let that happen."

—Jeanette

FEELING THE HEAT

"When I first started teaching fire-walking, I was very stubborn in my belief that I should always walk first. Since I wasn't walking purely for myself and was instead doing what I thought I should do, I often got burned. While walks are communal events, we must each listen to our own bodies and focus on our personal goals."

—Heather

HEATHER'S PICKS

BOOKS

:: *On firewalking:*

Firewalk: The Psychology of Physical Immunity by Jonathan Sternfield
A balanced, insightful account of the practice of firewalking, this book comes recommended by renowned firewalker Tolly Burkan and wellness guru Andrew Weil, MD.

Firewalking: A New Look at an Old Enigma by Larissa Vilenskaya and Joan Steffy
Traces the phenomenon of firewalking from ancient practice to modern personal development tool, with first-person commentary from firewalkers.

:: *On walking through fire in all aspects of your life:*

Clear Your Clutter with Feng Shui by Karen Kingston
Heather's favorite book on how to align your environment so it supports your highest purpose.

The Four Agreements by Don Miguel Ruiz
Describes how to improve all of your relationships—especially the one with yourself—by following four simple agreements: Be impeccable with your word, don't take anything personally, don't make assumptions, and always do your best.

The Four Elements of Change by Heather Ash
A practical, inspiring look at how we can create lasting change and harmony in our lives.

Nonviolent Communication: A Language of Life by Marshall B. Rosenburg, PhD, and Lucy Leu
Learn to communicate more constructively with others with this book from the founder of Center for Nonviolent Communication, a nonprofit that teaches peacemaking skills across five continents.

ORGANIZATIONS

Sundoor International Firewalking School
www.sundoor.com
Certifies walkers and lists upcoming workshops and seminars.

Toltec Center of Creative Intent
www.tolteccenter.org
Heather offers two firewalks here a year and sponsors other firewalk instructors.

CDS

Shamanic Tools for the Spiritual Journey by Heather Ash

Returning to Center: Meditations and Recapitulation by Heather Ash

Personal Ritual and Shamanism by Heather Ash

6 SPEAK UP

★ public speaking ★

SPEAK YOUR MIND, even if your voice shakes.

—Maggie Kuhn, founder of the Gray Panthers

So, what's your motivation? Take a moment. Dream a little, think big, and then complete this sentence: I see myself . . .

Imagine This . . . Your boss asks you to chair a panel at an upcoming corporate meeting. Fellow parents nominate you to introduce an important issue to the PTA. At a town hall meeting, your hand goes right up when a zoning issue you feel strongly about comes up for discussion. And when you have the chance to meet a fellow party guest who could help your career, you don't hesitate to introduce yourself. Gone are the days when you'd feel sick with anxiety, make excuses, and keep your mouth shut—only to berate yourself later. Once you've learned to manage your fears and discovered what an uplifting experience speaking can be, you'll have your audience hanging on your every word. We're all ears. *You can do it!*

The Payoffs

- **Understanding.** Knowing how to express yourself effectively goes a long way to making yourself seen, heard, and understood.
- **Dialogue.** When you speak with conviction, you'll fire up your audience. You'll often be thanked for saying what the silent couldn't manage to say, and you'll open up the possibility of meaningful two-way communication.
- **Freedom.** Fear of public speaking can keep us from pursuing life's possibilities: meeting fascinating people; pursuing promising careers, degrees, and promotions; and sharing our ideas, talents, and expertise. Don't let your gifts go to waste!
- **Domino effect.** Getting more comfortable speaking in public will help you overcome self-consciousness in all kinds of social situations that make you worry about your "performance"—reunions, weddings, professional mixers, and hot dates.

Meet Your Mentor

JANET E. ESPOSITO

What She Does: Janet is the author of *In the SpotLight: Overcome Your Fear of Public Speaking and Performing.* A licensed clinical social worker and practicing psychotherapist, Janet is the president of In the SpotLight, a company devoted to helping people overcome stage fright in public speaking and performing. In addition to leading group classes, Janet does individual coaching and consults with businesses.

© Mary Haggerty

Why She Does It: "I've been a psychotherapist for almost twenty years and, over time, developed expertise in working with a range of anxiety problems. But it was really my own personal experience that fueled my focus on this area: I had a severe case of performance anxiety for at least ten years. I kept it hidden because I was ashamed and embarrassed by it, and I don't think anyone really guessed that I had the problem. I was perceived as confident, assertive, ambitious, and accomplished, and when I had to get up in front of a group and speak, I could. But there was a huge personal cost internally. I suffered a lot in anticipation. Big groups were the worst, but the anxiety snowballed to the point when even speaking before three to five people made me very anxious. As with many people, my anxiety was especially high around people in positions of power or authority. I was really suffering, and because the condition worsened over the years, I began to develop methods for overcoming it."

Word from the Wise: "Public speaking is one of most people's biggest fears, so you aren't alone with it. But I'm proof that you don't have to live with it for the rest of your life or let it keep you from saying and doing the things that are important to you. My anxiety no longer stands in my way because I walk my talk, practicing the methods that I teach. They work!"

Overcoming my fears around public speaking has given me the confidence to do things that never would have been possible when I was busy playing it safe.

—Janet Esposito

BADGE STEPS

LISTEN AND LEARN

Take a cue from great talkers

You can read and occasionally listen to recordings of great speeches throughout history, from Lincoln's Gettysburg Address and Susan B. Anthony's suffragist speeches to Martin Luther King Jr.'s classic "I Have a Dream." (See Janet's Picks, page 45.) But you can also listen and learn closer to home. Do you have a coworker whom you look forward to hearing when she speaks at department meetings? Why is that? Does she use humor to make her points? Is she great at making eye contact with everyone in the room? Is there a political pundit who always persuades you? What's her communication style? When you listen to talk radio, pay attention to how speakers present their arguments, their tone of voice, use of humor or anecdotes, and the mannerisms and expressions they use to emphasize points, preface their remarks, and illustrate an idea.

1. Face your fears.

Having a fear of public speaking is normal, but avoiding it at all costs only compounds the problem. The debilitating effects of not facing the issue can snowball into low self-esteem and feelings of helplessness. But if you face your fears, you'll soon discover that gaining comfort in this arena creates a liberating, empowering ripple effect in other areas of your life.

For some people, preparation, practice, and experience are enough to get them over initial jitters and build confidence. But for others of us, like Janet, repeatedly squeaking through speaking situations does not resolve the issue. This kind of person can "pull off" the situation, but they don't feel better for having done so. They're relieved that they've survived, but they are no more confident that the skies won't fall next time around. Think about where you fall on the anxiety scale, and explore what's holding you back:

Mild. Do you speak when you have to, but wish you didn't feel so nervous beforehand?

Moderate. Is there a cringe-inducing public speaking experience in your past you want to shake off, or a venue you've long wanted to speak up in but never tried?

Strong. Does your fear keep you from attending events, speaking in meetings, or even changing jobs?

Once you've acknowledged your level of anxiety, you can overcome it using the tools in the steps and sidebars in this badge. So with that in mind, go ahead and line up a speaking engagement for yourself in the near future, giving yourself at least four weeks to prepare. Maybe you have an upcoming professional speech or presentation to make or are planning to make a toast at a wedding, anniversary celebration, or retirement party. Or perhaps you've been wanting to speak up at a PTA, city council, or club meeting. Whatever platform you choose to speak your mind, make a date on your calendar to step up and be heard. ***No more hemming and hawing—plan your speaking engagement.***

2. Know your purpose.

Janet suggests that one of the best ways you can bust anxiety and boost your performance is to access your truest self, the part that isn't concerned with ego and image, reputation or credibility. Think about what you want to say, not how you'll be perceived saying it. Whether you want to convey your convictions to a crowd, express love or appreciation in a toast, or urge others to sit up and pay attention to an important issue, thinking about your purpose helps you get the focus off yourself—and your sweaty palms. ***Get in touch with your message.***

3. Draft your speech.

Now that you know your own purpose and have picked up some tips from the pros, it's time to begin committing your thoughts to paper. Here are a few hints to get you started:

- Begin with a personal story or experience. This connects you with your listeners and establishes your expertise in your subject.
- Integrate gentle, inoffensive humor to vary your tone and provide moments of respite if your topic is weighty.
- As you write, build in time for natural speaking pauses.
- Practice reading your words out loud. As you do, underline the words or phrases you want to emphasize, and note pauses for audience responses and shifts in the tone of your voice to anticipate a change in mood.
- End with a clear statement of what you'd like your listeners to do or think about.
- Tailor your speech to fit the time available. If no limit is stated, err on the side of brevity. Time yourself reading your script aloud with necessary pauses, then ruthlessly edit your words to fit the time available.

Script your own immortal words.

4. Practice speechifying.

Once you've refined your speech, audiotape and/or videotape yourself giving your talk. What you see and hear will help you tweak and finesse the content and delivery of your speech.

While preparing for your upcoming speaking engagement, build your confidence and experience by speaking up in situations in which you would normally hesitate. For example, you might raise your hand to speak at a department meeting, ask questions in group settings, make a cold call, or send a bad meal back. As you practice, remember that you can't control everything, and shouldn't attempt to, either. Things may

TOAST TIPS

Here's to you!

- You really can't go wrong with short, sweet, and sincere.
- Make it personal rather than generic—but not too personal. Don't tell anecdotes that might embarrass the person you're toasting or reveal shared secrets or confidences.
- If you can't think of a darn thing to say, share a brief quotation by a great thinker.
- Resist the urge to apologize at the outset for being a lousy public speaker or for being nervous—you'll just invite closer scrutiny.

PEP TALKS

Psych yourself up

Janet stresses that it's crucial that we support ourselves with encouraging self-talk. You don't have to pull a Muhammad Ali and tell the world you're the greatest, but you can:

- Applaud yourself for taking this opportunity to speak up and be heard.
- Visualize your success.
- Silence the voice of doubt in your head. Any thoughts that begin "But what if . . . " are pure speculation and should be promptly ignored.
- Recall the encouraging words of a friend, colleague, or parent.
- Adopt an "I can do this!" attitude in all areas of your life—and notice how effective you become.

I DID IT!

"I volunteer with a numbr of issue-oriented organizations, and I've learned that while it's relatively easy to find people who are willing to write letters or hand out flyers or even attend marches and rallies, it can be extremely difficult to find folks who are willing and able to stand up at a city council meeting or make a speech. I wind up doing this quite a bit, and while I always get nervous beforehand, I also find it very rewarding. I've come to enjoy not just speaking up but also figuring out how to be persuasive. And it never fails: After I speak, someone invariably comes and tells me that they are glad I did—that I said what they didn't have the nerve to. That feels fantastic!"
—Patricia

VOICE-OVER?

"I wrote an essay in a writing workshop and the teacher encouraged me to send it to the local radio station, which plays three-minute pieces like the one I'd written. My essay was accepted and I had to go into the station to record it with an engineer. Yikes! Being in front of a microphone and all the knobs in the studio was intimidating, as was reading the thing to the engineer—a total stranger. Plus, I really hadn't paid much attention to how I'd read the essay, to emphasize the dramatic or funny moments. When I heard myself on the radio a few days later, I cringed. I really could have used a lot more practice and familiarity with the forum. Next time!"
—Bernadette

not go as planned, and you will have to stay flexible and gracious enough to handle unexpected interruptions, rapid-fire questions, or unanticipated reactions. Ask a friend to throw a few of these curveballs at you during your speech, so that you have practice dealing with them. Do your homework, but prepare to be flexible—not perfect. ***Prepare yourself.***

JANET'S EXPERT TIPS

EMBRACE THE SPOTLIGHT

Breathe. Slow, deep breathing has physiological as well as psychological effects. Consciously slowing the pace of our breathing helps our thoughts stop racing and regulates our heart rate. And focusing on something we can control, like our breathing rate, helps us feel less out of control in the situation. Janet suggests you simply work on being conscious of your breath and on slowing it down during every step of your preparation and practice.

Pause. While speaking, don't forget to pause. Accelerating your pace—usually to get the experience over with as soon as possible!—only fuels anxiety. "If you are carrying notes, write yourself reminders to 'pause and breathe' or 'slow it down,'" Janet says.

Ground yourself. When we're anxious or feel we're being watched, we can feel very alone, adrift, and disconnected. Counter this by feeling your feet planted firmly on the ground as you stand and speak or sit waiting for your turn. Feel supported by the ground. You can even visualize yourself as a sturdy oak tree with deep roots in the earth. You are solid and steady!

Stay in the here and now. Janet's grounding and breathing techniques serve another important purpose: They keep you in the present moment. "This is a very important part of managing anxiety," emphasizes Janet. "Most anxiety lives in the future and the past. We think about situations in which we were terribly uncomfortable, thus dragging those feelings into the present. Or we obsess about dire what-ifs in the future." Another way to stay present is to observe your surroundings, making yourself comfortable in this setting as you get familiar with it.

5. Be kind to yourself.

When we have everyone's attention, many of us tend to blush, our hands or knees shake, or our voice quavers. These responses may leave you feeling momentarily awkward, but remember: This too shall pass, and you don't have to let these perfectly natural reactions get to you. As Janet explains, "Our normal response to these physical symptoms—which are really a fight-or-flight response to our perceived threat in the situation—is to tense up further. We resist and try to control what our bodies are doing because it's so uncomfortable—and embarrassing."

The more we panic or resist the feelings, she says, the more power we give them. Instead, we need to acknowledge that we are feeling this way and accept it: "It's counterintuitive to accept something we don't like, but when we allow and accept, we relax. And, when the body begins to relax, the mind will follow."

Janet also reminds her clients to pace themselves and be kind to their bodies as they prepare to speak. You don't want to stay up half the night cramming in preparation, or "self-medicate" with big doses of sugar, caffeine, or alcohol. Make time for your favorite exercise, do a little extra stretching, or get a massage. And while it doesn't help to obsess about appearance, there's nothing wrong with wanting to look and feel your best. Wear something that makes you feel comfortable and confident. ***Relax, already—it's just a speech!***

6. Rise and shine.

Stand and deliver—and as you do, remember that if you never venture out of your comfort zone, you can't grow. As Janet says, "Nothing new is going to happen in the comfort zone. You don't want to shoot way beyond what's comfortable for you—that only sets you up for failure. After all, if you don't know how to swim, you don't dive into the deep end . . . but you do have to go into the water." So even if you feel fear, do it anyway! Once that initial flutter passes and your voice steadies, you'll find you get a charge of confidence. Feels good, doesn't it? ***Bask in the spotlight—you've earned it!***

CONGRATULATIONS!

Speech! Speech! Everyone wants to hear what you've got to say. Give yourself a round of applause. You did it!

I DID IT!

Name: ______________________________

Date: ______________________________

MOVIE MOMENTS

Great examples of cinematic oratory

- Sally Field speaking her mind about workplace conditions in *Norma Rae.*
- Jack Nicholson's "You can't handle the truth!" testimony in *A Few Good Men.*
- Katharine Hepburn redefining repartee in *The Philadelphia Story.*
- Gregory Peck's irrefutable closing argument in *To Kill a Mockingbird.*
- Renée Zellweger swaying the jury and public opinion in *Chicago.*
- Samuel L. Jackson's hair-raising "God's fury" speech in *Pulp Fiction.*
- Laura Linney's chilling rationalization for murder in *Mystic River.*
- Ewan McGregor's "Choose life" monologue in *Trainspotting.*
- Susan Sarandon helping a condemned man find peace in *Dead Man Walking.*
- Richard E. Grant's hilarious take on Hamlet in *Withnail and I.*
- Drew Barrymore learning to "Just breathe" and speak truth to power in *Ever After.*
- Kevin Spacey's riveting opening speech in *American Beauty.*
- Lauren Bacall coaching Bogie on whistling in *To Have and Have Not.*
- And last but not least, Halle Berry's unforgettable 2002 Oscar acceptance speech.

BEYOND THE BADGE

If you love it as much as you thought you would, dream on . . .

- **Be a Toastmaster.** Established in 1924, Toastmasters helps individuals deal with their public speaking anxiety and get comfortable giving speeches in a multitude of contexts. Built around local Toastmasters clubs, members meet regularly to practice giving both impromptu and prepared speeches, and then spend time evaluating each other's performances, as well as discussing general and specific tips to becoming an experienced and stellar public speaker. Go to their Web site (www.toastmasters.org) for more information about the organization and finding a club near you.
- **Get media-savvy.** If you're really serious about refining and rounding out your speaking skills, or are preparing for a press blitz, you might try a course in media training. Not only do media training courses teach you to be calm and cool while giving an interview, speech, or press conference, but they can also teach you how to attract the press in the first place (and how to deflect the kind of press you don't want), speak well on camera and the radio, handle negative and unexpected situations, take control of your public image, and create "power messages" to get your point across. See Face the Press for some available media training programs.
- **Speak up for your beliefs.** Many of the causes and organizations you believe in have lots of people who are willing to stuff envelopes or write letters, but they lack volunteers who are ready, willing, and able to spread their message through public speaking. Your skills can be put to work at local government meetings, lobbying political representatives, or reaching out to the public on the radio. Volunteer your now-polished vocal skills.

FACE THE PRESS

With the help of media training

Experience Media Consulting Group. Hands-on, experiential approach to media and presentation training. www.experiencemediaconsult.com or 323-465-5412.

Media Training Worldwide. Fifty-four separate courses in media and presentation training, and over one hundred media and presentation training books, CDs, and DVDs. www.mediatrainingworldwide.com or 212-764-4955.

MediaWorks. Billed as "modern media training," MediaWorks focuses on real-world-based strategies for dealing with interviews, press conferences, crisis management, and presentations. www.mediaworksgroup.com or 310-209-8384.

The Pincus Group. Offers courses in media training, presentation skill training, speech training, and crisis training. www.thepincusgroup.com.

JANET'S PICKS

BOOKS

Coping with Anxiety: 10 Simple Ways to Relieve Anxiety, Fear, and Worry by Edmund Bourne, PhD, and Lorna Garano
A general book about coping with anxiety through ten steps the reader can do in the moment. Tips include "thinking realistically" and "taking constructive coping actions."

Feel the Fear and Do It Anyway by Susan Jeffers, PhD
Jeffers discusses the crippling effect of fear in her personal life and explains how she created a course of action to conquer it. Includes case studies about careers and changes in personal life.

In the SpotLight: Overcome Your Fear of Public Speaking and Performing by Janet E. Esposito, MSW
Our expert's book provides methods and strategies for getting beyond stage fright and giving speeches, toasts, and presentations with ease.

No More Butterflies: Overcoming Stagefright, Shyness, Interview Anxiety and Fear of Public Speaking by Peter Desberg, PhD
A guide to overcoming public speaking jitters though a "presentation inventory"—helping readers to pinpoint their anxieties and work through them.

Overcoming Your Fear of Public Speaking: A Proven Method by Michael Motley
Focuses on speeches as communication tasks rather than performances, and offers advice on speech content and techniques for effective delivery.

The Portable Relaxer by Matthew McKay and Patrick Fanning
Simple exercises to reduce stress in the moment.

WEB SITES

www.bartleby.com
A huge reference site that allows you to search by keyword for great quotes and literary references for your next speech or toast.

www.mhhe.com/socscience/comm/pubspeak
McGraw-Hill's public speaking site has lots of free articles, tips, and advice.

www.performanceanxiety.com
Our expert's Web site, with Janet's top ten tips for handling stage fright and links galore.

www.public-speaking.org
The site provides more than one hundred articles on topics such as "genius tricks and gimmicks," "storytelling techniques," and "openings."

www.toastmasters.org
Find Toastmasters clubs near you.

www.ukans.edu/cwis/units/coms2/vpa/vpa.htm
This site, from the Communications Studies Department at the University of Kansas, takes you through the many steps in planning and making a presentation.

SPEECHES

Great American Speeches by Gregory R. Suriano (editor)

Great Speeches of the 20th Century (Audio CD)

The Greatest Speeches of All Time (Audio CD)

In Search of Freedom: Excerpts from His Most Memorable Speeches by Martin Luther King Jr. (Audio CD)

Lend Me Your Ears: Great Speeches in History by William Safire (editor)

Words That Shook the World: 100 Years of Unforgettable Speeches and Events by Richard Greene and Florie Brizel

World's Great Speeches by Lewis Copeland, Lawrence W. Lamm, and Stephen J. McKenna (editors)

www.historychannel.com/speeches
Another useful resource on speeches that made history.

www.pbs.org/greatspeeches/timeline/index.html
Who said what when? Find out with this Web resource.

7

CHAMPION A CAUSE

★ activism ★

You must BE the change you wish to see in the world.

—Mohandas K. Gandhi

Imagine This . . . You don't get riled up by what you see in the news—you get organized and start making your own headlines. A couple of phone calls to your phone tree later, and your volunteer network swings into action. Plans are made, a public awareness campaign kicks off, funds are raised, and lo and behold, lives are changed. Whether your immediate concern is Amazon rain forests or an HIV-positive family member, you don't stay up nights wondering what you can possibly do. Instead you awake each day inspired, full of ideas to make the world a place you can feel proud to call home. Maybe one day you'll concede that your place really is in the house—the House of Representatives, that is! *You can do it!*

So, what's your motivation?
Take a moment.
Dream a little, think big,
and then complete this sentence:
I see myself . . .

The Payoffs

- **Camaraderie.** Nothing bonds people together like a common cause. The people you meet at a city council meeting or at a casual café meeting you organize might be kindred spirits or lifelong friends, even (or maybe especially) if you don't always agree.
- **A better home.** Sometimes the world can seem like a real fixer-upper—but be it ever so humble, this is our home. Luckily, we all have the ability to make it a more warm and welcoming place to live.
- **A clear conscience.** "I'd like to give them a piece of my mind . . . " you mutter as you watch politicians make and break promises. So go ahead! With the support of others and personal strength you've discovered, you'll get your concerns off your conscience—and possibly into legislation.
- **Your true potential.** As Mother Teresa once said, "We can do no great things, only small things with great love." Every time your heart goes out to others, it grows.

Meet Your Mentor

JULIE SHAH

What She Does: Julie is a board member and former codirector of the Third Wave Foundation, an organization that shares a wealth of ideas and grants among young women activists nationwide. Known as a social innovator for her work with Jumpstart for Young Children, The Bank of New York's philanthropic division, W.E.R.I.S.E, Sakhi for South Asian Women, and AmeriCorps, Julie is now pursuing a new outlet for her activism: her first feature film, titled *AGIRLSGOTTADOWHATAGIRLSGOTTADO.*

Why She Does It: "My activism really started around the dinner table. I was raised in a mixed family in a predominantly white area in Oregon—my mother is Greek by heritage and my father is Indian—and we were always encouraged to discuss cultural differences and the lack of women's voices heard in our society. My first organized activist effort was in high school protesting against the first Gulf War, and it just grew from there. There was never just one issue that mattered to me, because it's all so interrelated, but in my first job at AmeriCorps in Seattle, I found that small, focused community efforts can have a really broad impact. Eventually I went on to get my masters in political science from NYU, and was lucky enough to get on board with Third Wave. Three years later, it's inspirational to see that projects we supported then are still around now—and many of those women have started initiatives of their own to support other women. Once you put even a small change in motion, there's no telling where the ripple effect will end!"

Activism provides a voice for people who wouldn't be heard otherwise.

—Julie Shah

Word from the Wise: "It's great to volunteer for underprivileged youth once a week, but it's just ironic if you leave those caring instincts behind in your daily life. If you can establish an understanding with teenagers behind the café counter or down the street regardless of religious belief or language barriers, that's a powerful political act."

BADGE STEPS

1. Ask questions.

As Julie says, it doesn't take superhuman powers to change the course of history—all it takes is a little healthy curiosity. "We all have so much to do that we walk right by problems every day," she says. "Maybe those workers are protesting outside your favorite restaurant because management decided to stop giving them health insurance—and probably as a loyal customer, you could do something about it. Start asking questions."

Pay close attention to the world around you for a week, and when you see something that puzzles you or doesn't seem quite right, give yourself pause to wonder. When is that rickety slide at the playground going to get fixed? Why are elderly people losing basic medical benefits? And why don't politicians pay attention to these things? Start asking around, and see if you can get some answers. ***Raise questions about what you see happening around you.***

WHAT'S WRONG WITH THIS PICTURE?

Now that's creative accounting . . .

In 1985, a group of women noticed that out of the 169 artists in the Museum of Modern Art's International Survey of Painting and Sculpture, only thirteen were women. This seemed shocking enough—but when they looked into the number of female artists featured in New York museums and galleries, they discovered this tiny percentage was not at all unusual. Instead of getting angry, they got gorilla masks and wore them while putting up posters all over New York listing the many art institutions that routinely featured fewer than 10 percent female artists. Their creative intervention prompted a major show of one hundred female artists to be organized, and the Guerrilla Girls have served as "The Conscience of the Art World" ever since, making sure that female artists and artists of color aren't left out of the picture. For information and inspiration see www.guerrillagirls.com.

2. Become a super sleuth.

If one particular line of questioning leads you to dead-end answers like "I don't know" or "That's just the way it's always been," start digging deeper into the subject. You never know where your investigation might take you. Here's how to start sleuthing:

Check out independent media sources. Most independent media outlets stake their reputations on in-depth coverage of local and international concerns that aren't covered so thoroughly in mainstream media. Look for independent perspectives in the media sources listed in Julie's Picks, page 53, and in free weeklies and the op-ed section of your local paper.

Hit the books. This doesn't mean you need to sign up for a class, as Julie explains: "I never took a women's studies class in college but instead learned a lot just by picking up books that intrigued me."

Look up related nonprofits. Seek out nonprofits that share your concerns by checking out Julie's Picks and using the Yellow Pages or an online search engine, limiting the responses to sites with addresses that end in .org (this designates a nonprofit).

Attend an event. Scan event listings in your paper, community bulletin boards, and online, and attend at least one event on the subject you're investigating.

Investigate an issue.

3. Rewrite a headline.

As you investigate your subject, you'll come across some stories and statistics that surprise, shock, or even scare the tar out of you. Pick out one that you think is especially troubling, and imagine an alternative headline you'd like to see on your chosen subject, such as: "New Wonder Drug for Alzheimer's Identified," "Women Now Earning as Much as Men in Most Fields," "Peace Declared in Middle East," "Music Program Back up and Running at Local School." Got it? Good—now your challenge is to make that vision real! ***Imagine the difference you can make.***

4. Share your thoughts.

Get the people power to make that vision of yours real by organizing a brainstorming meeting at a local café or community center. First, come up with a pitch that's simple and direct, such as: "What can we do to help earthquake victims overseas? Bring your ideas on [date and time] to [place], or contact [first name] at [e-mail or work phone]." That surprising statistic you've discovered might capture the attention of people new to the issue, so include it in your pitch too: "[X number] people in our sister city of [XXX] in [country] are having to rebuild their lives and homes from the ground up—and your help can make all the difference!"

To advertise your interests and ensure a good turnout at your brainstorming session:

Post flyers. Make a flyer and post it on community bulletin boards at cafés, the library, community centers, and other local haunts.

Reach out personally to those affected. "If a local paint plant is putting out toxins, consult with those who live closest to it," explains Julie. "Their personal insights and concerns will be your guide to make things better." In this case, you might reach people affected by pollution by visiting community centers, clinics, and hospitals where people come for toxin exposure treatment and posting meeting fliers on bulletin boards there.

Post personal ads. In rural areas, personal ads in local papers are a good way to rally people around a common concern. "When people live far apart, it's easy to start feeling like you're the only one who cares," Julie notes. "Getting people together can feel like a triumph in itself, because it makes everyone feel less isolated and fearful."

Take your concerns online. When you find an online forum where people share your concerns, join it so you can post your opinions, and

BEYOND BAKE SALES

Use group skills to put the fun back in fundraising!

- Make a quilt that expresses your shared hope for the world, and raffle it off at an appropriate charity event.
- Host a "Family Heritage" booth at a local street fair, and offer to help create family history albums in exchange for a nominal donation to an appropriate nonprofit.
- Plan a progressive dinner party with a sliding scale donation to raise funds and awareness. Julie suggests that you invite someone personally affected by the issue to make a short but meaningful slide-show presentation.
- If there are many varied skills represented in the group, plan a block party with booths where each person can put their skills to use for fundraising purposes. The amateur palm-reader can tell fortunes, the professional career counselor can tweak resumes, and the Italian speaker can pen love letters in Italian for would-be Romeos and Juliets.

I DID IT!

"I don't know how it happened, but I got nominated to head up a student-faculty committee in grad school. Basically I was supposed to be a figurehead and just sit in some room while a bunch of economics professors went through the motions of planning departmental events while they were rifling through their mail. So nobody was really paying much attention when I suggested that we invite a dissenting opinion on the subject of globalization at an upcoming academic symposium. Were they ever surprised when the dry academic panel turned into a hot debate, with the World Bank representative and free trade advocates on the panel facing an onslaught of pointed questions about debt relief for developing countries. It got me pegged as a bit of a troublemaker, but at least it shook everyone out of the usual thinking on the subject—and that day, I stopped being just a figurehead."

—Sahai

SUDDENLY SPEECHLESS

"I had an opportunity to meet a major international leader, and I was determined to use the opportunity to press him to do more to stop the AIDS crisis in South Africa. But I hadn't counted on my boss—who arranged the meeting—standing next to me, and I hadn't written anything down. When it was my turn to shake his hand and say my piece, I choked and mumbled something. To this day, I still regret not making better use of that opportunity. Okay, so it probably wouldn't have been the turning point in the epidemic, but at least I would know I'd done my best."

—Sally

invite local members to your brainstorming meeting. ***Start something big by convening a small group of people.***

JULIE'S EXPERT TIPS

DRIVE-THRU SERVICE

During the summers between 2000 and 2002, Third Wave roamed the country on its Reaching Out Across MovementS (ROAMS) tour, seeking fresh ideas for grassroots change and connecting like-minded organizations. Follow their cue, and make a few worthwhile detours of your own on your next road trip:

- Plot a route, leaving enough time for a few pit stops along the way.
- Look up local nonprofits in the places you'll be driving through. Check Julie's Picks, page 53, run an online search, or check the local Yellow Pages.
- Call or e-mail the organization and introduce yourself as an activist eager to learn more about their organization, and volunteer your skills for as long as you can spare.
- Extend an invitation to lunch. If they're too busy to bring a volunteer up to speed, ask if they'd be willing to let you take them out for lunch (your treat) to compare notes and brainstorm a few activism ideas—that way, you can sample local cuisine and local insights at the same time.

5. Come up with a plan of action.

At your brainstorming session, identify one thing you can do together to make a difference. This doesn't have to be the usual letter-writing campaign to elected officials, although that could be part of your plan. "Think creatively!" urges Julie. "Art auctions, music performances, and poetry slams are all great ways to express your concerns, educate people about issues, and raise funds for nonprofits that address them." To kick off your brainstorming session, try this exercise:

1. Ask people around the table to name one skill they each have and one favorite pastime.
2. Come up with a plan of action that best captures the skills and interests of group members (see Beyond Bake Sales, page 49, for ideas).
3. Ask everyone if they know of any nonprofits that do good work in your area of shared concern, and ask for volunteers to investigate the top three nonprofits named. That way, you can find out more about what they're doing, how you can best contribute, and where funds you raise might be the most useful.

4. Ask if anyone has resources they might be able to lend to make the plan a reality—a photocopier for flyers, a big backyard for an event, a table for a booth, etc.
5. Ask everyone to think of at least two people they could recruit to help implement the plan.
6. Decide on a date and time to hold your next meeting to put the plan into action.

Hatch your plan.

6. Show your support.

The details of your group's plan are coming together, and the moment of truth is near. Before your big event, be sure to:

- Check in with your fellow group members to be sure everyone is still on board. If someone has to pull out at the last minute, ask if they can recruit or recommend someone to take their place—a commitment is a commitment!
- Gather your resources. Make sure the group has everything you need so that your plan goes off without a hitch.
- Put your money where your mouth is. Before you ask anyone else for donations, pull out your pocketbook and write a generous check yourself. This will give you both personal satisfaction and the strength of personal conviction when you ask people to dig deep and give big.

One more thing: On your way out the door to put the final step of your plan into action, take a good look in the mirror. That's not just your average everyday citizen who votes when she can, keeps her head down, and hopes for the best—she's a mover and a shaker. ***Get out there and make some history!***

CONGRATULATIONS!

Thanks to you, this planet is a nicer place to be. You did it!

I DID IT!

Name: ______________________________

Date: ______________________________

GIVE UNTIL IT DOESN'T HURT

Make an investment in your future—and the world's

Is there a problem you find so personally heartbreaking that you're determined to see it solved in your lifetime, such as a military conflict, breast cancer, or landmines? Include nonprofit organizations that address these issues in your own annual giving plan, and organize a fundraiser at your workplace and/or in your neighborhood. "Giving money is an essential form of activism," says Julie. "If you can give even ten dollars every month to an organization you care about, that's a base of support they need to implement important programs." To make giving a lifelong habit and a valuable legacy, see Give Your Money Away, page 378.

BEYOND THE BADGE

If you love it as much as you thought you would, dream on . . .

- **Launch a movement.** What's the difference between your ideal world and the world as it currently stands? A passionate, experienced leader—hey, that's you! "Everyone has a voice," says Julie. "Keep speaking up until someone hears you, and you become the leader you were meant to be." Let your elected representatives in on your ideas and concerns with letters, calls, and e-mails—and if you don't get a satisfactory response, organize a group of people to head on down to city hall, the state capitol, or Congress and demand one.
- **Take it to the streets.** No matter how full your schedule is, there's time enough to make a difference. Here's what you can do with:

  A free evening. If there's a candidate for office you feel strongly about, volunteer with that candidate's election campaign. You can make phone calls, go door to door to get out the vote, hand out signs for residents and businesses to display in windows, or help out at a fundraiser.

  A nice day. Attend a rally nearby on an issue that concerns you in the morning, and volunteer to help out in the afternoon at a voter registration booth or a related petition drive.

  A long weekend. Pay a visit to your elected officials in the state capitol—or if you have a frequent flier coupon burning a hole in your pocket, drop in on your senators and representatives in Washington.

  A week or two. Go global with your concerns, and pursue them overseas (see Think Globally).
- **Start a nonprofit.** If there is no nonprofit that does exactly what you think sorely needs doing, maybe it's time you founded your own. Julie cautions that it can be a tedious process to apply for your official federal 501(c)(3) status as a nonprofit, which allows you to provide a tax exemption to donors and qualify for most grants. Instead, she recommends seeking a fiscal sponsor, a nonprofit that is willing to take you on as a pet project and allow you to raise funds using their good name and accounting staff. Julie explains, "Be sure to find an issue you care deeply about, involve the people directly affected by that issue who can keep everyone focused on the organization's reason for being, and find other organizations who connect to the issue."

THINK GLOBALLY

And act globally by taking a trip abroad

Attend an international conference. Most international conferences (including the UN-sponsored Women's Conference) allow nonprofit delegations to observe or even participate in the proceedings, so see if you can join or tag along with a local nonprofit group (paying your own way, of course).

Take a fact-finding tour. To get firsthand insight on the international affairs that affect our lives so personally today, join a fact-finding tour. Global Exchange offers Reality Tours to meet with leaders and activists and discuss local issues in several countries, including Argentina, Cuba, Haiti, India, Iran, Ireland, Mexico, and South Africa (see www.globalexchange.org/tours).

Work it on out. The American Friends Service Committee, the Nobel Peace Prize–winning Quaker organization, offers volunteers a chance to gain personal understanding of international issues while providing much-needed assistance to communities in Hunan, China, the Sierra Madre mountains in Mexico, and Namibia, among others. Commitments range from one week to a year—find out more at www.afsc.org/volunteering.

JULIE'S PICKS

BOOKS

The Karma of Brown Folk by Vijay Prashad

One hundred years after W. E. B. DuBois explored how it felt to be typecast by skin color in *The Souls of Black Folk,* Prashad examines how it feels for South Asians in America trapped by the "model minority" myth.

Killing the Black Body: Race, Reproduction, and the Meaning of Liberty by Dorothy Roberts

Northwestern University law professor Roberts recounts the history of African-American women's struggles to gain autonomy over their lives and reproductive choices.

MoveOn's 50 Ways to Love Your Country: How to Find Your Political Voice and Become a Catalyst for Change by moveon.org

A handbook on civic action by the flourishing online grassroots group.

Nickel and Dimed: On (Not) Getting By in America by Barbara Ehrenreich

Ever wonder how people get by on minimum wage? So did Ehrenreich, political commentator for *The Nation* and *Time*—so she took jobs as a cleaning woman, nursing home assistant, and Wal-Mart cashier, and captured it all in this breakthrough book.

No More Prisons by William Upski Wimsatt

The *Utne Reader* culture commentator brings caustic humor and hip-hop flair to observations on gated communities, home-schooling, and security systems, plus inspiring interviews with activists and politicos.

MEDIA SOURCES

Clamor Magazine
www.clamormagazine.org

Thoughtful perspectives from independent-minded commentators on politics, media, culture, and life as we live it.

Independent Media Center
www.indymedia.org

Offers independent media coverage for major metropolitan centers nationwide and Canada and Europe. Check listings for upcoming grassroots events.

MoveOn
www.moveon.org

The enormously successful activist group provides opportunities to get involved in local and national movements for change.

ORGANIZATIONS

Local Community Foundations

"Most major cities support community foundations that give grants to many amazing local nonprofits," explains Julie. "Find a community foundation near you, online or in the phone book, and take a look at who they fund."

Ms. Foundation
www.ms.foundation.org

This organization founded the Take Our Daughters to Work Day and supports the efforts of women and girls nationwide to govern our own lives and shape the world we live in.

National Gay & Lesbian Task Force
www.ngltf.org

Get the latest news on civil rights for women of all sexual orientations, read up on pending legislation on your area, and find out about events you can attend.

National Organization for Women
www.now.org

The nation's largest women's advocacy organization.

Planned Parenthood
www.plannedparenthood.org

Planned Parenthood provides women's healthcare and advances reproductive choices, but they're also involved in youth work and HIV/AIDS at a local level and international women's issues.

Third Wave Foundation
www.thirdwavefoundation.org

Provides funds, connections, and ideas to young female activists nationwide striving to overcome barriers due to gender, age, race, sexual orientation, or economic status.

8

ROCK OUT!

★ starting a rock band ★

Don't forget who you are, you're a rock-and-roll STAR!

—The Byrds

So, what's your motivation?
Take a moment.
Dream a little, think big,
and then complete this sentence:
I see myself . . .

Imagine This . . . The place is packed, the fans are screaming your name, and the amps are cranked to eleven. You grab the microphone, pick up your sticks, plug in your Fender, or take up the bass: "Hello Cleveland, are you ready to rock?!" Of course you are! Because, like Chrissie Hynde before you, you've plugged in and seen the amplified light. Whether you're in a hard-rock, alt-country, punk, or '80s cover band, you're living the dream. A crazy fantasy? Not at all. You may be rusty when you pick up your instrument—but hey, all you need to know is a few chords, and this badge will get you through the rest. There's a new girl on the rock block. *You can do it!*

The Payoffs

- **Instant gratification.** No other musical medium is as welcoming of the technically unskilled! In rock, the right attitude is more important than chops.
- **Stamina.** Rockers used to want to die before they got old, but when they didn't, they just kept on rockin'. Think Patti Smith and you'll think twice about retirement.
- **Influence.** Rock the Vote. Rock for Choice. Protest à la Ani DiFranco. And give little girls with Walkmans the role model they deserve.
- **Release.** The most buttoned-down amongst us sometimes wonder what power chords feel like.

Meet Your Mentor
STEPHANIE FINCH

What She Does: Sings, plays a variety of instruments, and writes songs in her band, Go-Go Market, which she formed in 1999; has done the same in her husband Chuck Prophet's band since 1990; tours and records with both bands; and teaches kids how to read and write when not on the road.

Why She Does It: "My first instrument was piano, and I was always singing somewhere or other, in church or school. I'm still learning to play the guitar. The first concert I went to was Fleetwood Mac, and I noticed that it was men and women in a band together. I wanted to be Stevie Nicks! I just kind of dreamed about it, singing in front of the mirror and such. I sang in public for real the first time with a girlfriend. We had a kind of folk duo and played around in Los Angeles. They were odd gigs because my friend was a bit of a movie star, Mare Winningham. We'd play and there'd be Michelle Pfeiffer or Rosanna Arquette or the entire Brat Pack in the audience. Then I actually fantasized about playing in a band with Chuck Prophet! I'd seen him play with his band, Green on Red, and had met him briefly, but mainly I think I was influenced by Richard and Linda Thompson, and Gram Parsons and Emmylou Harris. I had a feeling that Chuck and I could do something like that. It wasn't until I moved to San Francisco, though, that I felt I could really get started with my own thing."

Word from the Wise: "I think about packing it in and leading a more 'normal' life just about every day! But good things just keep coming up. If you stick with it and give it your all, they do. At this point, I've made sacrifices for my music and I'm invested in making it work. Making my own record made the pursuit seem all the more legitimate. Performing and making records is great fun. But it's also work that you have to choose over and over."

When I was a kid listening to records and going to concerts, I always knew I didn't just want to watch or listen; I WANTED TO DO IT.

—Stephanie Finch

BADGE STEPS

ROCK HERSTORY

Did you know?

Big Mama Thornton had a hit with "Hound Dog" three years before Elvis did.

The Go-Go's were the first all-gal band to top the album charts (with *Beauty and the Beat*).

Janis Joplin was banned from performing in Houston "for her attitude."

Chrissie Hynde's first musical instrument was the ukulele.

Kurt Cobain said, "the future of rock belongs to women."

1. Suss out the scene.

Maybe it's been a while since you played keyboards, or you first picked up drumsticks a year ago. Don't worry about perfection; many a band has been launched with little more than chutzpah and style. So:

Make like a teenager. Spend a few hours in your bedroom with the door locked and the headphones on! Think about the bands you love and why you love 'em. What will you do differently? What will make you unique?

Make yourself at home. Go to the places where live music is played, and talk to the people who are doing what you like.

Make friends. Chat with the folks at record shops and instrument stores—many of them are musicians as well. Look at the bulletin boards there, and read the entertainment and Musicians Wanted ads in the local papers. These are all ways to connect with the people you might want to play with and with the people who can clue you into rehearsal spaces, great new music, equipment for sale, opportunities to play live, etc. And these are the people you hope to one day have in your audience!

Take these steps to make yourself and your interests known:

- Go to at least five live shows.
- Pick out one local band to follow.
- Chat up at least three people at shows, record stores, or instrument shops.

Become a fixture on the local music scene.

2. Find some band mates.

It's easier than it sounds—really!

Join a band. If you'd like to step into a ready-made band, find a band that's hiring on record-store bulletin boards, in classified listings, or through a community Web site. Go to the audition with a prepared song.

Start a band. If you're a gal with a vision and want to found your own band, post an ad yourself and set up auditions. Stephanie placed an ad for a drummer in a local free weekly paper when putting Go-Go Market together. "We found a great female drummer that way and it was kind of fun getting all the calls. But be prepared for some characters. I didn't put my real name in the ad because you want to be able to hide from odd-balls if you need to!"

Talk it up. Talk to people everywhere you go about what you are trying to do—Stephanie met another musician in her band at a friend's wedding.

Once you've got your lineup lined up, you're ready to make beautiful music together—with a little practice. ***Schedule your first session.***

3. Rehearse.

Are you performing your own compositions, covers, or a mix of the two? Set a song list or agenda for each practice session.

Chances are you'll be paying for the space you rehearse in—unless you live a mile from your neighbors and have a big garage or basement—so you really don't want to waste the time you're paying for. You can find rehearsal spaces listed in the classifieds or phone book, but this is another time when your personal contacts can come in handy. Look for space you can share with one or more other bands to minimize costs.

Once you've got your song list and your practice space, rehearse twice a week until you have a kick-butt thirty-minute set you can play in your sleep. ***Rock nonstop.***

4. Record.

Now that you have that thirty-minute set, record it so that you can demonstrate your stuff to club bookers, radio stations, and perhaps even record companies.

The tape, or more likely CD, should showcase your best songs and live performance potential. Anyone with basic recording equipment can help you with this, or you can rent or borrow simple two- or four-track equipment. Ask fellow musicians how they made their demo tapes or what local studios offer these services. Don't worry about spending a lot of money on this recording. A tape of songs she recorded in her bedroom scored Liz Phair a record deal (a similar thing happened to Elvis Costello, too). If you want to do fancy remixing, ask a friend with a serious desktop setup for music production to help out or consider going to a professional studio.

Once you've got a master you like, burn fifty copies on CD—and don't give them all away to friends! You'll need some for the next step. ***Lay down some tracks.***

TALK TO MY MANAGER

If you want someone else to take care of business . . .

When you're just starting out, you don't need and probably won't have access to a high-powered manager or booking agent, but you can still get help. A friend or fan can become part of your team and act as your manager in the early days. They'll deserve a percentage of any monies you earn from a gig they secure for you (15 percent). It's ideal to find someone who really loves your music, believes in you as much as you do, and is willing to put in time and effort even when very little money is involved. Someone like this can become an indispensable, though nonperforming, part of the band. One advantage to not being your own booker/agent/manager is that you have a buffer between you, the artiste, and the inevitable rejections that will come your way.

I DID IT!

"I've always been comfortable being a 'sideman' in Chuck's band, just getting the spotlight a couple of times a night, but being the frontperson is completely different. Go-Go Market gigs have showed me I can do it."
—Stephanie

STAGE FRIGHT

"When I was twenty-five, a few of my girlfriends and I decided to form an all-girl band, with me on drums. I just sat down and started trying to channel Led Zeppelin's John Bonham. It was great fun and we even had a perfect name, the SugarBeats. But when we got an offer to play at a local club, I totally froze at the idea. I wish I'd stuck with it. We coulda been contenders—or at least the Bangles!"
—Yvette

STEPHANIE'S EXPERT TIPS

TOO COOL FOR SCHOOL?

- Rock 'n' Roll Fantasy Camp promises that "over the course of five days, you will become immersed in the world of rock, jamming, practicing, learning, and playing in a band." It features small group instruction with celebrities like Roger Daltrey, a chance to record and bring home a music demo and video, and seminars with industry executives. New York City. 800-252-3540 or www.rockandrollfantasycamp.com.
- Rock 'n' Roll Camp for Girls. Okay, you are probably too old for this—but you can send your daughter! This day camp for girls ages eight to eighteen in Portland, Oregon, teaches the basics of creating and playing rock on your instrument of choice. All-gal groups like Sleater-Kinney have been known to teach there. www.girlsrockcamp.org.
- Songwriting classes, workshops, and weekends are often offered through instrument stores or at local music or community schools. Do an online search or ask around your music community. Plenty of top-notch musicians augment their performing and recording careers by teaching such classes when they aren't on the road. Look for a class taught by someone with this kind of real-world experience.

5. Promote.

You have your own CD—great! Now you need to pull together a promotional package to show those music industry types you mean business.

Create some cool cover art for that CD sleeve. Some musicians like Peggy Honeywell (a.k.a. the painter Clare Rojas) actually do their own cover art, but those of us who aren't so creatively ambidextrous can always ask an artist, illustrator, or cartoonist friend to help out.

Take a photo of the band. It doesn't have to be Annie Liebovitz quality, but make sure it relates to you and your music in some way. If your sound is gritty but dreamy, for example, you probably don't want to dress up like a KISS cover band.

Create a brief bio of the band. If you have had experience playing, list it. If you are lucky enough to have had one of your demo songs played on a local radio station or if it has been reviewed in a local paper, mention this and send the clipping too.

Once you have promotional materials in order, send them out to:

Local college and community radio stations. If you know the name of any DJs who play your kind of music, send it directly to that person with a cover note saying that you like their taste in music and hope they'll enjoy yours, too. Offer to do a live set in the studio, if they'd like.

Music reviewers at local newspapers and music 'zines. Send it to writers whose columns you read regularly, along with a cover note making reference to a piece of music they reviewed favorably that is similar to yours in some way—e.g., "since I know you're a fellow Patsy Cline fan, I figured you might enjoy this torch-and-twang demo my band produced."

People who book local clubs. If you don't know who books your favorite clubs, call them and ask. Call the booking agents and ask what they would like to see from you, then promptly send them exactly what they asked for—no more, no less.

Follow up with e-mails to the music reviewers and phone calls to the radio stations and booking agents. Be persistent—and creative. ***Make yourself heard.***

6. Get a gig.

Once you've done your promotion, you've laid the groundwork to land a gig.

Ask friends. All your new band friends can help you get that first gig. A band you've gotten to know might offer you an opening slot at one of their shows.

Play anywhere and everywhere. Don't limit yourself to the radio and clubs. Offer to play for free at a party, school, gallery, café, street fair, farmer's market, or nonprofit fundraiser. Hey, all rock bands have to start somewhere. R.E.M. threw a party in an abandoned church. Nirvana played a backyard party.

Be an opening act. Cultivate professional friendships with the people who book shows. Pay attention to the club ads and note when a big touring act is set to play a date at the venue. If you know your band would be a perfect fit, lobby to get the opening slot. Local acts often get these gigs. (Stephanie and Chuck played their first shows together as an acoustic duo opening for big names like the Indigo Girls, Nanci Griffith, and Warren Zevon.) Even though you may not get paid a lot, you'll get to play for a lot of new people.

Play open mics. Play a couple songs on stage at a club's open mic night.

Find yourself a time and place to play.

ROAD TRIP

Rock out in Rochester

Take your show on the road, see the country, and establish a fan base in Kalamazoo. Stephanie and Chuck recently opened a bunch of concerts for Lucinda Williams, following her two tour buses in their van. And they, like many other American acts, are big in Europe, where promoters can line up strings of shows in Italy, Germany, and France. You can book a tour on your own with a little help from friends in a band who have done so and can share their itinerary and contacts with you. There's a whole network out there that revolves around small clubs, college radio stations, and fans willing to feed and house touring bands. Whether you or an agent books your shows, don't book more than you can do without dropping of exhaustion. And think about comfort. As Stephanie points out, "I'm around dudes so much, and being in a van for months with a bunch of them, no matter how great they are, gets old. I crave female companionship." Bring a laptop to stay in e-mail contact.

7. Debut.

You've got a gig lined up, you're rehearsing like crazy, and you know just what you'll wear. Here's the rest of your pre-gig checklist:

- E-mail everyone you know and put up flyers around town so that you get a good crowd.
- Make all your friends swear to show up and cheer, whistle, clap, and stomp so that you're sure to have a receptive audience. If you miss a note, they won't mind!
- The venue may do some advertising, but also make sure yourself that local papers and radio stations include the show in their listings.
- Send out a simple press release, so that all the local music journalists know about it.
- Put a mailing sign-up list by the front door, so that you can let your newfound fans know about upcoming gigs.
- Make sure everyone in your band is there on time for your sound check. Professionalism counts.
- If you're feeling ambitious and the venue okays it in advance, you could try to sell CDs and buttons after your set. Most people already have enough T-shirts, though, and they can be costly to design and print.

At the club, be on time, polite, professional, and friendly to everyone you encounter. Sound people, ticket takers, bouncers, and club owners never forget! Tune up, turn on, and take the stage by storm. ***Rock out!***

CONGRATULATIONS!

You've rocked and are on a roll. Rock on! You did it!

I DID IT!

Name: ______________________________

Date: ______________________________

ROCK MUSIC MECCAS

Cities that have made the scene

Athens, Georgia. College rock made good (R.E.M., B-52's).

Austin, Texas. Site of annual, influential South by Southwest music conference.

Detroit, Michigan. From Iggy Pop to the White Stripes, the Motor City rocks.

Minneapolis, Minnesota. Mid-'80s, indie rock breeding ground (Soul Asylum, The Replacements, Hüsker Dü)—and Prince!

New York, New York. Punk rock (The Ramones, New York Dolls, Blondie, Talking Heads) started here! And you can still go to (or play at) CBGBs.

San Francisco, California. The Haight-Ashbury. Enough said.

Seattle, Washington. Birthplace of grunge.

STEPHANIE'S PICKS

BOOKS

Christgau's Consumer Guide: Albums of the '90s by Robert Christgau
A decade's-end music review by one of Stephanie's favorite critics.

Dusty by Lucy O'Brien
Biography of '60s pop star and perennial cult favorite Dusty Springfield.

Lipstick Traces: A Secret History of the 20th Century by Greil Marcus
Musical musings by the legendary rock critic.

Lost Highway: Journeys and Arrivals of American Musicians by Peter Guralnick
Stephanie's favorite tales of honky-tonk heroes, hillbilly poets, and blues masters.

Rip It Up! Rock & Roll Rulebreakers by Denise Sullivan
Read more about how Finch and Prophet collaborate in life, love, and music. Stephanie also recommends Denise Sullivan's books on R.E.M. and the White Stripes.

MAGAZINES

Bust
www.bust.com
While not a music magazine, *Bust* has a rock-and-roll attitude and covers female musicians extensively.

Mojo
www.mojo4music.com
Stephanie particularly recommends the profiles by Sylvie Simmons.

Rockrgrl
www.rockrgrl.com
"No beauty tips or guilt trips."

Rolling Stone
www.rollingstone.com
The rock bible that launched Annie Liebovitz, Hunter S. Thompson, and Cameron Crowe.

Spin
www.spin.com
Industry standard on "all the music that rocks."

CDS

Blue by Joni Mitchell

Greatest Hits by Bobby Gentry

Hotel San Jose by Go-Go Market

The Pretenders by Chrissie Hynde and the Pretenders

MOVIES

Almost Famous
Worth watching to see Frances McDormand put the fear of mom into rockers.

Chuck Berry Hail! Hail! Rock 'n' Roll
Chuck Berry makes a comeback courtesy of Keith Richards.

The Clash Westway to the World
See why critics and fans still call the Clash "The Only Band That Matters."

The Decline of Western Civilization
Documents the Los Angeles scene circa 1980, featuring Exene Cervenka of X.

The Filth and the Fury
The Sex Pistols' rise to fame and infamy.

Still Crazy
The misadventures of an aging rock band that reunites for a tour.

Sugar Town
Alison Anders's bitingly humorous take on how to get ahead in the music business.

This Is Spinal Tap
The ultimate rockumentary spoof—deadpan hilarity at its best.

9

BE YOUR OWN BOSS

★ drafting a business plan ★

To business that we love
we rise betime,
And go to't with delight.

—William Shakespeare

Imagine This . . . People always told you that vinaigrette of yours could knock Newman's Own off the shelves or that your design sense is far more fabulous than any of those home makeover shows. And you've long suspected that you could go farther and faster solo than your company's glass ceiling would ever allow. So you sat yourself down and started turning your entrepreneurial vision into a game plan, a plan of attack—a business plan! Now you're putting all your skills to work: You've got business angles to work, numbers to crunch, and people to meet. Even when you were sorely tempted to sprint ahead and skip the hard or boring parts of planning, you knew that each careful, steady step you took brought you closer to being up and running. So step right up, and get down to business. *You can do it!*

So, what's your motivation?
Take a moment.
Dream a little, think big,
and then complete this sentence:
I see myself . . .

The Payoffs

- **Independence.** While you enjoy collaborating, partnering, and playing on teams, you really love knowing that, ultimately, you call the shots.
- **Quality time.** While you may actually work longer and harder than ever before, working for yourself makes it your time.
- **Innovation.** Great ideas can get bogged down in bureaucracy, stuck in committees, and drown while swimming through the proper channels. But when you're the boss, you don't need to wait for anyone else's approval to bring brilliant ideas to light.
- **Smiles all around.** Our expert finds little more rewarding than her product pleasing a customer. Even with tough customers, she has the power to turn frowns and bad days around by delivering the best possible customer service.

Meet Your Mentor

ANNA HERRERA-SHAWVER

What She Does: Founder, owner, and president of Apple Canyon Company, an Albuquerque-based specialty foods innovator. Anna's products have won international food competitions and appear under three labels: Orange Sesame, Holy Chipotle! and Puerta de Luna.

Why She Does It: "I started planning Apple Canyon well before I left my last job. I'd worked in marketing and as a product consultant for years but wanted to promote my own products my way. When I took my first salsa to a copacker to pack it, this guy basically said, 'What are you thinking? The world does not need another salsa.' What I found is that it is hard to market a salsa, but that people loved mine. It didn't hurt that my husband had a well-paying job, but when Greg's position was eliminated by restructuring, we just looked at each other and realized I had to start selling a lot of salsa! Another product line (Holy Chipotle!) and a phenomenally popular Orange Sesame dressing later, I'm happy to say that my accountant calls us a 'growing concern'!"

Word from the Wise: "It's important to be confident *and* to be willing to surround yourself with people who know what you don't. The graphic designer daughter of a neighbor ended up acing our logo after we'd been frustrated by other designs for months. And I bumped into a nutritionist while visiting my chiropractor who wound up giving me excellent advice about new marketing avenues for some of our products. While I've never worked harder, my bottom line is that I can't imagine ever being an employee again!"

I love people, and I love it when they love my products. That's the foundation of a good business—but it's also key to having a good time in business.

—Anna Herrera-Shawver

BADGE STEPS

1. Define your idea.

You can get an idea on Monday, quit your job on Tuesday, max out your credit cards on Wednesday, launch your business on Thursday, and hope for the best. But if you want to ensure that you don't lose your own shirt trying to sell novelty T-shirts or find out that your once-promising cookware line was just a flash in the pan, you'll need to come up with a business plan.

In this badge, we'll follow the lead of the Small Business Administration (www.sba.gov/starting_business) to explore the key areas of defining, marketing, financing, and managing your business. Essentially, a business plan describes your product or service, and explains how it fills a market niche by meeting consumers' needs or wants. If you aren't applying for a loan or seeking other funding, you may not show your plan to anyone for a while—but going through the process is an important step in taking yourself and your business idea more seriously.

Before you get down to the nitty-gritty numbers, spend some time answering these general questions:

- What inspired your idea—were you frustrated by a lack in the market place, or poor customer service, or excited by a new or underutilized technology?
- How does your product or service differ from what's already out there, and why is it better? Will you deliver it faster, smarter, cheaper, or easier?
- What makes you uniquely qualified to do this?
- Try to avoid jargon and technical terms; describe the biz in terms someone outside the field can comprehend.
- If you are writing a business plan to expand an existing company, you'll need to tell the history of the business as well.

Define and describe your business.

2. Find your market niche.

Which customers are most likely to buy your product or service, and how do you plan to reach them? This is the million-dollar question—or possibly more, if you analyze your market effectively. First, spend some time doing some market research, to figure out:

KNOW YOUR ASSETS

Have you got what it takes to succeed in business? Are you:

Self-motivated? Can you do what needs to be done without a boss, a set schedule, or external deadlines to prod you?

Ready to go it alone? Being the boss can make you feel isolated, even if you work with contractors or have frequent customer interaction. When you're in business for yourself, all the benefits, risks, gains, and losses are yours alone. If you'd prefer to share the celebrations and the setbacks with someone else, consider forming a partnership.

Willing to learn? If you know everything about numbers but lack people skills, or can brainstorm beautiful visions but are bored by details, you are going to have to add to your skill set—or partner with another professional who can complement your strengths.

Courageous? It is exhilarating—and scary—to fly solo. You don't have to be a daredevil, but if you aren't at least a bit of a risk-taker, your ideas may never make it off the ground, and you may be too easily rattled by normal business turbulence.

Able to persevere? Most businesses don't make much money their first (or second, or third . . .) year in business. You may find that you're paying your contractors more than you pay yourself! But if you can stick with it and learn from your mistakes, you stand to gain greater income—and true independence.

Who is your target market? Can you show that their numbers are growing, or that their need for your product or service is about to take off? What can you find out about their spending habits, daily routines, favorite publications, and favored shopping venues? Do some online searches to see what you find in the news, but don't stop there. Circulate a ten-question survey to your entire e-mail circle, inviting those who fit your customer profile to respond and to pass it along to others they may know. You should give people some incentive to respond—a sample of your product, say, or a coupon for a certain dollar amount in goods or services from your company. This will help you learn about your target customers and win them over at the same time. The better you get to know your customer, the better it is for your business—check out the Market Testing sidebar for more techniques.

What external factors might affect demand? Are there sustained economic developments, emerging trends, and technological advances that affect your particular arena now and down the line? Be careful to think long-term—if your business plan hinges on a trend that's already peaking, such as a hot real estate market or low-carb diets, your plan may be out of date before you have a chance to implement it.

Who is your competition, and how are they doing? Read trade publications, and peruse those business pages you used to use to line the bird's cage. Some advisors suggest getting a year-old Yellow Pages directory, looking for businesses similar to yours, and calling them to see if they are still in business. You might also call the proprietors of similar businesses in other cities or states—where you won't be seen as the competition—and ask how they're doing.

How can you do better than your competitors? Do an online search to find any press coverage they've received, customer reviews, and any annual reports or other publicly available financial statements. What have they done to get their product out? What has worked for them, and what can you learn from their mistakes? Try to find out what makes for a loyal, repeat customer in your business niche, and what makes customers shun a business.

How will you let customers know you exist? Don't just say "advertising." As Anna says, "Advertising is very expensive, and most of us can't rely on that route." Think about creative, free (or almost-free) marketing ideas. Anna sings the praises of press releases, because they have worked to get write-ups about her and her business into local and national

MARKET TESTING

Get to know your market with these proven methods

- Check out university marketing departments. Hire a student who is studying research methods to do some homework for you. Anna endorses this low-cost way to get data.
- Consult community experts, like chambers of commerce, banks, and real estate and insurance companies. It's their business to compile and keep stats.
- Marketing consultants such as ACNielsen (www.acnielsen.com) offer sophisticated market measurement services—but they usually don't come cheap.
- Internet. Great for demographic data, with sites like www.demographia.com.
- Surveys and focus groups are not just for big marketing consultants. Try surveying an online chat group that fits your demographic, and assemble a group of friends who represent your target market to collect their thoughts on your venture. Be sure to offer incentives for participation.

publications. She also "thinks outside the box" by taking her wares to home and garden shows, which not many people in her business do.

Outline a basic marketing plan.

ANNA'S EXPERT TIPS

BE RESOURCEFUL

Small Business Administration. In addition to offering clear instructions about all things entrepreneurial, the SBA features a special section for women, including links to an Online Women's Business Center and Women's Network for Entrepreneurial Training. www.sba.gov/starting_business/special/women.html.

SCORE. This "Service Corps of Retired Executives" is a nonprofit association dedicated to providing entrepreneurs with free, confidential, face-to-face and e-mail business counseling. Visit them online, or in 389 chapter offices. www.score.org.

Women's Venture Fund. This not-for-profit organization and microlender targets underserved urban communities. www.womensventurefund.org.

National Business Incubation Association. NBIA is the world's leading organization to incubate and grow small businesses. Incubators are regionally located, and Anna says they can really help you get on your feet. www.nbia.org.

3. Follow rules and regulations.

You know your business and your market—but is it legal? Even if you're not planning to become a bookie, there are probably regulations and guidelines that pertain to your line of business. If you're planning to run a food business like Anna, for example, you'll have to follow strict Food and Drug Administration guidelines about packaging, abide by strict Health Department standards for kitchen cleanliness, and apply for patents for your secret recipes.

"The importance of building your foundation slowly and well cannot be overstated," says Anna. "It's hard to undo early mistakes down the line . . . while ignorance may feel like bliss, it's not an excuse you can use with government officials or the IRS. They'll just tell you that if you didn't know, you should've found out!" And if you think regulations seem like a hassle, consider this: If it weren't such a hassle, you'd probably have a lot more competition! Here's what you need to know to get ahead in business while staying above the law:

I DID IT!

"I run my own business, and as scary as it was to leave the security of my 'day job,' I can't imagine going back. I work harder and closer to the bone than ever before, but the freedom (time, location, colleagues, and clients) is absolutely worth the trade. And I've found that, for me at least, survival anxiety is easier to deal with than traditional workplace issues. The whole thing requires a kind of faith that things will come your way as they need to—a revelation worth holding in all aspects of my life."
—Caroline

THE DEVIL'S IN THE DETAILS

"When I'm really busy—which is pretty much all the time—I have a bad habit of ignoring my computer's prompts to back up data. I learned my lesson when I lost several months' worth of correspondence and new customer information. I had to spend time and money on professional repairs and recovery efforts and now know that a few minutes taking care of details now can save you time—and money—later."
—Anna

- Check out Anna's Expert Tips and Anna's Picks, page 71, and consult the business-building resources listed there to find out about what bases you need to cover to secure a living for yourself and keep the government happy.
- As you begin to take advantage of business-building resources, you should also seek referrals to sound legal and accounting advisors.
- Seek advice (from the SBA and your local Chamber of Commerce) about how the following may or may not apply to you: business licenses and insurance; the pros and cons of sole proprietorship, partnership, and incorporation in your line of work; trademarks, copyrights, and patents; and other ways to protect your trade secrets.

Make the law work for you, not against you.

4. Prove it's feasible.

Even after you've described your product or service, created a marketing plan, and made sure it's legal, the question remains: Can what you're proposing actually be done? While your plan must convey your creativity, vision, and passion, it also needs to be down-to-earth enough to show you've thought through the nuts and bolts of the operation. You'll need to research and spell out how you will manage:

- Facilities, labor, and equipment.
- Product manufacturing, distribution, and development.
- The team that will help you deliver the goods. If you have a partner, backer, or advisor with an impressive track record, call that out. Mention the strengths and experience of your suppliers, designers, photographers, hotshot Web engineers, etc.

Detail your day-to-day operations.

5. Show me the money.

As hopeful as you may be about your proposed business idea, the financial section of your plan is no place for blind optimism. You might think you can start out with as much cash as you can beg or borrow, because you just know money will start pouring in soon—but that makes experienced entrepreneurs like Anna cringe. "It's impossible to control cash flow when you don't know how much to count on coming in," she says. "You need to learn how to forecast realistically, and most of us need help to do so."

KEEPING IT IN THE FAMILY

Good or bad for business?

Boundaries. When Anna and Greg were building Apple Canyon, they were glad to work on marketing, even on vacations—and on their honeymoon! But Anna admits that there have been times when "calculators have been flying" around their home office. Most small business people feel they have to work 24/7—but to avoid burnout and keep both your family and your business intact long-term, it pays to schedule some downtime.

Professionalism. If you are working with family or friends, be professional in your dealings. Draw up contracts for financial transactions, even if it feels weird. And even if you feel you understand each other perfectly, put on paper how decisions will be made, how disagreements will be resolved, and how profits (and losses) will be shared.

Honesty. To help maintain your relationships—not to mention your good name!—be honest with friends and family by sharing your business plan with them and being crystal clear about the risks involved with any investments.

In fact, the top reason small businesses fail is lack of enough capital to sustain the business. To be sure you escape that statistic, consult the counselors at SBA, SCORE, and other small business resource centers who can help you come up with more realistic capital investment requirements and growth projections (sometimes for a nominal fee). You might also try using spreadsheets to calculate growth rates at different cost and investment levels—many spreadsheet programs have built-in projection capabilities that allow you to consider how your profit margins will be affected if you limit your costs or investments up front. If you're planning to appeal to investors or apply for a loan, the financial section of your business plan will need to be lengthy and detailed (see Beyond the Badge, page 70). ***Calculate sound financial projections.***

6. Sum it up.

The Executive Summary appears at the beginning of your plan, but should be written last, because you can't write a decent one without having thought through each of the other plan components.

This short (generally one-page) introduction to your plan needs to grab people's attention and encourage them to read further—just like the jacket of a book. Think about what you'd say in two or three minutes if you were alone in an elevator with the person most vital to the launch of your business: You want to convey your excitement, inspire confidence, and engage interest. To do this:

Be concise and direct. Consider calling out important points in punchy, boom-boom-boom bullet points.

Sound confident but not naive. Avoid cliched hard-sell advertising terms and over-the-top projections. If you claim you're going to make a million bucks your first month of selling a revolutionary paper clip, you'd better have the numbers to back it up right away—and even then, you might inspire some skepticism. Savvy businesspeople know that if it sounds too good to be true, it probably is.

Pull out the most crucial points. Take them from the body of your entire plan to leave no question about:

- The precise mission of your business, what makes it so distinctive, and why you're just the person who can make this idea fly.
- The customer base for your business.
- How you will make it happen.

LET YOUR REPUTATION PRECEDE YOU

Create a winning brand

Name. Names are so important that big companies spend as much time and money naming products as they do developing them. Anna and her husband made lists of possible company names for about a year. Inspiration struck one day when they were driving and listening to a book on tape. "Apple Canyon" was the name of a town in the book—and as soon as they heard it, they knew they had their name.

Packaging. When Anna worked as a consultant on other people's products that weren't selling, she often found that the packaging, not the product, was the problem. "Packaging is what gets the product into people's hands the first time," she says, so consider yours carefully.

Logo. Anna spent months working with designers to create a logo. The quest for perfection paid off—she recently had a client tell her that she keeps her Apple Canyon business card on her desk because it's so unique and attractive.

• What investments, costs, and potential gains are associated with this venture.

While you continue to refine your business plan, you can use this *Cliffs Notes* version to introduce your idea to a variety of contacts. ***Summarize your bold venture.***

7. Take charge.

Look over all the documentation you have created in the course of this badge, and you'll notice two things:

First, you already have your first draft of an impressive business plan. You may already have all the information you need to get your business off the ground right in front of you! If there's any aspect of your plan you're not 100 percent sure about, consult the small business counselors at one of the state or nonprofit small business support services—by now, you're probably on a first-name basis. And if you need additional funding to get started, you should ask counselors to review your plan and help you fill it out as necessary to satisfy lenders and investors.

Second, business plans, marketing, financials—hey, you sound like an entrepreneur already! Whether or not you choose to take that next step and launch your business or just feel secure in the fact that you could if you really wanted to, you've opened up your career choices and become president and CEO of your own life. ***Create a master plan for your business or career, and put it into action!***

CONGRATULATIONS!

You're minding your own business—and loving it, too! You did it!

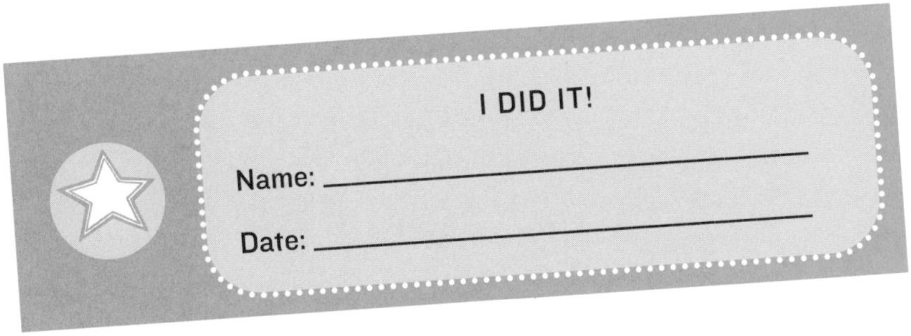

INVENT IT

If your dream business revolves around the better mousetrap you've invented, explore prototypes, patents, and licensing here:

Ideas, Inventions and Innovations. Available from the Small Business Administration, www.sba.gov.

PatentCafe. www.patentcafe.com.

Secrets from an Inventor's Notebook by Maurice Kanbar

The U.S. Patent and Trademark Office. www.uspto.gov.

BEYOND THE BADGE

If you love it as much as you thought you would, dream on . . .

- **Do your financials.** Unless you are completely comfortable with balance sheets, break-even analyses, and pro forma income projections and cash flows, you'll want to enlist qualified professionals to help you with this. Read up on the requirements for the financials section of a business plan using Anna's Picks, and ask your advising team (accountant, lawyer, small business resource center) every question that comes to mind. While you don't need to do this section all by yourself, you do need to understand every fact and figure.
- **Seek funding.** Most new businesses are financed through some combination of credit cards, savings, sales of assets, home equity loans, and friends and family. The eyes-wide-open budgeting and forecasting you prepare for your business plan is essential here, so that you know how much risk you and your investors can take. Your advising team can also give you insight about loans, arrangements with entities or people who will be repaid with interest over an agreed-upon amount of time:
    - Angel investors, who can be friends or relatives with deep pockets and/or a reason to believe in you, or successful strangers who believe in mentoring fellow entrepreneurs.
    - Equity investments, which involve your exchanging a piece of your business, profits, or products for cash.
    - Venture capitalists and venture capital firms who pony up for a share of your company.

FINANCING RESOURCES

When "pretty please" won't cut it, try

American Venture magazine. www.avce.com.

Financing the New Venture: A Complete Guide to Raising Capital from Venture Capitalists, Investment Bankers, Private Investors, and Other Sources by Mark H. Long

National Association of Small Business Investment Companies. www.nasbic.org.

Pratt's Guide to Venture Capital Sources. www.ventureeconomics.com.

Vcapital. www.vcapital.com.

ANNA'S PICKS

BOOKS

From Kitchen to Market by Stephen F. Hall
Tips on selling gourmet specialty foods.

How to Write a Business Plan by Mike McKeever
Covers all the basics, plus the hard stuff like estimating your profitability, financing options, and profit and loss forecasting.

Marketing without Advertising by Michael Phillips and Salli Rasberry
Learn how to attract clients, win over tough customers, plan marketing events, and more.

New Product Introduction: A Systems, Technology, and Process Approach by J. David Viale
Get insider know-how on managing costs, bringing products to market more efficiently, and turning profits.

The Small Business Bible: The Make or Break Factors for Survival and Success by Paul Resnik
Includes a CD with a business plan template.

Soul Proprietor: 100 Lessons from a Lifestyle Entrepreneur by Jane Pollak
Written by a businesswoman who turned a hobby she was passionate about into a successful business.

The Successful Business Plan: Secrets and Strategies by Rhonda Abrams
Contains handy worksheets.

MAGAZINES

Entrepreneur
www.entrepreneur.com
How-to guides, business opportunities, inventions, franchises, business plans, and more.

Gourmet News
www.gourmetnews.com
Food industry news, buyers' guides, and advertising info.

Gourmet Retailer
www.gourmetretailer.com
Breaking industry news, resource guides, and business connections for food-industry entrepreneurs.

WEB SITES & SOFTWARE

www.applecanyon.com
All about Anna's products, complete with recipes!

www.bplans.com
Read a selection of sample business plans.

www.brs-inc.com/business_plan.asp
Get free tips and white papers on business planning; you can also purchase PlanWrite software here.

www.businessplanpro.com
Check out sample marketing and business plans; you can buy Business Plan Pro software here, too.

www.sba.gov
The Small Business Administration has all things entrepreneurial.

ASSOCIATIONS

National Association for the Specialty Food Trade
www.specialtyfood.com
Offers food industry news, info, and opportunities, and hosts the annual Fancy Food Show.

National Association of Women Business Owners
www.nawbo.org
Provides networking opportunities for female entrepreneurs and hosts two annual conferences.

10

FLY SOLO

★ aviation ★

Flying is the finest kind of moving around, you know, just as poetry is the finest way of using words.

—Jessie Fauset

So, what's your motivation?
Take a moment.
Dream a little, think big,
and then complete this sentence:
I see myself . . .

Imagine This . . . You always believed the sky was the limit for you—but now that you can fly, you know better. When you're looking down from the comfort of your cockpit, suddenly all the obstacles in front of you are shrunk down to size. The traffic, the construction work on your street, your office and its politics—none of it has any power over you when you're hundreds of feet above it all. And when you land, you'll roll onto the tarmac with a fresh perspective on the world and a can-do attitude. Women account for just 6 percent of the pilots in the U.S. today—and once you beat those odds, there's no goal too high for you. Gravity's got nothing on you, girl. *You can do it!*

The Payoffs

- **Uplifting experiences.** Defying gravity is the ultimate high, says our expert Deanna: "One student told me piloting a plane was more thrilling than having her children!"
- **Freedom of movement.** "When my grandmother was ill, I could jump in the plane and get there right away, without getting routed through Denver or Newark," says Deanna. Plus when you're the pilot, you'll never have to worry about high-season fares or getting seated between a snorer and a colicky baby.
- **Camaraderie.** With moral support from your fellow pilots, your flying career is bound to take off—and you'll make some fast friends, too.
- **Higher aspirations.** Flying a plane will keep your spirits lifted and your mind racing ahead to the next challenge. "There's always something more to aspire to, whether that's deeper engineering knowledge or an aerobatic maneuver," explains Deanna.

Meet Your Mentor

DEANNA STRAND

What She Does: Deanna has been the owner and operator of Strand Flying School in Grand Junction, Colorado, since 1983, and is one of the few women to be named a Pilot Examiner for the Federal Aviation Administration (FAA). She has an illustrious career as a Certified Flight Instructor with specialized knowledge in seaplanes and mountain flying and was recently named FAA Flight Instructor of the Year. Deanna actively encourages young women to become pilots through aviation seminars at Mesa State College, programs for Girl Scout troops, and classes at local alternative high schools.

Why She Does It: "My parents owned a flight operation in Montana, so we took all of our family vacations and trips to Grandma's house by airplane. I did my first solo flight at seventeen, but my parents always encouraged us kids to pursue more stable careers outside aviation. So I studied linguistics in college, which taught me to think methodically and helped me discover my love for teaching. It just made sense to combine my passions and teach flying. I was only twenty-seven when the FAA made me a Pilot Examiner, and I was as surprised as anyone at the time—when we had our meetings, I was the only woman out of thirty to forty examiners from Colorado and Utah. But it's such a privilege to be a part of that pivotal moment in a pilot's career and issue that license. Sure, running an aviation business is hard work—my parents were right about that—but there's nothing like taking someone up over Aspen for the first time when the leaves change colors."

The best way to get around traffic is to fly right over it.

—Deanna Strand

Word from the Wise: "A plane is usually the fastest way to get from point A to point B, especially in the mountains. I take my dog for training in Denver, which is hours away by car. But it's a quick hop over the mountain by plane, and my dog loves to fly!"

BADGE STEPS

1. Find a flight instructor.

If you've always wanted to fly, stop leaving those grand plans up in the air and start by finding yourself a good teacher. To do this, Deanna recommends that you:

Look into flight schools. Look up "aircraft" or "airlines" in your local Yellow Pages to find flight schools near you, or run an online search to find a few nearby. You can also call local airports used by private planes, crop dusters, charters, and other small commercial planes, and find out if they have flight schools or freelance instructors.

Check instructors' credentials and references. According to the FAA, instructors are required to have their Certified Flight Instructor (CFI) credential. This guarantees they've earned their commercial pilot's license and logged 250 hours in the air. There are lots of CFIs out there, but Deanna cautions that many are only teaching to build up the 1,000 hours required to pilot larger aircraft. To find an instructor who actually enjoys teaching, Deanna recommends instructors who:

- Have already logged over 1,000 flight hours. "This shows they're really serious about teaching," Deanna says. (She should know—she has over 10,000 flight hours to her credit!)
- Teach ground school. The more experienced, professional instructors often do, and you can ask to sit in on their classes to see if you like their teaching style. (See Well-Grounded for more on ground school.)
- Can provide references. Before you commit, call a few former students and ask about their experience.

Trust your instincts. "Make sure you find a flight instructor who inspires your confidence," says Deanna. "Your instructor is also your copilot, and you need to trust that this person will be able to help you take off and land safely." Look for instructors who obviously like to teach as much as they like to fly.

Connect with an instructor and sign up for lessons.

2. Make a flight plan.

If flying alone seems like an impossibly lofty goal to you, now hear this: Deanna says it can be done in just two months. "To earn your student pilot certificate and make your first solo flight, you'll need to get in

WELL-GROUNDED

Get flight-wise at ground school

Deanna recommends that you check course listings at your local airport or community college to see if they offer "ground school," or classes that cover flight instruments, aerodynamics, meteorology, and other aspects of aviation before you climb into the cockpit. "You don't need to take a class in aerodynamics or meteorology to learn how to fly, but it will help develop your piloting skills," she explains. "Once you understand how the aircraft is designed to withstand turbulence, you'll have more confidence when you are in the air—and among your classmates, you'll discover that camaraderie pilots share."

about sixteen flying lessons, which will each run between an hour and an hour and fifteen minutes," explains Deanna. Some flight schools offer an intensive program of lessons that can even be squeezed into a long vacation, but Deanna suggests stretching your classes out over a longer time period: "If you fly twice a week, that will give you time in between to absorb lessons learned, and hit the books your teacher recommends so that you understand the basics of aviation."

To be sure you get in two sessions a week, you'll need to schedule three flight times per week. "Usually one session you schedule each week won't work out, either because the wind and weather won't cooperate or the airplane is in the shop for routine maintenance," Deanna explains. Early morning air tends to be the calmest for flying, so night owls may need to rearrange their schedules for a few months until they get the hang of flying. Some times of the year may be calmer than others, too: "In the Rockies, the winter is the best time to fly, but of course weather conditions change a lot by region," our expert says. "You'll want to find out about optimal conditions in your area and schedule flight lessons accordingly." ***Schedule three flight times per week over the next two months.***

3. Prepare for takeoff.

Before you climb into the cockpit, you should go over the basics of aerodynamics and safety with your instructor on the blackboard. "That way you'll have a better understanding of why it's not a crisis if your airplane bounces around, and why you're actually safer up in the sky than on a street," our expert explains. (See Rise Above Your Fears, page 77, for more.)

Your instructor should have all the equipment you'll need on hand, so all you need to do to prepare for your flight lesson is pay close attention and come mentally equipped to fly. Don't be daunted—just take these tips from Deanna:

- Keep an eye on the weather. Deanna advises keeping a close eye on weather reports in your area, and double-checking with your instructor about conditions before you drive to the airport for a lesson. You may be disappointed to miss your lesson, but you'll encounter less turbulence if you're flexible and responsive to changing weather conditions. If you're the least bit wary of the weather, ask pilots who have just landed what the flight conditions were like for them.

THE LEGENDARY NINETY-NINES

Taking aviation to new heights

Founded over tea and cookies on a New York airstrip in 1929, the Ninety-Nines (www.ninety-nines.org) is the world's first organization of female pilots. Amelia Earhart and the ninety-eight other female pilots who became charter members had been flying high and setting altitude and speed records for years—but until the Ninety-Nines came along, it was widely believed that women were naturally more inclined to china patterns than flight patterns. The Ninety-Nines set out to change the course of aviation history, and they've succeeded many times over: Ninety-Niners piloted enormous B-29s and set new aviation safety records during World War II; they founded the Flying Samaritans in 1961 to deliver humanitarian aid to remote areas in Latin America; they started "blood flights" in 1975 to deliver donated blood to hospitals; and the first American female astronauts were Ninety-Niners. Today the Ninety-Nines continue to initiate positive changes in aviation, including their "Airmarking the Skyways Like the Highways" safety campaign.

I DID IT!

"The first time I landed a plane by myself happened on one of the rare days I didn't feel like a complete idiot at the controls. My instructor calmly issued instructions, which I followed without any remark from him—a first. I talked to the tower, they gave me instructions, and the next thing I knew, we were on the ground. I was in shock; my instructor wore a big grin. I can still feel the rush, and that was eight years ago. I ran out of money before I could get my license—I was a single mom, trying desperately to establish my career—but it was a hoot and a half. To this day it surpasses anything else I've ever wanted to do."

—Fiona

KISSING THE GROUND

"Landing. Now there's a challenge! It sounds easy to get down, but it's hard to get down well. It's so counterintuitive: You actually pull up the front of the plane as you land. It's frightening—the fear of crashing to the ground overtakes my confidence that I've done this successfully before. But each landing gets better, and the feeling of relief after a safe landing takes over."

—Wendy

- Have some ginger an hour or two before you fly if you have a tendency toward motion sickness. "It really does help settle your stomach, and you can buy it in capsule form at your local natural foods store," explains Deanna. "At first the nervous excitement may get to your stomach, but air sickness is usually gone after a few lessons. In all my years of teaching, I've only had a couple of students actually use the airsick bags we provide." If you do start feeling queasy despite your ginger intake, just do what you'd do in a car, and look out toward the horizon until your stomach gets steadier.

Get ready to ease on down the runway.

DEANNA'S EXPERT TIPS

THE NEXT BEST THING TO BEING THERE

If you miss a lesson or two due to weather, Deanna recommends that you use the time you've set aside to:

Hit the books. "There's a lot to cover, and staying on top of your homework will help you make better use of your flight time."

Try out a flight simulator. "Microsoft Flight Simulator can be helpful to learn about airplane dynamics and hone your hand-eye coordination."

Play video games. "Nintendo is actually good practice for pilots because you learn to use your hands to control what you see onscreen. This can help you learn to pilot the aircraft just by looking at the instrument panel, which is an advanced skill."

Practice hand-eye coordination. "When you practice piano, play basketball, or operate heavy machinery, you're developing the kind of hand-eye coordination it takes to become a good pilot."

4. Get airborne.

"What, already?!" you say. That's right: Instructors defuse any lingering anxiety you might have about flying by putting you in the pilot's seat as soon as you've covered the fundamentals of flying—maybe even on your first day of lessons.

As soon as you feel ready, put on your headset and any other gear your instructor recommends, and make yourself comfy in your pilot's seat. Your instructor will have full controls on their side too, just to be sure you don't make any mistakes. But as you develop skills and confidence, your instructor will use those controls less and less, until you are actually flying the plane and your instructor is mostly there for moral support. ***Take to the skies with your instructor.***

5. Earn your learner's permit.

To get the student pilot certificate that you need to be able to fly solo, you'll need three things:

- A Federal Aviation Administration (FAA) medical certificate filled out by a doctor, showing that you have no history of heart or other medical problems and that your sight and hearing meet the minimum requirements for pilots. This helps ensure your own safety in the air and is an important assurance that you won't endanger anyone else, either.
- Fifteen to twenty-five hours of flight time. Deanna has noticed over the course of her many years of teaching that this is the average number of flight hours it takes students to put their textbook knowledge and hand-eye coordination to the test, gain confidence in their piloting abilities, and get the hang of takeoff and landing.
- Your instructor's signature on the back of your certificate. When you have your medical certificate and your instructor feels that you've developed the skills and confidence necessary to go it alone in the skies, she (or he) will sign the back of your student pilot certificate.

Get certified to fly alone.

6. Go solo.

You taxi down the runway, and you hear radio control say those words you've been waiting to hear for months: "You're cleared for takeoff." When your wheels leave the runway, you might think there's no greater thrill. But Deanna says the real joy is when you've navigated through the flight pattern and come in for a smooth landing, and your CFI gives you a pat on the back and a thumbs-up for your first solo. Once you hit the tarmac, Deanna warns, you'll want to do it all over again—"and that's when you'll know you're a real aviator!" ***Indulge your flight instinct!***

CONGRATULATIONS!

Check you out, fly girl! You did it!

I DID IT!

Name: ______________________

Date: ______________________

RISE ABOVE YOUR FEARS

Don't let your fears get the better of you

Flying is safer than driving. "On the road, you've got cars tearing along at sixty miles an hour in both directions, with only a couple of feet and yellow lines to prevent a head-on collision. But when you're flying, you hardly ever see another airplane, and you're usually miles from any mountains."

Fear of heights is rarely an issue for pilots. "I know a number of professional pilots who are afraid of heights to the point where they can't go to the edge of a cliff and look over. Flying is different because you're contained in a well-designed machine with an experienced instructor, and the door's closed and locked so you can't fall out."

When you're the pilot, you've got the best seat on the plane. "Even people who get anxious on commercial airplanes are usually okay in the cockpit—being at the controls makes you feel in control and a lot more secure than when you don't really know who's in that cockpit and have no idea how well they can fly."

Fears of flying are often exaggerated. "If you've got a fear of flying that really can't be overcome, you'll know right away because you won't be able to taxi down to the runway. Otherwise, you'll forget you were ever afraid after a couple of lessons."

BEYOND THE BADGE

If you love it as much as you thought you would, dream on . . .

- **Earn your private pilot's license.** Once you've learned to fly solo, you're well on your way to earning your private pilot's license. You'll need three things to reach that next level:

  More flight time. The minimum number of flight hours necessary to earn your license is forty, according to the FAA—but the Aircraft Owners and Pilots Association estimates that in actual practice, you can expect it to take closer to the average of seventy-three hours.

  A decent test score. You'll have to bone up on FAA regulations, aerodynamics, and meteorology to pass a computerized FAA knowledge exam at 70 percent or better.

  The A-OK from a flight examiner. You'll need to pass an in-person exam with a FAA-certified Pilot Examiner like Deanna, who will look over your log book and test results, ask you questions to check your knowledge, and do a final flight test with you. The ground and flight portions of this "Practical Test" take about four hours in all.

- **Fly higher.** Mountain flying is a special challenge, since the high altitudes and terrain require skill and a certain amount of courage to navigate. Deanna recommends the Rockies, northwestern Canada, Washington State, and Alaska as ideal places to pursue mountain flight training.
- **Glide through the air.** According to Deanna, gliders are especially fun and put your aerodynamics knowledge to the test. "There's no motor, so you have to make judgment calls based not on power, but on the amount of lift you can get on the wings," she explains. Locate a glider port near you, and find out how to sign up for a lesson or two.
- **Loop the loop.** If you've totally flipped for aviation, show off your skills with a few fancy tricks. Make sure your instructor and airplane are qualified in aerobatics. A basic loop or roll will get you started on aerobatics, a proud tradition among women "barnstormers" (stunt flyers) for almost a century.
- **Float away.** Even if you can't walk on water, you can land on it with a float plane. "It's the most fun flying I've ever done," says Deanna. "Once you get the hang of it, you can land on almost any lake or body of water." You can pick up this skill in the Pacific Northwest and in many tropical locations, too.

THE VIEW FROM ABOVE

Become an aerial photographer

Share your bird's-eye perspective on the world with others by snapping a few aerial photographs. You never know what you'll discover through the camera lens: crop circles, swirling mists, hidden waterfalls, even serpentine burial mounds. If it's inspiration you need, just watch *Winged Migration,* an amazing documentary that follows birds in flight, or check out the stunning book *Earth from Above* by ecologically minded aerial photographer Yann Arthus-Bertrand.

DEANNA'S PICKS

BOOKS

Jonathan Livingston Seagull by Richard Bach
For inspiration, Deanna recommends this poetic parable about a seagull who finds his higher purpose in flight.

Private Pilot Manual by Jeppesen Sanderson
Deanna considers this the leader in flight training manuals: "It's easy to follow and understand, explains key words, and has plenty of easy-to-follow illustrations." Check out the companion CD-ROM and video to watch and learn.

Stick and Rudder: An Explanation of the Art of Flying by Wolfgang Langewiesche
This classic text explains the aerodynamics of flying, inspiring understanding and confidence in generations of pilots.

MAGAZINES

AOPA Flight Training
www.aopa.org/flight_training
Full of useful flight training tips for new pilots. Sign up for a six-month trial membership to AOPA, and you'll get a six-month subscription for free.

Flying Magazine
www.flyingmag.com
Keep on top of developments in aviation with the flight reports and columns in this all-purpose aviation magazine.

Private Pilot
www.privatepilotmag.com
A key source of information on air travel, safety issues, aircraft ownership, learning to fly, and advanced aviation techniques.

ORGANIZATIONS

Aircraft Owners and Pilots Association (AOPA)
www.aopa.org
This organization brings pilots and advocates on their behalf together on air safety and other legislative issues. Check out their airport directory, training videos, and online weather information. Join and you'll get aviation tips galore in the AOPA magazine, *ePilot*, the AOPA *Pilot's Handbook*, and *Flight Training* magazine.

Civil Air Patrol
www.cap.gov
CAP is a United States Air Force Auxiliary that teaches about aviation and organizes volunteer-led efforts such as search-and-rescue, disaster relief, and drug enforcement reconnaissance.

Experimental Aircraft Association
www.eaa.org
If you're up to an even bigger challenge, try building your own airplane! This Web site will help you buy a kit, build it, and keep your costs down to the average of $100,000.

Federal Aviation Administration (FAA)
www.faa.gov
This is the official U.S. administrative branch charged with regulating airspace, air traffic, and licensing. Use the FAA's site to find schools, access educational resources, and find out what it takes to get your pilot's license and specialized certificates.

Strand Flying School
www.strandflying.com
Check out links to helpful aviation sites, and sign up to learn mountain flying in Colorado and Utah with our expert.

MOVIES & TV

Amelia Earhart documentaries
Take your pick—there are a million!

Discovery Channel specials
Their aerial photography is really impressive.

Discovery Wings
A channel devoted entirely to flying.

Never Cry Wolf
Those great aerial shots of Alaska might inspire a trip.

The Right Stuff
The earliest astronauts were cowboy pilots, not scientists.

Top Gun
This movie seems to inspire more pilots than any other.

11

SING YOUR HEART OUT

★ singing ★

To sing is to love and affirm, to fly and soar, to coast into the hearts of the people who listen.

—Joan Baez

So, what's your motivation?
Take a moment.
Dream a little, think big,
and then complete this sentence:
I see myself . . .

Imagine This . . . You take the microphone, cue the piano player, and wait for the audience to settle. You begin with just a phrase—but soon you have the audience eating out of the palm of your hand. No, they can't take this away from you! So whether you want to be the queen of your choir, conquer karaoke, or make life your cabaret, why not bring your singing out of the shower and take your place in the spotlight? This badge will help you find your voice, polish your pipes, and share your song. Sure, there are mountains to climb—but once you get there, the hills come alive with the sound of your music. Take a deep breath. *You can do it!*

The Payoffs

- **Self-expression.** No one croons quite like you do!
- **Poise.** Singing teaches you a lot about how to present yourself to the world. You'll notice that if you carry yourself with confidence and trust your own distinctive style, you can carry off almost anything—in or out of the spotlight.
- **Transformation.** As in acting, you get to be someone else for a few moments when you sing. When you interpret a song, you inhabit the story it tells and the emotions it describes. Your listeners share in this out-of-body experience, and everyone's the richer for it!
- **Showing off.** Singing "Happy Birthday," "Jingle Bells," or the national anthem need never again be cause for embarrassment!

Meet Your Mentor
BRENDA BONHOMME

What She Does: A soprano, Brenda is a graduate of the prestigious Oberlin Conservatory. Her wide-ranging singing credits include performances as an ensemble member and soloist with groups including the San Francisco Symphony Chorus, San Francisco Chamber Singers, VOCI Women's Vocal Ensemble, Coro Hispano, and the Oakland Jazz Choir. She appeared in a Bay Area production of *Sweeney Todd,* and was a featured soloist in the San Francisco Symphony performance of Wynton Marsalis's *All Rise*. Brenda also teaches voice at a range of age and skill levels.

Why She Does It: "My family was one of the first black families to go to a very German Lutheran church in Philadelphia. I sang in the children's choir at church and in my school's choir. In high school, my choir director told my mother that I should be taking voice lessons—to support my choir solos. Between city and church choirs and my voice lessons, I was singing seven days a week. I loved it, all the while being terribly self-conscious and shy. I was so glad to have choir robes so no one could see my knees shaking! I blended academics and music throughout high school and college—but when I went back to school for a business degree, I stopped singing (except at church) for almost ten years. Ultimately, I realized that I needed to express myself through singing and signed up for a little class at a private voice studio. I was like a fish back in water!"

Everybody's voice has a natural sound to it. You don't need to change that—just work with it.

—Brenda Bonhomme

Word from the Wise: "Everybody really can sing. It's not about having a gorgeous voice. Look at Louis Armstrong. His young voice was very pleasant, but as he got older he really didn't have much voice. He still made incredible music because he knew about expression and phrasing. It's about being in touch with how you physically produce sound out of your body, and then expressing yourself in a way that communicates with others."

BADGE STEPS

1. Decide what you really want to sing.

Tosca? "My Funny Valentine"? *South Pacific?* Do you see yourself as Billie Holiday, Celine Dion, or Maria Callas? Whether you want to carry a tune 'round the campfire or scat like Ella is important to know. Who do you like most, and what is it you like about them—their expression, technique, vocal quality, musical interpretation, repertoire? Keep in mind that pop, soul, jazz, gospel, classical, and opera singers all use distinctive vocal techniques. If you are a stone-cold beginner, you might want to try folk songs. Since they are traditionally sung by untrained singers, you may find them more straightforward and welcoming of your idiosyncrasies. Pick a song that represents the kind of singing you want to do, then learn the lyrics to that song. You might be able to find the lyrics online or in the CD booklet, or you may decide to invest in the sheet music. ***Select your standard.***

2. Find the right teacher.

You now know what you'd like to sing in the future—but in order to find the right teacher, you should also think about your singing history. Have you ever sung in school or in church? What did you like and dislike? What made you stop? You can find private instructors through the National Association of Teachers of Singing Web site (www.nats.org) and through music schools, music stores, and choral directors. The music teachers at community colleges may also teach privately, and don't forget to ask singing friends or musicians for personal recommendations. Whether you go for group classes or one-on-one lessons, chat with potential teachers a bit before signing up. Describe your goals, the song you'd like to learn, and how much experience you've had. Ask them about their experience and teaching style. ***Schedule a trial lesson with a teacher.***

3. Go to class.

Your teacher will ask you to sing a little so he or she can see how you breathe, how you've learned to use your voice, and how comfortable you are manipulating your voice. This is not a test, just a way to gauge your starting point. A good teacher like Brenda will take the time to find a study repertoire based on your interests. She'll find pieces of music that will work with your range, your personality, and your goals. After this initial class, consider: Have you met your match? If so, sign up for

HOW WE SING

Physically speaking . . .

The vibration of the vocal cords, which are inside the larynx, produce speaking and singing sounds. Air from the lungs moves through the windpipe and passes through the vocal cords, which then open and close to produce vibrations in the column of air that passes through the pharynx. The movements and shape of the mouth, tongue, and throat create variations in resonance.

VOCAL RANGES

Ask your teacher what yours is

- Soprano, mezzo-soprano, and contralto are the high-to-low female voices.
- Tenor, baritone, and bass are the high-to-low male voices.

weekly lessons. (If not, try another teacher.) Brenda recommends weekly lessons of forty-five minutes to one hour (less for children). ***Commit to voice lessons.***

BRENDA'S EXPERT TIPS

VOCAL STYLINGS

DO listen to lots of different singers and experiment—gently—with a variety of singing styles.

DO join a church choir or community group. Remember that in ensemble singing, your voice in used in the service of the whole. This takes discipline and direction—the instructor wants the entire piece to sound good, not just you.

DO learn to read notes and play keyboard at the most basic level.

DON'T judge yourself while finding your voice.

DON'T have false expectations. If visions of superstardom dance in your head, Brenda says you can't ignore the impresarios like Simon Cowell on *American Idol* who know what it takes to hit it big in terms of presence, style, and musical acumen.

DON'T give up!

4. Give it time.

Practice here, there, and everywhere at least once every day for three months, even if it's only in the shower. Don't be shy. Brenda remembers that when she was a kid practicing all the time at home, her neighbors told her parents how much they enjoyed hearing her. "People like to hear other people express themselves."

As you practice, you learn to consciously use the muscles in your throat and lungs. With repetition, you develop muscle memory, just as you do when you learn to play a musical instrument. We're less used to training our singing muscles than our fingers, so be patient. Don't overdo it: fifteen to twenty minutes a day is fine, and don't worry about taking a day or two off.

Brenda gives diction exercises as homework. "I have students concentrate on relaxing their jaw and using their lips to make the shape of words. In singing, we try to keep our mouths and jaws very relaxed and shape the words with our lips. I often use an Italian song to teach this. It has nice round vowels and teaches people a simple technique. It's also very emotional, and a little bit corny, but that brings the whole expression issue to the fore."

SINGING FUNDAMENTALS

Here's what you'll work on in class

- Posture, relaxed stance, open chest, free neck
- Coordinated breath intake with a relaxed jaw
- Tone focus and vocal "on-set"
- Breath support: full torso and abdomen, from the bottom up
- Breath management: measuring output for tone, musicality, and dynamics
- Musical phrasing and style
- Lyrics, meaning, and diction
- Expression
- Resonance: placement, vowel color, and consonants

I DID IT!

"I sang solo in front of 1,000 people when I was only nine, so I tend not to get nervous when I sing—not even at my own wedding. But one time I went with a couple friends to this hardcore karaoke joint, where they take singing very seriously and competitively. We'd had a bit too much to drink, so we weren't exactly in peak form—and when my friend started singing 'Besame Mucho,' she actually got dragged offstage! So I was kind of worried how it would go over when it was my turn to sing. But I psyched myself up, got up there, and sang the heck out of my song . . . and suddenly I was surrounded by all these serious karaoke fans clapping me on the back and saying, 'Hey, you should come here more often!'"

—Jenn

WRONG NOTE

"I was singing in a trio in front of Parkview Church of the Nazarene and, unbeknownst to me, the microphone cord was slowly lifting up my skirt. When I realized what was happening, I started laughing hysterically and literally slapping my knees. The whole congregation joyfully joined in . . . the place was in an uproar. They were both laughing at me and laughing with me! Cost of microphone? $200. Look of mortification on my mother's face? PRICELESS!"

—Carrie

Don't forget the song you picked at the outset. How's it coming? Ask your teacher if there are particular singers you might listen to who could help you master the skills you'll need to sing your song. Your teacher might also suggest special exercises, such as holding tones. When you're driving or riding your bike, just sing any old tone and hold it as long as you can. This strengthens your muscles and breathing technique. ***Train those vocal cords!***

5. Share your song.

Now that you've warmed up, tape yourself singing that favorite tune. Listen to the recording, and be proud of your progress. Wouldn't you like to show it off a little? Organize a karaoke night, recital, or lounge-lizard shindig with appreciative (or at least nonjudgmental) friends and family. Once you've gotten that first taste of applause, you'll want more! Here are some places to find it:

- If you know other students studying voice or have friends who sing or play instruments, host a hootenanny at home. Who knows—you might even decide to form a group.
- Singing as part of a group is a great way to get over singing-in-public nerves. Look into community college choirs or other local musical groups. If you go to church, sing in the choir.
- Volunteer to sing at a school, hospital, hospice, nursing home, or nonprofit benefit. Children are apt to sit in awe, while older folks are often taken back to happy times. It's not necessarily glamorous, but is oh so rewarding.

Go public, and bask in the limelight!

CONGRATULATIONS!

Take a bow and prepare your encore. You did it!

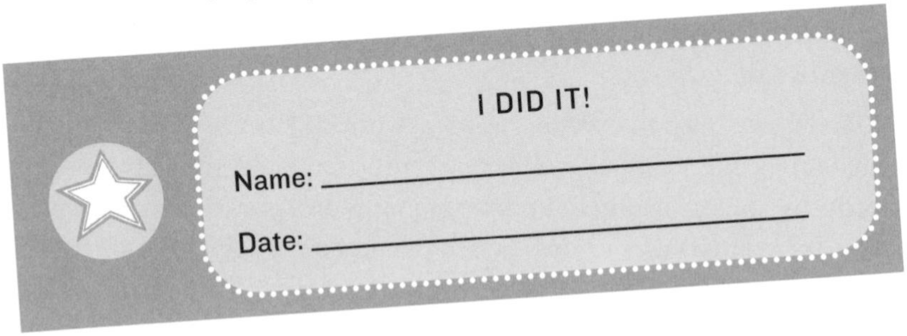

BEYOND THE BADGE

If you love it as much as you thought you would, dream on . . .

- **Try different types of music.** You learn different, useful techniques from every kind of singing. Brenda's experience singing spirituals in church has come in handy professionally. "I learned incredible technique doing that—which, of course, I wasn't aware of at the time."
- **Get serious about performance.** Now that you have "your song," you can audition for performance opportunities (musical theater productions, local choruses, gigging combos). Or work up a set, make a demo tape, and send it to restaurants or bars that feature live entertainment.
- **Be a happy camper.** If you want to solo, Brenda says music camps are ideal places to gain performing experience. This is the route she took when she wanted to work on her jazz singing. "After all my years of classical training, I was a beginner again, shaking in my boots. But people were great and supportive. I got experience singing in a combo and alone with an accompanist on piano."

  Brenda's jazz camp training came in handy in November 2002, when she earned a solo in Wynton Marsalis's performance with the San Francisco Symphony. She called on her jazz training, did the audition, and got the solo. "I thought I was just going to be singing up in the balcony, no big deal. But a week before the show, I learned that I'd be closing the show. I had to make an entrance and do a totally exposed solo in a sold-out hall for five nights. I was on cloud nine!"
- **Cut a demo.** Inexpensive, easy-to-use home recording equipment or small local recording studios make this less difficult than you might think. You can sell your tapes or CDs at performances or online.

EASY DOES IT

Once you find your voice, you don't want to lose it!

- Don't abuse your voice. Belting is really not a good technique for young or beginning voices.
- Avoid yelling and talking rapidly for long periods of time.
- Beware of medications, like some antihistamines, that can dry you out.
- Brenda steers clear of sad movies if she has to perform, because crying makes your vocal cords swell.
- Avoid singing in smoky or otherwise unhealthy environments.
- Stay healthy by getting plenty of rest, drinking lots of water, and avoiding colds (wash your hands!).

BRENDA'S PICKS

BOOKS

Foundations in Singing: A Basic Textbook in Vocal Technique and Song Interpretation by John Glenn Paton and Van Christy
Covers the basics with songs appropriate for beginners and a friendly approach.

Great Singers on Great Singing by Jerome Hines
Tips and inspiration from the likes of Birgit Nilsson, Joan Sutherland, Marilyn Horne, and Luciano Pavarotti.

A Soprano on Her Head: Right-Side-Up Reflections on Life and Other Performances by Eloise Ristad
Helpful advice for getting over stage fright and letting your voice rise to the occasion.

SHEET MUSIC

Any Score
www.anyscore.com/link.asp
Offers free classical scores and links to jazz, classical, and other sheet music sources.

Broadway Sheet Music
www.broadwaysheetmusic.net
Tunes from the Great White Way.

Sheet Music Plus
www.sheetmusicplus.com
Wide spectrum of sheet music covers Grammy winners (Nora Jones, India Arie, et al.).

CONSERVATORIES: INTERNATIONAL

Conservatoire de Montreux, Switzerland
www.montreux.ch/conservatoire
Study at the home of the legendary Montreux Jazz Festival.

Helsinki Pop and Jazz Conservatory, Finland
www.berklee.edu/international/helsinki.html
Enroll directly in the program, or through Berklee College of Music's exchange program.

Royal Academy of Music, London
www.ram.ac.uk
Offers musical theater, choral, music, jazz, and classical programs.

Seoul Jazz Academy
www.sja.co.kr and www.berklee.edu/international/seoul.html
Enroll directly in the program, or go through Berklee College of Music's exchange program.

CONSERVATORIES: NATIONAL

Berklee College of Music, Boston, Massachusetts
www.berklee.edu
The world's largest independent music college. Notable graduates include producer Quincy Jones and singer-songwriters Paula Cole and Melissa Etheridge.

Indiana University, Bloomington, Indiana
www.music.indiana.edu
A top-ranked program for decades in opera, jazz, and music education.

Stanford Jazz Workshop, Palo Alto, California
www.stanfordjazz.org
Brenda gives this one high marks.

Swannanoa Gathering, Asheville, North Carolina
www.swangathering.org
Where better to sing folk songs than nestled in the Appalachian foothills?

CLASSES AND TEACHERS

International Association of Schools of Jazz (IASJ)
www.iasj.com
Jazz in all four corners of the world and then some.

The National Association of Teachers of Singing (NATS)
www.nats.org
National Web site with local links.

MOVIES

When you need inspiration:

Cabaret

Funny Girl

Lady Sings the Blues

Moulin Rouge

Singin' in the Rain

The Sound of Music

A Star Is Born

Topsy-Turvy

create

To create one's own world in any of the arts takes *courage*.

—Georgia O'Keeffe

12

PAINT A PICTURE

★ painting ★

Cease to be a drudge,
seek to be an artist.

—Mary McLeod Bethune

So, what's your motivation?
Take a moment.
Dream a little, think big,
and then complete this sentence:
I see myself . . .

Imagine This . . . You crave that charge you get flinging pots of paint at eight-foot canvases or that sense of calm as you set up an easel at your favorite vista point. Maybe you brush ink onto paper in inspired swoops like a Zen master or painstakingly translate your favorite photo of a loved one into a portrait in oils. Is it art? Who cares?! The important thing is that you haven't had this much fun since kindergarten—when you didn't even know you were expressing with Expressionism or impressing with Impressionism. Do we have to paint you a picture? Nope. You'll be doing that all by yourself with this badge. So gather your brushes, prepare your palette, and commune with your canvas.
You can do it!

The Payoffs

- **Self-expression.** There's a reason people say a picture is worth a thousand words. You may find you're able to say things on canvas that you could never put into words and with a poetry you never knew you had in you.
- **Vision.** Even if you aren't trying to paint the most lifelike apple ever, the attempt to capture what you see in your mind's eye sharpens, clarifies, and crystallizes your powers of observation.
- **Adventure.** Every time you begin with a clean canvas or wrestle with a work in progress, you are venturing to places no one else can go. What will you discover?
- **Appreciation.** When you go to a museum or gallery, you will have a personal insight into how masterpieces are made.

Meet Your Mentor
SUSAN DORY

What She Does: An abstract painter who lives and works in Seattle, Susan is a winner of the prestigious *New American Paintings* competition (the painter's equivalent of winning an Academy Award) and her ethereal encaustic paintings have been featured in numerous solo and group shows around the country. Through the cloudy white layers of wax, vibrant patterns emerge—Susan calls them "the patterns of the domestic, the banal, the household ritual." *The Seattle Post-Intelligencer* calls it "beautiful" and "tough," "but with a bouncy, comic undertone." NextMonet.com says that Susan's "seamless craftsmanship continues a legacy of the art of the everyday, handed down through generations of women."

Why She Does It: "I loved my collages, crayons, and watercolors as a kid, and I also liked to make up stories. I was encouraged by my family but was definitely the unconventional, eccentric kid. I studied art in college, along with English, film, and journalism. After graduation, I studied art and German as a student in Vienna—but travel in and of itself was an enormous education. Painting is an emotional and cerebral necessity for me (though I also have a day job to augment the income I derive from my painting and from grants). I'm not sure you have a choice not to make art when you know the drive is there—artmaking finds you. When it becomes important and apparent, you'd better act! It's an amazing journey to delve into the self and actualize ideas."

Painting seems brave . . . and it is brave. It's also FUN. I suppose we are all artists inside, but only you can decide whether to make the journey into that part of yourself.

—Susan Dory

Word from the Wise: "The act of painting can become very mental—in a good way—especially if you are really open to the self-knowledge, risk-taking, and skill-building involved. What's the payoff? The possibility of a completely new perspective every day. Each day in the studio is a new beginning in many ways—even if you are working on the same piece for a year."

BADGE STEPS

PAINTING PATOIS

Speak the artist's argot

Brushes. There are hard and soft brushes made with bristle, fur, and synthetic fibers. Flats are long and rectangular, while filberts have a rounded end.

Canvas. Cotton or linen canvases are most popular. They can be bought already primed and stretched or you can prepare them yourself with stretcher bars.

Damar varnish. Can be used as a final varnish or to allow you to continue working on paint that has dried.

Gesso. This primes your work surface, preparing it for paint.

Palette. To hold and mix your paint.

Palette knives. Use to deposit paint on the canvas, scrape it off, and clean your palette.

Stand oil. A medium for thinning or thickening paint and for giving it transparency or gloss.

Turpentine. A solvent used to thin paint and clean brushes.

1. Make way for the muse.

Find yourself a place to paint. Many an artist has found inspiration in a garret, so clear out some of those boxes in your attic and voilà! You have a garret the greats would envy. Garages are good too, but Susan also knows people who paint in hallways, bedrooms, kitchens, dining rooms, and a friend's basement.

Wherever you paint, consider light, ventilation, and easy clean up. Obviously you want a spot with plenty of light. But don't forget about adequate ventilation—inspiration isn't the only thing that'll go to your head if you're working in a confined space with oil paints. Give yourself license to make a mess if the spirit moves you, but put down tarps on the floor and old sheets over any furniture. You'll also need plenty of rags to clean your brushes and any mishaps.

You don't need much in the way of furniture to get started—an easel is optional, though it may help you get into the rhythm of painting. If you're working with ink on paper, you may want to paint on a flat table so your colors don't run. Invest your money in paint, ink, canvas, and paper at the art supply store instead of fancy accessories: A few shallow tuna or cat food cans and chipped mugs and dishes will do to hold your paint and brushes.

Keep some comfortable clothing handy that you don't mind getting smudged with paint—pretty soon, you'll wear those smudges like a badge of pride. "Leave them in your painting area so that each time you begin to paint, you change out of your street clothes and into your studio gear—kind of like Mister Rogers!" notes Susan. ***Create a studio setup you—and the muse—can't wait to visit.***

2. Get art supplied.

Assemble your painting supplies so that you're ready when inspiration strikes. This includes:

Paint or ink

Water-based colors. With water-based paints and inks, you can create brushy textures and organic wash effects—and from a practical standpoint, they're often inexpensive and make for easy clean up.

Acrylics. Susan recommends latex for beginners, since it's usually cheaper and easier to clean up than oils. Use latex house paint leftovers you have lying around the garage, or buy quarts at the paint store (remainder paints or wrongly mixed colors can be really cheap!).

Oils. If you prefer to work in oils, start with less expensive student-grade oil paints. A good beginner's selection of colors includes primary colors and earth tones: black, white, red, green, blue, yellow, Naples yellow, burnt sienna.

Paint mediums, thinners, and primers

For watercolors and water-based inks. Water is really the only thinner you need to experiment with delicate ink washes and bristly brushwork, though other mediums are available that can make water-based colors more opaque and textured.

For acrylics. A range of acrylic mediums is available to give acrylic paint the transparent effect of watercolors, the glossy quality of oils, or even the grainy effect of glazed ceramics.

For oils. To change the consistency of oil-based paints, buy some already mixed damar varnish, turpentine, and stand oil. Try different ratios to create thick, frostinglike Van Gogh swirls, or pull a Cézanne with thin, luminous patches of color. You'll also need gesso to prime canvases before painting them with oils.

Tools

Brushes. To get fine details and cover vast areas of canvas, you'll want a variety of shapes—rounds, flats, and filberts—in a range of sizes. If you're using oils, get a house-painting brush for applying gesso.

Palette. A small square of plexiglass will serve as a palette on which to mix your colors—though nothing looks as impressive as a classic, paint-encrusted palette.

Extras. A palette knife is good for scraping off excess paint and plastering paint onto the canvas, and you can use a squeegee to apply paint in blurred, impressionistic strokes like Gerhard Richter.

Canvas and panels

Canvas. Prestretched canvases are available at any art store, but it's cheaper to stretch your own. "Canvas is cheaper at fabric stores, although art stores sell it too," says Susan. "You can even use other fabric, as long as it is cotton. I've used old burlap bags and tents!" Stretch your fabric of choice over store-bought stretcher bars or homemade ones made with 2-by-2-inch lumber and power tools.

Wood panels. These are readily available in art stores and lumber yards, but Susan offers this insider tip: "Cabinet shops have beautiful pieces of

SUSAN'S FAVORITE FOREMOTHERS

Look to these avant-garde women for inspiration

Hannelore Baron

Lynda Benglis

Louise Bourgeois

Vija Celmins

Sue Coe

Elaine de Kooning

Sonia Delaunay

Valie Export

Artemisia Gentileschi

Rebecca Gregory

Guerrilla Girls

Eva Hesse

Rebecca Horn

Frida Kahlo

Käthe Kollwitz

Lee Krasner

Barbara Kruger

Yayoi Kusama

Dorothea Lange

Agnes Martin

Joan Mitchell

Paula Modersohn-Becker

Anna (Grandma) Moses

Alice Neel

Meret Oppenheim

Bridget Riley

Susan Rothenberg

Nancy Spero

Ursula von Rydingsvard

Sue Williams

birch and fir plywood as scrap wood. Oftentimes they will give this to you for free."

Prepare your palette.

3. Get busy.

Where to begin? "Jettison any preconceived notions you may have about your capabilities and dive in!" recommends Susan. She considers classes good for learning basics (see Feeding the Muse sidebar), but stresses, "You can definitely *just start!* Starting is truly 90 percent of the work."

Watercolors require minimal preparation, but for oils you'll need to paint two to three layers of gesso onto your painting surface beforehand. Oils don't stick so well to plain canvas, but they adhere beautifully to canvas pretreated with chalky, stiff gesso. Let the gesso dry completely between each layer and lightly sand each coat. Then once the surface is well gessoed and dry, you're ready to paint.

For your first painting, Susan recommends "going hog wild with colors." You can also abstract real objects. Set up a still life—but instead of trying to paint that pear, treat it as a shape, pattern, or spot of color that serves as a starting point for your painting. Susan finds that working a series of thin layers into a final image provides a "great crescendo" and allows you to change or flesh out details as you go. The important thing is to get a feel for the paint, your brushes, and your surface. ***Don't wait for inspiration to arrive—meet it halfway.***

FEEDING THE MUSE

Inspiration is all around you

- There are many art centers in larger communities that have great beginner classes for the various painting media, plus there are extension classes at universities and individual artists who give instruction out of their own studios.
- Drawing classes are great for painters. There are often signs up at art stores that list meeting times for studio drawing sessions with models. Even if you plan on being an entirely abstract painter, drawing is an invaluable practice—and Susan insists that it is a learned skill, not an innate gift. "You can draw if you want to."
- Go to museums and look very closely, as a masterpiece is the ultimate teacher. Check out as many paintings as you can—look and learn!

4. Mix things up.

As you work, you'll notice the most amazing paint doesn't come in a tube—it's the stuff you mix yourself. Start combining primary colors, and see what happens: Red + yellow = orange! Blue + red = purple! Yellow + blue = green! Add white to any of these colors, and they become pale pastels. Check out a color wheel or color theory book, then put those color principles to the test in your own work. Feel free to experiment with texture, too: "Add turpentine to make it very washy," Susan suggests, "or mix in some damar varnish to make it runny and wonderfully fluid and sloppy." ***Go avant-garde.***

5. Get some perspective.

Begin to build relationships among the forms and colors on your canvas. Step back from your work from time to time, and consider the scale or size of each object that you paint. Do you want to create depth or flatness? Think about the relationship among the colors you are using and the lines you're making. Do they create tension or harmony? Does everything tie in together and make sense to you? "This is what is most important," says Susan. "Is it musical? Is it minimal? Is it like a jungle? A desert? A disco? Abstract painting can become very poetic." ***Learn as you work.***

6. Finish what you've started.

Push past the temptation to play it safe with hesitant gestures because you're afraid of "messing it up." "You often have to 'ruin' a painting many times to get to the real finishing point," asserts our expert. "It is super important in the beginning to see how far you can go. As you hone your own style and vision, you will make up your own rules (or lack of rules) as to your method to completion."

How will you know when you're done? "This becomes apparent as you paint more and more and figure out your personal vision," assures Susan. "You will come to just know. The painting itself has a voice in this department, if you are listening closely." ***Work until your painting tells you it's done.***

CONGRATULATIONS!

Step back, admire your art, and consider which heir you'll bequeath it to. You did it!

I DID IT!

Name: ______________________________

Date: ______________________________

I DID IT!

"As a young artist I was concerned with my paintings looking exactly as I had envisioned them. Then one day a painting teacher came over to me and turned my painting upside down. At first I was angry that he did this just as my grapes were taking form! Then I took a second look, and shapes emerged that I had not seen before. Now, I no longer try to control my images—I still start with an essential idea, but I let new shapes and colors emerge, form, and grow. Often my paintings become not as I had imagined them to be, but something completely different and more beautiful."

—Abra

DID I DO THAT?!

"Like most artists, I have moments when I feel I am 'in control' of my work and moments when I feel that my work is 'in control' of me. Occasionally, the work begins to show signs of change, often before I can identify, justify, or articulate the nature of the slight shift. It's as if it's evolving by itself, without my consent . . . this is unnerving and even paralyzing. However, I now realize that these feelings of fear and discomfort are in fact heralds of significant developments in the work. I have learned to welcome them, knowing that they are merely the symptoms of progress."

—Amy

BEYOND THE BADGE

If you love it as much as you thought you would, dream on . . .

- **Show your work.** Host an "open studio" event, where you invite everyone you know (and everyone they know) over to see your work. People who know you will be curious to see what you've been up to all this time, and you may find total strangers among your admirers if you circulate an e-mail announcement or put a listing in your local paper. Ask visitors to add their names, addresses, and comments to your guest book, so that you can learn from their observations of your work and invite them to future shows.
- **Bone up on your art history.** Read art books and attend lectures or classes that intrigue you, but above all make a habit of hitting your local galleries, museums, and art nonprofits—there's just no substitute for that firsthand experience of art history. So take the docent or audio tours at museums and pick up any free literature you find in galleries, and be sure to bring a notebook to sketch anything that captures your imagination and jot down any ideas that come to mind.
- **Scope out the art scene.** You don't have to live in a big city to find venues that show art—visit your local nonprofit spaces, schools, city hall, libraries, galleries, artists' cooperatives, and museums and check out the artwork on display there. If you like what you see at any of these places, there's a chance they may like what you do, too. Also, check out art magazines to find announcements for juried shows and open calls for artists to submit work on a particular theme—your work might be a perfect fit!
- **Hit the big time.** When you've created sixteen to twenty pieces that do you proud, have them shot by a photographer in slide format. If you want to submit your work to galleries or enter a competition, you'll need to submit slides along with a resume and artist's statement. Your resume should highlight any training or background in art and list any shows or publications where your work has been featured. The artist's statement should be a brief, thoughtful, and heartfelt statement about what motivated you to make the artwork you're submitting for review. Be aware that it's typically much easier to get your work accepted into a group show than in a solo gallery show—but while most reputable galleries do not charge fees for review, many juried group shows ask a modest review fee (typically twenty-five to thirty dollars for three slides) to defray the costs of putting on a show.

YOUR OWN SENSE OF STYLE

Try both of these on for size

Representational art. Depicts people, places, and things in recognizable ways, though their forms and colors may be distorted. But the goal here is not necessarily to create photo-realistic images. We all see reality differently to some extent, and our vision is altered by external factors like light and internal factors such as mood. So the idea of "accurate" representation can be quite nuanced.

Abstract art. Uses shapes, colors, lines, and textures that don't obviously correspond to things we see in everyday life, although these may be inspired by a real-world image or scene. Abstract artists draw on the symbolic and psychological meaning inherent in many colors and patterns. This can make it challenging for people to relate to, but also invites our active participation as viewers. We can draw our own conclusions, which may or may not correspond to those of the artist.

SUSAN'S PICKS

BOOKS

Any Dover books
These are terrific, inexpensive resources for patterns and designs from various eras and cultures.

The Woman's Dictionary of Symbols and Sacred Objects by Barbara Walker
Fodder for imagery and inspiration.

MAGAZINES

Art in America
www.artinamericamagazine.com
The granddaddy of art publications; publishes guide to American museums and galleries.

Artforum
www.artforum.com
Reviews, ideas, and conversations about art.

ARTnews
www.artnewsonline.com
Art world news and views.

Artweek
www.artweek.com
Check out the view of the art world from the West Coast.

Bomb
www.bombsite.com
For cutting-edge culture that's not afraid to clash.

Bust
www.bust.com
Provides sharp, insightful profiles of female artists.

Dwell
www.dwellmag.com
A must for anyone with a passion for modernism.

Flash Art
www.flashartonline.com
The international art scene on fast-forward: news, previews, insights.

I.D.
www.idonline.com
Ultra-sleek international design; publishes annual design review.

Index
www.indexmagazine.com
Aesthetic trends and trend-maker profiles.

Nest
www.nestmagazine.com
Minimalism brought home; domestic design quarterly.

New American Paintings
www.newamericanpaintings.com
A juried show and magazine featuring masterworks from painters' studios across America.

W
www.wmagazine.com
Popular culture gone highbrow.

Wallpaper*
www.wallpaper.com
Distinctive interior design from Britain.

MOVIES

An American in Paris

Artemisia

Basquiat

Carrington

Frida

High Art

I've Heard the Mermaids Singing

Lust for Life

My Left Foot

The Picture of Dorian Gray

Pollock

13

BE AN AUTHOR

★ writing ★

> The only certainty about writing and trying to be a writer is that it has to be done, not dreamed of or planned and never written.
>
> —Janet Frame

So, what's your motivation?
Take a moment.
Dream a little, think big,
and then complete this sentence:
I see myself . . .

Imagine This . . . You're reading your witty and instructive children's book to your niece; you spot a commuter reading your impassioned editorial on the bus; you're chatting with Terri Gross on *Fresh Air* about your creative process . . . hey, why not? There's only so long you can say to yourself, "If only I had a room of my own, an hour a day, or a friend in publishing . . . " before you realize that your love of words is too strong to be denied. Fact is, no one else can sit down and arrange those words your way except you. You owe it to yourself, to the reading public, and even to posterity to share. So take the plunge and get yourself a writing life. Come out and wordplay! *You can do it!*

The Payoffs

- **Your voice.** No one else can write what you can write. Someone else may have a similar idea or theme, but everyone has a unique voice.
- **Communication.** We write to be read. Writing itself may be a solitary act, but part of the pull is communication—with our deepest selves and with readers.
- **Adventure.** Even if you write your last sentence first, writing is filled with surprises. Your destination may be clear, but from inspiration to completion, you're headed for often delightful, occasionally maddening, but ultimately rewarding detours.
- **Writing.** Dorianne Laux put it, "writing begets writing." You can't finish what you don't start—but once you've gotten started, you'll never again wonder if you have it in you.

Meet Your Mentor

LAURIE HENRY

What She Does: A poet and novelist, Laurie is the author of *The Novelist's Notebook* and *The Fiction Dictionary.* She holds graduate degrees in writing from Johns Hopkins University and the University of Iowa, and her work has appeared in publications including *Poetry, Antioch Review,* and *The American Poetry Review.*

Why She Does It: "I was an art major in college, but an art major who had done a lot of writing. I decided to apply for graduate writing programs because I didn't want to get a 'real' job and because I knew that, with that degree, I could get a teaching job. I have done a fair bit of teaching but also got a job with Writer's Digest Books as the editor of what is now *Novel and Short Story Writer's Market,* and that led to my own two books. As an editor at *Story* magazine, I read submissions for years. While there are pitfalls that beginners can fall into (clichéd characters, excessive ambiguity), I regularly read wonderful stuff that I later learned was written by beginners, young people without a lot of training, and people writing in English as a second language. Making money, being a mom, teaching—these all make writing a challenge that I struggle with all the time. I keep doing it because, on some level, I have to. I'm working on a novel now, and I'm obsessed with my characters and with thinking up new things for them to do. I know how I want things to end, but it's an engrossing challenge to get the characters there in an interesting way. I care about the characters."

Your writing is YOURS—your ideas, your effort. That's what makes the process and the completion so satisfying.

—Laurie Henry

Word from the Wise: "Not all writing is done alone, but it is always personal. Even when I work with editors and get feedback, I'm essentially working with something that is mine, my perspective, my distinct view of the world. There's great joy in sharing that perspective with others."

BADGE STEPS

1. Write right away.

You probably know exactly what you yearn to write or write more of: poetry, personal essays, opinion pieces, short stories, a memoir, children's books, mysteries, the Great American Novel. Don't just commit that goal to memory—grab a notebook and write it down! Once you're done with this badge, you'll have that piece ready to send out for publication, whether it's a haiku, a 500-word op-ed for your local paper, or a chapter of that 75,000-word novel you have in mind.

The notebook you put your goal in is your official writer's journal, and you'll be carrying it with you everywhere you go. That way, you can always capture bits of overheard conversation, ideas you're afraid you'll forget before your next writing session, inspirational quotations, and more (see When You Aren't Writing). Laurie suggests you make at least one entry a day for a month. ***Start a writing journal.***

2. Learn your craft.

Commit to your endeavor by taking a writing class or joining a writing group or workshop, so that you can:

Get support. Writing may be solitary, but it doesn't have to be lonely! If you have a friend who is a writer, make a date to exchange writing and provide constructive comments once or twice a month.

Gather some expert feedback. When Laurie was a graduate writing student, revered novelist John Barth was her first teacher. "His lectures, reading lists, process tips, and, most importantly, comments on our student work were all detailed, careful, and helpful." You can up your chances of having this kind of simpatico teacher, either in a classroom or workshop setting, by looking for a teacher whose writing you admire and asking other writers about that person's teaching style.

Get some structure. Laurie suggests that you can make real progress by taking a class in your field at a local community college or adult extension program. For a nominal fee, you'll find a structured environment with a built-in time and work commitment.

Find and join a writing class or workshop.

3. Get a writing life.

A class or workshop should help get your juices flowing, but it's up to you to develop your writing habit. As Gertrude Stein put it, "To write is

WHEN YOU AREN'T WRITING

Read!

Read with attention and intention, making notes as you go as described in Get Well Read, page 216, but also:

- Read widely in your field of endeavor, and learn the conventions of the type of writing you want to do. Know the unwritten rules and expectations of your genre, even if you are only learning the rules in order to break them. Readers of mysteries expect crimes and clues; opinion pieces, a persuasive argument; memoir, significant life experiences. Note these in your writer's notebook.
- Cover the major titles in your genre. Reading won't only inform your writing, it can also aid your effort to be published. If there is a magazine, newspaper, journal, or book publisher that writers in your field aspire to, read it (or know them) well!
- List and revisit your favorite pieces of writing and write about why you like them in your journal.
- Analyze a piece of writing you dislike. Why? How would you revise it? Make a note in your writer's journal.

to write is to write is to write is to write is to write is to write." While they may also plan it, read about it, study it, and talk about it (not to mention finding very ingenious means of putting it off), writers write. There are many ways to get writing done, and it's crucial that you come up with the time, space, schedule, and tools that work for you. Chances are that if you already had these ducks in a row, you wouldn't be reading this—you'd be writing. So experiment with the following:

Timing. Set your alarm an hour earlier each morning for a week or lump those hours together for a marathon session on the weekend. Which works best?

Venue. Create a room or corner of your own for writing at home, but also try going mobile at a cafe, library, or even parked in your car at a favorite nature spot.

Tools of the trade. Index cards, tape recorders, yellow legal tablets, number 2 pencils, and laptops can all be useful tools.

Writing goals. These could be 250 words, three pages, one perfect image—all are common daily goals.

Program. Some writers warm up with exercises, while others guarantee themselves a fruitful starting point by ending each writing session with a clear sense of the next sentence or scene.

Structure. Do deadlines get your pen flowing? Classes and workshops are great for these, as are writing partners, people you take a solemn oath to exchange chunks of writing with each day or week.

For the next six weeks, commit to writing seven hours a week and experiment with different writing times, places, and tools. At the end of this time, evaluate what worked the best for you and make that your writing life. As Laurie says, "Take this routine seriously, protect it fiercely, and take solitaire off your computer!" ***Make a writing commitment: seven hours a week for six weeks.***

4. Stay inspired.

As you pursue your writing goals avoid the dreaded writer's block, by turning to these sources of inspiration:

Your writer's journal. By now, it's full of ideas, possible plot twists, and intriguing turns of phrase. Try a few!

Writing groups, classes, and peers. Your writing peers and instructors may be able to give you the feedback and encouragement you need to take your work in exciting new directions. Ask for what you want: Is the

GET SUPPORT IN WRITING

Ways to connect

Writing groups help cement your identity as a writer, keep your momentum going, and intersperse the isolation of creative work with community. Pick a regular carved-in-stone date so you don't waste time figuring out when and how. Meet at a conducive spot—one another's homes, a café, a workroom you can reserve at your library or at a community center. You could form such a group with fellow students in your writing class or with friends or coworkers, or seek out such a group by checking local bulletin boards, online listservs, and the classified sections of local publications. Formats can vary:

- Read and do the exercises in a how-to book together.
- Read and critique one another's works in progress.
- Support one another in another way such as writing silently together for an hour, discussing problems with your work, researching and sharing avenues for publication.

I DID IT!

"I was in a writing workshop and wrote a humorous personal essay about my family's devotion to See's Candy: How a holiday isn't complete without a box of 'Nuts and Chews,' how we gripe about people who bring the dreaded 'Soft Centers' assortment instead, how one of my boys has inherited his mother's chocolate addiction. My local newspaper publishes essays like this in the Sunday edition, so I sent mine in and it got published. This was great—but even better was when the president of See's saw my essay and wrote to ask me if they could reprint my piece in the company newsletter. My payment was a tour of the chocolate factory for me and my kids, and—get this—two pounds of candy delivered to my door every month for the rest of my life! Oh, the pleasures of publication!"

—Natasha

PUBLISH OR PERISH?

"I've taken a couple of writing workshops in which the ultimate goal was the instructor's red-ink 'SEND IT OUT' stamp on the top of your manuscript. At the end of the course, I had several of those coveted stamps, but I have a real block against taking the risk of sending my stuff out. I have at least a dozen pieces that teachers and trusted readers have said are more than ready, but they sit in my desk drawer. I guess I think the editors are going to knock on my door and beg for my writing—or that after I die, my heirs will find this treasure trove, and I'll be posthumously published!"

—Jeanine

LAURIE'S EXPERT TIPS

CLEARING CLOGS

Instead of packing it in when your writing isn't going well, try to unpack (analyze) the problem so that you can fix it.

- Don't like what you wrote? Put it aside for several days and then reassess your work.
- Were you unable to write a word? Try a writing exercise next time.
- Were you distracted? Can you try a different workspace or do you just need to unplug the phone?
- Are you hearing voices? Talk back to the internalized voice of your mother saying you should be organizing your linen closet or ending world hunger. Tell the English teacher who didn't like your style that you've learned a thing or two. Tell the friend who misses you that you'll catch up with her after your writing session.

ending too abrupt? Do they understand the heroine's motivation? If your group does not offer feedback, ask three well-read friends or acquaintances to read your work and provide constructive critiques. Tell them what you are trying to do with the piece, and ask them to let you know if it succeeds for them in that regard.

An outline. It may be helpful to outline your main ideas, so you can remind yourself where your story or poem is ultimately headed in moments of uncertainty.

Encyclopedias and other reference books. As you write, you may find you need to do a bit more research to fill in key details. Do you need to know more about homes in medieval France, shoe styles in the year you were born, or the symptoms of heart disease? Hit the reference section. Laurie suggests that phone books, baby name books, places on a map, and historical figures can be great prompts.

One word of caution: There's a fine line between preparation and procrastination. Don't let yourself get so involved with the preliminaries that you never get around to writing. Make sure you actually write during the time you've set aside for writing. ***Write your first draft.***

5. Revise.

You may dream of sharing your work by running into your office with *The New Yorker* in which your short story appears, but you'll have a better shot of getting into print if you learn to use the responses to your work to polish it to a high shine. Take in the feedback you've received, review the initial goals for your piece captured in your writer's notebook, and then play with your text. Experiment with the suggestions you've received from classmates, instructors, and peers, and see what you think.

As you make your revisions, take into account all the feedback you've received, even suggestions you're inclined to dismiss. Laurie says, "When I was in the program at Iowa, no one really liked the novel I was working on at the time! This was hard. When I look back now, I can still take issue with some of the particular critiques—but I also know that if a number of people are expressing doubt about a piece of writing, there's probably something wrong there. You have to take that in." ***Polish your piece.***

6. Write "The End."

When are you done? Getting anxious to begin a new piece of writing and reading your piece and smiling (rather than cringing!) are hints that the cake is baked. Stop working on the piece, put it aside for a few days or weeks, and reread it with fresh eyes. If you're still not happy, it could be that you have such a harsh "inner critic" or such an ingrained sense of perfectionism that you'll never think anything you write is good enough. Work with your trusted readers to help you know when a piece really is finished, and, if necessary, set a realistic deadline to complete your revisions.

When you've reached the end of your revisions, drop your pen or step away from the computer and go celebrate—you've got a piece you can send out for publication! For tips on sending your baby out into the world, see Getting Published, page 102. ***Finish with a flourish.***

CONGRATULATIONS!

Write on! You did it!

I DID IT!

Name: ______________________

Date: ______________________

WRITING EXERCISES

To warm up, find new ideas, and stay inspired

- Create a detailed biography for one of your characters or for a stranger you've observed. What was their childhood like? What kind of music do they listen to? Have they ever been in therapy? Do they believe in God?
- Write a letter to one of your characters, from one character to another, from the writer you are now to the writer you will be in ten years, or to yourself as a child.
- Go someplace you wouldn't normally go and describe it in great detail.
- Write down your favorite family story.
- Write with tools you don't normally use—for instance, try scrawling with pen and paper if you usually opt for typing at the computer.

extra credit

GETTING PUBLISHED

THE WAITING GAME

Tips for keeping cool

- Keep sending your writing out so that you always have an "iron in the fire."
- Know that rejection is just part of the publishing game. If you aren't getting rejections, you aren't sending stuff out—and if you aren't sending stuff out, you aren't going to get published.
- Don't linger on disappointments. "When I first started sending my writing out," says Laurie, "I thought it would be a good idea to pin all my rejections on the wall above my desk. It turns out that was a bad idea—too depressing!"
- Don't get too fixated on any one publication. As Laurie says, "If you repeatedly get a form rejection letter, with no personal note from the editor or reader, you might be barking up the wrong tree."
- Learn to recognize success. If your recipient takes the time to add a personal note, suggesting revisions or inviting you to send in other material, rejoice! Editors are busy, so this is a good sign.

How do we do it?

Seek out the right publications. What publications or publishing houses are publishing the kind of work you've written? Spend time studying the publications at a good newsstand or in your library's periodical section. Check the acknowledgments pages of books like yours for the names of publishing house editors—always address your submission to a specific editor so it doesn't get buried deep in a "slush pile" of unsolicited work. Don't ignore small or online publishers, since they are often the most likely to welcome newcomers.

Follow submission guidelines. In the publications themselves, at their online sites, or in the kinds of reference works noted below, you'll find detailed instructions about how to submit work. Follow these instructions to the letter.

Make some contacts. Do you need friends in high places? Not necessarily, but it helps. Ask teachers to put in a good word with publishing contacts, and don't be shy about asking for introductions to published writers from friends who might help. But don't stop there: Check out retreats and conferences to meet literary movers and shakers, and go to readings and mixers to meet fellow writers.

Check out agents. You may not need one for poetry or magazine writing, but it helps in book publishing. Without an agent, your manuscript may be more likely to wind up in the dreaded slush pile. Someone will eventually glance at your work there—bestsellers have been discovered this way by editorial assistants—but an agent can help you leapfrog the pile to the right editor. Laurie reminds us never to pay an agent to read your work: You want them to make money by selling your work, not for reading it. Ask writers and teachers to give you names of possible agents, and check these resources:

- *Literary Marketplace.* American and international versions of this directory of book publishers and industry yellow pages are published annually. www.literarymarketplace.com.
- *Writer's Digest* magazine. Markets, inspiration, instruction. Writer's Digest also publishes dozens of reference works for writers and online updates; visit www.writersdigest.com for details.
- *Writer's Market.* The bible for writers with the goal of getting published. Available in libraries or online at www.writersmarket.com.

LAURIE'S PICKS

BOOKS

:: *On writing:*

The Art of Fiction: Notes on Craft for Young Writers by John Gardner
In this classic book, Gardner offers pointers on such essential considerations as originality and audience.

Aspects of the Novel and Related Writings by E.M. Forster
The esteemed author of *A Room with a View* speaks his mind on the craft of writing.

Bird by Bird by Anne Lamott
A thoughtful, inspirational approach to writing as an invaluable means of understanding and an illuminating way of life.

How Fiction Works: The Last Word on Writing Fiction, from Basics to the Fine Points by Oakley Hall
Learn Hall's method for assessing what you read with an eye to craft, and you'll become a more astute writer and reader.

The Novelist's Notebook by Laurie Henry
Helpful tips, writing exercises, and extra motivation to help you write the American novel you always knew you had in you.

The Observation Deck: A Tool Kit for Writers by Naomi Epel
Stack the deck in your favor with tips from more than one hundred writers on overcoming writer's block.

A Primer of the Novel: For Readers and Writers by David Madden
"I can't begin to say what a wonderful book this is for a beginning novelist!" says Laurie.

Writing Down the Bones: Freeing the Writer Within by Natalie Goldberg
An excellent resource to help you start sifting through your words and focusing on the ones that matter most.

:: *Reference books:*

The Chicago Manual of Style by University of Chicago Press Staff
This is the bible for most publishing houses, so you'll want to be sure your manuscript follows these style guidelines religiously.

The Elements of Style by William Strunk Jr. and E. B. White
This slim volume by master wordsmiths Strunk and White (of *Charlotte's Web* fame) is an essential guide to composition, grammar, word usage and misusage, and writing style.

The Fiction Dictionary by Laurie Henry
Use this handy reference to sling literary terminology with confidence and put literary devices to work for you.

Guide to Literary Agents by Rachel Vater (editor)
Use this reference to stop envying writers with agents that land six-figure advances and start looking for one for yourself!

Novel and Short Story Writer's Market by Anne Bowling (editor)
Find out who might be in the market for your kind of writing with this reference, published annually.

MAGAZINES

Granta
www.granta.com
The British magazine that launches big ideas and great stories from established and emerging writers.

The New Yorker
www.newyorker.com
Essays, poetry, fiction, and cartoons galore from renowned writers and the occasional breakthrough literary star.

Poets and Writers
www.pw.org
Thoughtful interviews with authors and insightful first-person commentary on the writing life.

Publishers Weekly
www.publishersweekly.com
Book reviews, bestseller lists, major deals, and other breaking news from the publishing world.

WEB SITES

The Association of Authors' Representatives
www.aar-online.org
Learn more about what a literary agent can do for you and what kinds of questions to ask prospective agents from this key industry association.

Media Bistro
www.mediabistro.com
Helpful tips for breaking into the media business, from pitching stories to magazine editors to landing an agent for your great American novel.

Publishers Lunch
www.caderbooks.com
Get the inside scoop on the publishing industry with this informative, witty newsletter.

14 ROLL 'EM

★ filmmaking ★

I don't care if it doesn't make a nickel, I just want every man, woman, and child in America to see it!

—Samuel Goldwyn, referring to *The Best Years of Our Lives*

So, what's your motivation?
Take a moment.
Dream a little, think big,
and then complete this sentence:
I see myself . . .

Imagine This . . . Charlie Rose has assembled a roundtable to discuss your latest Sundance triumph; Bravo, HBO, and Showtime are fighting over you; and Bobby (De Niro) has agreed to do your next feature. Or maybe your friends have gathered around the table to toast your success at the local film festival, two of them are fighting over whose name should appear first in the end credits, and Joe at the video store has agreed to stock your next feature. It's official: You're in show biz! And by the end of this badge, you'll have a short film credit to your name to prove it. So whether you just want to tell a great story or actually deliver that imaginary Oscar speech one day, it's time to climb into that director's chair and yell, "Quiet on the set!" *You can do it!*

The Payoffs

- **Depth.** Turning your idea into a film requires you to delve deeply into your topic—a rare, almost luxurious level of absorption we often don't allow ourselves as adults.
- **Breadth.** Every phase of the filmmaking process will stretch you in ways you didn't think possible. You'll learn to brainstorm brilliant ideas on the fly, collaborate more effectively with others, and make the most of modern technology.
- **Leadership skills.** Why do you think actors say they've "always wanted to direct"? The control is behind the camera! You and your creative team call the shots—literally.
- **Snooping rights.** When you interview documentary subjects or put yourself in a character's shoes, you gain access into the human experience, into lives unlike your own.

Meet Your Mentor
JONA FRANK

What She Does: Jona's *Catholic School* premiered at the 1998 Sundance Film Festival, won the Best Bay Area Short Film award at the 1999 San Francisco International Film Festival, and was subsequently licensed by the Bravo network. Jona was commissioned by Bay Area PBS affiliate KQED to film *Paly High: Between Classes,* a thirty-minute documentary about life at Silicon Valley's Palo Alto High School. An award-winning photographer, Jona has traveled around the country visiting high schools and capturing diverse adolescent social groups for her *High School* photograph series. When we spoke, Jona was working on a series of still portraits of people in uniform.

Why She Does It: "As a thirteen- or fourteen-year-old, I'd look at photo books and think, 'That's what I want to do.' When looking at monographs, I'd think about the photos from the photographer's point of view—they got to go to all these interesting places and meet all these different people! I was always thinking of the stories behind the photos: If there was a jukebox in a shot, I wondered what song was last played. When I was a senior in high school, I told one of my teachers that maybe I'd go out to California and make movies since there weren't enough women doing that. I also knew that, while I loved photography, there were some things best conveyed by film. It's all about wanting to tell a story."

Word from the Wise: "Great character and content can go a long way, even if your film doesn't have flawless production values."

Be real, be sincere, and people will help you. Your seriousness and commitment are contagious.

—Jona Frank

AUTEUR ARGOT

How to talk like the director you are

Preproduction. Everything that happens before you start shooting: budgets, research, finding crew, etc.

Production. Shooting.

Postproduction. Everything that happens after you shoot: editing, music, titles, test screenings.

Composition. The spatial relationship of objects within the frame and to the camera.

Shot list. A written list of images you and your crew will set out to acquire. Essentially, a wish list for a day's work.

Storyboard. A visual guide of your shot list. Similar to a comic strip, your storyboards should represent in drawings or still photos what you hope to create in your film.

BADGE STEPS

1. Find your subject.

You may have a three-hour epic or nine-part miniseries incubating in your brain, but let's start with something more manageable. Your badge assignment is to choose an intriguing woman and make a ten-minute documentary about her—a video portrait—shot on digital video all in a single day.

First you need to find a subject with a compelling story to tell. You may not need to look far—it could be your next-door neighbor with hair-raising stories about growing up amid armed conflict in Kashmir or your sister who's having hilarious misadventures writing and directing an elementary school play. Listen for universal themes that can make the difference between a clever anecdote and a profoundly moving story. Even though not everyone lives in a war zone or writes plays in their spare time, anyone can appreciate the challenge of finding moments of grace in troubled times or watching children find their voice. ***Find a person with a story that deserves—or even demands—telling.***

2. Tap your community resources.

As you prepare to film your project, Jona suggests you take a class in basic filmmaking techniques at a community college or local nonprofit film and video workshop. This could be a one-day seminar or a semester-long course—whatever works for you. A course will help you become confident behind a camera, build your skills, possibly give you access to equipment, and introduce you to others who share your passion for film (and may be willing to help out on your crew, too).

Jona also advises checking out what your local public access channel and local arts nonprofits have to offer. They might have equipment you can borrow and can be a terrific resource for showing your finished work! As they say in the biz: It's not what you know, it's who you know. ***Get in the know.***

3. Assemble your crew.

You will do all your filming in one day, though preproduction and postproduction can each take several days or weeks. So to help develop your vision and make sure (most) things go off without a hitch on the all-important day of the shoot, you will need to enlist help. In order to do justice to your subject, you simply can't be everywhere at once: behind the camera, conducting the interview, capturing the sound, paying attention to details of continuity and lighting, and thinking ahead to editing, music, and titles.

You don't need experts in any of these fields to help—just someone ready to learn and to provide attention to technical details while you're focused on realizing the overall vision. A little enthusiasm goes a long way, since many essential filmmaking tasks can seem less than glamorous and tediously repetitive. It can be helpful to have experienced people to work with on some of the more technically demanding tasks in postproduction, such as editing and sound. If people are volunteering their time to be part of your crew, you'll want to make sure they feel appreciated. Provide them with lunch, snacks, and other amenities—and of course feature their names in the credits.

Recruit eager friends and family for straightforward tasks, and use your newfound filmmaking network to fill in the technically challenging positions (Jona has worked with several people from her film school days for years). Post calls for crew on community bulletin boards online and at your local schools, arts nonprofits, and cable access and public television stations. You may be surprised at the response you get—people get excited about a worthy movie project. And once you have talented people who believe in your film, there's no stopping you. ***Get your creative team together.***

4. Get geared up.

Jona says working with what you have and finding your way around your limitations is all part of the creative process of filmmaking. That said, try to get these basics lined up early on:

A digital camera. If you don't have a digital camera but have been wanting to buy one, now's the time. You can borrow one from a friend or family member, or possibly rent one. Visit a camera shop, electronics emporium, or manufacturer Web site to learn more about the cameras (see Jona's Picks, page 113).

A tripod. This will eliminate the shakiness that so often marks a home movie (and gives viewers motion sickness!). Tripods are easy to rent and not expensive to buy at photo supply rental houses.

A microphone. Sound issues can get complicated. Your camera's internal microphone will pick up unintended ambient sounds—including

DO IT DIGITALLY

Celluloid is so 20th century!

- Not everyone has a Hollywood budget. Shooting on digital video bypasses developing, processing, and splicing, so filmmakers (like you!) no longer need to spend months learning these skills—not to mention their life's savings on expensive equipment and facilities.
- Digital is by the people, for the people. In a way, digital has democratized film, giving more and more people a way to enjoy moviemaking.
- It's avant-garde. Some established filmmakers swear by it—Lars von Trier and the other award-winning directors of the Dogma school shoot exclusively in video, focusing on telling compelling stories without the frills of film. (Recent Dogma films include *Dancer in the Dark* and *Italian for Beginners.*)

I DID IT!

"I'm at the Sundance Film Festival. The lights go down and my movie comes up. The room is packed—sold out—and people are laughing and really into the film. When I made *Catholic School*, I had no idea that it would come to much. I had spent so much time alone with the project, and then to have it go public and be well received—an incredible feeling!" —Jona

CUT!

"I had had such an easy time interviewing second graders for *Catholic School* that I assumed the eighth graders would be similarly easy. Not. I went in with my questions, but one by one, they kept talking about an incident that had happened at the beginning of the school year. A student's brand-new and very expensive eyeglasses had been stolen, and as a result the whole class had to give up their senior trip. This event shaped their entire school year. But I had my questions all planned out and didn't want to hear about the damn glasses! I kept trying to change the subject. The glasses episode could have been its own great movie if I had just gone with it." —Jona

sirens and car alarms—while recording dialogue. Better to rent or buy a clip-on microphone compatible with your camera that you can attach to your interviewees to make sure you get their answers loud and clear.

Lighting. This can also get complicated, since digital video is best in daylight and digital cameras don't offer the best depth of field. So that you don't need to worry about too much lighting equipment, film in natural daytime light outdoors or well-lit, spacious indoor settings. You may need a light meter to check that the light stays relatively consistent throughout, and have a fill-in light on hand as the daylight wanes.

A computer. Working with digital means you may be able to edit and finesse your film on your home computer. There are a number of editing and effects programs for Macintosh, and many programs are now made for PCs, too. But if you have an ancient coffeemaker of a computer, beware: This can make editing slow going, and you'll need enough hard disk space and memory to accommodate both your editing program and your stored video. Still, don't despair—you should be able to rent time on an editing-equipped computer from a school, nonprofit arts facility, or film and video workshop.

Equip yourself for filmmaking success.

JONA'S EXPERT TIPS

MOVIE SUPPLY SIDE ECONOMICS

- Don't be intimidated by film and camera supply warehouses, even as a beginner. Chat about what you're doing, and make the clerks part of your team. Jona often finds her rental bills reduced because her suppliers have become so invested in what she's doing.
- Foster a collaborative spirit by inviting helpful suppliers to screenings or giving them a disk version of your finished project.
- Consider thanking your suppliers by name in the credits. That's free advertising for them and invaluable goodwill for you!

5. Finish preproduction.

It sounds intimidating—but this is actually the fun, creative part once you've done the hard work of finding a crew and equipment. Here's a creative to-do list for you:

Research your subject. Interview her at length, and get to know the woman you have chosen inside and out. Set a date with her for filming, and arrange ample time beforehand to observe her day-to-day world. What are the people, places, things, and ideas you associate with this person? Does her kitchen provide some intimate insight about her, or her CD collection, or her kids? What do these things say about her and her life experience? Make a list of ten things you'll film that you feel reveal something important about your subject.

Interview other people about your subject. Do they experience her differently than you do? What are the first five words that pop into their minds about her? Would you like to include the voices of any additional people in your film? (If so, feel free to add a second day to your shooting schedule during which you'll interview secondary subjects.)

Consider your story angle. As you've talked with your subject and done research, what's the most compelling aspect of the story that has taken shape in your mind? What do you want to convey with your film? If you're telling the story about your sister's play, maybe the touchstone is how your painfully shy sister has to help a shy kid overcome paralyzing stage fright.

Create a production shot list and storyboard. Your shot list describes in words each of the images you will film, and your storyboard is a visual version of the shot list (kind of like a comic strip—drawing expertise not required!). Jona sometimes uses still photos to create her storyboard, but stick-figure drawings will do. Keep your shooting schedule in mind as you plan your shots. It takes far more shots than you would think to fill ten minutes of screen time, so plan your time wisely to get them all in on production day.

Prepare for the big day!

6. Roll 'em!

Today's the day! Study your shot list and storyboard and review your interview questions. Make sure the lighting, microphone, and all other technical details are dealt with before you get started—you don't want to cut too often, because it interrupts the flow of your subject's thoughts.

As a beginner, don't feel you have to capture a lot of movement. Even with the built-in image stabilization devices in many new DV cameras, following your subject with a handheld camera can be dicey. (Remember audiences complaining about how *The Blair Witch Project* made them seasick?) If you want to experiment, resourceful filmmakers have been

FOR INSPIRATION

Some favorites

"Look at lots of photo books—they are a one-to-one cinema. Think about how the photos are arranged: There is a purpose and story behind the order." —Jona

The Americans by Robert Frank

Figments from the Real World by Garry Winogrand

In the American West by Richard Avedon

Mother exPosed by Bertha Alyce
Includes a DVD of a short film relating to the photographs.

Projects by Nikki S. Lee

Raised by Wolves by Jim Goldberg

known to use shopping carts or wheelchairs to give the camera stability while moving about.

In addition to capturing the shots on your shot list, be sure to get:

Establishing shots. A wide shot that sets the scene and provides maximum information about your subject's context.

Coverage. Getting coverage means photographing people and things from different angles and distances (sitting, standing, in action, close up, and from a distance) so that you can pick and choose while editing.

Cutaway shots. These provide the visual details that help to illustrate your story. For example, if your subject talks about her mother, you can cut away to still photographs of her mother to illustrate her story. Cutaways are a big help when editing, since they give you shots to cover the inevitable splicing as you transition between scenes and edit dialogue.

Bring your storyboard to life!

7. Edit, and then edit some more.

How can you possibly edit your precious footage down to a mere ten minutes?! Technically speaking, you'll use a computer editing system like Final Cut Pro (if you aren't set up to do this at home, local schools or community art centers are). But the real trick isn't technical, it's creative.

Study your footage over and over again. Make a list of the images you've captured and the subjects discussed in your interview. Which words and images add up to a visually appealing and meaningful story? Editing is crucial, and filmmakers routinely spend a lot more time editing than they do filming. You are really honing your craft here, so don't fret if the process is slow.

Try working with a more experienced editor to help you implement your vision. Rough out your own ideas and run them by him or her. Does the film make sense to your editor? Be open to suggestions and realize that you may have to sacrifice subplots or images that just don't serve your overall purpose—no matter how great they are. ***Make every second of those ten minutes count!***

8. Wrap up post-production.

This means finalizing the details of your film, including:

Music. If your film is destined for public consumption, remember that you need to pay to use even brief samples of most music written since

FILMING DOS AND DON'TS

Be a pro on production day

DO preinterview your subjects to establish rapport and help you develop your angle on your subject.

DO conduct interviews rather than having discussions with your subjects. Unless it is a stylistic choice to put yourself in the film, keep your voice out as much as possible.

DO sit right next to the camera when interviewing, so that your interviewee is looking at you and towards the camera—otherwise, your audience will wonder what the heck your subject is looking at! Jona says it's amazing how often filmmakers overlook this basic tip.

DON'T go into filming with a hard-and-fast agenda. Look for what's there, not for what you expected to be there.

DON'T let your subject dictate your content. Directors are supposed to direct—so feel free to gently steer them away from or towards topics and ideas.

the early 20th century in order to avoid copyright infringement. Maybe you can use songs from a local band or commission a classical piece from a musician friend?

Titles and credits. These are easy to add with home editing programs. Have fun with it and consider implementing different sound techniques, effects, or voice-over narration during your title sequence.

Color correction. Chances are you will also want and need to do some color correction with your editing program. You can fix video that is underexposed, soften, brighten, and achieve color continuity by making colors match in edited shots.

Make your movie into a mini-masterpiece.

9. Screen your film.

You've worked hard on your movie, so why not show it off? When you've got a final cut you're happy with, it can be burned onto a disk to play on a DVD player or projected onto a wall or screen with a digital video projector. Send copies to far-flung friends, stream part or all of it on the Internet, and enter your film in competitions or film festivals.

Host a preview screening with friends, family, crew, and your interviewees, and ask for constructive feedback. (Directors often recut their flicks after screenings like these.) Seek out local film festivals and nonprofit arts organizations that regularly screen beginning, offbeat, and experimental work—there's nothing like going to your own premiere. "Don't be afraid to submit your work to Sundance, either!" encourages Jona. ***Make your directorial debut!***

CONGRATULATIONS!

You ought to be in pictures—but hey, you already are! You did it!

I DID IT!

Name: ______________________

Date: ______________________

GO TO THE MOVIES

Take every opportunity to eat popcorn and study your craft

- Pay attention to film screenings at places other than the cineplex—film archives or schools, museums, community art centers, and repertory theaters.
- If a movie makes you think, see it again and take notes. Try to figure out why you remember dialogue from certain films or what makes images linger in your memory. Keep a journal of the movies you see and why you liked—or disliked—them.
- Check out the behind-the-scenes features on DVDs, even for lousy films. The director's commentary might reveal what camera was used for that one memorable shot, and checking out the storyboards can help you understand how to translate pictures to moving images.
- Jona watches the PBS documentary film series *P.O.V.* religiously. With public broadcasting, public access stations, and cable outfits like the Independent Film Channel, you don't have to look for parking to see an independent film.

BEYOND THE BADGE

If you love it as much as you thought you would, dream on . . .

- **Film school.** Jona attended the film production program at USC, where they have a strong documentary program. But she also has fond memories of seeing *Citizen Kane* and her first Fellini movie in a high school course. Your brother, best friend, and boss may think you have delusions of grandeur when you talk about your movie, but in film school, you're expected to! You'll meet people who can work as your film crew—and when classmates get paying work, they can often bring you in.
- **Grants, fellowships, festivals.** Jona had always thought *Catholic School* would someday be shown in a gallery in conjunction with the still photos she took of the students. She had to be persuaded to submit it to the Sundance Film Festival. Jona has also been the recipient of grants and artist-in-residence awards, which offer financial resources, technical support, and access to an artistic community. "Don't underestimate your work," she advises. "Believe in it, and other people will, too."
- **Write a screenplay.** You don't have to go to L.A. and work retail to write a script. Screenplays are written in a specific format and style, so if you have a story idea that you'd love to see on the big screen, check out a screenwriting book (see Jona's Picks) or take a class. You might apply for a screenwriter's workshop, which can help you shape and sell your script. You can also purchase the screenplays of your favorite films to study.

FILM SCHOOLS

If you're serious about the silver screen

American Film Institute. Features a directing workshop for women. www.afi.com/education/dww.

California Institute of the Arts, School of Film/Video. Offers courses in film and video, animation and directing. www.calarts.edu.

Columbia College Chicago. The largest film school in the U.S. www.colum.edu.

Hollywood Film Institute. A two-day crash course. www.hollywoodu.com.

New York Film Academy. Offers workshops for people with little or no experience. www.nyfa.com.

New York University. Offers degrees in film and TV. filmtv.tisch.nyu.edu.

University of Southern California School of Cinema-Television. Jona's alma mater and networking central for Hollywood. www-cntv.usc.edu.

JONA'S PICKS

BOOKS

Digital Filmmaking 101: An Essential Guide to Producing Low-Budget Movies by Dale Newton and John Gaspard
The title says it all.

How to Write a Movie in 21 Days: The Inner Movie Method by Viki King
Stop procrastinating and write that screenplay!

The Screenwriter's Bible: A Complete Guide to Writing, Formatting, and Selling Your Script by David Trottier
A poorly formatted screenplay is distracting and hard to read—be sure yours is good to go to agents and producers.

WEB SITES

www.2-pop.com
An extensive resource guide and forum for DV filmmakers.

www.ifilm.com
Has a large number of short films that can be viewed online.

www.lather.com/fsc
Insider tips on picking a school and what you'll find there, excerpted from the book *Film School Confidential* by Tom Edgar and Karin Kelly.

www.microcinema.com
Screening series shows all sorts of short films. Very accessible.

SUPPLIES

www.canondv.com

www.panasonic.com

www.sony.com

ORGANIZATIONS

Association of Independent Video and Filmmakers
www.AIVF.org
Publishes *The Independent Film and Video Monthly,* a good magazine resource for festival listings, and lists full festival listings for members online.

Squaw Valley Community of Writers
www.squawvalleywriters.org
Workshop your script in good company.

DIRECTORS/MOVIES

The key to great filmmaking—whether it's a short documentary or a Hollywood feature—is great storytelling. Watch and learn.

Amélie
Director: Jean-Pierre Jeunet

Basquiat
Director: Julian Schnabel

Fight Club
Director: David Fincher

My Brilliant Career
Director: Gillian Armstrong

Ordinary People
Director: Robert Redford

Streetwise
Director: Martin Bell

Sweetie
An Angel at My Table
Director: Jane Campion

Taxi Driver
Director: Martin Scorsese

25th Hour
Director: Spike Lee

15

TAKE A (REALLY GOOD) PICTURE

★ photography ★

SATURATE YOURSELF with your subject and the camera will all but take you by the hand.

—Margaret Bourke-White

So, what's your motivation?
Take a moment.
Dream a little, think big,
and then complete this sentence:
I see myself . . .

Imagine This . . . Your latest book of photojournalism is on the coffee table. *National Geographic* wants you in Kenya yesterday, *Vogue* calls you to make the fall line look good, and *Time* thinks only you can do justice to their person of the year cover . . . Or maybe you'd just like to take a family photo without lopping off anyone's head. Whether you dream of capturing the action on the Serengeti or on your kid's soccer field, globe-trotting with a Leica or hanging out in your own backyard with a zoom lens on the daisies, this badge will make you a hot shot. You'll take a professional-quality portrait of someone you adore and learn your way around a classic 35 mm camera in the process. Smile! *You can do it!*

The Payoffs

- **Vision.** The Talmud says we don't see things as they are, we see things as we are. In photography, that unique personal perspective is a good thing. Your photos let you document and share that vision.
- **Art.** The accomplished expert you're about to meet says she never felt like a creative person. She doesn't draw, paint, decorate, or cook fancy meals—but she does provide fresh insight on the world through her photos. You can, too.
- **History.** Photos that capture a moment, place, person, or event preserve your history, memories, and experiences in a way that lets them live forever.
- **Money!** Mastering a few basic skills ensures that more photos from every roll of film you develop will be worth saving.

Meet Your Mentor

LAUREN GREENFIELD

What She Does: Takes photos that appear in major periodicals like the *New York Times Magazine, Harper's Bazaar, Elle, Time,* and *National Geographic*. Has published two stunning and award-winning book projects: *Fast Forward: Growing Up in the Shadow of Hollywood* and *Girl Culture. American Photo* recently named Lauren one of the twenty-five most influential photographers working today. She lives in Venice, California, with her husband and son.

© Lara Jo Regan

Why She Does It: "I was exposed to photography early, at an alternative grammar school that had really good photography classes. Then my mom took me to France when I was twelve. We were on a biking trip in Brittany, and I was annoyed because she kept stopping to take pictures. She gave me her camera so I could try it myself, and I never gave the camera back! One of my school assignments was to take a portrait of a friend without showing her face. She was kind of punky, and I took a picture of this T-shirt she always wore and some of her stuff. I'm still doing that same kind of thing. I majored in Visual Studies at Harvard, and in my junior year I went on a program in which we traveled around the world, living with families and studying film and anthropology. That was when I knew I wanted to examine culture through film and photography. While doing an internship at *National Geographic,* I also learned that there were serious, rigorous jobs in which I could tell important stories as a photographer."

> You're the expert of your own life, your own world. Photography lets you share that expertise, that vision.
>
> —Lauren Greenfield

Word from the Wise: "You have to take tons and tons of pictures to get a good one! You have to be willing to experiment and use your intuition, and that means taking bad pictures on your way to the good ones, which are often accidental."

BADGE STEPS

1. Get a camera.

The camera Lauren grabbed from her mother was an all-manual 35 mm that was great to learn on and served Lauren well through college. You, too, should have a simple 35 mm camera that allows you to choose exposure and focus settings. While you can certainly have fun and take good pictures with an automatic or digital camera, Lauren says, "If you want to explore the principles of photography, you want to be able to make adjustments to your settings, whether your camera is automatic or manual." You may have one in your closet already, but if not, borrow or buy a new or used 35 mm manual camera. If you're feeling camera-store shy, ask a shutterbug friend to come with you and help you pick out the right camera. ***Get equipped.***

2. Get to know your camera.

Sit down with the manual for your camera and read it through, and pick up your unloaded camera to find the parts described in the manual. See Shutterbug Slang for help with mystery terminology. ***Learn what all those knobs do.***

3. Shoot your first roll of film.

Since black and white lends itself more easily to experimentation with timing, framing, and lighting and is less apt to fade over time, that's what we'll use for this badge. So go to a camera store, and stock up on six rolls of black and white film. (See Get It on Film for tips.)

Grasp the camera firmly in both hands with your elbows into your chest, and hold it still. If you're standing up, keep your legs a bit apart for good support. Leaning or sitting down can make holding still easier. Just make sure you're not covering anything important—like the lens! Now point your camera, and shoot.

To gain experience and learn about your camera, shoot a variety of things—objects, people, landscapes—under a variety of circumstances, both indoors and out, and with and without movement. As you click away, try experimenting with:

Orientation. Practice shooting horizontally, in landscape mode, then turning the camera ninety degrees to shoot vertically, in portrait mode. Try placing your subject in the center of the shot, and off to one side.

SHUTTERBUG SLANG

Technical terminology

Aperture. Sometimes called the "stop," this is the hole in a lens that admits light.

Bracket. To take a series of shots of the same subject at different exposures.

Fill flash (or flash fill). Flash that is used to fill in a subject's shadow area with light, reducing contrast. Fill light is supplemental light from a lamp or reflector that does the same thing.

Frame. This can either be the boundaries of the camera's viewfinder or something in a photo, like a doorway, that frames its subject.

Shutter. A movable cover for the lens that controls the amount of time that light is allowed to reach the film.

Zoom. Lens that allows you to vary focal length and stay in focus.

Proximity. Move in close to your subject. The most common mistake beginners make is not getting close enough to their subject. Lauren cites a Robert Capa saying, "If the picture's not good enough, you're not close enough." When Lauren showed a fellow photographer a shot she'd taken of a group of girls in a swimming pool, he rightly pointed out that she should have been in the pool in the middle of the action rather than on the periphery.

Aperture settings. Your aperture setting ("f-stop") establishes how much light you let into the lens. It may seem counter-intuitive, but in bright light, you want to use a high f-number to open the lens and in low light, a low number. Also try bracketing, which is taking the same shot at three different f-stop settings—one at the setting your light meter indicates, one an f-stop setting down, and one a setting up.

Focus. Adjust your focus to draw attention to that which attracts you to the scene. A smaller aperture (i.e., an aperture setting with a high number) will give you great depth of field, so that you have a large range of distance. A large aperture will give you a shallow depth of field, which allows you to use selective focus to bring the viewer's eye to your subject. Find the depth of field that will keep your subject sharp and clear.

Shutter speed. The shutter speed controls the duration of an exposure. Generally, use a slow shutter speed with a still object—like the moon—and a faster speed when shooting a moving target. However, these are not hard and fast rules—experimenting with different shutter speeds will yield interesting results.

Lighting. Photography is often described as "painting with light." If you set your meter according to the part of your subject that is in shadow, you should get an even balance of light and dark. Sunlight can pose problems at its peak midday hours by washing everything out. And when photographing a person, you don't want them to squint, but you do want the sun behind you and facing them. You may also want to try backlighting your subject with a fill-flash for a different look.

Shoot at least one of your rolls of film, practicing these manual adjustments and jotting down the settings used in each shot. Have the roll developed and note what did and didn't work. You can play around with two more rolls, but save the last three for your shoot. ***Give it your best shot.***

GET IT ON FILM

Choosing the right film

Get the right speed. Go to a camera store and ask the salesperson to suggest an appropriate film speed. The salesperson will need to know where and when you plan to take your photos to recommend the right ASA—generally speaking, strong midday sunlight outdoors requires higher-speed film, while interior light and twilight requires lower-speed film.

Color v. black and white. Since much of Lauren's work is about capturing popular culture in living color, she usually uses color film. But many serious photographers learned with black and white and still swear by it, finding it more versatile and creative. A war photographer friend of Lauren's chooses black and white to simplify and minimize distractions.

I DID IT!

"I have photographed several of my friends during their pregnancies. One of my favorite shoots involved a very pregnant Kathleen. Even though she'd always had a lovely figure, Kath had been so self-conscious that she never wore a bathing suit or even shorts to the beach! But at the shoot, in the lovely, secluded garden of a mutual friend, Kath surprised me by wanting to be photographed nude. Somehow her beautiful belly liberated her and the photos were just wonderful." —Kitti

NO FILM!

"Last week, while working on my documentary film, an incredible scene unfolded before my eyes, and by mistake, somehow my director of photography had turned her camera off. We didn't get the scene and both had a good cry about it. I felt like committing suicide! You can't re-create those moments—but it really does happen to every photographer, no matter how experienced, at one time or another." —Lauren

LAUREN'S EXPERT TIPS

PRACTICE MAKES PICTURE PERFECT

- "Keeping a photo diary is a great discipline and a way to record your life," says Lauren, who carries a digital camera for this purpose. Always having that camera at the ready to capture life as it unfolds is fun, and can also be helpful if you are going through a hard time. Pretend you are creating a "What They Were Thinking" section for the *New York Times Magazine* and jot down notes to accompany your photos. Lauren points out that the *Times* welcomes submissions from photographers for this popular feature of the magazine.
- Lauren says special occasions are great excuses to take pictures. Proms, weddings, and the like are situations in which people are comfortable being photographed and having a camera around. But you also have to take the time to get beyond the occasion. Look for the unexpected. You don't want to be governed by your subject's vanity.
- Focus on the details. In high school, Lauren did a photography project revolving around a community of elderly Jewish women who lived at Venice Beach. Her teacher suggested that she photograph only their hands. She did, and wound up winning the Jewish Historical award and a National Foundation for the Advancement of the Arts Achievement Award for her work!

4. Look for inspiration.

Think about who you might like to photograph at your photo session, then turn to the greats for inspiration. Check out books, museums, and galleries for masterworks by Irving Penn, Diane Arbus, Richard Avedon, Dorothea Lange, Sally Mann, Sedou Keita, Roy DeCarava, Herb Ritts, Margaret Bourke-White, Andrea Modica, Henri Cartier-Bresson, Judith Joy Ross, Imogen Cunningham, Annie Liebovitz, Robert Frank, and Mary Ellen Mark.

As you look at their photographs, ask yourself the following questions:

- Where do they direct your attention?
- Are photo subjects framed by other elements in the shot?
- What's in the background and foreground?
- What's in shadow and light?
- What's in sharp focus, and what isn't?
- What is completely in the frame, and what is left out of it?

- How are people's bodies and faces treated?
- Do props play a role?

Pick up a few tricks from the greats.

5. Plan your shoot.

Here's what you'll need to consider as you set up your shoot:

Model. Find someone you can spend several hours shooting—probably a friend or family member. You may want to ask your model to sign a model release form that grants you the right to capture their likeness, which you'll need in case you ever want to publish, sell, or display a portrait of that person. (See Lauren's Picks, page 123, for info on model release forms.)

Approach. Think about how you'd like to photograph your model. You can do a traditional "glamour" shot, with your subject in fancy dress and your goal to make her look as beautiful as possible. Or you can take the photojournalism approach, making a statement about your subject's life and personality.

Interpretation. Think about what kind of person your model is and what you want to say about that person. Is this individual defined by the work he or she does? If so, perhaps you should photograph that person doing some work-related task, in work clothes, or with objects used in their profession. Is there something in the eyes that reveals a personality trait? Or perhaps a way of sitting, or a gesture while talking?

Lighting. To avoid the need for lamps, reflectors, and backdrops, plan to photograph your subject outdoors in natural light or indoors by a window or in a very sunlit room. In addition to simplifying your shoot, natural light will make your subject look her best. The optimal natural light is found early in the morning or late in the afternoon.

Location. Scout locations, looking for simple but interesting backgrounds. Textured backgrounds on walls and shadows provided by foliage are especially nice. Try to find locations where the environment will say something about your subject.

Create your own photo op.

6. Loosen up and let loose.

At your shoot, hang out with your subject, chatting and giving her time to get comfortable with you and the camera. Ask questions that elicit

PICTURE THIS

Women who made photographic history

Imogen Cunningham (1883–1976) was a West Coast pioneer of modernism who opened a successful portrait studio in Seattle around 1910. She began working for *Vanity Fair* when they printed her photo of Martha Graham in 1932 and was working on a book of portraits when she died at age ninety-two.

Dorothea Lange (1895–1965) documented displaced farm families and migrant workers during the Great Depression and was hired by the War Relocation Authority to document conditions in U.S. internment camps for Japanese Americans in WWII.

Margaret Bourke-White (1904–1971) was one of the original staff photographers at *Fortune, Life,* and *Time* magazines. She covered the liberation of Italy and the German concentration camps during WWII, and is also known for her series on the rural South during the Depression, images of mining in South Africa, and portraits of world leaders.

Diane Arbus (1923–1971) began as a fashion photographer but went on to take controversial photos of unconventional subjects. Drawn to the disturbing, forbidden, and dangerous, she said, "I always thought of photography as a naughty thing to do—that was one of my favorite things about it."

smiles, laughter, and more serious expressions, snapping shots all the while. Your subject may start out posing for you, giving you what they think you want or what they want to project—but after a while, says Lauren, "they have to get back to the business of living their life. If you're patient and relaxed, they'll become less self-conscious and be themselves. When you become accepted as part of the furniture in their world, you can take real, spontaneous pictures."

Shoot three rolls of film, capturing your subject from various distances and at different angles. Try out:

- Facial close-ups, waist-up shots, and full-length ones
- Bird's-eye views from above, worm's-eye views looking up from below, and eye-level shots
- A tight focus on your subject as well as focusing on something behind your subject

Lauren insists that "there really are no rules to taking a good picture; if you follow 'the rules,' you'll wind up with a boring picture. Follow your heart instead, and think about how to express what you want to say. What's the essence of the person you are shooting?" ***Let the spirit move you to a photo finish.***

7. Develop and print your photos.

Have your film developed by a professional lab that works with black-and-white film and ask for a contact sheet rather than prints. Buy a loupe or small magnifying glass, go over the contact sheet with your subject, and choose a shot to have printed. You can give the developer instructions on how to print your choice, asking them to:

- "Burn" a spot in the shot that's too bright.
- "Dodge" an area that is too dark.
- "Crop" the shot, eliminating areas you can do without.
- Give you a glossy finish on the photographs rather than matte for optimal black and white contrast.
- Provide prints with borders (or not).
- Blow up your print to the desired size.

Print your portrait.

PRINTING POSSIBILITIES

Some developing styles defined

Chromogenic color print or "C" print. The most common color printing process.

Cibachrome print. A color print made from a slide or transparency (i.e., a *positive* rather than a negative).

Cyanotype or blueprint. Invented in 1842, cyanotypes were the first successful nonsilver photographic printing process. A contact print is made of a drawing, object, or other image and the resulting print is rendered in white lines on a blue background.

Daguerreotype. An early photographic process in which the image is created on a light-sensitive, silver-coated, metallic plate.

Digital print. A print that is made from a digital file. Digital files can be printed on high-quality ink-jet printers (IRIS, Epson) or on traditional photographic papers using a laser printer.

Gelatin-silver print. A term encompassing all photographic prints made on a paper sensitized with silver salts. Most black-and-white prints are in this category.

Platinum-palladium print. Considered by many to be the finest black-and-white printing process, these prints do not use a layer of gelatin (like most black-and-white prints), thereby allowing the metals to soak right into the photographic paper. These prints are capable of extremely rich tonal range and great detail.

8. Frame it.

You have lots of options when framing your photo—but whatever aesthetic choice you make, be sure to use a mat that keeps your photo flat and straight. You can also use a mat to crop a photo, covering extraneous elements. Acid- and lignin-free mats are best. Attach the photo to the mat with a bit of acid-free double-stick tape at the top. Black-and-white photos look classic and elegant in black frames with white mats. But remember that even framed photos are subject to fading from direct sun and fluorescent lights, and that heat and humidity cause deterioration. (See Organize It!, page 412, for photo storage strategies.) ***Wow your model with an artfully framed portrait.***

CONGRATULATIONS!

You've captured a moment in time, for all time. You're on a roll! You did it!

I DID IT!

Name: ______________________________

Date: ______________________________

DO WHAT YOU LOVE AND THE MONEY MIGHT FOLLOW

Making a living through the lens

Advertising. Magazines, billboards, and other ad agency assignments.

Commercial. Photographic work that is done for companies; can cover catalogs, products, and architecture.

Fashion. Someone has to convince us to buy all those clothes!

Fine art. Photos are exhibited in museums, sold through galleries, and published in books.

Journalism. Working freelance, for newspapers, or for news agencies.

Portrait studio. Weddings, portraits, and other work with the paying public.

Scientific. Medical, aerial, police, forensic, military, and natural history images.

Stock. Photographers can sell their photos to picture libraries and stock agencies who take a cut when they are licensed for use.

BEYOND THE BADGE

If you love it as much as you thought you would, dream on . . .

- **Sign up for classes.** Classes keep you doing the best thing you can do to boost your photography skills: taking pictures. Plus they provide a support network of fellow photographers and help you persevere with a personal project you care about that will ultimately showcase your strengths and style to the public.
- **Brave the darkroom.** Many amateur and professional photographers consider doing their own developing an integral part of their creative process. Again, the best way to learn is to take classes, though there are many good books and instructional Web sites if you'd rather go it alone. You can investigate community darkroom space that rents by the hour, develop at home in your bathroom, or even build your own darkroom—just be careful to dispose of the chemicals properly.
- **Go digital.** Lauren says that for most people, "the computer is the new darkroom, and while it takes a long time to get really good at something like Photoshop, the program is very accessible. Everyone can have fun with it." She also points out the wealth of new consumer products and online services that can help you edit, archive, and showcase your work, including one that actually produces a bound book to your specifications. "It took me two years (and sixty rejections) to find a publisher for my first book," says Lauren. "Now you can just make one yourself!"

GOING DIGITAL

Techno-savvy photography

- Digital cameras come with different resolutions or pixel counts. This determines the quality of the image. "Web quality" photos appear grainy when printed out but are fine for sending via e-mail.
- You can't print out a decent photo without a decent printer and photo-ready paper. Many retailers print digital images now or you can use a service such as Kodak's www.ofoto.com.
- How much memory do you need? If you don't want to have to download or delete while taking hundreds of images, you might want to invest in a supplemental memory card.
- Learn more about digital photography at www.dpreview.com.

LAUREN'S PICKS

BOOKS

:: *For instruction:*

Legal Guide for the Visual Artist by Tad Crawford
Includes standard model release form.

On Photography by Susan Sontag
Examines how photography has changed the way we look at the world and ourselves.

Photography by Henry Horenstein and Russell Hart
Great textbook combining how-to tips with a history of photography and a survey of modern photographers and photographic techniques.

Truth Needs No Ally: Inside Photojournalism by Howard Chapnick
An insightful look at the business and art of photojournalism.

:: *For inspiration:*

The Americans by Robert Frank
A classic of street photography.

Henri Cartier-Bresson: The Early Work by Peter Galassi
Cartier-Bresson's work is inspiring and exemplifies his idea of the "decisive moment."

Mary Ellen Mark: American Odyssey, 1963–1999 by Mary Ellen Mark
Mark is a portrait photographer par excellence.

Winogrand: Figments from the Real World by John Szarkowski
Garry Winogrand demonstrated that photography could comment on society; a great inspiration.

MAGAZINES

Aperture
www.aperture.org
Features distinguished fine art photography and insights from leading writers.

Blind Spot
www.blindspot.com
International sourcebook of photography-based fine art that publishes both established and emerging photographers.

Camerawork: Journal of Photographic Arts
www.sfcamerawork.org/journal.html
Leading thinkers take a close look at the photography that reflects our modern world.

DoubleTake
www.doubletakemagazine.org
Documentary photography features, articles, and interviews.

National Geographic
www.nationalgeographic.com
Documentary photography of culture, nature, and customs around the world.

Photo District News
www.pdnonline.com
News, product reviews, contests, and a community forum for photographers.

WEB SITES

www.editorialphoto.com
Events, educational support, and price estimator for photojournalists.

www.laurengreenfield.com and www.girlculture.com
Lauren's home on the Web.

www.shutterfly.com
Digital photo site.

WORKSHOPS

Eddie Adams Workshop
www.eddieadamsworkshop.com
Apply for a chance to be accepted to this prestigious, free, invitation-only workshop in New York.

ICP
www.icp.org
The International Center of Photography in New York offers more than 500 courses annually.

Missouri Photo Workshop
www.mophotoworkshop.org
An intense, weeklong immersion course in photography with leaders in the field.

Review Santa Fe
www.photoprojects.org
Get your work reviewed by the top curators, editors, and publishers in the field.

16

GO WORLD WIDE

★ building a web site ★

If you build it,
they will come.

—W. P. Kinsella

Imagine This . . . When you meet a potential client at a party, you impress her by saying, "Don't forget to visit my Web site." When friends ask how your trip to Jamaica was, you direct them to a Web address where your travel photos are set to a reggae beat. And when the holidays roll around, forget about stamps—you can cut and paste a few sprigs of holly onto your family Web site and e-mail the link in the time it takes to warm up some eggnog. Your site can be your business calling card, your baby's photo album, or the global stage on which you recite poetry, talk back to news headlines, or share lively reminiscences of the 372 Grateful Dead shows you've seen. All it took was some smart planning, a few tools, and a little patience. Construction zone ahead . . . no hard hat required! *You can do it!*

So, what's your motivation?
Take a moment.
Dream a little, think big,
and then complete this sentence:
I see myself . . .

The Payoffs

- **Visibility.** You have something to say, and your Web site lets you take it to the streets without megaphones or middlemen.
- **Connection.** Whether we want to amuse, touch, agitate, or sell, the Web lets us reach millions.
- **Community.** It may not be like strolling through the town square, but when you surf the Web, you join a community. With a site, you're the mayor.
- **Cool.** Your own Web site . . . how cool is that?!

Meet Your Mentor

ARIN FISHKIN

What She Does: The cofounder of the o2 Design Collective, Arin conceives, designs, manages, and produces print and Web graphics including Web sites, logos, banners, brochures, marketing, advertising, and illustration for a wide range of non- and for-profit clients in the San Francisco Bay Area.

© Dana Spaeth

Why She Does It: "When I got out of school, I started freelancing with a partner who had more experience than I did with print work. In order to add value to our team, I taught myself Web design. I almost didn't know how to turn a computer on when I started. The first thing I did was get a big fat book about the coding language HTML. With my arts background and the way my mind works, I didn't really take to it—I'm a visual person, and HTML is a text-based code. It's really a very simple language, and I did wind up creating a site just using what I'd learned about HTML coding, but I soon gravitated towards the more visual and professional design software out there. Today, there are so many ways for a newbie to put up a site. It doesn't have to be complex at all, but if you're motivated to learn the high-level stuff—as I was—and especially if you love design, you can work your way up and have a lot of fun with it."

Anyone can have a Web site, and it can be "about" absolutely ANYTHING.

—Arin Fishkin

Word from the Wise: "If you have patience and a sense of adventure, and you can word process and have an Internet hookup, you have what you need to put up a site. A Web presence is a tool. If you have a business, it's as essential as a phone book listing. And if you have a personal site, it can be a way to connect and share with infinite numbers of people."

BADGE STEPS

THE BIG PICTURE

Your map of the online world

The Internet. Draw a big circle. That's the Internet—a giant global network of computers.

The World Wide Web. Next, draw a smaller circle within the Internet. That's the World Wide Web, part of the Internet that is accessed using a Web browser.

Web site. Within the Web, there are many Web sites, which you can represent as a bunch of little circles within the bigger Web circle. Each Web site is a set of text and graphic files.

Web server. The site files that make up a Web site—stay with me—are stored on the hard drive of a Web server, a souped-up computer that's connected to the Internet around the clock. Draw a square around some of the little circles within the Web to represent Web servers.

Internet service provider (ISP). Most people with Web sites rent space on a server through an Internet service provider or other Web hosting service. When people visit your Web site, your ISP "serves" up your text and graphic files to them.

1. Decide what kind of site to build.

Maybe some of your favorite Web destinations are sites that people have created to post their opinions or share information about a hobby. Maybe you love visiting your sister's site to see the latest pictures of your nephew. Or maybe you've decided your fledgling business would really fly with some online visibility. Whatever kind of site appeals to you most, this badge will walk you through the basics of building it.

Think about what you'd like to do. Promote your business or service? Share family news and photos? Create a place where you and your fellow Toni Morrison, Colin Firth, or needlepoint enthusiasts can meet? If you want to share your thoughts with the world, maybe you'll want to develop your own "blog," which is a Web log or online journal. ***Set your sights on a dream site.***

2. Plan your site.

No matter what kind of site you want to build, sketching out your plan is an important preliminary step. "The biggest part of building a site—and the part that often gets short shrift—is everything you do before you start construction," says Arin. Get out good old-fashioned paper and pencil, and make a list of everything you want on your site:

Text. If your site will be personal in nature, you might include a personal introduction, favorite quotes, and commentary on subjects dear to your heart—movie reviews, political opinions, favorite books, snowboarding tips, you name it. If you're building a professionally oriented site, you might include resume highlights, portfolio samples, case studies of projects you've completed, and testimonials from happy clients.

Images. This might include recent vacation photos or family shots on a personal site, while a more professionally minded site might feature shots of recent projects and head shots of business partners.

Links to other sites. If you're planning a special event such as a wedding, you might include links to hotels where your guests might stay, or to museums, restaurants, and other places guests might visit. On a business site, you might want to link to vendors or client sites.

Now prioritize and group these items in a simple sketch, as follows:

Home page. What items should be featured front and center on the home page? List these in a box at the top of a sheet of paper.

Landing pages. Think of the top three or four places you want people to go from the home page. Perhaps you want your relatives and friends to have easy access to a page with the latest pictures of the kids, a page describing your recent holiday in Crete, and a page outlining your travel plans for your forthcoming high school reunion. Group these items in three separate boxes below the home page; these will be your three top-tier landing pages.

Second-tier pages. Think about other pages visitors to these landing pages might want to see. Visitors to the page with pictures of the kids might like to see a page of the kids' school photos or a page of pictures of their recent art projects from school. These two pages belong on the second tier, below the kids landing page. Then repeat the process for your Crete page and high school reunion page, adding one or two second-tier pages that might be of interest below these landing pages.

When you're done with this process, your sketch should look like a simple pyramid, with the home page in the box at the top and the secondary pages along the bottom. You can add to it later, but you now have what Web designers call your basic site architecture.

When you're planning where to put pictures, text, and links on each page, put yourself in the place of people visiting the site. "Your site has to be user-friendly or people will leave," Arin stresses. Visit lots of other sites to see how they achieve a natural flow from one page to the next. ***Sketch out your basic site design.***

3. Choose your host.

All Web sites need a Web server to call home. Lots of outfits offer these Web "hosting" services, and here are just a few choices:

- Your e-mail and Internet service provider (ISP) may offer a free personal Web site option.
- There are also dozens of free or almost free Web hosting services, including Yahoo! GeoCities, AOL, and Tripod. The catch with these free services (you knew there had to be one, right?) is that visitors may have to view ads from the service provider when they come to your site.
- For a more elaborate site or for a business site, you'll probably want to pay a monthly fee to a hosting service so that you can include more content and features without having your site cluttered with ads. Your ISP may set you up, or you can shop around at www.ispcheck.com.

Find a home for your site.

PHOTO FACTS

Tips to add images to your site

- Digital cameras import images directly into your computer.
- Film can be digitally processed to give you images stored on a disk or CD.
- Old photos can be digitized with a scanner.
- Consider Web-ready clip art. There are huge collections of often free images: try creativepro.com or mediabuilder.com.
- On Google.com, click on "Image," then type in a few words describing the image you are searching for. When you see what you like, right-click on the image, and hit Save. However, it's important to check to be sure the images you use aren't copyrighted.
- Experiment and get comfortable with your design tool's sizing, color correcting, and cropping capabilities.

BECOME KNOWN ON THE WWW

How to make your Web presence known

Of course you'll let friends, family, and business associates know about your site with an e-mail announcing its launch—but you may also want to increase the possibility that search engines will lead strangers to you.

- Go to search engine Web sites, and fill out their online registration forms.
- Search out Web sites related to your site's subject matter, and ask their Webmasters to link to your site. If the site is a good match, you might offer to provide a reciprocal link to their site.
- If you are a member in good standing of a newsgroup or mailing list relevant to the subject matter on your site, spread the word there.

I DID IT!

"I was a freelance journalist whose first book had been published at the height of the dot-com craze. I 'Googled' my name and hated what came up—links to a few old stories I'd written, a review or two of my book, and lots of weird mentions of other people with my rather common name. I wanted a site all my own. My Internet/e-mail provider offered a really simple way for me to put up such a site, and as a gift, friends registered my name as a domain. It was surprisingly easy to follow the instructions and build the site. Soon I had what I wanted: a place where people could find links to my best stories and news about my bookstore readings."
—Denise

WEB WOES

"My husband and I own a record shop, and for years we'd also run a thriving mail-order business through word of mouth and print ads. As people became more Web-literate, they started to ask us if we had a site. We decided to hire someone to build the site and weren't at all happy with what we got. The site was really flashy, took forever to download and move between links, and didn't really convey the vibe of our business. We're 'under construction' with a new site, and now know that we have to work a lot more closely with the designer up front in order to get what we really want and need."
—Nancy

ARIN'S EXPERT TIPS

HOW TO MAKE YOUR SITE USER-FRIENDLY

- Size matters. If you keep your graphics small, they'll take less time to download. If you build it, they might come—but they won't wait around forever. So put big graphics on a separate page, and give viewers a choice to click on them if they have time for the download. Also, use the "thumbnail" option in your design program to create a small version of your graphic that can be clicked on to view a larger image.
- Shape counts. Text in narrow columns is easiest to read; you don't want viewers to have to scroll sideways to finish a sentence.
- Colors and font styles can convey professionalism or frivolity. For instance, a financial planner probably wants to convey solid professionalism with colors like navy blue, a traditional typeface, and straight lines.

4. Name that Web site.

Free or low-cost hosting services generally come with a Web address like "geocities.com/your-Yahoo!-ID," which might be just fine for your personal page. But if you're building a professional site or have your heart set on something zippier for a personal site, you'll want your own snazzy domain name. You want it to be something intriguing enough to grab surfers or straightforward enough to direct information seekers. For a professional site, the name should be as close as possible to your established business name, reveal what your biz is about in a fun way (Netflix), or be otherwise memorable (Google). Before you get your hopes up about your dream name, steel yourself for the possibility that at this stage in the game lots of clever names are taken.

You can register for a domain name through www.networksolutions .com or www.register.com. You'll pay $35 a year for your name and pay for two years up front when you first register. ***Make a name for yourself online.***

5. Enter the construction zone.

Get out your tools: It's time to build that site! Basic, host-provided site-building templates walk you through the process of putting in text, creating background colors, creating links, adding an e-mail address, and putting in images. Templates are a great way to get your feet wet, overcome fear, and put up a site quickly and easily.

If you want to break out of the mold and create something more unique, your basic tool will be a Web page editor. This software lets you see the page either as code—in straight HTML (HyperText Markup Language)—or as WYSIWYG (What You See Is What You Get)—that is, as graphics. With HTML editors, you type in bracketed code, or "tags." To get comfortable with HTML, pick up a basic guidebook on the language or take an online tutorial such as Webmonkey. WYSIWYG tools let you work with a more visually oriented page layout approach.

The best way to experiment with HTML or WYSIWYG tools is to download a free trial version and test it out. For a handy grid of the various editors, go to About.com's "Choose the Web Page Editor That's Right for You" article at personalweb.about.com/cs/webpageeditors. Check your browser's home page, too, because an editor may come with your browser if you have Netscape or Internet Explorer. Once you've found a Web page editor, follow the instructions to build the components of the site you've outlined. ***Get your site under construction.***

6. Refine your site.

Once you have a draft of your site, send it to a few friends for review. Sites look different on computers with different operating systems and browser versions, and you want yours to be picture-perfect on every one. Ask for feedback on how colors look, whether the text is legible and the graphics clear, how long it takes to download, and whether your text needs editing.

Once you've made these changes, you can relax into maintenance mode. To attract repeat viewers, you should plan to update your site with new content to keep the site fresh. Change some text and/or images regularly, and periodically check to make sure links are current. ***Make yours a site to see.***

CONGRATULATIONS!

Outta site. You did it!

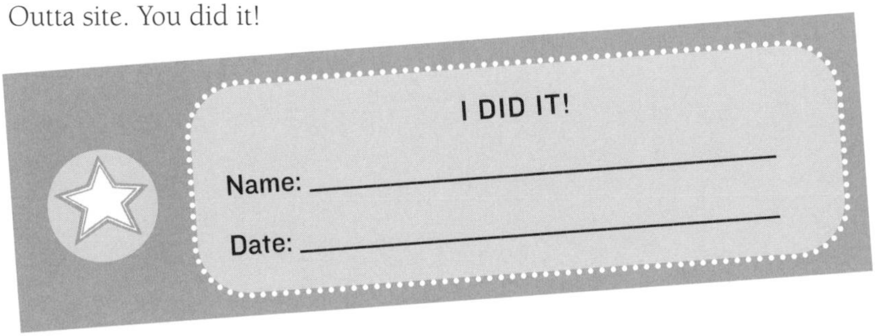

WORK IN PROGRESS

Don't let delays or obstacles get you—or your site—down!

Web construction delays are to be expected. When you get confused or frustrated, Arin says, "Your best resource is the Web. There's so much information out there." For starters:

- **Check the sites in Arin's Picks, page 131, head for the beginner's sections, and you'll find solid instructions.**
- **Take advantage of online builder communities. "Go to the Groups section of Google, and type in your question. You'll find dozens of postings from people who have faced—and worked through—the same issue."**
- **Borrow code. Arin also points out that when you see an effect you're after on another site, you can view that site's source code, the underlying instructions that make that cool thing happen. Go to the View menu in your Web browser and click on "Source." You'll see the code, and can cut and paste it into your own.**

BEYOND THE BADGE

If you love it as much as you thought you would, dream on . . .

- **Bells and whistles.** There are oodles of ways to up the ante on your site. Animation, visitor guest books, games, etc. See Advanced Building Tools for more.
- **Go pro—or donate your services.** If you get hooked on Web design, you can offer your services to people in need of your newfound skills. Your expertise may help you pay the bills or could make a world of difference to nonprofit organizations you care about in your community.
- **Conduct e-commerce.** Many e-businesses went from boom to bust in the last decade, but there is still money to be made online—as long as you learn from their hard-earned lessons about how important it is to be clear-headed and ultra-strategic about your enterprise. If you have a great e-business idea, take the time to develop a solid business plan (see Be Your Own Boss, page 62); make sure your site design is tailor-made for your customers; educate yourself about handling credit card transactions, shipping, tax, and security issues; and mastermind a marketing plan.

ADVANCED BUILDING TOOLS

Graduate from beginner to builder

Adobe GoLive. A good, professional-strength Web page editor.

Adobe Photoshop. Industry standard digital imaging program.

Dreamweaver by Macromedia. Another cool professional page editor.

Fireworks by Macromedia. Designs, integrates, and optimizes graphic art.

Flash by Macromedia. A leader in online graphics and animation.

Graphic Workshop. A graphics shareware product.

Paint Shop Pro. A graphics viewer, converter, and editor.

ARIN'S PICKS

BOOKS

Building a Web Site for Dummies by David Crowder and Rhonda Crowder
Web site construction 101.

Creating Killer Web Sites by David Siegel
A classic guide to good taste in Web design.

HTML 4.0: No Experience Required by E. Stephen Mack and Janan Platt Saylor
The basics of this most basic Web language.

Learning Web Design: A Beginner's Guide to HTML, Graphics, and Beyond by Jennifer Niederst
How-to for the complete beginner.

The Smallest Ever Guide to the Internet by Nigel Holmes
This handy book explains the Internet in real-world terms and with great graphics. Special order through www.arturan.com/store.

Web Design in a Nutshell: A Desktop Quick Reference by Jennifer Niederst
Browsers, graphics, HTML, Java, and more.

WEB SITES

www.freesitetemplates.com
Free, downloadable Web site templates for a variety of needs.

www.hotwired.lycos.com/webmonkey
Webmonkey is a Web developer's dream resource, with a beginners section that covers all the basics. Includes tutorials and good, functional examples.

www.lynda.com
This site from Lynda Weinman, author of Web design and software books, offers free tips and tutorials written in a clear, straightforward voice plus online training, training movies, books, and CD-ROMs.

www.personalWeb.about.com/library/bl_tutorial.htm
About.com's guide to building a personal Web site, including a section on why to build a personal Web site in the first place.

www.webdevelopersjournal.com/columns/abcs_of_building_web_sites.html
The ABCs of Building a Web Site. An extensive, free tutorial for the beginner, with a Web tools download page and beginner's discussion group.

www.webpagesthatsuck.com
Vincent Flanders teaches you how NOT to end up on his site, with articles like "What Would Amazon Do?," "Google Is God, Don't Piss Her Off," and "Don't Confuse Web Design with Sex." Also check out "Tools for Fixing Your Bad Design" and a featured "Daily Sucker."

www.webstyleguide.com/index.html?/contents.html
This Web Style Guide is an extensive, free online resource covering key topics such as organizing information, visual hierarchy, typography, frames, graphics, and multimedia.

17

DIG THIS

★ gardening ★

> If a blade of grass springing up in the fields has the power to move you . . . rejoice, for your SOUL IS ALIVE.
>
> —Eleonora Duse

Imagine This . . . The fern that seems to fear your footsteps and the violet you can't get to stop shrinking have been replaced by a pretty, practical container garden that you (yes, you!) planted and tended into full, fabulous bloom. Tender baby lettuce leaves, so much basil that the savory scent wafts in through the open windows, and cute-as-can-be cosmos flowers . . . you feel a memorable Mediterranean meal coming on! When your guests, special someone, or housemates arrive, you hand them a glass of wine—and a pair of scissors so that they can snip their own salad. Your homegrown basil pesto sauce is ready and waiting to be tossed with the pasta on the stove, and when you sit down at the table, a vase of colorful cosmos graces the table. Can you dig it? *You can do it!*

So, what's your motivation?
Take a moment.
Dream a little, think big,
and then complete this sentence:
I see myself . . .

The Payoffs

- **Good eats.** Really fresh and truly organic herbs and produce for your table.
- **Eye candy.** A rainbow-colored garden, a window box bursting with lush greenery, or even a simple pot of posies can be such a soothing sight!
- **Accomplishment.** When you can't get your team to work, your hair to behave, or the engine in your brain to turn over, you can pull weeds, plant a seed, or pot a plant and get an immediate, tangible sense of accomplishment.
- **Grounding.** You don't have to be an earth mother or tree-hugger to feel centered and connected when you work in tandem with nature to help something grow.

Meet Your Mentor
RENEE SHEPHERD

What She Does: Renee has helped pioneer the introduction of international specialty vegetables, herbs, and flowers for home gardeners and gourmet restaurants by founding Shepherd's Garden Seeds catalog in 1985 and, in 1997, Renee's Garden seed company. She is the coauthor of *Recipes from a Kitchen Garden* and *More Recipes from a Kitchen Garden,* writes often for publications including *Sunset, Fine Cooking,* and *Organic Gardening,* and lectures widely at national and regional garden shows and conferences.

Why She Does It: "My grandmother was an avid gardener, and I grew up visiting her every Saturday. The first thing we'd do is go out to her garden and harvest things. Then she'd make lunch from what we'd picked. I definitely got the idea of cooking from the garden from her. I started to garden in earnest when I moved to California and was surrounded by people with big, beautiful home gardens. The university where I was teaching also has a very famous organic garden, and I was able to get help from people there and from a few people I met who farmed produce for a living. I don't have a formal horticultural background, but I think that's been a good thing, because it helps me write seed packets for beginning gardeners. Ten or twelve years ago, if you were trying to convince people to plant radicchio or arugula, you also had to tell them what to do with it—so I started writing cookbooks."

Word from the Wise: "In modern life, one doesn't often get to do something from the beginning through to the end. Gardening lets you do that—and it always feels like a miracle to see a little, hard seed grow into something beautiful."

Gardening naturally makes you happy! Stewarding the earth to produce is fun, it's satisfying, and it's an art that ANYONE can practice.

—Renee Shepherd

BADGE STEPS

1. Pick your patch.

Don't worry if you don't have acres to plow! We've deliberately chosen container gardening to get you started: It's fun and simple, teaches you the basics, and (whew!) requires no weeding or hoeing. Even though Renee has large outdoor gardens behind and below her home, she loves to cultivate in containers on her patio. She even has a pal who lives on a boat, surrounded by water, who grows vegetables in pots on her decks. So as long as you have three to five square feet on a porch, balcony, rooftop, fire escape, or terrace that gets six hours of spring and summer sun each day, you too can get growing. Since you'll be planting your container garden outdoors to take advantage of fresh air and sunshine, early spring is the best time to think about planting. ***Pick a spot for your pots.***

2. Shop for sowing supplies.

To give you a feel for herb, flower, and vegetable gardening, we'll be planting three containers: one of basil, one of cosmo flowers, and one of mixed lettuces. While growing these plants will give you a solid introduction to gardening, the best thing about this container combo is that in a few weeks you can harvest your pots and turn their contents into a celebratory "Look what I did!" meal.

As Renee's customers will tell you, shopping for seeds can be the most fun part of your garden prep. "It's important to buy good quality fresh seeds—the packet should say that it's packed for the current year," Renee stresses. And make sure the planting and care instructions on the back of the packet make sense—those on inferior brands can leave you scratching your head. (Renee's Garden seeds are available at independent garden centers and nurseries, or you can buy them online at www.reneesgarden.com.) Check out the many seed options for each item in your container garden, as follows:

Basil. As Renee says, "It smells good, it flowers, and it draws butterflies!" It can also be used to season food, make pesto, or accent a salad. Basil varieties are bountiful. To make great pesto, look for "large-leaf Italian," "Italian pesto," or "dark green leaf" on the seed packet.

Lettuce. Look for a "mixed baby lettuce" seed mix. The end result will look like the salad at a chic cafe or the colorful premixed bags at your grocery. Mixed lettuce seed packets do the combining for you—the seed

GARDEN GLOSSARY

So you can talk the talk . . .

Annuals. Bloom and produce in one season. They tend to germinate and grow quickly, and you plant them anew each year. These are Renee's preference for the beginning gardener.

Broadcast. Disperse seeds randomly with your hand, rather than sowing in rows.

Deadhead. Removing dead or fading flowers from plants; it encourages them to flower longer and grow fuller.

Germinate. To begin to grow or sprout—what you hope your seeds will do!

Horticulture. The art and science of growing fruits, vegetables, flowers, and ornamental plants.

Hybrid. The offspring of two plants of different varieties.

Perennials. Unlike annuals, these last through several seasons and years.

Sow. To plant seeds.

varieties have been selected to grow well and taste good together. And buying "baby" lettuce seeds lets you start cutting and tossing sooner than you would if you were growing big adult heads of lettuce.

Cosmos. Look for the varieties in Renee's "Dancing Petticoats" specialty cosmos blend—Seashells, Psyche, and Versailles—or the Little Ladybirds, Sonata, or Snow Sonata varieties. These will give you easy-to-care-for blooms bountiful enough to cut for bouquets.

To get the rest of the goods you'll need for your container garden, Renee recommends you visit a local independent garden center, as opposed to a big chain store. Your local nursery is where you are most apt to find people who really know and love gardening and can spend time helping you. Head for the store with this shopping list:

Containers. Three twelve-to-eighteen-inch-wide plastic pots. Renee recommends plastic because it's lightweight, easy to maneuver, and dries out slower than clay pots. You can also use something funkier or fancier—clay pots, window boxes, wine barrels, etc. If you use pots too heavy for you to lift, consider placing them on wooden or plastic platforms with casters (available at garden centers) so that you can wheel them into or out of heat and sun. Whatever you use, make sure it has drainage holes (if it doesn't, put about an inch of stones in the bottom to allow for proper drainage), and that it's big enough to give full-grown plants room to breathe.

Tools. For this project, you'll need nothing more than a bucket for your soil, a trowel (use an old serving fork or spoon if you like), a watering can, and scissors.

Soil. Use a commercial potting soil mix. Dirt from your yard is too dense for a potted plant, and may contain weeds and pests.

Food. Renee says diluted fish emulsion makes an excellent fertilizer, though very strict vegetarians may prefer to explore other options with no animal by-products.

Gather your gardening gear.

3. Sow seeds.

To plant your seeds, first put the potting soil in your pots up to about a half-inch below the rim, then add the fertilizer in the proportions indicated on the bag or bottle. Some fertilizers you only need a little of to get your plants started. Then follow the instructions on your seed

JOIN THE GREEN THUMB CLUB

Avoid these common beginner boo-boos

- Not reading the seed packet for exact instructions on ideal planting seasons; sun, shade, water, and thinning requirements; planting depth; etc.
- Not keeping the seeds evenly moist while you are waiting for germination. "Keep the soil about the consistency of a wrung-out sponge," states Renee. "Look at the pots every day, and water gently."
- When the seeds germinate, it's often hard for beginning gardeners to thin out some of the small seedlings so that the remaining plants have room to grow above and below ground. As Renee says, this "often feels like murder." But if gardeners don't do this, "you'll wind up with a lot of thin, spindly plants that have to compete with each other and can't produce well. It's hard to do, but it's important—and it's what happens in nature."

I DID IT!

"When I bought my first home, I couldn't wait to decorate the interior. But I had no idea what to do with my front and back yards, since I could hardly keep a house-plant alive in my previous apartments. So I invited a gardening friend to visit. He suggested appropriate plants, took me to the garden center, and explained all the weird stuff there. Then we spent the rest of the weekend weeding and planting. It was exhausting but also exhilarating. Now I can't wait to put on my gardening gloves on the weekends. It's such a relaxing way to spend a few hours, and afterwards you get to stand back and admire the pretty results."
—Janice

BEWARE THE BUMPER CROP

"My father came to live with us after my mother died. He loves to garden, so he immediately set about transforming our backyard. It never looked better—but I have to say that my whole family came to dread strawberry season. Every morning he'd take my little boy outside with him, and they'd bring back a basketful. It got to the point where I'd just groan when I saw them . . . I had no idea a few plants could produce so many berries!"
—Sylvia

packets about how and when to plant. Optimal planting times will vary based on where you live; see below for necessary weather conditions:

Basil. Plant in late March through July or when you know the plant will get full sun and temperatures above fifty degrees Fahrenheit. Place seeds a half inch into the dirt and an inch apart. Firm and moisten the soil over the seeds. Remember not to plant until night temperatures are warm and settled and evenly in the fifties.

Lettuce. Plant in February through September. Germination is best at cool temperatures of sixty to seventy degrees Fahrenheit, so cool, early spring weather with full sun is ideal. Shake the seeds into the palm of your hand and then "broadcast" (scatter) them about a half inch apart over your entire surface. Cover lightly and evenly with a quarter inch of soil, and then water finely and evenly.

Cosmos. Plant in April through June or when you can promise the seeds lots of sun and no frost. Plant the seeds a half inch beneath the soil and one to two inches apart. Cover lightly.

Break new ground, and get gardening!

RENEE'S EXPERT TIPS

SEEDS OF WISDOM

- Plant more seeds than your desired number of plants, because not everything you plant germinates. Always read the packet back carefully, because it will give you information on exactly how to plant and grow each kind of seed.
- Most seeds you don't use now can be kept until the next planting season, if you keep them cool and dry. Renee says, "They'll be comfortable where you'd be comfortable—indoors, away from temperature extremes and humidity."
- The National Gardening Association Web site (www.garden.org/seedswap) administers a Seed Swap that lets you find seeds you've been looking for or share extras with others.

4. Tend your garden.

Remember when you were a first-grader who just planted bean seeds in half an old milk carton, and you couldn't wait to get to school to check on their progress? You need to pay this kind of attention to your containers. Container plants "are kind of like children," laughs Renee. "They're dependent on you, and you have to tend them carefully."

Check every day to see if your plants need water by putting your forefinger in the soil—if it's dry beyond the first joint, water immediately. Feed them fertilizer about every three weeks, because they use up the nutrients in the potting soil quickly. "Container plants need more attention than plants in the ground because they rely solely on the gardener to meet their needs," explains Renee. "Confined to a limited space, they will quickly become stressed if essential water or fertilizer isn't available regularly."

Nurture your plants daily for the six to twelve weeks it takes until harvest time, depending on climatic conditions in your area. Each of your plants requires slightly different care, so follow these tips to help meet their individual needs:

Basil. Keep the seed beds moist. Germination takes one to two weeks. When seedlings and leaves come up, thin the bed so that plants are about eight inches apart. (If you don't want to toss out thinned seedlings, transplant them into another container.) When plants become six to eight inches tall, pinch off growing tips to encourage branching.

Lettuce. Keep the seed bed evenly moist. Baby lettuces like mild, rather than hot, weather. Consider moving or creating light shade for your plants if it really heats up. And keep your eye on the birdies: Birds are often attracted to these seedlings.

Cosmos. Keep the seed bed moist. In five to ten days, when seedlings are large enough to handle, thin to eight inches apart. When the plants reach their mature height of three and a half to four feet, they can handle hot and dry conditions.

Now be patient—if they're getting the care they need, your plants will grow eventually. ***Handle your garden with care.***

5. Harvest your crop.

When your plants are mature, they look pretty in their pots—but you can also cut some or all of your basil and lettuce to eat, and a bouquet of cosmos to enjoy on the table. If you just want to thin out your patch and not use it all at once, consult the growing instructions provided and keep these harvesting hints in mind:

Basil. Plants are mature at one to one-and-a-half feet. Harvest sprays of leaves by cutting stems just above two new sprouting lateral branches to get lush regrowth. Pinch off flower buds to extend harvesting, and feed

HIT A ROUGH PATCH?

Get help from a garden guru

Renee heartily recommends you ask the personnel at your friendly local nursery for help or ask them to refer you to the local "Master Gardeners." With gardening gurus in all fifty states, these land lovers are volunteer members of the local community trained in everything from botany, entomology, and composting to diagnosing plant problems, flower gardening, lawn care, organic gardening, pesticide use, and vegetable gardening. One of their missions is to help beginning gardeners, so get to know your local Masters. Visit www.MasterGardeners.com to learn more.

the plants fertilizer regularly to promote new growth. Put stems of newly harvested leaves in a vase of water to keep them fresh in the kitchen.

Lettuce. About a month after planting, when plants are four to five inches tall, cut some leaves one to two inches above the soil level. Water well and fertilize lightly, and the plants will regrow for several more cuttings. You can even plant again in late summer for fall harvesting.

Cosmos. Cutting generous bouquets actually prolongs the blooming season. Harvest several times through June for a succession of fresh flowers. Do so in either the morning or the early evening, so that the blooms are not stressed by full sun.

Don't wait too long to harvest your crop—when the days get short and the weather cold, your plants will naturally wither up. (Not to worry: You can always plant again next spring.) ***Reap what you've sown.***

6. Enjoy the fruits of your labors.

Renee reminds us that "there's little as satisfying and rewarding as being able to cook with vegetables and herbs from your garden—they're fresh, they taste better, and you know how they were grown."

To get the most out of your containers, build a meal around them. How about your favorite pasta with Renee's basil pesto sauce (see the Eat It! sidebar) and a salad made from your baby lettuce mix, tossed in a simple vinaigrette that complements the sweet, delicate flavors of the lettuce? And don't forget to create a centerpiece of your smiling cosmos!

Serve a festive and flavorful garden-fresh meal with flowers from your own garden. ***Savor your success!***

CONGRATULATIONS!

You deserve two green thumbs up! You did it!

I DID IT!

Name: ____________________

Date: ____________________

EAT IT!

Cook from your container garden

Renee's pesto sauce.

In a food processor, combine:

3 cups of loosely packed fresh, washed basil leaves
½ cup chopped parsley
3–5 large garlic cloves
½ cup pine nuts
1 teaspoon fresh oregano
½ teaspoon pepper

Add ½ to ¾ cup of fruity extra virgin olive oil and process just enough to make a smooth paste.

Add one cup of freshly grated Parmesan or Asiago cheese and salt to taste.

Serve over hot pasta, using a little of the pasta water to help spread the sauce evenly.

You can also puree basil with extra virgin olive oil and freeze it in Ziploc bags, adding the other sauce ingredients when you cook it up. Enjoy a taste of summer with homemade, homegrown basil pesto year-round!

Makes two cups of pesto, enough for four servings of pasta.

BEYOND THE BADGE

If you love it as much as you thought you would, dream on . . .

- **Dig around.** If your green thumb is itching for wider pastures and you have space to spare in your front or back yard, consult with your nursery personnel, hire a local landscaper, or enlist a gardening friend (see I Did It!, page 136) to get your ground growing. If you don't have any dirt of your own and yearn to do more than container gardening, ask your local nursery to refer you to a nearby community garden. This is where you can rent a plot of land for a minimal amount of money and really grow wild! You can also get great ideas from your fellow gardeners there. For further inspiration, visit your local botanical gardens, or sign up for home garden tours in your area.
- **Become a garden-fresh chef.** Planting a small vegetable garden is a great way to up your intake of healthy produce. Seek out recipes for Mediterranean and Asian dishes, where veggies are often the featured attraction. Renee reminds us that there are also other, less obvious ways to cook from the garden. "Woody herbs, such as rosemary branches, bloomed-out basil stalks, sage branches, and thyme stalks can add wonderful smoky flavors to the barbecue process," she says. "When you are grilling meats, cut a big bunch of any of these herbs and throw them right on the coals for the last five or ten minutes of cooking. Cover your grill, and let the aromatic smoke add a subtle herb flavor to your meat." And don't forget edible flowers. Nasturtiums, petite violas, or calendulas are tasty and decorative.
- **Share your harvest with those in need.** If you're lucky enough to grow more than you can eat or you just want to share your bounty, call your local soup kitchen or other charities that feed the hungry. Or contact Plant a Row for the Hungry (www.gwaa.org/par), a program of the Garden Writers Association set up to distribute fresh food to those who need and want it.
- **Kid around.** Get your kids involved with your gardening. As Renee says, "They enjoy it, have a unique perspective, and it's a good way to get them to try new foods—they are likely to at least try what they've helped grow." See Gardening with Kids for more tips.

GARDENING WITH KIDS

Tips from Renee's Garden associate Alice Formiga

- Grow plants with playful appeal, multiple uses, and flavor or fragrance, such as pole beans, pumpkins, cherry tomatoes, snap peas, and sunflowers.
- Let your children help. Kids love to help you water or weed—give them their own "job" and show them how important their work is. Just steer clear of tiny seeds that can be a choking hazard, and teach kids not to eat what you haven't offered them.
- Keep your garden safe by keeping fertilizers, pesticides, manure, and sharp or motorized tools away.
- Visit the National Gardening Association's Web site for information and inspiration. www.kidsgardening.com.

extra credit

FLOWER ARRANGING

Grow your own art supplies! Follow these simple tips:

Cut. Cut blooms from your garden plants in morning or early evening using stem-cutting shears or sharp pruners, just above a joint in the stem or a dormant bud. Place cut stems in a bucket filled with lukewarm water.

Prep. Cut stems again at an angle, for maximum water absorption. Use your shears or a sharp knife instead of plain old scissors, which tend to seal part of the stem. Before arranging, let your stems soak up more water. Remove all foliage near or below the water line (to prevent destructive bacteria from breeding) and place the stems in water for a few hours in a cool, dark place.

Arrange.

- Narrow-mouthed vases are the easiest to arrange in because the mouth holds your stems in place for you. Other ways to hold stems in place include placing blocks of floral foam in your vase (provided it's not see-through) or creating a lattice across your vase's mouth with floral tape. (Tape and foam can be found at a craft supply store.)
- If you want to put heavy flowers in a lightweight vase, place a couple of inches of pretty pebbles, marbles, or stones at the bottom of the vase to weigh it down. (The stones can also help you keep stems in their place, much as blocks of floral foam do.)
- Rule of thumb: The height of a vertical arrangement should be one and a half times the height of the container. Horizontal styles should be one and a half times the width.
- Try imagining an overall shape to your arrangement—round, symmetrical or asymmetrical triangles. For daring artistic arrangements, pick up some ideas from books on the subject (see Be a Blooming Genius for suggestions).

Preserve. The National Gardening Association advises that freshly cut flowers have enough stored sugar to survive in a vase. But if you want to add a preservative to your water, try a teaspoon of sugar and an aspirin, *or* one cup of regular 7-Up to one cup of lukewarm water and one half teaspoon of bleach. Every few days, empty the vase, rinse it, replace the water, and recut the stems. This should prolong the life of your flowers.

BE A BLOOMING GENIUS

Take a tip or two from the professionals

Arranging Flowers: How to Create Beautiful Bouquets in Every Season by Martha Stewart et al.

The Complete Guide to Flower Arranging by Jane Packer

Enchanting Ikebana: Japanese Flower Arrangement by Reiko Takenaka

The Fine Art of Flower Arranging: A Garden Club of America Book by Nancy D'Oench, Bonny Martin, and Mick Hales (photographer)

Flower Power: Fresh, Fabulous Arrangements by Rebecca Cole and Helen Norman (photographer)

Flower Style: The FTD Guide to Flowers in Your Home by Pat Ross and Richard Felber (photographer)

Teach Yourself Flower Arranging by Judith Blacklock

RENEE'S PICKS

BOOKS

The American Horicultural Society Encyclopedia of Gardening by Christopher Brickell (editor) and the American Horticultural Society

As comprehensive as it sounds, this book covers gardening techniques and garden design, tools, and materials, and includes a glossary of plants, trees, shrubs, and perennials.

The New York Times 1000 Gardening Questions and Answers by Leslie Land (editor)

A nearly 700-page gardening bible based on the syndicated *New York Times* column, Garden Q&A.

Recipes from a Kitchen Garden and More Recipes from a Kitchen Garden by Renee Shepherd and Fran Raboff

Each illustrated book is an original collection of more than 300 easy to prepare dishes emphasizing fresh ingredients, wonderful flavor, and simplicity of style.

Trowel & Error: Over 700 Tips, Remedies, and Shortcuts for the Gardener by Sharon Lovejoy

A treasure trove of gardening smarts.

MAGAZINES

Better Homes and Gardens
www.bhg.com
Not just for your mother—*BHG* is a wealth of down-to-earth information on gardening projects, landscaping ideas, container gardening, lawn care, cut flowers, plants, seeds, pests, tools, and more.

Fine Gardening
www.taunton.com/finegardening/index.asp
Gardening basics as well as plans, projects, articles, tips, and lots of pretty pictures.

Garden Design
www.gardendesignmag.com
High-end garden magazine with great visuals, interesting articles (e.g., "More on Moss," "Sage Advice"), and a green marketplace.

Organic Gardening
www.organicgardening.com
Articles on organic flower and food gardening, as well as features on subjects from composting to building a bat house.

WEB SITES

www.avant-gardening.com
Info on composting, soil building, permaculture, creative garden design, and links to organic seed retailers.

www.garden.org
This NGA site is a treasure trove of information for gardeners in all areas of the country and at all skill levels.

www.gardenweb.com
Forums, info, plant database, regional listings, and a seed and plant exchange.

www.reneesgarden.com
Renee's site, with loads of info, including Master Gardeners in your state, planting advice, seed selection and descriptions, and botany.

ORGANIZATIONS

American Horticultural Society
www.ahs.org
Founded in 1922, the AHS is a nonprofit known for its educational programs and environmentally responsible gardening information.

National Home Gardening Club
visitors.gardeningclub.com
Features a members-only seed swap, *Gardening How-To* magazine, a members-only Web site with bulletin boards and gardening advice, and a directory of public gardens.

SUPPLIES

Extremely Green
www.extremelygreen.com
Environmentally friendly gardening wares.

Gemplers
www.gemplers.com
For the serious gardener—heavy-duty outdoor tools, chemical storage, hoses, spreaders, wheelbarrows, and the like.

Smith & Hawken
www.smithandhawken.com
Catalog, retail, and online supplier of gardening, yard, and home supplies and gifts.

Windowbox.com
www.windowbox.com
Specializing in container garden supplies.

18

REDO A ROOM

★ decorating ★

The house a woman creates is a UTOPIA.

—Marguerite Duras

So, what's your motivation?
Take a moment.
Dream a little, think big,
and then complete this sentence:
I see myself . . .

Imagine This . . . "I just love what you've done with your place!" your guests gush. You're getting used to the compliment. With a few creative touches, you've made yourself more at home in your home, and now it's the place everyone wants to be. You might enjoy your friend's cozy kitchen, or the vacation rental with that relaxing den, or the guest bedroom where you felt so pampered, but there truly is no place like home. It doesn't take a magic wand to turn your home into your castle—and you don't need tons of money or handywoman expertise, either. With a little time, basic skills, and creativity, you can make your home a truer reflection of you. *You can do it!*

The Payoffs

- **A positive outlook.** Your living space can leave you feeling comforted and cheerful, or unsettled and gloomy. Why not set a positive mood?
- **Practicality.** Successful decorating will make your space someplace you can actually use—it's functional as well as aesthetically pleasing.
- **A discerning eye.** With a little help from our expert, you'll develop an eye for design. When you look at your rooms (and other people's rooms!), you'll be able to pinpoint exactly what is—and isn't—working and why.
- **Style.** Once you know a few basic design principles, you'll be amazed at what you can do—and feel more assured in your tastes. As *Room Redux* states, "Style is confidence."

Meet Your Mentor
JOANN ECKSTUT

What She Does: The coauthor, with Sheran James, of *Room Redux: The Home Decorating Workbook*, and the author of *The Color Palette Primer*, Joann has designed spaces that range from private homes to very large projects such as the Smithsonian's National Museum of the American Indian in New York City. Her design business is The Roomworks.

Why She Does It: "I started out as a painter. My ex-husband is an architect, and many years ago, he asked me to help him with the colors and materials for his architectural models. This snowballed into all kinds of interior and exterior design work for me. It's no surprise that I do what I do, because one of my earliest memories is from when I was about three years old, and my mother gave me a time-out in the den as punishment for doing something naughty. I had to stay put, but I remember amusing myself no end by pretending the ottoman I was on was an island, and by coloring on the embossed white paper napkins I had with me with some crayons. Instead of feeling punished, I had the best time playing around with those colors and textures. That's a lot like what I still do! My work is so rewarding because, while I enjoy it immensely, it also makes other people happy."

Word from the Wise: "The space you are working with is going to tell you certain things. You have to listen—and when you do, it's great fun to experiment with what you hear."

Good design makes us happier because it's pleasing to the eye, and it makes our lives easier because it makes a space user-friendly.

—Joann Eckstut

MAKE HOME WHERE YOUR HEART IS

. . . with this Room Redux *exercise*

- Think of a word that describes the objects you'd save from a natural disaster—elegant, exotic, simple. This is a word that defines your personal style—so keep it in mind as you proceed with your plans.
- Think of a friend's home you love or a room you've admired in a magazine or on TV. Then define it in a word. Does this word describe your home too? If so, great—if not, perhaps this is a style you can aspire to.
- How would you redo your damaged room if money were no object—or insurance were footing the bill? This image represents your design ideal, your heart's desire.

BADGE STEPS

1. Find a room for improvement.

You may know exactly where to begin—maybe the living room that no one ever lives in, or the home office you shun in favor of the kitchen table. If you don't know which room you want to revamp, *Room Redux* includes a clever test to help you decide. Here's a quickie version.

A tidal wave is approaching your home. Answer the following questions quickly: Which room do you pray gets saved? This room is your haven, so think about which elements make it so ideal, and how you can repeat these successes elsewhere. Which room do you hope gets trashed? Think about starting here! ***Pick a room to redecorate.***

2. Take a good look around.

What do you like and dislike most about the room you've chosen? Survey the entire room in great detail, including its inherent architectural aspects and the furnishings you've placed in it. Ask the like/dislike question everywhere your eye falls, and jot down your answer on paper for future reference.

Next, write down all the things you want or need to be able to do in the room: work, entertain, relax, sleep, etc. If you can't seem to do those things in the room as is, think of possible explanations: Is there no place to sit, a cramped desk, inaccessible stereo, another problem? Make a note of it—and prepare for a change. ***Question the status quo.***

3. Gather your resources.

Clip photos out of magazines and catalogs and put them in a special folder, along with fabric samples and anything else you want to consider. "The more you look at and collect," says Joann, "the clearer you will get about your goals, because your eye is drawn to design elements that represent your sensibility. Plus, if you give yourself time to collect a lot of ideas, you'll often find that at the end, you'll discard your initial thoughts. Let yourself collect, and then edit, edit, edit."

Next, set aside some funds to make your dream room a reality. Do some preliminary pricing online or in person so you know how much you'll need for paint, shelving, fixtures, and furnishings, plus any professional help (plumbing, electricians, movers, etc.). ***Find your inspiration—and the funds to make it happen.***

4. Make a floor plan.

To save yourself from endlessly redoing your redo, start with an accurate rendering of how much floor space you really have before you start moving or buying things (you'll create a representation of your room to scale in Step 7). You don't need to be a great artist—just grab a blank piece of paper and:

- Turn toward the northwest corner of your room, and draw this corner in the top left-hand corner of your page.
- Continue outlining the floor until you get back to where you started.
- Sketch in every built-in protrusion or indentation, and leave small gaps for doorways.
- Mark windows—these too have to be taken into consideration.
- Use a tape measure to measure the spaces that correspond to the lines you've drawn.

Map out your room.

5. Make a surface change.

The floor, walls, and ceiling account for most of the surface area in your room, so changing them will make a dramatic difference. Furnishings and tchotchkes are fun, but you can reinvent an entire room with just a fresh coat of paint—and you can do it quickly, easily, and all by yourself.

Look through your design folder, and gather a few bright ideas to change the color of the walls, ceiling, and floor of your room. As you weigh your options, consider these helpful hints:

Ceiling. To create the illusion of a tall room, paint the ceiling a lighter, cooler color than the walls.

Walls. Painting walls a cool, light color can make a small room feel larger, and a dark, matte color can make it cozier. If your room is "boxy," consider creating a focal point by painting one wall a different color. Beware of major color transitions between rooms—changes should feel natural and complementary.

Floor. Floor color should either be neutral, or the scheme you build the rest of the room around. Stick with solids on the floor if you have patterned wallpaper or other prominent patterning on your walls. A bare wood floor can be refinished, stained darker, bleached lighter, or painted. Beware of transitions between rooms—changes should feel natural and complementary.

THE BASIC PRINCIPLES OF DESIGN

Five key design considerations

Balance. Furnishings distributed in a way that's comfortable to the eye. Think about the way we "naturally" center a light fixture above a table.

Emphasis. Highlights visual focal points. You might make the focus of your decor an ornamental fireplace, an attention-getting vase of flowers on a table, or the stand-out color contrasts of a painting.

Harmony. A consistent theme among furnishings and arrangements. Shoot for your own style, but realize that the room has a "mind of its own" to some extent. It would be hard to create a dark, cozy Victorian boudoir look in a sunny loft with high ceilings.

Rhythm. Orderly patterns among materials, objects, and placements. Just as repeated beats create rhythm in music, reprising shapes, patterns, and textures can create rhythm in a room.

Scale and proportion. How the dimensions of the furnishings relate to each other and their environment. You can play around with proportions, but if you put a tiny table in a big dining room or a big fabric pattern in a small space, you might make it look like something out of *Alice's Adventures in Wonderland.*

I DID IT!

"I was vacationing in Hawaii with two girlfriends, and one day we stumbled upon an amazing, out-of-the-way vintage/thrift/antique store. We spent hours exclaiming over our finds, and how the similar shops back home in San Francisco were either picked over or overpriced. My favorite find was a bookshelf filled with fabrics from the '40s, '50s, and '60s. I picked out a few yards with tropical themes, and made pillows for each of us when I got home. They're colorful, fun accent pieces for each of our homes—and best of all, they remind us of a great trip."
—Sherri

NOT SUCH A FLATTERING LIGHT

"While vacationing in Santa Fe, I went nuts for the color and decor schemes everywhere we went. I bought a big rug, a painting, and a blanket, with big plans to redo our den at home. Trouble was, all the stuff I bought looked horrible back home in Minnesota. The light coming through my windows was nothing like that New Mexico light."
—Theresa

JOANN'S EXPERT TIPS

LIGHT UP A ROOM

Light affects color. In fact, color is light, and both natural and artificial light change our perceptions. Look at your room at different times of day, both with and without the lights on. See the difference in the color? This is why you must try out carpet and wall colors in your room at different times of day, and under all lighting conditions. To try out wall color, try painting a four-by-eight-foot piece of sheet rock and moving that sample around your room.

Go for the glow. A fixture with an opening at the top and the bottom will provide the most general light, but the bulb should hang low in the shade for reading lamps.

Consider daytime lighting. Full-spectrum incandescents enhance daylight.

Ready to change the color of at least one wall, the ceiling, or the floor? Good! Here's how it's done:

- Go shopping for paint, stains, scrapers, rollers, brushes, blue painter's tape, plastic sheeting, and other gear recommended for your project by the helpful clerks at your local hardware store or specialty paint shop. Bring your floor plan with you so that you get enough paint, stain, or paint stripper to cover the dimensions of your wall(s), floor, or ceiling.
- Compare your clippings to the paint chips at the store to find a paint or stain that's as close to your desired color(s) as possible. If you don't see the exact color you're after among the paint chips, ask the store clerks if they can mix a custom color for you, and show a few paint chips that come close.
- Get home, empty the room of furniture, cover anything you don't want painted with plastic sheeting, tape off the edges of your painting surface, and get to work . . . or make like Tom Sawyer and enlist a few people to help you!

Change your room from top to bottom with color and texture.

6. Have fun with fabric.

As *Room Redux* says, "Fabrics give a room its personality and reveal as much about your personality as the clothes you wear." Remember the styles you defined in Make Home Where Your Heart Is, page 144, and imagine what fabric textures and colors convey that sense. Consult your inspiration file and examine the fabrics you find there.

Imagine ways to incorporate fabric as slipcovers, window treatments, seat covers, and pillows. Here are some hints to get you started:

- When considering adding a pattern to a room, note the patterns that already exist there, including artwork, wall treatments, floors, furniture, accents, etc.
- Decide if you want the color of a fabric to stay within the color scheme of the room or provide an accent. Again, always see how a swatch of fabric looks in your room, rather than guessing when you're in a store.
- Stripes can expand or contract a surface—horizontal stripes make a piece seem wider, while vertical add height.
- If your room has a period or historical feel ('50s, Southwestern, English country), consider patterns and fabrics used at that time and place.

Dress up your room with fabric.

7. Rearrange your furniture.

Your floor plan really comes in handy when trying new furniture configurations. Create a scale version of your floor plan on graph paper, so that each square on the graph paper equals a square foot (or half a foot or two feet) in your room. You can then make scale cut-outs of your furniture on graph paper and move them around on your scale floor plan to see what fits where. This will save you time, and a lot of lower back strain besides!

Good sources of inexpensive furniture include thrift stores—where you'll find authentic versions of vintage trends—and garage sales and sidewalk freebies. Get up early on heavy pick-up days, and you might discover a real find on the sidewalk. A door placed on top of two filing cabinets makes a great desk or work table.

And as you rearrange your furniture, consider the following hints:

- Remember that a room full of furniture will feel smaller. To open up small spaces, try removing an item or two.
- If you can't really afford brand-new furniture to go with your design scheme, go bargain-hunting and try sprucing up your old furniture with a new finish, new knobs, or a slipcover.

INSTANT STYLE WITH SLIPCOVERS

Give your furniture a new lease on life!

Slipcovers for chairs and sofas are an economical way to update your style, and they can be removed for cleaning.

- Medium-weight cottons, linens, or cotton blends tend to hang best.
- Look for a ready-made slipcover that comes in different sizes and has features to keep the cover in place, like elastic bands on the inside seams.
- Work the slipcover deep into crevices with a spatula or wooden spoon, but don't cover too tightly or the slipcover will twist when the furniture is used.
- For a better fit, you can bulk up the arms of a sofa or chair with foam quilting from a fabric store before covering.
- Leather surfaces can be problematic, since slipcovers tend to slide around on them. To fight this, lay down nonslip carpet padding on a leather chair or sofa before covering.

- To maintain a sense of balance and proportion, try to keep height lines consistent—a basket or stack of books on top can visually raise the height of a table or cabinet to match other furniture, and a low sofa or chair can be made to look higher than it really is with the addition of tall back pillows or even a painting on the wall behind it.

Make all your furnishings look fine.

8. Give your windows special treatment.

First take down whatever window treatments you currently have, clean your windows well, and live with the naked window for a few days. You may be surprised by how much you love it or would if you did something as simple as repaint the moldings. If that's not the case:

- Focus on your goal—privacy, less sunlight, a color accent, etc.
- Consult your inspiration file for specific styles of drapes and curtains, shades and blinds, shutters and screens.
- If you are aiming for a particular period style in your room, research appropriate window treatments.
- Take into consideration the type of window you have, its depth, and the way it operates.

Give yourself and your windows a whole new outlook.

CONGRATULATIONS!

Your place looks fabulous! Who's your designer? You did it!

I DID IT!

Name: ______________________________

Date: ______________________________

BEFORE SAYING IT'S FINISHED

Refinish!

- Veneers and stains can make an inferior wood look more expensive.
- Refinishing requires patience. You'll have to sand and wait for each coat to dry.
- Practice on wood scraps before tackling a piece of furniture.
- Consider spray-painting a piece with a single coat that doesn't cover all blemishes, and you've got shabby—and easy—chic.
- Educate yourself at a do-it-yourself home store or with a good reference book.

JOANN'S PICKS

BOOKS

The Color Palette Primer by Joann Eckstut
This book demonstrates how to coordinate color with hundreds of palettes, based on a foolproof color system for both beginners and design professionals.

All of Terence Conran's books, including **The Essential House Book, The Ultimate House Book, Terence Conran Small Spaces,** and **Terence Conran Kitchens.**

Room Redux: The Home Decorating Workbook by Joann Eckstut and Sheran James
Your handy all-in-one help manual, decorating diary, and reference book.

MAGAZINES

Architecture
www.architecturemag.com
Architect-designed buildings.

Dwell
www.dwellmag.com
Sophisticated, modern ideas for innovative and affordable housing.

Elle Decor
www.elledecor.com
International flair to make your home a showplace.

Interior Design
www.interiordesign.net
Residential and commercial design by major design firms.

Martha Stewart Living
www.marthastewart.com
Live in style with tips on decor and more.

WEB SITES

eBay
www.ebay.com
"I love it—it's fantastic!" says Joann. "You can find anything you want and usually get it at a good price."

CATALOGS

Crate & Barrel
www.crateandbarrel.com
A good mix of contemporary and traditional furniture and accessories.

Design Within Reach
www.dwr.com
The best of classic contemporary design.

Retrospect
www.retrospecthome.com
Traditional home furnishing styles, updated for modern living.

Room & Board
www.roomandboard.com
Contemporary home furnishings.

ASSOCIATIONS

The Carpet and Rug Institute
www.carpet-rug.com or 800-882-8846
Technical and educational info on flooring for consumers.

International Association of Lighting Designers
www.iald.org or 312-527-3677
Tips and lighting designer listings to help you set the mood with lighting.

National Paint and Coatings Association
www.paint.org or 202-462-6272
Advice on manufacturers and specific products, including environmental concerns.

19

BEAD IT

★ beading ★

> Nothing lasts except beauty—and I shall create that.
>
> —Thomas Wolfe

Imagine This . . . When you check the price tag on that gorgeous bracelet, you don't gasp and give up. You swing by the bead store on your way home and make it yourself that night. When *In Style* magazine features the lariat necklace that "everyone" in Hollywood is wearing, you rustle up a dozen to sell at next weekend's craft fair. And when your day has been filled with rough edges and chaos, you can finger the smooth items in your color-coded bead trays and escape into inspiration. You'll get used to hearing "Could you make one for me?" when you bead it yourself. So, make a beautiful necklace for yourself and bead happy. *You can do it!*

So, what's your motivation?
Take a moment.
Dream a little, think big,
and then complete this sentence:
I see myself . . .

The Payoffs

- **Originality.** In our day of mass production, your handmade, homemade trinkets are no trifles. They're one-of-a-kind, unique, and all yours.
- **Accomplishment.** Whether you spend an hour on earrings or a week on a six-strand pearl choker—and even if you take it apart and start over five times—your enterprise is rewarded with something you can wear, give away, or even sell.
- **Tradition.** Beads may no longer be used as currency or a method of counting, but when you sit down to do some stringing, you're tapping into a tradition that goes back to the Stone Age.
- **Beauty.** The lovely things you create with beads may not be displayed under glass at the Louvre, but they will catch the eye of passersby and make everyday life just a pinch prettier.

Meet Your Mentor

MELANIE PAYKOS

What She Does: Has run her own southern California graphic design studio for more than fifteen years (Melanie Paykos Design), is "addicted" to beading, and makes and sells elegant yet rustic jewelry at shows and in shops in and around both her California and Montana home bases.

Why She Does It: "A few years ago, one of my employees brought in these spectacular woven and beaded bracelets and necklaces. I got inspired—and hooked. It's all her fault! I took a one-session class at a bead shop. Then I discovered the wholesale outlets in the downtown Los Angeles jewelry district—unbelievable! I started to find the things I really like: antique glass trading beads, Ethiopian, Thai, and antique Indian silver, semi-precious stones. And I hadn't even been to the flea markets yet! I really enjoy the handwork aspect. I do creative work all day long, but much of it is done on computer. It feels so good to use your hands! You have to focus on what you're doing, but you also get lost in it. It's meditative. I do other kinds of artwork, but for that I need to go to a dedicated space where all the supplies are and where I can make a mess. That can be isolating. But my beading supplies are portable. I can hang out with other people while beading and be in the midst of things rather than removed from them."

Word from the Wise: "You can make something that you like and will wear forever on day one. It takes time to get good at mixing and matching, and there are new techniques and intricate patterns to learn all the time, but you really can make good stuff as a beginner. I still wear some of the first pieces I made."

Beads are just so beautiful. The combinations and juxtapositions you can make are literally endless. And the fact that you can create something really lovely in a relatively short amount of time is very rewarding.

—Melanie Paykos

BADGE STEPS

BEAD BASICS

Bead-dazzled by variety

- Beads come in an infinite array of shapes and are usually measured in millimeters, referring to their diameter.
- Beads are made of many things—minerals, gemstones, metal, ceramics, glass, plastic, and organic materials like amber, pearl, and bone.
- Many beaders collect (read: hoard) a favorite type of bead that they use as a base for most projects. Some of the most commonly collected bead types are tiny round seed beads (Czech, Japanese, and the Delica brand), Charlotte and true-cut beads, metal beads (silver, gold, copper, etc.), dazzling lampwork glass beads and Austrian crystal, and semiprecious beads and pearls.
- Know what you're working with. Ask the salespeople at the bead shop questions about how beads are made and whether they are dyed with fade-resistant dyes—and if they're made of glass, whether they are kiln annealed to ensure stability.

1. Find your muse.

Inspiration is everywhere—and once you start beading, you'll probably find it all around you. Melanie is inspired by other people's work all the time, whether it's the combination of materials or a new way of working with leather or an amazingly creative clasp.

What did Harry Winston loan out to the nominees on Oscar night? What's the trend in accessories in fashion magazines? Rip out pictures of necklaces you love, especially fabulous, simple, single-strand creations that might inspire your own. Get a copy of *Bead & Button* magazine for a comprehensive road map to the world you are entering. Check out Melanie's Picks, page 157, for books, catalogs, and Web sites. Head to the museum and library for tips from ancient cultures and trendsetters. Bring a sketchbook. ***Start an inspiration file or scrapbook.***

2. Buy your supplies.

Go to a bead shop or to the beading aisle of a craft supply store. Tell a clerk that you're a beginner, and ask them to help you find the things you'll need to get started with a simply strung necklace.

Beads

Let yourself get mesmerized and tantalized by the sizes, shapes, and colors. The options are truly infinite: a monochrome string, patterns involving several kinds of beads, a single accent bead in the center of a strand. For this exercise, you'll need three kinds of beads. End to end, these beads should span approximately 16 inches for a short necklace.

Shop for:

Primary beads. These will make up the bulk of your necklace, so buy a tube or strand full of something you like. (Since we're adding other beads to your necklace, you'll have some of these basic beads left over for another project or matching earrings!)

Accent beads. These beads will accent the primary beads at intervals, so buy eight to twelve of these beads. Choose beads slightly larger than the others and of a complementary color and shape.

Centerpiece bead. Finally, select a lovely, large bead to provide a focal point in the center of your strand.

Thread

After you've selected your beads, ask the clerk for help choosing thread. You should consider:

Hole size. Be sure to pick a thread that is thin enough to pass through the smallest bead hole you are stringing, and match the color to the beads (or use a shade lighter).

Strength. Silk thread is ideal for delicate beads such as pearls, nylon threads are a bit sturdier, and "tiger tail" steel thread is best for heavy beads.

Length. Some silk and nylon thread comes in lengths of a couple yards wrapped neatly around a card and pre-attached to a thin, flexible needle especially for beading. You will probably need just sixteen to eighteen inches for a short necklace, more for a longer one, less for a choker. But just to be sure your necklace fits you just so, you may want to measure a necklace that is exactly the right length for you.

Color. Think about whether you want the thread to be hidden or show. "Sometimes you may want to let the thread show, because colorful thread can be a pretty accent," says Melanie. If you want your thread to show, you could go with a matching color or one that provides a colorful contrast with your beads.

Tools

For this exercise, you'll need:

- Glue (or clear nail polish), to reinforce knots.
- Round nose and chain-nose pliers.
- Two bead tips.
- Enough spacers to go in between your beads, if you want to string them side-by-side.
- Big-eye needles for the thread (if you can't find thread with a flexible needle attached).
- A clasp.

Build your tool kit.

3. Organize your beadwork.

Creating and maintaining an organized beadbox is hardly essential to making your necklace, but it's one of the real pleasures of the craft, and

EASY AS 1, 2, 3

Melanie's tips for a simple, chic necklace

"A nice necklace doesn't have to be hard to make," says Melanie. Here are her instructions for a charming, rustic necklace:

1. Thread larger-sized beads onto soft-flex ("tiger tail") beading wire. "Beading wire is good for holding chunky or heavy beads, where you don't want the thread to be visible," says Melanie. Leave about two inches of beading wire on either end.
2. On either end, thread a crimping bead, which are small, soft-metal tubes. Push the crimping beads up to hold your beads in place, so that they are touching but not squeezed against one another.
3. Loop your beading wire through your clasp, then pull it back through the crimping bead. Now squeeze the crimping bead shut with crimping pliers to close the wire loop that holds the clasp. Ta-da!

STRINGING SUPPLIES

Know the beading class lingo

Bead tips and caps. Top off the end of a bead and hide the hole and final knot.

Beeswax. Gives thread extra body and makes beading easier.

Clasps. For securing the ends of necklaces and bracelets (lobster, spring, barrel).

Cones. At the ends of multi-strand necklaces, these hide the ends and knots.

Crimp beads. Small metal sleeves that hold beads in place once pinched.

Glue. For securing knots. Many beaders swear that clear nail polish works just as well.

Needles. Beading, big-eye, twisted-wire, and "sharps."

Pliers. To work with metal findings, making loops, and gripping wire. ("Findings" are the metal pieces used in jewelry making, like clasps and fasteners.) Needlenose, round nose, flat head, etc.

Separators. Disks or other shapes used to separate individual beads and add accents.

Thread. Waxed nylon, silk, tigertail, leather, elastic, hemp, etc.

Wire. Used to wrap, twist, and attach beads. Copper, sterling silver, gold-filled. "Memory" wire springs back into its coiled shape after being strung with beads. (Good for bracelets!)

the hallmark of any serious beader. There are divided boxes especially designed for bead supplies, or you can find similar boxes at a hardware store. Makeup, sewing, and fishing tackle boxes all work well, and you can improvise with household items like cupcake tins or egg cartons.

Pick a storage spot safe from curious kids and frisky cats and where you're not apt to knock the box over and spill beads and clasps everywhere. Beaders working on several projects at once often separate projects into their own boxes or Ziploc plastic bags (which are also perfect for grabbing on your way out the door!). ***Set up your bead box.***

MELANIE'S EXPERT TIPS

GETTING STRUNG ALONG

Once you get going with beading, you'll crave ever more unique and distinctive beads—and you won't always find them at bead stores. Here's where beaders in the know go to source spectacular finds:

- Your own jewelry box. Dismantle and restring one or more neglected strands from your jewelry box, plus that broken costume jewelry you saved from your Grandma's.
- Explore thrift stores, antique shops, and garage sales.
- The hardware store and your junk drawer. Make a statement about the utility of adornments with nuts, screws, or washers.
- Your sewing kit. Find sequins and buttons you can string.
- Check eBay and run a Google search for your bead of choice—look up "antique jade beads" or "African trade beads," and you may find an online treasure trove.

4. Learn the basics.

As with so many handcrafts, learning one-on-one and hands-on is ideal. Ask a friend who beads to show you the basics, which include stringing, knotting, and finishing. Ask her over so you can work side by side and pepper her with questions as you go.

Most bead shops also offer affordable classes. You'll meet other enthusiasts and get to know people at the shop, who can often be lifesavers when you have questions. Your parks and recreation department or community college may also offer a class. If you want to zoom ahead on your own, check out online resources or directions in books and magazines. ***Take a Saturday afternoon beginner's class with a friend.***

5. Make your necklace.

Get out your beads and other supplies, get comfortable, and find some good light to work in. Thread your needle and create a sturdy knot. String through a bead tip (it looks like a tiny basket with a hooked handle) from the inside to the outside. Now lay out your beads in the order you'll string them in. (There are trays designed for this, or you can fold a piece of cardboard into a makeshift one.) If your basic bead is small, you probably don't need to count them. Just lay them out, putting in your accent and center beads until the pattern is even and pleasing.

Start stringing, paying attention to how the beads lay side by side. If you find that your accent beads don't look right next to one another, you may need spacers—tiny disk-shaped fillers that separate beads slightly.

When done stringing your beads, string through a bead tip from the outside to the inside, cut off your needle, and tighten the beads on the strand, making sure there are no gaps but leaving enough slack so that they drape nicely. Knot the end of your thread. Glue or apply clear nail polish to both of your knots, and when the glue is dry, trim the thread. Press the halves of the bead tip together with chain-nose pliers, enclosing the knot. Use round-nose pliers to roll the bead tip hook tightly around the loop of your clasp. Voilà!

Before you close your bead tip, triple check that you like everything about your strand. Once you close off, the only way out is to cut and start again. (Not the end of the world, but avoidable if you are careful.) Melanie says she often redoes pieces two or three times for one reason or another, so don't worry if you find yourself needing to do the same. It's not a race to the finish—and in beading, as with so many things, the process can be even more fun than the completion. ***Make and remake your necklace until you love it. Wear it!***

CONGRATULATIONS!

You've got a new necklace and the know-how to bead on. You did it!

I DID IT!

Name: ____________________

Date: ____________________

I DID IT!

"A friend and I were shopping and saw some earrings that we thought were way too expensive. We figured we could make them and took a class. A few years later, I wanted to get my fake pearls re-strung. The shop was going to charge me fifty dollars—so again, I took a class (on pearl knotting) and did it myself. I love making things I've seen in a magazine or catalog, and now that I sell my stuff, I get a huge kick out of selling at craft fairs and having former customers seek out my table and my things."
—Mollie

52 PICK-UP

"I can't resist buying beads, so I usually have lots around. I keep them organized and sorted in those nifty compartmentalized boxes. Dropping the box and re-sorting its contents is not fun!"
—Mollie

ADVANCED TECHNIQUES

What you have to look forward to

Floating or "illusion" strands. Using knots or crimps around beads, and then leaving lengths of empty space on the thread.

Multiple strands. Some bead tips can accommodate more than one strand or you may need more than one.

Pearl knotting. Separates the beads and adds strength to the strand.

Stitching. Using a variety of stitches on your cord to achieve macramé-like effects.

Wire wrapping. For a more finished, polished look.

BEYOND THE BADGE

If you love it as much as you thought you would, dream on . . .

- **Branch out into clothing, accessories, and home decor.** Beads can be applied to just about anything. Think 1920s flapper dresses, 1950s sweaters, jeans, evening purses, gloves, or belts. Around the house, you can frame a beaded work of art, stitch the little suckers onto pillows, or even create beaded floral arrangements. (You can also explore other aspects of jewelry making by taking a class in soldering, casting, hammering, or molding.)
- **Make an art of it.** If you really want to branch out, and really love beads, they can become museum-worthy art. Liza Lou is an artist who has won a MacArthur "genius grant" for her installation works that merge fine art with age-old beadcraft. She spent five years creating her first major work, *Kitchen,* which is a three-dimensional, life-size, 168-square-foot replica of a typical American kitchen of the 1950s. Everything, including a cherry pie, dust balls under the fridge, and the kitchen sink are there—and they're all covered in brightly colored bugle beads! Her subsequent *Back Yard* features 250,000 blades of beaded grass. And you think your latest project is intricate!
- **Sell it.** Melanie sells her creations several times a year at shows held in various people's homes. (The hostess gets a nice piece of jewelry for her trouble!) Friends tell friends and these kinds of get-togethers can really take off, especially around holidays like Christmas and Mother's Day. You'll experience the joys of repeat customers, and may get commissions to create particular pieces out of beads your customer chooses or in a certain color or style. Mollie and her beading buddy, Jill, sell their work this way, as well as at fundraising craft fairs at their children's schools, in their offices, and at dinner parties. After all, you can't keep everything you make—though you might want to photograph pieces you sell to remind yourself of a winning technique or composition when it's gone. Shoot your creations digitally from the start so you can create a catalog of your work on your Web site and send pictures of samples to customers via e-mail.

WORK RETAIL

Marketing tips for ambitious beaders

- You can bring samples of your work into retail establishments in your neighborhood, especially the shops you frequent yourself.
- You may be able to set up a booth at a local craft fair for a nominal fee. Find out all the costs beforehand—some craft fairs have a jury process that charges a fee to review your work, or require you to pay a separate booth fee.
- If you don't have the inclination to sell your wares, ask a friend with sales experience or an outgoing personality to accompany you or be your "rep." Or you can seek out a professional sales representative who has his or her own regular clients. Ask the buyers at shops which representatives they work with and contact them.
- If you're a techie or know one, you can also sell your work online at your own Web site. The photos of your work will speak for themselves, but you'll have to find creative ways to direct people to that site.
- Carry business cards or brochures to hand out when someone asks you where you bought those great earrings, and advertise in local papers.

MELANIE'S PICKS

BOOKS

Collectible Beads: A Universal Aesthetic by Robert K. Liu
Instant savvy for the serious bead collector.

The History of Beads from 30,000 B.C. to the Present by Lois Sherr Dubin
Lovely coffee-table book tracing the history and importance of beads around the world.

Instant Gratification: Jewelry by Annie Guthrie
Simple, elegant jewelry projects with helpful illustrations.

MAGAZINES

Bead & Button
www.beadandbutton.com
The beading bible and a reliable source of direction on just about everything relating to the little suckers—suppliers, books, patterns, etc. Also hosts the largest bead show in North America annually.

Beadwork
www.interweave.com/bead
Helpful how-to tips on stringing, sewing, and sourcing beads along with fetching photos.

Step by Step Beads
www.stepbystepbeads.com
Features fifteen to twenty new projects in each quarterly issue, plus techniques and tips for anyone with beading on the brain. Also sponsors annual BeadFest.

ORGANIZATIONS

Bead Expo
www.beadexpo.com
This nonprofit hosts a twice-yearly beaders' extravaganza: workshops, lectures, historical research, and an international bead bazaar.

The Bead Museum
www.thebeadmuseum.com
The Bead Museum of Glendale, Arizona, offers information on beading traditions around the globe, from Bedouin dowry necklaces to Huichol masks.

WEB SITES

www.artgemsinc.com
Beads and findings from around the world.

www.beadshopfinder.com
Locate a bead store in your neighborhood.

www.beadwork.about.com
The lowdown on beading, from how-tos and artist profiles to research and design.

www.eebeads.com/Webzine
Webzine that offers free, detailed instructions for scads of fun bead projects.

www.gigagraphica.com/beadscape/beadscape.html
Beadscape is Mac-only software that helps you develop complex bead designs.

www.jewelrydesignermanager.com
Software to help beading professionals inventory their supplies and price their wares.

20

SEW FABULOUS

★ sewing ★

Success is following the pattern of life one enjoys most.

—Anonymous

So, what's your motivation?
Take a moment.
Dream a little, think big,
and then complete this sentence:
I see myself . . .

Imagine This . . . It's Saturday morning. You pull on the striped silk pants you whipped up Wednesday night, grab that great material you bought at a garage sale last weekend, and head to the fabric store. Your mission? A fun, easy pattern that will turn your fabric into a fabulous skirt. Mission accomplished, you return home, crank up a CD, and settle down to your scissors and seams. Afraid you'll hit a snag? That's what seam rippers are for! And even if you haven't threaded a needle since your tenth-grade home ec class, it's easier than you think to use a sewing machine, pick and follow a pattern, and stitch your way into something all new and all you. *You can do it!*

The Payoffs

- **Thrift.** It's much less expensive to indulge your passion for fashion if you do up your own versions of pricey boutique trends. Plus you can refurbish vintage or thrift store finds and save money by doing your own hemming, mending, and alterations.
- **Style.** Design your own unique clothes and personalize mass-produced, store-bought items.
- **Gifts.** Homemade gifts mean so much more because they come from your hands—and heart.
- **Decor.** Update your living space with decorative accents from charming place mats and pillows to eye-catching Roman shades and slipcovers.
- **Fine tailoring.** Once you know how to make it yourself, you'll never again be overcharged for a poorly constructed garment or pillow sham.

Meet Your Mentor
FRANCESCA STERLACCI

What She Does: Chairperson of and assistant professor in the Fashion Design Department at the Fashion Institute of Technology (FIT) in New York City, Francesca is also the author of *Leather Apparel Design* and ran her own successful freelance design business, Design Instinct, for ten years.

Why She Does It: "Back in the 1950s, in my Union City, New Jersey, hometown, my mother had a little cottage industry going. Material was delivered to her at home, and she'd cut out slip and panty patterns. I'd take the bits of material that fell to the floor and make Barbie doll clothes out of them. I made evening gowns out of these silky scraps and traded them to my friends for their store-bought Barbie outfits. My mother's sewing machine was strictly off-limits to me, but when I got a little older, I would sneak into the basement to use it—very slowly, so that she wouldn't hear its hum. I still smile when I think about designing my prom dress. This was the '60s, in a blue-collar Italian neighborhood. Most of the girls were wearing really ornate beaded things because, well, more was more! But I went in the opposite direction, designing and sewing a lacy peasant blouse and striped skirt—very hippie. A couple of girls came over to see it, said to hell with their beaded gowns, and asked me to sew dresses for them. It was exciting to go to the dance and see the other girls wearing 'my' dresses."

When you learn to sew, you'll find DOZENS of ways to use your skills and express yourself.

—Francesca Sterlacci

Word from the Wise: "When you love to sew, you'll find lots of opportunities to do it. When my son was born, he had tailor-made sheets, bumpers, and quilts. I also have a group of very crafty, creative friends. We have a lot of fun trying to outdo one another with our homemade Christmas gifts!"

BADGE STEPS

1. Sign up for Sewing 101.

Even if you already know the basics, you might want to sew up the gaps in your knowledge with a beginner's class. "A course commits you to learning your new skill," says Francesca. Once you have the basics under your belt, it's easier for your sewing friends or family to lend a hand, too.

Look for local high school continuing education or summer classes, or introductory courses at community centers or fabric stores. Many places that sell sewing machines also offer such classes. A beginner's course will generally run four to six weeks. Consider taking a daylong class if you're brushing up rather than starting from scratch.

A comprehensive introductory course should teach you:

- How to use a standard sewing machine (and its parts) efficiently
- How to use different needles to make basic hand and machine stitches
- Fabric fundamentals and considerations
- How to read, cut, and sew from a pattern

Find and take a beginning sewing class.

2. Shop!

To practice (and show off!) your brand-new skills, you're going to make a very simple skirt. Shopping for materials is one of the best things about sewing. Getting your hands on all those luscious fabrics, buttons, and trims, perusing patterns, and pulling together the essentials for the fabulous new thing you're about to make is half the fun!

There are lots of big fabric store chains, which are generally just fine. But you might also check around to see if there is an especially great store with very knowledgeable staff within reasonable driving distance. It's worth going the extra mile to find a better selection of fabric and patient advice from talented, creative people.

You don't buy patterns in the size you take in ready-to-wear garments; your pattern size is based on your measurements. You'll need waist, hip, and waist-to-hem measurements for your skirt. Take these while wearing underwear and shoes, holding the measuring tape snugly but not tightly. Your waist is the thinnest part of your middle. Your hips are measured at their fullest part (no cheating, or your skirt won't fit!). To

SEWING STAPLES

To keep you in stitches

Basket. To hold all your supplies, a specially made sewing basket is ideal. (It will have just the right compartments and holders.) But if you want something funkier or more personal, try out other toolboxes and storage containers.

Hem gauge. To measure while pressing a hem in place.

Marking pen, pencil, or tailor's chalk. These make temporary marks on your fabric.

Measuring tape. Get a good fabric one and replace it when it shows wear; it can become inaccurate with heavy use.

Pincushions. A classic (and cute!) tomato pincushion has a strawberry emery to sharpen and clean hand-sewing needles. A magnetic pin holder is perfect for straight pins.

Scissors. Invest in a quality pair, use them only for sewing, and they'll last forever. Buy a knife-edged bent scissor and a small sewing scissor.

Seam ripper. Comes in handy when you need to start over.

Sewing gauge. For measuring and marking everything from pleats to buttonholes.

Sharp needles. Basic hand-sewing needles with sharp points. Buy one packet with a variety of sizes.

get a waist-to-hem skirt length, measure from the middle of the back of your waist (you may need to ask a friend to help with this) to the desired point on your leg. Jot these down and take them with you to the fabric store.

At the shop, spend some time looking through pattern catalog books. In addition to getting fashion ideas, you'll learn construction details and get a pattern number or two. At some stores, you can just give that number to a clerk who will fetch the pattern; other stores are self-help. For this badge, look for patterns that are identified as "easy" or "for beginners." Most of the major pattern companies offer these "learn to sew" options. These patterns will have the fewest number of seams possible and call for simple finishing techniques. If you find something else you absolutely must have, be sure it has a simple zipper up the back, or a drawstring or elastic waistband—for now, you'll want to avoid pleats or other complicated details, though pockets are fine. The most basic designs can always be accented with decorative details like buttons and trims. Look for a style that you already know is flattering to your body type. When you have your pattern in hand, turn it over to find:

- A chart for your measurements—check that you've got the right size for you.
- A chart with the amount of fabric needed for your size. Double-check the fabric width when you find a fabric you like, since you'll need more yardage for fabrics that are less wide.
- Recommendations for the kind of fabric most suitable for the design. Don't deviate from this—you'll have plenty to choose from! So before you get carried away with taffeta or find yourself overly attached to some gorgeous knit, ask for help. Show your pattern to a friendly clerk, tell her you're a beginner, and ask her to direct you to the kinds of fabric recommended on the pattern. Francesca advises that you stick to woven cotton, lightweight denim, or chambray materials—anything that doesn't ravel and isn't too soft. Stay away from knits (which can be hard for a beginner to sew on), plaids and stripes that will require matching, and really big prints. (Small, all-over prints are okay.)
- The notions you'll need. Have your new clerk buddy help you select your thread, zipper, and any other notions you need and/or want as decorative elements. And while you're at it, stock up on the other items you'll need to fill an all-purpose home sewing basket.

SEWING STAPLES
continued

Straight pins. These come in different lengths. Those with glass or plastic ball heads are easy on the fingers, superfine flat heads are good for delicate materials, and nickel-plated steel pins are rust resistant and will stick to magnets. Ask a clerk to help you buy a good variety starter kit.

Thimble. Thimbles are optional and take a bit of getting used to. To see if you are a Thimble-ina, give one a try—it should fit snugly on your middle finger.

Thread. The basic and most versatile are cotton-wrapped polyester and 100 percent polyester. Buy four spools: black, white, khaki, and clear.

LEARNER'S LEXICON

:: Basic hand stitches:

Catch. For holding two layers of fabric together.

Hemming. Often used with seam binding; done on a diagonal.

Running. The most basic, used for basting, mending, gathering, etc.

Slip. Used for hemming, pockets and trims, and attaching linings, it has an almost invisible finish.

:: Some machine stitches:

Backstitch. When beginning and ending a seam, you want to secure it by moving forward and then backward for a quarter inch or so.

Straight. A simple, moving forward stitch.

Zigzag. Prevents unraveling and can be decorative.

:: Key sewing machine parts:

Bobbins. Either metal or plastic reels that hold thread. Keep several wound with the colors you use most frequently.

Feet. Straight-stitch and general-purpose feet allow you to do the basics. Zipper, hemming, gathering, and other specialized feet allow you to branch out.

Needles. Sizes and points (sharp, ball, rounded, wedge-shaped) will be specified in your sewing machine manual and are determined by the type of fabric you use. They should be changed frequently, as they can become blunt or damaged.

Spend a couple of hours at the fabric store, going through pattern books, selecting a pattern, and buying fabric and notions. ***Stock your sewing basket.***

FRANCESCA'S EXPERT TIPS

BUYING YOUR DREAM MACHINE

Unless you're determined to go the couture route and sew everything by hand or have a friend who is willing to share a machine indefinitely, sooner or later you will want to buy your own machine. When you do, keep these things in mind:

Know what you need. A very basic, inexpensive machine may be adequate.

Take your own thread and fabric to the store. Try out the features you want to use, rather than using the demonstration materials provided. Test drive several machines.

Try trade-in machines. People who sew often trade in good, basic machines when they upgrade to the latest models. Good shops will ensure that these trade-ins are in tip-top shape, so you can score bargain buys.

Don't be afraid of plastic parts. Metal parts require regular lubrication.

Know the latest features. If you know you want to branch out in your sewing, do some research on all the features that are out there (many!), then talk to retailers and try out the various features yourself.

State your price range. Look for a clerk who can find options within your price range and who gives you plenty of time to make your decision.

Find out what comes with your machine. Lessons? A good tool kit? A nice service package? This could make a slightly higher price tag worth your while.

Shop around online. Compare prices and features at manufacturer Web sites listed in Francesca's Picks, page 167.

3. Test drive your machine.

If you don't have Grandma's old Singer in the attic, you'll need to borrow a friend's machine or rent one from a sewing machine retailer to make your skirt. (To do the latter, you'll probably have to plunk down a refundable deposit and then pay a weekly fee.)

Review the terms in the Learner's Lexicon, review what you know about machines from your sewing class experience, and talk to your friend or retailer about the machine you'll use. Bring the machine's manual home with you if you can and make sure you know:

- What kind of needles the machine takes.
- How to thread the bobbin and needle.
- How to change the machine's feet. Are they for straight stitch only? A basic presser foot will work for straight and zigzag stitching, but you may need additional feet for zippers or buttonholes.

Play around with scrap material, trying out all the fun things you've learned in class and making sure you're comfortable with your machine before you start your skirt. At the very least, practice controlling the fabric as it is fed through the machine, sewing a straight seam, and sewing two pieces of fabric together. ***Rev up your machine.***

4. Sew it up.

Now a great new skirt is just four moves away!

1. Prepare your fabric. If the fabric you select is not preshrunk, you should wash, dry, and press it before cutting your pattern. Pressing before cutting is a good idea for all fabrics because it removes the wrinkles and crease lines that can affect accuracy.
2. Read your pattern. Before you do a darn thing, read through the entire pattern guide and make sure you understand each step. If you have concerns or get stumped, call a sewing friend or visit your new friend, the fabric store clerk.
3. Place and cut your fabric. Cut out your pattern pieces and arrange them on your fabric as directed in the pattern instructions. Pin the pattern pieces to the fabric along the inside perimeter of the pattern pieces, placing pins approximately three inches apart and pinning through all required thicknesses of the fabric. Cut along pattern lines, steadying the fabric with your free hand but trying not to stretch or lift the fabric from your cutting surface as you go. Follow the pattern instructions about transferring construction marks to your fabric with your pen, pencil, or chalk, then unpin your pattern pieces from the fabric, but don't crumple them up and toss them out. If you love your skirt, you'll want to reuse the pattern!
4. Start your engines and sew! The sewing guide in your pattern directs you every step of the way and often includes helpful hints. Consult the construction sketches that accompany written instructions. Take your time. Before finalizing the hem of your skirt, iron your skirt and try it on with the shoes you plan to wear with it.

Sew your skirt.

TAILORING TERMINOLOGY

Sew smart!

Baste. Preliminary stitching, either by hand or machine, to secure a construction piece before stitching a final seam.

Breaking the stitch. Stopping the stitching in a seam line by backstitching at the end and at a new beginning.

Clip seam. Cutting into the seam allowance to aid in construction (often used on curves or corners).

Grain. Refers to the crosswise or lengthwise threads in a woven fabric. A double-headed arrow on a pattern piece is called a "grain line," and should be placed on a lengthwise thread since these threads are sturdier. "On grain" fabric alignment—when crosswise and lengthwise threads are at perfect right angles—is important to the final appearance of a garment.

Press seam open. Using an iron to flatten seams and seam allowances.

Right sides together. Placing fabrics so that the finished, outside sides are facing each other. ("Wrong sides together" is—you guessed it—the opposite.)

Seam allowance. An excess amount of fabric beyond the seam line.

Selvage. The lengthwise finished edges on all woven fabrics.

5. Work that skirt!

Try on your skirt for size. What do you think?! Do you love it so much you'll wear it every day for a week? If your skirt doesn't fit your form exactly as you'd like, chat with a fellow sewer or fabric store friend about quick fixes. Maybe you can correct a minor problem by letting out or taking in a seam. Perhaps you'll need to double-check your measurements next time, or make minor adjustments to the pattern (see Beyond the Badge).

But for now, take a moment to admire your own handiwork. Remember that many an accomplished seamstress likens her first garment to that first Sunday morning waffle—fine, but slightly irregular. If that's the case, you've still learned a great deal—and as a result, your next one will be that much better! So sashay down the runway—whether that's your hallway or the sidewalk—in your new skirt. ***Strut your stuff!***

CONGRATULATIONS!

Are you wearing your work? Learn to take a compliment. You did it!

I DID IT!

Name: ______________________________

Date: ______________________________

I DID IT!

"I was at a flea market and bought a scrap of red Chinese silk that I thought I'd make into a pillow. But I wound up buying some cheap cotton lining and making a shoulder bag with it instead. I used it every day for years, even carrying it on a two-week tour of India because it was roomy enough to carry my guidebook, camera, and sunscreen. The whole thing cost me about five dollars, and I got more compliments on that bag than anything else I've ever made—or bought!"

—Denise

PASS THE SEAM RIPPER!

"I wanted the black pencil skirt I was making to be skintight and sexy, so I overlooked the concept of ease—the inches beyond your body's measurements that are added to a pattern that let you do things like walk and sit down! My skirt gave new meaning to the term 'fits like a glove'—until I ripped a seam and let it out."

—Sandra

BEYOND THE BADGE

If you love it as much as you thought you would, dream on . . .

- **Get the perfect fit.** As you learn to sew, you'll quickly find yourself altering—rather than tossing out—clothes that no longer fit properly or have gone slightly out of style. Depending on your level of expertise and attention span, you can do everything from changing a hem or sleeve length to moving buttons and adding darts. You can also learn to fit patterns more precisely. See Francesca's Picks (especially *Vogue Sewing*), page 167, for instruction.
- **Redecorate.** "I don't sew all my own clothes, but I do a ton of sewing for my home—all my own curtains and pillows, for instance," says Francesca. You can turn to books, magazines, classes, or the Internet for instruction, or just start experimenting.
- **Become a fashion designer.** One way to begin designing is to doctor up existing patterns. If you want to go further into design, Francesca advises studying pattern making in a class. "Drafting a pattern from your measurements is more difficult than you might think." She also advises her FIT students with entrepreneurial aims to spend some time working for another manufacturer. "Learn the ropes on someone else's dime! Plenty of people have had success by having a great idea, whipping up ten of them, and taking them to stores. But you have to be cautious. Your design can be stolen or you may never get paid for your pieces, since as a lone designer you are low on the totem pole of a retailer's accounts."
- **Sew for good.** You can put even rudimentary sewing skills to work for the common good in your community—create baby quilts for women's shelters, stylish caps for chemotherapy patients, or blankets for homeless centers.
- **Make a quilt.** See the following page for more details.

CREDIT FOR CREATIVITY

Get credit in design school

FIT is the largest fashion school in the world, with an illustrious list of alumni (including Norma Kamali and Calvin Klein). Francesca's design department serves almost 2,000 students in day and evening programs. Roughly 2,000 students apply each year for 200 entrance spots. One of the state universities of New York (SUNY), FIT requires a combination of a good GPA and creative spark. Applicants send in their portfolios and complete a mail-in home test that asks them to write an essay about their design goals and to design three garments for a career woman, a first lady, or a rock star. "I saw a student the other day who had taken a bunch of her grandfather's ties and sewed them together into the cutest halter top," said Francesca. "That kind of creativity is more important to us than sewing skills."

extra credit

QUILTING

There are as many reasons to quilt as there are quilting styles:

It feels good. Old time "quilting bees" were community affairs that strengthened the social fabric. Quilting en masse still brings people together, facilitating chit chat and forging connections. And as with other forms of sewing and handcrafts, quilting can be soothing and meditative. You take pleasure in your work as it progresses and pride in your finished product.

It commemorates something. A birth, a wedding, a life well lived—quilts can celebrate, honor, and memorialize. (The AIDS Memorial Quilt is one well-known example.)

It's art. Tell a tale or just plain express yourself through graphic design, your feel for fabric, and your eye for color.

How to get started:

Quilts are created by stitching through several layers of fabric in a decorative design or pattern. There are many different techniques, but the basic quilt sandwich includes a top (perhaps patchwork piecing or blocks), a middle layer of light padding or "batting" for warmth and body, and a backing.

- While you don't need to be a super-skilled seamstress—or own a fancy sewing machine—to quilt, you should be comfortable hand or machine stitching a nice straight seam.
- Take a class. Many towns, large and small, have quilting shops that offer classes. You can sometimes also take a class through chain stores like Jo-Ann fabrics or Michaels crafts stores.
- Look for quilting comrades. Folks you meet in a class or shop can become your quilting bee or "stitch-n-bitch" buddies. (Ask experienced quilters to put you in touch with your local quilt guild.) If you go online and search out quilting Web sites, look for message boards where you can post a "Hi, I just got started" message and get instant answers and support.
- Pick first projects that won't overwhelm you—a hot pad, sachet, pillow, or baby blanket.
- Check out local museums and craft fairs for the inspirational work of other quilters.

MEET YOUR QUILTING MENTOR

Denyse Schmidt founded Denyse Schmidt Quilts (www.dsquilts.com) in 1996. Denyse brings her background as a professional seamstress and graphic designer (she graduated from the Rhode Island School of Design) to her hip, hand-stitched quilts (with fun and funky names like "What a Bunch of Squares," "Lah Dee Dah," and "There Goes the Neighborhood"). Her quilts are made to order, hand-quilted by Amish women (after being pieced together by Schmidt and her studio assistants), and are signed and dated by Denyse like the works of art they are.

DENYSE'S PICKS

Abstract Design in American Quilts: A Biography of an Exhibition by Jonathan Holstein

Black Threads: An African American Quilting Sourcebook by Kyra E. Hicks

Denyse Schmidt's Quilt and Patchwork Projects by Denyse Schmidt

The American Quilter's Society
www.aqsquilt.com

C&T Publishing's jam-packed site
www.ctpub.com

FRANCESCA'S PICKS

BOOKS

The Complete Book of Sewing: A Practical Step-by-Step Guide to Sewing Techniques by Dorling Kindersley Publishing
Handy reference with step-by-step instructions for basic techniques through custom tailoring and couture finishes.

Easy Guide to Sewing Pants by Lynn MacIntyre
Get the perfect, flattering fit with guidelines from initial measurements to final pressing.

Easy Guide to Sewing Skirts by Marcy Tilton
Feeling bold after your first skirt? Follow this guide and try other skirt patterns.

Guide to Fashion Sewing by Connie Amaden-Crawford
An eighteen-step approach to sewing any garment, plus hints and detailed illustrations.

Reader's Digest Complete Guide to Sewing by The Reader's Digest Association, Inc.
Excellent reference guide, with clear instructions and helpful diagrams galore.

Sewing for Fashion Design by Nurie Relis and Gail Strauss
Introduces budding designers to the techniques and equipment used professionally.

Vogue Sewing
Instructions and advice on pattern adjustments and garment style, color, and construction.

DESIGNERS

For inspiration, Francesca recommends checking out these major labels run by women:

Laura Biagiotti. Luxurious, flowing, deconstructed.

Veronique Branquinho. Avant-garde austerity with luxe flair.

Coco Chanel. Those classic suits!

Ann Demeulemeester. Slick and sensual for the romantic.

Donna Karan. Confident, sophisticated, streamlined designs.

Stella McCartney. Dreamy yet tailored.

Jil Sander. Minimalism in elegantly draped fabrics.

Anna Sui. Fabulous with a fun, flirty edge.

Donatella Versace. Vavoom dresses and subversive chic.

Yeohlee. Strong, concise geometric designs.

SEWING MACHINES

Francesca recommends home sewing machines from these retailers:

www.brother.com

www.bernina.com

www.pfaff.com

www.singerco.com

MOVIES

For further inspiration, check out:

The Adventures of Priscilla Queen of the Desert
Arguably the most over-the-top fashion to ever grace the screen—the CD dress alone merited the Oscar for costume design.

Beat Street
A landmark in hip-hop style.

Blow-up
Antonioni's 1966 thriller set in the mod London fashion scene.

Breakfast at Tiffany's
Witness the Givenchy couture that made Audrey Hepburn a fashion icon.

Ciao! Manhattan
Psychedelic film featuring Warhol superstar Edie Sedgwick in outrageous '60s fashions by Betsey Johnson—check out the DVD for fashion commentary.

La Dolce Vita
Sunglasses and stunning shifts play key supporting roles in this Fellini classic.

The Great Rock 'n' Roll Swindle
Vivienne Westwood's designs defined the Sex Pistols' punk rock image and redefined fashion.

Grey Gardens
Check out the DVD special features, including Todd Oldham explaining how this strange 1970s documentary about eccentric Kennedy grand dames inspired his designs.

Pretty in Pink
If Molly Ringwald could sew her own funky prom dress, you can sew a skirt!

Unzipped
Documentary that captures Isaac Mizrahi in action, launching his 1994 collection.

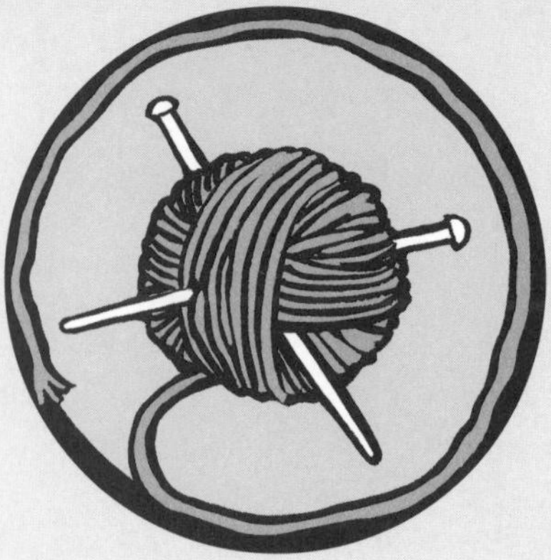

21

GET DOWN TO THE KNITTY-GRITTY

★ knitting ★

The only limits are,
as always, those of VISION.

—James Broughton

Imagine This . . . Curled up on the couch with a cup of tea and a soft, colorful ball of yarn, you couldn't be cozier. At your best friend's baby shower, your handmade booties elicit oohs and ahs. You notice trendy knit shoulder bags in catalogs and can't wait to create your own for half the price. Whether you're a trendsetter hankering for a hand-knit PDA cover or a traditionalist after a tea cozy just like Grandma's, this badge will have you in stitches—and a new scarf—in no time. As your fingers fly, you'll soothe your soul, relax your mind, and satisfy your creative urges. Get ready to get hooked. *You can do it!*

So, what's your motivation?
Take a moment.
Dream a little, think big,
and then complete this sentence:
I see myself . . .

The Payoffs

- **Stress relief.** Winding a new ball of yarn unwinds your mind. Casting and counting, needles clacking away, your mind and body are peacefully preoccupied with the project in hand. And there's no shame in watching trashy television when you're exhibiting such industriousness.
- **Higher ground.** If idle hands are the devil's playthings, a knitter has nothing to worry about. We're not making any promises, but actress Mary Louise Parker claims that knitting has taken the place of smoking in her life. As she says, "You can't do both at once!"
- **Creativity.** When you pick a color, select a yarn, and mull over designs, you're an artist. Could Picasso purl?
- **Bragging rights.** Whether you give it away or wear it with pride, you've got something to show (off!) for your efforts.

Meet Your Mentor
KRIS PERCIVAL

What She Does: Knits, teaches elementary school, and lives in Brooklyn, New York. Kris is the author of *Knitting Pretty: Simple Instructions for 30 Fabulous Projects.* She knits for family (including baby Simon), friends, and fine retail establishments like Barneys and the boutique Butter. She also teaches knitting to kids in an after-school program that uses needles and yarn to increase dexterity, develop math skills, and boost self-esteem.

© Doron Gura

Why She Does It: "My great-aunt Babe knit for the whole family, and she taught my sister and I how to knit as kids. A few years ago, I was sick in bed for days with a horrible flu. A friend of the family spent a lot of time with me, sitting by my bed, chatting and knitting. It looked so relaxing that I asked her to refresh my memory. I found it so soothing and meditative that I kept doing it after I got better. I give away most of what I knit. I always have several projects going—socks for my sister, sweaters for my little boy for next winter. I like everything about it: shopping for yarn, planning, and the actual knitting, which I do everywhere—on the subway, in meetings at work, when I visit with friends. I'm in a coed knitting group that meets once a month. Each gathering has a theme, like the Oscars or Mexican food. We have a great time and welcome people of every skill level, because we think it's important to help novices and share what we know."

You can walk into any clothing store and find beautiful knit scarves and sweaters. So why knit? The answer is simple: KNITTING IS FUN.

—Kris Percival

Word from the Wise: "People generally assume it's going to take a long time to learn, but it really doesn't. Then again, some people are way too ambitious at first and wind up discouraged. I've heard of people who have knit elaborate cable sweaters with a zip-up front as their first project, but I've never actually met one of them! Start with something simple."

BADGE STEPS

WHAT YOU NEED TO GET STARTED

The basics

:: Yarn galore:

Color. Most yarns are solid colors, but you can try variegated yarns and tweeds. If you're buying wool, get more than you think you'll need. Wool dye lots can vary, so you may have trouble matching your wool if you run out.

Fiber type. Kris recommends beginners practice on acrylic, which is inexpensive and won't fray as easily as wool.

Texture. Yarn without bumps, frizz, or elastic is best for just starting out—but you'll soon graduate to boucle, mohair, and chenille.

Weight. Ranging from heavy/thick to fine/light, yarn weights are: super bulky, bulky, worsted, sport, and fingering.

:: Know your needles:

Material. Kris suggests bamboo or wood for beginners, because they are less slippery.

Shape. Your pattern should specify single-point straight, double-pointed, or circular.

Size. Yarn packages and patterns often specify what size will work best with the yarn or specific pattern.

1. Fill your knitting bag.

You don't have to know how to knit to buy supplies! Check out yarn stores in your area and find one you like with salespeople you can talk to—they could be your new best friends. At least make sure to find a place you feel comfortable and welcome, a "there's no such thing as a stupid question" kind of place. Tell the salesperson you're a beginning knitter looking for the yarn and needles to make a scarf. Kris recommends:

- 4 balls (50 grams each) of worsted weight yarn in one color, or two if you're feeling adventurous.
- 1 pair of size 8 needles.
- 1 pair scissors, pointy and sharp.
- 1 yarn needle.
- 1 row counter (optional).

Yarn comes in balls and skeins, and you'll want to keep in mind that most yarn in skeins must be wound into a loose ball for knitting. Some yarn comes in pull skeins, so you can begin knitting immediately. Have fun picking your yarn colors, ask the salesperson when in doubt, and walk away from the store having purchased enough yarn and the appropriate needles for the job. ***Buy your materials.***

2. Learn how to use what's in your knitting bag.

"The best way to learn is to have a friend or relative show you, one-to-one, side by side, hands-on," says Kris. "But I also know people who sat down with a book and taught themselves. It depends on the kind of person you are, so seek out what you need." If you don't have an Aunt Babe or a friend who knits, the salespeople from your yarn shop are a good resource. They may well hold classes at the shop or at least direct you to another class or a good knitting book. Ask around or look online for a knitting group like Kris's that welcomes beginners, or check the course listings in your community schools. ***Find a teacher or class.***

3. Start your first project—a scarf!

Kris recommends starting with a scarf. This scarf will call upon your new skills at casting on, garter stitch, joining, binding off, and weaving in loose ends, and when you're finished, you'll have your own handmade piece of wearable art.

Here is a simple pattern for creating a basic scarf using four balls (50 grams each) of worsted weight yarn and size 8 needles:

1. Cast on 22 stitches.
2. Knit 44 rows of garter stitch.
3. If using two colors (you daredevil, you), join yarn 2 to yarn 1, leaving about a 6-inch tail of each.
4. Knit 44 rows of garter stitch in your new color, or vary the width of the stripes. Just make certain to always switch yarns on the same side of the scarf.
5. Repeat steps 3 and 4 until you're satisfied with the length.
6. Bind off.
7. Using your yarn needle, weave all loose ends into the edges of the scarf and trim them.

Variation: Knit two different yarns at the same time, such as boucle and worsted, holding them as one strand.

Don't fret if your knitting is lumpy or uneven. You'll get the hang of it. And don't be afraid to pull out some rows. If you get stuck, start over or get help. Some yarn shops post "The Doctor Is In" hours, when you can come in and get a knitting boo-boo diagnosed. Practice makes perfect. ***Let the knitting begin.***

4. Be sociable.

Sure, you can curl up with your knitting in front of the television—but Kris advises beginners to get out and about. Knitting with friends means there will always be someone at hand who can answer your questions. Meet at a café or at someone's home, and you'll have someone to turn to for help, inspiration, and resource information. Knitting in public opens you up to meeting new kindred knitting spirits, and knitting on the go gives you plenty of opportunities to make a little progress. (It makes waiting rooms more interesting than ancient issues of *National Geographic* and mass transit commutes fly by.) ***Knit all around town.***

5. Finish your project.

You're at the end of your scarf, and it's time to bind off and weave in the loose ends with your yarn needle. Remember: If you get stuck, consult a book, a friend, or the salesperson at your yarn shop. Once that last loose end is tucked in, try it on and admire your handiwork. ***Put it on, wear it out, or wrap it up and give it away.***

THE BEGINNER'S LEXICON

Chicks with sticks talk like this

American. Knitting style in which you hold and move the yarn with your right hand.

Binding off. What you do when you want to take what you've knit off the needles without letting it unravel.

Continental. Knitting style in which you hold and move the yarn with your left hand.

Casting on. All knitting begins with a cast-on row.

Gauge. Refers to the number of stitches per inch and rows per inch.

Knit and purl. The two basic stitches that make up almost every other type of stitch in knitting.

TECHNICAL ASSISTANCE

For purling perfectionists (you know who you are)

Crochet hook. To repair the inevitable dropped stitch.

Gauge aid. To determine the number of stitches in a swatch or a needle size.

Point protectors. To cover the tips of needles, so your work won't fall off when you put it down.

Stitch holders. Like safety pins that hold stitches you set aside.

Stitch markers. X marks the spot when knitting in the round.

Tape measure. Handy for patterns that tell you to knit a number of inches rather than a number of rows.

Yarn weight conversion chart. Because manufacturers use different units of measurement for their products (some use ounces, others use grams).

KRIS'S EXPERT TIPS

SHOP SMART

Price compare. Some projects, like the pillow covers in Kris's book, look fancy but are made of inexpensive drugstore yarn. Why pay more? Of course, you can buy cashmere if you like—just know you have options.

Be thrifty. Try garage sales and thrift shops for patterns, books, extra yarn, needles, etc.

BE A CLASS ACT

Classes at yarn shops. These are a great way to learn and meet people but can be expensive because they often require you to buy all your materials there. Buyer beware.

Network. Check the Web (see Kris's Picks, page 174) for groups in your area or people looking to start groups. Many meet regularly for the companionship, camaraderie, and skill-sharing. This is a great way to learn.

Fun fact. Waldorf schools teach all children to knit to cultivate dexterity, as well as spatial and math skills.

6. Begin your next project.

Your next project doesn't have to be a sweater or a hat. Of course you can try something more complicated, but it's also perfectly fine to make another scarf! The variety in color and texture of yarns means that knitting a scarf will never be boring. ***Go back to the yarn shop and restock your knitting bag.***

CONGRATULATIONS!

You know what you're giving everyone for Christmas next year, don't you? You did it!

I DID IT!

Name: ____________________

Date: ____________________

I DID IT!

"Being able to give handmade gifts to friends gives me a huge sense of satisfaction. Creating something for someone you care about is really rewarding. I guess I've become my Aunt Babe!"

—Kris

STITCH-N-BITCH

"We have a lunchtime 'stitch-n-bitch' at work. We swap patterns, knitting tips, and of course the obligatory office gossip. It's a relaxing break from the daily grind, a nice way to get to know my colleagues better, and when I botch a sweater, a great place to find a little sympathy. Every office should have one!"

—Mikyla

BEYOND THE BADGE

If you love it as much as you thought you would, dream on . . .

- **Hawk your wares.** Kris's husband approached shops on Kris's behalf and Kris followed up, calling on her old public relations skills. Once she got an appointment with a buyer, her stuff almost sold itself.
- **Improvise.** Everyone who knits works with the same basic set of tools, so a lot of the fun is in personalizing your projects. To spark your imagination, you might check out Kaffe Fassett's mosaic-inspired knitting patterns (www.kaffefassett.com), consider a pilgrimage to the Textile Museum in Washington, D.C. (www.textilemuseum.org), or even embark on a knitting tour of Europe, from the legendary Missoni in Milan (www.missoni.it/eng/index.html) to Ireland's famed Aran Isles (www.irishcultureandcustoms.com/aemblem/sweaters.html).
- **Volunteer your talents.** Get that warm fuzzy feeling by donating your creations to a worthy cause. Warm Up America donates afghans to homeless shelters—for details, visit www.warmupamerica.com.
- **Go retro.** Ask relatives for old knitting books or patterns, seek out the same at garage sales and thrift stores, or scour old magazines like *McCall's Needlework* or *American Home*. Many vintage knitting patterns are also available online—try www.yesterknits.com.
- **Expand your repertoire.** Challenge yourself with an intricate pattern, or create your own pattern. Once you get started, there's no end to what you can knit—witness *Dogs in Knits: 17 Projects for Our Best Friends* by Judith Swartz.

KNIT WIT

"There is no time for cut-and-dried monotony. There is time for work. And time for love. That leaves no other time."
—Coco Chanel, knitwear innovator

"I enjoyed talking to her, but thought nothing of her writing. I considered her a 'beautiful little knitter.' "
—Dame Edith Sitwell on Virginia Woolf (meow!)

"The web of our life is of a mingled yarn, good and ill together."
—William Shakespeare, *All's Well That Ends Well*

KRIS'S PICKS

BOOKS

Big Book of Knitting by Katharina Buss
Clear instructions and illustrations for basic knitting projects from darning socks to embellishing sweaters.

The Joy of Knitting: Texture, Color, Design, and the Global Knitting Circle by Lisa R. Meyers
Captures the culture, lore, and simple satisfaction of the craft.

Kids Knitting: Projects for Kids of All Ages by Melanie Falick
Easy instructions and dynamic photos covering the basic stitches.

Knitting Pretty: Simple Instructions for 30 Fabulous Projects by Kris Percival
Friendly, straightforward instructions and patterns galore, from bookmarks to halter tops.

The Knitting Sutra: Craft as a Spiritual Practice by Susan Gordon Lydon
The subtitle says it all.

Knitting without Tears: Basic Techniques and Easy-to-Follow Directions for Garments to Fit All Sizes by Elizabeth Zimmermann
Simple patterns and troubleshooting tips.

Stitch 'N Bitch: The Knitter's Handbook by Debbie Stoller
The editor of *BUST* magazine gives instructions and cool patterns targeted at Gen X knitters.

Vogue Knitting: The Ultimate Knitting Book by Vogue Knitting magazine
A veritable encyclopedia of knitting, with more than fifty contributors and some 1,000 illustrations.

MAGAZINES

Rebecca
www.rebecca-online.com
Practical, fun German pattern magazine; English translations provided.

Rowan
www.rowanyarns.co.uk
Elegant, modern British pattern magazine.

PATTERN SOURCES

www.knitting.about.com
Free patterns, advice, and explanations of the mysterious abbreviations in some patterns.

www.woolworks.org/patterns.html
Nonprofit featuring donated and copyright-free patterns.

YARN

If you don't like the selection in your neighborhood, try:

Artfibers
www.artfibers.com

Halcyon Yarn
www.halcyonyarn.com

Handknitting.com
www.handknitting.com/naturally_nzl.htm

Peace Fleece
www.peacefleece.com

Pine Tree Yarns
www.pinetreeyarns.com

COMMUNITY

Church of Craft
www.churchofcraft.org
Their statement of purpose reads: "By promoting creativity, we offer access to a nondenominational spiritual practice that is self-determined and pro-active." Groups in Los Angeles, San Francisco, and New York hold monthly Craft-Ons.

Craft Yarn Council
www.craftyarncouncil.com/knitoutbrochure.html
Provides information on Knit-Outs, held around the U.S. in the fall.

Knitting Guild Association
www.tkga.com
Locate a chapter near you.

learn

What we have to learn to do,
we learn by *doing*.

—Aristotle

22

GET YOUR WAY

★ negotiating ★

> Let us never negotiate out of fear. But let us never fear to negotiate.
>
> —John F. Kennedy

So, what's your motivation?
Take a moment.
Dream a little, think big,
and then complete this sentence:
I see myself . . .

Imagine This . . . You know what you want—a raise at your next performance review, a family gathering without a family feud, your hairdresser (and gardener) to embrace your definition of "trim." More importantly, you know how to get it—without making yourself sick with worry, implementing Machiavellian schemes, or calling Tony Soprano. You used to think it was easier to go along and get along, but now you know that "No" is a complete sentence. In the next few pages, you'll pick an outcome you need another person's cooperation to achieve. You'll learn to define and refine your bottom line, anticipate and address resistance, and hear and be heard. Get ready to give your goals the green light they deserve. *You can do it!*

The Payoffs

- **Stress less.** When you understand why negotiating makes you nervous, practice doing it in productive ways, and reap rewards for your efforts, you'll approach it with less anxiety.
- **Enjoy more.** Putting off asking for what you want may sometimes prevent unpleasantness, but it more often postpones getting your needs met. If you stop procrastinating, you'll have more time to enjoy the fruits of your persuasive labors.
- **Feel free.** The notion that you just aren't good at getting what you need locks you into the status quo. Knowing you can effect change frees your thinking, gives you options, and unlocks your dreams.
- **Be yourself.** Conveying your interests and concerns clues your listener in to the real you. We're often afraid this kind of directness will damage a relationship; it actually strengthens it, because it makes genuine cooperation and understanding possible.

Meet Your Mentor

SHEILA HEEN

What She Does: A graduate of Harvard Law School, Sheila teaches negotiation there, writes the Life Coach column in *Real Simple* magazine, is a coauthor of *Difficult Conversations: How to Discuss What Matters Most,* and is a founding partner at Triad Consulting Group.

Why She Does It: "Harvard is the conflict resolution mecca. The Harvard Negotiation Project, which is part of the Law School's Program on Negotiation, pioneered the research, development, and dissemination of solid methods of dealing with conflict. I took the negotiation course my first year of law school—and after contracts and torts and tax, it was like a glass of water to a woman in a desert. I liked the rigors of legal reasoning, but I really loved applying those analytical skills to thinking about how people interact and react to each other, and the challenge of finding ways around the mistakes we make when trying to get what we want. Roger Fisher, the founder of the Negotiation Project, is such an inspiration. When he reads the *New York Times* each morning, he looks at conflicts around the world and thinks about ways to help. No situation is hopeless to him, because he can see through the surface messes to how people are miscommunicating and missing solutions. It wasn't easy to forgo the legal career path I was on for the less-established world of mediation and conflict resolution, but I have never regretted it for a single second."

Negotiation is not about them or you; IT'S ABOUT WE.

—Sheila Heen

Word from the Wise: "My husband also teaches negotiation. Some people think this means we never fight. Truth be told, our training just gives us more ammunition: 'Nice listening, Little Miss Difficult Conversations,' my husband will say. All kidding aside, it's great. We get to work and travel together and also live out what we're trying to teach."

BADGE STEPS

1. Pick a fight.

Just kidding! Though asking someone to give you something you want—especially when you suspect they don't want to give it to you—can feel like arranging a rumble, think of the situation as an opportunity to understand one another and improve your circumstances.

Sheila invites those taking her courses to bring in their hardest negotiation situation. This is often talking about money—asking for a raise, negotiating a fee with a client, divvying up costs with a friend or family member. We'll use this typically nerve-wracking scenario as our primary example in the steps that follow. But you can use the format we describe for any negotiation conversation that's hard for you, including things like changing age-old family holiday traditions or getting a friend to stop bringing her truly terrible two-year-old to all your coffee dates.

Select a real-life challenge you want to address, and make a date for the talk within the coming month. ***Plan to negotiate a tricky situation.***

2. Negotiate with yourself.

Before you engage in a negotiation with someone else, sit down and have a little talk with yourself. The goal is to understand how your identity—the story you tell yourself about yourself—affects your thinking. Most of us care deeply about how we are perceived by others and about what we think of our own behavior. Both sides of this identity coin can be problematic. When it comes to money, for example, you may have been raised to think that talking or caring about it will make you look greedy. And if you want to change a family or friendship routine, you may wonder if you are being selfish.

If you've been procrastinating about negotiating, understanding your underlying identity issues should help you push past procrastination. And if you're cognizant of these button-pushers before your encounter, you'll be less vulnerable to derailment if they come up during your conversation.

To suss out your identity issues, grab a piece of paper and make four vertical columns. In the first, write down what you want; in the second, why you want what you want; the third, what this desire says about you; and the fourth, how you think this desire makes you look to others. If you find your thoughts look wacky on paper, stare them down and

ARE YOU PART OF THE PROBLEM OR THE SOLUTION?

Common pitfalls

Avoidance. Allowing the problem to continue unchecked by not addressing it—or complaining about it to a third party.

Being unapproachable. Keeping other people at bay by being uninterested, unpredictable, short-tempered, punitive, or hypersensitive.

Intersections. These are differences between two people (background, preferences, communication styles, assumptions about relationships). One person's preference for addressing conflicts straightaway can cause a head-on collision with someone whose family background taught them that doing so was unsafe. Understanding and acknowledging such differences creates a common ground for communication.

Role assumptions. Being the family drama queen may not be fun for you—or for anyone else—but the role has taken root because it works in some way. Everyone else gets to remain calm while you rant and rave for the group, for instance. When one person wants to change their role, everyone needs to play new parts.

write a red-ink rebuttal. For instance, is it really tacky/mean/insensitive to want to be paid the market rate for your work, spend some of your holidays in your own home, and have your friend's undivided attention once in a while? No! It's actually sensible, reasonable, and a sign of how much you value friendship. Don't just make a list—talk back to it. ***Know your hot-button issues—and your rebuttals.***

3. Find objective criteria.

One way to zap the subjective identity issues you've uncovered is to find objective reasons why your request makes sense.

If you are asking for more money, Monster.com has a salary database that can provide a starting point for your analysis. Check their figures, and then ask around in your community to get a sense of what your work is worth in a professional and geographical context. Also back up your request with a real-world understanding of your role and responsibilities. You may need more money because you have a mountain of credit card debt, but that won't be as persuasive in landing a raise as a list of the effective new methods you've implemented, clients your Rolodex has reeled in, or ways your multifaceted skill set saves money.

Your requests for behavioral changes can also be strengthened this way. Is traveling to Aunt Trudie's for Thanksgiving just too hard with your toddler or too costly now that you've moved out of state? Do you work hard to clear your decks and create one-on-one time with your friend? ***Build your case with facts and figures.***

4. Consider the other person's perspective and interests.

"You'll be more persuasive," says Sheila, "by being open to persuasion." In negotiations you need to state your case, but also anticipate and be interested in theirs because you "want to make it as easy as possible for them to say yes." Understanding their perspective gives you a better vantage point from which you can create solutions.

So put yourself in the other party's shoes. Think about the interests behind their positions. Does the person in charge of the purse strings have to consider precedents and fairness in terms of her other employees or contractors? Do you only see Aunt Trudie once a year? Is your girlfriend having a terrible time finding reliable childcare—or have you managed to make her think you want to see her son as often as you can? ***Remember the Japanese proverb: "Even a sheet of paper has two sides."***

FEELINGS, NOTHING MORE THAN FEELINGS

The good, the bad, and the ugly

Even though we'd often prefer to be calm, cool, and collected, strong feelings have a way of sneaking—or bursting—into our negotiations. So that you're not burned by the white-hot intensity of your own unexpected feelings, Sheila and her colleagues suggest you:

- Explore your emotional footprint, the uniquely personal way your upbringing has shaped the way you feel, express, repress, or rename your emotions.
- Accept that negative feelings are normal and natural—it's what we do with them that can be problematic.
- Recognize that good people (like you) can have "bad" feelings.
- Learn that your feelings are as important as theirs.
- Express your feelings without judging, attributing, or blaming. Beginning your sentence with "I feel" goes a long way toward accomplishing this.
- Don't assume that another party has intended to make you feel as you do.
- When you know feelings are central to a conflict, realize that they must be acknowledged before real problem-solving can occur. In fact, simply acknowledging one another's feelings can oftentimes resolve the problem.

SHEILA'S EXPERT TIPS

GREAT OPENING LINES

Begin with the "Third Story." Rather then launching into your point of view or second-guessing theirs, adopt the objective perspective of a keen observer. Start from a neutral stance with a line like, "My sense is that you and I see this situation differently. I'd like to share my perspective and learn more about yours."

Extend an invitation. Describe the problem in a way you think you can both accept, and then ask for help understanding and solving it. Make the other person your partner in figuring these things out.

Talk about how to talk about it. This is especially helpful if you have a track record of unproductive negotiating with someone.

5. Brainstorm options.

Your creativity in conceiving options and willingness to consider several different ways of meeting your goal can score you points and facilitate agreement. When you can suggest options, you change from someone who is complaining or presenting a problem to someone who is helpful and offering solutions. This approach puts you on the same team, rather than on adversarial sides.

If you want more money, would you be satisfied with more time off (during which time you might do freelance work), more vacation time, or work at home time? If the reason you want more money is because you are worried about your retirement, might increased 401(k) contributions on the part of your employer meet your need? In lieu of a raise, could you arrange an incentive plan that earns you a cut of clients or contracts you bring in?

Could you invite the gang to Thanksgiving at your home, or alternate at-home and out-of-town years? Can you schedule phone dates with your friend during Junior's nap time? Think of at least three options that may satisfy both you and the other party. ***Look for win-win situations.***

6. Know your walk-away cue.

You can improve your odds for a happy outcome by formulating several different ways of coming to a mutually satisfying agreement and by being open to the other person's needs and perspective. But it's also important to think about your personal bottom line. What will you do if

I DID IT!

"I really needed to earn more money, but my employer really couldn't afford to give it to me. Together, we brainstormed a solution. For several months of the year, when work at my firm is slow, I do freelance consulting work for outside clients. This satisfies me by bringing in the supplemental income I need, and allows my employer to keep me on the team. It wasn't my first choice, but still, we each got what we needed."
—Shawna

PICK YOUR BATTLES

"When I moved out of my last apartment, I had a conflict with my landlord: I felt I was owed my full security deposit plus reimbursement for some repairs I'd made. She refused to give me this reimbursement. We had long phone calls, exchanged lengthy faxes and emails, and even hinted around at small claims court. But I just wanted to get on with my life. So even though I thought I was right, and felt sure I could convince a small claims court judge, I signed off on just getting my security deposit back. My time (and sanity!) was worth more to me than having the last word."
—C.J.

agreement is elusive? How far are you willing to stray from your goal? How long can you wait? Answering these questions will make the negotiation situation less loaded for you—and make you less likely to agree to terms you might later regret.

"If you have solutions to every roadblock they set up, and they don't want to hear about them," counsels Sheila, "you know that you aren't talking to someone who wants agreement." Take a deep breath, continue to think creatively, and consider what you can do without their green light. Can you stick with the status quo or ameliorate the situation in other ways? Your "victory" may entail knowing when to walk away, having the courage to do so, and spending your valuable time and energy elsewhere. ***Know when it's time to leave the table.***

7. Go, girl!

Working through the above steps has laid the groundwork for a successful negotiation. It's time to have your talk. As you do, remember to ask questions and keep your ears open. Don't expect to hear, "Gosh, you're so right. I'll take care of that right away." Expect instead to hear their perspective. Since you've already thought about their point of view, you can ask them questions about it and hear the information in their answers that will allow you to create options that meet their stated needs.

Also remember that negotiations aren't usually one-shot deals. Be willing to think long-term. If you meet a red or yellow light, ask how it can turn green. If they can't agree to what you'd like now, ask what needs to change in order to make it possible, and when you can agree to revisit the negotiation. Keep the lines of communication open—and the doors too. ***Establish an understanding.***

CONGRATULATIONS!

You've found a way to get your way with less stress and more success. Way to go! You did it!

I DID IT!

Name: ______________________________

Date: ______________________________

GAME OVER

Rules are made to be broken . . .

If you think your boss, a car salesperson, or someone else expects you to haggle and you don't want to play that old-school game, be explicit about wanting to do things another way. Be transparent. In a salary negotiation, Sheila suggests, you can say, "I could start high and then we could counter offer back and forth, but frankly I'd prefer to talk about what we both think my work is worth." You can actually "lighten the moment by suggesting that if they prefer the game-playing, you could double your request first! Refuse to believe you have to learn the rules of some nonsensical game—and then help the other party understand what you are doing, so they know it's safe for them to stop playing as well."

BEYOND THE BADGE

If you love it as much as you thought you would, dream on . . .

- **Just say no.** Getting to no can be every bit as hard as getting to yes. Saying, meaning, and sticking by that little word brings up many of the same identity issues as asking for what we want and need. "If I'm a generous person, how can I turn down my favorite charity?" "If I were a good friend, I'd be more patient with her demands on my time." When your mind goes down those roads, remember that saying yes to even small requests of your time, talent, or money will cut into the other ways you might want to use those resources. This doesn't mean you should become a knee-jerk naysayer; it means you should strive to make every yes you utter what Sheila terms a "good yes." Here are her tips on saying no:
  - Say it when you want to, not when you'll feel guilty for not saying it—or when you are using selflessness as an excuse to put off your own tasks.
  - Before saying yes out of habit, fear, or nervousness, buy yourself time by saying you need to think about the request overnight.
  - Negotiate by saying, "Yes, I can do that, if you do . . . "
  - Realize that "No" is a complete sentence. In Melville's classic story of the same name, Bartleby the Scrivener never explained why he would "prefer not to." You don't have to either.
- **Keep talking.** If you've surprised yourself by finding you loved speaking up for yourself and advocating for your position, see Speak Up, page 38, and Champion a Cause, page 46. These will help you use and build on your powers of persuasion to speak up in public—even if your voice shakes—and practice issue-oriented activism with passion and pizzazz.
- **Create room for hope.** Follow the example of Sheila's mentor Roger Fisher, and look for opportunities for understanding and agreement in your world—then take action. If you don't agree with panhandling but you do agree that everyone deserves a chance to support themselves, why not volunteer at a job training program? See Give a Little Bit, page 476 to find opportunities to volunteer, and negotiate a better world.

I AM WOMAN

Hear me squeak?

Women are often perceived to be "softer," so people may push them harder. Even women will push other women because they expect they'll be able to without retaliation. However, softness can be a source of strength: As a woman, you are perceived as less rigid and more approachable, and people will engage with you. To be soft without being too soft, Sheila says, "You need to be persistent. If you are a woman who prides herself on her empathy skills, on being able to put yourself in the other person's shoes, don't forget to come back to your own shoes. Don't end the conversation on their issues and needs. End it by figuring out how to meet your interests while also accommodating their circumstances."

SHEILA'S PICKS

BOOKS

Difficult Conversations: How to Discuss What Matters Most by Douglas Stone, Bruce Patton, and Sheila Heen
The advanced course from the Harvard Negotiation Project for handling particularly challenging conversations—asking for a raise, giving negative feedback, saying no, or explaining to your spouse why you have to work late . . . again. This approach will help you tackle the conversation with less anxiety and achieve better results.

First, Break All the Rules: What the World's Greatest Managers Do Differently by Marcus Buckingham and Curt Coffman
A strong employee-supervisor relationship distinguishes teams with high productivity, employee satisfaction, and retention from teams with low productivity, dissatisfied team members, and high turnover. Learn the twelve factors that matter for getting the best from your team.

Getting to Yes: Negotiating Agreement without Giving In by Roger Fisher, William Ury, and Bruce Patton
Learn how to move beyond haggling over positions to discuss interests, create options, use objective criteria, and be mindful of your alternatives. A must-read in the field from the prestigious Harvard Negotiation Project.

The Seven Principles for Making Marriage Work by John M. Gottman, PhD, and Nan Silver
With twenty-five years of studying which marriages succeed and which fail, Gottman identifies strengths and warning signs to watch for—especially how couples handle conflicts.

ORGANIZATIONS

The Program on Negotiation at Harvard Law School
www.pon.harvard.edu
Books, courses, and teaching materials on negotiation and conflict resolution.

Triad Consulting Group
www.diffcon.com
Customized training, mediation, and consulting in negotiation and managing difficult conversations.

WEB SITES

www.crnhq.org/twelveskills.html
The Conflict Resolution Network offers a guide to their "12 skills" of conflict resolution, as well as a helpful checklist, information on how to contact conflict mediators, and other info.

Monster.com and other career sites have terrific databases of salary information, sorted for job, your level of experience, and region of the country.

WORKSHOPS

Harvard runs workshops open to the public several times a year:

www.law.harvard.edu/academics/pil/
Program of Instruction for Lawyers offers five-day courses each June; participants come from all over the world, and half are nonlawyers.

www.mwi.org
Mediation Works Inc. offers mediation and negotiation training, as well as mediator and facilitator services.

www.pon.execseminars.com
Program on Negotiation Executive Education Series offers one- to two-day workshops.

23

LEARN THE LINGO

★ speaking a foreign language ★

A word is dead
When it is said,
Some say.
I say it just
Begins to live
That day.

—Emily Dickinson

So, what's your motivation?
Take a moment.
Dream a little, think big,
and then complete this sentence:
I see myself . . .

Imagine This . . . Your Roman waiter smiles and nods as you flawlessly order *un bicchiere di vino rosso.* It's raining this weekend, and you plan to curl up by the fire and read Colette—*en français.* As you pack for that tricky business trip in Tokyo, you know you'll make a favorable first impression with your conversational Japanese. Language skills win friends, open doors, and give you options. And if you stumbled over the subjunctive in high school Spanish class, take heart. All you need to do is pick your language, and follow the steps below. Soon you'll be sitting in a restaurant of the region with a friend who speaks the language, making conversation and ordering in your newly acquired language with *gusto* and *panache*—so *kawaii!* Prepare to impress yourself and others. *You can do it!*

The Payoffs

- **International relations.** As you globe-trot, you'll spread goodwill if you make an effort to speak like the natives. And right here at home, many of your neighbors, coworkers, and fellow citizens have struggled to learn your language. Why not meet them halfway by learning a bit of theirs?
- **Travel savvy.** Never again will you inadvertently order organ meats, wind up on the wrong train, or unwittingly insult someone's mother. Once you're clued in to the local lingo and customs, the world is your oyster.
- **Worldliness.** You'll learn a lot about how different peoples see the world by learning their local idioms. Prepare to broaden your horizons, deepen your understanding, and acquire the multilingual *je ne sais quoi* of the upwardly global.

Meet Your Mentor
SUSAN CARVALHO

What She Does: Susan is director of the Spanish Language Program at the prestigious Middlebury College Language School. In addition, she is acting chair of the Department of Hispanic Studies and associate professor of Spanish American literature at the University of Kentucky. She is a recipient of the William B. Sturgill Award for excellence in teaching and is writing a book that explores issues of geography and power in women's fiction, including that of Isabel Allende.

© Robert Keren

Why She Does It: "My father is from Brazil and started teaching my sister and me Spanish when we were five and six years old. He quite rightly thought that Spanish, rather than his native Portuguese, would have great relevance to us in the States. He bought books and records, and we had tests on Sundays. We earned a dime if we knew our new vocabulary words! He also read us stories at night in Spanish. I was an avid reader, and I was thrilled to find out you could access whole other worlds by reading stories in different languages. Language learning is really about building bridges between worlds."

Word from the Wise: "You can be functional in a new language with basic grammar and a relatively small vocabulary. Use body language, and don't get hung up on not knowing a particular word or phrase."

EVERYONE who has learned English can learn ANOTHER language.

—Susan Carvalho

BADGE STEPS

ELOQUENCE AIDS

The basic tools of the language learning trade are

Language dictionaries. A portable paperback for traveling, an authoritative hardcover for home, and a guide to slang just for fun.

Auditory input. This could be provided by language tapes, but ideally comes from other speakers. You want to hear your language of study as often as possible. (See Susan's Picks, page 191, for dictionary and tape resources.)

Added incentives. This could be a class that pledges you to frequent participation, a handsome stranger on a train in Tibet, or a monthly foreign-language dinner party—find what works for you, and pursue it!

1. Pick your lingo.

What language are you yearning to learn? Do you want to brush up on your high school Spanish or communicate more effectively with relatives who only speak Cantonese? Perhaps your fondness for Indian food, South African art, or Brazilian soccer has sparked an interest in the language of their masters. If you're planning international travel for work or pleasure, you may want to attain specific language skills to help navigate transportation, lodging, restaurants, and conversation. ***Decide what language you'll learn.***

2. Find a teacher or class.

Many of us have unpleasant memories of language lessons when we were younger, because older teaching methods often emphasized memorizing rules of grammar and pronunciation out of context. This kind of teaching can leave you silently scrolling through your brain for the rules about how to pronounce double consonants before vowels—all while an angry mob forms in the line behind you in the Pisa post office. Current language learning leans toward getting students comfortable and talking before studying such rules.

When exploring private language lessons or classes at language schools or community colleges, ask the teachers how they teach and what they expect you to be able to do at the end of the course. Check out the course outline and textbook too, just to make sure the class will speed you toward your goal of ordering dinner in that language and holding your own in a basic conversation with a friend. Do they emphasize speaking practice and cover vocabulary you can actually use? If not, keep looking. Otherwise, take the leap and start learning. ***Sign up for class.***

3. Get your money's worth from class.

When taking a class or lesson, speak up. If you craftily find ways to say as little as possible, what will you do when you want a bottle of beer in Berlin? Supplement your class work with the following techniques:

Tapes. A friendly, precise voice on the tape will say a word or phrase and then give you time to mimic that perfect pronunciation. If you listen to tapes during your commute or while running errands in your car, you'll painlessly build your study time. Your goal here is to speak a foreign language, after all, so you don't need to fret about spelling. If you are an auditory learner, tapes are just the ticket.

Books. If listening to a foreign language without seeing it throws you off, books combined with tapes will better suit you. Susan considers herself to be this kind of visually oriented learner—she wants to see the word and know how it is spelled when she pronounces it.

Flash cards. Visually oriented learners may also benefit from writing words and their definitions on flash cards, then practicing with them.

Experiment. If you don't know whether you're an auditory or visually oriented learner, Susan advises you try both approaches: "You'll immediately see which is more comfortable." Whatever approach works for you, go with it.

Study with a buddy. Do you have a friend or partner who shares your goal? Is one of your children studying a language in school? Learning together will give you someone to gab with in your new language and give you the incentive to persevere. Make weekly study dates.

Speak up. Speak at least once in every class, and raise your hand even if you're not absolutely positively sure of the answer. You learn more from mistakes, so give yourself license to make them.

Do your homework—and then some.

4. Immerse yourself.

At the world-renowned language program at Middlebury, where Susan teaches, classes only take up four hours a day—but cocurricular, or outside the classroom, activities fill the rest of a student's waking hours. Every social interaction occurs in the language of study. Middlebury's approach makes perfect sense, because the most effective language learning occurs when it coincides with students' interests and passions. Activities like cooking, playing sports, dancing, and going to the movies, theater, and concerts make a new language less theoretical, more practical, and fun! And not incidentally, they also help maintain the linguistic and cultural immersion round the clock. Here's how you can put this principle into practice:

Chitchat. Embrace every opportunity you stumble upon for conversational practice—when a tourist stops you on the street, with local merchants, at ethnic restaurants. And if you have a friend or coworker who speaks the language you are studying, make a deal to speak only in that language.

TOTAL IMMERSION

The Middlebury method

The Middlebury language schools were founded just after World War I with the goal of promoting cultural and linguistic understanding. Middlebury is famous for promoting language learning in only seven weeks. The secret to their success is total immersion, backed up with a strict language pledge: Middlebury students sign a pledge to communicate only in the language of study throughout their program. No English television or Internet surfing is allowed, and family phone calls are kept to a minimum. "For the first two days students really don't say much at all," says Susan—but rest assured, this doesn't last for long. "By the third day, they can speak in complete sentences, and by the second week, they are talking in paragraphs. At summer's end, they are perfectly capable of surviving in the Hispanic world."

SUSAN'S EXPERT TIPS

PSYCH YOURSELF UP

Laugh at your gaffes. Who knew that turning down seconds at a French dinner table by saying you're full would make everyone think you're pregnant? Laugh it off, and chalk it up to experience—that's one mistake you won't make again, and now you have a funny story to tell the folks back home.

Try to understand your fears. Are you afraid of saying something incorrectly because you're used to being the top of your class? Are you afraid your sense of humor won't translate? What's the worst thing that could happen if you do find yourself at a momentary loss for words? Think about it.

Remember the words of our expert. "Victory is making yourself understood, and progress is doing just a bit better than you did yesterday."

Sing along. Susan also suggests you try listening to music performed in the language you are studying. Look at the lyrics as you listen, and you'll get a better sense of pronunciation. Listening to Edith Piaf roll her r's in a song sure beats phonetics drills! Sing along with Piaf, and you'll absorb the cadence of the language in a way that will carry over into more formal study.

Foreign cinema. Watch foreign films as often as you can. Work your way methodically through the foreign section of your video store. If you have a DVD player, turn off the English subtitles—even if you miss a few words, you'll figure out the plot from context and learn some new vocabulary (and useful slang!) in the process.

Have fun in another language outside of class at least twice a week.

5. Make a multilingual dinner date.

Think of friends you know that speak other languages. Is there anyone you know that speaks your target language? If so, great—this will be the person you invite to dinner, to test drive your language skills and earn your badge.

If you can't think of anyone in your circle who speaks your new language, don't despair. You will probably find a classmate who'd be game, but you could also check out postings at local cafés and community bulletin boards online to find one or two people that share your language interests and might be willing to go out for a multilingual night on the town. Find a restaurant that can accommodate you and your language

I DID IT!

"I had to pass a professional-fluency-level language exam to get my master's degree in international public policy. Problem was, I learned some of my French when I was little and some from a French boyfriend much later—which meant my vocabulary was stuck somewhere between 'I have to pee pee' and 'Kiss me, you fool.' Not exactly professional! So for a couple of weeks I read *Le Monde* religiously, especially articles about human rights. During my oral exam, every time the subject steered into areas where my vocabulary was shaky, I steered the subject back to human rights. Afterwards my examiner shook my hand and congratulated me, saying 'I've never met someone so passionate about human rights!' "
—Alison

THEY'RE LAUGHING WITH YOU

"I have an Italian cousin, Giuliano. I spent hours piecing together an e-mail to him in Italian and after he received it, he wrote back in English: 'I think your computer write better in Chinese. I and my family, when we are sad, we read your computer-note so we can smile again.' "
—Anna

pursuits. ***Set a time and place for dinner—in your new language, of course!***

6. Paint the town *rouge, rosso,* or *hong.*

A week before your dinner, think about the topics that are most likely to come up in the course of conversation, and make sure you have enough vocabulary to hold your own. If you need to, look up terminology for:

Polite expressions. You've probably covered these in class a thousand times, but it may be worth a quick review. Be sure you feel comfortable with formalities to address the maitre d', wait staff, and any newcomers at dinner.

Food and drink. You need to be able to read the menu and order with confidence.

Your interest in the language. Can you explain what piqued your interest to your dining partners and describe any related travel plans? Have a few sentences good to go.

Shared interests. If you know you share an interest in snowboarding, opera, or criminal law with your dining partners, bone up on your lingo accordingly.

Current events. Any big story in the news is likely to come up at dinner. If you have an opinion on the subject, you might want to prepare a few words in advance.

Now you're ready to dine in style, and in another language! A *bon appétit, salud,* or *prost* is definitely in order. ***Make a toast—and order your dinner—with your new terminology.***

CONGRATULATIONS!

You have the gift of gab in another language, so talk it up and bask in the bilingual. You did it!

I DID IT!

Name: ____________________

Date: ____________________

GET GUTSY

As grown-ups, it's pretty easy to do only things we are good or at least competent at, from playing sports we excel at to cooking only tried-and-true recipes. But learning a new language requires stepping into uncharted territory. As Susan puts it, "In another language, adult students can feel stripped of their intelligence, their history, and their sense of humor." So as you begin your study, recognize that it takes guts to confront the unknown—and congratulate yourself for being that gutsy!

BEYOND THE BADGE

If you love it as much as you thought you would, dream on . . .

- **Road test it.** Take your studies abroad. When you study Italian in Italy, there will be plenty of other foreigners studying Italian with you. The trick is to keep Italian as your common language, not English! You'll likely be tested at the outset to determine your class level and then begin four to six hours of daily classes in conversation, grammar, and culture. If you don't like school, plan your next "all Italian, all the time" vacation with Roam Where You Want To on page 14. Most overseas schools will help you find housing, sometimes with host families. Susan lived with a family in Spain during a college year abroad. The family had a ceramic dragon on their television set which they had named Ronald Reagan. This gave Susan incentive to read the local newspapers carefully and learn the vocabulary needed to engage in dinner table debates about the then-current U.S. president.
- **Read it.** If you love sports or music, visit foreign-language Web sites on the subject, or seek out newspapers and magazines that focus on your area of interest at an international newsstand or well-stocked library. Susan doesn't advise forcing yourself to read in your new language what you wouldn't want to read in English. But she also once had a student who never thought he cared for poetry until he read a Spanish poem in her class, and uncovered a dormant passion. Give it a go.
- **Work it.** If you just can't get enough of your new language, try finding a way to put it to work for yourself or others. Become ESL-certified to teach English as a second language, or look for work as a tutor or translator. Your skills may open new doors in your current career with overseas clients or underserved local communities. Fluency may bring moonlighting opportunities as a tour guide, working for ethnic media radio and TV stations, helping poets translate their work into English, translating for journalists conducting interviews, or showing visiting dignitaries around town. You could also volunteer your time, helping recent immigrants adapt to English-language classes, translating for doctors or patients at medical or legal clinics, or doing outreach for a community service organization.

BERLITZ BLITZ

Consider your options from the big-name language center

Go now or upon arrival. Berlitz has 400 centers in more than sixty countries.

Go solo or in a group. They offer group, semi-private, and individual instruction and promise courses for various interests, needs, and learning styles.

Go fast or slow. Weekly courses may work for you, but you might prefer intensive individual instruction seven and a half hours a day for two to six weeks.

Go multimedia or paperback. Instructional support materials include illustrated workbooks, review tapes, business supplements, and CD-ROM programs.

SUSAN'S PICKS

DICTIONARIES

Bantam pocket dictionaries
Susan's preferred for Spanish-English; available in all major languages.

Oxford Spanish Dictionary
Susan's recommendation for a Spanish desktop dictionary. Oxford offers similarly fine titles in other languages. Contains multiple examples of the words used in context, thus reducing the chances of using the wrong word for a particular situation.

COOKBOOKS

Look for titles in the language of your choice. In Spanish, consider:

100 recetas exquisitas sin carne by Rimondino Adrin
Recipes for vegetarians.

La tradicional cocina mexicana y sus mejores recetas by Adela Fernandez
An excellent Spanish recipe book.

POETRY

Again, look for titles in the language of your choice. In Spanish, check out:

Canto general and **Veinte poemas de amor y una canción desesperoda** by Chilean Nobel Prize winner Pablo Neruda

Poesia para todos los dias by Spanish poet Gloria Fuertes

All three titles contain relatively short and very poignant poetry.

NEWSPAPERS

When major world events happen, it can be enlightening to read about them from a different national perspective—in both news articles and editorials. At the same time, you'll be flexing your language muscles. For Spanish, try:

www.cibercentro.com
Click on the country of your choice to find local newspapers in Spanish.

El Pais
www.elpais.es
The Spanish national newspaper.

TAPES

Pimsleur series
A good set of tapes for oral practice and for accustoming your ear to a new language. There's a short and relatively inexpensive version for getting started, and then a comprehensive edition once you are addicted. Well-structured so as to move from more common, practical communicative needs to more sophisticated ones.

LANGUAGE SCHOOL LEADS

Look up your local college or university to find out what they have to offer, and consider these options, too:

Berlitz
www.berlitz.com
Language learning options worldwide.

Foreign Language Learning Guide
www.collegeapps.about.com/cs/languagestudy
About.com's foreign-language learning site links to language courses and discusses how to evaluate and choose a school.

I Love Languages
www.ilovelanguages.com
A guide to language-related Web sites and Internet resources, including language schools.

Language Course Finder
www.language-learning.net
Lists more than 6,500 schools in ninety countries and seventy languages.

Language School Explorer
language.school-explorer.com
Independent database of language schools around the world; features information on 2,500 schools in 1,000 cities and 120 countries.

Middlebury College Language Schools
www.middlebury.edu
Learn from our expert herself!

24

GO BACK TO SCHOOL

★ continuing your education ★

Not to know is bad;
not to WISH to know
is worse.

—African proverb

Imagine This . . . You're explaining what you learned in school today to friends and family when suddenly it hits you: You really know your stuff! Gone are the days when you lived vicariously through your kids' daily discoveries or colleagues heading back to graduate school—now you too are learning something new every day. Doctors are now discovering what you know from personal experience: Lifelong learners live longer, happier, more active lives. You don't need a tweed jacket, a pipe, and a PhD to be a scholar, either. With your love of learning and the wisdom you've gained over the years, you'll have no problem naming your goals, lining up support, and creating a study plan that works for you . . . and soon you'll earn yourself some impressive credentials, too. *You can do it!*

So, what's your motivation?
Take a moment.
Dream a little, think big,
and then complete this sentence:
I see myself . . .

The Payoffs

- **Advancement.** In many professions, getting ahead means jumping through certificate, degree, or training hoops. So limber up, and jump-start your career.
- **Change.** Whether you want to change the world, change jobs, or just change your mind, knowledge is power—and the quickest route out of a rut.
- **Choice.** If you don't know your options, how can you make wise choices? One reason we urge kids to stay in school is to give them opportunities we didn't feel we had. Education gives adults more life menu options, too.
- **Fitness.** "Use it or lose it" applies to the brain as well as the body. Recent research reveals that learning new things throughout life helps preserve mental strength and agility.

Meet Your Mentor

E. FAITH IVERY

What She Does: The founder and president of Educational Advisory Services, Inc., and author of *How to Earn a College Degree: When You Think You Are Too Old, Too Busy, Too Broke, Too Scared,* Faith earned an EdD degree in Educational Administration and College Student Personnel Administration, a master's degree in Human Development Counseling, and a bachelor's in Psychology.

Why She Does It: "I created Educational Advisory Services, Inc., to represent and help the adult learner. I wanted would-be students to know that there are a wide range of options available to them and a variety of ways to make education doable, no matter what their age or circumstance. It's important—and empowering—for students to realize that they are the consumers of a product called education. Looking at education this way encourages students to assess themselves and their goals and then find the program that's the best fit for them, rather than trying to squeeze themselves into an inappropriate template. I earned my graduate degrees as a working adult and used several nontraditional methods to do so. When I was an undergraduate, my mother was also working on her degree. I'd see her at the kitchen table late at night, typing or studying. At the time, I didn't realize how hard what she was doing was, but I do now—and it's very satisfying to help adult learners find realistic and effective ways to reach their goals."

Word from the Wise: "As my book says, adults usually think they're too old, too busy, too broke, or too scared to pursue education. One way or another, the fear boils down to 'I can't do it.' Statistics refute this idea. Adult learners have far better grade point averages than the traditional student. Not only can they do it, they can do it better!"

Half of all the people enrolled in colleges are adult learners. Adults need to know that they aren't alone on campus; they are increasingly the norm.

—Faith Ivery

FEAR 101

College takes courage!

When we're older and have been in the work world for a while, we develop a sense of proficiency, a familiar comfort zone. But going into class on day one means becoming a novice and throwing yourself headfirst into the unknown. It may not be as risky as white-water rafting, but you are heading into uncharted waters. This is a bold new adventure, and you should give yourself credit for having the courage to embark upon it. "The hardest thing is walking into that first college classroom," says Faith. "But after that first day, adults will quickly see how well they can handle it."

COMMUNITY PRIDE

Why a community college may suit you

"I've studied in seven colleges and universities, and I think I got my best education in community colleges. Don't assume that you'll get an inferior education there. In reality, you are likely to get one-on-one attention and have good access to instructors. The faculty focus in a community college is on teaching, not on research or publication, and by and large they share a real passion for teaching. The mission of a community college is to serve the broader community, so you will also find greater diversity there in terms of young people, seniors, and full-time employees."
—Faith

BADGE STEPS

1. Pick your area of interest.

Do you want to get the additional or advanced training that will propel you forward in your current career? Are you itching to make a dramatic career switch? Or do you yearn for the liberal arts education you've never had time to get? Whatever your reasons for heading back to school, it's important to zoom in on your needs and desires. To identify your educational goals, answer these three questions:

What do you want to be when you grow up? If you can't say for sure, take some time to assess your aptitudes and interests. What work, volunteer, or extracurricular projects have allowed you to really shine? Try matching your interests to a career using career-building tools like Faith's *How to Earn a College Degree,* the Myers-Briggs career assessment test, or employing the help of a professional career counselor.

What subjects are you most passionate about? Heed Faith's advice and avoid picking a path of study only because you've heard there are lots of job openings in the field, which may leave you qualified for work you don't enjoy. Take a moment to consider what discussions consistently get you the most excited and look for courses that allow you to pursue these lifelong passions and not just practical concerns.

What course of study would enrich your life the most? Don't assume that your desire to study medieval painting or existential philosophy is a waste of time. Studies have shown that employees with liberal arts skills tend to rise further in an organization than those with narrower education and training. As Faith puts it, "You learn skills in college—like organization, time management, problem solving, and how to write and speak effectively—that go beyond your area of study. Those skills are prized by employers."

Now take a look at your answers. Is there a field of study that pops up in all or most of your answers? Find the subject that's most promising in terms of career possibilities, lifelong passions, and learning potential. ***Choose your field of study.***

2. Find your learning style.

Think about the last few times you've learned a new skill or absorbed a new bit of knowledge and then list a few of these on a sheet of paper.

For each subject you learned, list one thing that helped you learn and one thing that got in your way. This list might read as follows:

WHAT I LEARNED	WHAT HELPED ME LEARN?	WHAT MADE IT HARD FOR ME TO LEARN?
Quilting	Could do it after kids go to bed	Going it alone
Refinancing mortgage	Having an expert on hand to consult	Not dedicating undivided attention to it
Russian poetry	Personal discussions with peers on subject	Having limited time to spend on it

Looking at the table above, for example, you might learn that you prefer a class structure where you're among peers, have an expert on hand, and can set your own study schedule. ***Define a learning style that suits you.***

3. Choose a study setting.

Once you know what you want to learn and how you learn best, you'll find it easier to pick a course of study that works for you:

In a classroom at a nearby school, college, or university. This is best for people who thrive on discussion and don't need a lot of one-on-one consultation.

With a tutor. One-on-one or small-group tutoring sessions can be useful if you need to pick up basic skills quickly, are looking to fill in specific gaps in your knowledge, or would rather proceed at your own pace.

Online. You can complete an entire degree online or opt for an online course when your schedule is particularly tight. If you want credentials, be sure the course is offered through a regionally accredited institution.

Telecourses. Many colleges and universities offer courses through public broadcasting and local cable stations. If you want to apply these courses toward a degree, check to be sure your credits are transferable.

Correspondence courses. Most allow you to set your own schedule and complete the course work within a year. If you want credit for your efforts, be sure your correspondence course is regionally accredited and affiliated with a reputable academic institution—there are some fly-by-night organizations that only offer bogus certificates of completion.

Find the class setting that works best for you.

FIND TIME TO LEARN

Three ways to discover time you never knew you had

- Try keeping a diary for a week, noting exactly how you spend your time. Include everything—work, chores, recreation, etc. Scrutinize the list for what you can and cannot give up, what can be streamlined, and what you might be able to delegate to others.
- Make a list of the people and institutions that can help you make time. Will your employer support your efforts with flextime? Can family members lighten your load at home? Make them part of your team from the get-go.
- Reclaim your time. You don't need to apologize for taking time out of your day to learn. Faith used to have a "Please Do Not Disturb" sign that she could hang on her door; now she has one that simply says "Go Away." This may sound extreme—but for active women, extreme measures may be necessary to establish that your alone time is just as sacred as your time with family and friends. As Faith points out, mothers who take the time to further their own educational goals show their kids the value of learning.

I DID IT!

"I was concerned that I'd be 36 by the time I finished law school. My sister very wisely told me that whether or not I went back to school, I'd turn 36—I could be that old with a law degree or without one! A number of attorneys tried to talk me out of going to law school. But these were people who'd gone straight from college, through law school, and into law firm jobs. They ended up feeling stuck and wondering 'what if . . . ' But I worked in a variety of fields for ten years before becoming a lawyer. That gave me a lot of confidence in my abilities and a sense of certainty about what I was doing and why I was doing it."
—Julia

THINK TWICE

"I had a plum job in book publishing, but one weekend I went to a convention in Chicago and spent the night at my niece's apartment. She was a med student at the time. Sleeping on her couch, I was surrounded by medical textbooks and journals. I woke up knowing—or maybe remembering—that I wanted to be a physician. A few hard but rewarding years later, I am. But it's crucial to have a realistic view of what you're doing. You have to talk to lots of people—you may think a medical career is one thing when it's really another. And you have to be completely realistic about the time and commitment involved and what that may do to your family life. Go into it with open—not starry—eyes."
—Joann

FAITH'S EXPERT TIPS

GET CREDIT WHERE IT'S DUE

Colleges are increasingly willing to give "credit for prior learning"—if you can demonstrate you've got experience. Here's how you might qualify:

Training. The American Council on Education (ACE) evaluates thousands of training courses offered by the military, major corporations, and professional associations, and assigns them equivalent college credit.

Testing. There are a variety of testing processes that let you prove you know the equivalent of what you'd learn in a college course. Ask your school about CLEP, PEP, and TECEP exams. Or you may be able to take a "challenge exam," which is typically the final exam in a course.

Portfolios. Many schools allow you to prepare and present a formal portfolio that demonstrates your expertise in a classroom subject area. A professor will evaluate your portfolio, and the school will provide guidelines for appropriate credit. The national portfolio average for an adult learner is twenty-one credits!

4. Finance your education.

Some employers offer tuition assistance to their employees, because they value an educated workforce and retaining good workers. If you're employed, make your firm's human resources department your first financial planning stop. Faith also suggests you consider the following funding resources:

Campus financial aid advisors. Seek out on-campus resources on loans, work study, grants, and scholarships.

Your bank. Find out if you qualify for low-interest federal student loans.

The Veterans Administration. If you've served in the military, you may be eligible for educational benefits.

The library and the Internet. Look for scholarship directories and listings for fellowships and grants, and apply to any that seem applicable.

Your tax advisor. Find out whether your educational expenses are tax-deductible. The tax dollars you save could lower your college costs.

Put some green behind your scheme.

5. Pick your perfect school.

Make use of every resource available to you—the Internet, your local library, your extended circle of colleagues and friends—to research schools, and find a few possibilities that seem to match your educational goals. Then pose the following questions to an admissions advisor at each school:

- Do you offer financial aid? How much, and what kind?
- Do you cater to adult learners who have family and workplace obligations?
- Do you offer the coursework options I want (such as online classes)?
- Do you accept transfer credits from other institutions, or offer credit for college-equivalent knowledge and experience?

When you find a school that best satisfies your criteria, collect course catalogs, application forms, and financial aid forms for the school. ***Find a campus to call your own.***

6. Apply to school.

Start filling out the appropriate application forms for your school(s) of choice. Application procedures for schools may vary from mailing in a simple form with a check for a noncredit course to a multipage application for full-time graduate programs. Most graduate schools will want admission test scores (such as the ACT, SAT, GRE, and GMAT), your past school transcripts, letters of recommendation from teachers or colleagues, and a personal essay describing your goals. ***Get enrolled.***

7. Go to school.

Stock up on school supplies, because you're headed for class! By taking each of the above steps, you're already on your way to successful completion of your educational goals—now all you need to do is show up for class, and start learning. ***Strut your student stuff.***

CONGRATULATIONS!

School is cool and so are you. You did it!

I DID IT!

Name: ______________________________

Date: ______________________________

APPLICATION EASE

Before you get too intimidated by any application, remember

- **Community or "junior" colleges are open admission.**
- **Many schools don't require that adult students take standardized admission exams.**
- **You can bypass the need to take the undergraduate admission tests (ACT, SAT) by taking a few community college courses and then becoming a transfer student.**
- **Don't be shy about asking for recommendations—most people will be more than happy to do you this small favor.**
- **Not every program requires a personal essay in the application. If writing an essay intimidates you, enlist an English grad student to help you edit and polish your ideas.**

BEYOND THE BADGE

If you love it as much as you thought you would, dream on . . .

- **Become a professional academic.** If you can't bear the thought of leaving campus, don't! There are any number of ways to make yourself at home in academia. You can go to the head of the class and teach, sharing your passion for a subject or field and inspiring others with your expertise and enthusiasm. Or you can work in an administrative capacity, advising students, doing public relations for the school, or performing some other vital student service.
- **Study (or teach) abroad.** If you missed out on that fabled junior year abroad as an undergraduate, make it happen now. (See Education Excursions for details.)
- **Volunteer.** Find a way to share your newfound knowledge or expertise. As an adult student you probably have an acute sense of how difficult it can be to pursue adult education. Consider the populations who face the most challenges (battered women, the working poor, immigrants, the incarcerated) and investigate ways to help. From your vantage point, you may also have a strong desire to help younger women further their education sooner rather than later. Why not mentor, tutor, or teach a girl whose environment puts her at risk? Inspiration is always better when shared.

EDUCATION EXCURSIONS

Some international study resources

GoAbroad.com. Program searches and travel resources, including a study abroad directory and information on overseas internships, volunteering, and teaching. www.goabroad.com.

IIEPassport. Offers a comprehensive search for study abroad programs by country, language, subject, and other criteria. Features a "Country of the Month" and an Advisor Center. www.iiepassport.org.

StudyAbroad.com. Lets you search for programs by country and subject and includes academic year, summer, and semester programs. Discusses adult and graduate study programs and features teaching, internship, and volunteer opportunities. www.studyabroad.com.

FAITH'S PICKS

BOOKS

Acing the College Application: How to Maximize Your Chances for Admission to the College of Your Choice by Michele A. Hernandez, EdD
Shows you how to describe yourself in your application in a way that will set you apart.

College Degrees by Mail & Internet by John Bear, PhD, and Mariah P. Bear, MA
Profiles 100 of the best accredited distance-learning providers in the world.

Do What You Are: Discover the Perfect Career for You Through the Secrets of Personality Type by Paul D. Tieger and Barbara Barron-Tieger
This career guide helps you identify your personality type and then use this information to find the right job.

The Fiske Guide to Colleges by Edward B. Fiske
This annual guide walks students through applying to appropriate schools, the application process, and obtaining scholarships and financial aid.

How to Be a Successful Online Student by Sara Dulaney Gilbert
What it takes to learn at a distance, essential tools and equipment, advice on setting up an independent study schedule, how to combine online learning with classroom work, and more.

How to Earn a College Degree: When You Think You Are Too Old, Too Busy, Too Broke, Too Scared by E. Faith Ivery, EdD
A step-by-step educational planning guide filled with worksheets, tips, and shortcuts to help adult learners create a cost- and time-effective road map to success.

New Beginnings: A Reference Guide for Adult Learners by Linda Simon
From how to choose a program and a course to drawing upon life experiences.

What Color Is Your Parachute? by Richard N. Bolles
This book has been the classic guide to choosing the right career for thirty years.

WEB SITES

www.Back2College.com
Articles and information for adult students. Faith is their volunteer "Ask the Expert" columnist.

www.e-a-s.com
Faith's Educational Advisory Services site features an Online Advisor with a comprehensive database of college/university programs for adult learners.

www.educationforadults.com
Contains a directory for adult education programs.

www.supercollege.com
Offers resources to help you pay for and get into college.

:: *For information on and help with financial aid, check out:*

www.adulted.about.com/cs/financialaid

www.finaid.org/otheraid/older.phtml

www.theoldschool.org

25

PLAY A TUNE (IN TUNE)

★ playing an instrument ★

I've started to take piano lessons (in my sixties). I'm a great seeker of pleasure. It's all about pleasure.

—Susan Sontag

Imagine This . . . All ears are on you as you strum your strings, tickle your ivories, or keep the beat. You're in "the zone," your trance finally broken by a burst of applause. Do you dream of Bogie leaning on your piano and asking you to "Play it again," or of raising the roof with your swinging sax solo? Whether you yearn to play violin concertos or bang out the blues, this badge will put an instrument in your hands and a song in your heart. No matter if you're starting from scratch or dusting off your drums, you'll integrate your instrument into your life and win over audiences soon enough. Get ready to meet your musical muse. *You can do it!*

So, what's your motivation?
Take a moment.
Dream a little, think big,
and then complete this sentence:
I see myself . . .

The Payoffs

- **Satisfaction.** You're bound to get some. Practice doesn't necessarily make perfect, but you'll see definite progress from week to week. You'll learn basic chords, practice scales, and finally master that Keith Richards guitar solo—and get plenty of satisfaction along the way.
- **Music appreciation.** You may have thought you were a music lover, but playing music dramatically increases your knowledge and deepens your appreciation in unexpected ways.
- **Staying power.** Seeing how your disciplined efforts pay off with tangible improvement reinforces your determination in other endeavors.
- **Altered states.** Musicians describe playing as a meditative activity that taps into another part of their brain (athletes call this "entering the zone"). When you play something well, it feels *sooo* good.

Meet Your Mentor

GEORGIA HUGHES

What She Does: Edits books nine-to-five (as editorial director of New World Library in Novato, California) and plays bassoon evenings and weekends with orchestras and chamber groups. She goes away for a week each summer to music camp, where the happy campers play, practice, and perform all day.

© Cathey Flickinger

Why She Does It: "When I was a kid and went to concerts with my parents, I was fascinated by the timpanist, who only played once in a while but who got to make a really big noise. Probably to spare my family the sound of my practicing, my mother steered me away from percussion. I played the flute at first, and when I was in the eighth grade, the band director asked if any of us wanted to learn to play the oboe. I said sure, but the following week the director came back with a bassoon. He had realized that the bassoonist at the high school was about to graduate! Musicians from the Indianapolis Symphony came to the schools and gave private lessons each week to those of us who played one of the 'wackier,' less common instruments. I played the bassoon, off and on, throughout high school and, to a lesser extent, college—hormones were raging, and I had other things on my mind! When I moved to the San Francisco Bay Area, I told myself I was either going to play the bassoon or get rid of it. So I went to a music store, got the name of a teacher, and started taking lessons again."

Word from the Wise: "My biggest misconception about learning to play an instrument was that you either had talent, or you didn't. If you had it, you could play really well—and if you didn't, you never would. That's just not true. It's all about time and focus, not something you were or were not born with."

'See,' I told myself, 'you couldn't do that a year ago!' Like the Little Engine That Could, I just kept chugging along, knowing with hard work, I could reach the next level. Who knows what I'll be able to play next year?

—Georgia Hughes

BADGE STEPS

1. Pick an instrument.

If you don't already have a fantasy of playing a particular instrument, pick an instrument based on the kind of music you love to listen to. Follow your ear. Country might lead you to the fiddle or banjo, classical to piano or French horn, Indian ragas to the sitar or tabla.

Once you've made your selection, you have another choice: rent or buy. Renting can be good for starters—but when you know you'll be playing consistently, you'll probably want to own your own. You can buy your instrument new or used. Most instruments don't depreciate very much, so don't expect your used instrument to come cheap. Check the stores, bulletin boards, ads, and the Web for options. Be sure to let people know what you're looking for so they can give you leads. ***Rent or buy your instrument.***

2. Find a teacher.

You want a teacher who not only plays your instrument, but is also knowledgeable about the kind of music that moves you. Ask other musicians for referrals, speak to the folks at music stores, contact local performance groups, and check out the course listings at nearby colleges. Be up-front about your time and money limitations.

Once you have your shortlist together, interview prospective teachers. The teacher is there to push and motivate you, so don't look for a buddy—look for a person who can bring out your best. For instance, Georgia's friend, Patty, had a hard time learning to read music when she took piano lessons as a child. She learned pieces by ear and memorized everything so her teacher wouldn't catch on. Needless to say, those lessons were a drag. But when she inherited the family piano, she found she could still sit down and figure out the basics of her favorite Steely Dan songs by ear. She found a teacher who valued this ability and now views her knack as an asset rather than a liability.

So, take the time to find the right fit. That said, you can always make a change if it isn't working out after a few lessons (see Making Beautiful Music Together sidebar). ***Interview maestros and sign up for classes.***

3. Find or create a practice space.

Where you practice can affect whether or not you care to practice. Some people find that renting a rehearsal space is ideal, especially if their in-

WHAT TO PLAY

Think beyond the usual marching band instruments, and try these orchestral options on for size

Strings. Violin, viola, cello, double bass, plucked harp. These predominate, playing almost continuously in most orchestral scores.

Woodwinds. Flute, oboe, saxophone, English horn, clarinet, bassoon. All harmonize with the strings and sometimes carry the melody.

Brass. French horn, trumpet, trombone, tuba. The French horn usually blends with the woodwinds, while other brasses can either play loudly and provide drama or contribute to subdued passages.

Percussion. Piano, kettledrums (or timpani), snare and bass drums, cymbals, triangle, xylophone. The piano often has solos, but most percussion is used sparingly for rhythm.

strument is loud. They don't have to worry about getting a noise citation, and paying for a space can goad them into using it. Check local colleges and music conservatories to see if they rent studio space.

But like Georgia, most people practice at home. "I've always told my neighbors that I'll stop if I'm playing at an inconvenient time for them," Georgia says. "I haven't had any problems—but my spouse did plead with me to try something new when I played a not-so-melodic Stravinsky passage for the twentieth time."

Wherever you practice, make it as pleasant as possible so you look forward to going there. Rent studio space near a favorite café, or set yourself up in a room with a view or art you love on the walls. Prop up a photo of your musical hero (or heroine) on your music stand, cover your TV with a scarf—whatever puts you in the mood to practice. Make sure you have easy access to all the gear you need, so you have no excuses to procrastinate. ***Settle into a practice space.***

4. Establish a practice schedule.

Commit to a schedule that really works for you, not a time when your favorite TV show is on or when you can't keep your eyes open. Look at practice time as time for yourself, a respite from the rest of your day—a pleasure, not drudgery. On weeknights after work, Georgia talks herself into playing by telling herself that she is just going to assemble her bassoon and play one piece of music. But once she starts, she rarely stops. She plays longer than she sets out to, just by tricking herself into getting started.

Ask your teacher how many times a week you should practice to master a simple song in a month, and stick to that schedule. Use incentives to stay dedicated—Georgia's mother used to bribe her by saying that if Georgia practiced, she'd do her household chores for her. ***Reward yourself for a month of faithful practice with a new CD.***

5. Perfect a song.

Once you've made it through that first month and can pick out a basic melody, you're well on your way to having your very own theme song. Play that tune until you own it, and you're not even tempted to sneak a peek at the score. Keep on practicing until you can play it from memory without a single mistake, from the first note right to the grand finale. To celebrate your achievement, treat yourself to a concert. And just think: That could really be you onstage. ***Carry that tune.***

MAKING BEAUTIFUL MUSIC TOGETHER

Find the right maestro

Don't be intimidated. "It took me almost a year to call a particular teacher because I was so impressed by how well he and his students played," says Georgia. "He became a great mentor, and I almost missed the chance to work with him out of pure fear and self-consciousness."

Make your wishes known. Ask for what you need, whether that's serious coaching or just supervised practice.

Don't suffer (too much) for your art. If you aren't connecting with a teacher, dread your lessons, and aren't making the kind of progress you'd like, make a switch. Try a teacher with a different technique, personality, or style of music.

I DID IT!

"I recently took my banjo plucking public for the first time. My advice? Start small. Play for your friends. Play in the background at family gatherings. Go to an open mic night or the kind of casual jam sessions often held in coffee shops and nightclubs. Play on the street. The more you do it, the more you'll want to do it!"
—Debbie

WHEN IN DOUBT, PLAY YOUR HEART OUT

"I was playing a concert where the clarinet and the bassoon had a little duet. I started playing it before the clarinet started. I thought I was right and couldn't tell what the conductor was doing—so I just kept playing, loud and proud! Well, I was wrong. I was sure the conductor was going to call me the next day and tell me never to come back, but he didn't. I've since learned that most conductors prefer to hear you make a mistake than to have you be timid and not play out."
—Georgia

GEORGIA'S EXPERT TIPS

GREAT PERFORMANCES

- Comfortable clothes are a must. Being able to breathe and move is more important than looking fabulous.
- Take a restroom break before taking the stage!
- Experiment and figure out what works for you as far as warming up and eating. If you are prone to jitters, avoid caffeine.
- Pick music you know and love for auditions. When you are auditioning at an amateur level, you usually get to pick what you'll play. Go with what you know, not something you've been madly trying to learn so as to dazzle them with your virtuosity. If you do have to fly by the seat of your pants, relax, trust your skills, and try not to psych yourself out. Once, when Georgia moved to a new town, she heard of an orchestra looking for a new bassoonist and was invited to come to a rehearsal. "They were doing Benjamin Britten's 'Young Person's Guide to the Orchestra,' which features all the instruments. The second bassoonist leaned over and told me, 'That bassoon part is really a bitch to play!' Meanwhile, the conductor was stopping every musician after they played to critique their performance. When it was my turn, I just nailed it. The conductor gave me a big grin and I knew I was in. It was a great moment!"

6. Take the stage.

Some musicians have no interest in performance—they just want to play for themselves, no matter how accomplished they become. But you may find performance prompts you to rise to the occasion. "I've played better than I thought I ever could in a performance with an orchestra," states Georgia. "There's an adrenaline rush and applause!"

Set a performance date, even if it's just a brief recital for a few friends. Here are some possible venues:

- Community groups, community colleges, theater groups, opera companies. You don't even have to wait for concert season to begin—many combos, duos, and quartets play several weddings a day during June.
- Recitals. Invite people over to your house, or seek out a performance venue—Georgia knows of a wealthy music lover who regularly hosts recitals in his home.

- Benefits, fundraisers, nursing homes, and church groups. As Georgia explains, you never know where you'll find an appreciative audience: "I was tuning up for a performance at a local church when a man approached me to ask if his wife, who was deaf, could touch my instrument while I was playing. I don't know precisely what it meant to her to do it, but it made me cherish playing and listening to music all the more."

Then practice like crazy. That way when you don't know what to wear, how to fix your hair, or are distracted (we hope) by sudden bursts of applause, your hands will still remember what to do! And take it from Billy Joel: "It's okay if you mess up. You should give yourself a break." ***Have a great time at your first gig.***

CONGRATULATIONS!

You've tuned up your instrument and turned on an audience. Let it go to your head. You did it!

I DID IT!

Name: ______________________________

Date: ______________________________

STAY INSPIRED

Watch these films and learn from the greats

Amadeus: Mozart

Buena Vista Social Club: various

Hilary and Jackie: Jacqueline Du Pré

Impromptu: Frédéric Chopin

Let's Get Lost: Chet Baker

Round Midnight: Dexter Gordon

Shine: David Helfgott

Songcatcher: Appalachian greats

BEYOND THE BADGE

If you love it as much as you thought you would, dream on . . .

- **Join a group.** Georgia found her first group through a newspaper ad. Your music teacher or music store can also hook you up with other musicians, and then they connect you with other people. It doesn't sound very nice to say, but one of the benefits of finding some playmates is learning from their mistakes—and discovering that you don't sound half bad in comparison! If you do feel a tad over your head, you'll have virtuosos on hand to ask for advice and plenty of incentive to improve. Play well with others.
- **Go to music camp.** There are jazz and classical music camps for people of all ages sponsored by colleges all across the country. You live in dorms, eat in a cafeteria, and experience total music immersion. "You basically play until your fingers—or lips—feel like they're about to fall off!" says Georgia. "Going to camp for a week is like a year's worth of lessons. Plus I've been exposed to tons of music I never would have found on my own." Send a postcard: "Having a great time, wish you were here!"
- **Play favorites.** Maybe that Aretha Franklin tune wasn't meant for clarinet—but how can you know until you try? And if there's a song that inspired you to take up your instrument, you owe it to yourself to learn it. Georgia has started a new round of lessons specifically to work the Mozart Bassoon Concerto, a piece she hopes to use in auditions to show off her soloing chops. Once more, with feeling.
- **Pack your bag (pipes).** Virtually every genre of music has its premier performance spaces, annual festivals, and pilgrimage sites. Many music-based travel destinations feature great performances and workshops, too. (See Georgia's Picks for starters.) Follow your bliss.

GET THE SHOW ON THE ROAD

Explore a world of music

:: Travel to hear these greats:

Société des Concerts du Conservatoire, Paris (1828)

New York Philharmonic (1842)

Boston Symphony Orchestra (1881)

Chicago Symphony Orchestra (1891)

London Philharmonic (1932)

:: Be festive. You have dozens of music festivals to choose from, including:

Glastonbury Festival. Alternative music in Wales

The New Orleans Jazz and Heritage Festival. Second only to Mardi Gras

The Other Minds Festival. Composers of new and unusual music flock to the San Francisco Bay Area

The Salzburg Festival. *The Sound of Music*, need we say more?

World Sacred Music Festival. In Fez, Morocco

:: Make a pilgrimage to:

Landmark locales. Motown, Graceland, or (dare we say) Dollywood

Musical crossroads. Appalachia, Australia, or West Africa

The origins. The birthplace of ska, samba, or Celia Cruz

GEORGIA'S PICKS

BOOKS

Concepts for Jazz/Rock Piano by Donald Fagen (video)
The Steely Dan cofounder shares his secrets.

How to Play Keyboards by Roger Evans (manual)
Sure beats playing "Chopsticks" forever.

How to Play the 5-String Banjo by Pete Seeger (manual)
That's right, Pete Seeger. Why not learn from a master?

MAGAZINES

All About Jazz
www.allaboutjazz.com
Monthly webzine.

Blues Revue
www.bluesrevue.com
The world's largest blues publication.

Down Beat
www.downbeat.com
News, merchandise, education, and sixty-five years of archives from the venerable jazz magazine.

Folk and Blues News
www.folkandbluesnews.com
An Internet magazine with reviews, interviews, features.

Gramophone
www.gramophone.co.uk
Classical music news, competitions, CD reviews.

Music and Vision
www.mvdaily.com
An Internet classical music magazine in daily digest form.

The Musical Times
www.musicaltimes.co.uk
The world's oldest continuously published classical music magazine.

Strings
www.stringsmagazine.com
Profiles, reviews, and news for violin, viola, cello, bass, and fiddle players.

GEAR

Apollo's Axes
www.apollosaxes.com
Offers an amazing array of musical instruments and other components, such as strings, picks, and such. If you're looking to wow your friends with an exotic instrument (bagpipes, fifes, tamburas from India, percussion of all sorts), look no further!

BMC Music Source
www.bmcmusicsource.com
Offers wind instruments of all types as well as method books (how to learn the instrument), fingering charts, and other accessories.

The New School of American Music
www.pianofun.com
Offers basic workbooks, tapes, and one-day workshops.

Weiner Music Catalog
www.weinermusic.com or 800-622-CORK
Sells saxophones, clarinets, other instruments, and accessories such as stands, music, method books, reeds, mouthpieces, and cases.

EXTENDED MUSICAL COMMUNITY

Amateur Chamber Music Players (ACMP)
www.acmp.net
An international network of amateur musicians. Use their directory to set up playing dates while traveling, connect with other musicians in your area, and learn more about available groups, music, and performance opportunities.

Music for the Love of It
www.musicfortheloveofit.com
Offers a guide to music workshops around the U.S., Canada, and Europe for classical, choral, big band, and jazz musicians of all levels. They offer links to other sites and publications, practice tips, and other information.

Musical Passages
www.musicalpassages.org
Plans travel abroad for chamber music players, usually to Europe.

26

BE A RENAISSANCE GAL

★ art appreciation ★

A good spectator also CREATES.

—Swiss proverb

Imagine This . . . Some people wait their whole lives for inspiration to arrive—but not you, because you know exactly where to find it at your favorite local gallery or theater. For you the thrill is not only the gala events and opening nights. You'd be a patron of the arts regardless, just for the chance to witness true greatness on canvas, stage, or screen. And when you share your passion for the arts with others, the whole room seems to light up—there's no better way to get to know other interesting people than an informed, spirited conversation about film, music, or dance. With this badge, you'll get to know your local arts scene, find artists that move you, and keep inspiration in your life by becoming an arts patron. You claim you're not artistically inclined? Fiddlesticks! With the strength of your insight and conviction, you can change the course of culture. *You can do it!*

So, what's your motivation?
Take a moment.
Dream a little, think big,
and then complete this sentence:
I see myself . . .

The Payoffs

- **Endless possibilities.** As Bell Hooks says, the arts are here to tell it like it is and "imagine what is possible." Art lifts the blinders of our own experience, and opens up an entire universe of possibilities.
- **Wonder.** There's no better way to add color, texture, sound, and feeling to a humdrum day.
- **Connection.** Artists wouldn't bother unless they had something to say about how happy, sad, furious, or awestruck they are. When we have these feelings, art assures us that we aren't alone.
- **Visionary leadership.** By making it a point to see, support, and enliven the arts, you become the kind of cultural mover and shaker our society needs to evolve and thrive.

Meet Your Mentor

ALISON BING

What She Does: An art critic, writer, and culture commentator, Alison reviews art for the *San Francisco Chronicle, Artweek,* and sundry other publications and catalog essays; has provided commentary about art and documentary film for PBS and NPR; and has authored two books about writing for Barnes & Noble.

© Marco Marinucci

Why She Does It: "Even though I grew up outside a very small town (Centerville, Indiana), my parents took us kids everywhere to see shows—they'd drive hours just to take us to the Indianapolis Museum of Art or the Art Institute of Chicago and to see art-house films, dance, and theater in Ohio and Michigan. I found that art could change the way we see the world, and I went on to study art history and work for galleries and at the National Museum of Women in the Arts. Eventually I decided there had to be a way to effect cultural change on a larger scale, so I went to graduate school in international public policy—only to discover that deep change truly doesn't come from the top down but rather through those profound individual moments of transformation that art makes possible. Art is talking about us, so no wonder we take it personally! What we see on gallery walls and in theaters and performance spaces is saying something about who we are and what we believe. A lot of it is going to be around in a hundred years and stand as a record of who we were. So do you really want your culture determined by other people? By participating—going to see art, supporting what we think has value, and talking about it—we can define our world."

If you want art to say something to you, get out there and strike up a conversation with it. PARTICIPATE!

—Alison Bing

Word from the Wise: "You shouldn't really expect to like everything you see—but there's a lot to be gained from pieces you don't immediately respond to. Don't let it end there. Why don't you like it? What disturbs you? Does it remind you of something you don't want to be reminded of? Getting stirred up is good!"

BADGE STEPS

BUT IS IT ART?

Some opinions

"Life is very nice, but it lacks form. It's the aim of art to give it some."
—Jean Anouilh

"I never paint dreams or nightmares. I paint my own reality."
—Frida Kahlo

"Art is not living. It is the use of living."
—Audre Lorde

"Any authentic work of art must start an argument between the artist and his [sic] audience."
—Rebecca West

1. Make the art scene.

Webster's defines "Renaissance man" [sic] as "a person who has wide interests and is expert in several areas." To become a true Renaissance woman, you should taste test from the arts buffet—try film, theater, dance, the visual arts, music, photography, and architecture. Afterwards, you'll know what you want to go back to for seconds.

To get a sense of what's on the menu in your community, take a close look at the arts section of your local newspaper and free community or neighborhood publications. The reviews, ads, and calendar listings will tell you what museum shows, gallery openings, auctions, special film showings, live performances, and architectural tours are going on all around you.

Pick four diverse upcoming events (such as a photography show opening, an architectural walking tour, a modern dance recital, and a community theater production), including one that kind of intimidates you, and plan to attend. If possible, enlist a friend to accompany you. ***Make four hot dates with the arts.***

2. Learn to discern.

When you arrive on the art scene, it can be hard to know where to look first—there's a lot going on out there! So at each event you attend, use these pointers to get oriented:

- Look long and hard, not only at what you immediately love but also at what puzzles or even troubles you. After all, scary movies can be very troubling—but many people appreciate their drama and cathartic value. So don't be put off by the equivalent in, say, dance or photography. Let yourself be stretched.
- Ask questions. You'll become less intimidated that way, and you'll find that the people who work at and attend cultural events are usually delighted to share what they know with enthusiastic novices. Film and music lovers may have to wait for intermission or afterwards to ask questions, but keep a notebook handy to jot down your queries.
- Find out what other people see in art. When Alison took her six-year-old niece to the Art Institute of Chicago and asked her what she saw in a painting, she replied, "A cat on top of a house about to jump

on a bald man's head!" Alison saw a square and a triangle—which just goes to show how an honest, exuberant reaction can enliven your experience of art.

- Don't worry about seeing every inch of a museum or zoning out in the third act at the opera—just be sure you ask at least one question and compare notes with at least one other person at all four events you attend. Then make up your own mind about what you saw or heard. Did it appeal to you or not? Why or why not?

Attend your four chosen events, and form your own opinions about what you've seen.

3. Specialize.

As you become familiar with a variety of art forms, remember that no one has time to be an authority on all of them. Think about the four art-world excursions you just took, choose the one you enjoyed most, and focus on that art form for now.

Now that you've chosen your major, take your pick of approaches to art appreciation:

Explore your human resources. Ask friends and acquaintances who know something about your chosen art form who they think the five most important artists in a field are and why. This will help you get through information overload and may lead to fascinating discussions, too. Then check out work by each of these artists yourself—if not at a show, then perhaps in books, CDs, articles, or online—and share your opinions with your friends.

Attend lectures. As Alison points out, speakers often talk about their subjects much more accessibly than they would write about them in a journal or book. And as an added bonus, you'll probably meet kindred spirits in the audience.

Take a class. Check out college extension courses, art schools, and arts organizations and look closely at the course descriptions. You might choose a broad survey course or zero in on something very specific like Chinese cinema, photojournalism, or the golden age of Mexican mural painting.

Read up on the subject. Run a subject search on the Web and at your local library, and check out any and all books and magazines that appeal to you. For a few starter suggestions, check out Alison's Picks, page 215.

MEET YOUR CREATIVE MATCH

Being a patron of the arts can have its perks . . .

When a group of single women gathered for a chat about their relationship "deal breakers," one of them said that she didn't care what kind of music a potential mate loved, but that he had to love some kind of music. If you feel similarly, act on your interests and advertise your inclinations. Alison knows dozens of people who, like her, have made friends, met a significant other, and created an extended family with fellow art lovers. As she puts it, "Meeting through a shared interest in art is like being introduced by a friend." Alison bonded with a handsome artist in her Tae Kwon Do class over art—and nine years later, they're still together. "Never underestimate the power of a shared passion," she says.

Try at least one and preferably two of the above approaches, and you'll soon expand your arts expertise. ***Dig deeper.***

ALISON'S EXPERT TIPS

WAKE YOUR SENSES

- Volunteering as an usher guarantees you a spot at sold-out shows and offers a peek behind the scenes of memorable performances.
- Does your town, or one nearby, have an art-house cinema or host a film festival? These can be great places to see movies that will never make it to the mall.
- Tune your radio dial to a new station, and check out the specialty music and arts programs on your local college or public radio station.
- Don't wait for out-of-towners to play tourist in your town. Take a day off and take in as many architectural monuments as you can.
- Take a walking tour of the murals in your hometown—and if you notice scruffy old walls where there could be murals, take it up with your city council.

4. Be a Bluestocking.

The first Bluestockings were women who held salons to discuss their artistic and intellectual pursuits. These kinds of conversations are still an ideal way to celebrate and learn about the arts. So gather a group of women you know share your artistic inclinations, and invite them to invite a few others along to your first Bluestocking Salon.

Plan a salon evening around your art form of choice. If film strikes your fancy, you could invite fellow cinema buffs over for a movie night. For dance, you might plan to catch a flamenco performance with fellow Bluestockings and meet up afterwards for discussion. Just be sure you meet someplace you can hear one another and be as loud as you like.

To get your Bluestocking conversation started, try this technique that Alison suggests to get those critical and creative juices flowing. "If you have a strong reaction to a piece of art, keep it to yourself and ask your friends what they think of it. See what they say, and then respond. You'll soon see how impassioned and articulate you can be! Conversation, debate, and argument fulfill the intention of art. The worst thing a work can be is forgettable, not worthy of further thought or discussion." ***Create a culture klatch.***

SALON SCENARIOS

Three ways to cultivate cultivated conversations

Start a film club. Pick a director and rent all of her (or his) films, focus on a genre like film noir or neo-realism, or explore Iranian, Italian, or Japanese cinema. Read critical essays on the works you watch.

Get season tickets with a group of friends. If you invest in season tickets for your local opera company, symphony, ballet, or theater troupe, you'll probably be exposed to a variety of old, new, traditional, and experimental productions over the course of the season. Season-ticket holders often have special access to pre-performance lectures, rehearsals, and opportunities to meet the performers. Go out for dessert after performances with your fellow season-ticket holders, and compare notes.

Invite an expert to a salon evening in your home. Does a friend of a friend teach drama, make documentary films, or collect sculpture? This friend can be your Bluestocking Salon's guest lecturer for an evening.

5. Invest in the arts.

Now that you know how the arts can inspire you, naturally you'll want to do what you can to keep the inspiration coming—for yourself and for generations to come. Here's what you can do:

Attend a fundraiser. When you purchase tickets to a fundraising event for your local arts organizations, you'll have a fabulous evening ahead—and help ensure you'll have more art to look forward to.

Get an inspiration insurance policy. At the end of a hectic work week, we really need recharging—so why not set aside some money to pay for that symphony ticket when you need it most? Alison says, "Buying one or two works of art that will be a lifelong source of inspiration can cost less than what many people pay for cappuccinos in a year. Great art is a lot more uplifting than any coffee buzz—and it lasts longer, too!"

Be an angel investor. Filmmakers, artists, and theater and dance companies always need backers for daring new projects, and it could be only a matter of a modest investment that makes or breaks a masterpiece. If you love performances, just imagine the satisfaction of sitting front and center at a world premiere knowing you made it possible.

Volunteer. Lend your time and talents to the arts by writing or designing a brochure, hosting a fundraising event, or volunteering to bring a musical group or art exhibition to a detention center or nursing facility.

Decide which of the above works for you, then make your move to keep the art you love in your life. Once art has shown you how much more there is to life than the daily grind, it's hard to imagine a more worthwhile calling than to share that moment of awestruck discovery with others. ***Follow your bliss—make a contribution and become an art patron.***

CONGRATULATIONS!

You've graduated from newcomer to connoisseur, found your inspiration, and made your mark on culture. You did it!

I DID IT!

Name: ______________________________

Date: ______________________________

I DID IT!

"I got a writing class assignment to go somewhere I'd normally not go and write about it. For me, this was my local museum of modern art. I nervously made my way through its many floors and tried to figure out why these works were in a museum while my nephew's finger paintings were only on the fridge. Then I stumbled into a room filled with feminist art that put things like big-rig mud flaps, rape whistles, and sanitary napkins to all kinds of playful and provocative uses. I loved it and would never have known that such art existed if I hadn't screwed up my courage to walk in the door."
—Dina

WHERE'S THE POPCORN?

"Two of my favorite things about going to the movies are the coming attractions and the popcorn. The first time I went to see a movie at Berkeley's Pacific Film Archive, I was bewildered to find no popcorn anywhere near the place. The theater felt like a museum. There was even a professor at a podium in front of the screen to give a short lecture before the lights went down—and when they did, there were no previews. It was actually a cool experience and I go there all the time now—making sure I eat first!"
—Marisa

COLLECTING SAVVY

Be smart about buying art

- If you see an artwork in a gallery that appeals to you, ask the gallerist if there's any other work by that artist in the back room. You never know what else you might find! And if the work you like best is sold or more than you can afford, ask the gallerist to keep an eye out for similar or smaller pieces by that artist, and ask about payment plans.
- In terms of monetary value, work by established and mid-career artists is more expensive and may keep more steady value over time, but art by emerging artists can be great bargains and may soar in value as the artist becomes more established.
- Think twice before haggling with an artist. Consider how you'd like it if your boss came to you and said: "Wow, you've done outstanding work here—but I only feel like paying you half your salary." You'd still need to feed yourself and your family, and so do artists! Pay the asking price or get a less expensive piece, and you'll have a pleasant transaction to recall every time you admire your art.
- Limited-edition photographs and fine art prints can be a great value. Etchings, woodcuts, and classic silver gelatin print photographs are time-intensive artworks created by hand mostly in small editions, so they tend to be more valuable than computer-generated Iris prints and photographs reproduced in larger editions.

BEYOND THE BADGE

If you love it as much as you thought you would, dream on . . .

- **Build a personal collection.** "If you wisely invest in beauty," said Frank Lloyd Wright, "it will remain with you all the days of your life." Alison considers it especially important to collect artists who are living and working today, because a collector's vote of confidence can help ensure that they keep making art in the years to come. As she says: "The Impressionists aren't exactly counting on your purchase to pay the electricity bill, and Chagall is pretty well established by now!" Alison also cautions that "If you don't truly enjoy what you buy and are only interested in its investment value, you might as well hang a stock certificate on the wall." So know what you're buying—educate yourself about the light-fastness of various types of photographs and prints, for instance—but above all else, buy work that amazes and awes you. Buy or commission affordable works by emerging local artists, save up for an editioned print, photograph, or sculpture by a mid-career artist, or splurge on a one-of-a-kind piece by an established artist.
- **Take a field trip.** Look beyond the usual suspects of New York, Paris, and London, and follow your passion wherever it leads you. Go to Ashland, Oregon, for its Shakespeare festival, study quilts in Paducah, Kentucky (a.k.a. Quilt City, USA), or follow Alison's favorite route in Mexico City and discover exceptional contemporary photography, prints, and sculpture at the Museo Rufino Tamayo, Centro de la Imagen, Museo de la Estampa, and Galería el Estudio.
- **Be a critic.** Writing down your impressions is a great way to get the most out of the experience of art and keep those memories with you. So keep a notebook handy to jot down your reactions, and note performers, directors, or artists you want to see more of—or avoid at all cost!—in the future. If something you see really gets you thinking, write a review of it and send it around to your e-mail list or submit it for publication to invite others into the conversation. "If you really like or dislike what art has to say to you, say something back!" says Alison. "Don't let an intriguing conversation drop right there." And if you disagree or agree strongly with a review you read, write a letter to the editor and say so. "Never let the critic get the last word!" says Alison.

ALISON'S PICKS

BOOKS

5001 Nights at the Movies by Pauline Kael
An anthology of reviews by the legendary movie critic.

The Grove Book of Art Writing: Brilliant Words on Art from Pliny the Elder to Damien Hirst by Karen Wright and Martin Gaylord
Inside takes on the art world—arguments, scandals, censorship, and all.

Nobody's Perfect: Writings from The New Yorker by Anthony Lane
Movie reviews by *The New Yorker* critic; spare, honest writing with insight and humor.

The Oxford Companion to Jazz by Bill Kirchner (editor)
Sixty essays by notable performers, writers, and scholars.

A Short History of Music by Alfred Einstein
Find out why Albert's brother Alfred is considered a genius in his own right with this concise book of music history from ancient Egypt through Béla Bartók.

Theories and Documents of Contemporary Art: A Sourcebook of Artists' Writings by Kristine Stiles and Peter Selz
An excellent sampling of artists' thoughts, including Marcel Duchamp on readymades, architect Maya Lin on surfaces, and Karen Finley on art and performance.

MAGAZINES

Artforum
www.artforum.com
Be sure to check out the online version for breaking news, reviews of current shows, and lively discussion forums.

Artweek
www.artweek.com
Take a tour of the West Coast art scene with reviews, news, and features.

Camerawork
www.sfcamerawork.org
Provocative thinking about provocative photographs.

Cineaste
www.cineaste.com
Wonderful film essays and in-depth interviews with the leading lights of cinema.

Contemporary
www.contemporary-magazine.com
British visual arts magazine with sharp thinking and plucky reviews.

Down Beat
www.downbeat.com
Like a classic jazz standard, this venerable jazz magazine always seems fresh.

Dwell
www.dwellmag.com
For lovers of modern architecture, this mag is an absolute fetish.

Kitchen Sink
www.kitchensinkmag.com
"The magazine for people who think too much," with independent thinking on art, film, literature, and music.

The New Yorker
www.newyorker.com
Pithy reviews plus in-depth features on architecture, dance, art, film, theater, and more.

Village Voice
www.villagevoice.com
Every issue takes issue with film, art, music, and more, with pithy, provocative articles.

WEB SITES

www.artnet.com
Event listings, news, reviews, and a database of 1,300 galleries and 16,000 artists.

www.artsjournal.com
The latest news and ideas from the art world; covers dance, music, theater, visual arts, and then some.

www.imdb.com
Comprehensive database every film buff should bookmark.

www.pbs.org
Check out the streaming video and behind-the-scenes looks at documentaries from the acclaimed PBS series *P.O.V.* and *FRONTLINE/World,* plus show times for *SPARK.*

www.sfgate.com/eguide/epicks/#art
San Francisco Chronicle ePicks; check out Alison's latest art picks every week.

27

GET WELL-READ

★ book lover ★

> Life-transforming ideas have always come to me through BOOKS.
>
> – bell hooks

Imagine This . . . You've run through all the usual small-talk topics—what do you do, where are you from, the weather . . . and just as the conversation is tapering off, you mention the terrific book you've just read. Suddenly a light goes on in the eyes of the person you've been chatting with casually, and the ultimate bonding words are spoken in a low, breathless voice: "I . . . loved . . . that . . . book!" Fast friendships are formed between people who recognize that a great book is more than a few well-chosen words—it's an experience that changes what you know, who you are, and what you believe. So put yourself at the top of your to-do list for once, and give yourself the rewarding experience of curling up with a selection of good books hand-picked for your reading pleasure. Settle into your favorite chair with a mug of cocoa, open to page one, and prepare to be illuminated. *You can do it!*

So, what's your motivation?
Take a moment.
Dream a little, think big,
and then complete this sentence:
I see myself . . .

The Payoffs

- **A window.** Books allow you to see the world in a completely different light, and offer a breath of fresh air when life as you know it seems a little stale.
- **A door**. Great literature is a glowing sign that shows you a way out of dark times, and ushers you into a bright realm of possibilities.
- **A castle.** Life's not always a fairy tale, but it's got to have a little magic! A great novel lets down the drawbridge, and invites you into a realm of wonder.
- **A world.** There is no barrier or border that can stop an avid reader from exploring new territory. If you don't think you can circle the globe and travel through time, then you just haven't found the right book yet.

Meet Your Mentor
CATHY LANGER

What She Does: Cathy is a buyer at Tattered Cover, the famed Denver, Colorado, independent bookstore that has earned an international reputation for selecting and promoting distinctive books by lesser-known authors that go on to gain widespread literary acclaim. Cathy is former president of the Mountains and Plains Booksellers Association and the Colorado Center for the Book, and is currently on the board of the American Booksellers Association. She feels blessed to have a job that brings her into contact with other rabid readers and gracious, gifted writers.

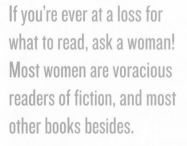

Why She Does It: "Reading was always a respite for me. I grew up in Washington, D.C., where it's really hot in the summer—and since I only had air conditioning in my bedroom, I shut myself in my room and read all summer. I went to the library every week and checked out the maximum number of books. Then when I was a teenager and wanting to be reclusive, I found I could hide behind a book. I took reading for granted until I was out of college, realized I had to do something for a living, and started thinking about law school. I was working in a law firm one summer, and when I complained to a friend that the work wasn't as interesting as I'd imagined, she suggested that I interview at Tattered Cover. I remember Joyce Meskis, the owner, asking me if I thought I could commit to a year because there was a lot of training involved, and I had to think about it before I said yes—when you're 22, a year seems like a long time. That was 1977. When you find a book you believe in and you get to see its effect on other people, that's an experience that bears repeating."

If you're ever at a loss for what to read, ask a woman! Most women are voracious readers of fiction, and most other books besides.

—Cathy Langer

Word to the Wise: "Even a small bookstore can be so visually stimulating that it's fairly daunting—but don't panic! Just head straight to the desk and ask staff for help. Believe me, there's nothing we enjoy more than the challenge of helping you find your dream book."

BADGE STEPS

BOOK BUFFET

What strikes your fancy?

African-American History
The Ancient Greeks
Armchair Travel
Art History
Buddhist Poetry
Christian Theology
The Civil War
Eastern Philosophy
English Mysteries
First Novels
Gunslingers
Latin American Poetry
Legal Thrillers
Literary Memoirs
Literary Science
Medieval History
Middle Eastern Politics
Natural History
The Occult
Presidential Biographies
Psychology
Pulitzer Prize Winners
Pulp Fiction
Science Fiction
Shakespeare
Short Stories
Social Commentary
True Crime
Women's Fiction
Young Adult Fantasy

1. Pick your subject.

Being well-read means different things to different people. It usually assumes some depth in a specific subject area or breadth across an "established" list of classics. But there is no right or wrong to reading, just as there is no right or wrong to any great love affair. The purpose of this badge is to open doors to a lifetime enriched by reading on your own terms, without literary presumption or prejudice. You can read whatever you like, and as much (or little) as you like, so long as you stay true to the call of what really interests and delights you. This is the real secret to becoming well-read.

In this badge, you will read one classic, one wildly popular book, and one "sleeper hit" that you discover on your own—but which ones? Good question. Even for lifelong booklovers, it can be hard to get past the piles of new arrivals in the front of your local bookstore or library to find the books that really interest you.

"You need to know what your goal is walking in," says Cathy. "Think about your real motivation for becoming well-read. Is there an area, genre, period, or author that's always intrigued you? Something you're dying to know more about? Years ago I discovered I had a hunger for spiritual texts. I was brought up in an agnostic household with no regular worship practice, no religious education, no vacation Bible school—and as a young adult, I realized if I ever was going to get all those Bible references and allusions you're supposed to get in books, I'd have to read up on the subject."

So give it some thought: What do you hunger for? ***Choose your subject.***

2. Go blank.

Make the first book you buy a sturdy and attractive blank book that will become your reading journal. This is how you'll remember which titles intrigue you while browsing, which ones you've been meaning to read for ages, and—most important of all—what you think of the books you read. In addition to your own thoughts, compare notes with reviewers to see if you agree with their assessments of the books you've read. "Just because critics get paid for their opinions, doesn't make them more valid than yours," says Cathy.

Your reading journal can also become what's known as a "commonplace book," a place in which you copy out the phrases or passages you want to remember from your reading. "Often you'll come across a phrase in a book that reaches your heart, something that makes you think, 'This is so important, I'm going to remember it forever!'" says Cathy. "But we just don't. Who can possibly remember the last five years' worth of words they've read? Keeping a book journal reminds you what you've gleaned from a book, so that it really does stay with you."

Lastly, if you have designs on collecting, donating, or trading your wares at used bookstores, using a book journal will preserve the resale value of your books. Best of all, it ensures that you'll never lose track of your great ideas again, even if you lose track of your books! Once you get your book journal going, you'll find it hard to imagine a literary life without one! ***Buy and begin your book journal.***

3. Read something tried and true.

In any field there's at least one book everyone admires and refers to, but few people have taken the time to read cover to cover. You're about to become one of that select few.

"Start with something that is high-profile, tried and true," recommends Cathy. "Pick a classic within the subject that interests you most." If you're not sure what qualifies as a "genuine" classic, Cathy suggests checking out the "100 Best" lists offered by the Modern Library and the Radcliffe Publishing Course, as well as prize-winners (see Cathy's Picks, page 223, for links to awards lists for fiction, fantasy, mysteries, and more). You can ask your favorite bookstore clerk, reference librarian, or a like-minded enthusiast for help, and most bookstores and libraries also feature book group sections, which often offer a sampling of books that are widely considered classics.

Once you find your classic, spend a few rainy afternoons reading it at your local café. Then check out the Web for serious reviews and compare notes in your book journal. No need to wear a beret—you're looking like literati already! ***Find out for yourself what makes a classic.***

4. Join the crowd.

When you read a book so popular that you spot three people on your commute carrying it, or hear the author on your favorite radio show, or keep bumping into reviews of it in magazines, you join a real-time

WHERE THE BOOKS ARE

Go visiting

Bookstores. A favorite bookstore can be a respite as well as a resource. Take some downtime hours to explore the stores near you. Find the one with the most knowledgeable and friendly clerks, and hang out long enough to know their names, chat a bit, and get the lay of the land. Check out the bulletin boards for upcoming events. Your local Yellow Pages may turn up the perfect specialty bookstore as well, and be sure to visit some used bookstores; these are a great source for cheap buys, out-of-print treasures, and trades.

Libraries. Visit several different library branches in your vicinity. Chat (quietly!) with a librarian or two. Where do you find the best selection, advice, reading chairs? Check out the bulletin boards for exhibits, author appearances, and other special events.

Go online. Even if you are already familiar with online booksellers, spend a few minutes browsing their Web sites to see what people are reading generally, and in your specific area. Reader's recommendations can be entertaining and informative—check them out (and add your own as you go through this badge!) **Tip:** Many authors have their own Web sites, which contain tour information, biographical information, news of forthcoming books, and the occasional readers' forum. Most publisher's Web sites feature extensive online catalogs, and many have "subsites" and online newsletters for specialized subject areas.

I DID IT!

"I always said I hated poetry, but what I really had was fear of poetry! (I think I was traumatized by some required memorization and recitation in junior high!) Then I saw the movie *Sylvia,* about the poet Sylvia Plath. I got really interested in learning more about her life, and as I read a couple of biographies about her, I got introduced to her poems. I learned that all poetry is not like the stuff that made no sense to me in school, the stuff that seemed to be written in a foreign language. Some of it speaks to me. Who knew?"

—Janet

SO MUCH FOR SHAKESPEARE

"About two years ago I decided I was going to read all of Shakespeare in order, because I felt that if this is the best writing in the English language, I really have to read it. Let me tell you, the first five plays are not easy, and I got completely bogged down somewhere in the middle of *Henry VI* parts I, II, and III. I've read ten plays so far, and there are about thirty to go. A lot of the comedies read like sitcoms, and in the tragedies and historical plays, basically everyone dies by being impaled by their best friends. I just don't feel compelled to get through it, but every few months I dutifully give it another try—and my husband teases me, 'How's that Shakespeare coming along?'"

—Debbie

cultural conversation. It's time to find out what everyone's reading—and raving about—even if it's only tangentially connected to your "specialty." This time, don't rely on award winners; broaden your scope by consulting other kinds of recommendations. Follow Cathy's advice for gaining a little assurance before you select your second book:

Hit the lists. Browse bestseller lists in-store, online, and in print (in magazines, journals, or newspaper book review sections). Books hit the lists for a reason! Consider books that might be great fun to read, even if they're a bit far afield from your subject.

Ask the experts. Ask your favorite bookstore clerk or librarian what their ten bestsellers are and what's new and hot in your area of interest. Is there any overlap? Are any of them "staff picks"?

Eavesdrop. Listen to the water-cooler buzz. Ask five friends and/or colleagues what they (or their reading group) are reading.

Sneak a peek. Try to stay open to recommendations outside your normal comfort zone, but do read the first few pages to see if you like the writing style. As Cathy says, "If I'm not hooked in the beginning, it's not happening."

Read what others are reading.

5. Discover a hidden gem.

What really distinguishes a well-read woman is her well-rounded taste in books. "Many of us who read a lot fall into a pattern of what we read," Cathy says. "We need to make sure we step out of our normal bounds every few books." To find a sleeper hit of a book on the subject that interests you most, check out:

Events at your local bookstore. Local bookstores are likely to offer readings by local and emerging authors, giving you the chance to discover unsung talent and hear authors describe their work in their own words.

Staff Picks. "Staff Picks" sections in bookstores often come with synopses and brief reviews by staff. "Most booksellers have no patience for books they're not captivated by," explains our expert, "so when we attach our names to a title, it means something."

Book reviews. To find out what books are generating the best buzz, check out some reviews in your local newspaper or your favorite magazine (see Cathy's Picks, page 223, for some of her favorite review sources). "Anytime you see a book reviewed favorably in more than one place, that's a good tip it might be worth your time," she says.

Anthologies. These are a great way to sample writings by a variety of authors on a specific subject, from a particular part of the country or the world, in a particular literary genre, or within a specific year (see Cathy's Picks).

Jackets. Spend a rainy afternoon deep in the stacks at your local bookstore or library. Go ahead and break the rules; do judge a book by its cover if the title, flap copy, or the reviewer's comments appeal to you.

Read a lesser-known find of your own.

6. Read on.

"If you're like most book lovers, you'll feel uneasy if you don't have at least one—if not two or three—books lined up to read when you're done with your current book," says Cathy. So look over the reading lists you've compiled in your book journal, and seek out three of the most appealing titles at your local library or bookstore.

To stay on top of the latest and greatest literature, Cathy recommends subscribing to one or two literary magazines and/or journals. See Cathy's Picks for a list of her favorites, or browse the magazine rack at your local bookstore to find your own.

Once you load up your nightstand with three books and a couple of literary magazines, you'll never be at a loss for what to read before bed . . . but with so much terrific reading material, you might not want to sleep! ***Stockpile a few books and magazines . . . and read on.***

CONGRATULATIONS!

Aren't you the bookish babe? Take a bow, bibliophile. You did it!

I DID IT!

Name: ______________________________

Date: ______________________________

READERS, DIGESTING

Get the most out of your read

Ever begin a book with great gusto, only to lose your appetite around page 67? Savor your book from start to finish with a few hints from our expert:

- Turn off the TV. You'll be surprised how much reading you can get done.
- Vintage Anchor, Penguin, and many other publishers offer reading and discussion guides to their books on their Web sites. These will help you follow along and get the most out of your book.
- Take a break. When you've read a book that means a great deal to you, sometimes it's hard to move on. If you find yourself dragging, try a "palate cleanser"—a comedy, rollicking adventure, or light mystery that allows you to savor the book you've just read and whets your appetite for the next.
- If you really don't like what you're reading, find another book! Life is too short.

BEYOND THE BADGE

If you love it as much as you thought you would, dream on . . .

- **Champion a book.** If you suspect other people would love your new favorite book, tell them so! Write a review and circulate it to your e-mail list, and consider submitting it for publication to the arts editor of your local newspaper, neighborhood newsletter, or free weekly paper. You'll be doing others a favor by recommending a good book, and yourself too, says Cathy: "When you explain succinctly why a book is important, it helps you explore what it means to you, and allows it to live in your memory that much longer."
- **Join a book group.** While the act of reading is solitary, many readers also find their reading is enriched through discussion. Chatting with a group of people who have all just read the same book, you'll get new perspectives and find your own sharpened as you debate or defend your interpretation. Group members often take turns suggesting titles to read and groups can have any kind of agenda they like—reading female novelists, reading in a genre, spending several months on a challenging work and inviting an expert to sit in, etc. Look for flyers at your local bookstore or start your own! Local bookstores, libraries, and newspapers often sponsor their own book groups, and there are also online groups, if you prefer. See Cathy's Picks for book group resources.
- **Re-read.** Book lovers don't spend all their time looking for something new and exciting to read. Some regularly return to old favorites. When you re-read a book you loved ten years ago, you bring your new life experiences to it and often gain a deeper appreciation for the book. You might sympathize or identify with a character you once "didn't get." You might interpret the ending differently. And then again, you may find that years later *The Fountainhead* no longer fires you up or Heathcliff seems like a heel. Discover what response an old favorite elicits in you now.
- **Book lovers, unite!** At fairs and festivals all over the country, readers and writers meet to discuss, debate, and share their passion for books. These events usually feature writers reading from their latest books, onstage interviews, book signings, Q&A sessions, great bargains in publishers' booths, and books hot off the presses just waiting to be discovered. See Living It Up with the Literati for some of Cathy's favorites.

LIVING IT UP WITH THE LITERATI

Cathy recommends these literary events

Local book festivals. These abound in almost every state, and are generally held in the spring or the fall. Check *Publishers Weekly* for listings of upcoming festivals.

Los Angeles Times Festival of Books. America's largest literary event, with two days of lectures, signings, storytelling, and writers' workshops. www.latimes.com/extras/festivalofbooks.

Miami Book Fair International. An entire week of literary events with hundreds of thousands of fellow book lovers—Cathy calls this one "incredible!" www.miamibookfair.com.

New York Is Book Country. A highly rated fair with hundreds of authors, hundreds of publishers and small presses, and a quarter of a million book lovers taking over the streets of New York. www.nyisbookcountry.com.

Writers Respond to Readers. Tattered Cover's own annual event features four authors whose book has just come out in paperback spending an entire day reading and responding to a small audience of about one hundred readers. www.tatteredcover.com.

CATHY'S PICKS

PRIZED BOOKS

www.literature-awards.com
In addition to the major literary awards, this site offers links to more specialized awards in dozens of categories, including science fiction, children's books, and more. Each site features a complete list of past award winners.

LITERARY MAGAZINES

The Believer
www.believermag.com
This monthly mag features contemporary writers writing about books, and their innerconnectivity to popular culture, politics, art, and music.

Granta: The Magazine of New Writing
www.granta.com
Luminary contributors tackling important and difficult subjects.

Iowa Review
www.uiowa.edu/~iareview
Published by the University of Iowa, home of the famed Iowa Writer's Workshop.

McSweeney's
www.mcsweeneys.net
Brainchild of Dave Eggers (*A Heartbreaking Work of Staggering Genius*). The spine of Volume 11 sports the following comment: "We are as surprised as you are."

The New Yorker
www.newyorker.com/
Fill your own Daytimer with poetry and articles from this esteemed literary publication.

BOOK REVIEWS

Bloomsbury Review
www.bloomsburyreview.com
Reviews books outside the mainstream and more regional books too; "a great place to find small-press gems," Cathy reports.

The New York Times Book Review
www.nytimes.com/pages/books
Cathy's favorite. You can subscribe online for free on their site.

Poets & Writers
www.pw.org/mag
Get wind of forthcoming books and what authors have to say about them; available online for free.

Publishers Weekly
www.publishersweekly.com
Reviews and sneak previews of forthcoming books.

Ruminator Review
www.ruminator.com/hmr
Covers books from small and independent presses.

Your favorite magazines and local newspaper
"Once you start looking for them, you'll find book reviews everywhere you look," says Cathy.

READING GROUPS RESOURCES

Good Books Lately: The One-Stop Resource for Book Groups and Other Greedy Readers by Ellen Moore and Kira Stevens
Everything you need to know to start your own book group (or enliven an existing one!). Great book lists, too!

You can also check out **The Reading Group Book, The Reader's Choice,** and **A Year of Reading** for additional reading group lists.

And for more inspiration:

Books That Changed the World by Robert B. Downs
The Bible, the *Iliad*, the *Republic*, *Civil Disobedience, Das Kapital, Silent Spring,* and many more.

How to Read a Book by Mortimer J. Adler and Charles Van Doren
Originally published in 1940, this classic on reading comprehension guides readers at all stages on how to read literature, history, poetry, and all kinds of nonfiction.

The New Lifetime Reading Plan: The Classical Guide to World Literature by Clifton Fadiman and John S. Major
This "classic about classics" has been in print for over forty years.

The Reading List Contemporary Fiction: A Critical Guide to the Complete Works of 110 Authors by David Rubel (editor)
Rubel illuminates the work of current novelists—each entry includes critical commentary on the author's published fiction by prominent reviewers, as well as thematic and plot synopses, and a short biography.

So Many Books, So Little Time: A Year of Passionate Reading by Sara Nelson
A memoir from the *Glamour* magazine contributing editor who set out to read a book a week for a year. What she finds is great rewards, deep frustrations, and that books chose her as much as she chose them.

28

DINE IN

★ cooking ★

One cannot think well, love well, sleep well, if one has not DINED well.

—Virginia Woolf

So, what's your motivation?
Take a moment.
Dream a little, think big,
and then complete this sentence:
I see myself . . .

Imagine This . . . When afternoon turns to evening and stomachs start to growl, you invite your friends to stay for supper—and bowl them over with your baked ziti. After dinner at your neighbor's house, you go home and plan a meal to return the favor. When you get an invitation to a potluck, you can't wait to prepare the Provençal potatoes you've perfected. Heck, you even get a kick out of hosting holidays for a standing-room-only crowd of family and friends. How did someone who used to find cooking for people intimidating turn into such a gracious gourmet chef? By keeping a panic-proof pantry, learning to rustle up a few reliable dishes, and refining your repertoire. Grab an apron. *You can do it!*

The Payoffs

- **Soul food.** Food may not be love, but you don't have to be an Italian mama or Jewish grandmother to know that a plate of scrumptious pasta or a steaming bowl of homemade chicken soup can warm anyone's heart.
- **Cash in pocket.** Dinner for six for less than $50. Need we say more?
- **Everyday creativity.** Cooking offers rewarding challenges and triumphs you can truly savor. When you succeed in blending colors, tastes, and textures artistically on a plate or magically whip up something out of just about nothing, it can turn your entire day around.
- **The good life.** Opening your home, sharing a meal, and lingering at the table chatting—now that's living!

Meet Your Mentor
SALLY SAMPSON

What She Does: Moves with ease from computer to Cuisinart. The author of numerous cookbooks including *The $50 Dinner Party: 26 Dinners that Won't Break Your Bank, Your Back, or Your Schedule,* Sally owned and ran From the Night Kitchen gourmet take-out in Brookline, Massachusetts, for nine years, writes about food for publications including the *Boston Globe, Bon Appétit,* and *Food & Wine,* and cofounded Sampsons Nuts with her husband, Mark.

Why She Does It: "When I was fourteen I became a vegetarian and stayed that way for ten years. My mother let me know that she wasn't going to do anything special to accommodate this, and that I should learn how to cook. While I had always liked cooking and my mother wasn't about to let me starve, I did learn more and more. I cooked a ton in college—for myself, for roommates, for my boyfriend. When I was twenty-five, I opened my gourmet shop. I loved making soup, and this wound up being the most popular thing in the shop and the subject of my first book. Every time I ate something, I imagined it as a soup! People are really intimidated by the idea of making soup, but it is really one of the easiest—and most forgiving—things you can cook. It's a lot easier than chocolate chip cookies, for instance."

Word from the Wise: "If a dish flops, order a pizza—or just give the dish a new name. I was at a friend's house once, and she made a soufflé that didn't work out. It tasted great, though, so I told her to call it something else!"

You should cook
because you love to,
and entertain because
you want to be with your friends.

—Sally Sampson

BADGE STEPS

1. Stock your pantry.

Having a well-stocked pantry, refrigerator, and freezer cuts down on your entertaining advance work and helps you heed the call of impromptu get-togethers. Consult Sally's Staples, and each time you shop over the next month, pick up some of the staples Sally swears by. ***Stock up on staples.***

2. Get equipped with the tools of the trade.

Sally insists that the best chefs don't necessarily have the best equipment. Much of what you need can be found in perfectly good condition at flea markets and garage sales—with the notable exception of knives, which should be bought sharp and kept sharp. If kitchenware seems like an investment, just think of how much you'll be saving by cooking at home instead of eating out! And if you're not about to get married just so you can score some decent kitchen equipment, consider creating a wish list of kitchen supplies at an online retailer so that your friends and relatives can get you something you need and want for your birthday or holiday gifts. Shoot for:

Prep gear. Glass and stainless steel mixing bowls, cutting board, stainless steel colander.

Knives. Eight-inch serrated for bread, ten-inch carving, four-inch paring, six-inch cook's, eight-inch chef's; plus poultry shears, knife rack, and knife-sharpening steel.

Other utensils. Rubber spatulas, wooden spoons, ladle, whisk, slotted spoon, stainless steel measuring cups and spoons, can opener, cheese grater, garlic press, lemon zester, stainless steel skewers, vegetable peeler, wooden citrus juicer.

Appliances and gadgets. Blender and/or food processor, grill, grill pan for the oven or hibachi with flue, kitchen timer, meat thermometer and oven thermometer, pepper grinder, salad spinner.

Cooking pots and pans. Nonstick shallow roasting pan, stockpot, two- and three-quart saucepans, eight- and ten-inch skillet or sauté pan, nine-inch cast iron skillet (check garage sales!), deep roasting pan with rack, eight-inch square baking pan, nine-by-twelve-inch baking pan, baking sheet without sides, bundt pan.

Get the goods you need to make good in the kitchen.

SALLY'S STAPLES, PART I

Larder essentials

Herbs and spices. Buy the best you can afford in small amounts, and use them within a year. Spices used often in contemporary American crossroads cuisine include: basil, bay leaves, caraway seeds, cardamom, cayenne pepper, chili powder, ground cinnamon, ground cumin, curry powder, fennel seeds, garlic, ginger, marjoram, nutmeg, Greek oregano, Hungarian sweet paprika, rosemary, tarragon, thyme, crushed red pepper flakes, and black and white pepper.

Fruits and vegetables. Including apples, carrots, celery, lemons, limes, potatoes, red onions, shallots, Spanish onions.

Canned goods. Beans, including chickpeas, dark red kidney beans, and white cannelini or navy beans; chicken and vegetable broth; whole plum and chopped tomatoes; tomato paste; anchovies packed in oil; capers in brine; assorted black and green olives.

3. Create your menu.

Why do meals out taste so great? Maybe because professional chefs put even more time and thought into menu planning than they do into execution. So make like a pro, and give yourself license to imagine, research, and experiment with your menu.

Before you start thumbing through cookbooks and gourmet magazines, consider which ingredients are most readily available and which are off-limits. Remember that while just about any kind of meat, fish, or produce can be found just about anywhere these days, using ingredients that are in season saves money and tends to make food more flavorful. And as Sally points out, "It's smart to ask guests in advance about anything they can't or don't eat, because you want them to be able to enjoy the food and not have to pick things out. My husband and I and three other couples have a dinner group that meets several times a year. One woman has a list of things she can't eat because she has rosacea, I have migraines so I have a different list, and one of the other women is on the Atkins diet!"

To make sure your delicious meal goes off without a hitch, invite enough guests to fill a table for four and ask them each to RSVP with any dietary restrictions. And even if you owe them a dinner, skip people who make you nervous or who you feel you have to impress. You'll have plenty of opportunity to wow them later!

For starters, aim for a delicious and balanced meal, with the following menu modified as necessary to accommodate seasonal items or dietary restrictions:

- Appetizer—see Sally's Expert Tips, page 228, for hints.
- Chicken and potatoes *or* a pasta dish. At future meals, fish, beef, etc., can be substituted for chicken; rice or couscous for potatoes; and hearty soup or stew for pasta.
- Vegetable or side salad.
- Bread—store-bought or home-baked.
- Wine—see Know Your Best Cellars, page 232.
- Dessert—store-bought, baked, or some assembly required; see Sally's Expert Tips.
- Coffee and/or tea.

Now it's time to find recipes that fit the bill. Resources include friends and family, cookbooks and magazines, and, in this online age, Epicurious

SALLY'S STAPLES, PART 2

More larder essentials

Sauces and condiments. Canola oil, extra virgin olive oil and regular olive oil; balsamic, white wine, and red wine vinegars; Dijon mustard and whole grain mustard; assorted chutneys; light and dark soy sauce; red and white wines. (Hint: Cook with wines you would drink.)

Pasta, rice, and crackers. Bread sticks; assorted crackers; dried pasta in various shapes and sizes; white, basmati, and Arborio rice.

Foods to freeze. Cut-up chicken, unsalted butter, vanilla ice cream, pecans, and walnuts (to maintain freshness).

Cheeses. Pecorino and Parmigiano-Reggiano—in chunks, not pregrated.

Baking staples. Baking powder and soda; unsweetened and semisweet chocolate, plus semisweet chips and unsweetened cocoa powder; unbleached, all-purpose flour; unsulfured molasses plus pomegranate molasses; old-fashioned rolled oats; white and brown sugar; vanilla extract.

I DID IT!

"I've worked as a caterer, prep cook for a PBS cooking show, and commercial food stylist. I also got to combine my love of food and rock and roll by cooking for musicians and crew backstage at the Warfield theater in San Francisco. Some musicians (Leonard Cohen, Bonnie Raitt) complimented the catering on-stage! But the moments that gave me the greatest satisfaction were when crew members would inevitably take the time to tell us our food was 'the best on the tour.' The backstage area felt like an extension of my living room. It was like hosting a really big dinner party several times a month!"

—Donna

PASS THE WATER!

"When I was in Italy, one of my aunts gave me a jar of the secret ingredient in her perfect spaghetti sauce: red pepper flakes. When I got home, I prepared an 'authentic' meal for my boyfriend. I put a few too many of those harmless-looking little flakes in, and after a few bites we were fighting over the S. Pellegrino water!"

—Francesca

(www.epicurious.com), which archives recipes from publications including *Gourmet* and *Bon Appétit*. Think about chicken or pasta dishes you've eaten and loved, beware of time-consuming or intricate techniques, and make sure that the ingredients of each recipe are available and affordable.

Look around until you find two recipes for each dish on the menu—and don't feel obliged to stick to one cookbook, either. "When I want to make something for the first time, I consult four or five cookbooks," says Sally. "Let's say I want to make beef stew. I might find that one recipe browns the beef in bacon fat. If I don't want that much fat, I move on. Another might use turnips, and since I really love turnips, I'll keep that one in mind." ***Put the mmmmm in menu.***

SALLY'S EXPERT TIPS

SCRATCH THAT

"Cooking a meal from scratch, from soup to nuts, is really hard, and not at all necessary," says Sally. "I would never bake my own bread, and I often use or tweak store-bought components."

For instance:

Appetizers. Serve a few dips, some marinated olives, flavored nuts, and a few cheeses. Put out toasted bread, bread sticks, crudités, and crackers, and let guests graze. You can find delicious premade hummus, salsa, and guacamole, or do something as easy as blend chopped scallions and curry powder into store-bought cream cheese and chutney.

Dessert. Set out vanilla ice cream and a variety of make-your-own-sundae toppings, or serve a plate of bakery cookies with grapes and melon slices.

4. Try out your recipes.

Now that you have two recipe options for each dish, you'll want to put them to the cooking test to determine the winners. But before you slice, dice, or boil, create a recipe box or journal to contain the secrets to your soon-to-be-signature dishes. Sally started her recipe book in college: "I would make something and then it went in the book, with notations about any adjustments I made to the recipe or ideas for doing so in the future. Now I keep these kinds of notes on my computer." Having one place where you note what you've cooked and how it turned out helps you build up a supply of signature dishes.

Try each of the recipes you've selected. As you test recipes, feel free to improvise a little. If a recipe calls for cilantro and you hate cilantro, try something like basil instead—and note your substitution in your recipe journal! But also pay close attention to the recipe. Sally once used two tablespoons of ultrastrong powdered thyme instead of two tablespoons of crushed thyme leaves—with inedible results.

Do a taste testing on each recipe, and invite family or friends to join in. Pick one winner for each course and finalize your menu, noting any tweaks you've made to the recipes. ***Dish it out and write it up.***

5. Plan ahead with painless prep.

After perfecting your recipes, the best way to feel confident on cooking day (and enjoy your own dinner party!) is to do as much in advance as possible.

- Clean your house (or at least the rooms people will see) the day before so you don't need to think about it the day of your party.
- Shop in advance. Carefully check your recipe ingredients and your pantry supplies. You should never need to run out to the market while cooking.
- Soups, stews, marinades, salad dressings, dips, and most desserts can be made a day in advance. If you want your guests to enjoy the scent of baking cookies or bread, make the dough in advance and bake shortly before they arrive.
- Lettuce-based salads can be assembled in the afternoon, but wait to toss them with dressing until right before serving so they don't get soggy.
- Mashed potatoes can be made early in the day and then gently reheated.
- Potatoes for roasting can be cut in advance and tossed in oil, garlic, and herbs.
- Spaghetti noodles can be cooked ahead of time and warmed up by running very hot water over them.

Be sure to check out the estimated cooking and prep time given on each recipe, and add ten to twenty minutes' grace just to be on the safe side. Then figure out what sequence you'll use for cooking. Be sure to leave yourself enough time to whip off your apron, shower, and dress before you put the finishing touches on your dishes and greet your guests. If you're nervous about timing, do a trial run of your entire meal so that you can perfect the cooking and serving schedule.

CARE FOR COFFEE OR TEA?

Piping-hot tips for piping-hot beverages

- No matter how you brew your coffee—in a single-cup filter, French press, espresso machine, or automatic drip—use fresh beans, and grind them just before brewing.
- Store coffee beans in an airtight container on the counter or in the freezer; they can absorb moisture and odors in the fridge.
- Use filtered water if your tap water is kind of funky.
- Use two tablespoons of ground coffee for every six ounces of water.
- If your coffee tastes bitter, grind it a little bit less.
- For tea, always fill your kettle with fresh cold water.
- If using a teapot, warm the pot by swirling in hot water.
- Use a teaspoon of loose-leaf tea or one small tea bag for each cup.
- Black, red, and herbal teas should steep for three to five minutes, green tea for one to three.
- Visit knowledgeable vendors of both coffee and tea, so that you can ask questions, taste test different varieties, and learn to pair the right tea with your dishes.

Think about the kind of ambiance you've most enjoyed at other people's homes—or even at your favorite restaurant. Are there aspects you can bring into your own house? Candles or soft lighting? Unobtrusive background music? Fresh flowers? Invest some time and money accordingly, but don't make yourself crazy. Sally says, "worrying too much about having everything matching or just-so can really make you crazy as a hostess—and can make your guests feel uptight as well." And to psyche yourself up for the big event, rent a culinary classic film: *Big Night, Babette's Feast,* or *Tampopo.* ***Be ready for your Big Night.***

6. Come and get it!

Something smells good in the kitchen—and since you've done your prep work and timed your cooking just right, you're relaxed when the doorbell rings. As your guests nibble on appetizers, you finish your last-minute touches. Serve your meal family-style in bowls and platters in the center of the table, so that you don't have to run back and forth to the kitchen when guests want seconds (which we know they will!). This will make your guests feel right at home—and most important of all, it will give you a chance to enjoy every moment of the wonderful meal you've created. ***Bon appétit!***

CONGRATULATIONS!

My compliments to the chef! Can I have your recipe? You did it!

I DID IT!

Name: ______________________

Date: ______________________

TASTY TRAINING

If you dream of a diploma . . .

The Cooking and Hospitality Institute of Chicago. Stars of the Midwest! Features a Cordon Bleu program that blends a traditional American culinary education with classical French culinary techniques. www.chicnet.org.

Le Cordon Bleu International. Twenty-two institutes in twelve countries. Founded in 1895, this landmark institution offers comprehensive training in cuisine and pastry to gourmet enthusiasts and culinary professionals, as well as degrees in several hospitality disciplines and a Master of Arts in Gastronomy. www.cordonbleu.net.

The Culinary Institute of America, New York. Offers twenty-one-month associate degree programs in culinary arts and baking and pastry arts, and thirty-eight-month bachelor's degree programs that include management training. www.ciachef.edu.

Tante Marie's Cooking School, San Francisco. One-week, weekend, one-day, and evening workshops and courses, plus a weeklong "Cooking Vacation in San Francisco" that is taught by Tante Marie herself and features a Wine Country field trip. www.tantemarie.com.

SALLY'S PICKS

COOKBOOKS

The classics:

Joy of Cooking by Irma S. Rombauer, Marion Rombauer Becker, and Ethan Becker
This classic, encyclopedic resource is suitable for both beginners and professionals.

Mastering the Art of French Cooking, Volumes 1 and 2, by Julia Child, Louisette Bertholle, and Simone Beck
Brought continental cuisine to the modern American kitchen–from Le Cordon Bleu straight to you!

Moosewood Cookbook by Mollie Katzen
The vegetarian classic.

The New York Times Cook Book by Craig Claiborne
1,500 recipes for gourmet home cooks, including crossroads cuisine and traditional dishes from many cultures.

The Silver Palate Good Times Cookbook by Julee Rosso and Sheila Lukins with Sarah Leah Chase
Great dishes for grand occasions.

For culinary specialists:

The Bake Sale Cookbook: 100 Quintessential American Desserts by Sally Sampson
There are seven recipes included for brownies alone!

The Classic Pasta Cookbook by Giuliano Hazan
Easy-to-follow directions to more than 100 pasta dishes from all regions of Italy.

Party Nuts: 50 Recipes for Spicy, Sweet, Savory, and Simply Sensational Nuts that Will Be the Hit of Any Gathering by Sally Sampson
Sally's tried-and-true recipes.

Reference books:

Culinary Artistry by Andrew Dornenburg and Karen Page
Great chefs offer insight and essays on the creative processes behind world-class cuisine.

The New Food Lover's Companion: Comprehensive Definitions of Nearly Six Thousand Food, Drink, and Culinary Terms by Sharon Tyler Herbst
The subtitle says it all: "Comprehensive Definitions of Nearly 6,000 Food, Drink, and Culinary Terms."

MAGAZINES

Bon Appétit
eat.epicurious.com/bonappetit
Great recipes, great pictures.

Cook's Illustrated
www.cooksillustrated.com
Recipes, articles, info.

Eating Well
www.eatingwell.com
Recipes and articles for healthy eating and living.

Gourmet
eat.epicurious.com/gourmet
Recipes galore and great articles about the culture of cuisine around the world.

ONLINE RECIPE RESOURCES

www.allrecipes.com
Thousands of recipes, plus newsletters, nutrition planners, and an online recipe box.

eat.epicurious.com
Recipes from the archives of *Bon Appétit, Gourmet,* and *Parade* magazine.

www.foodtv.com
Power search on recipes featured on the Food Network.

www.google.com
If you know what you want to make and are looking for a recipe, sometimes your best bet is just to Google it.

SUPPLIES

Crate and Barrel
www.crateandbarrel.com
Online, catalog, and in-store cooking gear.

Dean & Deluca
www.deananddeluca.com
Online, catalog, and in-store kitchenware.

Penzeys
www.penzeys.com or 800-741-7787
High-quality dried herbs and spices.

Williams-Sonoma
www.williams-sonoma.com
More cooking gear.

29

KNOW YOUR BEST CELLAR

★ wine appreciation ★

WINE is
earth's answer
to the sun.

—Margaret Fuller

Imagine This . . . When you order your favorite special occasion vintage at an upscale eatery, you sniff and swirl your sample sip like a pro. Your dinner guests flip for the Zinfandel you pull out of your pantry "cellar"—and you make a note of your success in your wine journal for future reference. And while you like a cold beer or cola as much as the next person, you know a nice glass of Cabernet or Chardonnay can make even fast food feel like a real meal. How did you change from someone who feared waiters bearing wine lists to someone with a particular preference for Pinot Noir? By educating and trusting your taste buds, you've found it's fun to buy, order, serve, and savor wine. Grab a corkscrew. *You can do it!*

So, what's your motivation?
Take a moment.
Dream a little, think big,
and then complete this sentence:
I see myself . . .

The Payoffs

- **Taste sensations.** Sure, you could drink water, coffee, or Kool-Aid with dinner, but sipping a wine that enhances the food and atmosphere can make a ho-hum meal memorable.
- **Social graces.** As any great hostess knows, the secret to a successful dinner is to have a constant flow of great wine and fun conversation. The more confidence you have with selecting wine, the easier it will be to order and serve well—so you can get back to your conversation.
- **Cold hard cash.** When you know what you like, you'll save money by avoiding the temptation to think expensive is better.
- ***À votre santé*!** (Translation: Drink to your health!) The French may not be healthy just because they like their Beaujolais, but studies do indicate that moderate wine consumption provides some real health benefits to most people.

Meet Your Mentor

CAILYN McCAULEY

What She Does: Worked with the charter members of Wine Brats, along with her husband, Joel, to take the organization national and is now starting her own venture. Founded in 1993, Wine Brats is the largest wine-consumer organization in the world, hosting informal wine tastings and wine and food events through chapters in cities nationwide.

Why She Does It: "I was in my late twenties and had only been living in California for a few years. I knew wine was important in California and had gone wine tasting once in Napa, yet I was really only a special-occasion wine drinker. I would never order wine in a restaurant because I didn't know how and was intimidated by the culture. Then a very good friend of mine was paid an abundant amount of wine for some work he did for the California Wine Fair. Somebody had to help him drink this stuff! When we first started sampling, I knew nothing about wine except that it was usually red or white. Slowly, after many weekend bottles, I started to notice other differences, like some whites are sweeter than others and some reds made my taste buds zing! I began to feel confident about which wines I liked, and wanted to learn more about wine in general. This same friend and my husband, Joel, were going to meetings of Wine Brats, which were just taking off locally. I started attending meetings too, and was able to help launch the group nationwide."

Learning what you like and a willingness to experiment is all you need to get into wine.

—Cailyn McCauley

Word from the Wise: "There's a difference between drinking wine and tasting wine. When you are drinking wine, it blends with the experience to become a poignant memory. When tasting wine, the process of swirling, sniffing, sipping, and spitting is educational—more like a chemistry experiment with your favorite lab partner!"

BADGE STEPS

1. Go where the wine is.

It's easier than ever to find good selections of domestic and foreign wines. Get to know your local wine resources, including wine shops or gourmet stores; or chains, such as Beverages & more!; grocery stores with a full aisle or more devoted to wines; and specialty markets like Trader Joe's and Cost Plus World Market.

At the store, ask the wine buyer or clerk to help you select one red and one white, and whether they ever hold wine tastings in the store. If they do, plan to attend with a friend. ***Pick up a couple bottles—and a few hot tips besides.***

2. Give it a swirl.

Good wine deserves a little extra appreciation. So take your cue from the professionals, and follow the traditional tasting procedure:

Swirl. Holding the glass by the stem, swirl your wineglass gently in a circle. This motion allows the wine to meet the air, enhancing the aroma and flavor. Don't swirl so hard that you get bubbles. Observe the wine, holding it up against a white wall or background. Note the depth and shade of the color—soon you will develop a sense of how the color of the wine relates to the flavors.

Sniff. After swirling, take a deep whiff. Our sense of smell is strongly linked to taste.

Swish. Take a substantial amount of the wine into your mouth to get the full effect of the complex flavors, and swish the wine around. Is the wine light or heavy? What flavors do you detect?

Swallow. As you do, breathe in through your mouth. Analyze the wine's aftertaste. Does it make you want to take another sip?

When tasting, an ounce of wine in the glass is sufficient. If you want to open and taste both of the bottles you bought, taste the white first, since lighter-bodied wines are less apt to linger on your taste buds. Remember to chill your white; thirty minutes in the freezer should do the trick in a hurry. Then take a bite or two of a plain cracker or bread before proceeding on to your red.

To save some of your wine for later enjoyment, you can recork and refrigerate both the white and red wine (not to worry: reds will return to

START WINING AND DINING

As you do, you'll meet . . .

:: Common whites:

Chardonnay. Fruit flavors, from citrus to tropical or fig-like. Fermentation in oak barrels gives this type of wine spicy, toasty, or even vanilla tones.

Pinot Grigio. A popular Italian white that often has melon-like flavors. "This is my favorite white wine currently!" says Cailyn.

Riesling. You might taste peaches when you sip this wine. Sweet and light.

Sauvignon or Fumé Blanc. Can be fruity or herbal, and tends to be less sweet than Chardonnay.

:: Common reds:

Cabernet Sauvignon. Rich and velvety, often described as tasting cherry- or blackberry-like.

Merlot. Less heavy than a "Cab," and sometimes has less alcohol. Should be soft and plum-like.

Pinot Noir. Ranges from light, silky red to a rich peppercorn flavor. Enjoy with the traditional "white wine" foods such as seafood, poultry, and pork.

Syrah. Weightier than Pinot Noir, often described as having spicy flavors such as licorice or anise.

Zinfandel. A full-bodied wine, Zinfandel is known for its "mouth-feel"—it slips across your tongue with bold, earthy flavors. Cailyn's favorite red.

drinking temperature a few minutes after pouring). That way, they should keep nicely for several days. ***Taste-test your purchases.***

3. Understand those labels.

Now that you've tasted the contents of your bottles, check out both the front and back labels for:

Grape variety. Merlot, Chardonnay, Zinfandel, etc. A bottle must contain 75 percent of a varietal to be labeled as such. Some wineries blend varietals for better flavor balance or to produce unexpected flavors.

Appellation of origin. Exactly where the grapes come from. This can be defined as broadly as a province or state; more specifically as a county, township, American viticultural area (AVA) such as Napa Valley; or perhaps even a specific vineyard. European wine labels sometimes give regional information in lieu of stating the grape varietal.

Terroir. This French term refers to the soil, climate, and other variables that affect a vine in its growing region.

Vintage. The year the grapes were harvested. Wines in which 95 percent of the grapes were not grown in a particular harvest year are marked NV for non-vintage.

Brand name. Could be the actual producer, but it might be a restaurant or grocery store chain that has made a "special label" purchase from a winery.

Copy the above label information for future reference into an attractive notebook, along with what you did and didn't like about the wine. Be as specific as you can: Note the wine's weight and texture, aromas and flavors, and aftertaste. This notebook will henceforth be known as your wine journal, and should come in handy the next time you need to explain to a waiter or wine salesperson what kind of wine appeals to you. (See Savor the Flavor for more hints.) ***Be label conscious and start a wine journal.***

4. Host a wine tasting.

To become familiar with a few more wines, host a blind tasting at your home to explore different types of wines free of prejudice.

- Invite half a dozen friends and assign each person (including yourself) a wine variety to bring, so that you wind up with one bottle each of the following: Sauvignon or Fumé Blanc, Chardonnay, Pinot

TO YOUR HEALTH

Something so good is good for you, too!

Wines contain antioxidants that neutralize the free radicals that can create a harmful kind of cholesterol and can lead to clogged arteries and heart disease. Dark red wines have more of the good stuff, because the skins and seeds of the grape are involved the longest in their wine-making process. As with most things, moderation is key. It looks like one glass of wine a day is optimal for most women (although you should talk to your doctor about your specific health profile). If you don't acquire a taste for red wine, purple grape juice and dark chocolate (thank you, God!) provide some of the same benefits.

SAVOR THE FLAVOR

Create a wine journal

Capture the occasion. Include a note or two about food you ate with the wine, the occasion, setting, and company. That way, the next time a friend asks, "Remember that great wine you ordered on my birthday last year," you can answer, "But of course!"

Paste in the wine label. Cailyn thinks "soaking off labels is too much trouble!" but offers this tip: If soaking the bottle in warm water doesn't slip the label off, try either one part ammonia cleaner to eight parts hot water or citric acid in warm water. After the label is dry, you can iron it to get rid of wrinkles.

Go high-tech. Cailyn finds that she and her fellow Wine Brats often plug wine data into their PDAs, so that after trying wine at a restaurant or social occasion, they can then go home, get online, and research the wine.

GLASS GUIDE

Raise your glasses in style, and enjoy!

Various styles of glassware are available to suit different wines; the shape of the glass can subtly affect the taste of the wine. Just try tasting the same wine from different shapes of glasses . . . it's strange but true!

- Wineglasses made for sipping white wine are tulip-shaped, with small bowls that keep the wine cool.
- Wineglasses for red wine are rounded, with a larger bowl than those used for whites in order to warm the wine and enhance its aroma.
- All-purpose wineglasses fall somewhere between the classic red and white shapes, and curve slightly inward at the rim to hold in the bouquet.
- Sparkling wine is best served in tall, thin flutes that keep their contents cool and bubbly.
- Use clear glasses so that you can admire the wine's appearance.
- Hold a wineglass by its stem. "It's there for a reason," says Cailyn. "You drink brandy out of a bowl-like snifter because you want your hands to gently warm the contents. Not so with wine. Stems also allow you to observe the wine's clarity and color without overheating it."

CAILYN'S EXPERT TIPS

RESPONSIBILITIES OF A RESPONSIBLE HOST

As the host, it's your responsibility not to let guests who show signs of intoxication to keep drinking or to drive themselves home. With one ounce per tasting glass, this shouldn't be a problem, especially if you:

- Provide food.
- Encourage folks not to finish any wine they don't love.
- Shift into coffee and dessert mode at least half an hour before anyone leaves.

Grigio, Pinot Noir or Merlot, Cabernet Sauvignon, Syrah, and Zinfandel. You can also assign a price range that will be comfortable for all your guests ($10 to $30, for example).

- Provide seven wineglasses for the wine; still and sparkling water; some plain crackers and breads; finger foods; and coffee and dessert to enjoy after the tasting.
- Uncork the reds fifteen minutes or longer before tasting to give them a chance to breathe. Some wine enthusiasts insist that older reds should be opened hours before drinking to appreciate their complex flavors.
- Place each uncorked bottle in a plain paper bag that covers the label completely. Arrange the bagged bottles on a table from light whites to heavy reds, then assign each bottle a number and write the appropriate number on the paper bag so people can discuss the wines by number—but don't give any other details away about the wines.
- Hand out slips of paper so that guests can fill out details about the wine they brought: the assigned variety of wine, where it was bought, and why they selected it. Also hand out rating cards to guests, and ask them to jot down a few words describing the flavor of each wine, then rate each one on a one to five scale in each of three categories: aroma, aftertaste, and overall flavor.
- Beginning with wine number one, pour a one-ounce glassful for each guest and ask them to taste and rate the wine. Before moving on to wine number two, guests should partake of the water and crackers to cleanse their palates. Provide a bucket where your guests can spit out or throw away any wine they would rather not finish.
- When everyone is done scoring, tally up the counts, unveil the wines, and chat about your opinions. Remember, there isn't a right

answer—everyone's taste buds are different, and it can be great fun to learn that you liked a really inexpensive wine or a wine that was produced locally. By the end of the evening, you will have discovered several new wines to buy and order in restaurants.

Host a blind taste test, and make an evening of it!

5. Pick your house reds and whites.

Restaurants often offer versatile, inexpensive house wines—and now that you've found a few wines you like, you can begin to stock your own house wines for dinner parties and special occasions. Bring your wine journal shopping, and see if you can find a wine you like at a good sale price. When you do, buy several bottles or a case and store them away. You don't need an actual wine cellar for storage; your wine cellar can be any dedicated place in your house that meets these criteria:

- No exposure to excessive light, heat, or movement (not next to the stove or in the water heater closet!).
- Relatively constant temperature, ideally 50 to 60 degrees.
- A little humidity to keep the corks from drying out and oxygen from getting in.
- An empty wine box from the store works to keep the corks moist and the bottles in a good position: either upside-down or on their sides (a wine rack also will do this).
- Basements are good, as are many closets.

Stock your own wine cellar with a few favorites.

CONGRATULATIONS!

Salute! Prost! Chin-chin! You did it!

I DID IT!

Name: ______________________________

Date: ______________________________

I DID IT!

"It sounds silly, but at a recent business dinner when I was assigned to entertain out-of-town clients, I was most nervous about ordering wine. I looked over the wine list, asked the clients what they liked, and then got our server to give me a little guidance. I really wound up being proud of myself because I remembered that the goal was just to have a nice time. Who really cares if the server doesn't think I scrutinized the cork properly?!"

—Angela

GRAPE GOOF

"At my local market the price on a bottle of Bordeaux seemed right so I put it in my basket. While I was checking out, I realized I hadn't seen the first number on the wine's price tag—which put it into a high-double-digit, outside-my-normal-price-range bracket. I was too embarrassed to say I didn't want the bottle after all, and so took it home and vowed to enjoy it with dinner after a particularly rough day. When I did, I found I didn't like the wine at all. I've since learned that some expensive/rare/prestigious wines are an acquired taste. Like organ meats and stinky cheeses, I don't plan to ever acquire such tastes!"

—Melissa

BEYOND THE BADGE

If you love it as much as you thought you would, dream on . . .

- **Try a daring pairing.** Food and wine pairings are really about complementary flavors, and conventional wisdom says that heavier food goes better with reds and more delicate flavors are accentuated with whites. But some people like to drink white wine with their steak, so it won't fight for power with the meat. Try both and see which you prefer. And if your fish or chicken is served with a dark sauce, try savoring it with a red. Sure, you could order the safe Chardonnay with your fish—but you might be missing out on a taste treat by making an unconventional choice of wines. And who says you have to drink sweet Rieslings and Muscats with dessert? Host a dessert and wines pairing party where you put bold pairings to the test. Take a bite of chocolate followed with a sip of fruity Muscat, and then take another bite and wash it down with a sip of spicy Syrah. Observe the difference! As the Wine Brats say, "You can enjoy whatever wine you like with your food—and tell anyone who gets huffy about your choices to stick a cork in it."
- **Visit wineries.** In addition to being fun, you get to connect the wine to the place the wines are grown, take educational tours and enjoy free or inexpensive pairings, and sometimes find special limited-edition bottlings at a winery that never make it into wide distribution. Designate a driver who swishes and spits instead of swallowing tastes of wine, and don't try to take in more than three or four wineries in a day.
- **Tour a wine region.** While traveling overseas, most of us love sampling the local cuisine; why not try some of the local wines paired with it? The local environment, culture, and traditions of wine making make for some great local wines, especially in France (the Bordeaux, Burgundy, Champagne, Loire, Alsace, and Rhône regions); Italy (Piedmont, Tuscany, Friuli); Spain (Rioja, Ribera del Duero, Penedes, Jerez); Portugal; Germany; South America; and Australia.

RESTAURANT REMINDERS

When ordering wine out

The sommelier or wine steward is the specially trained staff member at a restaurant who's in charge of recommending wines and serving them. Giving wine advice is their job—so take them up on it!

- If you are unfamiliar with the restaurant's offerings, or just want to try something new, ask your sommelier or server how their mystery wines compare to what you know you like—dry, sweet, heavy, etc.
- If your sommelier or server recommends a wine that's too pricey for your pocketbook, or if the markup on your favorite bottle seems too high, ask her (or him) to suggest something similar in a lower price range.
- If you're interested in trying a bold pairing, tell the sommelier so—chances are, it will be greeted as a welcome challenge to recommend something other than the obvious choices.
- When you are served, glance at the bottle to make sure it's what you ordered! If you are offered the cork, it shouldn't be dry and crumbly or soggy. Taste the wine before coming to any conclusions. Swirl, sniff, and taste your sample sip. If you think there's something amiss, ask the server to taste it as well, and feel free to refuse the bottle. Don't be too hasty to judge a red; they sometimes need a moment or two to breathe.

CAILYN'S PICKS

BOOKS

Parker's Wine Buyer's Guide 6th Edition: The Complete, Easy-to-Use Reference on Recent Vintages, Prices, and Ratings for More Than 8,000 Wines from All the Major Wine Regions by Robert M. Parker Jr. and Pierre-Antoine Rovani
Evaluates more than 8,000 recent vintage wines using a one hundred point rating system, with comments.

The Wall Street Journal Guide to Wine: How to Buy, Drink, and Enjoy Wine by Dorothy J. Gaiter and John Brecher
Practical advice to guide you through the wine aisle in the grocery store, assessments of specific wines, and tips on cork etiquette, how to impress your boss, and what to do about wine headaches.

The Wine Bible by Karen MacNeil
A great beginners' book, which teaches you about wine-growing regions, how different wines are made, and what flavor each grape is known for, along with specific information about different vintages.

The Wine Brats' Guide to Living with Wine by Jeff Bundschu, Jon Sebastiani, Mike Sangiacomo, and the Wine Brats Coalition
An irreverent guide to wine and wine culture, filled with fun and practical tips on everything from building a wine cellar to figuring out what goes with take-out pizza.

MAGAZINES

California Grapevine
www.calgrapevine.com
Tasting notes on and critical evaluations of new releases, plus essays, book reviews, and competition results.

International Wine Cellar
www.wineacess.com/expert/tanzer
Great tasting notes and vintage evaluations, interviews, technical topics, and recipes.

Wine Spectator
www.winespectator.com
Wine and lifestyle coverage in articles, restaurant reviews, profiles, and articles on varietals and regions.

WEB SITES

www.winebrats.org
Educational articles, resources, and info on becoming a Brat.

www.wineenthusiast.com
Online retailers of wine racks and cellars, glassware, corkscrews, and wine-oriented gifts.

www.wineloverspage.com
Wine notes, vintage charts, prices, glossary, lists of favorites, and user forums.

www.wine-searcher.com
Searchable database of wine prices and which retailers near you stock specific wines.

RETAIL

www.personalcellar.com
Specializes in limited distribution, boutique wines.

www.vino.com
Over 3,500 wines you can order online as well as a wine retailer locator and winery database.

www.wine.com
Online wine retailer that offers everyday wines as well as hard-to-find specialty wines.

winelibrary.com
Large selection of wines in all price ranges.

30 PARTY ON!

★ entertaining ★

> Well, did you evah!
> What a swell party this is.
>
> —Cole Porter, *Well, Did You Evah*

Imagine This . . . You enter your living room and see a couple dozen of your favorite people laughing and smiling. Your best friend is deep in conversation with your sister, another friend is telling an obviously fabulous story to three or four rapt listeners, and your next-door neighbors have put on a '70s disco CD and are doing the hustle. Before your college roommate can corner you for your crostini recipe, you take a moment to savor the scene. As you do, a wave of happiness and goodwill sweeps over you. Was your planning, preparation, and attention to detail worth it? Absolutely! With a few simple ingredients, you've gathered good people, given them a good time, and pulled off one of life's perfect moments. *You can do it!*

So, what's your motivation?
Take a moment.
Dream a little, think big,
and then complete this sentence:
I see myself . . .

The Payoffs

- **Love.** Orchestrating special experiences for your friends honors them and shows you care. If your goal is to have fun and celebrate one another, your party will be a success.
- **Networking.** One of the great joys of entertaining is bringing people together and witnessing personal and professional relationships flourish.
- **Play.** Once you learn to relax when it comes to entertaining—playing around, feeling free to be yourself, and riding with the inevitable faux pas—you and your guests will all have more fun.
- **Memories.** Your guests will thank you for the memories you give them, and you'll be able to look back fondly yourself.

Meet Your Mentor

ERIKA LENKERT

What She Does: The author of *The Last-Minute Party Girl: Fashionable, Fearless, and Foolishly Simple Entertaining*, Erika Lenkert is a veteran food and wine journalist for such magazines as *In Style, Travel & Leisure, Bon Appétit,* and *Food & Wine.*

Why She Does It: "I grew up in San Francisco and my mother was an avid cook who did a lot of home entertaining. She took me to all the restaurants in town, large and small, funky and fancy. I also learned to cook while young, partly because I had a single, working mom. When I was little, I loved having other kids come to my house, and I soon realized I could lure them there if I whipped up something good to eat, like garlic bread. I also realized that making something for someone makes them feel good and makes me feel good, too. One of my first writing jobs was working on *Frommer's* guides. I got to spend a lot of time in restaurants and learned a lot about entertaining—restaurants are really all about professional entertaining. I was right out of college and wasn't making a ton of money, so my roommate and I had a lot of parties on the cheap at home—much less expensive than going out. One of my first magazine assignments was a cover story for *Los Angeles* magazine reviewing the top caterers in L.A. I went to parties for forty days! Entertaining at home is really all about spending quality time with people you love. That makes it worth doing, even if it makes you a little nervous at first."

Good entertaining has nothing to do with perfection. So relax—things going a little bit WRONG makes them more memorable.

—Erika Lenkert

Word from the Wise: "A comfortable environment and people you love is all you really need. How complicated is that?"

BADGE STEPS

THE HOSTESS WITH THE MOSTEST

This means you!

- Make meaningful introductions. Introduce people to one another one-on-one, instead of all at once in a large group, and provide some insight on each person. Examples: "You should see Rebecca's amazing photographs." "Julio is a fellow kayaker." "Karen just got back from Belize—weren't you there last year, Eric?"
- Work the room, not just the buffet table. Consider hiring someone to serve and clean, especially for larger parties when it's a challenge to spend any quality time with guests. A local caterer or restaurant can set you up with a waiter for around twenty dollars an hour. (You might be able to pay the teenager next door a little less!)
- Don't fret—about the food, forgetting someone's name, or not having time to blow dry your hair. A great party is about good company and a comfortable environment. Enjoying yourself rather than rushing around with a furrowed brow inspires your guests to follow suit.

1. Make up a good excuse for a party and get it on the calendar.

If this is your first time hostessing in a while, steer clear of major events like wedding showers, New Year's Eve, or your best friend's law school graduation. These events usually come with lots of expectations and long guest lists. Does someone have a birthday coming up? Is Oscar night approaching? The first day of spring? The start of summer? Pick a casual occasion and a party date four to six weeks hence.

Now pick a time. We suggest either three to six or nine to midnight. Kick-off times tell your guests what to expect. For instance, a 7:30 P.M. start implies dinner will be served, while 3:00 P.M. tells guests to eat lunch before coming. If you want to be able to load the dishwasher and curl up with a video later on, specify a party cut-off time.

Planning food, drink, and decor around an event or theme will put your guests in a festive mood. A theme can be as simple as cozy comfort foods during the winter months, a Latin fiesta to spice up an otherwise blah month, or a retro cocktail hour that gives you a chance to wear that fab vintage dress. Think about the kinds of parties you most enjoy attending, and aim for that kind of ambience. ***Decide why, when, and what.***

2. Make a list, and check it twice.

Your first instinct may be to invite scads of friends, but the party particulars, budget, and size of your home will inevitably rule some of them out. Since this is likely your first party in a while, it's a good idea to keep your guest list down to thirty people or less—this isn't the only party you'll ever have. True, it can be dicey to invite some coworkers/relatives/friends and not others, but hey, it's your party. Feel free to specify no kids, ladies only, or no extra guests.

Mix things up a little. If you've always wondered if your friend from the gym would like your friend from your book group, invite them and assume they'll find common ground. Just try not to invite the Hatfields and the McCoys, and it'll be fine. "As the hostess, it's your job to try to diffuse situations that are uncomfortable for your guests," says Erika. "But generally speaking, if you invite nice people you can pretty much rely on good behavior from everyone involved." You may also want to consider the networking possibilities, and invite that interesting woman you met at a business meeting or ask that perfect couple you know to bring that single friend they've been talking about. Who knows—you may cinch a career deal or meet your dreamboat. ***Write your guest list.***

3. Spread the word.

The next order of serious party business is the invitation. In addition to the obvious time and place info, tell your invitees if you'd like them to RSVP, bring a bottle or six-pack, and whether they can bring a guest.

Be as creative as you like with your invitation. Erika has been known to send:

- Inscribed flip-flops as invites to a pool party
- A swizzle stick that can be redeemed for a drink for a cocktail party
- Individual monkeys from a Barrel of Monkeys to guests she was inviting to hang out
- A baggie filled with plastic ants, a plastic fork, and a square of gingham tablecloth for a picnic

You don't have to use snail mail to get the word out—e-mail can be very effective. Erika loves the Evite online service because people tend to lose written invites, and Evite makes it easy to include a map. But whether you're counting on the Internet or the postal service, be sure to send out your invitations four weeks in advance for a formal party or two to three weeks beforehand for an informal gathering. If you haven't heard back from everyone a week before the party, follow up with phone calls or e-mails. ***Issue those invites.***

4. Hey good lookin', what's cookin'?

Finger foods, of course! An abundance of snacks and drinks on the premises will keep your guests busy and circulating. Ask friends and family for tried-and-true recipes, and seek out inspiration from magazines and books— Erika's book offers dozens of doable recipes, many from five-star chefs. When planning your menu, be sure to consider:

Variety. Offer a range of foods to accommodate different palates, vegetarians, and Atkins diet diehards, and go for a mix of savory dishes and sweet treats.

Quantity. Make more of the dishes you know from experience are popular favorites. If you're famous for your homemade brownies with crème de menthe frosting, be sure to make enough to go around.

FUN WITH FOOD

Finger foods rule (only small plates and napkins required!)

- Bruschetta sounds fancy, but it's really just chopped tomatoes on toasted bread with olive oil and a little garlic rubbed in for pizzazz.
- Fill the bases of endive leaves with crumbled blue cheese, toasted nuts, and a drop of honey, and arrange decoratively on a platter.
- Chef Suzanne Goin starts diners at L.A. hot spot Lucques off with bowls of oven-toasted almonds tossed with olive oil and salt, then combined with Lucques, Picholine, or nicoise olives and thyme.
- Fill a wood cutting board with oven-toasted baguette rounds, cheeses, tapenade, and cured meats like salami and prosciutto.

I DID IT!

"My friend Judy invented a brilliant birthday party tradition. One year she invited thirty friends, who were fun, interesting women of all ages and backgrounds. The second year she invited the original thirty, and asked them each to bring one of their best friends. The third year she asked the second group to bring a guest, and so on. The party is up to 120 amazing women this year—by far the best party of the year. This year she'll be asking everyone to leave twenty dollars at the door for her favorite charity, which she will generously match in lieu of fancy party favors!"
—Caroline

IT'S MY PARTY AND . . .

"At 3 A.M. on the day of my thirtieth birthday party, I knew I was crazy. In ten hours I would welcome fifty guests for an afternoon of wine and seven different homemade finger foods. But after eighteen hours of cooking, I was covered in chocolate praline pastry filling and wondering whether burns from caramelized sugar would scar. The event went well and my guests flipped for the food. But more important was the lesson I learned: Throwing a great party is not nearly as fun when you're too stressed and overworked to enjoy it."
—Erika

Cooking time. Make one or two recipes you can whip up with no stress, and complement these with purchased delicacies such as sushi, Vietnamese spring rolls, artisan cheeses, breads, spreads, crudités, olives, or a gourmet bakery dessert.

Serving suggestions. Serving is a cinch with a self-serve buffet accessible to guests from all sides. Group napkins, plates, and utensils together and arrange sweets and savories separately.

Once you've set your menu, make a shopping list, and shop two or three days in advance. And whatever you serve, don't stress. As Erika says, "A failed or flawed recipe has nothing to do with the success of your party." Laugh, smile, and order takeout at the last minute if you must. ***Whip up a little something***.

ERIKA'S EXPERT TIPS

PARTY GIRL DO'S AND DONT'S

DO greet each new arrival and offer to stash their coats and purses away from the action.

DO make sure to introduce people who share a particular passion or interest.

DO send handwritten thank-you notes to guests who help you prep or clean up (and to the hostess when you are a guest!).

DON'T feel party favors are essential. You're doing plenty by giving the party! But if you are so moved, Erika suggests kitschy items like gumball machine toys, a lollipop for the road, or a small item in keeping with your overall theme.

DON'T encourage or initiate mean-spirited gossip. Depending on who's present, politics, religion, and money matters can also be conversational taboos.

5. Make like a bartender.

You don't need a fully stocked bar in order to entertain. Ask guests to bring a bottle of wine or six-pack of beer, buy a case of your own favorite wine, and don't forget nonalcoholic options like sparkling water, sodas, ginger ale, lemonade, and coffee. Just in case people don't bring much in the way of drink, have enough on hand to supply a couple of drinks per person. Shop a week ahead of time for drinks, and make sure you have enough glasses to go around. Erika offers these bartending tips:

- For cocktail lovers, consider serving one specialty mixed drink along with wine and beer basics. Go with something that matches your food or theme: classic cosmopolitans for a swanky cocktail hour, say, or margaritas garnished with jalapeño in hot weather.
- Set up a bubbly buffet with inexpensive sparkling wine rather than pricey champagne. Then give people a choice of mixers, such as fruit juices and liqueurs like Cointreau and Chambord.
- Buy your booze at discount stores, and don't be afraid to go for the economy-sized bottles. Your guests will be glad you haven't run out.
- Create a freestanding bar, separate from the food. Keep glasses, napkins, coasters, and bottle openers there.

Bartend with the best of them.

6. Add some ambience.

Don't let a lack of space cramp your style. Swinging soirees have been held in tiny studio apartments, backyards, patios (weather permitting), and even the laundry room of an apartment building (true story!). Put your guests at ease with a few minor adjustments:

Clear a path. Guests should be able to move about, access food and drink, and sit down easily. Move furniture out of the way if need be.

Find extra seats. Separate ottomans from their chairs to create additional seating, and borrow a few folding chairs or bar stools.

Provide trash cans. Erika has learned to keep a trash can and a recycling bin handy so that she can concentrate on playing hostess, not maid.

Create mood lighting. Warm lighting at nighttime events provides a sense of intimacy, so switch on side lamps, light a few candles, and dim those overhead lights.

Add flowers for flair. You don't need to spend a fortune—a simple arrangement of one dramatic bloom, such as a cala lily or tulip, adds elegance to any affair. Or fill a large, shallow decorative bowl with water, and float Gerber daisies or orchids surrounded by loose flower petals. Tight, tiny flower arrangements also add flair to side tables.

Select your music. Facilitate conversations with quiet jazz, classical, or bossa nova, or boogie down with funk, salsa, or pop. Load up the CD changer, or record your perfect party mix, in advance.

MARTINI MADNESS

Serve the classic cocktail

A traditional martini. One and a half ounces of gin and three-quarters of an ounce of vermouth.

A standard dry martini. Two ounces of gin and one-quarter of an ounce vermouth (but proportions, like taste, can certainly vary).

1. Chill gin, shaker, and glasses in the freezer. Chill vermouth in the refrigerator.
2. Pour gin into a shaker of cracked ice.
3. Let the gin get comfortable with the ice for a minute or two.
4. Pour in your vermouth.
5. Shake until shaker is frosted.
6. Pour into a glass and slip in an olive.

Beautify your bathroom. Along with essentials such as extra toilet paper, clean hand towels, and a fresh bar of soap, add a scented candle and a single flower or elegant bouquet.

Make your place the place to be.

7. Prepare to party.

Do as much of the prep work as you can before the day of your party. If you must do some cooking the day of, do it in the morning. If a dish requires lots of chopping, marinating, or simmering, start it first—don't be afraid to leave things like cheese trays or salad dressing until the last minute. You can put early bird arrivals to work helping with these. Better yet, enlist as a sous-chef a friend who can come a little early, provide good company in the kitchen, and whip up something tasty in a flash if need be!

Clean as you go to minimize post-party cleanup and keep counters clear. Erika suggests you resist popping a cork until major kitchen chores are accomplished but highly recommends treating yourself to a little preparty mood music. Pace yourself so that you have a few moments to primp after your kitchen duties are done, too. ***Is someone at the door? It's show time. Party on!***

CONGRATULATIONS!

You've played hostess with savoir faire to spare. Collect your kudos. You did it!

I DID IT!

Name: ____________________

Date: ____________________

PARTY MUSIC

Erika's favorite mood setters

***The Best of the Song Books,* Ella Fitzgerald.** Sets a perfect dinnertime scene.

***A Charlie Brown Christmas,* Vince Guaraldi Trio.** The jazzy soundtrack from the beloved TV special spreads nostalgic holiday cheer.

***Chez Moi,* the Baguette Quartette.** Parisian music of the 1920s through 1950s.

***Play,* Moby.** Smooth techno grooves.

***Sister Bossa,* Volume 2, various artists.** Happy, sexy, and perfect for a pool party.

***Songs for Swingin' Lovers!* Frank Sinatra.** For when you're pouring martinis.

BEYOND THE BADGE

If you love it as much as you thought you would, dream on . . .

- **Learn to cook.** If you want to make culinary delights a highlight of your home entertaining, consider cooking classes, collecting recipes and tips from cookbooks and magazines, and going for the cooking badge (see Dine In, page 224). One of Erika's favorite ways to enhance your skills in the kitchen is to take cooking classes while traveling. She's also been known to ask in restaurants how a special dish or effect was accomplished.
- **Learn to be spontaneous.** Wouldn't it be nice to invite people back to your place after an outing or feel free to call a few friends at the last minute to keep you company on a free Saturday night? With a little confidence, creativity, and the right kitchen supplies, you can. (See The Party-Ready Pantry.)
- **Go pro.** If you find you have a knack for making functions fun, you can make a career or sideline out of fiesta planning. Do it all yourself, or hook up with cooks, organizing gurus, and designers, and work as a team to orchestrate parties of all kinds for hostesses who can pay for your services.

THE PARTY-READY PANTRY

Supplies for instant party success

- Blender, food processor, timer, and more than one corkscrew
- Serving platters and utensils, glasses of all shapes and sizes, and ceramic ramekins (ideal for dips, olives, nuts, and the like)
- Breadsticks, crackers, nuts, tortilla chips, pasta
- Chocolate, coffee, tea, mints
- Frozen foods, from mini quiches and potstickers to ice cream
- Good vinegar and olive oil
- Olives, roasted red peppers, salsa, salami, sun-dried tomatoes
- Ice and ibuprofen!

ERIKA'S PICKS

BOOKS

The Fannie Farmer Cookbook by Marion Cunningham
A cornerstone cookbook and resource for everyday American cooking and baking.

Good Things for Easy Entertaining by Martha Stewart Living Magazine
A great little book filled with lots of tabletop ideas, pretty pictures, and creative inspiration.

The Joy of Cooking by Irma S. Rombauer, Marion Rombauer Becker, and Ethan Becker
The bible for cooking basics for American standards (think hollandaise sauce, club sandwiches, baked chicken, and sugar cookies).

The Last-Minute Party Girl: Fashionable, Fearless, and Foolishly Simple Entertaining by Erika Lenkert
"Yes, this is shameless self-promotion—but I really can't think of another book that is as approachable, fun, and practical, and offers endless tips and nearly one hundred recipes."

MAGAZINES

Bon Appétit
www.eat.epicurious.com/bonappetit or www.bonappetit.com
An overall casual style makes this a friendly choice for the beginner as well as the more experienced cook.

Food & Wine
www.foodandwine.com
Get it out for straightforward and easy recipes seasoned with a little style and glamour. Their wine coverage is some of the most approachable out there.

Gourmet
www.gourmet.com
Adventurous and confident cooks will like the sophisticated recipes and food-related stories.

In Style
www.instyle.com
Their entertaining section stylishly covers everything from hip decor to racy recipes.

Martha Stewart Living
www.marthastewart.com
Check out this mag for crafty do-it-yourself decor ideas and tasty recipes.

WEB SITES

www.cooking.com
Kitchen equipment.

www.crateandbarrel.com
Tabletop decor.

www.deananddeluca.com
Food and gifts.

www.epicurious.com
Recipes, food dictionary.

www.evite.com
Send invites online.

www.lastminutepartygirl.com
Personalized answers to your party-planning questions.

www.marthastewart.com
Recipes, tabletop decor, and kitchen products.

www.mixologys.com
Barware.

www.potterybarn.com
Tableware.

www.urbanoutfitters.com
Home and tabletop decor.

www.webtender.com
Cocktail recipes.

play

How we spend our days is,
of course,
how we spend our lives.

—Annie Dillard

31

EXERCISE YOUR OPTIONS

★ fitness ★

I am persuaded that the greater part of our complaints arise from want of exercise.

—Marie de Rabutin-Chantal, Marquise de Sévigné

So, what's your motivation?
Take a moment.
Dream a little, think big,
and then complete this sentence:
I see myself . . .

Imagine This . . . Hike Kauai's rugged Na Pali Coast? Of course! You wouldn't want to miss those views. Help out with your groceries? No thanks, you can handle it—even when you buy bleach *and* kitty litter. Sit out a jungle gym play date with your favorite five-year-old? You wouldn't think of it—and now you know you won't pay for it later with sore muscles. How'd you get so fit? Once you realized exactly what your body needed, the many ways you could satisfy those minimum fitness requirements, and how much better you felt when you gave your body what it craved, you found it surprisingly simple to ring the recess bell regularly and get a little exercise. Feel like getting fit for your life? *You can do it!*

The Payoffs

- **Sanity.** In addition to stress management and mood enhancement, the expert you're about to meet loves the way exercise lets her busy mind "go blank." While some think deep thoughts and get bright ideas, many also make movement a meditative experience.
- **Let's talk about me.** Many of us look forward to our exercise time because it's practically the only time that's completely our own.
- **Health.** Heart, lungs, bones—exercise is good for every part of our bodies, including the reproductive system (easier periods and pregnancies, increased libido).
- **Weight management.** Exercising solely to achieve some pie-in-the-sky body standard isn't any fun, but workouts help many of us eat more of what we like (including pie!) while maintaining a healthy body weight.

Meet Your Mentor
SARAH BOWEN SHEA

What She Does: A freelance health and fitness writer, Sarah writes often for publications including *Real Simple, Shape, SELF, Living Fit,* and *Parenting* (she has a three-year-old daughter). She runs, swims, does Pilates, works out at a gym, and has completed several marathons, triathlons, and adventure races.

Why She Does It: "My dad always said, 'Let your avocation be your vocation,' and I think I'm successful writing about health, fitness, and athletics because I actually *do* what I write about. That said, I wasn't much of a jock when I was an editor at *City Sports.* In fact, when I was getting ready to do a century (one hundred mile) bike ride, an event where something called a 'sag wagon' picks up the exhausted, my supportive coworkers said 'sag' stood for 'Sarah's a goner'! My family was all about reading, and I didn't really get exposed to sports as a kid. I'm also really tall and was kind of uncoordinated, so I always felt dorky in P.E. class. I accidentally got into crew in college. The crew coach sent me a note—which I'm sure he did to everyone five foot ten and over—and because I wanted to get into the school, I went for it and wound up *loving* it."

If I have an inner jock, EVERYONE does!

—Sarah Bowen Shea

Word from the Wise: "When I'm going up a hill or pushing out a heavy rep, I always tell myself that this tough or maybe even slightly unpleasant moment is just a *moment.* I felt fine five minutes ago and will again in another five. Workouts have taught me that, and I remember it in every aspect of my life—when something goes wrong in my work or even with things like my first husband leaving me. We are all a lot stronger than we think we are."

BADGE STEPS

1. Take an honest look at your health.

The goal of this badge is to help you understand—and get—the exercise you need for overall health. We'll give you the minimum weekly requirements that support your heart, bone, muscle, and mood health (and which can jump-start your efforts on personal goals like weight loss, sport performance, cholesterol management, etc.). To assess your current fitness, a good personal trainer (see Sarah's Expert Tips, page 256) would recommend you do the following:

- Check in with your doctor and let her know that you're planning an exercise program. This is especially important if you haven't exercised in years, are considerably overweight, or have chronic conditions like high blood pressure, diabetes, heart disease, or lung problems. Your doc may suggest specific dos and don'ts based on your health issues. Ask for a blood pressure reading.
- Get to know your heart rate. Take your pulse at rest. (With your index and middle fingers, find your pulse on the underside of your wrist. Count the beats for fifteen seconds and multiply the number by four.) Then take your pulse after exertion. Jog in place, jump rope, or climb steps for two minutes, rest for a minute, and then take your pulse again. (We'll talk more about your target heart rate while exercising.)
- Can you touch your toes? Do a push-up or sit-up? (How many without pause?)

Dedicate a new notebook to your fitness plan and note your answers to the above—blood pressure, pulse rates, etc.

LOG YOUR JOGS

And notice your progress!

When Sarah started working out as a teen (to those Jane Fonda aerobic albums and clipped-out magazine articles like "Six Moves to a Better Butt"), she kept a log of her activities: "Did Jane, thirty minutes," "Ran around the reservoir twice." Knowing you get to make such an entry makes the effort easier. Writing down what you do also motivates you to push yourself. It's great fun to note that you walked that mile faster than last week, added another loop around your block, managed three more sit-ups or another bicep curl. For all these reasons, keeping such a diary is especially helpful at the outset of an exercise program.

2. Get to know your fitness needs.

Depending on your overall fitness levels and specific health issues, the training you'll need to get into tiptop shape will most likely include:

Cardio. Thirty minutes, five to six days a week. Cardio training is often accomplished with one of the -ing words—walking, biking, swimming, jogging—but an activity you enjoy more (see Step 3) could provide your cardio, as long as it gets your heart rate up to 60–80 percent of your maximum. Your max heart rate is 220 minus your age. So if you're forty, that's a max heart rate of 180, and a good target workout rate would be 108–144. Take your pulse while exercising, wear a heart monitor (available at sporting goods stores), or give yourself the talk test. Sarah says you should be working (that's why it's called a workout) but still able to carry on a conversation. Regular cardio activity will not only make you look and feel better, it provides some long-term health benefits (see Give Me One Good Reason!).

Strength. Fifteen to twenty minutes, twice a week. Strength training involves resistance and includes plenty of things you can do at home (leg lifts, push-ups, ab crunches, lifting free weights, using exercise bands or balls). Strength training helps prevent weak bone breakage and osteoporosis. Bonus: Strength training activities boost your metabolism.

Flexibility. Five to ten minutes, three to four times a week. Some activities, like yoga, build in stretching, but if your preferred activity doesn't, stretch for a few minutes before and after your cardio and strength routines. Slowly and gently stretch out your hamstrings before a walk or run, extend your arms overhead and side-to-side before lifting weights, etc. While simple to do, gentle stretching is part of a sound overall fitness routine because flexibility helps prevent everyday aches and pains and exercise-related injuries.

In your notebook, jot down your current fitness activities. Note things like the brisk ten-minute walks you take to the bus each morning—they count! Brainstorm ways you can maximize the impact of what you already do and what activities you could add. ***Evaluate your fitness strengths and needs.***

3. Pump up your daily routine.

If you can't imagine finding twenty- to thirty-minute chunks of time in your schedule for workouts (or if you feel like calling a paramedic after exerting yourself for this length of time!), know that studies show that several ten-minute periods (the time it takes to brew a cup of coffee or write an e-mail) are more than fine. Also know that we find the time and energy for activities we genuinely enjoy (don't force yourself to jog if you hate it) and that some activities satisfy more than one fitness requirement. (Yoga is strength and flexibility; tennis and rowing are cardio and strength.) To get you thinking about the many ways to use it or lose it, check out the chart on the next page. Augment your current activities with at least one new activity to create a regimen that fulfills the fitness requirements outlined in Step 2. ***Pick a fitness kick.***

GIVE ME ONE GOOD REASON!

Here's three

- Cardiovascular disease is the cause of death for more than 40 percent of American women. Cardio exercise fights this, as well as lowering blood pressure and "bad" cholesterol, and reducing the risk of diabetes and some cancers.
- Weak bones break more easily and develop osteoporosis; strength training fights this.
- Everyday aches and pains, not to mention more serious injuries, restrict us. Stretching fights these things.

ACTIVITY	CARDIO	STRENGTH	NOTES
Dance	X		Swing, modern, square . . . you can even do it with friends, a date, or your partner.
Racquet sport	X	X	Tennis, racquet ball—run for that ball and keep moving between points.
Water sports	X	X	Find an irresistible indoor or outdoor pool. If laps bore you, try water aerobics or water polo—or stay drier with rowing or kayaking.
Martial arts	X	X	Karate, tae kwon do, Wing Chun, tai chi, capoeira, etc.; boxing; and self-defense training can be one-stop shopping for cardio, strength, and flexibility.
Skating	X	X	Roller, inline, ice—get outdoors, perfect your figure eight, or even join a women's hockey team.
Team sports	X	(some)	Softball, soccer, basketball: All mean competition, uniforms, camaraderie . . . and post-game pizza and beer!
On-the-job training	X		Walk or bike to work, trade the elevator for stairs, add exercise to your lunch break, use the copier on the other side of the office, and skip e-mails in favor of a walk to a coworker's office.
Homework(out)	X	X	Yes, you can invest in a treadmill, but you can also work out by raking leaves with gusto, turning chores like vacuuming and dusting into a circuit by putting on some music and dancing between rooms, and doing crunches or lifting dumbbells while watching TV.
Sex	XXX	XXX	Think about it: cardio, strength, flexibility . . . you can do it!
Kid stuff	X	(some)	What left you happily huffing and puffing as a kid before you knew you were "working out?" Fly a kite, do gymnastics, explore the neighborhood on your bike.

YOUR LIKES AND DISLIKES

Make exercise personal and fun by taking the following into consideration

- What exercise plans have you tried in the past that didn't stick?
- Was there something that kept you active as a kid (or at another point in your life) that you miss?
- What do you already do that is so fun that it doesn't feel like exercise? (Swing dancing is cardio!)
- Do you want to be alone or be in a group or on a team?
- Do you like to be outdoors or do you feel, like Fran Leibowitz, that "the outdoors is what you must pass through in order to get from your apartment into a taxicab"?
- Do you feel like a fish in water?
- Does music keep you moving?

4. Schedule it.

Get out your calendar for the coming month. Go over the requirements spelled out in Step 2, then highlight times when you'll meet those cardio, strength, and stretching requirements by doing the activities you've outlined in Step 3 (three different colored highlighter pens are ideal for this). Spell out what you'll do in those highlighted time slots. Write down dance class, not just cardio—and call to register for the class. Make dates with the friend you'd like to walk with, put air in your bicycle tires, rent the movies you'll distract yourself with as you do your free weights routine, etc. Get to it, and don't forget to stretch! A typical week might look something like this:

Sunday. Family bike ride or hike, one hour (one cardio, one strength).

Monday. Yoga class at lunch, forty-five minutes (one strength).

Tuesday. Walk briskly to work, or to distant bus stop in each direction, forty minutes (one cardio).

Wednesday. Crunches, push-ups, etc., while watching favorite TV show, thirty minutes (one strength).

Thursday. Walk/run errands at lunch time, forty-five minutes (one cardio).

Friday. Evening jog with neighbor, thirty minutes (one cardio).

Saturday. Yard and housework in the morning and swing dancing at night, one hour total (one cardio).

Exercise physiologists say it takes six months for a new habit to take root, but Sarah assures us that "most people are going to notice some kind of positive change—more energy, better sleeping, having more patience—in ten days to two weeks." Sticking with your program may help you reap the benefits, but feel free to make adjustments to activities, playmates, and times of day to prevent boredom. To keep the benefits coming, increase the duration, frequency, or intensity of what you are doing when a cardio workout no longer sets your heart aflutter.

Get your fitness requirements for a month, and log your activities in your notebook. Now answer the fitness assessment questions in Step 1 again—see what a difference a month can make?! ***Feel great about feeling fit!***

WALKING TALL

The best exercise is right at your feet

Sarah says, "Walking is a perfectly legitimate form of exercise for beginners and the more advanced alike. You don't have to drive to a gym or pool or buy any fancy equipment (other than comfy and supportive shoes). You can make walking enjoyable in so many ways—by exploring new settings or walking with friends, for instance. You can do it just about anytime and anywhere—on your lunch break, by walking instead of 'running' errands, first thing in the morning to jump-start your brain and body or at the end of the day to unwind. You can start walking at any age and keep doing it as you age. And you can build in challenges by walking faster, seeking out—rather than avoiding—hills, or incorporating jogging intervals."

I DID IT!

"When I was a teenager, I stumbled across a book on weight lifting for women. This was in the late '70s, way before we all went nuts for Linda Hamilton's arms in *The Terminator.* The book was for everyday folks, not competitive lifters, and let you use soup cans and jugs of bleach as weights. But I loved how serious dumbbells made me feel, even though my family thought I was nuts! More than twenty years later, I still use weights at home several times a week. The best thing about weights is that you see results quickly—and while I know I'm doing something good for my bones, I have to admit that I do it more for how good it makes my muscles look." —Vanessa

FITNESS FAUX PAS

"It was one of those New Year's resolutions: I was going to go to the gym three days a week for two hours each time, no matter what! I joined a gym, bought workout clothes I wouldn't be embarrassed to be seen in—and made it to the gym three times in three months! What was I thinking? I much prefer playing sports outdoors, and with a little help from a couple of visits with a personal trainer, I've also figured out quick and simple things I can do each day in between my weekends of tennis and hiking. I thought you had to go to a gym to get fit, but though many of my friends love their workouts there, it's just not for me." —Katie

SARAH'S EXPERT TIPS

FITNESS SAVVY

- Set personal and attainable goals—a lower heart rate, a bit of definition in your upper arms, being able to keep up with your toddler at play, doing a charity walk, skiing better, etc.
- Effective workouts aren't about "no pain, no gain," but do entail pushing yourself beyond your comfort zone. Learn to listen to your body while exercising. You know the difference between discomfort and pain, and unless you are having a sharp, shooting pain or can't speak for lack of breath, you are probably doing something that's good for you when you push the exercise envelope.
- Personal trainers can be a wonderful resource. They can help you reach goals, make friends with the mystery machines at a gym, motivate you to push yourself, and teach you new moves that can help keep you interested and surmount plateaus. Remember that you don't have to make a lifelong commitment; many women work with a trainer for three to five sessions when beginning or just setting out to reinvigorate their routine.

CONGRATULATIONS!

Your inner jock is on the move. You did it!

I DID IT!

Name: ______________________________

Date: ______________________________

SARAH'S PICKS

BOOKS

Complete Guide to Walking for Health, Weight Loss, and Fitness by Mark Fenton
This comprehensive, well-written book tells you step-by-step how to develop a walking routine.

Om Yoga: A Guide to Daily Practice by Cyndi Lee
Strike a pose or two from this book every day to strengthen and harmonize your mind and body.

The Stretch Deck: 50 Stretches by Olivia H. Miller
Got ten minutes to spare? Try this magic trick: Pull out a card or two from this deck, and try out the stretches illustrated there to ease the body and the mind. Presto, change-o!

Swim 30 Laps in 30 Days by Jane Katz
"This was the book that taught me how to swim with my face in the water and alternate breathing, and set me up for my love of swimming," says Sarah.

The Ultimate Body: 10 Perfect Workouts for Women by Liz Neporent, MA
Easy to follow and completely illustrated with photos, this how-to book offers up programs like "The Perfect No Crunch Abdominal Workout" and "The Perfect Gym Workout."

The Ultimate Workout Log by Suzanne Schlosberg
This useful log lives up to its name, giving you designated space to record your cardio, strength, and mind-body workouts, along with your eating habits. Plus, it is filled with interesting fitness factoids, prompting you to keep turning the pages—and keep working out!

Weight Training for Dummies by Suzanne Schlosberg and Liz Neporent
Two renowned fitness writers deliver wit and wisdom about how to navigate the weight room, do a wide range of strength training moves, and develop a comprehensive lifting program.

MAGAZINES

SELF
www.self.com
Fitness is a big part of the equation in this women's publication, and the articles usually have an intriguing spin, such as real-women comparisons of yoga and Pilates.

Shape
www.shape.com
This is the workout bible for fit women, whether looking for new tricep-toning moves, motivation, health news, or a more effective cardio workout.

WEB SITES

www.halhigdon.com
For do-able marathon training programs for all levels of runners. "I swore by this for my third marathon," says Sarah.

www.ideafit.com
Features a personal trainer locator along with interesting news from a leading health and fitness association.

www.myexerciseplan.com
Developed in part by a noted exercise physiologist, this site offers for-a-fee personalized fitness plans and support, plus free clever animated demos of a new move each week.

WORKOUT SPOTS

Ladies Workout Express
www.ladiesworkoutexpress.com
Upwards of 1,000 gyms worldwide for women only. Offers a full-body workout in just thirty minutes. Great for exercise novices, but intermediates and above might get bored—and unchallenged.

24 Hour Fitness
www.24hourfitness.com
Most of the several hundred facilities are open round-the-clock. Bare-bones clubs—you have to bring your own workout towel and might have to wait a few minutes for a vacant treadmill—but loads of class options.

VIDEOS

A.M. and P.M. Yoga for Beginners
The gentle, basic yoga poses and simple stretches in the eighteen-minute morning program and twenty-three-minute evening routine are a simple, sane way to start or end a hectic day.

Crunch: Fat-Burning Pilates
No need for a machine: This fast-paced, forty-minute workout mixes cardio with ab-strengthening moves.

Donna Richardson's 4 Day Rotation Workout
Four fifteen-minute routines: Do them all at once for a challenging hour-long workout, or pick and choose when time is tight.

Going Ballistic
Let a down-to-earth instructor guide you through strengthening and toning moves on a fitness ball; she offers continuous encouragement and modifications for all experience levels.

32

STRETCH YOURSELF

★ yoga ★

Each body has its art.

—Gwendolyn Brooks

Imagine This . . . You've spent some quality time on your yoga mat, and it shows. But it's not just your posture that seems different lately; it's your entire outlook. When the world seems a little upside down, you don't let it throw you off balance anymore: You just ease into an inverted pose and put the world back in proper perspective. You don't bend over backwards for just anyone, of course—but you could, if you were so inclined. Once you stretch yourself with yoga, you'll never need to snap back into the same old stressed-out, hunched-over shape again. So take a deep breath, and prepare to walk tall. *You can do it!*

So, what's your motivation?
Take a moment.
Dream a little, think big,
and then complete this sentence:
I see myself . . .

The Payoffs

- **Stress relief.** The breathing techniques, stretches, and restorative poses you'll learn will help you handle life's tests, from blind dates to boardroom presentations and even labor pains.
- **Strength.** The poses may feel good, but make no mistake, this is serious exercise. Stick with it, and you'll soon gain muscle tone, improved endurance, and better balance.
- **Concentration.** If you're impressed at how far you can stretch your legs after a couple months of yoga, just wait until you see what it does for your attention span!
- **Self-acceptance.** When you pay closer attention to your body and recognize that you are capable of much more than you'd imagined, you'll learn to stop judging yourself and respect the woman you are.

Meet Your Mentor

NORA ISAACS

What She Does: Nora is a senior editor at *Yoga Journal* as well as a sought-after private yoga teacher. She writes regular features for *Yoga Journal,* as well as articles for *Salon.com, Natural Health,* and *San Francisco* magazine.

Why She Does It: "My parents practiced yoga and started teaching in our basement when I was growing up. In suburban New Jersey, our family definitely stood out. I didn't know too many other kids who went to ashrams on weekends! Like most kids, I went through a period of being embarrassed by my parents as a teenager and actually dropped yoga for a while because I didn't want to stick out. But I got back into it after I moved to New York for graduate school because I started getting panic attacks. Thanks to yoga, I knew I had the tools I needed to manage my stress; it was just a matter of using them. Eventually I moved from New York to California, where I started teaching yoga in addition to freelance writing. Then I got the call from a journalism school friend that *Yoga Journal* was looking for a journalist who taught yoga, and I thought, 'This is perfect.' It's a blessing that I can pursue two things that I love at the same time."

© Jen Molander

Word from the Wise: "One of the most rewarding aspects of teaching for me is watching beginners gain an awareness of what their bodies can do. The first day when I ask beginners to move their right shoulders, you can see they really have to think about it. But after a couple of weeks, it becomes second nature."

> Our bodies actually learn very quickly, once we start paying attention to them.
>
> —Nora Isaacs

BADGE STEPS

1. Explore your options.

If you know what you want out of a yoga class going in, you're more likely to leave it with that bona fide, yoga-fied look of serenity on your face. So ask yourself: Do you want to relieve stress, regain your strength after an injury or illness, lose weight, or gain flexibility? "Yoga can help you meet all these goals," says Nora. "The trick is finding the type of yoga that's the best match for your interests." Pick the type of yoga that most closely matches your personal goals.

Iyengar. Expect to hold poses for a long time while you make small adjustments to achieve ideal body alignment and greater awareness of your anatomy. This type of yoga helps improve your posture and relieve stress, and is less aerobic than other disciplines. If you have any injuries, you'll need to work closely with your teacher so that you don't strain yourself while working on some of the more challenging poses.

Bikram or Ashtanga. You'll perform a specific sequence of postures in rapid succession, and after a few classes, you'll fall into the rhythm of movement. This type of yoga is highly aerobic and hypnotic, too! If you have blood pressure or heart problems, you should probably choose a less strenuous type of yoga. Bikram yoga is taught in a very hot room to warm the muscles, so be careful not to let yourself get dehydrated.

Integral, Sivananda, and Kripalu. These practices are more meditative and focus on inner strength in addition to outward movements. You'll learn to relieve stress with deliberate movements, plus breathing exercises that help strengthen the body as they clear the mind.

Anusara. This type of yoga focuses on maintaining body alignment and seeing the divine nature within each person. It's a serious workout and physical discipline, but the teaching approach is lighthearted and playful. "Anusara is fun, so it's gaining popularity," says Nora.

Next, track down yoga studios that offer classes in the type of yoga that seems right for you, with some help from friends who do yoga, listings on community bulletin boards, and Nora's Picks, page 265 If you come across class listings for Pranayama and Hatha yoga, don't be confused. Pranayama is breathing exercise, which is a component of most types of yoga, while Hatha is an umbrella term that includes all yoga with physical poses—and technically, all the types listed above fall under this rubric. ***Find a few yoga classes that promise to meet your needs.***

YOU TOO CAN BE A YOGI

Forget the usual excuses!

"I have tight hamstrings." "I hear lots of people say, 'I want to try yoga, but I'm not flexible enough'—but that's exactly why they should do it!" Nora says.

"I like to eat meat." A recent *Yoga Journal* poll found that only 10.8 percent of readers are vegetarians—"And these are people who are really into yoga!" says Nora.

"It's too trendy." Yoga is a practice that is over 5,000 years old. It's been practiced in the West for nearly a century and has really gained momentum here over the past forty years. "By now it's a cultural movement, not a trend," says our expert.

"That tantric sex stuff sounds weird." "Tantra is a very deep philosophy that doesn't have much to do with sex, and it's distinct from yoga," explains Nora.

"I already have a religion." No conflicts here! "Yoga is not a religion," explains Nora. She describes it as "a meditative practice" that inspires reflection and complements religious belief, much like writing in a journal or taking a long walk.

2. Try out a few classes.

Beginning classes should last an hour and a half, with a brief meditation at the beginning, warm-up stretches, a series of standing poses, forward bends, back bends, a resting pose, and a meditation at the end. As you become more advanced, your teacher may add in headstands and other inversions. Spend a month trying out a few of the most promising class options you've found, taking into consideration:

Level. "It's very important that you take a class specifically for beginners at first, rather than a mixed-level or advanced class," says Nora. "You don't want to get overwhelmed or hurt yourself trying poses that are really too difficult."

Schedule. Look for beginning classes that are convenient to attend at least twice a week. Be realistic about your schedule. If you know you'll be working late in the coming months, don't count on making that 6 P.M. class—especially if you'll have to fight traffic to get there. Yoga is meant to relieve stress, not create it!

Location. Classes close to home or work will make it easier for you to fit yoga into your regular routine.

Limitations. If you have any injuries or other physical constraints, be sure to consult the instructor beforehand to make sure the class won't overstrain you (see No Pain, Just Gain). You'll probably still be able to take the class, but the instructor may advise you to modify or sit out certain poses during class.

Before you go to class, ask what you might need to bring with you. Depending on the type of yoga, you'll need:

Clothes that move with your body. Avoid restrictive clothing that might limit your range of motion or make you uncomfortably hot.

A yoga mat. This ridged foam mat will keep you from slipping while you're holding poses. You might want to buy your own, so you can practice at home.

Blocks and a strap. These props can be used to help you stretch, and they're usually provided by the yoga studio.

Go to four or five different yoga classes in a month.

3. Commit to one class.

Once you've been to a few different yoga classes, you'll know what a difference a teacher can make. "Do you prefer teachers that are more or less

NO PAIN, JUST GAIN

Feel those muscles—without the sprains and strains

After your first few classes, "muscles you never knew existed will be aching," says Nora. But after your first couple of weeks in a class, you'll find you can hold poses for longer and that your flexibility has increased: "You might be surprised how easy it is to touch your toes!" Whatever you do, though, don't force it. "As in any physical activity, there's a possibility of injury, especially when you push yourself too far, too fast," she says. "Too often, we apply our Western ideals of competition and perfection of the physical body onto yoga, which is about being attentive to your mind and body." In other words, "No pain, no gain" does not apply—when you feel pain, stop.

NORA'S EXPERT TIPS

YOGA WITHIN YOUR LIMITS

Yoga gives you plenty to do, even when you're:

Recovering from a sports injury. "An instructor who specializes in therapeutic yoga may be able to work with you one-on-one to help you rebuild your strength," advises Nora. "As always, pay attention to how each pose makes your body feel, and avoid any poses that give you sharp pains. The tendency is to do what everyone else is doing in class, but if something doesn't feel right, it's not."

On your period. The conventional yoga wisdom is that women should avoid upside-down poses when they're menstruating. "Many believe that this reverses the *apana,* which is the downward flow of the body's energy," says our expert—but others just call it uncomfortable. On the other hand, she says, "Restorative, nonstrenuous poses and certain forward bends can be great for easing cramps."

Pregnant. Seek out a trained prenatal yoga specialist. "Prenatal yoga focuses on squatting and breathing to get ready for labor and forward bends that strengthen the lower back," she explains. "Recently a student of mine had a baby, and she told me yoga made her labor much easier—it strengthened her pelvic floor, and she knew how to breathe." Nora recommends avoiding new poses, backward bends, twists, and inversions after your first trimester and steadying yourself with props, such as blocks for standing poses and a chair for support during forward bends.

strict? Do you feel more comfortable with an instructor telling you what to do or a hands-on teacher who will adjust your body for better alignment? Does it matter to you if the teacher is a woman or a man?" asks Nora. "Before you settle on a class, be clear about what kind of teacher works best for you."

If you know you'd have more confidence in a more experienced teacher, Nora suggests you find out if your instructor has been certified by the Yoga Alliance with 200 or 500 hours of training. "You also might want to find out who your teacher trained under, so you can have a better understanding of their style," she says. But she cautions that credentials aren't everything. "There are plenty of great teachers who aren't certified by Yoga Alliance, so your best bet is to discuss your specific goals with your teacher and talk to other like-minded students about their experience."

I DID IT!

"I remember watching more advanced yoga students and thinking, 'Not me, no way!' I had a hard time keeping my balance even doing basic bending poses because they gave me a head rush every time. But one day I stopped listening for the blood rushing in my ears and started concentrating on the teacher's instructions instead. Lie down: Hey, I could do that. Raise your hips: No problem. And before I thought about it too hard, I found myself lifting off from the floor and pulling my feet off the wall. I can't tell you what a triumph that was! I guess I'd always resigned myself to the equilibrium problems that run in my family, but that day I realized I could find my own sense of balance."

—Zoe

GETTING OUT FROM UNDER

"When I first started doing yoga, I was so focused on getting myself into the poses that I didn't think about how I was going to get out of them. I would do a pose, hold it, and then yank myself out of it as quickly as possible so I could get into the next one. I wound up with a lot of sore muscles, and I could never figure out why everyone said yoga was so relaxing! Then I found a teacher who told me that what I was doing wasn't yoga—instead, I was becoming a contortionist. Once I became more focused on the process instead of just the end goal, I really began to stretch myself."

—Alison

Once you find a teacher you feel good about, sign up for eight weeks of classes, and go at least twice each week. Going regularly will keep your muscles stretched and limber and help you remember the basic poses. ***Sign up for eight weeks of class.***

4. Strike a pose.

After just eight weeks of classes, you won't be just a poseur with your yoga poses. Sure, you'll know a sequence of stretches and poses you can practice at home, and you may already be working on more difficult poses like a headstand or a "dropback," where you come into a backbend from a standing position. But better yet, you'll know what it means to pay attention to yourself for a change and trust that inner voice that tells you to relax, believe in yourself, and let yourself stretch farther than you ever thought possible.

"Yoga changes you," confirms Nora. "The things that used to obsess you drop away. Your cravings will evaporate, all that concern and weight you've been carrying around will start to taper off, and you'll find you want to take better care of yourself and the people around you. And don't be surprised if you get the urge to go to bed early, so you can get up and do yoga!" ***Reach a whole new level with yoga.***

CONGRATULATIONS!

Now that you've stretched your mind and your muscles, you know your own strength like never before. You did it!

I DID IT!

Name: ______________________________

Date: ______________________________

IT'S ALL RIGHT TO CRY

Get a load off your mind with yoga

How is it that without any warning or physical pain whatsoever, people are suddenly moved to tears in the middle of a backbend? Ask a yoga teacher, and you'll get this response: "The issues are in your tissues." As Nora explains, yoga poses stretch out and open up entire sections of your body and your mind that are usually defended and tightly closed—think of how often you fold your arms across your chest, cross your legs, and push unresolved issues to the back of your mind. "Over the years, yoga instructors have noted that certain poses tend to facilitate emotional release—in particular, backbends and movements that open the hips," she says. "It happens all the time, and it's embraced as a natural part of yoga practice."

BEYOND THE BADGE

If you love it as much as you thought you would, dream on . . .

- **Take a yoga break.** Smokers take breaks throughout the day to indulge their habit, so why shouldn't you take a few minutes out of your day to enjoy a much healthier habit? Nora practices breathing exercises on her morning commute to work and says it's a great way to start the day: "Take five minutes in the morning before you get to work to just sit and breathe." To rejuvenate yourself before and after a big meeting, close the office door, throw down your mat, and do a few poses—or flee your cubicle, and step outside or use the hallway. If you work at home, you could practice breathing while vacuuming and add a few forward bends. So what if your neighbor catches you in the act—who cares how it looks if it feels great?
- **(Re)treat yourself.** When those daily breaks just aren't enough and that deep relaxation at the end of class feels like it's over far too soon, treat yourself to a yoga retreat for a day, weekend, or even a week or two (see Great Escapes).
- **Go deeper.** "There are eight limbs of classical yoga, and physical yoga is only one of them," Nora explains. "There's a lot of mental work to be done, too." To make the mindfulness you gain from yoga part of your daily life, she suggests writing in a journal. To explore this practice and other forms of reflection further, check out Get an Inner Life, page 420. But not all yoga practice is inwardly focused, as Nora points out: "One of the ideals of yoga is to be more compassionate toward the world." To make compassion part of your everyday practice, why not complete the Champion a Cause and Give a Little Bit badges, pages 46 and 476?
- **Mind your health.** Check out Care for Your Health, page 334, to take charge of your health maintenance plan, challenge old habits with the Eat It and Quit It badges, pages 326 and 344, and work toward physical fitness goals with badges like Hang Ten, page 266, and Head for the Hills, page 274.

GREAT ESCAPES

Renowned yoga retreats

Inner Harmony in Brian Head, Utah. Offers intensive yoga classes in a down-home, rustic setting with good vegetarian meals. You'll spend a fair amount of time in class, but there are also hikes and field trips.

Kripalu in West Stockbridge, Massachusetts. This idyllic Berkshires retreat offers yoga, rest, and relaxation in a converted monastery. For a truly spectacular experience, go in the fall when the leaves are changing color.

Maya Tulum in Mexico's Yucatán Peninsula. Take a couple of yoga classes a day, and you'll still have time to enjoy swimming, snorkeling, the nearby nature preserve, and complete spa services . . . this is the life!

Parrot Cay in Turks and Caicos Isles, British West Indies. A Shambhala holistic spa in a splendid setting surrounded by Caribbean blue waters, featuring special "Healing Weeks" plus yoga classes and legendary massages year-round.

Rancho la Puerta in Tecate, Mexico. This yoga center and spa attracts yoga teachers from around the world to teach a variety of classes. After class, you can look forward to a hot tub, sauna, and other spa amenities, plus exploring Tecate.

NORA'S PICKS

BOOKS

Light on Yoga by B.K.S. Iyengar
The classic reference book for learning and understanding yoga postures.

The Shambhala Encyclopedia of Yoga by Georg Feuerstein
A necessary yogi's companion, whether you are beginner or advanced.

Yoga and the Quest for the True Self by Stephen Cope
Delves into the history of America, along with a personal story of the author's experiences living at Kripalu Center for Yoga and Health.

The Yoga Sutras of Patanjali by Swami Satchidananda
An accessible translation of this classic yoga text.

Yoga: The Spirit and Practice of Moving into Stillness by Erich Schiffmann
A must-have for yoga students looking to understand the deeper meaning of yoga, as well as the basic poses.

MAGAZINES

Yoga International
www.yimag.org
Put out by the Himalayan Institute, *Yoga International* delves into the spiritual and physical applications of yoga.

Yoga Journal
www.yogajournal.com
A source for yoga information and inspiration, covering lifestyle, meditation, poses, and life issues. Web site features comprehensive pose finder, articles, and a teacher directory.

WEB SITES

www.yogasite.com
Clearinghouse for information on retreats, schools of yoga, products, articles, and teachers.

www.yrec.org
Created by yoga scholar Georg Feuerstein to uphold the classical teachings of yoga, the Yoga Research and Education Center Web site is chock full of writings and information.

ORGANIZATIONS

Himalayan Institute
www.himalayaninstitute.org
Spiritual organization that offers retreats, workshops, and classes.

Yoga Alliance
www.yogaalliance.org
Alliance of diverse yoga organizations that sets voluntary standards and provides support for yoga teachers; a good place to find a certified teacher.

Yoga on the Inside
www.yifoundation.org
Nonprofit that brings yoga to incarcerated youth and adults; a great place to volunteer!

33

HANG TEN

★ surfing ★

The best surfer in the water is the one having the most fun!

—Surf Diva motto

So, what's your motivation?
Take a moment.
Dream a little, think big,
and then complete this sentence:
I see myself . . .

Imagine This . . . You stride purposefully down the beach, board under your arm, sun on your back, smile on your face. Heads turn as bored, boardless sunbathers watch you wistfully—they'd throw down their paperbacks and join you if only they could. When you reach the water, you gracefully throw down your board, ease yourself onto it, and begin paddling into the clear blue of sea and sky. Thoughts of deadlines and duties recede with the shoreline. You have just one thing on your mind: catching a wave and riding it sure and strong. If this is your beach-chair daydream, this badge will get you up, out to sea, and on a board. *You can do it!*

The Payoffs

- **Body.** Surfing works your arms as you paddle out and pop up, your abs and legs as you stand and balance, and your heart the whole darn time as you move through preparation, exertion, and exhilaration.
- **Mind.** Wave time goes a long way toward erasing "I can't" from your head's hard drive.
- **Spirit.** There's something magical and mysterious about the ocean. Big and strong, it can also be gentle and serene. The effect on humans tends to be simultaneously energizing and calming.
- **The cool factor.** The surfer-dude stereotypes may be on their last legs thanks to all the surfer dudettes out there, but until they are gone for good, it's still rad to master a traditionally male sport like surfing. They think you're hot, you know you're cool—everybody wins!

Meet Your Mentor

ISABELLE "IZZY" TIHANYI

What She Does: Izzy is the diva, founder, owner, and CEO of Surf Diva, Inc., the world's first surf school for women and girls, which she runs with her twin sister, Coco. Izzy earned a National Scholastic Surfing Association scholarship to the University of California, San Diego (where she earned degrees in communications, literature, and writing), and was the National Collegiate Overall Surfing Champion. A professional longboarder, Izzy is the recipient of numerous awards, including the 2003 Surfrider Foundation Waterperson award, the 2002 Inspiration Award from the Pacific Women's Sports Foundation, and the 2001 Cool Woman of the Year award from the San Diego chapter of the Girl Scouts.

© Todd Peterson

Why She Does It: "My father taught my sisters and I how to surf when I was eight. A one-foot wave can look pretty big when you're so little, but the great thing is that you are too young to worry about what other people think of you—as opposed to when you're sixteen. Surfing wasn't popular for girls when I was a teenager, and when I started competing at age seventeen, it was—and still is to a certain extent—very male-dominated. The first surf shop I worked in wouldn't let me sell boards because they thought men would never take advice from a woman seriously. For our company, I wanted a name that was feminine and strong. Divas are confident and competent, at the top of their class and classy."

Word from the Wise: "Being a beginner is great, because you remember every single wave and get a real sense of accomplishment as you improve. Surfing is one of those things where getting good is fun. But no doubt about it, surfing is also a real physical workout."

> Surfing is better than a roller coaster, sex, drugs, you name it. Everybody can do those things—
> but not everybody surfs.
>
> —Isabelle Tihanyi

BADGE STEPS

SURF SCHOOLS

Learn to catch a wave while seeing the sights here

Big Island Girl Surf Camp, Hilo, Hawaii. Seven-day, weekend, private, and group camps and lessons. www.bigisland girlsurf.com or 808-326-0269.

Las Olas Surf Adventures for Women, near Puerto Vallarta, Mexico. Operates late October through early June. This "un-finishing school" seeks to "make girls out of women." www.surflasolas .com or 707-746-6435.

Richard Schmidt School of Surfing, Santa Cruz, California. Coed programs, several women instructors. Group and private lessons year-round and weeklong camps May through early August. www .richardschmidt.com or 831-423-0928.

Surf Diva, La Jolla, California. Surf Diva instructors have hosted guided travel and instruction trips in Costa Rica, Hawaii, Mexico, and Canada. www .surfdiva.com or 858-454-8273.

1. Get schooled.

Izzy hears from students all the time that their boyfriends/husbands/ brothers tried to teach them and it just did not work—kind of like trying to learn to drive from your dad. Professional teachers have far more patience and can break their skills into doable steps so students don't get discouraged. Learning from and with other women is important to many of Izzy's students, although Izzy knows a few excellent male instructors out there whom she considers honorary surf divas. (She even employs a few!) But if you know you'd be more comfortable in an all-female setting, they're increasingly easy to find.

Teachers are also important for safety reasons, so think twice about just renting a board and giving it a go on your own. Izzy says that you might be able to get away with this with skiing or snowboarding—maybe you'll end up having to walk down the mountain, no big deal. "But when you're dealing with the ocean, self-taught is a bad idea," she warns.

Ask around at surf shops to find a school with a solid reputation. The surge in the popularity of surfing has given rise to some fly-by-night instructing operations. (Izzy calls these "man in a van" schools.) There is not currently a national licensing board that regulates schools in the U.S., so you'll have to do your own background check. Your school should:

- Be a member of the Better Business Bureau and the local chamber of commerce.
- Have permits to operate where and when they do. Permits ensure that the school is properly insured.
- Have instructors who are certified in CPR, lifesaving, and first aid. Your instructor needs to be a competent lifeguard—don't just rely on the lifeguard on the beach.
- Keep a ratio of one instructor to no more than five students.
- Be a member of the Surfrider Foundation, an important environmental organization. (See Izzy's Picks, page 273.)

Sign up for surf school.

2. Flex some muscle.

A little presurf prep will go a long way toward building your confidence and preventing undue soreness after your first lesson. Warm up with:

Swimming. The Divas recommend being able to swim 200 yards in the ocean. If you haven't frolicked in the sea for a while, refresh your memory.

Skateboarding. What do surfers do when they're landlocked? They skateboard! These surfboards on wheels actually help you practice your stance and balance.

Push-ups. Popping up on your board after paddling out on your stomach is a lot like doing push-ups. Doing some push-ups daily will make this move easier.

Sit-ups. These are also good training—you'd be surprised how much strong abs will help you maintain your on-board stance.

Yoga. A few Warrior poses on your mat for strength and flexibility can help you be a warrior on your board. ***Tone up before you suit up.***

3. Get geared up.

Here's your basic gear:

Swimsuit. Whether your swimsuit is one- or two-piece is up to you—just make sure it's comfortable and easy to move in.

Foam boards. The Divas teach with friendly foam boards. If you get hooked on the sport and want to buy your own board, see Izzy's tips in Beyond the Badge, page 272.

Rashguards. These are snug Lycra shirts that keep you from getting a rash. "Rashies" also keep your bikini top on and provide varying degrees of SPF.

Wet suits. In warm-water months (May–September), wet suits are optional and surf trunks or boardshorts with your swimsuit suffice. If you decide to purchase your very own wet suit, Izzy likes those by Hotline, a woman-owned company, as well as those by Billabong and O'Neill.

Leashes. These keep you and your board connected.

Beach gear. Pack whatever you normally would for a day at the beach: waterproof sunscreen, towel, hat and hair ties, sunglasses, sweatshirt, drinking water, and a light snack.

Eyewear. Surf Divas who wear contacts suggest wearing disposables—put in an old pair and close your eyes tightly underwater—or using swim goggles.

LOOKING THE PART

Diva duds

Yes, it matters. Surfing apparel for women isn't just a fashion statement. It goes a long way toward encouraging and allowing women to perform up to their potential. If wearing shorts and guards tailored for men, you might not feel comfortable or welcome in the sport.

Historically speaking. In researching an article, Izzy found plenty of evidence that traditionally, in the Polynesian cultures, surfing was a coed pastime. She hypothesized that a lot of women got out of the water when religious missionaries objected to their bare-breasted boarding. You can't really surf in a muumuu or grass skirt!

Where to buy. Chickabiddy sells a range of items for female surfers and athletes of all sizes. They cater to a slightly older and curvier customer than do the Billabong and Roxy lines. Surf Diva apparel is sold at Sport Chalet stores and on the Diva Web site, www.surfdiva.com.

I DID IT!

"Heather was an MBA with a corporate job at Ford Motor Company in Detroit. She came to Cali on vacation, took a lesson, and got so hooked on surfing that she quit her job, moved out here, and became a massage therapist. She makes her own schedule now, reads tide charts instead of pie charts, and gets to surf whenever she wants!"
—Izzy

THE RINSE CYCLE

"Surfing should be fun, not scary. A four-foot wave can pummel you into the sand effortlessly, so it's important to be respectful of wave size. I took a lot of waves on the head and swallowed buckets of water before swearing off waves that were too big for me. When you do get worked by a wave, learn to relax your body and cover your head (so you don't get bumped by your board). You'll pop up eventually, and the less energy you waste thrashing, the more energy you'll have to catch the next wave."
—Sarah

Like most schools, Surf Diva provides students with wet suits, boards, and leashes—other gear you may have to buy, borrow, or rent. ***Gather your Gidget gear.***

IZZY'S EXPERT TIPS

SAFETY FIRST AND LAST

DO surf with a friend—it's safer and more fun.

DO surf in front of a lifeguard.

DO keep your eye on the horizon—to avoid crashing into other surfers.

DO the stingray shuffle. Stingrays are the satellite dish-shaped creatures that glide along the ocean floor. If you step on one, they will instinctually sting in reply. Shuffling your feet along the sand lets 'em know you're coming and moves them away.

DO remember what it was like to learn when you're out there surfing like a true diva. Stay humble and be tolerant and sharing toward newbies.

DON'T caddy a board. This means retrieving another surfer's wayward board which is usually the result of someone not using a leash. Keeping tabs on your own board is your first priority.

DON'T have a tea party. This is surfing in a cluster, and though it sounds sociable and festive, Izzy says it's really an accident waiting to happen.

DON'T tailgate. Riding too closely behind another surfer is dangerous.

DON'T snake a wave, or cut in front of another surfer who has already nabbed the wave you want. (According to the Divas, this rule has an unspoken qualifier: ". . . unless he's really cute.")

4. Class is in session.

Surf Diva beginning classes start out with the absolute basics. Yours should, too. How to carry the board, how to lay on it, and how to paddle might seem rudimentary, but it's important to learn these fundamentals accurately. You'll also learn how to handle a board under and over a wave, to read tides and currents, to get into a standing position, and to "wipe out" safely. Be sure to pick up etiquette pointers about how to share the water with other surfers, too.

Standing up on your board is not emphasized by the Divas because no one should feel pressured to do so before they're ready and because everyone begins with a different level of fitness and daring. Diva instructors emphasize that getting up on the board is frosting and that the rest of the cake is just as good. Try to focus on fun and enjoyment, not performance or goals. (If you feel your instructor has gone drill sergeant on you, you might want to find another class.)

A reputable surfing class will take place at a reliably advantageous spot for the sport. Izzy urges beginners to remember that you're only as good as your conditions—pro skiers are not going to ski their best on sheer ice, and surfers can't exactly freestyle on flat seas. You can't control the weather, so cut yourself some slack if the perfect waves don't show up when you do. Just slather on some sunscreen, and paddle out to class anyway. ***Surf's up—so what are you waiting for?!***

5. Maintain your tan—and your enthusiasm.

When you've mastered the board basics, you're apt to yearn for as much wave time as you can get. If you live on the coast, you can:

- Find the surfing beaches and ask local enthusiasts which are best for your skill level. Make sure your choices feature supervision by county lifeguards.
- Find a surf buddy and make regular dates. (You should always surf with a friend.)
- Watch the weather report and learn how to read a tide chart (which you can get at your local surf shop) to determine optimal surf times.

If you can't stray far from your desk for a while or have to head home to the Midwest, schedule some vacation time so you can hit ideal surfing weather locally or at a world-famous beach. (See Beyond the Badge, page 272, for locations.) Meanwhile, pop in one of the videos listed in Izzy's Picks, page 273. This will refresh your memory about the skills you've learned, the fun you've had, and what you have to look forward to on your next ride or surf vacation. ***Stay stoked!***

CONGRATULATIONS!

Hey there, surfer girl, you shred! And you did it!

I DID IT!

Name: ______________________________

Date: ______________________________

SURF SLANG

Surfer girls say

Catch a wave. When you don't have to paddle, kick, or swim any more to maintain your speed, you've caught a wave.

Hang ten. Popping up on your board and then walking to its very tip, hanging your ten toes over. The wave breaks on the back of the board, balancing you like a teeter-totter. An advanced skill. (Divas are equipped to hang twelve, depending on how far they care to lean over!)

Pop up. The push-up move that gets you off your stomach and upright on your board.

Wipe out or the rinse cycle. Falling off the board.

BEYOND THE BADGE

If you love it as much as you thought you would, dream on . . .

- **Surf around the world.** Happily, the best waves are also in some of the prettiest travel destinations in the world (Hawaii, Costa Rica, Australia, California, Mexico). Plan your next trip around surfing or build it into your vacation. Make your next reunion with your college roommate a surf camp reunion, meet your sister at a weekend surf session, or talk your company into having its next corporate team-building clinic at the beach. So much nicer than fire walking, no? (But if you want to try that too, go to Walk on Fire, page 32.)
- **Buy a board.** When buying a board, consider your budget, skill level, and the spots you are likely to surf. Izzy advises you to walk away from any clerk who tries to sell you a board without asking you about these criteria, and walk out of any shop that doesn't make you feel welcomed and respected (see Board Scores).
- **Compete.** The major sponsors of amateur competitions are the National Scholastic Surfing Association (www.nssa.org), Eastern Surfing Association (www.surfesa.org), United States Surfing Federation (www.ussurf.org), and Hawaii Amateur Surfing Association (www.hasasurf.org). These organizations may be able to help you locate a coach if you're serious about competition. Check out an event or participate yourself—your local YMCA may sponsor some if you live in a beach community.

BOARD SCORES

Catch a wave and a sweet deal

- Bargain surfboards can be found at garage sales—although if the board needs repairs, it may not be such a bargain. You can also find gently used boards on the used rack at surf shops. If you can afford to spend more, a new or custom board can be yours.
- You don't have to buy a board made specifically for women, but Izzy does advise you check them out. The best are shaped to accommodate female arm widths, centers of gravity, and upper body strength.
- Izzy advocates shopping for brands that promote women's surfing, so that your dollars can support the sport and its athletes.
- Izzy recommends these board vendors: Wahine Blue (Miami, Florida), Ocean Outfitters (Wildwood Crest, New Jersey), Ron Jon's (online at www.ronjons.com), Hansen Surfboards (online at www.hansensurf.com), Aquahine (Mission Beach, California), and of course, Surf Diva (online at www.surfdiva.com).

IZZY'S PICKS

BOOKS

Girl in the Curl: A Century of Women in Surfing by Andrea Gabbard
A Diva-endorsed history.

MAGAZINES

SG, a.k.a. Surf Snow Skate Girl
www.sgmag.com
Skewed for a young audience but fun for all ages.

Surf Life for Women
www.surflifeforwomen.com
Izzy writes for them regularly.

ORGANIZATIONS

Boarding for Breast Cancer
www.b4bc.org
A nonprofit, youth-focused awareness and fundraising foundation. BBC spreads information about good health practices and the importance of early cancer detection through sports, music, art, and events.

Surf Diva
www.surfdiva.com or 858-454-8273
An organization dedicated to women's surfing, offering classes and gear for women who rule the waves.

Surfrider Foundation
www.surfrider.org
A nonprofit environmental organization working to safeguard the world's oceans and beaches. They have sixty chapters around the world, and Izzy is a lifetime member.

MUSIC

Ben Harper
What's not to like about this rootsy reggae, rock, funk, and folk poet?

Jack Johnson
He's a surfer and all the surfers love him.

Israel "Iz" Kamakawiwo'ole
Traditional Hawaiian music that captures the aloha spirit.

MOVIES & VIDEOS

Blue Crush
Izzy has seen it five times, and some of the stars and crew prepared for filming at Surf Diva.

Heart of the Sea
A biographical documentary about Hawaiian Rell Sun, one of the founders of the first women's professional surfing tour and an international surfing champion, who waged a fourteen-year battle with breast cancer.

North Shore
Hilarious and one of Izzy's all-time faves.

Roxy's Surf, Now
Gorgeous cinematography.

Tropical Madness
Inspirational footage shows what it's like to be a female pro surfer.

Yoga for Surfers with Peggy Hall
To prevent injury and increase strength and flexibility. Includes moves you can do on a board.

34

HEAD FOR THE HILLS

★ climbing ★

> Great things are done when men [sic] and mountains meet; This is not done by jostling in the street.
>
> —William Blake

So, what's your motivation?
Take a moment.
Dream a little, think big,
and then complete this sentence:
I see myself . . .

Imagine This . . . Some days, climbing out of bed feels like climbing Mount Everest. But on those flat-footed, nose-to-the-grindstone days, you daydream about your next ascent. Maybe you'll scale a nearby peak or the walls at a local rock-climbing gym. Or perhaps you're preparing for a trip to Machu Picchu up the Inca Trail; to Nepal's capital, Katmandu; or to New Zealand's postcard-perfect Mount Cook. Once you start climbing, nothing can stand in your way. The disciplines and delights of the endeavor spill into your daily life, giving you the confidence to set goals, solve problems, and overcome any obstacle. With this badge to walk you through your first climb, you'll soon reach new heights. *You can do it!*

The Payoffs

- **Body.** No doubt about it, this is exercise! Climbing strengthens and tones your muscles and increases flexibility and agility.
- **Mind.** Physical strength, stamina, and dexterity are great—but to get to the top, you'll need to use your head to solve logistical puzzles, exercise good judgment, and pace yourself.
- **Spirit.** Spirits are sure to soar when you master the elements and terrain, glimpse panoramic vistas that only a climber sees, and enjoy the camaraderie of fellow climbers (as a smart hiker, you'd never climb alone).
- **Pride.** When you stand on the top of a mountain with the clouds at your feet, you know you've really achieved something.

Meet Your Mentor

ARLENE BLUM

What She Does: Has made more than 200 ascents, led more than twenty successful mountaineering expeditions, and taken part in climbs of Everest and Mount McKinley. She led the first American climb of Annapurna and completed a 2,000-mile, nine-month trek across the Himalayan regions of Bhutan, Nepal, and India. She is the author of *Annapurna: A Woman's Place* and *Breaking Trail: My Path to High Places,* and her articles and photographs have appeared in publications including *National Geographic, Smithsonian,* and the *New York Times.* As an academic (she has a PhD in biophysical chemistry), she was instrumental in banning Tris, a cancer-causing chemical once used as a flame retardant in children's sleepwear. Today, Blum conducts multicultural understanding workshops in California and Bangalore, India; leads adventure travel trips; and presents motivational lectures and workshops.

Why She Does It: "I grew up in the Midwest and did not have an adventurous or athletic upbringing. When I was an undergrad at Reed College in Portland, my chemistry lab partner suggested we go climbing. He was handsome, so I went! I was completely incompetent and wound up sliding down the ice and rock of Mount Adams, but I was also exhilarated and hooked on the sport. On most of my early trips, I was the only woman. In 1970, when I was twenty-five, I was the assistant leader on the first all-women's climb of Alaska's Denali. My academic career was successful and rewarding, but after taking my nine-month Himalayan trek, I left it behind. How can you stay in the lab once you've seen the Himalayas?"

A woman's place is ON TOP.

—from the cover of Arlene Blum's *Annapurna: A Woman's Place*

Word from the Wise: "The trick is small steps. If you look at a mountain, it seems impossible—but if you just think about whether you can lift and lower your foot, one step at a time, you can do it."

BADGE STEPS

1. Find a class.

Depending on your local terrain and personal inclinations—no pun intended—you might take to ice climbing, mountain trekking, or peak scaling. To explore your options and get a firm grasp of the climbing basics, find yourself a comprehensive beginner's class, where you'll learn the fundamentals of techniques, equipment, and safety, then put them into practice. Beginner climbs are often on "walk-up" mountains, which can be challenging but don't require special equipment beyond boots and appropriate apparel.

Schools and universities in communities with nearby mountains will probably offer classes—Arlene learned the basics at a Reed College P.E. class in Portland, Oregon. Local mountaineering and climbing clubs may be able to refer you to an experienced teacher and can give you the lowdown on local guides and outings. Mountain climbing takes practice and perseverance, so look for a class that gives you a chance to put in a few hours at a time over several days or weeks to build up your skills. If you don't live near a mountain range, head for the high country on your next vacation and sign up for an introductory class. ***Sign up for climbing class, and start moving up in the world.***

2. Gear up for the uphill climb.

Ask your class instructor to explain and give shopping instructions for required class gear. Here are the basics:

Boots. The classic mountain climbing version is made of leather, but lighter-weight leather, nylon, and Gore-Tex models can be less expensive and are easier to break in. Either way, look for high uppers to protect your ankles and good traction on the sole. Tell your outfitter where you'll be climbing so that they can advise you about different boot heights. Try on boots with appropriate socks and in the evening, when your feet will likely have swollen a bit—as they will during a climb.

Socks. Look for wool or synthetic blends instead of cotton for the best cushioning, insulation, and absorption.

Clothing. Your apparel will vary based on your weather conditions, but layering is key. You may want to wear a sports bra and spandex undergarments to feel comfortable with the range of movement. Then add a layer of warm, snug clothes for insulation, and at least one outer layer

BEFORE YOU HEAD FOR THE HILLS . . .

Curl up with a good book

Mountaineering: The Freedom of the Hills is the book Arlene turned to when she was getting started forty years ago and the book she has all newbies read before they climb or trek with her. This authoritative reference is assembled by Seattle's Mountaineers, a nonprofit organization founded in 1906 "to explore, study, preserve, and enjoy the natural beauty of the outdoors." (See Arlene's Picks, page 281, for contact information.) With both introductory and advanced information on all aspects of mountaineering, *The Freedom of the Hills* is all about combining "the simple joy of being in the mountains with the skill, gear, and strength to travel where we will without harm to ourselves, others, or the environment." A must-read.

that you can remove if you get hot—a lightweight sweatshirt, fleece pullover, or flannel shirt should do the trick. Since the weather can be changeable at high altitudes, be sure to put on protective outerwear over it all to protect yourself from wind and rain.

Food and water. Be sure you have some nourishment and water with you, even if you don't think you'll need it. You don't want to have to turn back an hour or two into your climb because the altitude or exertion has gotten the better of you, and you're suddenly lightheaded or dehydrated.

Packs. You'll want a lightweight daypack to carry your food and water, plus any other climbing equipment. For longer climbing or trekking, you'll want a bigger backpack filled with the "Ten Essentials" detailed on page 438 in Commune with Nature.

Climbing equipment. Your class will provide or advise you about ropes, harnesses, and carabiners, plus ice axes and crampons as needed for climbing in snow and ice.

Get equipped.

3. Move up the learning curve.

In class, you'll learn how to make your way in the great outdoors and pick up some key climbing skills, including:

Tying knots. A strong knot can make all the difference in the world between a safe rappel and unintended free fall, so pay attention!

Making sound decisions about when to rappel. Mountaineering is not a race, and knowing when to go with a slow and deliberate descent is the sign of a true pro.

Navigating weather and routes. The wilds can get very wild with unexpected weather, so you need to be prepared to think on your feet and map out a sound course of action.

Taking responsibility for yourself. Only you can know when you've reached the limits of your ability and knowledge, and a good teacher will help you develop instincts about when to head back or call it a day.

In addition to teaching you the basics, a class experience will introduce you to other people at a similar skill level. "When I first came to California," says Arlene, "I did a couple of Sierra Club trips, and afterwards I had friends to climb with." Climbs are best celebrated with friends. ***Learn what it takes to be upwardly mobile.***

MOUNTAINEERING MUMBO-JUMBO

Explained at last

Anchor. How the belayer is connected to the rock or mountain face.

Belay. The length of rope that runs from a climber to another person, the belayer, who is at the ready to brake the rope and stop a fall.

Carabiner. Metal snap links of different shapes used for belaying, rappelling, securing rope, etc.

Harness. The rope is tied into a harness, which fits around your legs and/or waist. In the bad old days, rope was simply coiled around the climber's waist—but harnesses protect the back and ribs in the event of a fall.

Pitch. A section of a climb between two belays.

Rappel. Sliding down a rope to descend.

Rope. Should be synthetic and approved by the Union Internationale des Associations d'Alpinisme (UIAA).

I DID IT!

"I finally conquered all my fears and finished a climb. Before that, I'd get about 90 percent of the way to the top and be satisfied (or scared), which drove my partner, an avid climber, crazy. We were at Owens River Gorge, in the Eastern Sierra, and the view at the top was just spectacular. I stayed up there for quite a while to appreciate where I was and what I had accomplished."
—Arin

DOES THE FIRE DEPT. MAKE MOUNTAIN CALLS?

"When we began to make our way down the mountain, the sun had started to set. So instead of hiking down the steep path, my partner suggested lowering me off the rock with ropes. I trusted him, so I put my harness back on and he started lowering me off the edge of this huge rock. As he did, I realized that because of the way the rock side curved, I'd be dangling in the air. All my training and understanding about how secure the gear was vanished. I asked my partner to let me up and he laughed, not seeing any problem. Having nothing to hold on to, I started clawing at the rock face to get back up—like an animal! It felt like an eternity, but eventually my partner realized I was serious and brought me back up. That was the first climb I completed—and the last!"
—Arin

ARLENE'S EXPERT TIPS

WORK YOUR WAY TO THE TOP

Different mountains pose different challenges, largely based on altitude and terrain. A very high mountain that's not all that technically difficult to climb may pose a challenge because of its altitude, while a lower peak may be trickier because its topography is more daunting. In order of their difficulty, here are some variations:

Novice. These climbs don't require special equipment but can still get you up high.

Snow-capped. You'll need ice axes and crampons plus training on how to use them to make it up these "glaciated" peaks, which are often volcanoes.

Expedition. Handling high altitudes, serious weather, and at least a week of climbing requires training and fortitude.

The fourteen 8,000-meter-high Himalayan peaks. High and difficult, these are the stuff of dreams—and nightmares. Only those with years of training should attempt these.

4. Be safe up there!

Review the safety recommendations in Commune with Nature, page 441, and don't doze off or pass notes to your classmates during this portion of your instruction. As *The Freedom of the Hills* states, the most common causes of mishaps are climbing without a rope, climbing beyond one's abilities, and being ill-equipped for the conditions at hand. These scenarios are all avoidable—and avoiding them won't impede your fun and adventure one bit. ***Remember: Safety first, last, and everywhere in between.***

5. Get into climbing condition.

As you take your class and get comfortable with your skill set, set a climbing goal. You may need to focus on specific skills for this climb—snow, ice, or rock, for instance. Ask the leader of the climb to help you prepare.

In addition to learning specific techniques, spend some time on general physical conditioning. Arlene once had a New Yorker on one of her adventure trips who said the only exercise he got was running for subway trains. As it turned out, he would have had a much better time if he'd been in good overall condition. So take a lesson from the subway-chaser,

6. Rise above it all.

Before you set out on your ascent, do a final check:

- Make sure you're heading uphill early in the day, so that you give yourself more time than you think you'll need to enjoy the view up there and get back down before dark. The way down won't necessarily be faster than the way up, and as daylight grows dim, a downhill climb can swiftly go, well, downhill.
- Double-check your equipment to be sure you have everything you need. You don't want to be dangling on the side of a mountain when you discover you're missing an essential tool.
- The company you keep on your climb is also your safety and support network, so go over safety and emergency procedures once more before you set out together. Know exactly what you'll be doing and who you'll be doing it with.

As you make your way slowly and steadily uphill, "Synchronize your walking and breathing, and go at your own pace," advises Arlene. "Once when I was climbing Mount St. Helens, I ran into a woman stopped and gasping for breath at the side of the trail. She'd been trying to keep pace with her boyfriend, who was running and stopping in spurts. I told her to follow me instead. She did—and by keeping a slow and steady pace, we got to the top before the boyfriend!"

Incorporate the "rest step," a pause built into each step. After one foot is brought forward, support your body on the rear leg while relaxing the forward leg. If you find your own comfortable rhythm with this step, you'll avoid huffing and puffing—and as Arlene says, "You wind up almost meditating your way up the mountain!" ***Enjoy your time on top of the world!***

CONGRATULATIONS!

The hills are alive with the sound of your achievement. You did it!

I DID IT!

Name: ______________________

Date: ______________________

WOMEN ON TOP*

They did it without Gore-Tex

Marie Pardis. The Frenchwoman who climbed Mont Blanc in 1808, becoming the first woman to do so and the first woman mountaineer known to Western history.

Alexandra David-Neel. Made a series of journeys across the high Tibetan plateau from 1911 to 1944. When she was fifty-five, she disguised herself as a Tibetan beggar woman and walked 2,000 miles across high snowy passes to reach the forbidden city of Lhasa.

Annie S. Peck. This professor climbed the Matterhorn when she was a young thing of forty-five. When she was fifty-eight, she made the first ascent of Huascarán South in the Peruvian Andes.

*Cited in *Annapurna: A Woman's Place*

A REAL CLIFF-HANGER

Find inspiration from thirteen trail-blazing women

Arlene's *Annapurna: A Woman's Place* is an adventure classic that tells the story of the first American expedition up the world's tenth highest peak. The time was 1978, when female climbers were routinely turned down for expeditions because the prevailing belief was that they would distract, impede, or generally discombobulate the male climbers. So Arlene organized thirteen women to participate in the American Women's Himalayan Expedition to Annapurna and attempt to become the first Americans and the first women to scale the notorious peak. Arlene's story is a true page-turner, capturing grueling months of trekking, treacherous ice climbing, and the constant threat of avalanche.

BEYOND THE BADGE

If you love it as much as you thought you would, dream on . . .

- **Make it harder on yourself.** This could mean taking a harder route on a local mountain, experiencing a new type of terrain or weather condition, climbing higher, or taking a longer trip. Approach each new challenge as you did your first—with plenty of advance preparation and skill-building.
- **Adventure climbing or trekking travel.** There are plenty of worthy challenges in this world, even if you don't have the urge to mimic Arlene's nine-month Himalayan trek. Make intercultural study, language basics, and environmental awareness part of your training, and you'll make yourself welcome on mountains worldwide. (See Going Up?)
- **Join an expedition.** Expeditions vary in length, depending on time needed to travel to the peak, hike into base camp, and take essential rest breaks. The routine climbing challenges of terrain and weather are amplified by duration. Do extensive research to find the right match for your abilities and to find team members with compatible personalities and climbing styles.
- **Rock climbing.** If you think you've got a grip on mountaineering, try your hand at rock climbing. In rock climbing, strength and strategy work hand in hand—or to be more accurate, hand and foot—to give you a superhero's ability to climb a sheer rock face. Rock climbing can be pursued as a separate activity from mountain climbing, make up a portion of a mountain ascent, or take place on the artificial climbing walls of a gym. Climbing gyms provide a safe and controlled learning environment for sport climbing, in which you'll use ropes and be belayed by someone on the ground. Some gyms also give you a chance to try bouldering, which is done without a rope and not too far from the ground. Crash pads are placed on the gym floor to cushion falls.

GOING UP?

Help getting there

Alpine Ascents International. Offers climbers at all levels the opportunity to achieve personal goals through challenging, safe, and enjoyable expeditions. www.alpineascents.com.

Aventuras Patagonicas. An international climbing guide service, running high altitude mountaineering expeditions throughout the world. www.patagonicas.com.

Expeditions International. An adventure travel, mountain guide service, and climbing school leading trips throughout the United States and around the world. www.mtnguides.com.

International Mountain Guides. Since 1975, they have conducted over 300 expeditions to destinations around the globe. www.mountainguides.com.

Mountain Madness. Combines the physical challenge of climbing and trekking with the cultural and aesthetic experiences of the last wild places on earth. www.mountainmadness.com.

ARLENE'S PICKS

BOOKS

Annapurna: A Woman's Place by Arlene Blum
Thirteen women set out to blaze a trail up one of the world's highest peaks at a time when female mountain climbers were considered excess baggage on major expeditions. A true tale of passion and courage.

Beyond the Limits: A Woman's Triumph on Everest by Stacy Allison
This is the account of Stacy Allison, the first American woman ever to reach the highest point on Earth.

Breaking Trail: My Path to High Places by Arlene Blum
Arlene combines memoir and adventure to explore why and what she has climbed.

Mountaineering: The Freedom of the Hills by The Mountaineers
The climber's bible.

Tents in the Clouds: The First Women's Himalayan Expedition by Monica Jackson and Elizabeth Stark
The story of a triumphant 1955 climb by a three-woman British team.

ASSOCIATIONS

Appalachian Mountain Club
www.outdoors.org
Twelve chapters offer numerous climbing programs from two to five days. They also publish excellent outdoor guides.

The Colorado Mountain Club
www.cmc.org
Sponsors trips and classes, including national and international outings.

Mazamas
www.mazamas.org
Founded in 1894, this organization based in Portland, Oregon, is on a mission "to provide a comprehensive climbing program with allied activities that enhance and protect the participants and the environment."

The Mountaineers
www.mountaineers.org
This venerable organization publishes guidebooks and adventure literature and sponsors outdoor activities.

Sierra Club
www.sierraclub.com
With 700,000 members working together to protect the planet, "The Club" is America's oldest, largest, and most influential grass-roots environmental organization.

GEAR

Eastern Mountain Sports
www.ems.com
Helmets, harnesses, packs, shoes, and clothing.

REI
www.rei.com
All-purpose Web site specializing in high-quality outdoor performance wear.

Title 9 Sports
www.title9sports.com
Inspired by women, created for women, and run by women, Title 9 Sports is women's athletic apparel.

WEB SITES

www.cruxed.com
Informative articles plus features to help you locate climbing gyms around the world.

www.mountainzone.com
Personal stories, trip reports, route finders, and world mountain facts.

www.nps.gov
The portal to the National Park Service.

www.7summits.com
Detailed info on the world's highest mountains. Plan a trip, or just fantasize!

CLIMBING SCHOOLS

Adventures in Good Company
www.goodadventure.com
An outfitter that offers women-only rock-climbing excursions to all ages and ability levels.

Eastern Mountain Sports Climbing School
www.emsclimb.com
Ice climbing, mountaineering, rock climbing, expeditions, and treks.

Exum Mountain Guides
www.exumguides.com
Since the 1920s.

International Mountain Climbing School
ime-usa.com/imcs
Courses, trips, and expeditions.

35 JUMP!

★ skydiving ★

Impossibilities
are merely things which we
have not yet learned.

—Charles W. Chestnutt

So, what's your motivation?
Take a moment.
Dream a little, think big,
and then complete this sentence:
I see myself . . .

Imagine This . . . You're falling but it feels like floating. You feel small compared to the wide blue yonder all around you, but you also feel sturdy and strong as you steer and balance. And though you thought you had a sense of your senses, you now know how heightened they can be as you hear air and feel silence. When, all too soon, you feel the earth beneath your feet, you still feel like you're walking on air, flying high, giddy and grinning. You always wondered what training, skills, and equipment you'd need—and if, when you got right down (or up!) to it, you could actually push yourself out of a plane and into the sky. Now you know! Gonna fly now? *You can do it!*

The Payoffs

- **It's thrilling.** Well, duh! To get an idea of the rush, think sitting on a cloud, riding a really steep roller coaster, and drinking a triple shot of espresso—all at once!
- **It's challenging.** Even on heavily supervised beginner jumps, you have to do something completely counterintuitive: Leap out of a plane! And more advanced solo jumps require great concentration and precision.
- **It's fear-conquering.** Like so many of the *You Can Do It!* badges, learning you can take that leap vaporizes old stumbling blocks and makes new challenges feel like a piece of cake.
- **It's special.** As a skydiver, you join an elite club. Our continent-hopping expert likens it to a family; you can go to any "drop zone" in the world and feel at home.

Meet Your Mentor

JILL SALO

What She Does: Jill is a skydiving instructor with about 1,800 skydives and 250 BASE (Buildings, Antennas, Spans, Earth) jumps to her credit.

Why She Does It: "It was something I had wanted to do since I was twelve, when I saw a photograph of skydivers in a magazine. I remember running to my parents to tell them that this is what I wanted to do. They nodded in polite acknowledgment and said that I would have to wait until I was eighteen. As the years went by, I grew ever more determined, and on my eighteenth birthday, I asked permission to go. In South Africa (where I was living) one had to be eighteen, with signed parental consent, or twenty-one to jump as an individual. My parents, who had always prided themselves on keeping their word, said that they could not sign for me because they would never forgive themselves if something happened to me. So I waited another three years and, at twenty-one, signed up for a course at the local parachute club. That first jump was amazing and opened up a whole new world for me. I was so excited and couldn't stop babbling about my experience—this coming from a normally quiet girl. My dad said, 'The good news is that she lived; the bad news is that she loved it!' It was the most challenging and empowering thing I had ever done, and it changed my life. From that weekend, it was all I could think about, and I spent every moment I could at the 'drop zone.'"

I love being able to do something that we should not physically be able to do: Jump out of a plane!

—Jill Salo

Word from the Wise: "It's a mental challenge and physical adrenaline rush in one package. It feels a bit like swimming but is a *lot* more liberating."

BADGE STEPS

1. Drop by a drop zone.

Though it's called the United States Parachute Association, the USPA Web site (www.uspa.org) is the perfect place to begin your skydiving adventure no matter where you live. Use the site to locate drop zones (diving sites) around the world. You can also check your Yellow Pages—under "parachute" or "skydiving"—but you'll want to make sure any site you find is a USPA "group member," and that its instructors are certified and rated members of USPA.

You can call the drop zone to ask about the different options they offer for beginners, but why not visit the site to make your inquiries? Seeing is believing, and it'll give you a feel for the place and its people. Make a day of it—ask if there's a training video you can watch, observe a few jumps, and talk to a first-timer after her first dive.

Some drop zones require a tandem jump the first time around, while others will give you a choice of:

Tandem. You are connected via a harness to a tandem master, who calls the shots from plane exit to landing. You share a heavy-duty parachute which the master opens. Your prep time for this is minimal, often about thirty minutes.

Static line. In this technique, developed by the military, your parachute is attached to the plane by a (really strong!) cord. The chute opens for you almost immediately after you deplane. You'll get landing signals from the ground or via radio contact. This requires a four-to-six hour training class.

Accelerated free fall (AFF). Two instructors jump out of the plane with you and hold onto you during the forty-five seconds or so of free fall. Your instructors monitor your ability to pull your own cord and open your own chute. When you do so, they let go of you, and you get about a five-minute float to the ground. Ground or radio signals direct your landing. For this, you'll need an all-day or weekend training.

Jill suggests that tandem is just the ticket for your first jump. "You won't have much to learn or remember—and since you're attached to a tandem master during the jump, you can pretty much just enjoy the ride, relaxing and taking in the view." ***Find and visit a drop zone—and sign up for a tandem jump.***

DIVE TALKIN'

Diving definitions

Automatic activation device (AAD). Opens the reserve parachute automatically. Often referred to by its brand name (Cypress) and usually required at drop zones.

BASE jumps. BASE stands for Buildings, Antennas, Spans (bridges), and Earth (like mountains)—and you know what jumping means.

Canopy. Cute word for parachute.

DZ. Abbreviation for drop zone.

Free fall. What you do during the first forty-five to sixty seconds of your dive, before opening your parachute.

Jump Master (JM). A jumper trained and certified to supervise students.

Main. The primary parachute.

Pit. Intended landing area at a drop zone.

Reserve. Secondary (backup) parachute.

2. Predive checklist.

As you anticipate your jump, be aware of these preliminaries. At the drop zone, you'll register and sign a liability release form. Skydiving is really very safe, but you are, after all, jumping out of a plane! You usually need to be at least eighteen (some schools admit sixteen-year-olds with parental consent) and should be in good health (heart and respiratory problems and some medications don't mix well with skydiving). Your gear rental is part of the cost of training. Here's what to expect:

Parachute system. One main and one reserve, packed into a backpack with chest and leg straps.

Jumpsuit. Various fabrics and tailoring are used in different types of jumps.

Helmet. Required for students.

Goggles. To protect your eyes during the speedy (120 to 150 mph!) free fall period.

You'll also want to dress comfortably and wear sneakers (no boots or sandals). Think about who you'd like to invite to your diving debut. Most people enjoy having a cheering section to celebrate with post-jump. ***Prepare to fly.***

JILL'S EXPERT TIPS

WAYS TO KEEP FLYING

Dive differently. Jill says, "There are so many disciplines within the sport that it's almost impossible to get bored. There's relative work (flying on your belly relative to four, eight, or sixteen other jumpers); free-flying (a newer form of flying in different positions, mostly on one's head or in a sit position); accuracy (landing on a specified target); style (individually performing a set of predetermined moves in the fastest time); and canopy relative work (building formations while under an open parachute)."

Become a licensed diver. The USPA offers four classes of license: basic, intermediate, advanced, and master. Visit www.uspa.org to learn more.

Dive around. Crave a change of scene? Click on "Drop Zones" at the USPA Web site to find descriptive listings of diving centers throughout the U.S. and around the world. Think Swiss Alps, Hawaiian Islands, or diving Down Under.

WHAT IF?

Why you can trust your parachute

- Modern parachute materials are incredibly durable (zero-porosity nylon, if you really want to know).
- In the unlikely event that your main canopy malfunctions, you have a reserve parachute as backup. (These reserves are regularly inspected by Federal Aviation Administration–certified "riggers.")
- In the even more unlikely event that you—or your tandem master—are unable to open your parachute, an automatic activation device calculates rate of descent and altitude and deploys the parachute at a preset altitude.

BIG THINGS

Can come in tiny packages

Georgia "Tiny" Broadwick (four feet tall, eighty-five pounds) was the first woman to jump from a plane, in 1913, above Griffith Park in Los Angeles. She was also the first to make a free fall from a plane, during a parachute demonstration for the U.S. government in 1914.

I DID IT!

"None of my coworkers could believe it when I told them that my sister and I were going skydiving that weekend. Maybe they could believe her wanting to do it, since she's the type to get a tattoo or go white-water rafting, but I'm the sensible older sister—or so everyone thought! We found a beautiful training center in northern California, with views from the plane of the Pacific Ocean, the Sierra Nevada Mountains, and the San Francisco Bay Area. I wasn't even nervous, just really psyched. We had a blast and still giggle about our wild adventure. Sisterhood really is powerful!"

—Margery

SO SOON?

"I guess I didn't realize how fast the dive would go—not how fast you fall, but how quickly the whole jump is over. I've since learned that it's common for people not to really remember their first jump all that well. You're nervous and trying to remember all your safety instructions. I wish someone had told me to work on relaxing and really observing and savoring every second I was up there. Maybe that's just not possible during your first few jumps, but that's what I'll try to do more of next time."

—Elena

3. Dive day.

Almost all drop zones will offer a professional video of your jump. (The cameraperson jumps just before you to capture your every move.) Jill highly recommends that you take advantage of this option! There's no way you'll forget your jump, but the video will let you replay it forever—plus you can use it to scare your mother, wow your dates, and impress your teenage nephew. The video will also give you a different perspective on your experience. You might not believe your own eyes!

Before your jump, you'll receive basic safety instruction and get briefed on the jump procedures your tandem master will follow, including exiting the plane, controlling the parachute, steering, and landing.

You'll have about a twenty-minute plane ride to reach diving altitude, typically 10,000 to 13,000 feet. Once you're there and situated above the drop area, the pilot will cut the engine while you deplane. Your tandem master "rides" on your back. During the initial forty-five to sixty seconds of free fall, you'll really hear the wind. Your guide monitors your altitude, deploying the parachute at about 4,000 feet. At that point you'll feel a gentle tug upward and begin a four- to five-minute float to the ground. Now you can hear and even chat with your instructor on the way down.

Finally, you'll come in for a landing just as you've been trained to do. Landings these days are more gentle than jolting, due to the rectangular shape of modern chute canopies. Once you're back on *terra firma*, do you want to kiss the ground like the Pope, or dump the tandem master and fly solo? ***Jump, smile, celebrate—and watch your video!***

CONGRATULATIONS!

Jump for joy! You did it!

I DID IT!

Name: ______________________

Date: ______________________

JILL'S PICKS

BOOKS

Eyes in the Sky by Patrick Passe and Wendy Smith
Photographs from around the world by two premier free-fall photographers cover the range of diving techniques and styles.

Jump: Skydiving Made Fun and Easy by Tom Buchanan
A wealth of information for the novice.

Parachuting: The Skydiver's Handbook by Dan Poynter and Mike Turoff
From first jump through advanced techniques, a comprehensive and well-illustrated basic text.

Skydiver's Information Manual
Published by the USPA and available at their Web site.

MAGAZINES

Parachutist
www.uspa.org/publications/parachutist/online_index.htm
The world's largest and most widely read skydiving publication. Published monthly and sent by mail to USPA members. (You are sure to find a copy or two at your drop zone.)

Skydiving
www.skydivingmagazine.com
The latest news on equipment, events, techniques, and the people and places of parachuting. Published monthly.

WEB SITES

www.afn.org/skydive
Provides links to virtually every information source about skydiving on the Internet.

www.dropzone.com
A wide range of features and services, including forums, gear reviews, and photo galleries.

www.uspa.org
The United States Parachute Association's site. This is the place for beginners and experts. Features everything from information on the history of skydiving, safety, and equipment to up-to-the-minute news and event listings.

VIDEOS & SOFTWARE

Flying Your Body
This instructional DVD helps new divers master the correct free-fall body positions (English, German, and French text).

From Wings Came Flight
A video filled with dramatic footage filmed on three continents.

Skydiving: A Multimedia Reference
Contains *Parachuting: The Skydiver's Handbook* (referenced above), fifty-six minutes of video, and searchable, hyperlinked text from the USPA's *Parachutist* magazine. (PC with CD drive required.)

36

GO FOR THE GOLD

★ triathlon ★

I am convinced that life in a physical body is meant to be an ECSTATIC experience.

—Shakti Gawain

Imagine This . . . Your body glistens with sweat and your muscles glow with the definition of exertion. You thought you were running on empty, but the sight of your friends, family, and fellow athletes waving and clapping up ahead gives you a surge of adrenaline. You raise your arms high, and grin from ear to ear as you cross the finish line. Never has your mind and body felt so in sync, so strong, so beautiful. For hours afterwards, you can't stop beaming, and you now know exactly what the phrase "tears of joy" means. Best of all, while the race becomes a memory, its effects on you never fade. You'll never again doubt your ability to push past self-imposed limitations. Who, me? Yes, you! *You can do it!*

So, what's your motivation?
Take a moment.
Dream a little, think big,
and then complete this sentence:
I see myself . . .

The Payoffs

- **Attitude adjustment.** Exercise acts as a natural antidepressant as endorphins are released and your serotonin uptake is increased.
- **Communion.** Triathlons are group affairs; even while competing, racers form a community. You strive alone yet together, with mutual understanding and respect.
- **Self-appreciation.** We are used to criticizing the way our bodies look, but this event lets us experience and celebrate what our bodies can do.
- **Glory.** At most tris, an announcer shouts your name out loud and clear as you take that last step to triathlon triumph. There's something about crossing a finish line to the cheers of onlookers . . . how many of our accomplishments are so tangibly recognized?

Meet Your Mentor

NANCY REINISCH

What She Does: A licensed clinical social worker and triathlete, Nancy "prescribes" exercise as a foolproof way to bust depression and boost self-esteem. She is the codeveloper and co-coach (with Judy Haynes) of the Roaring Fork Women's Triathlon Training Group in Glenwood Springs, Colorado, the race director of the Mother's Day Mile fundraiser, and a triathlon guide for blind triathlete Nancy Stevens.

Why She Does It: "I completed my first triathlon at age thirty-four, a product of what triathlete Sally Edwards has called AOA, or adult onset athleticism! I've since completed some forty short course and sprint events. I was not an athlete when I started, but I watched a friend finish our local Glenwood Triathlon and thought that if she could do it, so could I. I gave myself a year to train and taught myself to swim in local pools. Then I got out the old Schwinn bicycle. I trained to the distance of each component of the race, until I knew I could do what I'd have to on race day. But before the day of the race, I had never put all three events together, so I didn't really know if I could do them back to back. I did it—and at the finish line, when they called my name, 'Nancy Reinisch from Glenwood Springs' . . . well, I still tear up thinking about it! I didn't know any of the other competitors that day, but at that moment, for the first time in my life, I felt I was one of the athletes."

START WHERE YOU ARE. Everything begins with one step. Triathlon is a lifestyle of fitness that lasts a lifetime.

—Nancy Reinisch

Word from the Wise: "After training for a triathlon, you will always know that you can dig deep, that you can do what you had no idea you could. I've trained with women who are starting from square one at age fifty, women who could barely walk a mile, let alone run one, and women who don't know how to shift gears on a bike. Wherever we begin, we wind up learning lessons—about goal setting, patience, perseverance, competition, and teamwork—that we carry into every aspect of our lives. As they say at the Danskin event Web site, the woman who starts the race is not the same as the woman who finishes it."

BADGE STEPS

1. Get equipped.

Read Go for the Gold Gear and assemble your supplies. But don't stop there. To complete your first triathlon, you need to gear up mentally as well. To do so, take a cue from Nancy's Roaring Fork Women's Triathlon Training Group and write down your goals. Your own personal "Why tri?" goals make training easier because you have something concrete to shoot for—or cling to on those "I don't want to get out of bed" days. Keep your goals simple, attainable, and positive. Nancy suggests you complete the following sentences:

- Three things I want to accomplish in training (including specific swimming, cycling, and running goals) are . . .
- Three things that will help me accomplish this are . . .
- Three things that may get in my way are . . .
- Three strategies I'll use to combat these barriers are . . .
- Three ways others can help me meet my goals are . . .

Next, share your goals with a training buddy or team. Even if you tend to be a lone wolf, your tri experience will be enhanced if you buddy up. It's harder to weasel out of a workout if someone's waiting for you at the track or pool! So seek out a group like Roaring Fork, convince a friend or two to try a tri with you, or line up three friends to train with you: a swimmer, a runner, and a cyclist. (You can also ask the organizers of triathlon events for referrals to training groups; see Step 2.) ***Gear up with equipment, goals, and teammates.***

2. Pick an event.

Your first triathlon is not just an athletic challenge, it's a major life event, so choose a triathlon that will make it really special for you. To find tris, check out the Web sites and magazines in Nancy's Picks, page 295, and take these factors into consideration:

Location. You might be most comfortable at a local triathlon, since you are more likely to be accustomed to the terrain and weather conditions where you train. On the other hand, one of the benefits of triathlons is the opportunity to make the most of wonderful weather and splendid natural surroundings. If you live in blustery Boston or rainy Seattle, your first tri is the perfect excuse to head for sunnier climates. If you decide

TRI TYPES

There's something for everyone—including you!

Ironman Triathlons. 2.4 mile swim, 112 mile bike, 26.2 mile run. Also available: Half Ironman.

Olympic Distance. 1.5 km swim, 40 km bike, 10 km run. This event made its actual Olympics debut at the 2000 summer games in Sydney, Australia.

Short Course. Typically about half the distance of an Olympic race.

Sprint. ½ mile swim, 12–17 mile bike, 2–3 mile run

Team Triathlon. Different athletes do each leg of the event.

to make a trip for your triathlon, just be sure to leave yourself enough time to recover from jet lag and train locally before the big event.

Women's events. Some triathlons are specifically for women, and those sponsored by Danskin are legendary, including its Team Survivor events for women at all stages of recovery from cancer. One of the great things about Danskin events is that tri guru Sally Edwards goes to each race, rallies and inspires the "troops," and then comes in last in the race—so you don't have to fret about pulling up the rear.

Sprint triathlons. As you can see in Tri Types, triathlons come in many shapes and sizes. The short sprint triathlon is ideal for your first time out. You'll still need at least twelve weeks to train, so be sure to find one that's taking place a few months from now.

Register for a triathlon that is at least three months down the road.

3. Cross-train.

Careful cross-training is the key to any triathlon—in fact, triathlon was invented in the early 1970s by the San Diego Track Club as a varied, balanced workout method. Since you practice three sports, you are less apt to injure one overused, repeatedly stressed muscle group. "The swimming, cycling, and running/walking that make up a triathlon are each great, accessible sports that you can do most anywhere for the rest of your life," Nancy says.

But tri training requires mental as well as physical rigor. "The three events are also a metaphor for the different roles you juggle in your life," says our expert. "If you spend too much time in any one sphere, the others suffer. You learn this clearly in training. If you swim too much, you are taking time away from running and biking. You are forced to learn a great life lesson: balance and moderation."

For your physical training regimen, Nancy offers these tips:

- Start where you are. For Nancy (and Sally Edwards) this includes heart rate training and wearing a heart monitor so that you build endurance and strength at your own pace.
- To begin, build your base, getting to the point when you can swim, bike, and run the distance of your tri.
- When you can do this, build in "bricks"—two sports back to back.
- Place your training emphasis on your weakest sport.

GO FOR THE GOLD GEAR

What you'll need for a triathlon

:: For swimming:

Goggles

Swim cap

Towel

Wet suit or swim suit (according to pool or open water conditions)

:: For biking:

Bike

Bike shoes and socks

Bike water bottle

Helmet

Mini repair/tool kit

Sunglasses

:: For running:

Hat or visor

Running shoes

Water bottle

:: Miscellaneous:

Backpack to carry everything in

Food

Post-race clothes

Sportwatch with stopwatch capability

Sunscreen

Warm-up suit

I DID IT!

"When I turned fifty, I started training just to prove to myself that my physical life was, for sure, beyond salvation (too many cupcakes, too little exercise). To my amazement, little by little, I began to get more fit and actually enjoy all phases of training (well, almost all). Guess what? I did it!!! Next year I may be even faster, but regardless, the journey to the race—friendships, moments of personal truth, the joy of training—is a journey I intend to continue taking."

—Carol

TRI AGAIN

"I'd moved to a beautiful, coastal community with jogging/bike paths galore and, of course, lots of water. I was fit but wanted to exercise more and challenge myself, so I went online and found some training regimens for an Olympic distance triathlon. That was my goal. Swimming is often the toughest thing for people, but that and cycling were my strengths. I had the most trouble with the running! I trained steadily for several months—but when my work life started heating up, my training gradually ground to a halt. In retrospect, I think I should have set my sights on a shorter race and found people to train with. That's what I'll do next time!"

—Annie

- Strive for weekly training distances that equal three times the race distance. If your tri includes a 1 km swim, shoot for 3 km per week.
- Taper down the week before the race, giving yourself two complete rest days right before race day.

To train your brain:

Affirm. Quickly zap negative self-talk with positive thoughts and repeat them often. "I'm too nervous" becomes Nancy's "It's okay to have butterflies—just teach them to fly in formation." "I'm not good enough" becomes "I am strong, I am trained, I'm a can-do woman."

Visualize. Picture yourself meeting your training goals and overcoming obstacles in each sport. Visualize the entire triathlon, from race-morning jitters to the finish line. See yourself smoothly transitioning between sports, and feel yourself being carried along by the other racers.

Pump it up. Nancy suggests that the women she trains make a "pump you up" music tape or CD—the Pointer Sisters ("I'm So Excited"), Aretha Franklin ("R.E.S.P.E.C.T."), the *Rocky* theme, whatever gets you going. Watch inspiring movies about athletes—because that's what you are!

Train your mind and body.

4. Tri for success.

The day before your tri:

- Pack your own supplies. Map out the entire event in your mind to anticipate everything you may need or want.
- Call in reinforcements. Ask friends and family to take up a position at regular intervals along the course, or even follow alongside you from the sidelines during particularly difficult legs of the race. This will help keep up your energy and spirits.
- Eat balanced meals and drink plenty of water.
- Check and prep your bike.
- Watch an inspirational movie, and get to bed early.

On race day:

- Begin drinking water two hours before the start, and eat a light but nutritious breakfast.
- Don't inquire about anyone else's workouts that week so you can't psyche yourself out for not doing "enough."
- Don't try out any new gear or products right now.

- Arrange to have someone take a photo of you at the finish.
- Don't forget your sunscreen!

During the race:

- Pull over when necessary. Food, fluids, and first aid will be provided at official pit stops all along the course, but don't hesitate to ask for help in between if you need it. You may not even have to stop—just move to the side and shout out or signal what you need. Supporters and bystanders alike will be eager to help and get you on your way.
- Stay fueled. Nancy tries to consume 120–240 calories per hour or 30–60 grams of carbohydrates. She also reminds us that drinking 5–10 ounces of a sodium- and carb-rich sports drink every 15–30 minutes can ward off dehydration and enhance performance.
- Remember: Triathlons mean never having to say you're sorry. Racers bump into and jostle one another at close quarters; it's not meant to be malicious. When you feel a nudge, just be assertive or even aggressive about your turf, and stay focused on your performance.

After the race:

- Refuel within thirty minutes of finishing and have a celebratory dinner (and dessert!) that night.
- Book a massage for the day after.
- Don't say you could have done better "if only . . ." With a tri, just being a competitor makes you a winner.
- In the days and weeks after a race, do make sure to mention as often as possible and to anyone within earshot that you just did a triathlon. You deserve the awe and admiration you'll get!

On your marks, get set, go!

CONGRATULATIONS!

Your personal best just got better! You did it!

I DID IT!

Name: ______________________________

Date: ______________________________

FREE ADVICE

You don't have to hire a personal trainer to be a triathlete!

- Nancy uses a regimen culled from the books of Sally Edwards. For a free tipsheet outlining Sally's methods, check out www.danskin.com/triathlon/trainstartline.html.
- Once you register for an event, you can usually attend a free prerace training information seminar that will give you tips on cross-training, nutrition, and expected race conditions.
- Danskin also offers a free online tri-training discussion group and mentorship program, so that you can get training tips and answers to your questions from seasoned triathletes (for more, see www.danskin.com/triathlon/traininginfo.html).

BEYOND THE BADGE

If you love it as much as you thought you would, dream on . . .

- **Raise money.** Sport offers plenty of ways to flex your earning potential as well as your muscles. Call the local or national charities you support to find out about existing walks, runs, and bike rides, or follow Nancy's lead and start your own fund-raising event. Nancy was on the board of a local domestic violence shelter and suggested they do a one-mile race on Mother's Day: The Mother's Day Mile. "I hoped we could get 25 to 50 people there and charge ten dollars a person," she recalls. "Well, 325 people showed up that first day! This has now snowballed into a whole Glenwood Charity Race Series."
- **Up the ante.** Better your time, try to win your age group, or take the mental and physical training discipline you experienced with tri-training into another sport. Nancy had just run her first ("and last!") marathon when we spoke; her tri experience helped her know she could do it. And while she was at the bottom of her age group when she did her first tri at age thirty-four, in 2002 she won her age division in the same event—and got a commemorative tattoo to celebrate!
- **Mentor.** In the Roaring Fork Training Group, women who have already done a tri are called "tri-umphs" and mentor the inexperienced "tri-babies." You're a tri-umph now, so why not share your wisdom and experience? Ask triathlon event coordinators about opportunities to do so. You never know what form this might take. Nancy is now guiding a blind athlete: "I'd never ridden a tandem bike before, and I've also never done an Olympic distance tri, so we're going to do one together!" See www.challengedathletes.org for opportunities and inspiration.

GO FOR IT GOALS

The two largest North American triathlons

Mrs. T's Chicago Tri, Chicago, Illinois. Both sprint and Olympic distance races. More than twenty years old, this popular event includes a children's tri and features downtown Chicago as its spectacular setting. www.caprievents.com.

Wildflower Triathlon, Lake San Antonio, California. Offers long course, Olympic, and sprint distance races. Boasting North America's biggest field, this is a "three-day tri Woodstock" with a tough but beautiful course in Monterey County. www.tricalifornia.com.

NANCY'S PICKS

BOOKS

Endurance Sports Nutrition by Suzanne Girard Eberle
Tips on food, fluids, and vitamin supplements to build strength for endurance sports.

A Kind of Grace by Jackie Joyner-Kersee and Sonja Steptoe
The autobiography of perhaps the world's greatest female athlete.

The Measure of Our Success: A Letter to My Children and Yours by Marian Wright Edelman
Wisdom from the president of the Children's Defense Fund; inspiration to see you through life trials.

The Mental Game Plan: Getting Psyched for Sport by Stephen J. Bull, PhD, John G. Albinson, PhD, and Christopher J. Shambrook, PhD
A program of mental training that will help you maintain performance consistency by concentrating on the key psychological principles of success.

No Finish Line: My Life as I See It by Marla Runyan and Sally Jenkins
The inspiring story of the first legally blind athlete to compete in the Olympic Games.

Peak Fitness for Women by Paula Newby-Fraser and John M. Mora
Tips from this eight-time Hawaii Ironman champ to attain the total mental and physical fitness needed to reach that finish line.

The Runner's Guide to the Meaning of Life: What 35 Years of Running Have Taught Me about Winning, Losing, Happiness, Humility, and the Human Heart by Amby Burfoot
Insights from the champion marathoner and executive editor of *Runner's World* magazine.

Seven Mountains: The Inner Climb to Commitment and Caring by Marilyn Mason, PhD
Messages of courage, strength, and self-esteem.

Starting Out Triathlon: Training for Your First Competition by Paul Hudle and Roch Frey
All about training for your first competition.

Triathlons for Women by Sally Edwards
Triathlon training for all levels, from beginner to advanced.

MAGAZINES

american TRI
www.americantri.com
"The triathlete's performance magazine." Features on training, gear, nutrition, and even an article on the best dogs to train with!

Inside Triathlon
www.insidetriathlon.com
"The journal of multisport." Departments include "Water Log," "Coach's Corner," "Body Shop," and "My Turn" personal stories.

Triathlete
www.triathletemag.com
The "largest triathlon magazine."

WEB SITES

www.active.com
Register online to participate in sports events around the country, including triathlons. Offers tips on gear, workouts, and prep for your next challenge.

www.cdifferent.com
Established to promote the participation of blind and visually impaired athletes in competitive sports.

www.danskin.com/triathlon
Danskin sponsors tris for women of all abilities who want a supportive, noncompetitive environment.

www.heartzone.com
Sally Edwards and Kathy Kent's Heart Zones site has information on heart rate training, seminars, resources, and triathlon training programs.

www.trifind.com
Listing of triathlon and multisport events worldwide.

www.usatriathlon.org
A national membership organization for triathletes that coordinates and lists events and organizes the U.S. Olympic triathlon team (this could be you!).

MOVIES

Bend It Like Beckham

Breaking Away

Cool Runnings

Everest

The Long Run

Radio

Triathlon: Through the Eyes of the Elite

Without Limits

37

DIVE RIGHT IN

★ scuba diving ★

Water . . . Not necessary to life, but rather life itself; you fill us with gratification that exceeds the delight of the senses.

—Antoine de Saint-Exupéry

So, what's your motivation?
Take a moment.
Dream a little, think big,
and then complete this sentence:
I see myself . . .

Imagine This . . . You're weightless, and you glide with strength and grace amidst gorgeous reefs and Technicolor fish in a crystal-blue world. A sense of peace pervades the scene—you can't even remember the office politics or family feud that had your stomach in knots yesterday. Tortola? Belize? Papua New Guinea? You'll make a splash there, too. Perhaps you were hooked on *The Undersea World of Jacques Cousteau* television show as a kid, or maybe you think you know exactly where the sunken treasure is. Could be you just want to get away from it all. Once you're certified, you know all you need to do is be current on your knowledge and skills, strap on some gear, and dive in. Come on in—the water's fine! *You can do it!*

The Payoffs

- **Change of scenery.** There's an entire world to discover underwater, and the company doesn't get much more spectacular!
- **Escape.** "No matter what else is going on in your life," write our experts, "it ceases to exist the moment you drop beneath the surface."
- **Accomplishment.** Learning about equipment, the physics of diving, and the skills necessary to dive takes effort and application. If you can learn to breathe underwater, who knows what else you might be able to do?
- **New life.** You may not be able to talk to these animals, but you can get up close and personal. Did you know eels are shy? Or that octopi are more scared of you than you are of them? Fascinating!

Meet Your Mentors

ELLA JEAN MORGAN AND ERIN O'NEILL

What They Do: Ella Jean and Erin are the authors of *When Women Dive* as well as Women Divers Hall of Fame Inaugural Honorees. They are longtime National Association of Underwater Instructors (NAUI), Los Angeles County diving instructors, and international divers with a wide variety of underwater experience, including photography, video, and film industry work. Ella Jean is vice president of academics at the College of Oceaneering (a commercial diving school) and Erin writes, gives seminars, and prepares programs on virtually every aspect of underwater life.

Why They Do It: Ella Jean: "I was raised in the Caribbean, and the first time I looked underwater was through a fisherman's bucket. He'd placed a pane of glass at its bottom so that when he paddled out to the reef, he could place the bucket in the water and see the fish. I was captivated! I bought snorkeling gear and explored and enjoyed the water. But much later, after a divorce, I decided not to put off my interest in scuba. I met Erin in an advanced leadership course—we were the only two women in the class, and the only two students who finished the course!" Erin: "I grew up as a water baby on the Gulf of Mexico—swim team, lifeguard, water skier, body surfer. I didn't realize my true passion until I finally put a mask on my face and peered down into the blue, blue water of Catalina Island to discover the astonishing world of the golden, graceful kelp forest. I'm hooked for life!"

> If you have never been underwater, you are missing a world of great beauty and peace.
>
> —Ella Jean Morgan and Erin O'Neill

Word from the Wise: "Men tend to naturally assume they will do well when learning to dive, while women tend to assume they won't. We've found that to be very far from the truth! And there's been a great evolution in equipment. Manufacturers have started actually designing equipment for women rather than just coloring men's equipment pink and designating it as female gear."

BADGE STEPS

GET THE GEAR

Snorkeling stuff

"Get this at a dive store, not a Wal-Mart!" say our experts. "You'll need good guidance in this."

Booties and gloves. For warmth and protection.

Fins. These enable you to maneuver efficiently in the water. Although there are different kinds for cold and warm waters, you can use your cool-water fins anywhere. Experiment in the water to see if a small, flexible fin or a larger fin works best for you. This will depend on your leg strength and kicking skills.

Mask. The lens should be made of tempered safety glass, and the strap should be easy to adjust. The plastic skirt of the mask needs to form a comfortable seal around your face.

Snorkel. Experiment to find the right size and shape for you, so that you get enough air during exertion and are easily able to clear it of water. A silicone mouthpiece is comfortable and flexible.

1. Qualify.

You aren't qualifying for the Olympics, but scuba diving is a rigorous sport with some risks to consider. So let's look at some prerequisites:

Swimming. You don't have to be Esther Williams, but you should know how to swim, feel safe and comfortable in water, and have (or be willing to get) the experience of being in the water for longish periods of time.

Health. You should be in good general health. Your doctor can inform you about conditions that might possibly preclude you from diving, including a cough, nasal congestion, asthma, diabetes, a heart condition, and epilepsy. Also consult your doctor about any prescription or over-the-counter drugs you take regularly. You must consult your physician if you're pregnant or trying to be.

Temperament. Keeping a cool head is mandatory. If you panic, you endanger yourself and your buddy (see The Buddy System, page 301).

Evaluate your qualifications.

2. Get your feet wet.

Becoming scuba certified takes class time, and buying or renting scuba gear is not cheap. So before investing tons of time and money, try:

Snorkeling. You observe while floating on the surface of the water and watch the ocean go by beneath you.

Skin diving. You take a deep breath and dive down beneath the surface, getting closer to the reef and its inhabitants.

In addition to letting you explore underwater life, snorkeling and skin diving introduce you to some of the gear involved in scuba diving. Even after years of scuba diving, Ella and Erin continue to enjoy both snorkeling and skin diving. You may be perfectly content to pursue one of these activities—but if you want to go deeper and stay there longer, read on . . .

Give snorkeling and/or skin diving a try.

3. Jump in the baby pool.

If you've been snorkeling or skin diving for a while, you may be ready to sign up for a scuba certification course. But there are at least two more ways to "try it on" (including the gear!) before committing:

A minicourse. In a pool or other quiet water, you'll use a mask, fins, and scuba gear to experience breathing underwater. Minicourses are usually a couple of hours long. The National Association of Underwater Instructors has been known to cosponsor Scuba Tours in which a self-contained mobile pool lets the curious check out the sport (see www.thescubatour.com).

A resort course. You'll get to dive in the ocean, usually in a warm water location, and get oriented on the basics under the watchful eye of an instructor. These courses are usually a single day or a weekend long. Insist on a low instructor-student ratio.

Being a woman will affect your diving. Take note of how some distinctive female features can affect you underwater:

- Women tend to have less upper body strength than men, and scuba diving equipment is heavy. When still on land, instead of struggling to lift and carry the tank to water (thus risking injury and expending energy), wear the tank in its backpack, or use a cart for hauling gear.
- Women's natural dexterity, balance, grace, and stamina count underwater, allowing us to keep kicking, adjust to gear that can feel awkward, and manage our fins well.
- Since women have a higher percentage of body fat for their body weight than men, we have to wear proportionately more weight on our belts to keep us underwater.
- Women's smaller lungs mean that the same size air tank will last you longer than an average man, so you may be able to use a smaller tank.

Try scuba on for size.

4. Sign up for certification.

Scuba certification courses combine classroom learning, pool practice, and actual dives. The goal is a certification card. You'll need this "C-card" to purchase or rent equipment, take dive trips, and fill your tank with air.

A number of associations and agencies offer certification courses and issue C-cards. They require different things of their instructors and students. To find certification options in your area, consult retail dive shops, check your Yellow Pages for colleges and professional teaching facilities, and go online and visit the National Association of Underwater Instructors at www.naui.org.

GET THE GEAR

Scuba stuff

Air tanks. These vary in size, weight, capacity, working pressure, and buoyancy.

Buoyancy compensation device (BCD). This vest includes the tank pack, allows you to control your buoyancy, and can act as a flotation device on the surface.

Dry suit. This keeps you warmer in colder waters; it insulates with air.

Regulator. This is the gadget that makes diving possible—it takes the air from the tank and provides you with breathable air at whatever depth you are.

Weights and belts. Since a wetsuit is very buoyant, you must compensate by wearing weights. Your goal is to wear just enough to allow for neutral buoyancy at ten to fifteen feet of depth at the end of your dive. Over-weighting is common, uncomfortable, and hazardous.

Wet suit. If properly fitted, this neoprene rubber suit allows a thin layer of water to be trapped between your skin and the suit, and your body warms this layer. Don't compromise on fit, thickness, or comfort.

I DID IT!

"I've snorkeled in Israel, Bora Bora, Cozumel, and Maui. The best was in Mombasa, Kenya, when I was eleven, in the Indian Ocean—gorgeous, gorgeous fish! No, I changed my mind: The best was in Bora Bora. We took an outrigger, got in the water on the reef, put on the mask and snorkel, held on to the rope, and swam among all the fish that showed up—every color and size you can imagine!"

—Meg

WET BLANKET

"I'd been diving for a while, and went into a shop to buy a regulator. I'd done a lot of research on the subject and knew just what I wanted. The owner of the shop tried to talk me out of it! He said it had more features than I needed and seemed to think they would just confuse me. It's hard to believe this kind of sexism still exists, but this guy was definitely keeping it alive. Not just a condescending jerk, but a lousy businessman—he lost my business that day!"

—Cynthia

Erin and Ella Jean suggest that you:

- Choose the available course with the most required dives.
- Pick a course that covers skin-diving skills as well as stressing emergency procedures.
- Search for a low student-to-teacher ratio.
- Meet with the instructor before making a class commitment. They should be happy to chat and answer questions. You'll want to feel perfectly comfortable and confident with this instructor.
- Understand what is and isn't included in the course fee—equipment rental, textbooks, boat fees, the C-card. What purchase will be obligatory?
- While you will likely need to purchase some gear for your class, rent as much as you can at the outset. Before making purchases, read Rodale's *Scuba Diving* magazine (www.scubadiving.com), the *Consumer Reports* of diving equipment.
- Recognize that an entry-level course prepares you for a limited number of situations. Ocean and freshwater diving are not the same, for instance, and some things you might want to do—like deep, wreck, or night dives—require additional training.

Take a certification course.

ELLA JEAN AND ERIN'S EXPERT TIPS

SAVE YOUR STRENGTH

Use your head to conserve and maximize your body's power:

- Always keep something in reserve; slow down before you get tired.
- Smaller bodies lose heat faster than large ones because of a greater surface-area-to-body-mass ratio. Don't skimp on wetsuit fit or thickness to maximize your comfort. Terminate a dive if you're uncomfortable.
- Maintain your physical skill with regular diving and by engaging in aerobic conditioning and strengthening exercises year-round. If you haven't dived in awhile, take a short refresher course.

5. Earn your dive credentials.

Your certification course will feature some in-depth and important book learning, covering health issues, diving physics, how to use dive tables, and other key knowledge. You'll learn all your water skills in a pool, including crucial water survival and safety training. In open water, perhaps the ocean, you will put your new abilities into practice. To get certified, you will demonstrate your ability to dive safely during four to eight dives, which will cover setting up your equipment, using hand signals, descents and ascents, and much more. Also on the syllabus:

Fin kicks. Important to snorkelers, skin divers, and scuba divers alike. A good kick is from the hip (not the knee), and deep rather than shallow. Some classes teach you as many as five separate kicks for different situations; a good thing to learn.

Ear clearing. You need to clear your ears, or "equalize," more often than you do on a plane. You'll be taught the passive methods like swallowing, yawning, and wiggling your jaw, and the active method of Valsalva. The key words to remember about equalizing are early, often, and gently.

Surface dives. They get you below the surface. Learn feet-first descents for scuba and pike and tuck head-first dives for skin diving.

Buoyancy control. You're aiming to control buoyancy throughout your descent, arrival at depth, and your ascent. Achieving neutral buoyancy throughout your dive will involve adding or subtracting air to your BCD at various depths if you're wearing a wetsuit.

Take your time and learn well. "It's very important that divers are not equipment-dependent," says Erin. "Your skill development is the most important part of your training. If you have a rare equipment malfunction, you'll know you have the skills to see you through." ***Get certified!***

CONGRATULATIONS!

Dive on! You did it!

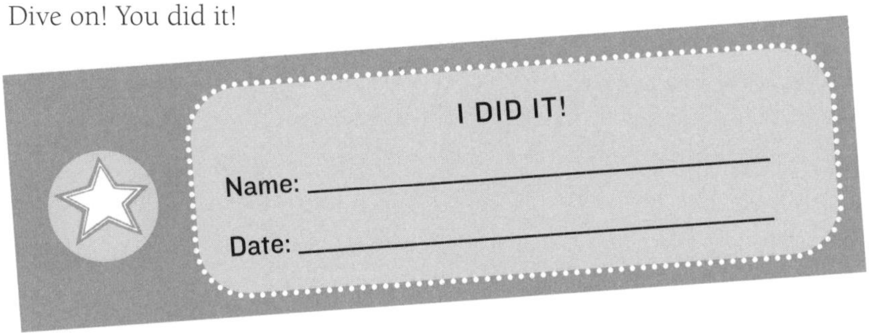

SCUBA SMARTS

Did you know?

- SCUBA stands for Self-Contained Underwater Breathing Apparatus.
- Most early research into the apparatus revolved around its potential military uses. Jacques Cousteau was in the French Navy when he began his underwater explorations and perfected the Aqua-Lung, which allowed divers to locate and remove enemy mines after World War II.
- In 1954, Los Angeles County began to train instructors to teach safe scuba-diving techniques. Zale Parry was the third woman to graduate from this program. She set a woman's depth record in 1954, was the first female president of the Underwater Photographic Society, and became well recognized as the underwater damsel in distress (harrumph!) on the television series *Sea Hunt*.

THE BUDDY SYSTEM

Two is better than one

You should always have a buddy while diving. This is someone who you'll remain near and keep an eye on, and they'll do the same for you. You'll learn to signal and communicate with this person during training, and how to help each other in case of an emergency with techniques such as "buddy breathing" from a single air tank. Once out of the class setting, Ella Jean and Erin advise choosing a diving buddy with compatible interests: "If you hate the sight of dying fish, don't look among hunters for a buddy." Before you dive together, be sure to discuss the pace, depth, and duration of your preferred dives.

BEYOND THE BADGE

If you love it as much as you thought you would, dream on . . .

- **Get in deeper.** Now that you know the ropes, try specializing. Go reef diving to discover a variety of spectacular creatures amid colorful coral, or wreck diving to explore sunken ships and other artifacts that house schools of fish and sponge formations. And why not join the creatures that go bump in the night on a night dive? You'll never know what you'll find on the other end of that flashlight!
- **Travel.** Dive travel destinations vary widely. Dive resorts cater to divers, and you'll find these aplenty in such legendary dive destinations as Egypt's Sharm el-Sheikh, Australia's Great Barrier Reef, and Belize's Barrier Reef and Blue Hole. If you are interested in a more generic travel resort, inquire in advance about the diving facilities available. Live-aboard boats offer serious divers easy access to sites, and virtually unlimited dive time (see Follow that Fish!).
- **Take some pictures.** If you think no one will believe what you've seen down there, document it on film! Visit www.divernet.com for *Diver* magazine's extensive links to photos, information on equipment, and beginner's guides.
- **Learn about underwater life.** As Ella Jean and Erin write, "Unlike a zoo, there are no fences between you and the interesting and intriguing creatures who inhabit the reef. You can get close to untamed critters and observe their behavior in their natural habitat." Learning about the marine life everywhere you go through dive cards, books, and classes is not only fascinating but can actually help you be more aware and safe while diving. Visit the Marine Life Learning Center at www.fishid.com—and while you're there, check out the marine life links and New World Publications Inc.'s catalog of fish identification and reference books, including titles on reef fish, coral, and creatures.

FOLLOW THAT FISH!

Find Nemo with this dive travel resource

Visit NAUI's worldwide travel connection at www.naui.org/travel. They can hook you up with adventures in the Caribbean, Florida, Asia and the Pacific, South and Central America, Mexico, Africa, the Indian Ocean, and the Red Sea! Try wreck diving in the Atlantic, Indian, or South Pacific oceans, where WWII relics have become artificial reefs teeming with sea life, or paddle around a Caribbean reef with giant turtles and angel fish galore. If you like what you see and want to keep the reef in its pristine state, look into eco-tours led by marine biologists that can help you become a more welcome and conscientious underwater visitor.

ERIN AND ELLA JEAN'S PICKS

BOOKS

Scuba America: The Human History of Sport Diving, Vol. I by Zale Parry and Albert Tillman
All about the roots of diving in America, by one of its female pioneers.

The Underwater Photography Handbook by Annemarie Kohler and Danja Kohler
For underwater photographers of all levels (still photography and videographs).

When Women Dive: A Female's Guide to Both Diving and Snorkeling by Erin O'Neill and Ella Jean Morgan
A comprehensive guide that looks at diving subjects from the standpoint of how they affect women.

MAGAZINES

Dive Training
www.dtmag.com
Geared toward new divers.

Rodale's Scuba Diving
www.scubadiving.com
The *Consumer Reports* of diving equipment.

Undercurrent
www.undercurrent.org
A dive travel newsletter that takes no advertising and shoots from the hip. Also features good safety and equipment information.

WEB SITES

www.divegirl.com
Feature articles for female divers.

www.diverlink.com
"Your connection to the world of diving: A comprehensive resource for scuba divers and dive businesses."

www.naui.org
Features an online reading room packed with articles and essays on all things scuba.

www.womenunderwater.com
A resource dedicated to inspiring and promoting the accomplishments of female divers.

ASSOCIATIONS

NAUI, National Association of Underwater Instructors
www.naui.org
Founded in 1960, this not-for-profit sets high standards for certifying divers.

PADI, Professional Association of Diving Instructors
www.padi.com
Founded in 1966, this for-profit proponent of the sport is the largest certification agency in the world.

38

HIT THE SLOPES

★ snow sports ★

You don't have to see where you're going, as long as you GO.

—Lorita Bertraun, blind skier

Imagine This . . . Driving to work on Friday, you hear the weather report: six inches of fresh powder in the mountains. You speed dial your best ski buddies, coordinate your after-work schedules, and head for the hills. When your teenagers grab their snowboards and tell you they'll see you at dinner, you surprise them by grabbing your own snowboard and telling them to wait up. And when you hear about a pristine meadow just over that pass on the right, you strap on some cross-country skis and make your own tracks. You still enjoy sipping hot toddies by the lodge fireplace, but now that you have a few lessons under your belt, you love knowing you can be a good snow sport, too. Can we give you a lift? *You can do it!*

So, what's your motivation?
Take a moment.
Dream a little, think big,
and then complete this sentence:
I see myself . . .

The Payoffs

- **Fear busting.** You don't need a steep slope to feel brave. Just being willing to land on your butt in public is life lesson enough.
- **Confidence boost.** We didn't learn to walk with sticks strapped to our feet, so getting the hang of skis or a snowboard is quite an accomplishment—and once you can move gracefully in a down parka, you'll know you're cool!
- **Change o' pace.** Why do kids love romping in the snow? That sparkling white blanket makes the world feel like a magical place.
- **Sociability.** Whether you're showing off, just learning the ropes, or feeding the appetite you've worked up after a day in the mountains, there's a wonderful camaraderie to be found in the shared exertion, challenge, and play of snow sports.

Meet Your Mentor

STEPHANIE SLOAN

What She Does: A former World Champion Freestyle skier and the founder of the Stephanie Sloan Woman Only Ski Program at Whistler Blackcomb, British Columbia, Stephanie runs and teaches in the "Women on the Edge" program. A longtime resident of Whistler, Stephanie has served as a town councilor and was very much involved in the town's Olympics planning and negotiations.

© Greg Edmunsen

Why She Does It: "Skiing was part of my parents' lives, and they tell me they got me on skis when I was two. We went to the Osler Bluff Ski Club north of Toronto every weekend, and I loved it from the beginning. I was in ski programs and raced all through high school. Competing evolved naturally out of my enjoyment of the sport. My fifteen-year-old daughter is following in my footsteps now—and while I worry, I'm supportive because she loves it as much as I did. I broke my ankle badly when I was seventeen, which took me out of alpine ski racing for a bit. I went to university, and then while traveling in Europe, I saw a Europa Cup freestyle competition. It was a brand-new sport in Europe, and there was one woman competing against the men because there wasn't even a women's category yet. I looked at her and thought, 'I can do that.' So I did!"

Word from the Wise: "When I retired from competition and started teaching, I ran a bump (mogul) clinic. I wondered why more women weren't in my classes—and when I asked, women said they couldn't do it, weren't good enough, and didn't want to slow everyone else down. Women-only classes can feel less intimidating and more supportive. Look for the encouragement you need, because believe me, women can do it!"

There's something for everyone in snow sports: great exercise, beautiful scenery, and, if you choose, thrilling challenges.

—Stephanie Sloan

BADGE STEPS

1. To ski or not to ski . . .

Alpine skiing. Gravity gets you from point A to point B. While you don't have to tackle giant slaloms, you are moving downhill and need to master speed control, stops, and turns. (Technically, snowboarding falls into this category.)

Nordic skiing. Includes cross-country skiing, both classic and skating. Stephanie suggests that if you aren't really athletic, you should probably go with classic cross-country, in which you make diagonal strides, like walking. "If a woman is a bit more into aerobic exercise and likes to push and get her heart rate going, then she should take up skate skiing," she says.

Snowboarding. Uses one board, instead of two skis—and look, Ma, no poles! Stephanie says, "You can get up and running as a snowboarder fairly quickly—basic skills are a bit easier to learn than all the technicalities of downhill skiing—but you have to be willing to get bumped around a bit."

Pick a snow sport to try.

2. Get ready to go.

Before you head for the hills, make sure you have these bases covered:

Destination. You're probably familiar with the snow spots near you. If you aren't, check www.GoSki.com and search by country or state. Call the resort at your destination, and they'll connect you with ski schools. Tell them you are looking for a beginner's learning package. "Mountain resorts are good at accommodating your needs, because the more new skiers they can get on the mountain, the better their business will be down the line," Stephanie explains. "They want you to have a good time and get hooked, so beginners are often treated like royalty." Look for package deals that include lessons, equipment rental, and lift fees.

Gear. Your learning package should include gear rental, and the person outfitting you will work to ensure your ease and comfort, with, for instance, short skis. Give yourself two hours before a lesson to get outfitted so you aren't rushed. To get the right fit, be sure to wear the socks you'll ski in when trying on boots.

Body. You'll enjoy your snow sport more and have less soreness the day after a first lesson if you're fit and flexible. Stephanie suggests you add

SNOWSPEAK

Talk like a snow bunny

Bumps. Just what it sounds like! (Also known as moguls.)

Crud. Chopped-up snow.

Mashed potatoes. Wet, heavy snow.

Piste. French for trail. (Off-piste refers to uncharted ski areas.)

Powder. Fresh, fluffy, untracked snow, either natural or machine-made. Knee-deep or at least above your boots is best.

Packed powder. The same as above, only it's been packed down by skiers or grooming machines. (Also known as hardpack.)

Slalom. A race with tight turns around obstacles.

Steeps. Anything vertical enough to require good speed control.

GEARSPEAK

Outfit yourself for the slopes

Bindings. Keep your boots connected to your skis or board while also releasing in a safe way.

Boots. Snowboarding boots are softer and less clunky than ski boots.

Poles. Look for a comfortable grip and weight, and speak with your outfitter about the kind of skiing you plan to do.

Skis. Vary depending on the kind of skiing you plan to do. Recent technological and design changes make it worth your while to at least try newer models.

Snowboards. Come in a variety of lengths, waist widths, and degrees of flexibility.

squats to your daily routine for a few weeks before skiing. Also consider upping your aerobic activity a bit, working with weights, and stretching.

Clothes. Try a three-layer approach for staying warm and dry:

1. Long underwear and polypropylene socks (warmer and drier than cotton).
2. Wool or fleece sweaters that provide insulation but can be peeled off.
3. Waterproof jacket, pants, and gloves. (Gore-Tex good, denim bad.)

Don't forget something on your head to keep in body warmth and sunglasses—or better yet, goggles. ***Prepare to hit the slopes.***

3. Go to class.

Different snow sports—and snow bunnies—have different learning curves. Stephanie suggests that three to six lessons are ideal for beginners. Consider weekend packages that feature all-day lessons on Saturday, with time for you to practice what you learned on Sunday, and try to do this several weekends running.

Remember to relax, laugh at your mistakes, and not get hung up about your performance (or lack thereof). Every snow sport enthusiast has been a beginner who has spent a significant amount of time on their butt! Savor the thrills (first time on a ski lift) and victories (first time you get on a lift gracefully) that are built in to the learning process.

At first, you may feel like you're wearing clown shoes or that you keep slipping on banana peels. But if you persevere, the slapstick comedy routine will end and you'll feel the rush when it all comes together: your body, your equipment, and the terrain are one as you swoosh downhill or glide cross country. Try not to gloat when you get back to the lodge. ***Go to class and have a blast.***

CONGRATULATIONS!

Whoosh! Pretty cool, eh? You did it!

I DID IT!

Name: ______________________________

Date: ______________________________

I DID IT!

"Though I grew up near the Sierras, I never understood the appeal of snow sports. The cold, the wet, the unflattering clothes that keep you from getting cold and wet—not to mention speeding down slippery slopes with foreign objects strapped to your feet. I just didn't get it. Then I went cross-country skiing. I loved the way my arms and legs powered me along at a pace at which I could really see and enjoy the landscape. It felt great physically and mentally."

—Gabrielle

NEED A LIFT?

"Snowboarding? The teacher had us get up the little hill by unclamping one of our feet from the board and dragging the board behind us. It's like dragging a ball and chain up a mountain—a ball and chain that scoops up snow as you go. Then the humiliation really began! By the end of the lesson, I was actually getting to the point where I was able to keep from falling when I did the toe turn, only to fall flat on my bum doing a heel turn. And don't even get me started about nearly knocking over a four-year-old at the ski lift when my legs gave out and the snowboard slipped out from under me. 'Hey lady, you're pushing me!' "

—Justine

BEYOND THE BADGE

If you love it as much as you thought you would, dream on . . .

- **Invest in equipment.** "When snowboarding came along, the ski industry took a close look at those boards. They're kind of fat, with narrow waists; they grab well; and they carve beautiful lines in the snow with less skidding," says Stephanie. "So the ski companies have now developed new skis that are easier to turn with, are shorter and fatter, and almost float on powder and crud. Learning to ski has never been easier!" Take advantage of free demos before buying, look for end of season sales, and go to a ski-specific shop (rather than a multisport outfitter) for the best advice.
- **Travel.** If you want to mountain-hop, the destinations are endless (see Travel Destinations). Ski travel packagers in regions where resorts are grouped even offer "ski safaris" that shuttle skiers between several resorts. Gourmet food and aprés-ski pampering can also be yours in most top ski areas.
- **Challenge yourself.** As with any sport, there's always something new to learn, a challenge to rise to, and a skill to finesse. If you're skiing or snowboarding and you've gotten comfortable on green runs, you can shoot for the intermediate blue runs, and then the black diamond runs. If you're doing classic cross-country, think about tackling tougher terrain and making longer excursions.

TRAVEL DESTINATIONS

Stephanie's slope suggestions

Australia, New Zealand, South America . . . "I wish I'd traveled to these locales when I was competing!"

Austria and Switzerland. Home to what many people consider the most beautiful resorts in the world.

Mont Blanc, Chamonix, France. "So beautiful, and amazing skiing!"

Mont Tremblant, Quebec, Canada. Enjoy French food and culture without a trans-Atlantic flight.

Stowe, Vermont. The pride of New England.

Vail and Aspen, Colorado. A favorite for movie stars and hard-core skiers alike.

Whistler, British Columbia, Canada. Stephanie's top choice, natch.

STEPHANIE'S PICKS

BOOKS

Inner Skiing by W. Timothy Gallwey
A book not just about technique but about the fundamental relationship between the snow, the mountain, the skis, and you.

The Rough Guide to Skiing & Snowboarding in North America by Tamsin Murray-Leach, Stephen Timblin, and Christian Williams
A guide for everyone—budget skiers, resort-seekers, families, thrill-seekers, and singles.

Women Ski by Claudia Carbone
Helps women to ski better and enjoy skiing as a lifelong activity.

MAGAZINES

Ski
www.skimag.com
"The magazine of the ski life"—snow reports, travel tips, mountain cams, and then some.

Ski Canada
www.skicanadamag.com
Tips on where to ski in the Great White North, snow reports, training tips, and more.

Skiing
www.skiingmag.com
All the makings of a winter adventure are here: a resort locator, new equipment reviews, snow reports, and even party guides.

WEB SITES

www.goski.com
So you want to ski Turkey? This site will show you where to go. Specs on ski mountains and ski travel around the world.

www.onthesnow.com
Daily snow reports and weather conditions across the United States and selected international locations (including Chile!).

www.skicentral.com
This site is chock-full of info on everything from summer skiing, the history of skiing, ski patrol, disabled and extreme skiing, ski clubs and teams, to telemark, cross country, skiboarding, snowboarding, and more.

www.skinet.com
Snow reports, info on gear, resorts, and travel, as well as news, forums, and an interactive gear-finder that will recommend the gear that's right for you.

WOMEN'S SKI SCHOOLS

Jackson Hole Women's Ski Camp and Clinic
www.jacksonhole.com/skiing/women_clinic.html or 800-450-0477
Learn to ski with wild women in wild Wyoming.

Stephanie Sloan's Women Only and Women on the Edge Ski Programs
www.whistler-blackcomb.com/school/womenonly.asp or 800-766-0449
Learn at the world-famous Whistler resort from our expert. Stephanie has been running women's-only ski programs for twenty-one years, and has taught over 5,000 women how to ski better.

Women's Edge at Aspen Snowmass
www.aspensnowmass.com/schools/adult or 800-308-6935
A four-day clinic with female pros in amazing Aspen.

GEAR

eBay
www.ebay.com
Find great deals on used and almost-new equipment.

Gear Direct
www.geardirect.com
Skis, snowboards, boots, clothing, and accessories online.

REI
www.rei.com
Online and brick-and-mortar retailer for all kinds of snow sport gear.

Rossignol
www.rossignol.com
This venerable maker of skis, bindings, poles, boots, snowboards, and clothing gets Stephanie's stamp of approval for gear and duds.

Snowshack
www.snowshack.com
Online retailer specializing in ski and snowboarding accessories.

39

BEAT THE BOYS AT POOL

★ billiards ★

You know, this is my table, man. I own it.

—Fast Eddie (Paul Newman) in *The Hustler*

So, what's your motivation?
Take a moment.
Dream a little, think big,
and then complete this sentence:
I see myself . . .

Imagine This . . . It's girls' night out and you're at your favorite watering hole, the one where the only thing better than the jukebox is the pool table in the back corner. As you and your friends play, the number of respectfully silent onlookers increases. It could be because you're all so cute, but it's really because you can play. At the start of your game, a smirking, cue-wielding tough guy challenges the winner. You always enjoy winning—but now you're determined. You pocket two balls on your break, catch the stunned expression on that pool shark's face, and leave your friends a bit bewildered about what's gotten into your game. Now aren't you glad you spent a few hours learning and practicing the basics of shooting pool? Rack 'em up, and watch jaws drop. *You can do it!*

The Payoffs

- **Physical.** "You walk miles around the table without realizing it," says Shari. "You're bending and straightening, and because you are holding positions as you aim and shoot, you really work your leg and butt muscles!"
- **Mental.** When you calculate just how much spin to put on the ball to make it ricochet into the side pocket, you're exercising mathematical logic. That's why the kid's show *Big Blue Marble* has used pool to teach kids geometry.
- **Networking.** As your mentor Shari points out, pool now often takes the place of golf as a way for business associates to socialize while wheeling and dealing. Whether it's a date or a night out with clients, pool is a way to mingle, connect, and impress.
- **The cool factor.** Cue equals cool. Woman plus cue equals hot!

Meet Your Mentor

SHARI STAUCH

What She Does: The owner and editor of *Pool & Billiard Magazine* (a publication she launched with her dad, Harold Simonsen, back in 1983) and the coauthor of *Precision Pool* and *Pool Player's Edge,* Shari "The Shark" Stauch began playing—and winning—on the Women's Professional Billiard Association Tour in 1980. She was instrumental in getting the sport recognized as an official Olympic sport, was founding president of the Billiard Education Foundation, and has received several awards from the Women's Professional Billiard Association.

Why She Does It: "When I was growing up, we had a pool table in the basement. My mother used to joke that when my father came home from work, he kissed the table before kissing her! My father loved the sport and eventually opened a billiards club in Chicago. I actually hated it as a kid, but by the time I was in high school, I realized boys were intrigued when a girl could play pool—until you beat them, of course! There weren't a lot of competitive opportunities for women when I started. A few of us with a passion to play helped out on the Women's Professional Billiard Association Tour. My father, my husband, one of my younger brothers, and I were all in *The Color of Money.* Dad and I consulted with Martin Scorsese and his production team and wound up reviewing the screenplay for technical stuff, setting up the final tournament scene, and bringing in people to be extras. My daughter likes to brag that she was in a movie with Tom Cruise because I'm in it—briefly—and I was pregnant with her at the time."

> Pool is a sport, a game, and a form of recreation that can challenge and delight you your entire life.
>
> —Shari Stauch

Word from the Wise: "Pool is definitely a sport, but you get to look good while playing it. You aren't sweating, your hair doesn't get messed up, and no sports bra is required!"

BADGE STEPS

THE NAME OF THE GAME

Shari on the interchangeable terms "billiards" and "pool"

"Billiards began as a lawn game, kind of like croquet. The French word for ball is 'bille,' hence billiards. The game moved indoors and many variations developed. The British brought the word 'pool' into usage, because their version was a gambling game and it referred to pooling your money. The film *The Hustler,* with its depiction of big money, underworld connections, and even violence, threatened pool's reputation. To battle this perception, the industry began marketing billiard clubs as family centers and poshed up the term *pool* to a more official sounding 'pocket billiards.' But the American public still loved it as pool. We call ourselves *Pool & Billiard Magazine* because if we called ourselves *Pool Magazine* people would think we were about swimming!"

1. Find a pool hall.

If you don't already have a favorite bar or rec center with a table, or a friend or relative with a table at home, check your phone book for billiard clubs and pool halls. "Clubs want women to be regular customers," says Shari. "We bring in a whole new segment of the population, and these days you will often find that women make up 40 to 50 percent of the patron population on any given night."

At the club, you can ask a friend to show you the basics and find out if there's a teacher on staff or someone who offers lessons on the premises. If you want some pointers before you go in, look at Shari and Gerry Kanov's step-by-step *Precision Pool* and other resources listed in Shari's Picks, page 317. To get you started, here's a look at the basic equipment:

Balls. Eight of the balls are solid colors, and the other seven are "stripes," with white tops and bottoms—these are the object balls that you are going to try to hit into the holes (or "pockets") of the table. Each ball has a number on it, one to fifteen, and the eight ball is black. The all-white cue ball is the ball you'll hit with your cue stick to pocket the object balls.

Cue. While the standard cue stick is fifty-eight inches long, cue sticks range from fifty-six to sixty-two inches long. Your "limb length" will determine the right size for you. Weights range from eighteen to twenty-one ounces. As you gain proficiency, you can experiment with different weights and tip sizes. Make sure you feel comfortable with the weight, and that your cue is long enough that you don't "run out of cue" when you're sliding the cue forward to hit your cue ball.

Table. These vary in size and are traditionally covered in green wool as a nod to the game's origin as a lawn sport. Shari suggests you beware of pretty but potentially hard-on-the-eye table colors like red and purple.

Establish your billiards base of operations.

2. Get a grip and build a bridge.

Grab a cue, and learn how to use it with your basic grip and bridge:

Take your cue in hand. Put one hand on the thick, back end of your cue, and the other on the front. Your back arm and hand (also known as your "grip hand") really control your cue, so if you're right-handed, this should be your right hand.

Easy does it. "Ease up on your grip," says Shari. "The word best used is 'hold.'" Find the balance point of your cue by holding the stick lightly with the index finger and thumb of your grip hand until, like a scale, it tips neither to one side nor the other. You'll hold the stick several inches behind this point.

Hold it right there. Hold the cue using your two middle fingers and thumb, and then wrap your index and little fingers around the cue.

Find the right angle. Try holding the cue so that the upper part of your arm, from your shoulder to your elbow, is parallel to the floor, while the lower part of your arm is perpendicular to the floor. Fine-tune a little bit up or back from here, and stay loose!

Next, you'll need to build a bridge—the support formed by the front hand where the front of the cue stick rests. Experiment and learn if the open or closed bridge is more comfortable for you:

Open bridge. Place your bridge hand flat on the table, putting pressure on your palm and slowly raising your knuckles above the bed of the table so that the pressure is now equally distributed between your fingertips and the palm of your hand. Spread your fingers as far apart as they will go, and keeping your thumb next to your index finger, allow the cue stick to rest between the thumb and first knuckle of the index finger. (Honest, this isn't as complicated as it might sound!)

Closed bridge. Place your hand flat on the table and spread your fingers as in the open bridge. Then form a loop with your thumb and index finger through which your cue will slide. Your hand will naturally raise up on its side, but the heel of your hand and remaining three fingers will rest on the table for support.

Also ask your teacher to help you master some of the bridge techniques to use when the cue ball is on or near the table's rail, and how to use a separate piece of equipment called a mechanical bridge. ***Learn how to handle your cue.***

3. Take a stand and make your move.

Once you've got a handle on your cue, it's time to get the rest of your body in on the action with the right stance and stroke:

Stance. Different body types will dictate different positions for comfort, but here are the basic nine steps to the proper pool stance:

1. Stand up straight behind a shot at the table.

THE VISION THING

Optimize your playing vision by

- Managing stress, which can affect how we process visual information. Try deep breathing and simple stretching.
- Strengthen your eye muscles with an exercise like this: Straighten your arm out in front of you while holding a pencil. Keep your eyes focused on the eraser as you slowly pull the pencil toward your nose and back out until your arm is fully extended. Do ten to twenty times, once or twice a day.
- Avoid cigarette smoke. Smoking results in constriction of the blood vessels, and many of these vessels at the back of the eye contribute to optimum vision.

I DID IT!

"Gary and I were hanging out as friends. We met at my apartment on the Upper West Side and headed to the Amsterdam Billiard Club. I paid for the table, and he was in charge of the drinks. The music was pretty good, and I was inspired enough to win the first game. Gary got a little competitive and won the second. As it got a bit later, we decided that the third game would serve as the tiebreaker. After the last game, Gary said, 'I like a girl that can beat me in pool.' We started dating a month later!"
—Gena

DO THE HUSTLE

"I was in a bar I'd never been in before, and the level of play was pretty high and very competitive. I was happy just to watch, but then a fellow who seemed to be at my kind of intermediate level asked me for a game. As soon as we started, I knew he'd been hiding his skills. I guess he really wanted the beer we'd wagered, because he really slaughtered me . . . I thought hustlers were only in the movies!"
—Adeline

2. Line up the little toe of your back foot with the cue and object ball.
3. Hold the cue stick with your back hand.
4. Let your arms hang naturally down at your sides.
5. Place the tip of the cue stick about an inch behind the cue ball.
6. Pivot your back foot—that is, swing your heel in toward your body.
7. Step your front foot to a comfortable position.
8. Bend at the waist and lock or slightly bend the back leg.
9. Allow your front leg to relax and bend slightly.

Stroke. The most important thing to remember while taking your shot is to keep your cue parallel to the table. To do so:

1. Put your bridge hand on the table eighteen inches in front of the end rail.
2. Make a bridge.
3. Let go of the stick with your back hand, and allow the cue stick to come to rest on the end rail.
4. Your cue stick is now parallel to the table.
5. Resume your hold on the butt end of the stick without moving the cue out of its parallel position. You are now in position to deliver a level shot.

Limit your backswing to five to six inches, and practice shooting right through the ball as though it weren't there. Then follow through, dropping your elbow as you do. Try to let the cue move through contact with the ball and then stop by itself. Your follow through should be at least a couple of inches on all shots, and a foot or more to break (more on this in Step 5). ***Take your best shot.***

4. Pocket a few.

Now that you know the basics, you're ready to practice hitting using your cue ball to hit those stripes and solids into any of the six pockets of the pool table. You'll want to aim for the center of the pocket, and the angle you choose to hit the ball will vary depending on where you are shooting from on the table and what pocket you're aiming for.

There are dozens of aiming techniques that you can investigate or be taught, but the most common is the "ghost ball" technique. Simply visualize a line through the middle of the object ball to the center of the pocket. Then imagine a "ghost" cue ball positioned at the spot where the actual cue ball must hit the object ball in order to send it into the pocket. Line up your stance behind your cue ball to hit it to the place where you've positioned your ghost ball. Now just stroke the cue ball into position, so that it hits the object ball right where you imagined it and sends it right into the pocket. ***Chalk a few up to experience.***

SHARI'S EXPERT TIPS

SWIM WITH THE POOL SHARKS

- Chalk your tip before every shot. It maintains friction, preventing the cue tip from sliding off or mis-cueing. Place chalk on the tip with a feathering motion, making sure the tip is covered but not caked. You'll look cool doing it, too!
- Beginners can improve their game dramatically by learning to stay down on the shot, says Shari: "Imagine a brick on your head, and resist the temptation to immediately jump up after shooting to see where the balls end up."
- Do some form of stretching before you play. It will help you relax mentally and physically, reduce tension in your muscles, and help you develop better body awareness.

5. Give yourself a break.

Before you can take a break shot, you have to "rack 'em up," or arrange the balls into a triangular rack, alternating stripes and solids. Once all the balls are in the rack, push the balls forward and together so that all are touching. The front ball in the rack is centered on the "foot spot" of the table, which is a small white circle at the end of the table.

To break with power:

- Spread your legs a little farther apart than for a normal shot, placing at least 60 percent of your body weight on your front leg.
- Adjust your grip by holding the cue stick roughly three to six inches behind where you normally would.
- Experiment—many people find that the open bridge allows for the most power.
- Remember that it's more important to hit solidly than with great velocity.

Break it up.

STRIKE A WINNING POSE

Make a proper stance second nature

Check your position regularly while playing, so that you:

- Feel balanced
- See your shot easily with your chin directly over the cue stick, and your cue, chin, and swinging arm in line behind the shot
- Swing the cue freely, without hitting any part of your body on your follow-through
- Bend over low enough for aiming accuracy, but understand that standing up a bit offers more power

6. Shoot some Eight Ball.

There are numerous games of pool—Eight Ball, Nine Ball, Straight Pool, etc. Here are the basic rules of Eight Ball, one of the most popular versions of the game:

- After racking the balls, flip a coin to see who will break. Opponents switch turns until someone sinks a ball.
- If this is you (why not?), follow up by pocketing all the balls of the kind you first pocketed—solid or striped. If you sink two balls on your break (why not?), and one is solid and the other striped, you get to take your pick.
- Your goal is to get all of your own balls in the pockets before your opponent. Whenever you sink a ball, you get another turn.
- "Scratching" is knocking the cue ball into a pocket (not good), hitting the other player's ball into a pocket (codependent), or not hitting any balls at all (missing the cue ball completely). If you scratch, your opponent gets to reposition the cue ball anywhere behind the foot spot—a nice advantage.
- When you've pocketed all your balls, you must "sink" (pocket) the eight ball before your opponent. Beware: If you sink the eight ball before pocketing all your other balls, you LOSE. You also lose if you scratch while trying to sink the eight ball.
- When you do take aim on the eight ball, you have to say which pocket you will sink it into (referred to as calling your shot). If it goes into another pocket, you guessed it—you lose. But if you get it right, you win!

Rack up some experience, call your shots, and play to win!

CONGRATULATIONS!

You're on the ball. Nice shot! You did it!

I DID IT!

Name: ______________________________

Date: ______________________________

GET INTO THE GROOVE

Find your sense of rhythm and timing

In pool, rhythm refers to the overall cadence of your game as you move from shot to shot. Timing refers to the actual steps you take in executing a shot, including your warm-up strokes and actual shot. To develop steady rhythm and good timing:

1. Line up a series of balls.
2. Find the right stance to shoot the balls one by one into a corner pocket.
3. First look at your target (the corner pocket), then take three practice strokes before shooting the ball. If three strokes feels uncomfortable, try two or four.
4. Continue to experiment until you feel natural in your approach, and neither too rushed nor too slow in your attempt to pocket the balls.

SHARI'S PICKS

BOOKS

The Billiard Encyclopedia by Victor Stein and Paul Rubino
Stein is the historical consultant at *Pool & Billiard Magazine*.

The Complete Idiot's Guide to Pool & Billiards by Ewa Mataya Laurance and Thomas C. Shaw
Authored by *Pool & Billiard Magazine* staffers.

The Ewa Mataya Pool Guide by Ewa Mataya and Bob Brown
Mataya is an instructional columnist for *Pool & Billiard Magazine*.

Mental Training for Peak Performance: Top Athletes Reveal the Mind Exercises They Use to Excel by Steven Ungerleider
Because pool is physical and mental.

Precision Pool and **Pool Player's Edge** by Gerry Kanov and Shari Stauch
Shari knows what she's talking about, and so does Gerry, an accomplished player and coach.

Sport Stretch by Michael J. Alter
Shari and Gerry's favorite book on the subject.

MAGAZINES

Pool & Billiard
www.poolmag.com
This is the sport's oldest monthly magazine and boasts the largest readership of billiard businesses, players, and fans.

WEB SITES

Easy Pool Tutor
www.easypooltutor.com
The fundamentals, the advanced game, rules, equipment, pool halls, and forums.

Pool & Billiard OnLine Expo
www.poolmag.com/expo.htm
An ideal place to learn about the sport and its equipment.

Shari's Web Site
www.sharitheshark.com
Find out where your pool mentor will be appearing next, whether on book tour or giving clinics, and learn more about women's pool from a straight shooter.

Women's Professional Billiard Association
www.wpba.com
Official Web site of the Women's Pro Billiard Tour. News, events, top player profiles, and instruction tips.

MOVIES

Bad Boy
A 1935 kitsch classic of a pool hustler redeemed by love.

The Baltimore Bullet
James Coburn and Omar Sharif star in this pool-hall camp classic.

The Color of Money
Paul Newman chalked up an Oscar for his role as Tom Cruise's pool-room mentor in this Martin Scorsese classic.

The Hustler
Young hustler Fast Eddie (Paul Newman) gives the legendary Minnesota Fats (Jackie Gleason) a run for his money—the ultimate pool player's flick.

Io, Chiara e lo scuro (The Pool Hustlers)
Italian movie about gambling it all on love and pool.

Poolhall Junkies
Check out the great trick shots in this indie film.

Stickmen
Three amateur pool sharks rack up trouble when they take on the mob.

40

TAKE THE REINS

★ horseback riding ★

You may have my husband, but not my HORSE.

—D. H. Lawrence

So, what's your motivation?
Take a moment.
Dream a little, think big,
and then complete this sentence:
I see myself . . .

Imagine This . . . The wind is in your face, you have true horsepower at your disposal, you are . . . free. Will you gallop across the Mongolian steppes, trot through Tuscany, or out-dude the dudes at a ranch in Wyoming? Or maybe you're content to saddle up at the local stables a couple sunny Saturdays a month. Whether you are putting foot to stirrup for the first time or getting back in the saddle after growing up, this badge will have you sitting tall in the saddle with a lot more grace (and a lot less fear) than you have right now. You'll find the horses in your 'hood, learn your way around a stable, saddle up, and take the reins into your own hands. *You can do it!*

The Payoffs

- **Strength, flexibility, balance.** Riding builds leg strength and your overall balance and flexibility. Trotting really works your hamstrings, quadriceps, and glutes.
- **Confidence.** Horses are big, and riding them is a confidence-boosting challenge.
- **Patience.** Riding takes physical and mental discipline. Working with your horse teaches you to stop champing at the bit.
- **Exhilaration.** When you're on horseback, riding high with the wind in your hair . . . there's just nothing else like it!

Meet Your Mentor

LINDA RUBIO

What She Does: Runs the Miwok Livery Stable, located in the gorgeous 680-acre Golden Gate National Recreation Area that borders the Pacific Ocean and Mt. Tamalpais just a few minutes north of San Francisco. Linda teaches riding at all age and skill levels and takes groups on horseback riding excursions in Europe.

Why She Does It: "I joke that I don't know how to do anything else, but the truth is, I wouldn't want to do anything else! Girls are often fanatical about horses; I know I was. Riding gives girls a sense of accomplishment at a time when many other things feel out of their hands—which can feel just as true at forty as it does at fourteen! Plus, riding is something that we can do as well as, or better than, boys. While it may not be politically correct to say, 'female' traits like flexibility, empathy, patience, emotional generosity, and nurturing give us a real leg up in mastering one of the key essentials of the sport: developing and maintaining a close relationship with your horse. Many women give up riding as they get older. These women often come back to it at a point in their lives when they want to reclaim something they love, just for themselves. I also teach total novices who are getting ready for a dude ranch vacation. It's really never too late to start or start over."

Riding is joyful;
and who can't use a little
more JOY in their lives?

—Linda Rubio

Word from the Wise: "Some people think riding is just about getting on the horse and yelling, 'Giddeyup!' But it's really about learning to speak a new language. Using hand, leg, seat, weight, and voice techniques, you learn to communicate with your horse. While riding is a sport, horses are not pieces of athletic equipment. They aren't tennis racquets or golf clubs! They're alive and you need to relate to them. And finally, fancy manicures, beware! Riding is not for fastidious fashionistas, though the outfits can be pretty cute. You'll get dirty, smelly, and maybe a little (or a lot) sore. But that's rarely anything that a hot bath and a little Ben Gay won't fix."

BADGE STEPS

1. Find a horse, of course!

Ask around, check the phone book ("Riding Academies"), go online. Call and make an appointment to stop by and look around. ***Find a stable and schedule your appointment on your calendar—in ink.***

2. Visit the stable.

Look for a place that has healthy-looking horses. Good facilities care about their horses, exercising them regularly, tending to injuries, and sending them out to pasture if they need a break. Take a good look around to see if the horses look well kept, if the facilities are clean, and if the riders and teachers seem to be having a good time. Then ask the following questions:

- Do they have a variety of horses, of different ages and temperaments? It's best if there are a number of choices, so that your instructor can match your skill and comfort level with an appropriate horse. Forty-two horses live at the Miwok Livery Stable. Twenty-three of these Appaloosas, Arabs, quarter horses, Morgans, and ponies are used in lessons. Linda advises, "We like our riders to reach the point where they are comfortable riding different types of horses." Look for a stable that offers these kinds of options.
- How long have their instructors been teaching, and what kind of certification do they have? How do they promote and maintain rider safety? The U.S. doesn't require teacher certification, but good stables have instructors who are certified by a reputable organization, such as Centered Riding, the American Riding Instructors Association, or the British Horse Society.
- What do their classes include? You want to ride at a stable where you learn to groom and tack up your horse before riding it. Private lessons are good for fine-tuning a specific problem, but Linda generally recommends small group lessons because they are more cost-effective and allow you to learn by watching your classmates.
- What riding style do they teach? English or Western? Linda likes lightweight English saddles for teaching a secure seat and perfect balance, but can provide the Western variety. Choosing one style or another is largely a matter of where you are, what you were raised with, or what seems more natural to you.

THE BEGINNER'S LEXICON

So you don't sound like a greenhorn!

Bit. Horse's mouthpiece.

Bridle. Horse's headgear; includes reins and bit.

English. Style of riding where you use a lightweight saddle with a shallow seat and hold the reins in both hands (think Princess Anne).

Gaits. The various speeds and foot movements of a horse: walk, trot (or jog), canter (or lope).

Halter. Equipment used for leading or tying a horse.

Post. Bouncing, up-and-down movement done in rhythm with the horse's trot in English riding.

Tack. Equipment worn by the horse, including saddle and bridle.

Western. Style of riding where you use a heavier, deeper saddle than English riding and hold the reins in your left hand (think Annie Oakley).

• What do they supply, and what will you need to buy?

Are you satisfied with the answers? If not, try other stables until you find one that fits. ***Sign up for an evaluation lesson.***

3. Get your gear.

Stables will often supply what you need to take a class, or tell you exactly what and where to buy what they don't have. Visit a tack and feed store for your supplies, or if you know exactly what you want, use mail order or online catalogs (see Linda's Picks, page 324). You don't have to spend a lot of money to get started, but if you get serious, you might want to invest in boots, breeches, half-chaps, and even equestrian underwear. ***Assemble your ensemble.***

4. Take an evaluation lesson.

Most stables offer these so they can determine the right class level for you, and so you can get a feel for the instruction. ***Have fun!***

LINDA'S EXPERT TIPS

BUYING A HORSE

- Consider leasing or sponsorship. It's a win-win situation, since the owners have you to groom and exercise their animal, and you get to try on the concept of ownership without all the responsibility and expense.
- Know what you want in a horse, then shop around and get lots of input from people more experienced than you. And remember, pretty isn't everything. Linda cautions: "Buy with a professional, and with the same kind of vigilance you'd use with a used car salesman!"
- Find a boarding situation that works for you. Some barns require you to take lessons from their trainers, which might not work for you or your horse. And you need to be able to trust the onsite caregivers.
- Be realistic about your time and money. How many times a week will you really be able to ride? Horses, boarding fees, equipment, vet, and horseshoeing fees add up. Do the math.

5. Sign up for a series of weekly lessons.

It's important to commit to a series of six to twelve classes, because there's a lot to learn. Good beginner or refresher classes teach you slowly and carefully, building your skills week to week. If you stick with it and embrace the challenges as well as the thrills, your solid skill set will pay off down the line . . . or trail!

HORSE SENSE

Wise up before you saddle up

- You don't have to fall madly in love with your horse, but you do need to respect and understand it. Ask your teacher about the basics of horse psychology.
- "I teach students stretching exercises while on horseback, but stretching beforehand is good, too," says Linda. Strength training can minimize your chance of experiencing knee or back pain. Yoga and Tai Chi are great to do if you ride, because they emphasize proper breath during movement.

WHAT TO WEAR?

Head-to-toe dos and don'ts for the equestrian set

Boots. You need footwear that won't let your foot slip through the stirrup, so sneakers and hiking boots won't do. Ask your teacher if something in your closet will suffice, or buy shoes or boots especially designed for riding.

Breeches. Jeans are fine, and the leggings of choice for many riders—but you'll probably find that cotton/Lycra riding breeches are more comfortable.

Gloves. These protect your skin from chafing and keep your hands nice and warm, too.

Helmet. You may not like what it does to your 'do, but it will protect you if you take a tumble. Wear one approved by the Safety Equipment Institute.

Tops. Depending on the weather and your level of exertion, you may want to add layered sweatshirts and jackets to your giddeyup getup.

I DID IT!

"I was thirty-seven. My best friend had just died of breast cancer, and I had recently completed law school—at night, while working full-time as a paralegal. I'd forgotten how to have fun. Then I remembered hearing about some riding stables not too far away. Before I started riding again, a couple of my girlfriends went to a toy store and bought me a model of a smiling girl on horseback. I put it on the bookshelf in my living room. I'm not sure if it goaded me or inspired me . . . but not too long thereafter, I made that first information-gathering call to the stable. A few months of riding later, I took a weeklong riding trip in France."

—Julie

SADDLE SORE!

"I was hanging off a tree somewhere in Canyon de Chelly, not exactly feeling like Barbara Stanwyck. I'd been bouncing uncontrollably for six hours straight, with a huge camera and about forty-two extra lenses banging around my neck. (No, I didn't listen when the guide suggested I skip the Annie Liebovitz routine that day.) When my horse, 'Little Boss,' veered off on (yet another) hostile detour designed to decapitate me, I grabbed the branch before it hit my neck, spun around like a rebus monkey, dropped to the ground, and screamed at the top of my lungs, 'TAXI!'"

—Wendy

If you are taking classes in preparation for a riding trip, start well in advance of your departure. Three months is ideal. Take back-to-back lessons to build your stamina. Since most riding trips are on country trails, make sure that you get plenty of trail (not just ring) experience beforehand. Dude and guest ranch vacations can generally accommodate inexperienced riders, while working ranch stays blend practical activities like roping and herding with recreational riding. Make sure your classes prepare you for your destination. ***Book your dates.***

6. Complete the series.

"Learning to ride is more of a process than a goal," says Linda. "Relax, have a good time, and be willing to laugh at yourself. If you enjoy the process, the goal will follow. Remember: Every hour in the saddle increases your ability and confidence exponentially." ***Show up for class.***

CONGRATULATIONS!

You've gotten on—or back on—your horse. How is the air up there? You did it!

I DID IT!

Name: ______________________________

Date: ______________________________

BEYOND THE BADGE

If you love it as much as you thought you would, dream on . . .

- **Get fancy.** Try specialized types of riding: trail, ring, dressage, jumping, etc.
- **Horse fans, unite.** Investigate riding clubs or organizations in your area.
- **Take in a show.** Check out a derby, amateur riding event, or go to a rodeo!
- **Try a fresh approach.** The goal of Centered Riding is perfect harmony with your horse. The CR Four Basics—soft eyes, breathing, centering, and "building blocks"—aim to help riders discover their inner balance, serenity, and control. This approach promotes freedom of movement, suppleness, and coordination in the rider and increased balance, poise, and forward motion in the horse. To try this approach, make sure your instructor is Centered Riding certified.
- **Own your own.** As a kid, Melanie rode horses a few times at Camp Fire Girls. Then she spent her college senior year studying in Scotland, took riding lessons, and "got hooked." She and a friend, Lisa, decided to buy a horse together and share the expense. Inexperience and some not-so-hot advice led them to buy Ariel, a thoroughbred "off the track." Horses like this are gorgeous, but they're fast because they're high-strung and skittish. Ariel promptly threw Lisa and treated Golden Gate Park as his personal track, charging about and nearly getting hit by cars. Many years, stables, and trainers later, Melanie says she "wouldn't trade Ariel for the world." But she also says her next horse will be a sturdy, mellow, and homely mule. "Looks are overrated in this world!" (See Linda's Expert Tips, page 321.)
- **Be a real globe-trotter.** Melanie has taken two "fantastic" riding trips in Ireland. Julie just got back from a seven-day frolic in France, where long, sunny days of riding were punctuated by five-course lunches and dinners. Linda takes groups trotting through France, Italy, and Ireland. She considers France—the Loire Valley, Provence, the Périgord—an ideal destination because the weather is great, the countryside stunning, the food amazing, and there is a time-honored trail network.

HORSING AROUND (THE WORLD)

Consider these adventure locations for your riding trip

Darhat Valley, Mongolia. The annual Naadam Festival features horse races and wrestling matches.

Killarney, Ireland. Emerald-green farmland, seaside cliffs, gregarious pub-goers, friendly bed and breakfasts.

Snowy River, Australia. Wild horses, kangaroos, and wombats in the Australian Alps.

Yellowstone National Park, Wyoming. Acres of stunning scenery where you can get away from cars and commune with moose and elk.

LINDA'S PICKS

BOOKS

Centered Riding by Sally Swift
The basic text for this distinct discipline. The sequel, *Centered Riding 2*, is Linda's bible.

Fitness, Performance, and the Female Equestrian by Mary D. Midkiff
Tips on health, nutrition, safety, and more.

Happy Horsemanship by Dorothy Henderson Pinch
Okay, it's a kid's book—but this makes it easy for beginners to understand. Linda recommends it to all her new students.

Horse Lovers Vacation Guide by Lynne Johnson
Horseback vacations to suit every riding style and personality.

The New Encyclopedia of the Horse by Elwyn Hartley Edwards
Useful reference covering basic equestrian terminology and techniques.

Of Women and Horses by GaWaNi Pony Boy
True stories by horsewomen about the steeds they admire.

Seabiscuit: An American Legend by Laura Hillenbrand
The true story of a great racehorse. A classic.

TRAVEL

Adventure Rides, Inc.
www.goadventureriding.com

Equestrian Vacation
www.equestrianvacation.com

Equitours Worldwide Horseback Riding Vacations
www.ridingtours.com

GEAR

Country Supply
www.countrysupply.com

Dover Saddlery
www.doversaddlery.com

State Line Tack
www.statelinetack.com

MAGAZINES

EQUUS
www.equusmagazine.com
Monthly articles and links to equine sites and equestrian community sites.

Horse and Rider
www.horseandrider.com
Articles on training, horse care, and trail riding with a focus on Western horsemanship.

Horse Illustrated
www.animalnetwork.com/horse
Articles and tips galore. Linda's favorite.

The Trail Rider
www.trailridermagazine.com
Articles about trail riding (billed as "America's fastest-growing sport"), including info on horse care, wagon train rides, and product reviews.

ASSOCIATIONS

American Endurance Ride Conference
www.aerc.org
Governs long-distance riding in North America.

American Riding Instructors Association
www.riding-instructor.com
Provides certification for instructors.

Centered Riding
www.centeredriding.org
An approach promising perfect harmony with your horse.

MOVIES

... and while you're nursing sore muscles:

All the Pretty Horses

Black Beauty

The Horse Whisperer

The Mask of Zorro
Catherine Zeta-Jones swashbuckles!

National Velvet

Seabiscuit

Yellow Rose of Texas
Roy Rogers and Dale Evans, the ultimate cowgirl.

deal

I'll tell you why I did all these things.
It is very simple.
I did all these things because they
needed to be done.

—Marie Grace Augustin

41

EAT IT

★ nutrition ★

Everything you see I owe to SPAGHETTI.

—Sophia Loren

So, what's your motivation?
Take a moment.
Dream a little, think big,
and then complete this sentence:
I see myself . . .

Imagine This . . . You've been known to catch a chill while standing in front of your refrigerator with the admonitions of diet gurus, yesterday's newspaper headlines, and your mother running through your head. Meals used to feel like battles. Good fats v. bad fats. Fast food v. slow food. Carbs: friend or foe? You had questions. Soy what? To supplement or not to supplement? And those supposedly helpful Nutrition Facts labels? They made you feel like a freshman trapped in a senior's chemistry class. Then you found that nutrition know-how could actually make food fun—nourishing your body, easing your mind, pleasing your palate, and restoring your faith in one of the finer things in life: food, glorious food! Come and get it. *You can do it!*

The Payoffs

- **Health.** You have a better shot at maintaining or regaining yours if you eat well-balanced, nutritious meals.
- **Happy tummy.** An empty stomach can make you crabby and contentious—but when you've got a healthy, pleasing meal in you, your entire outlook changes for the better.
- **Conflict resolution.** Many of us are conflicted and confused about the way we eat—but who needs all the guilt and anxiety the media feeds us? A little nutrition knowledge can give us the clarity we need to feel more serene.
- **Joie de vivre.** Eating well is not about rules (eat your vegetables!) or deprivation (no dessert for you!). It's about satisfying both your needs and your desires—for comfort, pleasure, and even joy.

Meet Your Mentor

CAROL ANN RINZLER

What She Does: Carol is the author of more than twenty (yes, twenty) books on nutrition and health. They include *Nutrition for Dummies, Controlling Cholesterol for Dummies, Weight Loss Kit for Dummies, The New Complete Book of Food, The Book of Chocolate,* and the pioneering *Estrogen and Breast Cancer: A Warning to Women*. She is the nutrition columnist for the *New York Daily News* and frequently writes articles on health, food, and diet for a number of newspapers and magazines.

© Stanley Schulman

Why She Does It: "I love explaining scientific issues in ways that ordinary human beings can understand. I choose to write about subjects I want to know more about myself—partially because I'm the kind of person who can't rest until I understand an issue and get my questions answered. I'll never be 'done' with nutrition, because we are at the very beginning of our understanding of the subject. I've updated *Nutrition for Dummies* three times, and once a year in the *New York Daily News,* I do an 'Oops!' column of nutrition bloopers. The great thing is that with what we do know about nutrition, you can do a great deal to make your life more adventurous and fun. You can learn about your body, your history, and your culture."

Everything you don't know can be used against you!

—Carol Ann Rinzler

Word from the Wise: "What you eat says a great deal about you—whether you are adventurous, what allergies and conditions you may have, and quite a bit about your genetic makeup. When George H.W. Bush said he hated broccoli, he might have been letting us know that he has the gene that makes some people sensitive to one of the flavor chemicals—phenylthiocarbamide—in cruciferous veggies. And food is an incredible adventure, a continuing journey of self-discovery."

BADGE STEPS

1. Know thyself—and thy diet.

Before embarking on any significant change to your diet, get the facts about your dietary needs from a reliable source: your doctor. But your doctor can only help you if she has accurate information about exactly what you eat and what your health issues are. So make an appointment to see your doctor at least a week from now, and in the meantime:

- Keep a complete food and drink diary for a week, noting everything you eat and drink alongside accurate portion sizes. Be honest—this is the really illuminating part.
- Get a handle on your medical history. The Health History you created for Care for Your Health, page 334, will come in handy! If you haven't yet earned that badge, list your medical conditions, major illnesses, and medications, plus any medical conditions you know your parents, siblings, and grandparents have had.
- Make a list of questions for your doctor about your diet. Here are a few to get you started: Is there anything obviously missing in my diet? Should I be taking a dietary supplement? (See Carol's Expert Tips, page 330.) Do I need to lose weight? Does my health history indicate that I should modify my diet in some way? Diabetes/high cholesterol/osteoporosis is common in my family—are there any dietary changes I can make to help prevent these problems? Is the rash/headaches/nausea I've been having the result of a food allergy?

Take your food diary, medical history, and dietary questions to your doctor. She'll be impressed—and it will help you both get a handle on your nutritional needs. If you'd like specific meal-planning pointers, ask your doctor to refer you to a dietician (see Beyond the Badge, page 332). ***Go to your doctor prepared to make a difference in your health.***

2. Follow the Guidelines.

In addition to the input you get from your doctor, spend an afternoon reality-checking what you think you know about what you should eat. The U.S. Department of Agriculture and Health and Human Services' Dietary Guidelines for Americans and Food Guide Pyramid are ideal for this. Go to www.nal.usda.gov/fnic/dga and there you'll find:

Rules of thumb for shopping and menu planning. Stick the Food

COMPARISON SHOPPING

Before you buy, check the Nutrition Facts panel

- Ingredients are listed in order of their prominence in the food. If corn syrup is item number two after water, that "juice drink" is more like soda pop than juice.
- Pay attention to serving sizes; they are often smaller than you think (or wish!).
- "% Daily Value" helps you determine how an item will help meet your body's daily needs for vitamins and minerals, and how much fat, sodium, and cholesterol you're in for with each serving.
- "High" means that one serving provides 20 percent or more of the Daily Value of a nutrient. For example, a juice might read "High in Vitamin C."
- "Low" means you can eat several servings without going over the Daily Value of this nutrient. The FDA strictly monitors items that claim to be "low-fat."
- "Good source" means one serving gives you 10–19 percent of the Daily Value, for instance when a cereal advertises that it's a "good source" of fiber.
- "Light" (or "lite") refers to calories, fat, or sodium. Items that claim to be "light" must have one-third fewer calories, 50 percent less fat, or 50 percent less sodium than is usually found in that type of product. But be sure to double-check serving size on "lite" items—sometimes they are smaller.

Guide Pyramid on your fridge, and take the information in the Pyramid Pointers sidebar with you shopping. Carol quips that "It's hard to believe anything concocted by a committee is this sensible! The best thing about these guidelines is that they seem to have been written by real people who actually like food."

Serving suggestions. The Food Guide Pyramid tells us the numbers of servings we should shoot for from each food group and reminds us what healthy serving sizes really are.

Tasty options. The Guidelines are big on variety, with Mediterranean, Asian, South American, Native American, and Vegetarian Food Pyramids to please any gourmet palate.

Reliable research. Dubious about that article you read in *National Enquirer* about donuts being the cure for cancer? Consult the Guidelines to research food and lifestyle choices that promote health, provide energy, and may reduce the risk or severity of chronic illnesses, including heart disease, diabetes, and cancer.

Commonsense reminders. About aiming for a healthy weight and exercising regularly. (See Exercise Your Options, page 250.)

Put the Guidelines to work for you.

3. Make a meal plan.

Using the Pyramid and your doctor's recommendations, create your own eating plan for a week. Remember that while the Pyramid allows for a great deal of variety, you should:

- Emphasize whole grains in the "Bread, Cereal, Rice & Pasta" base of the Pyramid. This includes oats, brown rice, whole-wheat or durum semolina pasta (which includes most Italian pastas), and whole-grain baked goods.
- Use fats and oils sparingly, and try to use mostly unsaturated fats.
- Trade up to lower-fat, lower-cholesterol dairy and proteins in place of high-fat, high-cholesterol items. A serving of lean beef, skinless chicken, or low-fat yogurt is better than a serving of beef hot dogs or whole milk. (See Comparison Shopping.)
- Go for balance. An easy way to balance a meal is to imagine four sections on your plate. Fill one with protein, one with a whole grain starch, and the other two with fruits and vegetables.

Make a meal plan for the week.

PYRAMID POINTERS

Ripped from the Guidelines

- Eat a variety of whole grains, fruits, and vegetables daily. These plant foods make you feel full with few calories, are low in fat, have no cholesterol, are high in fiber, and are filled with the phytochemicals believed to reduce your risk of heart disease and cancer.
- Mind your serving sizes. The suggested minimum of five servings of fruits and vegetables may seem like a lot, but in actual practice this amounts to some veggies at lunch and dinner plus a fruit snack in between. (No, ketchup doesn't count!)
- Aim for a diet low in saturated fat and cholesterol and moderate in total fat. Unsaturated fats are found in: olive, canola, and vegetable oils; avocados, pecans, almonds, walnuts, and flaxseed; fatty fish like salmon, tuna, mackerel, sardines, and lake trout; and vegetables. Saturated fats (including butter, cheese, lard, and palm and coconut oils) are associated with increased cholesterol, heart disease, high blood pressure, blood clots, and some kinds of cancer.
- Go easy on the sugar and the salt.
- Moderate your intake of highly processed foods. This means frozen entrees, "instant" box mixes, and meal-in-a-can dishes like chili or baked beans. These tend to be high in salt, sugar, fats, and multisyllabic mystery ingredients.

I DID IT!

"My work requires me to drive around seeing client businesses several days a week. Though I'm not a junk food junkie, I did find myself eating fast food on those days because it's so convenient and, well, fast! Trouble was, I quickly put on ten pounds and felt guilty for eating the stuff I try to keep my kids away from. I started ordering off the children's menu to get smaller portions, sticking with grilled chicken or plain burgers, and substituting side salads (with low-fat dressing) for fries and water for soda. It's still fast and convenient, but I no longer feel guilty—and I lost the weight."
—Rikki

INDIGESTION

"In an effort to lose weight, I eliminated sugar and wheat from my diet. I did lose weight this way—but since I was eating quite a bit more protein and fat, my cholesterol counts went way up. My doctor was concerned, and I'm now trying to eat more grains. It's a struggle, and I'm still trying to find the right balance for me."
—Sondra

CAROL'S EXPERT TIPS

SUPPLEMENT SAVVY

It's best to get nutrients from food, rather than from pills or powders. But there are certain situations that call for supplementation, such as when:

- You're pregnant or nursing. Ask your doc for specifics.
- You take prescription drugs. Ask your doctor if the nature of the drug makes supplements prudent.
- You smoke. Smokers use up vitamin C. (Also see Quit It, page 344.)
- You're approaching menopause. This is time for extra calcium.
- You're a strict vegetarian (or vegan). You may need extra vitamin B12, calcium, and iron.

When buying your supplements, choose a well-known brand, check the label for exactly what you are getting in each dose, check the expiration date, and follow storage instructions.

4. Shop for taste sensations.

Once you've got your square meal plan squared away, it's time to make up a shopping list. In addition to any ingredients you need for your meals, add these items to your list:

Condiments and spices. Eating veggies, beans, and grains is much more fun when you throw on a little wasabi (Japanese horseradish), salsa, fresh herbs, spices, olive oil, balsamic vinegar, or a sprinkling of sharp, freshly grated cheese.

Fresh produce. Even if your lettuce occasionally wilts before you get around to using it, having produce on hand makes it a lot more likely that you'll eat enough fruits and vegetables. If your supermarket doesn't inspire you, go to your local farmer's market or natural food store and take your pick of ripe, seasonal local produce.

Healthy snacks. This includes nuts, fruit, string cheese, hard-cooked eggs, dill pickles, raisins, and small cans of tomato juice. Instead of frequenting the vending machine, stock that snack drawer in your desk and the office fridge with these items.

Dark chocolate. Satisfy sugar cravings and get health benefits (it's true!) with a one-ounce portion of dark chocolate. Why dark chocolate? No milk = no cholesterol.

To make room for all this good stuff, go through your food supplies at home and at your office, and ditch a few items that don't sit well with your newfound nutrition knowledge. If they're not expired, you might donate them to a local food pantry. Easy does it, though: You can't expect to change your family's eating habits overnight, and you don't want anyone to feel deprived. Implement healthful changes gradually, and you'll avoid cravings and rebound bingeing. ***Stock up on healthy eats and treats.***

5. Play with your food.

Now that you've enjoyed a week's worth of tasty, healthy meals, you'll know what eating well can do for your mood, your body, and your spirits. So make a habit of it! Spend a month exploring healthy food options by trying three of the activities listed below at least once:

Make every day a picnic. Bring your lunch to work in a cool lunchbox or a brown bag your kids have decorated, and soak up some sun on your lunch hour. It's easier to control what you eat at work if you pack your own lunch and snacks. (You'll probably save money, too.)

Throw it into a stew. Stewing tenderizes meats, which means you can use lower-fat cuts of beef. When the stew is done, let it cool in the fridge for a day to marry the flavors and skim any leftover fat off the top.

Get wacky with a wok. This round, deep pan distributes heat evenly, so you don't have to use much oil to make sure your meats and veggies get cooked to perfection in minutes. Works great with a steamer and cover, too.

Food fight!!! Come on, what else are you going to do with all those old marshmallows you found in the pantry?

Eat well for a month—and have a blast doing it!

CONGRATULATIONS!

Feeling merrier as you eat and drink? Here's to your health! You did it!

I DID IT!

Name: ______________________

Date: ______________________

SEALS OF APPROVAL

Here's the deal with all those seals

Certified organic. Your produce is guaranteed by the USDA and state certification agencies to be free of pesticides, and genetically modified organisms (GMOs) are not used in their production.

Fair Trade Certified. A guarantee that the farmer got paid a fair price for their produce and that your purchase supports responsible farming practices.

Free range. A term usually applied to eggs or meats, implying that the animals were not reared entirely in cages, but were instead put out to pasture or allowed to roam on fenced-off land. However, this claim is not certified by the FDA or any other agency.

GMO-free or (GE-free). Implies that the food was not genetically modified or engineered to grow faster or develop other traits (such as a thicker peel for easy transport). Because the public health consequences of GMO foods are unclear, there are strict European Union labeling requirements on GMO foods. However, the U.S. Food and Drug Administration does not currently require labeling for foods produced with GMOs or monitor "GMO-free" claims.

Hormone-free. Implies that the item has been raised without growth-promoting hormones that can make animals grow larger faster or produce more eggs or milk. The long-term effect of exposure to these hormones on humans is not known. Although the FDA does not currently require foods produced with hormones to be labeled accordingly, the agency is cracking down on false "hormone-free" claims.

BEYOND THE BADGE

If you love it as much as you thought you would, dream on . . .

- **Consult a specialist.** When should you see a dietician? Carol puts it this way, "If you have diabetes, you require a special diet. Your doctor may hand you a diabetes-friendly diet plan, but a smart doctor will also send you to a dietician. The dietician will help you translate that diet into terms you can live with in your real world." Dieticians can also be helpful when you are trying to lose weight safely and for the long haul (see Weight Loss). You can find a dietician in your area by going to the American Dietetic Association's Web site, www.eatright.org. Click the "Find a Nutritional Professional" link, enter your zip code, and voilà.
- **Grow your own.** Instead of worrying about how organic, natural, or pesticide-free your grocery's produce is, why not take matters into your own hands and grow at least some of it yourself? See Dig This, page 132, to learn more about why and how.
- **Cook it up.** In addition to controlling ingredients and portion sizes, cooking helps us slow down and really appreciate food. For more on the pleasures of cooking, see Dine In, page 224, and for lots of fascinating facts about how the ways we cook affect nutrition, see Carol's *Nutrition for Dummies.* While cooking up a storm, implement the following practices to minimize germs and bacteria (there are 76 million cases of food poisoning each year in the U.S. alone!):
    - Wash your hands before and after touching food and wash all fruits and vegetables.
    - Follow the directions on packages for storing and preparing foods, and cook foods thoroughly.
    - Use one cutting board for raw meat, fish, and poultry; another for other foods.
    - Keep sponges dry, or microwave them for a few minutes—long enough to dry but not burn them!
    - Keep hot foods hot and cold foods cold.
    - Never eat or drink anything containing raw eggs.

WEIGHT LOSS

What works?

If you're curious what health and science professionals—rather than fashion magazine editors—consider "overweight," visit the Weight Control and Obesity section at www.nal.usda.gov/fnic to see charts and assess your Body Mass Index. Consider consulting a dietician about your needs and struggles, and if you just want to fit into your skinny jeans, remember this common sense from Carol: "The Food Pyramid offers so many choices that you can eat that way for the rest of your life. Weight Watchers also doesn't exclude any foods, which is extremely important. Most people can stay on a restricted diet for a short period of time, but eventually say, 'To heck with this; I can't do this!' and gain weight back." Eating fewer calories (rather than excluding entire food groups) and exercising is what works long term.

CAROL'S PICKS

BOOKS

Controlling Cholesterol for Dummies by Carol Ann Rinzler
Confused about identifying "bad cholesterol" v. "good cholesterol"—and keeping both within healthful limits? No problem: *Cholesterol for Dummies* explains it all.

Eat, Drink, and Be Healthy: The Harvard Medical School Guide to Healthy Eating by Walter C. Willett, MD
Harvard's Dr. Willett offers an alternative to the USDA Food Pyramid.

Healthy Women, Healthy Lives: A Guide to Preventing Disease, from the Landmark Nurses' Health Study by Susan E. Hankinson, ScD, Graham A. Colditz, Joanne E. Manson, and Frank E. Speizer
Based on a thirty-year study of thousands of nurses, researchers from Harvard Medical School have assembled a straightforward medical guide focusing on the major preventable diseases that women are susceptible to.

The New Complete Book of Food: A Nutritional, Medical, and Culinary Guide by Carol Ann Rinzler
What makes this book special? It treats more than 200 foods as individual health products, complete with medical benefits, side effects, and interactions.

Nutrition for Dummies by Carol Ann Rinzler
This user-friendly book made Amazon.com's "Ten Best Health Books" list, and it was an *L.A. Times* health bestseller.

Our Bodies, Ourselves for the New Century: A Book by and for Women by Boston Women's Health Book Collective
Although this famous book covers many aspects of women's health and sexuality, it has great sections on body image and nutrition.

WEB SITES

The American Cancer Society
www.cancer.org
Type "food and cancer" in the home page search box, and you'll find answers to your questions about the connections between the two.

The American Heart Association
www.americanheart.org
Everything you ever wanted to know about diet and heart disease; includes "Cholesterol Lowdown" and "Exercise and Fitness."

The Food Allergy and Anaphylaxis Network
www.foodallergy.org
A nonprofit membership organization that provides education about food allergies and coping strategies.

The Food and Drug Administration
www.fda.gov
Carol calls this site "the world's biggest nutritional information toy store."

National Women's Health Resource Center
www.healthywomen.org
National Women's Health Resource Center offers comprehensive, unbiased information on women's health topics, including specific nutrition information.

Transfair USA
www.transfairusa.org
Find out about Fair Trade products and how your purchases support family farmers, their communities, and the environment.

The USDA National Nutrient Database
www.nal.usda.gov/fnic/cgi-bin/nut_search/pl
Allows you to enter a food item and get a calorie count and nutrient analysis.

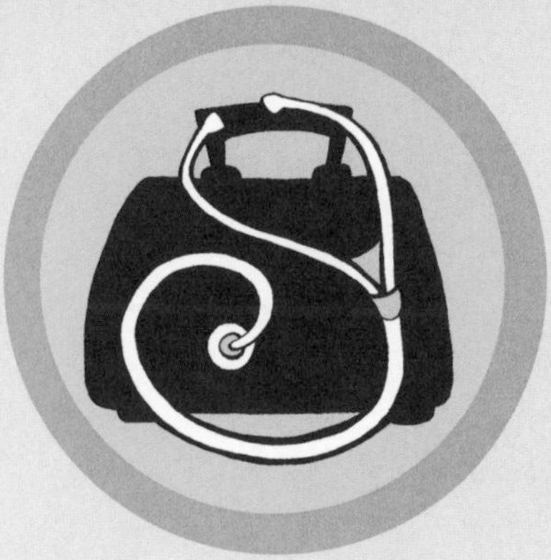

42

CARE FOR YOUR HEALTH

★ healthcare ★

The day you decide to do it is your LUCKY DAY.

—Japanese proverb

Imagine This . . . You give your health the care it deserves by being a savvy consumer of information and an active partner with your doctors. You've picked your doctors at least as carefully as your babysitter or hairstylist and wouldn't dream of putting off appointments and tests because you know they're important preventive measures—like saving your computer files or tuning up your car. You have regularly scheduled annual exams and don't wait to address nagging health concerns. And when you come out of the doctor's office, you feel confident that you got the medical attention that you need and deserve. Insurance? You've got it covered, complete with organized records. After all, it's your body, your self, and your job to take charge of your healthcare. Begin by making an appointment with this badge and getting a handle on your healthcare options. It won't hurt a bit, and you'll feel so much better knowing you've done it. *You can do it!*

So, what's your motivation?
Take a moment.
Dream a little, think big,
and then complete this sentence:
I see myself . . .

The Payoffs

- **Peace of mind—and body.** When you have your healthcare act together, you've swept a major dust bunny out from under your bed—and no longer have to lie awake nights worrying about putting it off.
- **Empowerment.** When it comes to your health, ignorance is not bliss, and knowledge really is power.
- **Choice.** The more you know about what you need, when you need it, and how to get it, the more options you have.
- **Change.** When you know better, you can do better. And major changes in your health and well-being can often be made with minor investments of time and effort.

Meet Your Mentor
JUDY NORSIGIAN

What She Does: The executive director of Our Bodies Ourselves and coauthor of *Our Bodies, Ourselves* (the book by the same name), Judy is the organization's primary public speaker (did you catch her with her daughter on *Oprah*?) and plays a major role in fund-raising, administrative functions, work with interns and volunteers, and collaborations with other groups. *OBOS* is produced by Our Bodies Ourselves, a nonprofit organization devoted to education about women and health, and over the past thirty-five years, the book has become the bible for women's health. Since its original publication in 1970, *OBOS* has sold more than four million copies and has been translated into twenty languages.

© Jane Pincus

Why She Does It: "I joined the group in 1971 and was part of our incorporation process and decision to go with Simon & Schuster to create a commercial book of what had been a 193-page, typewritten, newsprint publication. Earlier I had lived as part of an intentional community in upstate New York, and a friend of a friend knew someone at OBOS. This group of lay women was continuing to research topics in women's health, including the gathering of women's personal stories. They shared this information in pamphlets and at community workshops. I met the group and liked what they were doing. Since I was interested in nutrition as a result of some experience with organic gardening, and as I was concerned with the connections between nutrition and health, I took on the cowriting of the first nutrition chapter ever written for *OBOS*. I wanted to make eating healthfully fun and delicious, not a chore or a mystery."

> We really have come A LONG WAY from the early 1970s—when physicians were 92 percent male and obstetrician/gynecologists were 98 percent male.
>
> —Judy Norsigian

Word from the Wise: "Good-quality sources of information can improve the decisions we make about our healthcare. Beware of hype and hidden agendas. Our mission at OBOS is to get balanced information out there and to help women discern the good from the hype."

BADGE STEPS

1. Collect your health info.

This badge will take some of the guesswork out of healthcare, so that you have a clearer picture of your own health, your doctor has a better sense of how to treat your health concerns, and your next visit with your primary healthcare practitioner doesn't cause you to break out in a cold sweat. First things first: Get your medical records in order.

When it comes to our medical records, most of us figure they are tucked safely away in a file in some doctor's office. But in actuality, your medical records may be a scattered paper trail. How many doctors have you seen in the last ten years? How many times have you drawn a blank when filling out your immunization history at the doctor's office? And would the doctors be able to get hold of your complete medical records, should you find yourself in an accident or emergency room? Don't wait to find out—a little organization and record retrieving can help ensure you get the prompt, appropriate medical care you deserve.

Here's how to clean up that paper trail and keep your comprehensive healthcare information in an accordion file or three-ring notebook divided into six sections, labeled as follows:

Physicians. Create a complete contact list of all your current healthcare practitioners—your OB/GYN, physical therapist, primary care doctor, dentist, dental surgeon, dermatologist, chiropractor, optometrist, etc.—with full name, address, telephone, and fax. Add the name, address, and phone of the emergency room nearest your home. Put these in the front of your file.

Medications. List all the medications you take, giving the drug name, dosage, how often you take it, and when you started taking it. Don't forget to include herbal remedies, nonprescription medications, and vitamins. Note any allergies or adverse reactions you have had to medications. Add this to your file.

Health history. Make a complete list with descriptions and dates of serious illnesses or conditions you've experienced, any surgeries you've had, and accidents or emergency care. Include a record of your immediate family members' (mother, father, siblings, grandparents) health, since many conditions have a genetic component. What health issues do they have, and if applicable, what did they die of? Be sure all this info is in the file.

AN OUNCE OF PREVENTION

Common screening recommendations

Consider the following general age-based schedules, checking in with your healthcare provider for any new information that may come available.

Twenties. Pap test, clinical breast exam, self-breast exam, blood cholesterol test, blood pressure, lung scan if you smoke (see Quit It!, page 344), and mole-mapping by a dermatologist, especially if you are fair skinned.

Thirties. All of the above, and if there is an immediate family history of breast cancer, your doctor may advise a baseline mammogram.

Forties. All of the above plus screening for glaucoma and diabetes.

Fifties and forward. All of the above plus thyroid function and screening for colorectal cancer. You may also want to discuss the pros and cons of routine mammography screening with your provider as this has become a controversial area in recent years. Routine bone mineral density should be considered in the early sixties (in the absence of any risk factors).

Medical records. To get copies of your medical records from your healthcare practitioner, you will likely have to mail or fax a written request for these and may be asked to cover the cost of photocopying. These records will indicate results and dates for tests like Pap smears and mammograms, any X-rays or other diagnostics, and what your last blood pressure and cholesterol counts looked like. Make it a new habit to ask for copies of your records immediately following your doctor's visit. Your health care providers now have to comply with a complex healthcare privacy law (HIPAA) that may require certain forms to be filled out in order for you to obtain these records, so be prepared to do the necessary paperwork.

Health concerns. Note and date any nagging, pesky health concerns you've been experiencing—a sore neck, a ticklish throat, sleeplessness, you name it. That way, you'll remember to bring it up with your healthcare practitioner on your next visit. Also, be sure to note any new symptoms that may develop after you begin taking a new drug. And be sure to take notes about what the doctor says to you about your health in general, any specific diagnoses, and any prescriptions and health maintenance recommendations.

Screening schedules. Make a list of what you need done in the coming year. Your healthcare providers can advise you when to have routine checkups and tests (An Ounce of Prevention provides a general idea of what screenings are likely to be recommended). Your history and your family history may affect any particular screening schedule, as will your general health and symptoms. The National Women's Health Information Center (www.4woman.gov) and the U.S. Department of Health and Human Services (www.pueblo.gsa.gov/cic_text/health/personal/personal.txt) also provide recommendations about various routine preventive screenings.

Keep this file updated and accessible, and be sure someone in your family knows exactly where it is in case of emergency. ***Keep tabs on your healthcare.***

2. Understand your insurance coverage.

Anyone who has insurance, whether purchased individually or through an employer or partner, knows it isn't exactly self-explanatory—there's usually lots of fine print. Now's the time to locate your insurance coverage handbook, and make sure you understand what you're entitled to.

WHO YOU GONNA CALL?

Meet your healthcare practitioners

Primary care physician (usually an internist or family practice physician), nurse-practitioner, nurse-midwife, or physician assistant. These primary care providers provide preventive care, treat everyday ailments, and refer us to specialists as needed. Some of them also attend women in childbirth.

Obstetrician/Gynecologist. This is a surgical specialist who sometimes has additional training in providing general well-woman care. She can diagnose and treat diseases of the reproductive organs and is trained to handle complications during pregnancy and childbirth. If you don't plan to make use of obstetric care, a gynecologist's practice is likely a better fit for you. Many women prefer nurse-practitioners and midwives for their basic OB/GYN care and are referred to physicians as necessary.

Dentist. To monitor our teeth and gums. Oral hygiene is about more than having cover-girl white teeth. Gum disease has been linked to heart disease, diabetes, premature births, and a range of other ills.

Opthalmologist. Medical doctors who specialize in eye care and diseases. Optometrists examine eyes and prescribe glasses, but do not provide drugs or surgery.

OPTIONS FOR THE UNINSURED

Getting the healthcare you and your family need

If you are uninsured or know someone who is, explore these resources:

Group plans. Investigate organizations you might join that offer low-cost group plans. Many professional or common interest groups do, including many guilds and unions.

Medicaid. You may also be eligible for the government's Medicaid program. Guidelines vary from state to state, and most are stringent about how much money you are allowed to earn while remaining covered. Most private hospitals and some doctors won't treat Medicaid patients, though many states do have special Medicaid programs to treat women with breast or cervical cancer. See www.cms.hhs.gov/medicaid or call 877-267-2323.

Clinics. Many communities have clinics that serve the uninsured at low or no cost, and some clinics are especially for women. Clinics may offer services on a sliding scale payment based on income, including treatment for illnesses, screening tests, and discounted prescriptions. Check your local phone book, plus www.phf.org/links.htm and www.nachc.com.

Patient assistance. Pharmaceutical companies also have patient assistance programs. See www.disabilityresources.org/RX.html; www.needymeds.com; and www.rxhope.com.

If you look through your coverage handbook carefully, you'll probably find things you weren't aware of. Some "alternative" or "holistic/complementary" services may be covered, such as acupuncture, and some discounts may be offered if you follow certain procedures for preventive care. You may also find that you have access to free health consultations over the telephone or prescription advice services and that you are paying extra for coverage you don't need, such as maternity benefits. (We'll discuss making sure your health insurance makes financial sense in Grow Your Money, page 372.)

Give yourself a quiet hour or two and read through your insurance handbook. Make notes of anything you don't understand or any questions it raises. To get answers, talk to your firm's human resources person, visit your insurer's Web site, or call your insurer's customer service line. Make a note of the answers in the margins of the handbook for future reference, then file your handbook alongside your comprehensive health file for easy access. ***Benefit from knowing your insurance benefits.***

JUDY'S EXPERT TIPS

CONSIDER THE SOURCE

You Can Do It! can't give you medical advice or answer all of your healthcare questions, but it can point you in the right direction:

- Assembled by and for women, *Our Bodies, Ourselves* is a mainstay on many women's bookshelves for a reason: It provides comprehensive, straightforward, and honest information you'll turn to again and again, whether you're preparing for a doctor's appointment, following up on a news story, or dealing with a diagnosis.
- As *OBOS* states, the best information is the kind that is backed up by "research that uses rigorous scientific methods to evaluate medical care and that is free of commercial or professional biases." If a news story reveals research findings, look for how big the study was, how it was conducted, and who sponsored it. Are the health benefits of banjo playing being touted by the Banjo Manufacturers of America, Inc.?
- If you are surfing for health information online, check out the source's URL to determine the nature of the organization. Is it an accredited research institution, or is it a commercial enterprise that aims to sell its product or services? The designation .edu stands for educational institution, .org for nonprofit organization, .gov for government agency, .com for commercial company, and .net for network (.ca points to Canada and .uk to Great Britain).

3. Put your healthcare team to the test.

In Step 1, you listed all the healthcare practitioners you consult; now it's time to evaluate them and make sure they're meeting your healthcare needs. Many patients don't believe that they have the right or the expertise to assess their providers, but your health may depend on it. And as the coach of your own healthcare team, you're entitled to make any necessary cuts or replacements. So fill out the following checklist for every healthcare practitioner you consult. Does your provider:

- Explain exactly what she (or he) is doing and why?
- Allow time for and encourage your questions?
- Ask questions about your health history, medications, and life circumstances?
- Inform you of the possible side effects of and alternatives to suggested treatments?
- Have a professional, responsive, and detail-oriented staff?
- Maintain an open line for communication between visits, both for emergencies and for advice?
- Recommend an ongoing preventive care program appropriate to your age and specific condition(s)?
- Consider holistic options as part of your overall care?

If you feel your providers fall short on any of these levels, bring up your concerns. If you are not satisfied with the results, consider a change. In the current medical care climate, where providers are often required to limit the time they spend with you, it may be difficult to find an ideal situation, but do consider trying. To find a new healthcare practitioner, seek referrals from other physicians, from friends, and from nurses or other health workers. A longstanding relationship with a healthcare provider you trust can improve communication, diagnosis, and treatment. ***Set your standards for excellent care—and get it.***

4. Schedule your appointments.

Once you've identified the healthcare practitioners who pass your test, pull out your datebook and call to schedule visits and screenings for the coming year. Routine annual exams often need to be scheduled months in advance. Some women like to group these into a few days, so they can schedule the time off and get everything out of the way at once. But

GYNO KNOW-HOW

Tips to help you feel more comfortable in those stirrups!

- Pap smears are lifesavers; don't avoid them. They should begin at age 18 or whenever you become sexually active.
- Empty your bladder and bowels before your pelvic and Pap. It makes the procedures more comfortable and helps your doctor be more accurate.
- Don't rely on your Pap and pelvic to rule out sexually transmitted diseases. Raise your concerns with your provider so she can test you thoroughly.
- Pay attention to the breast exam, and if you have any questions about your monthly at-home self-exams, ask.
- Use this visit as a time to assess your contraceptive choices, if appropriate.
- It's natural for these exams to make us feel vulnerable and fearful. Do what you can—including asking to speak to the doctor for a few minutes with your clothes on!—to get the information and reassurance you need.

just getting the dates down in your book will go a long way toward helping you feel organized, responsible, and on top of things. And if you schedule them now, you can plan the rest of your activities around the most important one of all: taking care of your health.

In the future, pick a time of year when you will remember to make a round of appointment calls. Some people use their birthdays or the first of the year as a prompt. Whenever you choose to make your calls, put a big bold reminder to do this in your calendar. ***Make time for your health.***

5. Make your appointments count.

Now that you have healthcare practitioners you trust, know what your insurance will cover, are more aware of your health history, and have a schedule for your health maintenance, going for appointments will be much easier. Look at it this way: If you can commit to this badge, you can commit to a half-hour checkup! You're no longer a patient—you're a participant. When you do go to your provider, take these tips to get the most out of your visit:

- Make a list of the specific symptoms and issues you want to discuss, and bring your list of ongoing health concerns from your comprehensive health file.
- Bring your list of current medications and health history from your comprehensive health file. Your healthcare practitioner will want to know about these.
- Take notes while your provider talks or bring a friend to do so. (Sometimes a provider may want to take you aside to make sure that it is truly your desire to have the second person present.) Be sure to record any specific diagnoses, treatments, medications, and health maintenance recommendations your healthcare practitioner offers.
- Be honest. Don't expect someone to read your mind or intuit your fears—let them know your questions and concerns.
- Summarize your understanding of what you are told before you leave, to make sure you are both on the same page.
- Ask for copies of your records and book your next appointment before you leave the office.
- Update your files.

Go prepared to your next checkup.

TIME TIPS

Because yours is valuable

When you need to see a healthcare practitioner about an ailment between scheduled appointments, here are some ways to make sure you get the time you need to cover your concerns.

- **Tell the receptionists why you are coming in, so that they can pencil you in for enough time.**
- **Try to get the first appointment of the day, before your provider has had a chance to fall behind schedule.**
- **Feel free to call the office in advance to make sure your provider is on schedule.**

6. Explore your alternatives.

A broad range of holistic healthcare methods is increasingly available and covered by many insurance plans. Many women swear by herbal medicine, massage, acupuncture, and other alternative healthcare practices to complement conventional Western medicine, or "biomedicine." Even the government is getting involved: In 1992, the Office on Alternative Medicine (now called the National Center for Complementary and Alternative Medicine) was established at the National Institutes of Health to study and research the efficacy of a range of these methods.

To find out if alternative healthcare practices might work for you, do a little research. *OBOS* counsels, "When you are seeking any form of care or healing, be as informed and assertive as you can." So go into any appointment with an alternative healthcare practitioner knowing what you want to get out of it: improvement in your health or quality of life and clear treatment objectives. Also, be sure to let your conventional medical care provider know about any alternative therapies you are pursuing, and vice versa—some conventional and alternative treatments are complementary, but some are not. For example, some herbal remedies may not be taken in conjunction with certain pharmaceutical drugs.

Consider your full range of healthcare options. Even if the cost of alternative therapies is not 100 percent covered by your insurance plan, you may still want to try out a particular practice to see if it's worth the investment for you and your well-being. ***Take good care, and be well!***

CONGRATULATIONS!

Here's to your health! You did it!

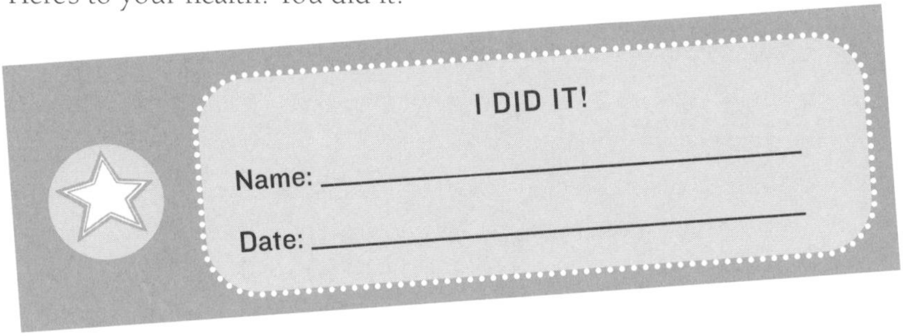

I DID IT!

"Friends now marvel at my close relationship with my current doctor and my ability to talk back, question, and disagree with him and his colleagues. He respects me and trusts me to tell him what is going on, and I in turn trust him to listen, make suggestions, and consult with me before any action is taken . . . I have finally after many, many years found someone willing to take into account my whole medical history and apply it to my current situation."
—Anonymous *OBOS* reader

HEALTHY SKEPTICISM

"I followed the 'best' medical advice and took the high-dose contraceptive pill for a decade . . . I had many habits based on unchallenged beliefs: for instance, that bingeing on sugar was okay as long as my weight was normal [and] that only heart attack-prone men had to worry about cholesterol or cardiovascular fitness."
—Gloria Steinem, in *OBOS*

BEYOND THE BADGE

If you love it as much as you thought you would, dream on . . .

- **Rise to the wellness challenge.** Eat right, exercise, and relax once in a while. Yeah, right. Easier said than done. Getting a handle on your routine preventive healthcare by earning this badge will go a long way toward promoting your health and well-being. But, what you do—and don't do—day in and day out is crucial. Good healthcare providers will talk to you about all of these things, but your self-care initiative and follow-through are key. See Beyond the Badge Badges for more badges in this book that address overall health.
- **Find out how powerful sisterhood can be.** If you are grappling with a particular health issue in your own life or feel drawn or connected to an illness or cause for other reasons, hooking up with a self-help or advocacy group can empower you and help others. Whether it's coming face-to-face with a life-threatening diagnosis or joining others to find a cure for Alzheimer's, many women find meaning, comfort, and aid in numbers. Look in your phone book, go online, and ask other women about organizations and efforts in your community. Many groups simultaneously focus on helping individuals one-on-one and addressing larger societal ills through public education and legislative advocacy.
- **Make healthcare a right, not a privilege.** One in seven Americans do not have health insurance—and many of those left uninsured have jobs but no coverage. For more information on this important issue of our time, visit www.covertheuninsured.org. Julie Winokur, coauthor (with her husband, photographer Ed Kashi) of *Denied: The Crisis of America's Uninsured,* is an expert on this subject. Visit their Web site, www.talkingeyesmedia.org, to learn more or to order their book.

BEYOND THE BADGE BADGES

Because there's more to your health than doctor's visits, earn these badges

Eat It. As *OBOS* states, food "affects how we feel physically and emotionally. By eating we take care of ourselves at the most basic level." Fran Lebowitz put it this way: "Food is an important part of a balanced diet." This badge demystifies ye olde Food Pyramid, looking for fun and easy ways to eat right and well.

Exercise Your Options. Find ways to meet your minimum daily fitness requirements that work for you, and develop a personal plan that feels more like play than work.

Get an Inner Life. No mumbo jumbo, just ways to soothe and relax your mind, body, and spirit.

Quit It. If you have a bad health habit—or three—this badge will provide some tools and techniques to help you become a winner by being a quitter.

JUDY'S PICKS

BOOKS

The first three books below are by members of the Boston Women's Health Book Collective.

Our Bodies, Ourselves for the New Century
The updated and revised seventh edition of the classic.

Nuestros Cuerpos, Nuestras Vidas
The Spanish-language cultural adaptation of *OBOS*.

The New Ourselves, Growing Older
A comprehensive manual about older women's issues.

The Five-Minute Herb and Dietary Supplement Consult by Adriane Fugh-Berman, MD
A useful tool for understanding alternative medicine.

Women's Health on the Internet by M. Sandra Wood and Janet M. Coggan (editors)
Gathers together information about the best Web sites in women's health.

WEB SITES & ORGANIZATIONS

www.cdc.gov
The Centers for Disease Control and Prevention site offers practical information on diseases, health risks, and prevention guidelines and strategies.

www.citizen.org/HRG
Public Citizen Health Research Group is Ralph Nader's watchdog organization. Monitors drugs, doctors, and federal agencies, and publishes *Health Letter* and *Worst Pills, Best Pills News.*

www.cspinet.org
Center for Science in the Public Interest offers excellent resources and publishes Nutrition Action.

www.feminist.com
Women's resources and links promote awareness, education, activism, and empowerment.

gateway.nlm.nih.gov/gw/Cmd
The National Library of Medicine Gateway is a fantastic resource that provides a simple way to search Medline, an index of thousands of medical journal articles.

www.healthywomen.org/content.cfm?LI=3
National Women's Health Resource Center offers comprehensive, unbiased information on women's health topics.

www.nwhn.org
The Web site of the National Women's Health Network, a national membership organization that works closely with Our Bodies Ourselves.

www.omhrc.gov/omhrc/index.htm
The Office of Minority Health Resource Center site holds a database of materials on specific health concerns.

www.ourbodiesourselves.org
Features original content and links to reputable sources.

www.seekwellness.com
Created by consumers and healthcare professionals. Provides evenhanded treatment of both Western and alternative medicine.

43

QUIT IT

★ breaking bad habits ★

Habits are at first cobwebs, then cables.

—Spanish proverb

So, what's your motivation?
Take a moment.
Dream a little, think big,
and then complete this sentence:
I see myself . . .

Imagine This . . . You couldn't face your desk without a giant cup of coffee, which you thought made you productive—until you realized it made you twitch. Or maybe you couldn't get to sleep until every kid toy was put away, and your living room looked like a *House Beautiful* photo spread. It's not that you actually wanted to do these things, but you felt like a helpless marionette, with habit pulling your strings. Once you cut those strings, you can finally stop being a meek creature of habit and be a truly independent woman. Maybe you'll up and quit smoking or start to reclaim the sunny weekends and oodles of cash you used to spend shopping on the Web . . . anything's possible! Prepare to square your shoulders, analyze your behavior, and transform your thoughts and actions for good. *You can do it!*

The Payoffs

- **Time.** Do the math: how many minutes did you spend last year keeping up this habit, even though you gained precious little from it? Aren't there lots of ways you'd rather spend that time?
- **Money.** Even if your habit isn't costly (lucky you), you've probably spent cold hard cash trying to cover it up or keep it in check—hello, breath mints, dieting books, and debt consolidators!
- **Freedom.** Our habits can keep us from going places, trying new things, and being with people we enjoy; they restrict our freedom and cramp our style.
- **Pride.** Because getting out from under an old habit can feel like climbing Mt. Everest, you deserve to feel proud and exhilarated when you finally make it!

Meet Your Mentors

CHERRY PEDRICK

What She Does: Cherry is a registered nurse and the coauthor of several books, including *The OCD Workbook: Your Guide to Breaking Free from Obsessive-Compulsive Disorder* with Bruce Hyman, PhD, *The Habit Change Workbook: How to Break Bad Habits and Form Good Ones* and *The BDD Workbook, Overcome Body Dysmorphic Disorder and End Body Image Obsessions* with James Claiborn, PhD, *Helping Your Child with OCD: A Workbook for Parents of Children with Obsessive-Compulsive Disorder* with Lee Fitzgibbons, PhD, and *Loving Someone with OCD: Help for You and Your Family* with Karen Landsman, PhD, and Kathy Parrish, MA, MS.

Why She Does It: "I worked as a nurse for twenty years and have always been interested in healthcare and helping people. Then I developed obsessive-compulsive disorder at age forty and began researching the condition. One thing led to another, and I began to write, which had always been a secret ambition but one that didn't seem practical as a career when I was a student. I wrote several articles about OCD and published a continuing education course on the subject for fellow nurses. I also wanted to point people with OCD in the right direction through a book, so I went to an Obsessive-Compulsive Foundation conference and joined up with my first coauthor, Bruce Hyman, PhD. While habits are not the same as obsessive-compulsive behaviors, some aspects intersect—so *The Habit Change Workbook* was born, along with a Web site (www.cherrypedrick.com). Basically, the more I learned, the stronger my desire to share hope with others became."

> If we can develop a habit, we can CHANGE a habit.
>
> —Cherry Pedrick

Word from the Wise: "Habits are often formed because we use the behavior as some kind of reward. But eventually, changing that behavior can make us feel better than the habit ever could—it's a far better reward, and the self-esteem and confidence that ensue are tremendous; they definitely spill over into other areas of one's life."

BADGE STEPS

1. Define your habit.

If you are reading this, you probably have a habit that you'd like to change. Being late, eating sweets, biting your nails, even overexercising—just about anything can feel like a bad habit. What all these behaviors have in common is that they initially serve a purpose—like relieving tension, alleviating boredom, getting attention, etc.—but we keep doing them after they outlive their usefulness. The behavior stops being rewarding once our health, finances, career, relationships, self-esteem, etc., have started to suffer, yet we can't seem to stop doing it.

Habits aren't the same as addictions or disorders like obsessive-compulsive disorder (OCD), though they can be every bit as harmful and demoralizing. How can you tell them apart? Check out the Addiction and OCD sidebars, and make sure your concern isn't more than just a habit. The steps that follow can be a critical part of your recovery from any habitual behavior—but if a chemical substance or obsessive-compulsive disorder is involved, you will likely need additional help. ***Select one habit you'd like to break.***

2. Monitor your habit.

While you may spend a lot of time indulging in your habit, you may not understand it all that well—and since it's become part of your routine, you may not even realize exactly how or how often you do it. So get a notebook and describe your habit: What is it? When did it begin? Has it changed over time? How do people react to it? Then, for a week, record every time you engage in the behavior. Next to each notation, write:

- What else you were doing at the time: Where were you? Who was there with you? What time of day was it?
- What you were feeling: before, during, and after.
- What you were thinking: This can be hard to discern, since we are often robotic about our habits. Slow down so that you can hear your mind say things like, "I deserve this," "I'll feel better after this," "I don't want to do this, but I'll worry about it later."

Cherry says you shouldn't be surprised if this simple act of record-keeping reduces the severity of your habit. But don't worry if it doesn't, and don't stop now. If you really want to rid your life of a habit, keep going. ***Spend one week getting to know your habit inside and out.***

ADDICTION

Coming to terms

If you even suspect that chemical addiction to drugs, alcohol, or nicotine may be a problem for you:

- Speak frankly with your family doctor. Your health is at stake, and there are medical interventions that can make quitting easier.
- Call Alcoholics and/or Narcotics Anonymous, or the local council on alcohol and drug dependence. You are not alone, and they are there to help—without shame or blame.
- Bring concerns about sexual or spending/gambling behaviors that feel "out of control" to one of these resources as well.

OCD

Coming to terms

OCD is characterized by obsessions, which are "persistent ideas, images, impulses, or thoughts that intrude into a person's thinking and cause distress, anxiety, and worry," and by compulsions, or "repetitive behaviors or mental acts performed in response to obsessions." As *The Habit Change Workbook* states, "A person with OCD feels he or she must perform these compulsions in order to prevent or avoid a dreaded event such as illness, death, or perceived misfortune." While the steps that follow can help with OCD, further help in the form of therapy and/or medication will probably be necessary. Talk to your doctor, and see Cherry's Picks, page 351, for additional resources.

3. Consider a change.

Even if you're already convinced you want to change, thinking your decision through will reinforce your efforts. So take some time to consider your answers to these questions:

- Does the habit interfere with your family or social life? With your work life? With your finances?
- Do you think you'd be happier without it? Why?
- Imagine your life without this habit, and describe the differences.

Devote at least one entire page in your notebook to writing about the advantages of keeping the habit, and another page to the disadvantages. Your reasons for wanting to change should now be crystal clear. Review these pages often, and make copies that you can post in places you'll see throughout the day. ***Detail your reasons for wanting to change.***

4. Commit to change.

A commitment is more than a desire. Back up your resolve with these actions:

- Write in your notebook about any past efforts you made to break the habit. Give plenty of details: What were the circumstances? What tools did you use? How did you stumble?
- Write about exactly what you'd like to change. Be specific and realistic by setting both long- and short-term goals. If your long-term goal is to tame your sweet tooth, your short-term goal may be to substitute fresh fruit for pastry, cookies, or ice cream each night for a week.
- Pick and write down a change date that's at least one week away (so that you have time to line up the resources that follow), but not more than two weeks from now. Don't wait for the time to be "just right," or your time may never come.

Make a commitment and set the date.

5. Don't go it alone.

Discuss your habit and your plans to change with one or more friends or family members. Let them know that nagging, criticizing, guilt, and "shoulds" don't work, and ask them for support, praise, and positive reinforcement. Show them your notebook if you like. If someone in your life is not supportive (for reasons of their own, some people in our lives

DECLARE A GUILT-FREE ZONE

Guilt is a lousy motivator

Guilt is one of the major consequences of bad habits for most people. You might think this would be a potent impetus toward change, but it's not. As Cherry points out, well-meaning friends and family members have probably already tried to use guilt to get you to change, and how did that work for you? Probably not so well. Here's why: Guilt adds to our feelings of helplessness, compounding the sense that we are out-of-control losers who will never be able to modify our behavior. It can actually demoralize you to the point of giving up the whole idea of change, so as to avoid the guilt of failure afterwards. What's more, many of our habitual behaviors serve to soothe and comfort our bad feelings. Guilt is a pretty bad feeling—so when we feel it, we might find ourselves triggered right back into the habitual behavior. So before it gets to you, give guilt the boot!

I DID IT!

"I usually smoked by myself, so I thought I could quit by myself. But after several failed attempts, I decided to try a new way. I 'fessed up to my doctor—who wound up being a former smoker—and she suggested I start taking a prescription medication several weeks before I wanted to quit. I also bought some books on the subject and followed their directions for writing about my habit. Then I found a twelve-step group for people trying to quit cigarettes. I found so much support there and learned a lot about how other people had kicked the habit—and about the many ways people relapse. I hated to admit that I needed all this help, but I did. And by getting it, I became a nonsmoker."
—Pat

SLIPPERY SLOPE

"I'm the kind of all-or-nothing person who thinks that if I succumb to eating one potato chip, I might as well eat the whole bag because, what the heck, I'm a weak-willed schmuck. When I was trying to stop shopping each payday, I had to change my thinking. I've slipped to one degree or another several times. Once, instead of saying, 'Well, you're in the parking lot, so you might as well go into the mall and charge up a storm,' I actually stopped the car, thought about whether I really, really wanted to be there, and left. Instead of berating myself, I got to pat myself on the back and reaffirm my goal. I realized it's up to me whether I slip a little or a lot."
—Jennifer

may prefer we not change) take them out of your loop to the extent that you can. Also:

- Ask someone who has made a similar change to mentor you. Check in with this person regularly.
- Read true-life stories of people who have made inspiring changes or accomplished challenging goals in magazines, and check out books about changing habits (see Cherry's Picks, page 351).
- Seek out a support group or consider one-on-one work with a therapist. You might want to find an online chat group as well or form your own.
- If you are a spiritual person, says Cherry, "maintaining and growing in your faith will help you build resilience."

Create a change support system.

CHERRY'S EXPERT TIPS

CH-CH-CH-CHANGES

James Prochaska, PhD, has developed a model of the stages of change. Change is a process and most of us don't progress smoothly from one stage to the next in a straight line—we hop around. View this as part of your process, not as being back at square one. Where are you now?

Precontemplation. The intention to change has not yet been formed.

Contemplation. A problem has been recognized and the desire to work on it formed.

Preparation. You want to change and have perhaps made some efforts to do so.

Action. You are actively trying to change.

Maintenance. Every bit as active as the "action" phase, this is our ongoing effort to prevent relapse.

6. Prepare for challenges.

Review your writings about your habit, and see if you can notice any situations and feelings that seem to trigger your habitual behavior. Then, consider what you could do differently in these circumstances to prevent that same old behavior from kicking in:

Relax. Deep breathing can be done anywhere, anytime, as can some forms of meditation (see Get an Inner Life, page 420). To increase your overall well-being, pay a little extra attention to exercising regularly, eating well, and sleeping enough.

Develop a competing response. This is something incompatible with your habit that you can do when the urge to engage in your habit hits. If you tend to eat sweets in the evenings, can you take a yoga class or walk with a friend instead? If you bite your fingernails while watching TV, can you sew, knit, or bead instead?

Talk back to yourself. In Step 2, you identified what you were thinking when performing a habit. When those thoughts creep up, stop, listen, write them down—and write down a snappy comeback.

Innovate. Remember that behaviors often become habitual because they relieve stress, reward our accomplishments, or soothe our disappointments. If you have identified these as triggers, create new methods of meeting those needs. How about a meal with a friend instead of a box of chocolates? A bubble bath instead of a shopping binge?

Know what you'll do when temptation strikes.

7. Call it quits, and get a fresh start.

You've approached your change date with preparation that paves the way for success. Review your notes often to remind yourself of what you are gaining by losing that habit and to remember the coping mechanisms you have brainstormed. The time has come to change, and you're ready! Make your quitting day celebratory, a beginning rather than an ending. Plan some pampering, and do what you can to minimize the number of personal triggers (stress, boredom, loneliness) you'll face. Think of the change you are making as a journey rather than a destination, and stay on the road even if you do encounter potholes or detours (see Oops!). ***Greet your change date with a smile.***

CONGRATULATIONS!

It's easier to get around without a monkey on your back, no? You did it!

I DID IT!

Name: ____________________

Date: ____________________

OOPS!

I did it again . . .

Lapses and relapses happen even to people who have abstained from a habit for long periods of time. A relapse is a return to an old pattern, while a lapse is a brief episode of problem behavior. But any lapse or relapse can be reversed—it's never too late to make a course correction. If you slip up:

- Don't let yourself free-fall into a shame spiral. Challenge the thought that since you slipped, you'll never be able to get back up.
- Write about your slip and identify the triggering circumstances. Plan how you'll deal with similar circumstances in the future.
- Review the advantages, disadvantages, and consequences of your habit.
- Develop new "competing response" strategies.
- Amp up your support. If you've resisted seeking outside help, give it a try.
- Remember: "There is never a time in the future in which we will work out our salvation. The challenge is in the moment; the time is always now." (James Baldwin)

BEYOND THE BADGE

If you love it as much as you thought you would, dream on . . .

- **Cultivate a happy habit.** The competing responses you created to help you break a bad habit just might be habit-worthy—especially if they are healthy, relaxing, and affordable. The steps for change that you completed above are every bit as helpful for adding a good new habit as for subtracting a bad old one. Here's how it works:
  - Identify and write down the advantages, disadvantages, and consequences of this new habit you'd like to develop.
  - Keep a journal as you try out the new behavior so that you can easily spot and either boost or counteract the feelings and circumstances that make it easy or hard.
  - Find allies and people who will support you—or maybe even engage in the habit with you (ideal for exercising).
  - Make it convenient. If you are trying to eat more fruits and vegetables, for instance, shop where the selection is good, keep your fridge stocked, and fill a bowl where you can't miss it.
- **Make it a family or group affair.** Every member of your family may not have the same habit they'd like to change, but you can still create a positive, supportive team atmosphere by encouraging them to work through the steps you are taking to address their own goals. Any group of people can provide this kind of camaraderie by meeting regularly in person or online and working through the change process together. Consider forming such a group with friends, coworkers you can meet with over lunch, or with members of your church, gym, etc.
- **Support someone else's change.** As we've all probably learned by now, you can't change another person. But you can be an aid rather than an impediment, as noted in Step 5. You can take this role a step further by mentoring someone struggling with an issue you too have grappled with. Twelve-step programs for addiction recovery consider this so important that they've made it one of their steps and an integral part of their program (see Help and Be Helped). Supporting another person's efforts is good for them and good for us. It can help us to feel useful and remind us (lest we get cocky and forget) of the steps essential to success.

HELP AND BE HELPED

The Twelve-Step Way

Anonymous Twelve-Step programs exist to help people recover from a variety of addictions and behaviors, including alcohol, narcotics, nicotine, caretaking, overeating, gambling, and sex. Information and group meetings are available around the world.

- Check your local phone book.
- Do a Google search for the Web site of the group you are interested in (Alcoholics Anonymous, Gamblers Anonymous, etc.).
- If you are grappling with the addiction or behavior of another person, consider Al-Anon, www.al-anon.org.

CHERRY'S PICKS

BOOKS

Active Wellness: Feel Good for Life by Gayle Reichler
A practical guide to developing a healthy lifestyle.

Changing for Good, A Revolutionary Six-Stage-Program for Overcoming Bad Habits and Moving Your Life Positively Forward by James O. Prochaska, John C. Norcross, and Carlo C. Diclemente
Detailed information on the process of change and the stages of change, based on the authors' many years of research.

The Complete Idiot's Guide to Breaking Bad Habits by Suzanne LeVert and Gary McClain
Provides helpful pointers about breaking bad habits.

Consuming Passions: Help for Compulsive Shoppers by Ellen Mohr Catalano and Nina Sonenberg
A compassionate book that helps readers uncover why they shop too much and develop plans for controlling their spending habits.

Dieting with the Duchess: Secrets & Sensible Advice for a Great Body by Sara Ferguson
Just one of Sara Ferguson's great books, it combines the sound advice of Weight Watchers with the real-life, real-woman, common sense of the Duchess of York.

The Habit Change Workbook by James Claiborn, PhD, ABPP, and Cherry Pedrick, RN
An interactive workbook that gives detailed guidance for overcoming a variety of habits.

Health and Fitness in Plain English by Jolie Bookspan
An easy-to-understand, thorough book about health, nutrition, and fitness.

Keep the Change: Breaking Through to Permanent Transformation by Becky Tirabassi
A good book for those wanting to add a spiritual dimension to their habit change journey.

Life Management for Busy Women: Living Out God's Plan with Passion and Purpose by Elizabeth George
A useful book for women needing to get organized.

Living the Good Life: Simple Principles for Strength, Balance, and Inner Beauty by Ruth McGinnis
Sound advice on developing a healthy lifestyle and strengthening your mind, body, and spirit.

The OCD Workbook: Your Guide to Breaking Free from Obsessive-Compulsive Disorder by Bruce Hyman, PhD, and Cherry Pedrick, RN
An interactive workbook that gives detailed guidance for breaking free from OCD.

Virtual Addiction, Help for Netheads, Cyberfreaks, and Those Who Love Them by David N. Greenfield, PhD
A good resource for those who wonder if they spend too much time on the Internet.

ORGANIZATIONS

American Heart Association
www.americanheart.org or 800-242-8721
This Web site is packed with information on healthy living, much of it specifically designed for today's woman.

The Center for Internet Studies
www.virtual-addiction.com or 860-233-9772
Good information for people hooked on the Internet.

Debtors Anonymous General Service Office
www.debtorsanonymous.org or 781-453-2743
A great starting place for people having problems with overspending.

Weight Watchers
www.weightwatchers.com/index.aspx
Good advice and support for sensible weight loss and fitness; their Web site offers an alternative for those who don't want to join a group.

44

LOOK SHARP

★ personal style ★

As we let our own light shine, we unconsciously give other people permission to do the same.

—Nelson Mandela

So, what's your motivation?
Take a moment.
Dream a little, think big,
and then complete this sentence:
I see myself . . .

Imagine This . . . You walk down the street with a strut in your step, because you know the world can see you for the woman you really are. You don't dress just to impress, or to have a safe disguise to hide behind—you actually have fun with your wardrobe, like you did when you were a kid. Gone are the days of arriving late to parties because of all that time you wasted staring at your closet, chanting, "I have nothing to wear." Now you're right on time, and you make quite an entrance. Girl, you look fierce—and you're living proof that looking sharp isn't about spending a fortune on nonstop primping, nipping, and tucking. Glossy ads have no power over your self-esteem—who needs a personal stylist to look their best? Not you. You've got your own signature style, thank you very much! *You can do it!*

The Payoffs

- **Time.** When your closet is filled with fashions that work for you, you have more time to get out there and be you.
- **Money.** The customer is always right when she knows what's what before she enters those seductive, style-landmine-strewn, credit-card-gobbling places we call stores.
- **Self-expression.** It's no fun to feel like a funky free spirit but look like a downtown drone. Dare to look on the outside the way you feel on the inside, and be admired for who you are.
- **Freedom.** Whether you want to say yes to a spur-of-the-moment invitation or make a splash at your high school reunion, having faith in your style will supersize your sense of independence and confidence.

Meet Your Mentors

LAURIE HENZEL AND TRACIE EGAN

What They Do: Laurie is the copublisher of *BUST* and Tracie is a writer for the magazine, which describes itself as the magazine "for women with something to get off their chests." *BUST* has been around for more than a decade, pulling themselves "up by their bra straps" to grow from underground 'zine to move-over–*Marie Claire* newsstand fare. *BUST* isn't in the business of telling its readers they should be a size six or spend a week's salary on shoes. Instead, its forward-thinking fashionistas are beloved by millions for making fashion and beauty fun, witty, and very accessible.

© Debbie Stoller

Why They Do It: "In the very beginning of the magazine, we didn't do any fashion stories," says Laurie. "After a few issues we decided to give it a try, but only according to our own rules: We would not use models or feature designer clothes. We wanted to picture real women of every age, shape, and color and talk about clothes that people like us—without tons of money—could buy. We're also the kind of people who wouldn't spend $3,000 on a purse, even if we could afford to! It's not that we don't appreciate the beauty of high fashion, but our whole philosophy is very do-it-yourself. If you love that Marc Jacobs skirt, we encourage you to buy a cheaper version, find its inspiration in a thrift store, or learn to sew it. And as for models, well—who do you know who looks like that? We sometimes write about hair and makeup products that we like, usually by new, small, and/or women-owned companies. And our interns review mainstream products in the *BUST* Test Kitchen to give readers an honest sense of what they're like."

We believe women everywhere deserve to know that they are just as VALID and as VISIBLE as any mythological *Cosmo* girl or *Glamour* gal.

—BUST

Word from the Wise: Tracie says, "No matter what your career, shape, and budget look like and what other people say about how you should look, you can be yourself. Find your comfort zone, stretch it a little to emphasize your one-of-a-kind strengths, and work that look!"

BADGE STEPS

FLAUNT IT

Know your sartorial strengths

Forget those fashion rules that are all about hiding "flaws"—because that kind of logic is flawed, not you! Show the world what you're working with:

- **Stop being self-conscious about your bust, already—all women have one! Stand tall and proud, and give yourself permission to wear V-necks and scoop Ts.**
- **Pregnant women used to hide their bellies, but no more. The most current, comfortable maternity styles stretch to accommodate those beautiful bulges—why hide a good thing?**
- **If lifting boxes, babies, or barbells has given you powerful arms, show them off in snug T-shirts and strapless, sleeveless, or halter tops and dresses.**
- **Don't be shy about having beautiful eyes, a perfect smile, or a lush mane. Play them up! The world should never begrudge beauty.**
- **If you run around a lot and have the strong legs to prove it, work that skirt!**

1. Confront your closet.

Let's be honest here: Over the course of a lifetime, many of us will spend entire days (okay, weeks!) worrying about such seemingly critical style issues as whether these shoes match that skirt. But the far more relevant fashion question is: Do your clothes match your life? Start by comparing your wardrobe and your life:

- Take a "before" photo of yourself as you are right now: regular clothes, regular makeup, everyday hair. Put it away in a "style file" as your point of reference.
- Think through a day, a week, and a typical year in terms of how and where you actually spend your time. Are your days filled with office politics, pitching your freelance wares, or ferrying kids to school and soccer? Do you date a lot, enjoy opera, or head for the hills to hike every chance you get? Write down your major activities.
- Check in your closet to make sure you have clothes to match each activity that feel good on you and fit. Hint: For regular clothes, if you haven't worn them at least ten times in the last six months, it's probably because you don't feel your best in them. As for party duds: If you haven't worn it in the last year and didn't feel fabulous the last time you did, it may have outlived its purpose. A good fit is one that follows the curves of your body without swamping you with extra fabric, but that isn't so tight that you fear the seams might pop with any sudden movement.
- Notice which activities on your list aren't reflected in your closet. Forget about your budget for now (we'll get to that later!), and list the wardrobe items you need to match these activities. Add this list to your style file.

Now you have a list of must-haves in your style file—a sensible first step for any wardrobe makeover. ***Match your style to your lifestyle.***

2. Build your wish list.

Now that you know your fashion facts, it's time to explore your fashion fantasies. Changing your personal style can be scary, but it can also be fun. Remember playing with paper dolls? Or that scene in the movie *Clueless* where Alicia Silverstone mixes and matches outfits on her computer? Or that obligatory scene at the mall in just about any '80s movie, where the stars try out new looks? Now it's your turn to consider the possibilities:

Find your own personal style icons. You probably already know of several people whose fashion sense you admire: a good friend, a great aunt, or that stranger on your commute with the amazing hats. Take a good long look at these fashion mentors next time you see them, and make a note in your style file about what you like in particular. There may be some celebrities whose looks you admire, too: Halle Berry, the Donnas, Venus Williams. To jog your memory, leaf through a few fashion, sport, and celebrity rags—you might even clip some pics, and throw them in your style file.

Go retro. As *BUST* reminds us, today's designers often use past points of reference to inspire their design. So catch some classic movies, and pick up some old fashion mags and photo books while thrift or garage sale shopping. What catches your eye? Try to isolate the elements that make a look work. Be realistic: If you have a broad bustline, Audrey Hepburn's straight sheaths might chafe. But be adventurous, too: Wanna try on some movie-star sunglasses, red lipstick, or a new hair color? Add these ideas to your personal style file.

By the time you're done, you'll have a style file full of fashion ideas to try on for size. Dare yourself to try at least three of these. ***Be your own genie, and grant yourself three style wishes.***

3. Shop in your closet.

Crank up some music to set the mood, grab your shopping list of needs and wants, and start going through the rack in your closet as though it were a rack at a store. With each item, ask yourself: If you had to pay for this item all over again, would you buy it? Then take action accordingly.

If yes, take a good look at it. What is it you particularly like about it: the color, the fabric, the feel, the way it drapes? Make a note of it in your style file—these will be your personal fashion dos. And move these items to the front of your closet where you can reach them easily.

If no, put the item in a big box or bag. And be sure to note what you didn't like, so you won't make the same mistake twice.

If maybe, give yourself a fashion reality check. Ask yourself:

- What do these clothes say about you? Is it something you still want to say, or are you ready for something new?

ICON INSPIRATION

The BUST seal of approval goes to . . .

Morticia Addams
Little Edie Beale
Exene Cervenka
Cherie Currie
Angela Y. Davis
Catherine Deneuve
Divine
Marianne Faithfull
Pam Grier
Françoise Hardy
Chrissie Hynde
Joan Jett
Pippi Longstocking
Sophia Loren
Rita Moreno
Nico
Yoko Ono
Edie Sedgwick
Penelope Tree

I DID IT!

"I always thought the perfectly made-up women at makeup counters would take one look at me and say, 'How did you leave the house looking like that?!' But one day I let a saleswoman do my make-up. She listened when I told her what I did and didn't want. I learned some basic techniques and walked out feeling like a million bucks without spending a million bucks. I bought a couple of products I never really used—but even that was educational, because it taught me to be supervigilant in the future."
—Nicky

READ MY LIPS!

"I thought my hairdresser and I spoke the same language, so I made an appointment for a cut and color immediately before my lunch with Chris—the hip, handsome, and always well-coiffed boyfriend who I hadn't seen since he'd dumped me five years before. I guess I didn't make myself perfectly clear to my stylist, because I wound up going to lunch with Auburn Sonata dye stains all over my forehead and a haircut that made me look like my fondest wish was to anchor the local six o'clock news."
—Kathy

LAURIE AND TRACIE'S EXPERT TIPS

MAKE OVER YOUR MAKEUP

- If you have chronic skin problems, get a referral from your primary care physician or a friend, and make an appointment with a dermatologist. If you're feeling flush, schedule a facial.
- Cruise the makeup counters at your local department store. The best clerks will listen to what you want, and load you up with free samples. Remember that you don't have to buy what you try! But because makeup counters and clerks can be intimidating, Laurie likes Sephora stores (www.sephora.com) where "you can go wild and try everything."
- Make a play date with a friend, pretend you're thirteen, and do each other's makeup. You'll get to try products without buying them, try out looks you never would have imagined, and probably learn a trick or two.
- Don't forget drugstores. You can't always try the packaged products there, but then again you won't make costly mistakes. Many makeup artists and fashionistas swear by low-cost drugstore staples—Laurie loves Maybelline eyeliner, and Tracie likes Wet 'n' Wild's fun nail polish colors.

- Can you mix and match them in new ways? Try on some combinations you've never tried before, and see if you can make up a couple new outfits to liven up your usual rotation. If they're still not working, say bye-bye!
- Can you get them tailored to fit you better, or update the style? If so, put them in a box to take to the tailor, or fix them up yourself with the skills you learned in Sew Fabulous, page 158.
- Are you attached to them for purely sentimental reasons? Put treasured clothing items that you'll never wear again in a special trunk destined for your daughter, dear friend, niece, or granddaughter. (If you want to make a gift of it right away, write a gift tag explaining what made each item so special to you.)

Now look at that—your closet is beginning to shape up already, and you haven't spent a dime. Cross the items off your shopping list that you've acquired just by repurposing old clothes or getting them tailored. ***Become a closet shopper.***

4. Swap 'til you drop.

One woman's trash is another woman's treasure—so before you start dropping dough to fill the gaps in your wardrobe, trade those throwaways for items you actually need and want at your very own swap party. All you do is set aside a few hours, assemble some snacks and drink for stamina and courage, and create a changing area or room. *BUST* calls them Naked Lady parties, because when we women start eyeing each other's clothes, we strip in record time to try them on!

Tell your guests to bring the clothes they don't like or need anymore. The only rule is that everyone leaves with a new addition to their wardrobe.

After the swap, get rid of your leftovers by selling them at consignment or secondhand stores or donating them to charity. And be sure you cross the items off your shopping list that you scored for free. ***Go for broke without going broke—host a swap party.***

5. Shop strategically.

Chances are you didn't fill in all the gaps at your clothing swap. So now, some shopping is in order:

- Learn the local retail landscape so you don't spend days searching for clothes that suit you. Look at your list of needs and wants, and ask around: Where do your fashion mentors buy their clothes? What is the best discount shopping in town? Check out your city magazine (and other local rags) for store ads.
- Next, window shop. Your goal is to comparison shop without making any impulsive mistakes, so leave your credit card at home. Grab your shopping list and spend a few weekend days lunching, trying things on, and checking price tags. Visit at least a couple vintage and/or discount designer stores on your travels, and find three or four places that have clothes you need, love, and can afford.
- Back home, pause and prioritize without cash burning a hole in your pocket and salespeople breathing down your neck. What can you afford to buy now, and what can wait? Unless you have a special occasion coming up, start with the clothes you need most and will wear most often.
- Venture out with a fashion-forward friend. She can give you reality checks when you try things on, help you cope with the sensory overload, and share her secrets. If you're visiting vintage or thrift shops for the first time, a veteran of this world can be very helpful. But whatever you do, keep your defined goals and lifestyle in mind. You

HAIR APPARENT

Make a splash with a new cut and color

Although *BUST* avoids issuing beauty dictums, Tracie says, "No matter what you do to your hair, you should color it!" Laurie agrees. "If you're doing a makeover, it will give you instant change gratification. And it's not permanent—it will grow or wash out."

- **For longtime hair colorers, a change of pace might mean giving up the goo and learning to love your natural color or letting yourself become a gray panther.**
- **Get the salon treatment for a fraction of the cost by volunteering as a hair model for new stylists, who work under the supervision of more experienced teachers. Laurie says, "I got great cuts and colors that way. I never let them do anything too drastic and was always clear about what I did and didn't want."**
- **Try to venture out of your comfort zone once in a while. Laurie didn't love the bangs she tried, but as she says, "That's the beauty of hair: it grows out!"**

want to wind up you, not someone else's notion of you. *Vogue* magazine once styled Laurie and *BUST* editor-in-chief Debbie Stoller for a photo, and Laurie wound up in a beige cowl-neck she'd "never wear" in real life. Tough love while shopping will make a noticeable difference on your bank balance, so you'll have more resources to commit to enhancing your innermost self: a much-needed tropical vacation, a weekend journal-writing retreat, photography classes.

Shop wisely.

6. Debut the new you.

If you've been preparing for a special event, you're good to go—and if you can't wait for a film festival to premiere that full-length gown you acquired at the clothing swap, host your own video film festival at home with your girlfriends, complete with a fabric-remnant red carpet, champagne, and popcorn. If you've been shooting for a new everyday look or workaday wardrobe, have a mix-n-match session at home with a friend where you lay out new outfits for a week.

When you're working that new look, take an "after" photo or two to compare with your Step 1 photo. See the difference? A distinctive personal style cranks up the dimmer switch on your individuality, lighting up your face and any room you're in. ***Shine on!***

CONGRATULATIONS!

Hey good-lookin', I like your style! You did it!

I DID IT!

Name: ______________________________

Date: ______________________________

CLOSET CLASSICS

Get gussied up on the go with these standards

Black slacks. Ideal when you don't have time to think about what to wear.

Black turtleneck sweater. Make it mod with big hoop earrings or superfly with a leather jacket.

Jean jackets. They can be worn with just about anything (including that little black dress) and only look better with age.

A little black dress. It can make dressing up a no-brainer.

Shoulder bag. A good one will last forever, so make sure it's comfortable to carry and won't weigh you down . . . bigger is not necessarily better!

A suit. The right suit gives you pulled-together polish, and it doesn't have to be boring—try a vintage houndstooth number. Suits also give you lots of mix-and-match options.

T-shirt. When you find one you love, stock up.

White shirts. They are as versatile as can be. Take the time to find one that fits perfectly.

TRACIE AND LAURIE'S PICKS

BOOKS

The Bust Guide to the New Girl Order by Marcelle Karp and Debbie Stoller (editors)
Features the best writing from "the magazine for women with something to get off their chests."

The Looks Book by Rebecca Odes, Esther Drill, and Heather McDonald
Written by the cocreators of the girl-positive gURL.com, this guide to style for teens can also help grown women of all body shapes and sizes experiment with styles from "ice queen" to "girl Goth."

Making Faces by Kevyn Aucoin
Makeup tips galore from the makeup artist to the stars, including step-by-step illustrations for recreating the look of glamour queens from Isabella Rossellini to Cher.

We're Desperate: The Punk Rock Photography of Jim Jocoy by Jim Jocoy
Jocoy's glorious photos capture new wavers and punks in the act of smashing every fashion rule back in the 1970s and early '80s, with essays from designer Marc Jacobs and punk icon Exene Cervenka.

MAGAZINES

BUST
www.bust.com
"Keep abreast of the latest developments" for women in life, liberty, and the pursuit of fabulous fashion.

Cutie
www.tkj.jp/cutie
A Japanese fashion magazine "for independent girls"—this means you!

The Face
www.theface.co.uk
British fast-forward fashion and culture mag.

Lucky
www.luckymag.com
"The magazine about shopping"—bargains, fashion hints, the latest looks.

Any French or British fashion mag—a new view for a new you!

WEB SITES

www.bust.com
Check out The Lounge forum, Girl Wide Web links, free sassy e-cards, girly gear, and more.

www.cutxpaste.com
A DIY fashion dream come true.

www.dailycandy.com
Articles, tips, and yes, nonpromotional product reviews for women on beauty, fashion, travel, and culture events.

MOVIES

Beyond the Valley of the Dolls

Black Tight Killers

Bonnie and Clyde

Breakfast at Tiffany's

Desperately Seeking Susan

Grey Gardens

Polyester

Valley of the Dolls

West Side Story

MONEY, MONEY, MONEY

budgeting
saving and investing
estate planning

Dear Reader,

Getting your financial affairs in order many not sound like a whole lot of fun, and you may not want to spend the first sunny Saturday of spring doing it. But wouldn't it feel great to scratch it off your to-do list?

We've broken this big (but not bad!) subject into three badges to keep things manageable and reward you as you go. You can choose to work through these badges in the chronological order listed here, but consider taking Janet's tip and turn to the one thing that is making you most anxious. That's a fine place to start. Then read all our expert's wise words through these three badges. If you do, you'll soon get a handle on everything you wish you knew, thought you knew, and had no idea about money management.

Money changes EVERYTHING.

—Cyndi Lauper

Imagine This . . . You listen sympathetically when friends complain about their messy finances—and afterwards you breathe a sigh of relief, because yours are finally in order. These days you sleep soundly: No more waking up at three A.M., fretting about your credit card debt, your disorganized financial records, and securing your family's future. Why panic? When your car, your roof, or your trick knee gives out, your rainy day fund will help you weather the financial storm. You've taken a calm, cool look at what you have and what you owe, organized your records and attacked your debt, started saving in the present and investing for the future, and planned ahead to share the wealth and leave a legacy behind you when you go. You're not worried about winding up a bag lady, because you've got financial planning in the bag. *You can do it!*

The Payoffs

- **Sweet dreams.** Nights should be spent dreaming about upcoming trips to Bali, not having nightmares about money.
- **Security.** No one can plan for everything, but knowing you've done all you can to save, invest, and plan ahead is as comforting as a security blanket.
- **Options.** Money doesn't give you absolute power or unlimited freedom, but it can dramatically increase your choices.
- **Independence.** You feel like a million bucks just knowing that you needn't rely on the kindness of strangers, and that you're not a financial burden on loved ones.

Meet Your Mentor
JANET BODNAR

What She Does: The author of books including *Think $ingle! The Woman's Guide to Financial Security at Every Stage of Life* and *Dollars & Sense for Kids,* Janet is the executive editor of *Kiplinger's Personal Finance* magazine. Her weekly "Money-Smart Kids" column appears in many newspapers, and she appears regularly on television programs, including *The Oprah Winfrey Show,* the *Today Show,* and *Good Morning America.* Last but certainly not least, Janet is a wife, mother, and household manager.

Why She Does It: "After getting a journalism degree, I started working as a copyeditor and general assignment reporter on newspapers. In an effort to make a niche for myself, I volunteered to cover business and economics. Since this was the '70s and there was inflation, skyrocketing interest rates, and lines at gas stations, my area became front-page news. I eventually went back to Columbia for my masters in journalism, and then got the Knight-Bagehot Fellowship in Economics and Business Journalism at Columbia. I went to work for *Kiplinger's* straightaway after that. All of this professional work and learning definitely affected my approach to my personal finances—and conversely, I could bring my feelings as an individual and as a woman into my work. I can relate to feeling intimidated or overwhelmed by financial subjects, and those are the people I write for. It's my intention to cut to the chase, giving busy women the answers they need and helping them overcome the fear of the unknown."

When you're financially independent, you can approach life's twists and turns with assurance, secure in the knowledge that you can handle any curves.

—Janet Bodnar

Word from the Wise: "Keep it simple. You will be overwhelmed if you try to do everything that people like me, or my magazine, tell you to do! You do not have to do everything at once. Make a list and then prioritize. What is the one thing that keeps you up at night? Paying off debt? Buying a house? Being a bag lady when you retire? Start with that and you'll get a great feeling of relief and accomplishment, plus you'll be encouraged to keep going down your list."

45

FIND YOUR MONEY

★ budgeting ★

Change yourself,
and fortune will change.

—Portuguese proverb

So, what's your motivation?
Take a moment.
Dream a little, think big,
and then complete this sentence:
I see myself . . .

1. Clean up your desk.

To get comfortable with your finances, first you need to get comfortable at your desk. Piles of paper can hide, confuse, and overwhelm, so tackle your paper trail:

Banking. Toss ATM receipts after reconciling them to your bank statements. Same goes for canceled checks, except for those you need at tax time to verify charitable contributions, business expenses, or home improvements.

Taxes. Keep the returns, but toss supporting materials after three years, unless you are self-employed or have supplementary income. In that case, you should hold onto them for six years.

Credit card bills. Safe to toss after your payment is posted on the next month's bill, except for credit card receipts you need for tax purposes (same as for canceled checks above).

Utilities. Chuck, unless you deduct home office expenses.

Mutual fund and brokerage statements. Keep cumulative year-end reports and your first and most recent transaction records. (When you sell, you need to know your original cost.)

Home improvement records. Keep if you rent out a portion of your home or use it as an office, or if you think you'll live in your home for less than two years and will earn a big profit when you sell.

Purge and organize your financial records.

2. Know your steady cash flow.

Before you can improve your future money situation, you have to understand your current state of affairs. And while you might think you have a clear sense of your big financial picture (maybe because you worry about it so much), Janet has learned that laying it all out on paper (or on a computer screen) "makes it more concrete and helps you spot hidden surprises."

So turn on some soothing music, close the door to prevent interruptions (or opportunities to procrastinate!), and spread out the following information in front of you:

- Checkbook balance log (or canceled checks) for last year and current year to date.
- Credit card statements for this year, plus previous year-end reports.
- Investment statements from the end of the previous year and the most recent quarter.
- Plus: Paper, pen, calculator, chocolate (optional).

Once you're ready, fill out the chart on the pages 364–365 with information you know about your predictable income and expenses.

Once you've filled out this chart, you should have a handle on predictable, relatively steady income and basic expenses. Often these expenses are referred to as "fixed expenditures"—but when it comes time for budgeting, you'll find that there are ways to trim some of these line items without feeling the pinch. So don't panic if your expenses subtotal is larger than your income subtotal, because you can and will reconcile those numbers! ***Get a handle on your basic cash flow.***

3. Discover hidden variables.

If your income subtotal above is larger than your expenses subtotal, congratulations! But don't celebrate with a fancy dinner out just yet, because you still have to account for your variable expenses—which includes expenditures on all of life's little extras, including fancy dinners, plus any one-time or infrequent expenses. Then again, your variable income may offset your variable expenses. There's only one way to find out: Fill out the chart on pages 366–367. Just add up your income and expenditures over the past year in each of the variable categories defined, then divide that lump sum by twelve to come up with a prorated monthly amount.

Once you see these incidental expenses and income streams as lump sums, they may not seem so incidental after all. Some line items may jump out at you as being larger or smaller than you expected—you're getting budgeting ideas already, aren't you? ***Add up the incidentals.***

FORTUNE TELLERS

What are your strengths and weaknesses when it comes to money?

Janet emphasizes that "there is no money gene that makes men inherently more financially astute than women." When it comes to handling money, it's your personality, not your gender, that makes the difference. In *Think $ingle!* Janet identifies the following common personalities, and the strengths and weaknesses associated with each.

Accountant. Money means security to you, so you take it very seriously—balancing your books to the penny, never (ever!) spending impulsively, and saving religiously—sometimes to the point of hoarding.

Social worker. Money means affection to you, and you lavish it on the people and causes you care about. While you might have a "save this, that, or the other" bumper sticker on your car, you don't save money and feel uncomfortable handling it.

CEO. Money means success, so the right clothes, house, and car are essential—whether you can afford them or not.

Entertainer. Money means esteem. You always pick up tabs and host gatherings. Being Lady Bountiful is more important to you than being Lady Practical.

Predictable Income and Expenses Chart

NET INCOME (after taxes)	ANNUAL	PRORATED MONTHLY	WHAT THE NET INCOME COLUMN SHOULD COVER
Take-home pay			Salary (after taxes)
Investment income			Steady income streams only; don't count stocks sold or mutual funds cashed in
Rental income			From residential and commercial properties
Last year's personal draw from your own or family business			As reported on your taxes
Trust fund payments			From parents, grandparents, etc.
Other			Must be steady, ongoing income streams
SUBTOTAL			

PREDICTABLE EXPENSES	ANNUAL	PRORATED MONTHLY	WHAT THE EXPENSES COLUMN SHOULD COVER
Housing			Renters should list rent plus annual increases allowable under local law, and home owners should list: • Monthly mortgage payment • Remaining mortgage balance • Current interest rate • Term/type of loan • Original down payment • Portion of your payments that are allocated to interest
Property taxes			Find out whether there are property tax hikes scheduled to go into effect, and if so, when; list the increase here
Home maintenance			• Repair • Cleaning supplies • Housekeeping services • Gardening/landscaping services • Plumbing/electrical/appliances

Predictable Income and Expenses Chart *(continued)*

PREDICTABLE EXPENSES *(continued)*	ANNUAL	PRORATED MONTHLY	WHAT THE EXPENSES COLUMN SHOULD COVER
Groceries			• Grocery store bills • Farmer's markets • Warehouse retailers/clubs • Specialty food retailers
Utilities			• Water • Gas/Electric/Oil • Garbage/Recycling • Phone
Insurance			Name every type of insurance you carry: medical, car, life, umbrella, house, dental, vision, etc. For each type list: • Basic coverage • Co-pays • Deductibles • Any steady, ongoing, out-of-pocket expenditures you incur
Credit card payments			List each card, along with current remaining balances and interest rates
Loans/other debt			List remaining balances and current debt interest rates
Car/transportation			• Gas • Parking • Tolls • Other commuting expenses (bus passes and tickets for public transportation) • Registration
Child care			Day care, babysitters, etc.
School			Tuition and other school fees, for yourself (if applicable) and each of your children (if applicable)
SUBTOTAL			

Variable Income and Expenses Chart

VARIABLE INCOME	ANNUAL	PRORATED MONTHLY	WHAT THE INCOME COLUMN SHOULD COVER
Dividends			Fluctuating dividends from investments
Capital gains			Gains on investments, as reported on taxes
Inheritance			One-time or short-term inheritance, rather than longer-term trust funds
Freelance income			Earnings and honoraria from side projects and moonlighting
Annual bonus			Variable bonus, based on performance
Last year's per diem and reimbursements			For travel, hotel, dining, with clients, etc.
SUBTOTAL			

VARIABLE EXPENSES	ANNUAL	PRORATED MONTHLY	WHAT THE EXPENSES COLUMN SHOULD COVER
Dining out and entertaining			• Business lunches • Dinner dates • Café purchases • Grocery bills for parties • Package store bills for parties • Party supplies (decorations, dishware, candles, etc.)
Capital improvements			Check with your accountant to find out what's considered a deductible capital improvement to your home under current law; this may cover landscaping, cabinetry, flooring, etc.
Health and wellness			• Short-term needs/treatments (medicines, arm splints, short-term physical therapy, etc.) • Massage • Acupuncture/holistic healthcare not covered by insurance plan • Health club dues
Vacations and travel expenses			Including summer, holidays, and that weekend house, if you're lucky enough to have one

Variable Income and Expenses Chart *(continued)*

VARIABLE EXPENSES *(continued)*	ANNUAL	PRORATED MONTHLY	WHAT THE EXPENSES COLUMN SHOULD COVER
Hobbies and lessons			Piano, skiing, yoga, singing, riding, etc., for you and your children
Arts and entertainment			• Movies (ticket and rentals) • Books (purchases and library fines, too!) • Music and art events (price of admission, catalogs, CDs/downloads, stereos) • Tickets to performances (plays, dance, opera, musicals) • Clubs/bars (cover, bar tabs) • Cable/satellite TV • Internet (including monthly DSL or dial-up service)
Gifts			• Birthday • Holiday • Special occasion
Apparel			• Clothing • Shoes • Outerwear
Beauty			• Hair (including cuts, color, shampoos, products) • Makeup • Skincare
Charitable contributions			• Community organizations • Fundraiser donations • Political campaign contributions
Decorating			• Furniture • Art (including framing costs) • Small appliances (lamps, mixers, grill, food processor, etc.) • Plants and flowers
Subscriptions			
Other			
SUBTOTAL			

4. Know your bottom line.

Now you have a better sense of where your money comes from—and where it goes. To get a handle on exactly how much you've earned and spent, add your predictable and variable subtotals together as follows:

INCOME	ANNUAL	PRORATED MONTHLY
Subtotal predictable		
Subtotal variable		
TOTAL		

EXPENSES	ANNUAL	PRORATED MONTHLY
Subtotal predictable		
Subtotal variable		
TOTAL		

Add up each column, then take a deep breath and subtract your total annual expenditures from your total annual income. Do you have a surplus or a deficit? ***Find out if you are operating in the red or the black.***

5. Budget.

A budget tells you what you can and can't spend in the future, but you don't have to think of it as "tightening your belt." No one's asking you to go hungry here! Budgetary spending caps can actually be more liberating than confining because you are managing your money, rather than letting it manage you. Be realistic about how much you need to cut in order to at least break even, and which expenses you can cut back on without agonizing too much about it.

If you're in debt, you may have to rethink some nonessential expenditures in the short-term that at first you might not be thrilled about cutting back on, such as cable TV, lunches out, or expensive makeup. But you might be surprised how little you notice the difference, and it may even enrich your life to read more, cook more, and spend less time getting ready in the morning. Budgeting can be rewarding in many ways!

To create a budget that gives you money to spare, revisit each of your expense categories from housing and insurance to food and clothing, and look for areas where you know you could save some money. Once you've lowered some of your expenses, forecast a projected total spent for the month in each category on the chart on the next page:

DOES THIS COMPUTE?

Financial software options

You don't have to use a computer to track your finances. Software won't work for you unless you're actively interested in setting it up and updating it faithfully. "There's no point in investing in nifty software," says Janet, "if you know you'll never sit down and key in the numbers. Know your personality, what you do and don't like to do, and then proceed accordingly, without guilt, using either a computer or an old-fashioned bookkeeping ledger." If you are digitally inclined, consider:

- **Quicken or Microsoft Money.** These software packages help you track your spending and monitor your investments. They can also help you forecast and see the results of different "what if I did this" scenarios.
- **Financial institutions.** Your bank or brokerage house may provide a variety of online tools to help you track and plan. Log on to find out.

EXPENSES	ANNUAL	PRORATED MONTHLY
Housing		
Property taxes		
Home maintenance		
Groceries		
Utilities		
Insurance		
Credit card payments		
Loans/other debt		
Car/transportation		
Child care		
School		
Dining out/entertaining		
Capital improvements		
Health and wellness		
Vacation travel		
Hobbies and lessons		
Arts and entertainment		
Gifts		
Apparel		
Beauty		
Charitable donations		
Decorating		
Subscriptions		
Other (define)		
TOTAL		

Create a budget you can live on—and live with.

6. Make ends meet for a month—and then some.

Now that you've made a budget, the trick is to stick with it. To stay within a budget, we have to spend less than we make. (Sorry, credit card companies!) Here are four strategies for striking a better bank balance:

- Spend less on nonessentials like designer clothes, gourmet meals, subscriptions or memberships (especially those you rarely take advantage of), three-dollar coffees, and (ahem) that daily pack of cigarettes. (See Quit It, page 344, on dropping the habit.)

ASSESS YOUR ASSETS

Figure out your net worth

Your checkbook balance isn't the sum total of your personal finances. That would be your net worth, which you can calculate by comparing your assets and liabilities.

:: Assets include:

- Cash in checking and savings accounts
- Certificates of deposit and U.S. savings bonds
- Cash value of life insurance
- Equity in pension, 401(k), and profit-sharing plans
- Market value of IRAs or Keoghs and of securities like stocks, bonds, and mutual fund shares
- Market value of house or other real estate and of possessions like your car, furniture, appliances, jewelry, collectibles, and recreation equipment
- Money owed to you (loans receivable)
- Interest in a business, etc.

:: Liabilities are:

- Outstanding bills
- Credit card balances
- Car and other loans
- Taxes due
- Balance due on mortgages, etc.

Add 'em up, subtract liabilities from assets, and you have your net worth.

I DID IT!

"When I stopped to think about it, I realized I often went out to restaurants I couldn't really afford—and even picked up the tab for the whole table—just to see my friends and feel good about myself. Many of these friends earn a lot more money than I do. When I honestly said I had to spend less money when we went out, or suggested we get together but stay in, my friends were happy to oblige. I didn't lose my friendships, and I didn't feel like a loser either. I actually felt smart and honest."
—Elizabeth

IGNORANCE IS . . .

"My freelance income varies from month to month, and I have no idea what my routine monthly expenses add up to. Why should I do the math? It will only depress me! Somehow—usually with a good deal of help from credit cards—I manage. I know my head is buried in the sand, but I'm too afraid to pull it out!"
—Janelle

JANET'S EXPERT TIPS

FINANCIAL PLANNING SAVVY

Janet says, "You can feel—and be—on top of your finances without a planner. You want to do as much as you can for yourself to be empowered and independent. My goal is to help people feel able to manage their own finances *and* know how to seek good help. I don't want someone to go to a planner and say, 'I don't know what to do—so here, you do it for me.' I want you to know the issues, ask the right questions, and really understand the whole process." If you seek out a planner, Janet advises:

- Seek referrals from other women you trust and respect.
- Your planner should have several years of experience in financial planning and/or related fields like accounting, securities analysis, trading, or law.
- Look for credentials. They don't guarantee you'll get sound advice but do show the advisor takes the business seriously. At a minimum, look for the certified financial planner designation (CFP).
- Consider how the planner is compensated. Fee-only (by the hour or plan), commission-only (on products they sell), or a combination of the two. All are fine, but if you work with a commission-only planner, evaluate the products they suggest very carefully.
- Interview several planners in person before deciding on one. Ask to see Parts I and II of the registration they are required to file with the Securities and Exchange Commission. And trust your gut—you need to be very comfortable with this person.

- Do it yourself. Why not pay yourself to wash the car, give a manicure, do the laundry, garden, houseclean, and mow the lawn? You'll win back your own money and a sense of accomplishment besides.
- Earn more by making a case for the raise you deserve, moonlighting, or starting a home-based business.
- Get repaid for some of your expenditures by keeping track of expenses that your employer might reimburse (check with your accounting department about policies on out-of-pocket expenses and work-related travel), writing off tax-deductible expenditures (including monetary and in-kind donations, capital improvements, and small business expenses), and applying for a grant to fund a pet project or go back to school.

Janet also suggests you:

- Go to the ATM no more than once a week, and stretch that cash!

- When you make a credit card purchase, immediately subtract the amount from your checking account.
- Give yourself a twenty-four-hour pause-and-reflect period before buying nonessentials.
- Track your expenses in each category for a month, and at the end of the month, note what you actually spent. Did you stay under or go over budget?

Our individual needs and goals vary, but we all need to have rainy day, retirement, and discretionary cushions socked away—so keep your eyes on the prize, and keep reading. ***Live on your budget for a month, and reap the rewards!***

CONGRATULATIONS!

Look at you with the financial savvy! You've put money in the bank and a big smile on your face. You did it!

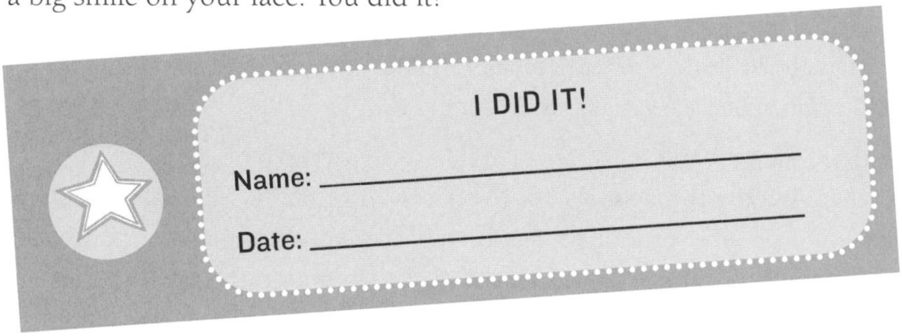

CUT DOWN WITH CLASS

If Holly can do it...

Remember *Breakfast at Tiffany's*? In this classic movie, the Audrey Hepburn character, Holly Golightly, regularly visits a financially astute mobster, Sally Tomato, in prison. After learning that Holly is trying to save money, Sally tells her to write down all the money she earns and spends in a little notebook, and after reviewing her general finances, which he terms "heartbreaking," Sally advises Holly to "operate on a cash basis." So when you feel like a drudge for trying to cut your costs, think of Audrey and:

- Write down everything you spend until spending less is second nature.
- Pay cash (and don't carry around wads of it) or use your debit card.
- Window shop! Holly swore that just looking in the windows at Tiffany's relaxed her.

46

GROW YOUR MONEY

★ saving and investing ★

From saving comes having.

—Scottish proverb

So, what's your motivation?
Take a moment.
Dream a little, think big,
and then complete this sentence:
I see myself . . .

1. Pocket the difference.

Now that you've got a working budget that you can stick to, it's time to really scrutinize your expenditures and see if there is any excess in there that may not be quite as obvious as your insatiable desire for shoes. Some simple comparison shopping on items you listed in your "predictable expenses" column might save you a nice chunk of change. Start with a closer look at your everyday financial transactions, and you'll soon find many easy ways to save, including:

Banks. Pick a bank with lots of ATMs so that you don't get zapped by the surcharges at machines not owned by your bank. Comparison-shop for low fees on overdraft protection and free checking or savings if you maintain minimum balances. If you have access to one, credit unions often have low fees and high interest rates for savings accounts.

Credit cards. Call your current companies and ask for a lower interest rate, transfer balances to lower-rate cards, and comparison-shop for low rates at www.cardweb.com.

Student loans. Some lenders will reduce your interest rate if you have your payments automatically debited from your checking account.

Mortgage. When rates fall a half a point or more below that of your current loan, it pays to look into refinancing.

Telephones, Internet, cable. Figure out the kind of service you really need by asking yourself whether you really have a reasonable need for DSL, or could live with a dial-up connection; when and where you make calls most often, and if you could live with fewer cell phone minutes or (gasp) no cell phone at all; how many sport or movie stations you can actually watch on an average day before your eyes glaze over. Then make providers earn your business by comparison shopping with several different companies.

Insurance is another area where you can find big savings with a little research. Shop around for insurance policies in the following areas:

Health. Read or reread Step 3 in Care for Your Health, page 339. While you may be eligible to extend your health coverage after a job loss through COBRA, a stopgap health plan may be more economical. (Fortis Health, 800-211-1193, and Golden Rule, 800-444-8990, are the leading providers.) Group plans through your employer—or if you are self-employed, through a professional organization—are almost always cheaper than individual plans. You can cut costs in individual plans by raising your deductible or passing up expensive options (prescriptions, maternity, etc.). Comparison shop!

Disability. Don't assume you are covered adequately through your employer. You should be covered for eighty to ninety percent of take-home pay. See if your employer will let you buy individual coverage at their group discount.

Life. You don't need this if you don't have dependents who count on your income. If you have children, it's a priority. Are you covered through your employer? Go to www.kiplinger.com to figure out how much insurance you need, and buy term insurance for the best deal.

Homeowners. You needn't insure for the value of your mortgage, since mortgages often include the value of your land. You can often get the best rate by insuring with your auto insurer, but always comparison shop with at least three providers. To save money, boost your deductible and invest in safety devices like alarms.

Renters. If you rent, get renters insurance to cover household valuables like computers, stereos, art, and jewelry; insure you against fires; and provide liability coverage in case anyone happens to get hurt in your home.

Auto. Again, it pays to shop around periodically for the best rates. Also, before you buy a car, check on its rates. If your car is worth less than $4,000, consider dropping collision/comprehensive coverage.

Start saving on essential services.

2. Tackle your debt.

If you think it's expensive to pay off credit card debts and loans, consider the alternative.

Take a look at the big monthly finance charge figure (in an itsy-bitsy

SHOP AROUND

To ensure you're getting the best possible deal

www.consumerquote.com. Online quotes and essential data on over 300 life insurance providers.

www.instantquote.com. Input some simple information about yourself, and this site will provide a number of life insurance policies with ratings, applications, and policy details for you to choose from.

www.insure.com. Instant quotes and impartial information on the top 200 insurers for health, life, home, auto, travel, and renters.

www.insweb.com. Comparison shop for life, health, auto, homeowners, renters, and critical illness insurance.

www.masterquote.com. Instant, online life insurance quotes.

typeface) on your credit card statements. The cash register is ringing up interest every month. Consider how much that sale sweater will actually cost you if you take six months of such charges to pay it off . . . maybe that bargain isn't such a bargain after all! Do the math for all your cards, and calculate how much more of your hard-earned dough you spend just paying the minimum on several card or loan balances over a year. Staggering, isn't it? Don't get mad about your finances—get even! Here are six things you can do to get out of debt and ahead of the game:

1. Stop using credit cards, unless you pay off their total balances each month—no more minimum monthly payments! Cut them up if you must, and switch to a debit credit card that takes the money for every purchase you make directly out of your checking account. The only financially savvy way to use credit cards is to pay them off monthly and rack up frequent flyer miles or other perks in the process.
2. Compare the rates on your credit cards and auto and student loans and deal with those debts with the highest rates first.
3. Pay off your credit card balances. Your new saving strategies have freed up some funds to do so, so pay off credit debt first.
4. If you can't pay off an entire balance right away, move that balance to a lower rate card or ask the folks at your current card if you qualify for a lower rate.
5. Limit yourself to one or two cards, with low rates of interest and low or no annual fees.
6. Consider selling something you can live without on eBay or through a classified ad. Do you really need all that furniture you have in storage? What about that designer dress you haven't worn for a year? (We'll discuss the wisdom of selling stocks or raiding savings accounts to clear balances next.)

Cut your debt down to size.

HELP WITH DEBT

You may feel alone, but you really aren't

The Consumer Credit Counseling Service. One of the largest nonprofit counseling services in the U.S. www.cccsintl.org.

Equifax. Experian. TransUnion. These are the major credit bureaus. Contact them for copies of your credit report annually to ensure its accuracy. www.equifax.com, www.experian.com, and www.transunion.com, respectively.

The National Foundation for Credit Counseling. Member groups help you get lower rates, consolidate your payments, and may also help you create a budget. www.nfcc.org or 800-388-2227.

Sallie Mae and Nellie Mae. For help dealing with student loan debt. www.salliemae.com. www.nelliemae.com.

3. Plan ahead.

Now that you're coming to terms with your financial past and stopped accruing credit card and other high-interest debt, you should start thinking about your financial future. Saving for retirement, a kid's college fund, or a tropical vacation takes planning:

Dream vacation. This might just be a matter of earmarking ten dollars or one hundred dollars a month. Try creating a separate saving account for it and having an automatic deduction made from your paycheck or checking account each month.

Schooling. To save for a child's college expenses or plan ahead to go back to school yourself eventually, learn all about state-sponsored college saving plans at www.savingforcollege.com and investigate education IRAs or Coverdell Education Savings Accounts through a mutual fund company.

Retirement. To consider your retirement needs, turn to the worksheet in Janet's *Think $ingle!*, try one of the online planning tools in Janet's Picks, page 383, and remember these rules of thumb:

- In order to maintain your standard of living in retirement, you'll need 70 to 80 percent of your preretirement income.
- If you are in your twenties or thirties, aim to save at least 5 percent of your income for retirement; women in their forties should increase this to at least 10 percent.

Add slots for your specific saving goals into your budget, and juggle the numbers until you can fit in your forecasted savings requirements. If the budget numbers aren't working, weigh your immediate desire for that new sofa against your need to get away from the office for a week . . . that slipcover is sounding better all the time, isn't it? ***Set a savings goal, and factor it into your budget.***

ADDING UP THE INCENTIVE

What are you saving for?

The secret to making budgetary changes stick is to keep your eye on your own personal financial goals. Janet writes a lot on the subject of kids and money and has learned that simply telling kids that it's a good idea to save money doesn't work as an incentive. Adults are no different. You aren't alone if "living within your means" doesn't cut it for you in the motivation department. Think about why you'd really like more money—to buy a house or a weekend getaway, take a trip around the world, work less, contribute more, or spend more time with your kids. Focus on getting closer to these future goals as you streamline and save in the present.

4. Create a cash cushion.

While you're working toward your long-term financial goals and dealing with debt reduction, it's also important to build an at-the-ready rainy-day fund. Standard wisdom says you should have enough cash tucked away to cover three to six months' worth of living expenses in case of emergency. No surprise, most of us don't come anywhere near this.

But rather than letting yourself feel overwhelmed by this goal, Janet suggests you begin by socking away a month's worth of expenses. She also notes that creating this personal emergency fund is every bit as important as paying off debt and saving for retirement, because you don't want to have to finance emergency expenditures with credit cards or by borrowing against your retirement plans.

This SOS money has to be safe and available. This doesn't mean under your mattress (silly), in the stock market (not safe enough for emergency money), or in a bank certificate of deposit (time restrictions). Instead,

I DID IT!

"I was paying a small fortune each month for long-distance telephone service, because I call out-of-town friends regularly, and my boyfriend travels to Europe frequently. But I work for myself at home and always have so much to do that I put off comparison shopping for a new plan. One day I decided that saving money was just as important as making money, so I scheduled shopping for a better phone plan into my datebook; that was my job for the day. I called three different companies and wound up with a plan that saves me about one hundred dollars a month. I got so fired up by this that I tackled my health and car insurance plans next. Saved big there too—just by taking the time to shop around."

—Dana

SNOOZE AND LOSE

"I was going through a rough time and fell behind paying my credit cards. The next month I not only had thirty-five dollars in late fees, but my interest rates had also gone through the roof. I had no idea that I could be penalized that way. I've since automated my credit card payments so that I can never let that happen again."

—Rose

choose a bank or credit union savings account, a money market account at your bank, or a money market mutual fund. Research the perks, interest rates, and various restrictions on each of these, including penalties for early withdrawal. (Research money market mutual funds at www.Imoneynet.com.) ***Plump up your cash pillow to cushion possible falls.***

5. Invest wisely.

Relationships should be reciprocal, right? So instead of just working for your money, make your money work for you, too. But first, you may be saying, "Hello! I've still got debt, and I'm struggling to create a cash cushion, too. Am I supposed to be investing at the same time?" Janet says there are a couple of ways to answer this question. "One is the mathematical answer. Standard wisdom is that you should put your money where it gets the greatest return. So if your money is sitting in a bank account earning 1 percent, and you have credit card debt on which you are being charged 18 percent, then it makes sense to take money out of the bank account and put it toward that debt. But if the money you have in the bank is your cash cushion, I wouldn't say it's wise to apply it all toward your debt. There's psychology to money, not just math. You'd probably feel vulnerable without an emergency fund.

"But if your cash cushion is sufficiently plumped up, start putting the money you had been putting there toward the debt. Or put a chunk of the cushion toward debt . . . it doesn't have to be all or nothing! Same goes with retirement saving and investing. If you have none, you could start putting a little aside even before all your debt is gone."

You don't have to be a Wall Street broker to invest wisely. You'll get a good start just by looking into the following investment types:

Retirement account saving/investing. If you don't have access to a workplace 401(k) or 403(b), or even if you do, you can also open a Roth IRA (Individual Retirement Account). You can put in up to $3,000 a year, won't have to pay taxes on your earnings as they accrue, and won't owe taxes when you begin to withdraw this money at retirement. What's not to like? If you are self-employed, there are IRAs for you as well—SEPs, Keoghs, and SIMPLEs. Learn more at www.individualk.com.

Short-term saving/investing. Like emergency fund money, this is money that you know you'll need to access in five years or less, so it should be safe and readily available. You need it to be there when you need it—which is soon—so you can't take risks with it—or reap the potential rewards of risk-taking. These funds should go into bank savings accounts, money market mutual funds, CDs (bank Certificates of Deposit, not Neil Young), short-term bond funds, or treasury bills.

Long-term saving/investing. Janet believes that money you won't need for a while (five to ten years) should be in the stock market (in stocks and/or mutual funds). Historically, stock market growth has been reliable. Despite plunges like that in 1929 and recent booms and busts, over the long term, you can expect an average annual return of about 10 percent. Janet likes broad stock market index funds that let you "buy a share in virtually every company that's traded," so that you spread your investments, and your risk, over the entire market.

To explore your options in detail, talk with an investment planner and/or read through Janet's book and some of the additional resources in Janet's Picks, page 383. In general, though, the keys to sound investing to meet your retirement, short-term, and long-term goals are:

Diversification. Put your money eggs in a variety of investment baskets: bonds, mutual funds, stock, real estate.

Your age. Sometimes—sorry!—this matters. The sooner you need access to your money to retire or the less time you have to rebound from losses, the less risk you should take with your portfolio. Ask retirement-age dot-com investors about this one, and you'll hear a collective groan.

Regularity. Invest regularly in small amounts—it adds up faster than you think, because your interest and gains compound over time.

Invest now, and enjoy a comfortable life for years to come!

CONGRATULATIONS!

You're well on your way to a nice nest egg. Who needs luck when you've got smarts? You did it!

I DID IT!

Name: ______________________________

Date: ______________________________

DEFINING KEY TERMS

There's no such thing as a stupid question!

Bond. An IOU from a company or government: You lend them your money and they pay you an agreed-upon rate of interest for a set number of years.

Mutual funds. Groups of stocks, bonds, or other investments managed by a professional fund manager.

Stock. A share of ownership in a company. While stocks tend to be riskier than bonds and other forms of investments, some stocks are riskier, with more volatility (ups and downs) than others.

AUTOMATIC SAVINGS

It's hard to spend what never gets into your hot little hands, so

- Have your bank automatically deduct a certain amount from your pay each month and put it in your savings or money market account rainy-day fund. Once you've saved your three to six months of living expenses in that account, you can start automatically putting that same amount into a retirement fund instead.
- Take full advantage of your workplace 401(k) or 403(b) accounts. This is another automatic deduction, and one filled with tax savings to boot. Try to contribute enough to get all the matching dollars your firm offers. That's free money!
- You can also empower a mutual fund company or brokerage firm to automatically deduct a set amount from your bank each month to put into your investments.

47

GIVE YOUR MONEY AWAY

★ estate planning and philanthropy ★

He [sic] that fears not the future may enjoy the present.

—Joseph Fuller

So, what's your motivation?
Take a moment.
Dream a little, think big,
and then complete this sentence:
I see myself . . .

1. Look into the future.

Now that you're budgeting wisely and saving for your long-term plans, there's every reason to expect you'll be financially secure in your lifetime. But what then? How will you be sure your well-earned wealth is passed on to those you love? Not to worry—Janet has two words that will put your mind at ease: "estate planning."

What is estate planning, exactly? Estate planning has several possible components: life insurance (see Step 1 of Grow Your Money, page 373), a will, powers of attorney, a living will, trusts, and long-term care insurance. It's a widely misunderstood term, but Janet's here to clear up a few misconceptions:

- Estate planning isn't inherently complex; it just means distributing your property and planning for your children and other heirs after your death.
- Estate planning is not just for rich people.
- Estate planning isn't just about money; it can be about possessions that have no significant monetary worth, and if you have kids, it's definitely about their care and well-being.

As Janet puts it, estate planning is about:

- Whom do I love and want to show my appreciation for?
- What people and organizations do I want to help?
- What do I want to have happen if I die, retire, or become disabled?
- When do I want to transfer property, so that the recipients aren't hit quite so hard with taxes and other complications?
- How do I want to accomplish all of that?

We'll address all of this and more, so set aside a date and time to consider your master plan for your estate. ***Set a date to shape the future for generations to come.***

2. Use your will power.

You might think of preparing a will as gloomy, but instead consider it as an empowering way to make informed choices about how to spend your hard-earned money, to show how much you care by saving beneficiaries trouble, and to lend your support to people and causes that are meaningful to you.

Having children prompts many parents to get around to drawing up a will, because the will lets parents choose who will act as guardian to minors if need be. You simply must put your wishes in this regard in writing.

But there are other reasons to draw up a will. You may know that your estate includes your stocks, bonds, retirement accounts, pension, home, car, artworks, etc. But if you think about it, there's much more you might want to say through a will. Do you want to leave a ring to the friend or niece who has always admired it? Your George Eliot first edition to the writer in your life? A chunk of change to the ASPCA? If you don't put it in writing, a judge will decide what happens to what you leave behind. Who wants that?

Attorneys don't charge much for basic wills and can help you to be thorough. Do-it-yourself resources also exist (see I Will). If you want to make elaborate or unusual bequests or have oodles of money and assets, use a lawyer with estate planning expertise.

To prepare for drafting your will with the help of a lawyer or kit:

- Make a list of your assets. Revisit your list from the Assess Your Assets sidebar in Find Your Money, page 369.
- Designate beneficiaries (whom you want to get what) and review whom you designated as the beneficiaries of your retirement plans and insurance policies.
- Pick an executor, who is the person who will execute your wishes and settle your debts and taxes. To spare your spouse these tasks at such a difficult time, Janet suggests a trusted friend or family member.
- Choose and consult with a guardian for your children, taking into account shared family values, the comfort of your children, and financial stability.

Draft a will.

I WILL

If you want to prepare your own

The Complete Book of Wills, Estates & Trusts by Alexander A. Bove Jr., Esq.

www.legalzoom.com
Will help you create a will online.

Nolo's Simple Will Book by Denis Clifford

Quicken WillMaker software

I WILL REVIEW

Examine your will for needed updates when you

- Have a child
- Amass significant assets
- Get divorced
- Remarry
- Retire and move to another state
- Experience the death of a spouse

3. Make arrangements for life.

A will is all you need, right? Not exactly—there are a number of arrangements you should make to transfer your wealth while you're still alive, ensure that you and/or your beneficiaries can enjoy significant tax benefits, and accommodate your wishes in the event that you should become incapacitated. These arrangements are:

- Trusts. A number of kinds can be set up to carry out your wishes. Consult with an attorney well versed in estate planning to carefully consider their costs versus their benefits. Relatively small, simple estates may not warrant a trust.
- A durable power of attorney for finances appoints someone to handle your finances—pay bills, access accounts, make decisions—if you become incapacitated. Name your spouse or adult child or a trusted friend, sibling, or longtime financial advisor in this document to avoid legal hassles for everyone involved.
- A durable power of attorney for healthcare names someone to make medical decisions for you if you become unable to do so for yourself.
- A living will spells out your wishes regarding the kind of medical treatment you do—and do not—want if you become terminally ill and cannot communicate your wishes.
- Long-term care insurance is especially important for women, notes Janet, because we are statistically likely to outlive our husbands. "A well-chosen policy that pays for both nursing-home care and at-home care can protect the assets you've spent a lifetime accumulating and buy priceless peace of mind." Janet suggests you begin looking at this type of insurance around age fifty-five, and that you shop carefully (see Long-Term Care).

Make your wishes known in the necessary documents.

LONG-TERM CARE

Put yourself in good hands

To best evaluate your options and factor in the specifics of your medical history, seek out a specialist in the field who deals with several insurers. For help:

The Corporation for Long-Term Care Certification. Offers a professional designation and a Web site to aid you in finding a specialist in your area. www.ltc-cltc.com.

Weiss Ratings' Shopper's Guide to Long-Term Care Insurance. Provides a personalized list of many company prices and coverage details based on your age and area code. www.weissratings.com or 800-289-9222.

4. Be a philanthropist.

As noted above, estate planning is also about helping people and organizations we care about. Being able to participate in this kind of philanthropy can be one of the deepest rewards of accumulating assets and living a financially sound life—and you don't have to be a Rockefeller to touch many lives in these small ways:

Charitable contributions. Many people get the most immediate satisfaction from giving lump sum donations of cash or goods, and there are often tax benefits, too. Revisit Give a Little Bit, page 476.

Annual gifts. You can give $11,000 a year to as many individuals as you like without paying gift tax. This can be cash, stocks, or partial ownership of a home. The benefits to the recipient are clear, and the gift may save them considerable inheritance taxes. There's also a tax benefit to the giver that comes with decreasing the size of her estate while living, not to mention the warm glow of gratitude from the recipients.

Appreciated stock. Donating $5,000 worth of such stock can make more sense to you than donating the same amount in cash, since you would owe capital gains tax if you sold the stock in order to donate the proceeds in cash. If you donate the stock, the charity can sell it without incurring a tax bite.

Give now—and then.

5. Store your words.

Complete your planning by storing all your legal and financial documents in their proper places:

Lawyer's office. Copies of will, medical directives, powers of attorney, trusts.

Safe deposit box. Stock certificates, Social Security cards, birth certificates, list of bank and brokerage accounts, marriage licenses and divorce decrees, deeds and titles.

Safe place at home. Wills and trusts, powers of attorney, medical directives, insurance policies, list of bank and brokerage accounts.

Store your documents away for safekeeping.

6. Share your best intentions.

By now you will have discovered for yourself what an expert like Janet knows: Handling estate planning gives you a sense of security and accomplishment. It's a way of caring for others so that they won't have to wonder and worry about what we would have wanted, and of caring for ourselves by ensuring that our wishes are carried out. It's the responsible thing to do for those who survive us, and we should encourage our parents and significant others to be similarly responsible.

In addition to doing the planning, it's important to let the important people in your life know you've done it. Some will have been consulted if you've named them as guardians or executors or given them power of

INHERITANCE INSIGHT

If you find yourself on the receiving end

- To defuse the sadness, guilt, or confusion that may come with inheriting (especially sizable inheritances), sit tight for several months and don't touch it, except to put the money in a safe spot like a money market fund.
- Deal with debt before investing or spending. Evaluate your debt as described above, paying down or off those with the biggest interest rate bite. Then proceed to round out the gaps in your financial planning (rainy-day fund, retirement). In this way, you'll feel better and more responsible about using remaining funds to realize a dream like home buying or travel.
- Get help. If the inheritance is lottery-sized, or if you simply find yourself paralyzed by fear and indecision, consult with a financial planner.

I DID IT!

"I had several fights with my live-in boyfriend about his not having prepared a will or chosen guardians for his children and about his being totally unwilling to talk about his last wishes. I think he thought that talking about such things would hasten their coming! Finally I just decided to take care of my own paperwork. I don't have a lot of assets, but I do have prized possessions, and I actually enjoyed thinking of who I'd like to pass them on to. I even went into written detail about the kind of memorial service I wanted. When I showed my work to him, it made it easier for him to sit down and do the same. We both felt great afterwards and no more fights—at least about that!"

—Janice

EASY COME, EASY . . .

"When the mother of a dear friend passed away, I was shocked to learn that she'd left me several thousand dollars. She'd been ill for a long while, as my own mother had been before dying. And I think the bequest was made, at least in part, to recognize the hard work and pain of such situations. Plus, I think she knew that I really needed the money to make ends meet! I wish I'd thought more carefully about how I spent the money. I really don't know where it went—just out the door on daily expenses, I guess. It would have meant more to her and to me if I'd approached it more logically—using some on debt, investing some, and using a bit to treat myself with the love she showed with the bequest."

—Louise

attorney. But in addition, you should talk to your immediate family, your parents, and siblings to:

- Let them know what you've set forth in your living will—and ask about their wishes.
- Let them know how they can access your important papers—and ask the same about theirs.
- Exchange the names of your pertinent attorneys, accountants, and financial advisors.

Make your intentions known, and they will be duly appreciated!

CONGRATULATIONS!

You're leaving a legacy that will do you proud, and you've made your wishes known. You don't let concerns about your family's future give you the blues, because you've got a plan to spread the green around. You did it!

JANET'S PICKS

BOOKS & PUBLICATIONS

The Budget Kit: The Common Cents Money Management Workbook by Judy Lawrence
An easy-to-use budget-creating tool.

Living Together: A Legal Guide for Unmarried Couples by Ralph Warner, Toni Ihara, and Frederick Hertz
All about the legal—and financial—implications of living together.

S & P Stock Reports
Standard & Poor's provides data and commentary on stock for more than 1,000 companies. (See also www.spoutlook.com, or call 800-852-1641.)

Take Control of Your Student Loan Debt by Robin Leonard and Deanne Loonin.
Sound strategies for getting out from under as you get on with your life.

Taming the Paper Tiger at Home and Taming the Paper Tiger at Work by Barbara Hemphill
A professional organizer helps you declutter and set up a sound financial record-keeping system.

Think $ingle! The Woman's Guide to Financial Security at Every Stage of Life by Janet Bodnar
Everything discussed above and much, *much* more.

Value Line Investment Survey
A one-stop encyclopedia on 1,700 U.S. companies that can be consulted at your public library. (See also www.valueline.com or call 800-833-0046.)

Your Family Records Organizer by the Kiplinger Washington Editors and PARS International Corp.
Offers a convenient means of writing down and identifying where important information is located. Comes in either CD-ROM or print version. (See also www.yourfamilyrecordsorganizer.com or www.kiplinger.com/organizer.)

ORGANIZATIONS

The American Savings Education Council
www.asec.org
Offers an easy-to-use worksheet to help you plan for retirement.

The Institute for Divorce Financial Analysts
www.institutedfa.com or 800-875-1760
Can assist you and your attorney in handling the finances of divorce.

WEB SITES

www.ameritrade.com
Ameritrade is an online stock broker with a low commission (as is Scottrade).

www.individualk.com.
For information about individual 401(k)s.

www.kiplinger.com
"Trusted financial advice and business forecasts for more than eighty years," including tips and tools on investing, planning, spending, and more ways to build your financial know-how.

www.morningstar.com
Morningstar has nifty retirement-planning tools and access to data on thousands of mutual funds.

www.savingforcollege.com
Everything you need to know about state-sponsored college savings plans.

www.schwab.com
Charles Schwab is one of the discount stock brokers (like Fidelity Investments and TD Waterhouse).

www.ssa.gov
The Social Security Administration. Information for women is at www.ssa.gov/women or available by calling 800-772-1213.

www.troweprice.com
Where T. Rowe Price offers free retirement-planning advice.

48

POP THE HOOD

★ car care ★

If you want a thing
done well,
DO IT YOURSELF.

—Napoleon

So, what's your motivation?
Take a moment.
Dream a little, think big,
and then complete this sentence:
I see myself . . .

Imagine This . . . Your hubcaps gleam, your engine purrs, and when you take the wheel, you are one with your machine. Put on a tire? Of course. Change the oil? Sure. Buy a vintage convertible and retrace Route 66? Why not? Whether you dream of taking your lead foot to the local speedway or doing more than nodding when your mechanic is talking, this badge will fill your tank with supreme car confidence. You will pop the hood and perform basic maintenance, equip yourself for emergencies, and know that you're in the driver's seat at auto shops and dealerships. *You can do it!*

The Payoffs

- **Street smarts.** Feel safe, sound, and confident by knowing your car is in good shape and that you have emergency roadside skills.
- **Savings.** Save money and optimize your car's performance, longevity, and resale value by following owner's manual instructions, handling some maintenance yourself, and developing an ally at your auto repair shop.
- **Confidence**. When you have a clue about your car, it's easier to find a mechanic you can trust.
- **Fun!** Women may not be as inclined as men to see their cars as an extension (ahem) of themselves, but the freedom and exhilaration of the road are open to everyone. So after you've done your homework, why not take a tip from Bruce Springsteen's "Thunder Road," and "roll down the window and let the wind blow back your hair"?

Meet Your Mentor

PATTI CRITCHFIELD

What She Does: Owns and operates Patti's Auto Care in Berkeley, California. At this certified Bay Area Green Business, the "Team Patti" mechanics "Patticare" your car while you wait in a kid- and dog-friendly waiting room stocked with *House Beautiful* as well as *AutoWeek* and *Motor* magazines.

Why She Does It: "I've worked in auto repair shops for more than twenty years. There aren't many women in this business and I got more attention at first for being young and wearing mini skirts! But I got another kind of attention when I asked intelligent questions and showed myself to be serious, capable, and motivated."

Word from the Wise: "Walking into an auto shop can be uncomfortable and nerve-wracking, especially for women. You wonder if you're being taken advantage of, getting charged a fair price, etc. I don't want my customers to just take my word for it. I want them to understand enough so that they know they can trust me and the decisions we make together. You shouldn't feel stupid if you don't know much about cars—and you shouldn't tolerate being made to feel dumb at a shop. You're not stupid, just inexperienced in this area. You gain experience by asking questions and being willing to try new things."

I like being a woman who knows her way around a car.

—Patti Critchfield

BADGE STEPS

1. Read your owner's manual.

Many of us only consult this treasure trove of information when daylight savings time forces us to adjust our car's clock, but giving it a thorough read at least once is essential. You'll finally learn to decipher the mystery graphics on your controls, and maybe how to defrost your windshield without freezing your feet. Plus you'll get valuable information on driving your car, maintaining its appearance, and handling emergencies. So grab a cup of coffee, head out to your car, pop the hood, and follow along with the manual. Once you know your way around the engine and your dashboard controls, program your radio to your favorite stations—just to show your car who's boss. ***Establish a working relationship with your car.***

2. Check the fluids.

Reread the section of your manual that tells you how to check your fluid levels, how often to check them, what kinds of fluids to use, and how to add them. Pay special attention to instructions about which fluids to check warm and cool. Check the optimal octane rating for your car. In general, it pays to look under the hood and check your brake and clutch fluid, engine coolant, power steering fluid, engine oil, and washer fluid levels each time you gas up. Try it out, and stock up on the right fluids for your car. Once you get the hang of it, it takes only minutes. ***Perfect your dipstick technique.***

3. Keep an eye on your gauges.

Your dashboard gauges and warning lights are designed to help you ward off emergencies, from running out of gas to overheating. During your morning commute, is your tachometer needle reaching into the red zone? Is your water temperature gauge doing something ominous as you enter Death Valley? What does it all mean, and what the heck should you do? You'll know the answers if you take a few minutes, check the manual's description of every gauge, understand what each gauge measures, and note what to do if it lights up, blinks, or runs in the red. Make it your habit to scan the dash regularly, whenever you check your rear- and sideview mirrors. ***Know what to do when you see red.***

LIGHTS AND DIALS

What's going on on your dashboard

:: Gauges

Fuel gauge. Shows how much fuel is in your tank.

Odometer. Records the total distance the vehicle has been driven.

Speedometer. Indicates your speed.

Tachometer. Shows engine speed in thousands of revolutions per minute (rpm).

Water temperature gauge. Shows the temperature of the engine coolant.

:: Warning Lights

Brake system. Lets you know if your parking brake is on; if the brake light is on while you're driving and the parking brake is off, your brake fluid and/or braking system needs to be inspected.

Charging system. Indicates a malfunction of the alternator or charging system.

Check engine. Indicates a problem with the engine function or, on some cars, the transmisison.

Engine oil pressure. Reveals low engine pressure.

4. Check your tire pressure.

The proper inflation of your tires is determined by the weight capacity of your vehicle, so trust the manual, not what's written on your tire or what the gas station attendant tells you. Driving with over- or under-inflated tires is dangerous, so note the correct tire pressure for your car on a little sticker and paste it to the inside driver's door. Have your tires rotated and checked for wear as instructed in your manual. Buy one of those little pen-like tire gauges and check all your tires when they're cold, including your spare. Keep the gauge in your glove compartment and check your tires monthly. ***Be sure you and your tires can handle the pressure.***

5. Inspect your windshield wiper blades.

Getting stuck in a downpour or snowstorm with worn blades is no fun and can be perilous. Check to see if your blades are worn or cracked. Just a few months of hot weather can do a set of blades in, and insects, tree sap, and the commercial waxes used by some car washes can create a buildup. If your blades aren't worn but still aren't working efficiently, gently clean them and your windshield with a mild detergent and rinse well with clear water. ***Clean or replace your blades as needed.***

6. Assemble an emergency kit.

What supplies should be in your car at all times? Here's Patti's list:

- Flares.
- A flashlight.
- Rope.
- A gallon of water.
- A couple of quarts of oil.
- First-aid kit.
- Tire changing equipment.

Patti also recommends that you sign up for roadside services, either through your auto insurance or by joining AAA. Finally, she advises every woman on the road by herself to have a cell phone. AAA has phones designed purely for emergency use—but only in emergencies, since using a cell phone while driving can be unsafe. ***Be prepared—safety first!***

YOUR GLOVE COMPARTMENT

Not just for gloves anymore

AAA or other roadside assistance cards

Auto insurance info

Health insurance info

Pen and paper

Regional maps

Tire gauge

Travel-size packet of wet wipes

Your owner's manual

Your car registration? No! This should be kept in your wallet, with a copy in your file cabinet at home, in case your car is stolen.

I DID IT!

"I freaked out a bit when my daughter became old enough to drive. I realized I really didn't know more about my car than how to start, stop, and steer it, so I decided we should both visit Patti for an Auto 101 lesson. We got hands-on experience, got our hands a little dirty, and actually had a ton of fun! I was surprised at how simple some things were, like checking fluid levels, and while I'm not the least bit interested in tuning up my own car, I'm proud that I—and my daughter—now know what to do, when to do it, and when to call for help."

—Mary

SPEED BUMP!

"I had a customer whose car blew up because he had a prayer, ironically enough, taped over his dashboard warning lights! He had no idea that his charging system and oil pressure warning lights were on and trying to tell him something."

—Patti

PATTI'S EXPERT TIPS

SHOP TALK

- Get a second opinion whenever you are quoted a high price and whenever you get a gut feeling that you aren't getting the "straight story." If you've been going to a shop for a while and suddenly start to see a lot of new people, beware and ask what's up. "High employee turnover means something's going on," says Patti.
- Let the shop know your financial limitations. "A good shop should prioritize the work you need done, telling you what you must do now and what can wait." Shop owners need to make a living, and they absolutely need to maintain vehicle safety—but that doesn't mean they can't take customer finances into consideration. "I've even worked out trades. A single mom who was strapped for cash traded bookkeeping work for repairs."
- Stick with a good shop. That way, they get to know you and your car over time. This helps them predict and prevent future repairs and breakdowns, and will make them more likely to go that extra mile in meeting your time and money needs.
- Record your car's repair history. Many shops keep computerized records, but you should have your own. Keep a file of your itemized bills.

7. Start a relationship with a shop (or improve the one you have).

If you're not involved in a mutually rewarding long-term relationship with a repair shop, circulate and find the mechanic of your dreams. Get recommendations from friends and from people who drive the same kind of car you drive.

"Start the relationship before the car breaks down," urges Patti. Don't try to "interview" the shop over the phone. Drop in and check it out instead. Look for a shop that is clean and well organized. Are the employees courteous and polite? "If they aren't willing to talk to you during a drop-in, they won't be willing to when you have a car problem, either," says Patti. Ask to see their stock, too. "If they hesitate, they probably aren't using factory parts, and you don't want after-market parts. Go in as if you are looking for a doctor. Car safety is a matter of life and death. Shoddy work can get you killed."

If they say something you don't understand, are they willing to slow down, speak in plain English, or draw you a diagram? "Most shops have computers these days. They should be willing to pull up pertinent images for you from their Mitchell Manual database and/or print out a diagram for you." They should also be willing to explain exactly why something costs what it does or takes the time they quote.

If your current shop doesn't stack up to the above criteria, break up, and find one more deserving of your business. ***Meet your mechanic match.***

CONGRATULATIONS!

Take your rightful place in the driver's seat, crank up the radio, and cruise with confidence. You did it!

I DID IT!

Name: ____________________

Date: ____________________

CLEAN UP YOUR ACT

Apply some elbow grease

Road grime isn't just a nuisance; it can eat away at metal, causing rust and deterioration. Clean it yourself, and pocket the cash you'd part with at a car wash.

- Use floor mats to protect your carpeting.
- Give your back tires a break by cleaning out your trunk.
- Try electrostatic dust cloths on dashes, vinyl, and plastic surfaces. A mild dishwashing liquid works well on unwaxed finishes, and to avoid streaks, wash in the shade.
- Try two parts water to one part white vinegar to clean windows and headlights to a high shine.

BEYOND THE BADGE

If you love it as much as you thought you would, dream on . . .

- **Learn to drive stick shift.** Patti teaches teens (and older drivers) on the shop lift so they can gain confidence before facing road distractions. "I rented a Pinto wagon with a slipping clutch and no hand brake, and taught myself to drive stick shift over a weekend. My bosses at the shop were impressed and gave me an extra $1 an hour!"
- **Perform minor maintenance.** Try changing the engine oil and filter or some other modest task, paying strict attention to the instructions in your manual and never proceeding if you're unclear about any details and descriptions. Consider asking a more experienced friend to help you, or booking an appointment at your service shop so that they can give you a lesson. If you do this with a friend, you'll have someone to high-five at the end. "Books and classes are fine, but hands-on learning is best, and if you're like me, watching someone else do what you're trying to learn is ideal," says Patti.
- **Go speed racer, go!** Even if you don't look for sponsorship and assemble a pit crew, racing school will make you a better, safer, and just plain cool driver. Most schools offer one-, two-, or three-day programs. You'll probably start in a classroom discussing general concepts, but make sure you also get plenty of time behind the wheel. Track time will emphasize different braking techniques, downshifting, double clutching, passing, and overtaking. See www.racingschools.com for a school near you, and check Patti's Picks for other ways to connect with your fellow female racing enthusiasts.

BUYING TIPS

Life may give you lemons, but your car dealer shouldn't!

Don't play their games. Go in knowing what you want to pay, give them a reasonable amount of time to accept or reject your offer, and be willing to walk away. Don't let salespeople leave you alone in a room while they "talk to their boss." There's no reason for the whole experience to take more than an hour.

Do your homework. Once you have an idea what you want and have test driven the models you are considering, do your online research. You can compare safety ratings and learn the invoice prices of models and features.

Time your visit. Try visiting the lot a half hour before closing time, since the salespeople will probably want to get home and would undoubtedly like to squeeze in another sale before they do.

Shop at your convenience. Patty has a friend who sells cars and is willing to quote prices over the phone, fax people forms, and otherwise expedite the whole process. Look for salespeople like this.

PATTI'S PICKS

BOOKS

Ladies, Start Your Engines: Women Writers on Cars and the Road by Elinor Nauen
Essays and stories from the likes of Eudora Welty, Gertrude Stein, and Joyce Carol Oates.

Mitchell Manual
For hardcore, mechanic-friendly repair information and diagrams; published each year and available at library reference desks.

The Savvy Woman's Guide to Cars by Lisa Murr Chapman
Good for beginners; includes illustrated instructions for six basic car maintenance skills.

The Woman's Fix-It Car Care Book: Secrets Women Should Know about Their Cars by Karen Valenti
Explains all the basic car parts and their care.

WEB SITES

www.cars.com
Check the value of new and used cars for sale.

www.cartalk.com
Yes, this is the site for the ever-popular National Public Radio show "Car Talk," hosted by Tom and Ray Magliozzi, a.k.a. Click and Clack, the Tappet Brothers.

www.cybergrrl.com/fun/womenandcars
Includes practical auto insurance tips and advice on how to deal with your mechanic.

www.herauto.com
Useful links, accessories for the serious car enthusiast.

www.racerchicks.com
Fast cars and fast women: This could be you.

www.shedrives.com
Become a road scholar with maintenance and car care tips.

www.thundervalleyracing.com
Race reports and breaking news on female racers.

www.womanmotorist.com
Community forums, car reviews, and price quotes.

BUYER'S GUIDES

For new and used car pricing, and information on buying and selling a car:

Edmunds Car Buying Guide
www.edmunds.com

Kelley Blue Book
www.kbb.com

MAPS

www.aaa.com

www.mapquest.com

maps.yahoo.com

MOVIES

While your car is in the shop, watch:

Bullitt
Steve McQueen!

Fast Women
A documentary about female racers.

The Great Race

The Gumball Rally

Hands on a Hard Body
True Texas story: Last person with a hand on a new truck wins it!

Heart like a Wheel

Speed

Thelma & Louise

49

SPEAK GEEK

★ computer care ★

A ship in port is safe, but that is not what ships are for. Sail out to sea and do NEW THINGS.

—Grace Hopper

So, what's your motivation?
Take a moment.
Dream a little, think big,
and then complete this sentence:
I see myself . . .

Imagine This . . . Your computer does what you want when you want. More than a gadget or tool, it acts as a valued coworker and personal assistant, sparking new ideas, streamlining tasks, and helping you achieve goals. Hard to believe that there were times when you used to fear the thing. Maybe it had a tendency to freeze up and ignore your requests. Maybe it came down with a virus and started to behave erratically. Maybe you felt you just weren't speaking the same language. But those days are long gone—whew! Now you understand your machine. You give it the maintenance it needs, and know how to treat and troubleshoot the technical glitches that used to tie you in knots. Ready to cross the digital divide? *You can do it!*

The Payoffs

- **Confidence.** If we don't know a darn thing about how our computers work, we're at their mercy. Knowing a thing or two—including who to call for help—makes us feel more confident and less vulnerable.
- **Transferable skills.** Computers are everywhere: workplaces, libraries, airports, schools, you name it. You'll have a leg up if you can walk right up to one and interface with ease.
- **Time.** Yes, there's a learning curve whenever you face a new gizmo. But once you've turned that corner, you'll learn why they're such useful time-saving devices.
- **Thinking big.** Whether you dream of launching a business, traveling across South America, or starting a grassroots movement, the tools on your desktop can help you research, develop, and realize your dream without delay.

Meet Your Mentor
DENISE SHORTT

What She Does: The coauthor of *Technology with Curves: Women Reshaping the Digital Landscape*, Denise studied technology and gender studies at Harvard and MIT, founded the Toronto chapter of Wired Woman (www.wiredwoman.com), and teaches, consults, writes, and lectures on technology around the world.

Why She Does It: "I don't have a technology-oriented bone in my body! I did my undergraduate degree in English and didn't have a computer until I was working as an editor at a publishing company. As an editor, I worked on the first educational CD-ROM in Canada. When I knew I wanted to go back to school and do a master's degree, I heard about the brand-new Technology in Education program at Harvard. It was perfect for me, because in addition to hands-on experience with emerging technologies, I could explore my interest in women's issues by working with Carol Gilligan, the pioneering researcher into the psychology of women and girls. I cross-registered at MIT and began to focus my research on gender and technology. I was staggered when I learned there were so few women in computers. With all the work that women were doing to achieve equity, find their voices, become part of the literary canon, etc., here was technology encompassing every single profession, and there were very few women embracing it."

A computer can really be a lifeline, a window to the world that enables you to do things personally and professionally that would otherwise be IMPOSSIBLE.

—Denise Shortt

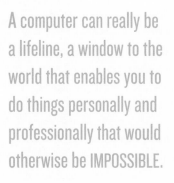

Word from the Wise: "Computers jump-start communication, connection, collaboration, and community. This is especially important for women who juggle so many personal, professional, and family roles every day. Computers let you work at home while still being connected to the rest of the world. They can help you join supportive communities or collaborate without taking you away from other priorities. Technology can move you beyond the geographic or economic limitations that stymied previous generations. That's why it's so important—and so empowering—for women to get in there and make technology their own."

BADGE STEPS

1. Get to know your machine.

If you're like most people, your computer is kind of like your car: You use and rely on it to get you from point A to point B almost every day. You know you shouldn't take its smooth operations for granted, but in general you do—ignoring warning signs, assuming ignorance is bliss, and crossing your fingers. Then, when it makes a funny noise or refuses to budge, you're baffled, afraid, and stuck. You don't have to become a computer engineer to escape this fate. Once you pick up some basic know-how and maintenance savvy with this badge, you'll be a more comfortable, competent, and confident computer user. But first you need to get to know your computer inside and out. Here's how:

Know your vital statistics. If you're using Windows, right-click on the My Computer icon with your mouse and select Properties from the menu. This area has all the information you need about your computer model, system, and performance. This is vital data you'll need to give anyone you call for tech support, repair, or upgrade information.

Create a tech support notebook or file. In it, write down:

- The computer model name and number.
- The operating software, including the version number.
- What applications you use, including version numbers for each. For example, knowing what version of Netscape Navigator or Internet Explorer you use will help a tech support person fix any technical glitches you're experiencing with the program.

Crack open that computer manual. You don't have to read it cover to cover—but at least skim the sections where your knowledge is thin, and keep the manual handy in case you experience technical difficulties. If you don't have a manual because you bought your computer used, spend some time familiarizing yourself with the Help menu on your computer and the tech support section of the Web site for the company that made your computer.

Get better acquainted with your computer.

2. Line up your tech support team.

Even computer whizzes occasionally bump up against a glitch they can't solve, or a computer feature that is less than self-explanatory. But with a

TECH TERMS

How to talk like a techie

Application. A piece of software that does a particular thing, for instance, Word for word processing, or Quicken for finances. Also called programs.

Boot. Starting the computer.

Browser. Software application used to navigate the Web.

CPU, or central processing unit. Refers to the number of chips on a computer's system board that do the main processing or perform the actual computations inside any computer.

Crash. When your computer suddenly stops functioning, and refuses to respond to your commands (or pleas!).

Desktop. What you see on your monitor when you turn your computer on.

Download. Copying files from the Internet to your computer.

Hardware. The physical parts of a computer.

Motherboard. The main circuit board in your computer.

Operating system. The software, like Windows XP or Mac OS X, that runs your computer and supervises the overall operations of your computer.

RAM. Random Access Memory—the amount of memory your computer has available to run programs.

Software. A set of computer programs that enables the hardware to process data.

Spam. Junk e-mail.

tech support team, you'll never have to face it alone. On the inside cover of your tech support file or notebook, jot down the contact information (phone numbers, e-mail addresses, Web addresses) of the following tech support resources available to you:

Tech-savvy friends. When trouble or confusion strikes, making this kind of call first is a lot more soothing than calling an anonymous tech support hotline and listening to Muzak as the clock ticks and your blood pressure rises.

The tech support team of the company that manufactured your computer. You may have to wait a while to be connected, but it may be worth the wait—tech support staff can walk you through solutions to many technical glitches. If the problem requires a replacement part and your computer is under warranty or came with a service plan, the tech support person may dispatch a repair person to fix what ails your computer.

The tech support contact for Microsoft or Apple. Common problems are often caused by your operating system, so if you're using Windows, be sure to have Microsoft's support number handy, and if you're on a Mac, Apple's support info. Some problems are caused by conflicts or bugs in a software application you're using, or a problem your Internet Service Provider (ISP) is experiencing—so you'll also want to keep tech support numbers for your ISP and the manufacturer of programs you use often.

Online user forums and technology support groups. Many software manufacturers' Web sites include support databases and user forums where your questions have probably already been asked and answered. If you don't find an answer, you may be able to join the group and post your question. Add these Web addresses to your list.

Computer repair professionals. Ask friends and colleagues to refer you to a reliable repair person who can help you fix a computer that's not under warranty, or help you recover information lost due to a crash, virus, or other damage. Look in your local Yellow Pages and newspapers for other options. Make note of a few whose services are right for you: some make house calls, some invite you to bring in your computer for a free diagnosis, and others have a specialty in dealing with specific platforms (such as Mac or PC).

Make sure tech support is never more than a phone call away.

FYI—YWIA

Standard abbreviations keep e-mail short and sweet

F2F: face to face

FWIW: for what it's worth

FYI: for your information

GMTA: great minds think alike

IMHO: in my humble opinion

IRL: in real life

LOL: laughing out loud

ROTFL: rolling on the floor laughing

TTFN: ta-ta for now

YWIA: you're welcome in advance

I DID IT!

"I'd been word-processing for years when I took a temporary job at a law office, revising huge legal documents all day long. The day I learned how to make universal changes in a one-hundred-page document—changing every '$150,000' to '$200,000' in one fell swoop—I almost stood up and clicked my heels in the air. Who knew? Not me! Taking the time to learn can really save you time down the line."

—Meg

SAVING GRACE

"I was working at a fancy art gallery in the early '90s. I didn't remember to do a full backup every night, and one night I pulled a cable out of the back of the server without turning it off first. The computer simply never turned back on again. The entire database for the gallery was lost—15 years of inventory, client and mailing lists, correspondence, exhibition lists, and everything else. The gallery spent hundreds of dollars and many hours having experts piece together lost data, and eventually most of it was recovered. That damaged hard drive still retains a place of honor (and warning) as a paperweight on my desk. Advances in technology have made it harder to damage or destroy data, but it still pays to remember the words of my father, a computer geek from way back in the '70s: 'Emulate Jesus: Save early and often!'"

—Deborah

DENISE'S EXPERT TIPS

EASY ERGONOMICS

Once you're comfortable with computers, be sure you stay that way! Because Denise is at the computer all day most days, she has invested in an ergonomic keyboard and mouse designed to minimize repetitive strain. At the very least, take these head-to-toe precautions:

- Set up your monitor at eye level.
- Hands and wrists should be straight and relaxed as you work. To prevent "mouse shoulder," a bursitis-like pain in the shoulder of the arm with which you use your mouse, keep the mouse level with your keyboard and a tad lower than your elbow.
- Use a chair that provides back support.
- Make sure your feet rest comfortably on the floor.
- Get up and stretch every half hour or so if you are at the computer for long periods of time.

3. Take security precautions.

We've all heard the horror stories about computer viruses, lost files, and identity theft—but don't let that scare you off your computer. A lot of this technical trouble is avoidable with just a few simple precautions:

Get antivirus software (a.k.a. virus protection software). Your computer may come equipped with this software, but if not, you can buy it at an office or computer supply store or download it from the Internet. The software you purchase from the big names in the field—Symantec (makers of Norton software) or McAfee—warns you when your virus protection is getting outdated and offers automatic upgrades.

Back up your files regularly. When you work in an office, chances are that the computer network is set to back up data automatically. When you work at home, you have to do this yourself. Duplicate your work on an ongoing basis using a secondary storage device like an external hard drive, diskettes, CD-ROM, DVD, etc. Some especially careful users store their backup copies off-site or send them to a friend; that way if their house burns down, that great American novel in the works isn't lost forever! Don't worry about backing up software—as long as you keep the original installation disks, you can always reinstall any software that gets damaged or lost in a computer crash.

Guard your privacy. Be just a little bit paranoid and at the very least, use common sense when it comes to online privacy. You wouldn't give your e-mail address, credit card number, or social security number to a stranger on the street, so don't do it online, either. Denise advises you to stick with recognized, established retail sites that guarantee privacy and to provide as little personal information as you can when you do make a purchase online.

Safeguard your computer.

4. Avoid the crash and burn.

When your computer freezes up so that your cursor won't budge no matter how wildly you move your mouse, and punching the keys seems to have no effect, your computer is letting you know that it's experiencing technical difficulties. And when your computer abruptly shuts itself off when you're in the middle of typing an e-mail, this is a not-so-subtle hint that your computer needs attention. So don't ignore the warning signs and hope for the best—take action!

As Denise will tell you, the best way to avoid getting burned by computer crashes is to avoid them in the first place. Here's how:

- Make sure you aren't running too many applications at one time. Close programs that you aren't currently using.
- Make sure you have enough disk space. When your screen freezes, it could be a sign that you are running out of disk space. You can check this by highlighting your C drive, right-clicking, and selecting Properties. If you are running low (less than 500 megabytes of storage left), delete some software that you never use or transfer some old files to backup disks.
- Update your virus protection software regularly. You can usually download the latest versions online. You may have to pay a fee, but it's worth it to avoid crashes caused by viruses.
- Save and back up your files often. When you reboot your computer after a crash, unsaved data usually goes missing. So be sure to save your e-mails and files as you work, every few minutes. Major crashes can damage the disk, which can affect or even erase multiple files—but if you back up your files often, you'll have copies of your files to fall back on.

WHO KNEW COMPUTERS COULD DO SO MUCH?

These women did!

Ada Byron, Countess of Lovelace. To balance the artsy tendencies of her father, the Romantic poet Lord Byron, Ada's mother saw to it that Ada studied mathematics. When she was just seventeen, Ada met Charles Babbage, a mathematics professor and inventor, and together they developed the Analytical Engine, a device now recognized as an early general-purpose computer. Ada has been recognized by the U.S. Army, which named its universal programming language Ada in honor of the woman called "the world's first programmer" and "the inventor of the first computer language."

Admiral Grace Murray Hopper. Hopper made history as the programmer of the world's first large-scale digital computer and the developer of the COBOL computer language. After joining Navy WAVES in 1943, she was assigned to the Bureau of Ordinance Computation Project at Harvard where she put together the operating manual for the Automatic Sequence-Controlled Calculator, outlining the fundamental operating principles for computing machines. The term "computer bug" originated with Hopper's team at Harvard in 1945, when they identified a computer glitch as a moth trapped in the machine and promptly "debugged" it. For her achievements, "Amazing Grace" was the first person to receive the (ahem) Man of the Year award in computer science from the Data Processing Management Association back in 1969.

• Upgrade. Newer operating systems crash less than older ones, so consider movin' on up to the most recent version.

Buckle up against crashes.

5. Learn computer CPR.

Even if you take precautions, occasionally an unexpected glitch will cause your computer to freeze or crash. When this happens, don't panic—or get physical. Though most of us have tried it in moments of desperation, thumping your computer usually does more harm than good. Instead, consult your computer manual, and follow the instructions it provides to get your specific computer up and running.

Generally speaking, the routine will probably go something like this:

End task. Hold down the Ctrl, Alt, and Delete buttons on your PC at the same time. This will bring up Task Manager, where you can select the Not Responding option and then click on the End Task button. (The Mac equivalent of the Ctrl-Alt-Delete key combination is the Apple key plus the Option key plus the Escape key.)

Reboot. Simply turn your computer off using the power switch. Give it a time-out minute or two to consider the error of its ways, and then start it up again.

Scan disk. To prevent this problem in the future, make use of the software in your computer that pinpoints glitches. ScanDisk on PCs can be found by going to Programs, then to Accessories, System, and Tools. Disk First Aid on Macs is in the Utilities folder.

Undo. Whenever your computer starts misbehaving, think about what you did right before the meltdown. Did you just install new software? If so, uninstall it. (Some Windows versions come with System Restore—which you can find either in the Help menu under Support, or by looking in Accessories for System Tools—to help you do this.) Even plugging in a new mouse has been known to wreak havoc, so retrace your steps.

Learn how to revive your computer.

6. Make yourself at home.

If your computer is a little sluggish or a particular file or e-mail is hard to find, don't get mad—get organized!

Take out the trash. Disk space can be used up by applications downloaded but hardly ever used, or big video or image files e-mailed to you

TECH-NICOLOR

Films in which machines rule (or try to!)

The Computer Wore Tennis Shoes (1969)

Hackers (1995)

Johnny Mnemonic (1995)

Jurassic Park (1993)

The Lawnmower Man (1992)

Logan's Run (1976)

The Matrix (1999)

The Net (1995)

Sneakers (1992)

Total Recall (1990)

Tron (1982)

2001: A Space Odyssey (1968)

Wargames (1983)

Weird Science (1985)

You've Got Mail (1998)

by friends or family (of course, you should always run a virus check on files before opening them and avoid opening files from unknown senders). Also, clear out those temporary Internet files and clear your cache in your Internet browser—keeping tabs on all those Internet files and addresses can take up a chunk of your computer's memory.

Tidy your desktop. First thing Monday morning or last thing Friday afternoon, Denise takes some time to delete outdated files and put strays in folders. "If I can't see it, I forget I have it!" she says. Denise says that the My Documents feature on your computer desktop allows you to file documents and keep the ones you use most handy, as you would in a filing cabinet.

Clean out your inbox. Even people who keep their word processing documents neatly organized in folders are occasionally guilty of letting their e-mail inboxes overflow. If you let your inbox get too full, e-mails headed your way may be rejected and returned to the senders until you create some room for new ones. So throw some of those old messages away, already, and put old e-mails in compacted or archived files using the File feature in your e-mail application.

Control spam. Spam is the junk e-mail that floods your in-box, promising everything from overnight financial success to pills that hold the secret of eternal life. Don't let these advertisers waste your time and your in-box space—take action! See Ad Busters for tips.

Get comfy in your very own digital domain.

CONGRATULATIONS!

Clap your computer-literate hands, digital diva. You did it!

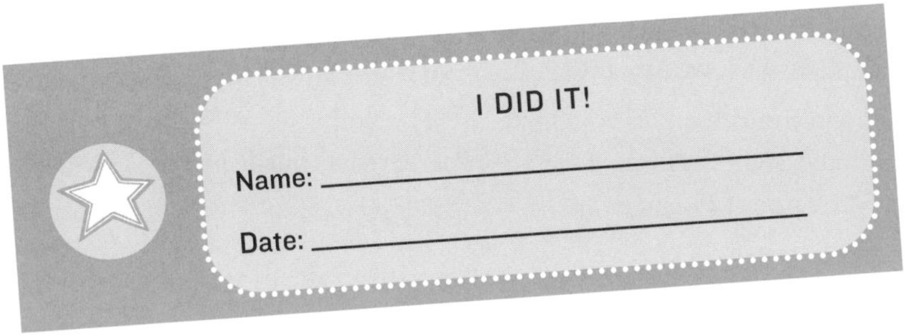

AD BUSTERS

To minimize your distractions

- Set up a separate e-mail account to use for online shopping or subscriptions, so that the bulk of e-mails from commercial interests goes to one account. If a commercial site asks you if you want to receive e-mail messages from them, just say no.
- Check to see if your e-mail program can help you weed out junk e-mails by searching its Help area for "filter" information.
- Investigate the various "Windows washer" programs or the Ad-aware download. These can find and disable the data-mining tactics that are the root cause of spam.
- To avoid Web-based pop-up ads, download the Google pop-up blocker. Go to www.google.com, then locate the blocker under Services and Tools.

BEYOND THE BADGE

If you love it as much as you thought you would, dream on . . .

- **Learn a new program.** Once you are making full use of the software capabilities on your computer, you may want to explore additional software to make your life that much easier—for example, Quicken to manage and record financial information, Adobe Photoshop to edit photos, PowerPoint to create persuasive presentations. Friends and colleagues can recommend programs that worked well for them, and computer magazines and many daily newspapers review new products (see Denise's Picks). You might also download some shareware—software you can try for free or almost free—and true freebies called freeware. But remember: Newer is not always better, and you don't want to clutter your computer with applications you'll never use. Before investing in software or a new computer, Denise suggests you sit down and get clear about your needs. She does just fine with word processing, a fast Internet connection, and PowerPoint: "That's it for me, because I only want and have time to learn the technology that suits my needs." When you do install new software, be careful—follow directions to the letter, and make sure your system meets all requirements for running that software.
- **Think outside the box on your desk.** As Denise emphasizes, computers and the Internet are wonderful tools for interacting with the world, forging connections, and even fomenting action. If you aren't great at the meet-and-greet of professional networking or at making "cold" telephone calls, perhaps you'd be more comfortable introducing and marketing yourself online. If you're frustrated that no one is marching in the streets in your neighborhood, use the Internet to connect with like-minded activists. The possibilities are truly endless.
- **If you build it . . .** If you'd like to create your own Web site to post photos, share your manifestos, or market your business, see Go World Wide, page 124.

SOFTWARE SOURCES

To learn more about available programs

:: Software reviews:

PC World magazine. www.pcworld.com.

PCAnswer.com. www.pcanswer.com.

CNET. www.cnet.com.

:: Software resources:

CNET's downloads. www.download.com.

CNET's shareware. www.shareware.com.

DENISE'S PICKS

BOOKS

. . . For Dummies (authors vary)
The place to begin, with titles on everything from Microsoft Office applications, Windows and Mac operating systems, Photoshop, networking, using e-mail, surfing the Web, AOL, eBay, graphics, doing business online, investing, and even programming.

Mastering Mac OS X by Todd Stauffer and Kirk McElhearn
For the Mac users out there, here's a basic guide to the new operating system.

Microsoft Press (authors vary)
Chances are you are using some kind of Microsoft product on your computer, such as the Windows operating system and Microsoft Office applications (including Word). Microsoft's Inside Out and Step by Step book series guide you through their programs.

Technology with Curves: Women Reshaping the Digital Landscape by JoAnn Napier, Denise Shortt, and Emma Smith
An informative, entertaining look at the lives and work of women who are breaking down barriers and driving our high-tech world.

MAGAZINES

Macworld
www.macworld.com
All things Mac.

MaximumPC
www.maximumpc.com
Their motto: "Minimum BS." Articles range from "How to Quiet Your Noisy PC" to "Ultimate PC Toolkit" and "How to HTMLify Your Desktop."

PC World
www.pcworld.com
What to buy and where to buy new products.

Smart Computing
www.smartcomputing.com
Articles, reviews, tips, and advice.

WEB SITES

:: *For women:*

Cybergrrl
www.cybergrrl.com
Community and guide for women online, offering free e-mail, chat, forums, and articles on current topics and technology tips.

DigitalEve
www.digitaleve.org
Digital Eve encourages women to get creative and form communities using technology.

Institute for Women and Technology
www.iwt.org/home.html
Learn more about great female and technology advocates, such as pioneer and founder Anita Borg.

Wired Woman Society
www.wiredwoman.com
WWS encourages women to explore opportunities and build successful careers in information technology and new media.

:: *For tech tips:*

www.howstuffworks.com/bytes.htm
Useful how-to information.

www.learnthenet.com/english/index.html
Covers the online basics: e-mail, searches, security.

www.members.aol.com/shobansen3/
"The basics of computing for people over 50"— and other beginners, too. Tutorials on attaching a file to an e-mail, downloading from the Internet, and installing software, plus other general tips.

www.microsoft.com
Learn about and buy Microsoft products, search their huge database for answers related to their products, and ask questions in user-to-user forums.

www.netforbeginners.about.com
Learn your way around the Internet with an expert guide, whom you can e-mail with questions. Covers AOL, e-mail, browsers, HTML, downloading, search engines, shopping, and a useful guide to computer viruses and virus hoaxes.

spam.abuse.net
A site dedicated to fighting online spam with lots of information, places to report spam, and software to stop spam.

50

MAKE YOURSELF HANDY

★ home maintenance ★

Nothing will work unless you do.

—Maya Angelou

So, what's your motivation?
Take a moment.
Dream a little, think big,
and then complete this sentence:
I see myself . . .

Imagine This . . . You're installing a new smoke detector when the phone rings: It's your brother, calling for your advice on how to fix the leaky faucet that's keeping him up nights. Good thing he's related to a handywoman! Then your best friend calls: Can she pop by with her two adorable toddlers? Sure thing—your home is fully childproofed, and it's your haven, too. Blown fuse? No problem. Overflowing toilet? Under control. With your newfound maintenance savvy, your toolbox stocked, and your home maintenance team at the ready, your home is more snug and safe than ever. Ready to repair with flair? *You can do it!*

The Payoffs

- **Savings.** Once you can manage and diagnose maintenance problems yourself, you can shop around for reasonable estimates—and you and your checkbook won't be at the mercy of that Mercedes-driving plumber every time the sink is clogged.
- **Security.** Every woman wants to feel safe in her own home, and getting a handle on a few home safety measures will allow you to rest that much easier.
- **Power.** We're not just talking about power tools here! Knowing you can make quick fixes around the house will give you a real charge.
- **Peace.** Who wants to wrestle with a leaky faucet after a hectic day? Knowing you've got a comfortable, snug place to go home to brings real peace of mind.

Meet Your Mentor

TERRI McGRAW (A.K.A. MRS. FIXIT)

What She Does: Mrs. Fixit is a nationally syndicated home improvement expert whose television news segments can be seen in more than one hundred cities across the United States and Canada. She has appeared on national television shows such as *LIVE with Regis & Kelly*, ABC's *The View*, and the Discovery Channel's *Home Matters*. She gives two hundred radio interviews a month, and her user-friendly maintenance tips also appear in *Redbook*, local newspapers, quarterly trade magazines, and her own book, *Mrs. Fixit Easy Home Repair.*

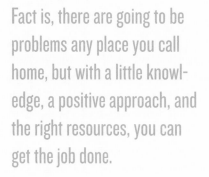

Why She Does It: "I became Mrs. Fixit when I married Mr. Break It. Don't get me wrong, he has so many wonderful qualities, but his first response to home maintenance issues is to hire it out. One day when I was calling a handyman to change a tricky lightbulb in our cathedral ceiling, it suddenly occurred to me: 'I bet it would be much cheaper if I just bought a ladder and did this myself.' Once I realized that I saved time and money by doing it myself, I started tackling other jobs around my home: replacing the hoses on my washing machine, fixing squeaky door hinges, replacing light switches, and weatherproofing. I started telling my friends and family about my successes, and they asked me to show them how to make repairs in their homes. From there I started doing a home improvement segment on a local TV news station. These days, Mrs. Fixit is on television nationwide, makes personal appearances throughout the country, and shares home repairs and household hints through the Mrs. Fixit Web site."

Fact is, there are going to be problems any place you call home, but with a little knowledge, a positive approach, and the right resources, you can get the job done.

—Mrs. Fixit

Word from the Wise: "Armed with a can-do attitude, some basic tools and know-how, you really can tackle many repairs and household problems that crop up around your home. It's just that simple!"

BADGE STEPS

1. Take a tour of your home.

Whether you own or rent, this badge will help you feel right at home with minor home repairs. But first things first: Do you know where your electrical panel is? How about the shutoff valve for your sinks, tubs, and toilets? Do you know where the gas line comes into your home? These are things that you should know to take action in an emergency, prevent a small problem from getting worse, and save yourself from some whopping repair bills. "Once you know these basics for plumbing, electrical, and gas," says Mrs. Fixit, "you'll already be a safer, smarter homeowner or renter." When you tour your home, note the following points of home maintenance interest:

Plumbing. Find the water shutoff valve for every sink, toilet, and bathtub. If you live in a house, check the location of the main water shut off as well—this is the valve that controls all the water that enters your house.

Electrical. Find the circuit breaker box or fuse box. This box is the control panel for your home electrical system. It's usually located in the basement or a hall and contains a series of circuit breaker switches (some panels in older houses still contain fuses that need to be replaced when they "blow"). Each breaker switch controls the electricity for a particular room or group of electrical outlets, known as an electrical circuit, and should be labeled accordingly. If your switches aren't labeled, try this: Plug a radio in a room outlet and set the volume as high as it will go. Go to the power box and flip your switches until you hear the music turn off, then label the circuit. Next, repeat the process for each outlet throughout your home. This is a great way to map out all of the circuits in your house. That way, next time your power goes off because you've tripped a switch or blown a fuse, you'll know right where to go to turn the electricity back on. And if you need to fix a dodgy light fixture, you must make absolutely sure the power is switched off before you start tinkering with it (see Step 3).

Gas. Most gas companies will come out to your house and show you how to shut off your gas, light your gas appliances, or maintain them at no charge. If you ever smell gas in your home, leave and call your gas company immediately.

Get to know your home from the inside out.

FIRE SAFETY

Where there could be smoke, there should be . . .

Smoke detectors and carbon monoxide detectors. Make sure they meet the latest federal safety standards, and test them regularly to make sure they are in working order. Change the batteries in your smoke detectors at least twice a year; try to come up with an easy way to remember, like every Christmas and the Fourth of July. Don't remove the batteries to cook bacon or another smoky dish—turn on the fan and open the windows instead.

Fire extinguishers. Every home should have extinguishers that are less than five years old handy near the kitchen, fireplaces, and laundry room and on each level of your home.

2. Stock your toolbox.

You've already proven you've got the commonsense smarts to take on home repair in Step 1; now all you need are the tools. According to Mrs. Fixit, the tools that will come in especially handy for this badge are:

Basic hand tools. A curved claw hammer pounds any size nails. A multi-tip screwdriver usually comes with both Phillips and flatheads in different sizes, to accommodate most sizes and types of screws. (A flathead screwdriver is used for screws with the single slash on their heads; Phillips screwdrivers are for the screws with a plus on the head.)

Wrenches. An adjustable wrench or a set of crescent wrenches will come in handy for turning nuts and bolts on plumbing and other fixtures. A ratchet set is also handy to tighten nuts in small spaces.

Pliers. Needle-nosed pliers, slip-joint pliers (with bolt in center to adjust), and channel-lock pliers (also adjustable) are great for fixing wiring on electrical appliances and fixtures.

Cutting tools. You'll want a razor-sharp utility knife with a retractable blade for safety and wire cutters for electrical projects.

Tape measure. To take measurements for replacement parts.

Toolbox. Keep all your tools in one place.

Because your safety should always come first, be sure you also have these home maintenance safety musts on hand:

Safety glasses, air filter masks, gloves, and ear protection. Keep yourself safe from harm when working with tools.

First aid kit. You may not need that snakebite kit, but the gauze, disinfectant, and eyewash could come in handy for maintenance mishaps.

Flashlights with extra batteries. Having flashlights available for a power outage seems obvious, but do you know where yours are in your home? Do they have working batteries in them? It is best to keep a flashlight in every bedroom and check the batteries every month, so you know they'll work when you need them. A good way to make sure you can find your flashlight is to put some glow-in-the-dark tape on the handle.

Keep your tools handy.

3. Check for faulty wiring and fixtures.

Ever plug in a lamp, flip the switch, and nothing happened? Armed with a circuit tester, circuit analyzer, continuity tester, and a couple of basic

CHILDPROOFING

Make your home kid-friendly

Mrs. Fixit's advice:

- "Sit on the floor so you're at their level, and see if you spot any danger areas," she advises. Is there anything within reach that is sharp, pointed, breakable, or small enough for kids to pop into their mouths? If so, move it out of harm's way.
- Cover your electrical outlets with child safety covers.
- Wind lamp cords around table legs so that little ones won't pull on them.
- Kids have a way of getting into places they shouldn't. "Screw safety latches on the inside of cabinet doors and drawers," recommends Mrs. Fixit.
- Make sure all your household cleaners and any other potentially toxic chemicals are out of reach of children and pets.
- If you have blinds, finish off the cord ends so that they don't make a loop. Install a small cleat or two cup hooks spaced a few inches apart to wind your cord around, so little ones don't get entangled in them.
- Pick up stove guards so curious kids can't turn the knobs on your stove. This is also a good safety precaution if you have cats!
- Have a list of emergency numbers by the phone, and let even the smallest family members know how important it is. List 9-1-1 first and include doctors, close family, and poison control. If you have smaller children, you may even want to put pictures by the number, so kids know exactly who they're calling.

hand tools, you can diagnose wiring problems and fix those fixtures. Just remember: When in doubt, consult a licensed electrician. Here's how to identify uncooperative outlets and faulty lighting fixtures:

- If your outlet doesn't seem to be working, grab your circuit analyzer. This tool will test an outlet for improper wiring, and may prevent serious electrical shock. To use your circuit analyzer, simply plug it in to an outlet. The analyzer will detect common wiring problems, like reversed connections and open wires. If you detect these problems, it could be an easy fix—check out www.mrsfixit.com for instructions.
- If the outlet is working, but your lamp isn't, grab a continuity tester to see if the circuit is complete and power is running into your appliance through the cord as it should. To use the continuity tester, unplug the cord from the outlet and turn on any switches on the item. Attach the alligator clip on the tester to one prong on the plug, and touch the tip of the continuity tester to the other prong. If the tester lights up, the cord is working. If it doesn't, there's a problem.
- If the wiring for your lamp is faulty or the cord is frayed, you can follow the instructions for rewiring a lamp on Mrs. Fixit's Web site (www.mrsfixit.com). Just make sure that you unplug the lamp from the wall before you start your repair!
- If you want to replace an entire light fixture, just search for "change a light fixture" at www.mrsfixit.com and follow the instructions provided. Remember, before you tinker, shut off the power and test the circuit. Remove your light fixture and use your circuit tester to check all wire combinations to make sure there is no electricity running through the line before you start working. "A circuit tester is a simple Y-shaped tool with a light and two leads that tells you the power is completely off for that outlet," explains Mrs. Fixit.

Sort out your home's wiring.

GET WELL GROUNDED

Prevent shocking events with GFCIs

Mrs. Fixit recommends installing ground fault circuit interrupters (GFCIs), the outlets with test and reset buttons in the center that help you prevent electrical shock: "At $10 to $20 a piece, replacing outdated outlets with GFCIs is a worthwhile investment to keep your home safe!" GFCIs monitor the amount of electricity to an outlet; if there is a problem, they cut off the power supply. So if you happen to drop an electrical appliance you're using into a tub or sink full of water, the GFCI automatically shuts off power to prevent shock. Building codes typically require GFCIs in all garages and outdoor installations, but you may want to install them in other places where electricity and water are in close proximity, such as kitchens, bathrooms, and laundry areas. If you install GFCIs yourself, just be sure to shut off the power supply, use your circuit tester to be sure the power is really off, and carefully follow the installation directions that come with your GFCI.

4. Check for clogs and leaks.

Now that you've got some home repair knowledge under your tool belt, you're ready to deal with plumbing issues. "There are really just two basic plumbing problems," explains Mrs. Fixit. "If it won't go down, you've got a clog. If it won't stop running, you've got a leak."

If it won't go down

Speed up your slow drains. "Pour a cup of baking soda down the drain, followed by a cup of white vinegar," advises Mrs. Fixit. "The two ingredients will bubble up. When the vinegar and baking soda stop foaming, pour a gallon of boiling water down the drain. This will flush away all of the gunky buildup." Use this formula once a month to keep drains flowing freely. Cola is another handy solvent for clogs.

Clear stubborn sink or bathtub clogs. Use a wet washcloth to cover the overflow vent, the hole located near the plug lever in a bathtub, and across from the faucet on a sink. Then clear the clog by fitting a bowl-shaped plunger over the drain with a tight seal, and really pump that plunger up and down. If it's still clogged despite your best efforts, see Solve Your Plumbing Problems, page 408, for instructions on using a wire hanger to clear the pipes.

Unclog your toilet. If the toilet is about to overflow, don't use the plunger yet! First, turn the correct water shutoff valve you located in Step 1. Phew! Now you can unclog the drain in peace. Grab a sturdy bulb-shaped plunger designed especially to fit into toilet bowls, and put some power into your pumping action. If your toilet is still clogged, Mrs. Fixit recommends using a good-quality snake, a long tool that reaches deep into your pipes. Pick one up at your hardware store and follow the instructions provided, as they may differ slightly from brand to brand.

If it won't stop running

Notice any leaky pipes or wet spots on your walls? Get a licensed plumber to check it out. It could be a sign of greater problems in your plumbing system and breed mildew and airborne bacteria. If you can find the source of the leak, cover the leaky pipe with a rubber patch secured with a hose clamp until the plumber arrives (both available at your hardware store). Check out the plumbing section at www.mrsfixit.com for more detailed quick fixes for leaks.

Diagnose your leaky toilet trouble. Take the ceramic top off the toilet tank, add a few drops of food coloring into the water tank, and let it sit for an hour or two. When time's up:

- Look into your toilet bowl. If you see food coloring in the water, says Mrs. Fixit, "Your flapper valve is leaking and probably needs to be replaced." (Your flapper valve is that round rubber contraption in your toilet tank that opens and closes whenever you flush.) But before you replace it, try lifting up the flapper valve and scrubbing the underside. This will get rid of any mineral deposits that are getting in the way of a tight seal.

FEEL THE POWER

Of power tools!

Power tools are optional, but as Mrs. Fixit says, "They may save you some sweat if you're contemplating serious repairs"—plus you'll look way cool once you know how to use them! Be sure to follow the directions provided in the tool instruction manual, and remember to put on your safety glasses before you so much as pick up any of these tools:

Variable-speed drill. A combination power drill and screwdriver. This tool makes everything from changing cabinet hardware to installing a deadbolt a breeze.

A random orbit sander. Makes short work of furniture refinishing and house-painting prep (see Redo a Room, page 142, for more on redecorating projects).

A circular saw and jigsaw. If you get involved in carpentry projects, these will save you a lot of time and are more precise than a handsaw.

SOLVE YOUR PLUMBING PROBLEMS

With help from your dry cleaner!

Take one of those flexible wire hangers that you got from your dry cleaner, and use it to clear a clogged U-joint under your sink using these instructions from Mrs. Fixit's gold mine of a Web site, www.mrsfixit.com:

1. **Turn off the water supply.**
2. **Put a bucket under the joint to catch the muck and water. You may also want to put a few towels around to catch any splashes.**
3. **Some sinks have a plug at the bottom of the U-bend that you can unscrew to drain the trap. If your sink has this, just loosen it up and let any water drain out. Then use a flexible wire hanger, bent at one end, to fish out the clog.**
4. **If the clog is too big or you don't have a plug, you'll have to remove the entire joint. Loosen the slip nuts on the U, and slide them away from the junction. Once the nuts on both sides are loose, carefully pull the joint away from the drain. Turn it over so all the water drains out, and then use that hanger to fish out the blockage.**
5. **When the clog is out, scrub the bend with some cleanser and a bottle brush.**
6. **Put the pipe back into place and secure all of the fittings. (If your connection requires rubber washers, it's a good idea to replace them with new ones before reassembling.)**

- Look behind your toilet. Notice any colored water dripping out the back of the toilet by the pipes? If so, the seal between the tank and the bowl needs replacing. You can do this yourself, but if you're not sure, call a plumber, explain the problem, and (as always) ask for an estimate. (See Step 6 for tips on selecting a plumber.)
- No color in or behind the toilet? Flush and look at the base of your toilet. Is there a puddle of water there? If there is, the wax ring is cracked and needs to be replaced. Check out www.mrsfixit.com on how to replace a wax seal, or call a plumber if it's more than you can handle.

Keep the water supply flowing as it should in your home.

MRS. FIXIT'S EXPERT TIPS

FIX THAT FAUCET

The most common problem with a two-handled (one for cold and one for hot) or compression faucet is a worn-out washer or stem, but it's usually an easy fix. Follow these steps from the www.mrsfixit.com Web site:

- Turn off the water supply to the faucet. The shut-off valve should be located under your sink.
- Remove the index cap (the little disks that are marked "h" or "c"). Remove the screw that you find under that disk and lift off the handle.
- Use a pair of slip-joint pliers to loosen the bonnet nut, which is the nut that's holding the stem assembly in place. Then, pull the stem out of the faucet. Worn parts in the stem assembly are most likely causing the leak. The part is pretty inexpensive so just replace the whole device. Bring it with you to the store so you're sure you're getting exactly the right one.
- Slip the new stem assembly into place, making sure that it lines up straight and it fits snugly. Twist the nuts back into place, securing them with slip-joint pliers. Replace the handle, making sure to tighten down the screw snugly, but not too tight.
- Replace the index cap, turn the water back on, and then test the faucet.

5. Get savvy about gas safety.

- If you smell gas when you open your front door, walk right back out and call your gas company from a cell phone or a neighbor's house. Gas fumes are toxic and highly flammable.
- Take your gas company up on its free services. Most gas companies will evaluate your home for gas leaks and provide gas safety tips at no

charge. This is especially important for older homes, where a combination of outdated electrical wiring and leaky old gas pipes could prove dangerous.

- Check your furnace to make sure it's running safely and efficiently. If you have an efficient new gas furnace that heats your home, you may only need to get it checked every other year. If you have an older gas system, you'll need to get your furnace checked annually. Most likely you have a forced-air furnace that uses filters, which need to be replaced every three months or so in the wintertime.

Get a handle on gas safety.

6. Take charge of your home maintenance team.

By now, you may have discovered you need to consult a number of different professionals about home repair issues from time to time: A licensed electrician, a licensed plumber, your gas company, and possibly a general contractor or professional handyperson who can handle electrical and plumbing in addition to carpentry and cleanup. Sure, your Uncle Jim or handy neighbor Colleen might help in a crisis, but their well-meaning stopgaps may not solve the real problem. Even the handiest handywoman should still have phone numbers for maintenance professionals on hand in case emergency strikes. To assemble a reliable home maintenance team with affordable rates, Mrs. Fixit offers the following suggestions:

- Talk to your friends, neighbors, and colleagues about the repairs you need, and ask them to recommend reliable professionals. Let everyone know you're looking for professionals who will:
  1. Come quickly when you call in a crisis.
  2. Explain the problem clearly, in terms you can understand.
  3. Provide a fair estimate that they will stick to.
  4. Discuss with you bigger problems that could not be foreseen at the beginning of the project before simply proceeding with the repairs.
  5. Make the necessary repairs expertly and efficiently.
  6. Inspire your confidence and trust, so that you feel safe allowing them into your home.
  7. Get the job done without leaving a mess.
- Once you have a few recommendations for each type of home repair professional, give them a call or meet to discuss their services. Be

I DID IT!

"Our utility bills shot up last winter, and instead of just chalking it up to short days and cold nights, I decided to see what I could do about it. I went around the house sealing off areas where cold air was leaking in, switched to energy-saving fluorescent lights in our closets, and took up our electric company on their offer to analyze which appliances were gobbling up the most energy. To my surprise, our old refrigerator was the biggest culprit! We'd put off buying a new one because it seemed like an extra expense—but our new energy-efficient fridge is saving us so much on electricity, it's actually paying for itself. I can't believe I never bothered to do this stuff before . . . all it takes to save money on your bills is a can-do attitude."

—Michelle

REINVENTING THE FLAPPER VALVE

"I knew just enough about home repair to know that my toilet kept running because there was something wrong with the flapper valve. Turns out a little knowledge can be a dangerous thing . . . I wasted hours on a sunny Saturday inventing all kinds of contraptions that I was convinced could get the valve to open and shut properly. Finally I gave up and called a plumber, only to discover I really could have done it myself if I'd just gone to the hardware store and bought a new chain, instead of trying to fashion one out of bobby pins and rubber bands!"

—Julie

sure to confirm that they are licensed plumbers and/or electricians, ask for references, and actually call a couple to make sure your positive first impressions are justified.

- When you have cause to consult your top-choice home maintenance professional for the first time, be sure to ask for a written estimate for the job before you commit, and get competitive bids from one or two other professionals who rank high on your list.
- After you've had repair done by a professional, take time to think about how it went. If you were happy on all counts, this could be the beginning of a beautiful home maintenance friendship.

Get your team ready and raring to tackle any home repair—this means you, too!

CONGRATULATIONS!

How handy to have you around the house. You did it!

STAY SAFE AND SNUG

All year round!

Keep your house warm in the winter, cool in the summer, and safe and dry throughout the year:

- Check your need for weather stripping and storm windows. How were your heating bills last winter? Call your utility company and find out what is average for a house or apartment the same size and age as yours, and ask what steps you could take to conserve energy (and lower your bill!).
- Notice a water stain on your wall? Chances are it's caused by a leaky pipe, a damaged roof, or clogged gutters on the roof. Get it fixed now, before it becomes a moldy mess and a big-ticket repair.
- Check your home for potentially toxic radon emissions, carbon monoxide, and lead in paint and water. Self-testing kits are inexpensive and can be found at your home improvement store, and may be available for free from your city's Department of Health. Testing will put your mind at ease, and it could be a lifesaver.
- Drastic shifts in temperature can cause your pipes to burst, so take precautions in extremely hot or cold areas. Insulate pipes in colder climates to keep them from freezing, and have your pipes checked for overheating in the summer.
- Have a professional clean your chimney once a year to keep it clear of buildup and debris, which could cause a chimney fire. In the meantime, Mrs. Fixit says, you can loosen up and burn off accumulating soot by periodically burning dried potato peels in your fireplace . . . strange but true!

MRS. FIXIT'S PICKS

BOOKS

Better Homes and Gardens Home Improvement and Repairs Series

These books are clear and concise with easy-to-follow instructions to get you through your projects.The "Step-by-Step," "Start-to-Finish" and "All About" series (among many others!) are available on their Web site, www.bhg.com.

Mrs. Fixit Easy Home Repair by Terri McGraw

Our expert's book with over two hundred easy and practical do-it-yourself home repairs and household hints that anyone can tackle.

Books from Yankee Magazine by (or edited by) Earl Proulx

"You'll find a wealth of information—my Dad always used these books. Mr. Proulx spent his life in the repairs business and offers tons of advice derived from personal experience," says Mrs. Fixit. Look for titles such as these: *Yankee Magazine Vinegar, Duct Tape, Milk Jugs & More: 1,001 Ingenious Ways to Use Common Household Items to Repair, Restore, Revive, or Replace Just about Everything in Your Life; Earl Proulx's Yankee Home Hints: From Stains on the Rug to Squirrels in the Attic, over 1,500 Ingenious Solutions to Everyday Household Problems; Yankee Magazine's Make It Last: Over 1,000 Ingenious Ways to Extend the Life of Everything You Own;* and *Yankee Magazine's Home Fix-It Book.*

MAGAZINES

Better Homes & Gardens

www.bhg.com

Not just recipes! *BHG* has decorating, home improvement, and home repair advice galore.

Real Simple

www.realsimple.com

Better living with less hassle in all areas of your life.

Redbook

www.redbookmag.com

Check out Mrs. Fixit's home improvement tips, plus articles on family and food.

WEB SITES

www.hgtv.com

Home & Garden Television's great all-inclusive site that offers everything from specific and comprehensive remodeling to repair information. Curious about fireplace maintenance? Look no further.

www.mrsfixit.com

Hundreds of home maintenance problems solved here!

51

ORGANIZE IT

★ organizing ★

ORDER is the shape upon which BEAUTY depends.

—Pearl S. Buck

So, what's your motivation?
Take a moment.
Dream a little, think big,
and then complete this sentence:
I see myself . . .

Imagine This . . . In your closets and cupboards, purse and pantry, there's a place for everything and everything is in its place. There's room for guests in your guest room, you can actually dine off your dining room table, and that receipt or recipe is right where you thought it was. You're the Organizer Bunny! This badge will give you organizational expertise that you can apply to every cluttered nook and cranny. You'll declutter one area, establish order there, and learn to keep the chaos from coming back. We predict you'll be inspired to carry on throughout your home. Don't know where to begin? Right here . . . *You can do it!*

The Payoffs

- **Time.** By putting in a little organizing time now, you'll save hours hunting things down later. And cleaning is quicker when you know where to put things, and can maneuver with ease.
- **Space.** Decluttering can dramatically increase your living space, whether you live in a studio apartment or 10,000-square-foot home.
- **Serenity.** How can you relax in the midst of clutter? Practitioners of the ancient art of feng shui believe that when you put your external life in order, your internal life becomes clearer, too.
- **Money.** Have you ever bought a CD, jar of relish, or black turtleneck twice because you couldn't find the one you already had? Never again!
- **Reliability.** People who can keep appointments and locate client files in a snap tend to inspire confidence.

Meet Your Mentor

MERYL STARR

What She Does: Meryl Starr has been a professional personal organizer in New York for more than twelve years—but she's been an amateur organizer her whole life. As a kid, her room was always neat. Her clothes closet was so precisely color-coded that her brothers called it "the museum." Meryl is the author of the *Home Organizing Workbook*, has been the subject of feature articles in *In Style*, *Woman's Day*, and *Rosie*, and taught "The Nanny" everything she knows about organization. (Fran Drescher is her cousin!)

Why She Does It: "I've always loved order, organization, and simplicity, and I thrive on helping people get what they want out of life. I didn't realize I could make a career of this until a weekend spent at the home of friends, when I was trying to whip up a nice breakfast for everyone. My friend's kitchen was so cluttered and chaotic that this little task became a major project. So after breakfast, I suggested I organize the kitchen. Fifteen garbage bags later, the cabinets, drawers, pantry, and fridge were so sensibly ordered that my friend's husband suggested I charge for my services! 'Let's Get Organized' was born." Meryl recently worked with a 9/11 widow who was pregnant when her firefighter husband died. She wanted to organize and store all the memorabilia she'd been sent and the accounts of the tragedy she'd accumulated for their child. This gave her some sense of control in the midst of uncontrollable events.

Organization doesn't just look good. It FEELS good.

—Meryl Starr

Word from the Wise: "We all have clutter—it's what we do with it that's important. Clutter muddles your thinking, impedes your energy, breeds procrastination, and blocks enjoyment of your home. At its worst, it makes us hide and keep people out of our homes—and lives. I call myself a personal organizer rather than a professional organizer, because it's not just about organizing your stuff. It's about transforming your life."

BADGE STEPS

1. Choose a space.

Select an area that is small enough for you to organize in one hour, one afternoon, or one day. What are you waiting for a rainy Saturday to tackle—is it the hall closet, your desk, family photos? What causes you the most daily frustration: your clothes closet, kitchen shelves, home entertainment center? Thinking about a whole room can paralyze the best of us. One pile, drawer, or corner is a good way to get started—and inspired. ***Pick a problem area.***

2. Gather supplies.

You'll need garbage bags, cleaning materials, containers for sorting, and any organizing products you might want to use. But don't just run out to the container store at the mall and charge up a bag full of cute boxes. This is actually a better way to procrastinate than get going! You can probably make do with items on hand. Once you clear the decks, you'll have a better idea of what you actually need and will use. Also, consider the supplies that will make your task relaxed and fun. A pot of tea? Your favorite music on the stereo? ***Get geared up and get going.***

3. Clear the decks.

Remove everything from the cabinet, drawer, or closet. If you are working with a pile of papers, move them to a workspace. Clean the space you've emptied. Wipe down, put down paper liner, vacuum—whatever you need to get a fresh outlook on that space. ***Start with a clean slate.***

4. Sort.

Go through the stuff you've cleared out. What have you found that you haven't seen in years, thought you'd lost, or forgot you had? Make piles of items you'll keep in the space, throw out, and put elsewhere.

Throwing things out is the toughest thing for most people, but it's also the most liberating. As Meryl says, there's a place for everything—and for some things, the garbage bag is that place! We've all heard the rules: if you've never used it or haven't in years, toss it. If you don't really like it, bye-bye.

But also, consider your emotional ties: Does the item make you feel guilty, or bring back bad memories? Do you think you should keep it

TOOLS OF THE TRADE

With the right gear, anything is possible

Double rods. Either built-in rods or hanging rods that hook over your existing rails will double your clothes closet space.

Files. Think beyond files for bills and records. How about a file for those haircut ideas you tear out of magazines? What about restaurant reviews, decorating ideas, travel tips?

Lists. Keep a memo pad on the fridge so you never find yourself without a key ingredient. Keep one notebook that includes your to-do lists and schedule, so you don't forget commitments and don't have notes to yourself in half a dozen places.

Multitaskers. Look for end tables with drawers or shelves, or use a chest as a coffee table. The tops of file cabinets can double as workspaces.

because it was costly or a gift? Divide your discards into donations and trash, and stick at least one bag in the back of your car to drop off at Goodwill. Remember: You can hang onto the memory of your first love, college trip to Spain, or childhood love of science without hanging onto the physical mementos.

When considering what to return to the space, use common sense. In general, items with a similar purpose—kitchen implements, office supplies, makeup—belong together. And things should be stored where you use them: spatulas near the stove, stapler near your printer, mascara near the mirror. ***Divide and conquer!***

MERYL'S EXPERT TIPS

GETTING PROFESSIONAL HELP

- Look for people to help who are honest, supportive, and compassionate. You need someone who knows what they are talking about—what financial papers and documents can and can't be tossed, for instance. And you need someone who can give you a little nudge, but they should do it with a smile on their face and without judgment.
- A professional should take the time to get familiar with you and your needs. They shouldn't impose a system on you but rather suggest customized options that might work. And they shouldn't push organization systems you can't afford and don't need.

5. Organize your space.

Now that you have a clean, empty space and a pile of items that rightfully belong there, consider your organizing options. Is the space really big enough for the items? (If you've been good about tossing things out, chances are you'll have more than enough space.)

Also, how do you want the space to look? What containers, dividers, or hooks would be helpful? Here are some choices:

- Baskets, woven or wire, come in all shapes and sizes. On shelves, wire baskets keep towers of sweaters or purses from toppling over.
- Hooks on the underside of kitchen shelves can hold cups while freeing up the shelf space below for plates. On office walls, hooks hold supplies that would otherwise monopolize your desk space. On a closet door, they can hold tomorrow's outfit or belts.

NEAT FEATS

Clever clutter solutions

Cold storage. If you want to keep something that you only use once or twice a year, put it in "cold storage"—up, out, or away from what you use regularly.

Pegboards. Julia Child's husband built a giant pegboard in their kitchen for hanging up pots and pans, outlining each pan with a black marker so it could be easily returned to its proper place.

Vacuum-sealed storage bags. These can be used to store and protect sweaters and blankets from moths during the warm months and reduces their bulk by 75 percent. (Your vacuum sucks out the excess air.)

I DID IT!

"I was so worried about putting documents in the right place that I never put anything away. Now I have a serious filing system. My energy company recently asked to see my bills for the last six months, and I just went to the file. That kind of thing would have taken me hours of searching before. When you're organized, life runs more smoothly."
—Diana

EMBARRASSMENT OF RICHES

"A friend of mine gasped when I told her that I had ten stuffed storage boxes under my bed. Very bad feng shui, she insisted. So I rented a storage space, dragged the boxes into it, and felt pretty good about myself. Trouble is, I keep tossing stuff into it. I don't really even remember what's there—and every time I unlock the door, something tumbles down on me. It's out of sight but not out of mind . . . and I'm paying for it every month!"
—Marie

- Divider trays used to keep knives and forks apart in your kitchen can organize any drawer.
- Boxes for shoes and documents are great, but today you can also find inexpensive, attractive versions sized to store CDs or photos, archival boxes made out of materials that preserve treasured letters and keepsakes, and slim versions that can slide under sofas.
- Repurposed household items make great personalized storage solutions. If you have a fun ashtray collection, use it to collect hairpins, earrings, or paper clips. If you never bake cupcakes but have a cupcake tin, use it for tacks, nails, or beads. Tote bags you rarely use can house beach, gardening, or athletic gear, or be kept by the door as a repository for library books or videos to be returned. (Keep your list of books to check out or movies to rent in the bag.)

Put things back.

6. Celebrate.

Step back, look at your work, and feel good about it. Chances are, this is something you've put off for a long time—so even if it's just one drawer, pat yourself on the back. Better yet, take a picture. This will remind you of what you've accomplished and what you always want the space to look like. ***See how organized you are?!***

CONGRATULATIONS!

You've created order out of chaos. Doesn't it feel good? You did it!

I DID IT!

Name: ______________________________

Date: ______________________________

BEYOND THE BADGE

If you love it as much as you thought you would, dream on . . .

- **Have a garage sale.** Believe it or not, it can be as much fun to sell your stuff as it was to shop for it.
- **Keep your collections in check.** There's nothing wrong with them, but even museums rotate what's on view. Put some of your collections in storage. Rotate what's on display every once in a while. You'll have less to dust, never tire of them, and give visitors new treasures to admire. If you really don't want your mint-condition *Rolling Stone* magazine circa 1982 or your Malibu Barbie anymore, there's surely someone who does: Check out online auctions.
- **Get help.** The biggest and most dreaded projects can be fun if you involve friends or the whole family. Invite someone over whose opinion you trust, so you can get advice on what to toss. Make a deal to do your clothes closet one week, and your best friend's the next. Have organizing parties in each other's kitchens. If you envy a friend's home office, buy her lunch in exchange for help organizing yours. Cleaning and straightening the basement can be a family day, with dinner out as a reward. Help can also be found in professionals like Meryl.
- **End photo frustration.** Once you've dealt with the pile-up, it's easy to maintain order. Decide on boxes or albums, and which shots you want to frame. Separate photos into categories, like family vacations and holidays, or go chronological. Designate a box or album for each category and label. Discard duplicates and duds, create a separate box for labeled negatives, and run to the store for frames or bulletin boards for photos you want to display. When you pick up developed photos, promptly put them in one of these places!

MAINTENANCE STRATEGIES

Keep a clean conscience

- **Deal with incoming mail on a daily basis, putting bills in a "to be paid" tray or file, filing financial statements, and putting magazines and catalogs you want to look at in a basket or rack.**
- **Teach your kids—and yourself—to "put that back where you found it when you're done."**
- **Create rituals and routines. Rotate your clothes seasonally—and when you do, refresh your closet and toss, toss, toss. When you put things in the fridge, check what's ready to go. If you routinely order doubles when you have photos developed, give away the duplicates immediately.**

MERYL'S PICKS

BOOKS

Creating Sacred Space with Feng Shui by Karen Kingston
Organizing can be a spiritual experience, with this guide to "space clearing" and other feng shui principles that help bring harmony to your home or workspace.

Home Organizing Workbook: Clearing Your Clutter, Step by Step by Meryl Starr
Friendly, step-by-step guidance for every room in your house, with beautiful pictures to inspire your organizing efforts.

Smart Storage: Stylish Solutions for Every Room in Your Home by Joanna Copestick and Meryl Lloyd
Tips to maximize your living space, stash your stuff, and pare down your possessions.

The Ultimate Guide for Professional Organizers by Maria Gracia
If you're so organized you could be professional, why not try it? This book explains how.

WEB SITES

www.getorganizednow.com
Monthly organizing checklists and articles disclosing professional organizing secrets.

www.interiordec.about.com/cs/homeorgarticles
About.com's guide to home organizing, with links to recommended articles.

www.merylstarr.com
Learn more about Meryl Starr and the importance of organization and decluttering your life.

www.onlineorganizing.com
Check out the "clickable house" and "clickable office."

www.organizedhome.com
Articles on such topics as organizing kids' rooms and identifying your clutter personality type.

ORGANIZATIONS

National Association of Professional Organizers (NAPO)
www.napo.net
Get a referral or locate a chapter near you.

MAGAZINES

Real Simple
www.realsimple.com
Regularly features detailed articles on organization.

TOOLS

Bed Bath and Beyond
www.bedbathandbeyond.com or 866-462-3966
Home and storage organization.

CD Storehouse
800-829-4203
CD storage solutions.

The Container Store
www.containerstore.com
Storage solutions galore; frequently recommended by *Real Simple*.

Easy Closets
www.easyclosets.com or 800-910-0129
Customized closet systems.

Exposures
www.exposuresonline.com or 800-222-4947
Photo storage and archival boxes.

Hold Everything
www.holdeverything.com or 800-421-2264
Closet storage products.

Levenger
www.levenger.com or 800-667-8034
Home office organization.

Rubbermaid
www.rubbermaid.com or 888-895-2110
Home and storage organization.

connect

Act as if what you do
makes a difference.
It does.

—William James

52

GET AN INNER LIFE

★ meditation ★

It is those who have a DEEP and REAL inner life who are best able to deal with the irritating details of outer life.

—Evelyn Underhill

So, what's your motivation?
Take a moment.
Dream a little, think big,
and then complete this sentence:
I see myself . . .

Imagine This . . . Whenever the world seems loud or mean and all its inhabitants are getting on your last nerve, you have a serene haven to call your own. When you lose sight of your priorities and dreams, you have a surefire way of reconnecting with them. And when sadness and grief visit, you know comfort and peace of mind are still possible. Have you achieved sainthood? Nope, you've simply started devoting a sitcom's worth of time each day (okay, most days) to shoring up the foundation of your life. Whether you use writing, breathing, or reading as your meditation technique, you've made sitting still for a few minutes as habitual as running around for hours. Why? Because finding your own peace makes keeping the pace—and everything else in your life—so much easier. *You can do it!*

The Payoffs

- **Direction.** Inner knowledge is a trusty compass that brings clarity and focus to everyday decision making and big picture priority setting.
- **Confidence.** When you develop your own inner strength, you won't worry so much about what others think of you. As Anna Freud once said: "I was always looking outside myself for strength and confidence, but it comes from within. It is there all the time."
- **Compassion.** A deeper understanding of who you are gives you greater empathy and compassion for others. With sharper insight, you'll see right through superficial differences.
- **Health.** Meditative practices have been shown to diminish stress, insomnia, and high blood pressure while boosting mood, energy, and the immune system.

Meet Your Mentor

THE REVEREND BETH HANSEN

What She Does: Beth's duties as associate rector at St. Mary the Virgin Episcopal Church in San Francisco include advising people (like you!) who want to enrich their inner lives.

Why She Does It: "I studied psychology as an undergraduate and then went into the seminary, not knowing if I would be a professor or a priest. What I did know was that I wanted to learn more about spirituality—faith, religion, scripture—and that I was good at making such things fresh and fun for other people. My inner life then guided me into becoming ordained as an Episcopal priest. While the mission of my work is to reconcile people to God, you don't have to believe in God to have an inner life. Belief is about your intellect, whereas awaking to your inner life is about heart and soul. The world we live in does not teach us to listen to what's inside. It encourages us to listen to all the voices out there in the world, so it takes practice to be able to tune in to an inner life. But whether we call it inner wisdom, the collective unconscious, or God, it's the voice that lets us know the truth—and the truth really can set you free."

Word from the Wise: "The goal is an inner life—not an inner visit! You can't expect to pop in every once in a while and pick up a great insight, solution, or hit of serenity. Tuning in needs to be a regular part of your life. The rewards will come when your soul knows you've made a place for it, when you listen to it consistently."

When you develop an inner life, you will feel more centered, grounded, creative, and even more SEXY!

—The Reverend Beth Hansen

BADGE STEPS

TAKE THEIR WORDS FOR IT

To keep you company on your inner journey

"If we go down into ourselves, we find that we possess exactly what we desire."
—Simone Weil

"Who looks outside, dreams; who looks inside, wakes."
—Carl Jung

"Knowing others is intelligence; knowing yourself is true wisdom."
—Lao Tzu

"Mindfulness helps us regain the paradise we thought we had lost."
—Thich Nhat Hanh

"What lies behind us and what lies before us are tiny matters compared to what lies within us."
—Ralph Waldo Emerson

1. Schedule some quality time—with yourself.

Before you try out the following three approaches to meditation—a writing meditation, a breathing meditation, and inspirational reading—you need to clear out some time every day to make it happen. Since each of these paths leads to the same place (you!), you can't really go wrong or get lost! Here's how to get started:

Set a time. Commit to thirty minutes a day (but don't beat yourself up if you only manage ten minutes on some days). Unless otherwise specified, choose a time that feels right to you and that you can commit to consistently over time. Many find mornings optimal because the mind is refreshed and the strains of the day have yet to take hold. But if you're an evening person or crave a midday time-out, set your inner schedule accordingly.

Create a sanctuary. You may have a particularly lovely place to sit during your work lunch hour, or enjoy getting to your sunny office before anyone else arrives. Or you may choose to create a special "room of one's own"—a cozy corner, favorite porch swing, or a private nook that you empty of distractions or fill with meaningful objects.

Think long-term. The rewards of a meditative practice come over time—and once they do, finding time will no longer feel like a burden. As Beth explains, your first few inner encounters can feel chaotic. "You may feel like you're in a hectic open-air market in a foreign country, surrounded by unfamiliar sights and sounds," she says. "If you hang in with it, you'll soon get the lay of the land." In the meantime, vow to keep these dates with yourself, because you must be present to win!

Choose your sacred space and time.

2. To start your day off right, write.

The first exercise Beth usually recommends is a meditative, first-thing-in-the-morning writing ritual developed by Julia Cameron in her best-selling book *The Artist's Way.* Cameron refers to these "morning pages" as "spiritual windshield wipers" that give you a clearer view of the day ahead, plus a "strong and clear sense of self."

Beth says that even if we don't do any other inward exploration, if we write our morning pages consistently, we will wind up with a richer inner life. Although the morning pages practice is specifically designed to be an A.M. ritual, she points out that writing or journaling can be done at any time (see Be an Author, page 96). Morning pages are simply three pages of longhand writing, done on any kind of paper you like. Here's how you get started:

Let it flow. Let your hand move briskly across the page and write in an uncensored stream of consciousness. Try not to pause or lift your pen from the paper. Just dump whatever is in your brain onto the page—even if it's a list of life worries or groceries to buy. The writing doesn't need to be neat, organized, or profound.

Be honest. If you're self-conscious and don't know what to write, write "I'm self-conscious and don't know what to write." The idea is to get this stuff—whatever it is—out of the way and off your mind.

Never look back. Don't read back over your pages after you write them, just write them. (You can even toss them out after doing so if you like—the less attached to the result you are, the better.)

Write morning pages daily for a month.

3. Take a deep breath.

To meditate, you don't have to go to an ashram, light incense, or chant in a foreign language. Beth suggests we try nondenominational meditation that calms us down and focuses our attention on what's bubbling up inside. It doesn't have to be complicated. Try this out for starters:

Make time. Set aside five to ten minutes a day at first, and work up to twenty or thirty. You can add this meditation to your morning pages ritual, or try it after you've completed your month of morning pages—whatever works for you.

Find a safe haven. Choose a place where you won't be interrupted.

Sit still. Settle into a comfortable and relaxed but alert position, and close your eyes. Most of us find it much easier to do something (anything!) than to do nothing—hence the title for Sylvia Boorstein's popular book about meditation, *Don't Just Do Something, Sit There*. You may fidget or fall asleep at first, but you'll get used to it.

Breathe. By focusing your attention on your breath, meditation brings you into the present moment, allowing you to stop rehashing the past and worrying about the future. For just a few minutes, live fully in the moment. You can count your inhalations and exhalations, if that helps; try breathing in through your nose for four counts and out through your mouth for eight. Concentrate on the air moving through your nostrils,

WRITE ON

In addition to morning pages, experiment with other forms of writing or journaling

- Journaling about a problem or situation is different than thinking or talking about it. Writing imposes a structure and provides a safe place to let it all out.
- If a fancy pen and elegant blank book inspire you, indulge in them. If facing a blank page intimidates you, try writing on a private home computer.
- Try different writing techniques. Script a dialogue between you and another person, or your inner and outer selves; write with your non-dominant hand; describe yourself or a situation in the third person. Writing letters to your old, current, or future selves can be especially enlightening, too.
- Write on and on about your goals. Therapists, career counselors, and life coaches advise this because they know that committing goals to paper commits us to working toward them.

I DID IT!

"I felt like just about every area of my life—my work, my relationship, even my exercise routine—was off track, and I couldn't seem to get anything going in the right direction. A therapist friend suggested I spend one hour a week writing about each of the areas in my life that I found problematic. I resisted taking the time until I remembered a cute blank book I'd gotten as a gift, and started writing in it at my neighborhood café once a week. Without consciously trying, I started to make changes. Maybe I just wanted to have something other than whining to write in my journal, but one way or another, the writing really helped."
—Miranda

ACHOO!

"I was in my first meditation class, sitting in silence with about twenty other people. Even though everyone had their eyes closed, I was terrifically self-conscious. Then I felt a sneeze coming on. I put it off as long as I could, so I wouldn't draw attention to myself or jolt my neighbors out of the nirvana I was sure they had all achieved. But I finally had to give in and sneeze—loudly! Maybe I learned something in the class after all, because you know what? The world didn't end, no one gave me a dirty look, and I realized that I can't control everything all the time."
—Kate

your lungs expanding and contracting, or your tummy rising and falling. That's it. Sounds easy, right? Now here comes the hard part:

Stay focused. We're so used to multitasking that even when we aren't doing three things at once, our minds tend to race around. But when your mind starts to get ahead of you, just bring your attention back to your breath. That way, you'll give yourself a chance to catch up with your thoughts. If you're having trouble focusing, try some of the alternative meditation techniques suggested in Meditation Variations.

Let it go. When you take this time to suspend your worries rather than getting carried away by them, you'll be reminded that you exist beyond all the concerns that seem so pressing. Whether the thoughts that come to mind as you meditate are trivial ("Will the cleaners give me my skirt without my receipt?") or profound ("My mother does not approve of me"), remember: They are just thoughts. Thoughts come and go, and they become less insistent and troubling if you calmly acknowledge them, take a deep breath, and sigh them out of your system.

Meditate daily for a month.

BETH'S EXPERT TIPS

POTHOLES ON THE ROAD TO ENLIGHTENMENT

- Expect to get fidgety. Depending on what your current life looks like, the first few months of a meditative practice can be uncomfortable. "If someone starts going inward and they don't feel good, I say perfect!" says Beth. "You're right on target, because you are seeing the truth of where you are."
- Let your conscience be your guide. When you tune in to your inner voice, how do you know that the voice you're hearing isn't just an echo of someone else or your own never-satisfied inner critic? "If it's talking English," quips Beth, "don't listen to it!" She explains that "when your consciousness is resting deeply in your soul, it's another language, beyond words. You don't have to listen to your inner voice. You *are* your inner voice. It will naturally move and guide you."
- During meditation, expect your thoughts to, um, wander a little. "It's great for your sex life!" laughs Beth. "After a few months of inner listening, people often come to me and report that during their meditation, they've gotten a surge of sexual energy. They often feel guilty about this, but it's really typical—because when you let go of all the junk and clutter in your life, you will feel stronger and more whole. Fears drop away, and sex is great when you feel complete and fearless."

4. Read up on the subject.

Another meaningful way to use the quiet, private time you've scheduled is to read the writings of spiritual seekers. Incorporate spiritual or inspirational readings into your daily routine, either adding them to your writing and breathing rituals or devoting fifteen to thirty minutes every day for a month solely to this practice. Just a few minutes of reading and reflection each day can illuminate and inspire, whether you choose to explore the mysteries of Tao Te Ching, selected Bible verses, the spiritual ruminations of Rumi, Zen riddles (koans), or the Big Book of AA. (See Beth's Picks, page 427 for further reading resources.) ***Read and reflect.***

5. Make it a way of life.

In trying the meditative practices above, you've likely learned what does and does not work for you—and you may have begun to reap some real rewards. But remember that the goal is to stay in touch with your spirit, not just bump into it occasionally. Once you get acquainted with your inner self, Beth says, you'll want to be sure you make time to cultivate the relationship. Pick one or more of the meditations you've learned above and particularly enjoy—writing, breathing, reading—then make a daily ritual of it. At the same time every day for at least three more months, go to your chosen sanctuary spot and do your meditation. You'll find your most reliable source of insight, smartest mentor, and best friend will always be there for you—because you've had it in you all along. ***Keep your spirit strong.***

CONGRATULATIONS!

You're living life to the fullest—from the inside out. You've created a moment's peace in this crazy world and nourished the spirit that guides you. You did it!

I DID IT!

Name: ______________________________

Date: ______________________________

MEDITATION VARIATIONS

Because one size does not fit us all . . .

- Instead of using your breath as a focal point, use a centering word, phrase, or prayer. Whenever the chatter starts up in your mind, bring yourself back to this recitation.
- Visualize a word, image, or color. Choose something you honor, respect, or find has the power to bring you back to a deep, sacred place.
- If you don't want to close your eyes, focus on a candle flame, meaningful icon, or special object. Beth initially found Transcendental Meditation (or TM) difficult, because closing her eyes made her feel off balance—but focusing on an object helped.
- Total silence is not a prerequisite. Some people enjoy the soothing sounds of nature or simple, repetitive music or singing. Others ring a bell to symbolize their coming into or out of the outer world of action and thought.
- Walking meditation focuses the attention on the rhythmic physical sensation of taking steps.
- For a close reading of spiritual writings, you might try the *lectio divina* or "sacred reading" approach in which passages of a religious text (such as the Bible), blessing, or prayer are examined word-by-word or even syllable-by-syllable; each is read, repeated, and given pause for careful reflection. Using this technique can make evocative words that we thought we understood (or are used to skimming over) shimmer with new meaning.

RETREAT RESOURCES

Plan your own spiritual quest

Fodor's Healthy Escapes: 288 Spas, Resorts, & Retreats Where You Can Relax, Recharge, Get Fit, & Get Away from It All (Eighth edition). An encyclopedic listing of spas and retreats.

www.nardacenters.org. A Web site sponsored by the World Council of Churches.

www.retreatsonline.com. Guide to spiritual, healing, nature, business, and women's retreats worldwide, including journeys to sacred lands.

Sanctuaries: The Complete United States. A Guide to Lodgings in Monasteries, Abbeys, and Retreats by Jack Kelly and Marcia M. Kelly. Several editions of this book are available, featuring sanctuaries to visit in various regions of the country.

Silent retreats. For information on silent retreats and links to other possibilities, Beth recommends: www.retreatsintl.org, www.mercy-center.org, and www.franciscanspiritualitycenter.org.

Spirit Rock Meditation Center, Woodacre, California. Offers meditation retreats with noted teachers, such as Sylvia Boorstein and Jack Kornfield. www.spiritrock.org or 415-488-0164.

BEYOND THE BADGE

If you love it as much as you thought you would, dream on . . .

- **Can we talk?** Some of us may like our first steps inward to be guided. Beth considers the various forms of therapy, counseling, and twelve-step work (through the numerous programs based on the tenets of Alcoholics Anonymous) to be helpful and sometimes essential. (A serious trauma or active addiction can be a powerful block to an inner life.) If you suspect you need such guidance, consider counseling with a religious counselor in your faith, psychiatrists (they can prescribe medications), psychologists, psychoanalysts, social workers, and marriage and family therapists. To find the right person:
  - Seek referrals from someone you trust.
  - Interview several providers over the phone, asking about their experience with your issues, the nature of their licenses and credentials, and their working methods.
  - Agree on a treatment plan and time frame, and feel free to make a change if you are not experiencing benefits after several months.
  - Understand what your health insurance will and will not cover, and if the costs are a hindrance, ask if your therapist will work with you on a sliding scale.
- **Check out to check in.** Getting away can help you get in touch with your inner self, providing a respite from your everyday sensory overload in order to see, hear, and feel more acutely. Beth considers retreats an advanced practice, something to try after having a good bit of experience paying attention to your inner voice. When you're ready, let your spiritual inclinations lead you to a cabin in the woods, an ancient pilgrimage site, a weekend yoga workshop, a work/study program or tour abroad, or a holistic health spa and wellness center. (See the Retreat Resources sidebar for more.) Your spirit doesn't necessarily require deluxe accommodations, either. A friend's seaside cottage might be free for the asking, and many faith-based retreat centers are inexpensive—sometimes downright cheap, if you're willing to put in a certain number of hours of volunteer work while you're there.

BETH'S PICKS

BOOKS

The Artist's Way: A Spiritual Guide to Higher Creativity by Julia Cameron
Even if you're too wiggly to sit in silence, at least take up her discipline of morning pages.

Care of the Soul: A Guide for Cultivating Depth and Sacredness in Everyday Life by Thomas Moore
Good guidance for the beginner in a soulful journey.

Centered Living: The Way of Centering Prayer by M. Basil Pennington
Practical guide for living your outer life led by your inner life.

Companions on the Inner Way: The Art of Spiritual Guidance by Morton T. Kelsey
If spiritual direction sounds too "directed," read Kelsey and learn about the value of companions on the Inner Way.

Concerning the Inner Life by Evelyn Underhill
A classic source and spiritual guru from Great Britain.

The Courage to Teach: Exploring the Inner Landscape of a Teacher's Life by Parker J. Palmer
A must-read for any type of teacher wanting to tap her inner strength.

Don't Just Do Something, Sit There: A Mindfulness Retreat with Sylvia Boorstein by Sylvia Boorstein
A delightful guide toward the benefits of silence.

Inner Compass: An Invitation to Ignatian Spirituality by Margaret Silf
For the intellectually rigorous and independent-minded.

New Seeds of Contemplation by Thomas Merton
A classic from a deep contemplative.

The Other Side of Silence: Meditation for the Twenty-first Century by Morton T. Kelsey
Kelsey makes silence so appealing, how could one resist!

The Tao of Contemplation: Re-Sourcing the Inner Life by Jasmin Lee Cori
Excellent first book for inner-life newbies.

Writing Down the Bones: Freeing the Writer Within by Natalie Goldberg
There is no better guide to journaling than this!

WEB SITES

"Inner life on the computer . . . are you kidding?!" says Beth. "It would be better just to unplug your computer and go be silent! But if you are looking for Web sites with some discussion on the inner life, you could try these."

www.anamchara.com
Interesting resources and commentary on the mystical life in the Celtic tradition; offers an interesting blend of inner life with Christianity, the Goddess, and nature.

www.belief.net
Multifaith e-community designed to help you meet your own religious and spiritual needs—in an interesting, captivating, and engaging way. It is not affiliated with a particular religion or spiritual movement, but definitely sports the more liberal side of spirituality.

www.explorefaith.org
Online resource for those desiring to grow in their inner life and explore how that connects to a spiritual life with God.

www.tricycle.com
Buddhist magazine which offers a "daily dharma." No inner life should be without it.

53

SHARE WHAT YOU KNOW

★ teaching ★

The one who teaches is the giver of eyes.

—Tamil proverb

Imagine This . . . You're helping a kindergartner learn to hold a pencil—maybe she'll write a bestseller in twenty years. Your yoga classes stretch and soothe stressed-out student bodies three days a week. Painting gives you so much pleasure—and now that you supplement your commissions with what you earn teaching workshops for senior beginners, you've learned that those who can, can also teach. Teacher of the Year? Even if you never get such a trophy, you know the profound thrill of watching people take the skills and understanding you've imparted and run with them. Area of expertise? Check. Desire to help others? Check. Experience teaching? Read on. *You can do it!*

So, what's your motivation?
Take a moment.
Dream a little, think big,
and then complete this sentence:
I see myself . . .

The Payoffs

- **Purpose.** Even on a not-so-great day, good teachers know there's meaning and purpose in what they do.
- **Perks.** Who else gets to watch a smile form on the face of a student who solves a problem, and see eyes light up when a new idea is understood? Lucky you!
- **Posterity.** Teaching is an investment in the future. You're planting seeds and influencing lives, and your words and actions will live on in a tangible ways.
- **Perspective.** When it comes to teaching, giving really is getting. When you give of your expertise, your own understanding is deepened and refined in ways that never could have happened if you'd kept it all to yourself.

Meet Your Mentor
JENNIFER BERNE

What She Does: Jennifer has a PhD in literacy education. She teaches at the University of Illinois in Chicago, educating those who want to teach elementary school in urban settings and people pursuing teaching certification alongside master's degrees in education. She is now beginning a job educating future teachers at National-Louis University's venerable College of Education.

Why She Does It: "I taught struggling adult readers and writers at a community college for nine years. Then I became the chair of my department and supervised other teachers. I wanted better tools for helping these teachers, so I went back to school myself. The greatest reward—and curse—in teaching is realizing that every word you say can affect your students for a long, long time. If a teacher tells a student, 'You're good at this,' they believe you. I could say the same thing a hundred times to my own children, and it would not affect them the same way. When a teacher says that to you, you are really lifted up and redefined. That's a huge amount of power, and it should be treated very gently. People often think that if you've been a student, you know what it means to be a teacher—yet no one thinks they could be a heart surgeon because they've had heart surgery! You also can't think that because you love reading or science or math that you will automatically be a success at teaching that subject. You have to learn to teach."

It's amazing to be able to encourage people, to change the way they see themselves and help give them options.

—Jennifer Berne

Word from the Wise: "Education is not disposable; people can't live without it. Yes, teachers are underpaid, teaching is not the most respected profession, and there are numerous frustrations and challenges—but at the end of the day, I know that what I do matters."

BADGE STEPS

1. Define the course of your dreams.

If you're reading this badge, you've probably already thought about teaching as a way to make a meaningful difference—in your life and in the lives of others. Perhaps you want to introduce young minds to your love of learning. Or maybe you want to share a skill you've mastered with peers or elders, much as the mentors in these pages have done through *You Can Do It!* You might also be thinking of teaching as a career switch, a way to supplement your income, or as a way to volunteer.

Whatever your goals, this badge will give you indispensable teaching experience. You will prepare a curriculum on a subject of your choosing, find students, and teach one small group (four to six people) a short (two- to three-hour) class. While this won't mimic the process of earning a teaching credential and entering a school system (see Your Credentials), you'll get to experience the thrill of teaching and get a head start on a course you could offer in a variety of venues. Here's how to get started:

- Define your teaching dream by answering the following questions: What is it you're teaching? Who's the teacher? (Describe your expertise in the area.) What will students in your class walk away with? Given the nature of the class, where will it ideally be held—your living room, a local community center, a craft supplies store, someplace else?
- Turn your answers into a one-paragraph course description in which you outline the skills or knowledge you will impart during your lesson. (Don't worry too much about getting it just right, you'll be finessing this first draft in the following steps.)
- Give your class a catchy and descriptive name, like "Grease Monkey: How to Tune Up Your Own Car."
- Consider your student base. Are you targeting a specific age group? Is your class for absolute beginners? If not, what background experience will you require? If you aren't sure, read on—Step 2 will help you define your class.

Outline a class you'd like to teach.

2. Watch and learn.

Think about your best teachers, including people who have helped you learn outside of classrooms. What made them so good? What pointers

YOUR CREDENTIALS

A few words on formal and informal qualifications

- Teaching credentials are required in public elementary and secondary schools, but not in all private or preschools. State requirements vary (see Get Certified, page 434). Jennifer reminds us that if you are considering teaching in an elementary school, you should know that you will be teaching a variety of subjects—and can't dodge the ones you aren't wild about. (If you have a passion for science or literature, consider teaching just that subject to older kids.)
- A master's degree in a subject area (English, Communications, Computer Science) often allows you to teach in junior or community colleges, without a teaching credential.
- TeachersCount is a nonprofit that supports educators. Their Web site is an excellent one-stop source of information about certification and job-seeking. Visit www.teacherscount.org.
- Your professional accomplishments—like the business you grew, the book you've published, or other achievements in a sport, art, or craft—can earn you students in private classes and open-to-the-public workshops.

or encouraging words helped you master that new computer program or quilting stitch? Your homework is to observe teachers at work:

- Find at least two different classes on the subject (or one similar to it) that you plan to teach. You might locate classes at: elementary schools where you can shadow a teaching friend or volunteer as a guest reader; literacy programs—most colleges where teachers are trained run these; community adult education programs; local businesses, such as craft, home, wine, sporting goods, or garden stores; or senior centers or community nonprofits.
- Sit in on two different classes, and analyze the teachers' methods. Think about each teacher's goals and strategies, pay attention to how the class is structured from start to finish, and watch student reactions to get a sense of what is (and isn't!) working.
- Look around at your fellow students in each class, and consider the challenges and rewards of working with this particular student body.

Observe, and take note of your many options as a teacher.

3. Complete your curriculum.

Jennifer reminds us that great teaching starts in "the empty classroom," since that's where behind-the-scenes planning happens. Apply what you learned in Step 2 to revisit the course description you wrote in Step 1, and start filling in these details:

Outcome. This should be a goal that's realistic (given your time constraints) and appealing for students. A beginning genealogy class goal might be a simple family tree.

Steps. What knowledge and skills do the students need to achieve this goal? Do you need to define terms like "genealogy," explain and demonstrate research methods, and provide templates or handouts? Check to be sure you have all the skills, knowledge, and resources you need to cover these bases.

Materials. What will you provide, and what will you ask students to bring with them?

Methods. How will you teach each step? Will you lecture, have a question and answer session, provide examples and exercises, or offer handouts? Don't forget your class experiences in Step 2. What worked well and held student interest? How did the teacher build in variety?

Become a class act with careful course planning.

PREREQUISITES

Good teachers excel at these three P's

Passion. You need to be as passionate about helping people learn as you are about your subject. A love of Shakespeare alone won't make you a good Shakespeare teacher.

Patience. As Jennifer says, "To be an outstanding teacher, you have to be in touch with what it feels like not to know. You must continually put yourself in the shoes of the student." This requires patience.

Processing. Jennifer says that good teachers are able to be "ruthlessly self-critical," creating objectives, implementing methods for meeting those objectives, and then evaluating their practice and changing their approach as needed.

JENNIFER'S EXPERT TIPS

MISS CONGENIALITY: NOT.

Teaching is not a popularity contest. "If you're a good teacher," stresses Jennifer, "everyone isn't going to love you all the time." How come? "Good teachers create dissonance, replacing their students' existing ideas with new ones. That can be uncomfortable." This doesn't mean you have to be an ogre, but you do have to get over a desire to be liked above all else and can't expect to coast on your charisma. It's much better for a teacher to hear, "You made me so mad when you did such-and-such, but I now get what you were doing," than "you're my favorite teacher."

4. Do a dry run.

Before you step into the classroom, run through your material:

- Practice teaching your entire class from start to finish once. (You can do this on your own, or enlist a few practice students.)
- Time yourself running through component parts separately—you'll want to make sure that you'll have time to cover all your bases and leave time for class questions and detours.
- See Speak Up, page 38, if you find yourself getting anxious about being a focal point. But also remember that teaching isn't public speaking. "Shy" people can be great teachers: focus on your subject, your materials, and your desire to share what you know.
- Prepare an evaluation form that you will ask your students to fill out at the end of the course. The form should be short and specific to your class. Include: What do you know about [the subject] now that you did not know before the class? Did you learn or do what you expected in class? What do you still want to know? What was your most and least favorite part of the class? What about the instruction did and did not help you learn?

Prepare for class.

5. Get the word out.

Now that you have a class, it's time to set a date, time, cost (if any), and place. When you've nailed down the above, you can seek your students. Remember to limit your class size to between four and six students the first time out. You could just invite friends and acquaintances by e-mailing them your course description, but you might also consider posting

I DID IT!

"I've taught elementary school for more than thirty (gulp!) years. There's a saying in my field: Don't smile until after Christmas. Of course, that's a wild exaggeration, but the point is that being everyone's best friend isn't the point. That said, there's another saying: You have to reach before you can teach. You do that by letting your students know how the classroom is going to work. Kids feel safe and comfortable when they know there's structure, they understand how it works, and they see that you are always fair and reasonable. When you lay that foundation, you can teach—and smile!"
—Yvonne

PASS OR FAIL?

"I'm a journalist, I've been a publicist, and I've published three books about music. I've been asked to teach or speak to students on each of these subjects. It's important that I'm prepared and know what I'm talking about, but I've also learned to find out what the students know so I don't bore or mystify them. I've watched teachers lecture—'Bob Dylan was a folksinger . . . ' I think it's much better to ask questions, get a show of hands, and get people talking. If you ask what people know about Dylan, you can fill in the holes. It'll be a much livelier class, and the students are more likely to retain the information. It also helps students who might not otherwise engage become participants in their classroom."
—Denise

flyers in appropriate businesses or at the community center, library, or church where you are using a room. ***Advertise your class.***

6. Teach, and make course corrections.

As you head for the head of the class, keep these tips in mind:

Be flexible. Tune in to subtle shifts you might need to make during class. Spend more time on a portion of your class that is proving especially successful, and move right along on slower portions. If the information you are giving is sounding dry, tell a brief anecdote that illustrates the "lesson" or ask the students to share their own experience. If you invite questions and don't get any, ask students questions of your own.

Learn on the job. Even though you're coming to class well prepared, a student may ask a question you don't have a sure or full answer for or point out something you didn't know. Be willing to learn, find answers, and solve problems together. You're facilitating a learning process, not delivering wisdom from on high.

Cut yourself some slack. As Jennifer gently reminds us, most new teachers are a little shaky at first.

Collect evaluation forms at the end of class. These will help you think about what you'll do differently next time.

Evaluate and refine your teaching practice. After class is over, go over the completed evaluation forms and curriculum criteria you spelled out in Step 3. Did the students learn what you hoped they would? How did what you did aid or impede that learning? Are you on track to achieve the goals you set? Jot down any notes or adjustments in your curriculum, and feel proud of yourself for feeding those hungry minds.

Teach—and learn.

CONGRATULATIONS!

Hey teach, give yourself an apple. You did it!

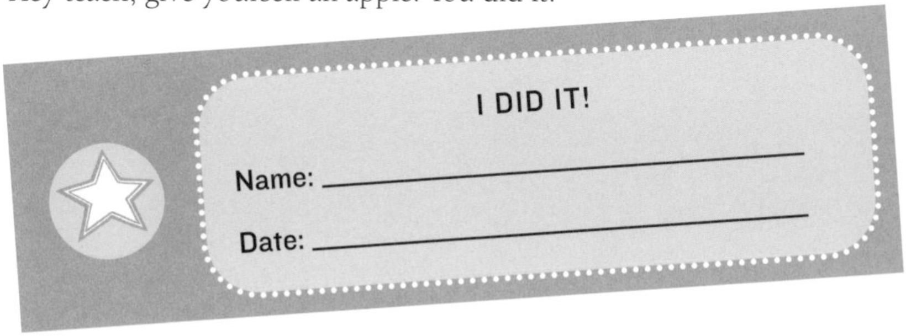

TEACHING OPPORTUNITIES

Here are two to try

AmeriCorps. More than 40,000 members each year serve in every part of the U.S. through national groups like Boys and Girls Clubs and local community centers and places of worship. After completing a term of service, which can be full-time, part-time, or reduced part-time, members are eligible to receive an education award to pay for higher education or training or to repay qualified student loans. www.americorps.org.

4-H. This one-hundred-year-old organization relies on local volunteers to teach fun and practical skills that range from community gardening and photography to riding horses and designing Web sites. They are always looking for new leaders and welcome new club ideas. Their established courses will teach you a great deal about interactive learning as well. www.4-h.org.

BEYOND THE BADGE

If you love it as much as you thought you would, dream on . . .

- **Get new students.** Now that you've taught a class, evaluated it, and have some ideas for improving it, teach it again. Seek new students in the way you did before, or sell or offer your class in a new venue—an after-school program, adult education program, senior center, or appropriate business. Don't forget to solicit testimonials from the students you have taught to add to your course description!
- **Go back to school.** Get a teaching credential (see Get Certified), learn to teach Special Ed, become a Montessori teacher, get an advanced degree in your subject area, or learn to teach ESL (English as a second language). Now that you've gotten a taste for it, there's no telling what you might learn—and teach!
- **Teach one-to-one.** If you like the personal interaction of teaching, try tutoring. Jennifer reminds us that research has shown that such intensive and personal instruction is highly effective. You might sign up as a tutor with a not-for-profit organization that teaches adults to read, through a business such as a language school or tutoring center, or by advertising your services through flyers and classified ads.

GET CERTIFIED

How?

Teaching credential requirements vary by state (and are sometimes modified by states to deal with temporary teacher shortages). Learn about your state's requirements by:

- Contacting your State Department of Education in the government pages of your telephone directory.
- Typing in your state at www.uky.edu/Education/TEP/usacert.html. This University of Kentucky College of Education site collects and presents the teacher certification requirements for all fifty states.
- Calling, visiting, or logging on to the Web site of local colleges or universities with a school of education.

JENNIFER'S PICKS

BOOKS

:: *Core reading for teachers:*

Jennifer recommends the following cycle of books to her students to gain insight into teaching at various levels. In addition to offering practical information, they are at turns funny, poignant, and inspiring reads.

Educating Esme: Diary of a Teacher's First Year by Esme Raji Codell
Esme is a twenty-four-year-old fifth grade teacher in an inner-city Chicago public school.

Lives on the Boundary: The Struggles and Achievements of America's Underprepared by Mike Rose
Written by the director of the writing program at UCLA, this memoir shows the power educators can have on a developing mind.

Schoolteacher by Dan C. Lortie
The first text to look demographically at who teachers are and why they choose to teach.

Small Victories: The Real World of a Teacher, Her Students, and Their High School by Samuel G. Freedman
Follows a teacher through a year at a high school on Manhattan's Lower East Side.

White Teacher by Vivian Gussin Paley
Shadows a kindergarten teacher and her multicultural class.

:: *Other useful books on teaching:*

Becoming a Teacher by Forrest W. Parkay and Beverly Hardcastle Stanford
Helps aspiring teachers answer the questions "What does it take to become a professional teacher?" and "Do I want to teach?"

Developing Life Skills: A Learning Resource Manual for Trainers and Educators Working in Nontraditional Learning Environments by Gillian Squirrell
Specially developed for use in nontraditional learning environments, this resource organizes activities to help the user customize their curriculum to specific individuals or groups.

Teaching Your Occupation to Others: A Guide to Surviving the First Year by Paul A. Bott
A survival guide for new teachers, offering numerous methods for instruction not specific to any one subject or content area.

Those Who Can . . . Teach! Celebrating Teachers Who Make a Difference by Lorraine Glennon and Mary Mohler (editors)
Celebrates unforgettable educators through personal reminiscences from contributors—including writers, entertainers, business leaders, religious figures, politicians—and of course, teachers themselves.

WEB SITES

www.education-world.com
Education World is billed as "The Educator's Best Friend." Lots of original content on teaching and integrating technology, plus hundreds of links.

www.sitesforteachers.com
Sites for Teachers offers thousands of links to education Web sites and resources.

www.teacherscount.org
Teachers Count is a nonprofit dedicated to supporting educators.

54

COMMUNE WITH NATURE

★ camping ★

When you consider things like the stars, our affairs don't seem to matter very much, do they?

—Virginia Woolf

So, what's your motivation?
Take a moment.
Dream a little, think big,
and then complete this sentence:
I see myself . . .

Imagine This . . . You're as comfortable in a sleeping bag under the stars as you are in a four-poster bed. You've dined at a chi-chi restaurant on top of a downtown skyscraper, but it couldn't compare to that memorable meal of apples and cheese on top of a mountain that scrapes the sky. And while you love the hustle-bustle that surrounds you every day in the city, you sometimes crave the sounds of silence and the sights and scents of a more natural, less electronic world. That's when you grab a little gear and head for the hills, desert, or shore. Because with a little help from this badge, you can get around the great outdoors and stay in touch with nature. Even if only for a weekend, you're one happy camper. You can do it!

The Payoffs

- **Mental health.** "Getting away from it all" is a common phrase because it's such a common yearning. You needn't go too far or too wild to feel the benefits.
- **Physical health.** It's easier to exercise, breathe deeply, and avoid fast food and fast living in a natural outdoor setting.
- **Adventure.** No matter how many maps and guidebooks you consult, there are always variables (like the weather) in nature. When you embrace the unexpected, you'll find great adventure and greater self-reliance.
- **Experience.** Bird-watchers keep lifelong lists of the species they've spotted. Others log the miles they've hiked or state parks they've slept in. Even if you're most proud of doing without a blow-dryer, spending a couple of days outdoors will add to your list of life experiences.

Meet Your Mentor

KAREN BERGER

What She Does: A multifaceted outdoorswoman, Karen is the author of numerous books on hiking, backpacking, adventure travel, and even scuba diving. She has been a contributing editor for *Backpacker,* the outdoor expert for GORP.com, the "outdoor smarts" columnist for *Scouting,* and a technical consultant for the PBS television show, *Trailside*. Her outdoor adventure stories have been published in newspapers and magazines too numerous to mention.

Why She Does It: "I was born in Manhattan and grew up in the New York suburbs. I went to summer camp as a kid, and my childhood passions quickly became books, music, travel, and the outdoors—the same loves that fuel my professional work now. I studied music at Northwestern and got into journalism through an internship. At the same time, my summer camp experiences led me into environmental issues and gigs as a supervisor at my old childhood camps, as an outdoor educator, and with the Sierra Club's Inner City Outings program. There are hiking trails and ways to get out from under concrete everywhere. I lived in Bronxville, New York, for thirteen years, and even there, there was a trail within minutes of my house. There are state parks, there are county parks, there are rail trails. Within an hour's drive of just about every city, you can really be outside. Eventually, my husband and I decided to hike the 3,000-mile Continental Divide. We wrote *Where the Waters Divide* about that trek, and the positive attention it received led to lots of other projects."

A view is better
when it is EARNED.

—Karen Berger

Word from the Wise: "I begin one of my books by telling readers why I'd rather walk to the top of a mountain than drive there. The same applies to getting outdoors in general: 'Because the world looks different at two miles an hour. Because spring comes one flower at a time . . . Because of the way wind cools the skin and a snowflake stings the tongue . . . Because it's a way to reconnect with a simpler world, and with ourselves.'"

BADGE STEPS

TEN ESSENTIALS

Back to nature and back to basics

Karen recommends you bring the items on the following list, first assembled in the 1930s by The Mountaineers, a Seattle-based hiking, climbing, and conservation organization.

1. **Map.**
2. **Compass.**
3. **Water.** The Mountaineers advise outdoor travelers to bring not only water but a way to purify water (a filter or iodine or Potable Aqua tablets, available at outfitters).
4. **Food.** To simplify your outing, forget cooking stoves or fires. Simply load up on sandwich fixings, beef jerky, candy or granola bars, apples and oranges, peanut butter, and other food that doesn't require refrigeration. If it's hot or you are car camping, you might bring a cooler. And don't forget raisins, nuts, and dried fruit—it's called trail mix for a reason!
5. **First-aid kit.**
6. **Warm clothing and waterproof outerwear.**
7. **Firestarter and matches.** In case you need to set an emergency signal fire to get help—which, obviously, can only be safely set in a clear and contained area.
8. **Army knife.**
9. **Flashlight.**
10. **Sunscreen and sunglasses.**

1. Make a date with the great outdoors.

An ideal beginner's outdoor excursion can be done over a weekend, with not too much time required to get there and back, and plenty of time once there to hike, observe the wonders around you, or just sit by a babbling brook with a good book. We suggest you plan an overnight outing so you can watch night fall, hear nature sleep, and feel blanketed by the stars. Take a friend along on your first outing; you are likely to feel safer and more comfortable this way.

Where to go? Check one of the directories or Web sites in Karen's Picks to learn what's accessible and appealing within a two- to three-hour drive; go to your local outdoors outfitter (like REI) and look at the guidebooks devoted to local outings; or ask outdoorsy friends about their favorite spots nearby.

Spend some time comparing the attributes of various destinations. Would you like one that doesn't allow RVs or one that offers showers? Once you find the perfect spot, make a reservation by phone, through the Web site, or through one of the online reservation services in Karen's Picks, page 443. Also buy or borrow a guidebook, and read up on the area. ***Plan to go wild.***

2. Pack light and right.

Karen advises that as a beginner you should beg, borrow, or rent gear. You can invest in your own stuff once you've decided you definitely want to spend more time camping and have a better sense of what you really need. The basics:

Tent. Unless you are using the cabins, huts, or lean-tos available at some sites, you'll want a tent. Beggars and borrowers can't be too choosy, but if you are renting, you may be spoiled for choice. Ask the outfitter to recommend one, explaining where you are going and that you are a beginner. Practice putting up your tent a few times before you go, and don't forget to use a ground cloth under the tent to protect the tent bottom from roots and rocks.

Sleeping bag. Know the nighttime temperature at your destination so you can bring a bag that will keep you toasty but not too hot (most bags list the temperature range they serve right on the tag). Don't assume that because you're headed for the desert, you should buy a light bag—it can get cold out there! Consider bringing an air mattress or foam pad for under your bag, to make roughing it a little less rough on your back.

Daypack or backpack to bring on hikes. Bring one big enough to hold your rain gear, one more layer of clothing than you think you'll need, a hat, water, snacks, and your first-aid kit. A pack with a waist belt will keep your stuff from bouncing around.

In addition to the items on the Ten Essentials list, consider bringing:

- A sketchbook or notebook.
- Your guidebook and small pocket or fold-out guides to birds, stars, or plant life.
- Binoculars and/or a camera to spot wildlife.
- A fully charged cell phone in case of emergency. You won't be able to count on the phone working everywhere, but climbing a ridge can improve your wilderness reception.

Get geared up to camp out.

3. Get your bearings.

You will probably get more out of your trip if you do a little homework on the front end:

- Read up on your destination, including the kinds of plant and animal life you may encounter.
- Refresh your memory about first-aid techniques, and familiarize yourself with the contents of your first-aid kit.
- Learn to identify poison oak, poison ivy, poison sumac (less common), and stinging nettles.
- Practice using your compass. Outdoor primers like Karen's include clear, complete directions—or you can always ask your outfitter or a compass-adept friend to show you the ropes.
- Familiarize yourself with maps of your destination. You'll find them in guidebooks, at your outdoor outfitters, and probably at the ranger station at your destination as well.

Prepare yourself for a great adventure.

4. Set out on your adventure.

If there is a ranger station at your destination, you'll check in, receive instructions, and pick up maps. Now what?

WHAT TO WEAR?

On the trail, practicality is paramount!

- A rain jacket of some kind—or a cheap waterproof poncho—is essential because you never know when a little rain might fall.
- Hats are important since covering or uncovering your head is the best way to warm up or cool down.
- Bring enough clothing to layer on or off as needed.
- Sneakers or running shoes should be just fine for your feet. If you plan to hike off-trail, bring lightweight boots made of fabric and leather. Break in new shoes before you go!
- Choose nylon or nylon and wool socks instead of cotton for an added layer of cushioning and to absorb and keep water away from your skin (which can cause blisters).

TOPO TIPS

Learn the lay of the land

Topographic maps, or "topos," aren't essential unless you are venturing into really remote or wild terrain, but they are fun! In addition to the usual roads, rivers, and borders, topos show cliffs, passes, mountains, depressions, ridges, and ravines. The U.S. Geological Survey will send you a free index of its maps for every state, and outfitters carry handy waterproof versions that show campgrounds, ranger stations, and backcountry campsites. Landscapes are not static, so it's important to check the date on topos. The best way to get comfortable with topos (or any map) is to take one on a well-marked trail and compare what you are seeing to what's on the map.

I DID IT!

"I'd been camping and hiking for years, so I thought I'd challenge myself with an organized wilderness trip. One of our assignments was to make camp and sleep alone one night. I really enjoyed setting up my tent, cooking myself dinner, and then reading by candlelight for a while. But once I'd put all my little fires out and gotten into my sleeping bag, the night sounds started to fray my nerves. When I heard what sounded like Big Foot stomping around right outside my tent, I screwed up my courage and pulled back the tent flap just a crack. I saw a deer just a few feet away, gorgeously lit by the full moon. We made eye contact, I nodded 'Hey there,' and then I fell asleep with a big grin on my face."

—Marcella

DRINK UP

"I was with a bunch of friends in Yosemite. The weather was warm and gorgeous, and I ran around with my three ecstatic kids and two never-happier dogs all day. This is how I spent most days at home, so I wasn't worried when I was tired. But even I knew something was wrong when I got a horrible headache and every muscle in my body felt like Jell-O. My husband wound up speeding me to the nearest emergency room. I wasn't dying, just dehydrated. When I run around now, I run around with a nice big bottle of water."

—Louise

KAREN'S EXPERT TIPS

BE KIND TO MOTHER NATURE

Do nature and your fellow nature lovers a favor by treading lightly on the land. Karen says it's like kindergarten: Remember to pick up your toys, clean up your mess, and leave things as you found them. Here are a few hints:

- Garbage? "Pack it in, pack it out!"
- Even if you have biodegradable soap, don't wash yourself, clothes, dishes, etc., directly in a stream, lake, or spring.
- Be conscious of noise pollution. Only listen to a radio with earphones, and reserve your cell phone use for emergencies. Even if the campers at an adjacent site are whooping and hollering, most people venture out to get away from such annoyances—so be considerate.

Hit the trail. As Karen enthuses, "Hiking is great, low-impact exercise—and best of all, it's exercise that doesn't feel like drudgery." That said, stick to marked trails for now, don't forget your daypack, and take it easy. Karen cautions that "all miles are not created equal." Is it hot or cold? Is the hike uphill? What's the elevation? Is this the first time you've ever worn a backpack? Stay in your comfort zone and build cushion time into your hike so that you have time to savor a gorgeous view or ponder a pine without worrying about being on unfamiliar turf at nightfall.

Talk to the animals. You can often get quite close to birds in the wild, and Karen says you can call a bird to you even without a fancy whistle or technique. Try loudly kissing the back of your hand, or calling "pish, pish, pish" several times. Aside from birdcalls, remember that noise keeps most animals away—so tone it down if you want to raise your chances of an encounter.

Observe. With your handy pocket guides at your side, sit in one spot and see how many different flowers, plants, and signs of animal life you can note. Or go on a scavenger hunt, looking for the specific birds, plants, rocks, etc., that you've read might be at your location.

Sketch and take notes. Draw or describe the size, shape, texture, and surroundings of what you see. As Karen says, "Sketching is a great idea. I recently started doing this even though I can't draw well at all, because if you try to sketch what you are seeing, your attention to detail is heightened. Plus, things you draw become much more imprinted on your memory." ***Explore and enjoy your surroundings.***

5. Goodnight, moon.

Your nighttime routine in nature is a little different. With a day of hiking behind you, you might find yourself getting sleepy earlier than usual, but before tucking yourself in, make your foodstuffs inaccessible so as not to attract unwanted critters while you sleep. Don't keep them with you in your tent; your car's trunk is a much better bet. If your car is far away, you can bag your food and hang it from a tree branch. If you're in bear country, toss anything with a food-like scent (including toothpaste) into a bag hung from a high branch or a locked bin. Also remove anything edible from your daypack and put your shoes and clothes out of harm's way—your salty sweat can attract some animals.

What's there to look at when there's no TV and no Internet? Check out what our ancestors watched: the sky. Get out your flashlight and pocket guide to the stars, and prepare to be star-struck:

- Identify constellations, stars that appear to be in groups when looked at from Earth. Many constellations are named after Greek gods and goddesses—see if you can find these, and recall any mythical tales about them.
- Learn which planets are visible to the naked eye, and see how many you can identify.
- See if you can discern slight differences in the colors of stars, and look up what that means about their age and temperature.
- Look for shooting stars—summer meteor showers are more visible without the interference of streetlights.

Wish upon a star and have sweet dreams.

CONGRATULATIONS!

Aren't you the natural wonder?! Happy trails to you . . . You did it!

I DID IT!

Name: ______________________________

Date: ______________________________

STAYING SAFE

As Karen writes, "If you are going to spend any time where there is no access to medical help, you need to have first-aid training." Your local American Red Cross chapter can tell you where and how to get trained.

- If you get hooked on wilderness adventures, take a course on wilderness first aid.
- Bear in mind (no pun intended!) that if you get into trouble out of ignorance, by being reckless, or by not being prepared, you also endanger those who will work to get you out of your jam.
- Remember that hypothermia, or the inability of the body to keep itself warm, is a bigger outdoor threat than bears, snakes, Lyme disease, and the host of other things we fear "out there." Hypothermia is not just a problem in the winter. Especially if you are hiking and generating a bit of body heat, cold can creep up on you. So can wind and rain.
- Always carry a hat, an extra layer of clothing, and rain protection.
- Don't go far without water, snacks, and a first-aid kit.
- Drink lots of water to avoid dehydration and prevent altitude sickness.

BEYOND THE BADGE

If you love it as much as you thought you would, dream on . . .

- **Add adventure to your life.** Go farther, stay longer, add activities—these are all things you'll want to try when you get bit by the outdoor bug. Take your cue from one of Karen's books and go on a backpacking trip where you carry everything you need on your back. Trek the Appalachian Trail, climb the Himalayan foothills in Nepal, or follow the footsteps of medieval pilgrims in the Pyrenees. Add rafting, kayaking, or rock climbing through a wilderness school like Outward Bound. (See Adventure Schools for more.)
- **Bring it on home.** Instead of going to the gym, hike, jog, or bike in the wildest spot in your town. Take your sketchbook and binoculars into your backyard or local park, and play naturalist there. Investigate opportunities to preserve and protect nature in your neighborhood. What local species or plants are endangered? Your local humane society can clue you in to opportunities to learn more about work with wild animals, from orphaned fawns to injured shorebirds. Community volunteers often maintain local trails and creeks. You don't need special skills and will likely enjoy meeting kindred spirits during the hours you volunteer.
- **Star search.** You may not have majestic redwoods, grazing elk, or watchful owls at home, but you do have the stars. Invest in a home telescope, visit a nearby planetarium to learn more, and see if a local astronomy club ever hosts "star parties"—friendly and educational gatherings where enthusiasts watch the sky together. (For a list of some of the biggest annual star parties, go to www.skyandtelescope.com.)

ADVENTURE SCHOOLS

Learn as you go

Adventure Travel Society. Promotes sustainable adventure travel and provides planning info. www.adventuretravelbusiness.com.

Backroads. Destinations around the world. www.backroads.com.

GORPtravel. The adventure travel resource section of Great Outdoors Recreation Pages. gorptravel.away.com.

National Geographic Expeditions. Many of these are headed by a National Geographic expert. www.nationalgeographic.com/ngexpeditions.

KAREN'S PICKS

BOOKS

:: *Directories:*

Coleman National Forest Campground and Recreation Directory
From popular destinations to seldom-visited gems, there are over 4,300 National Forest campgrounds across the United States, all of which are mapped out and described in this guide.

Woodall's 2004 North America Campground Directory
Considered the "most widely used and respected campground directories," Woodall is known for its accurate, reliable, and up-to-date rating system.

:: *Guide books:*

The Complete Guide to America's National Parks: The Official Guide to All 384 National Parks by Fodor's
This guide lists everything to see and do in America's parks, and if the 600-page guide is too big for your pack, pick up Fodor's guides to National Parks of the West or East.

National Geographic Guide to the State Parks of the United States
More than 200 state parks in all 50 states skillfully covered in classic *National Geographic* style.

Trailside Guide: Hiking and Backpacking by Karen Berger
Introduction to hiking and backpacking with color photos.

:: *Field guides:*

National Audubon Society Field Guide to North American Butterflies
A handy field guide with more than 1,000 photographs, measurements, and descriptions of North American butterflies.

National Audubon Society Field Guide to North American Mushrooms
Most comprehensive photographic field guide to identifying more than 700 mushrooms in North America—with tips on cooking and eating, too!

Newcomb's Wildflower Guide by Lawrence Newcomb
The perfect guide for quickly identifying wildflowers, flowering shrubs, and vines.

The Sibley Field Guide to Birds of Western North America by David Allen Sibley
The new standard of excellence in bird identification guides; this guide covers more than 810 North American birds in amazing detail.

ASSOCIATIONS

American Hiking Society
www.americanhiking.org
Dedicated to promoting hiking and preserving the great outdoors for future generations.

Federal Recreation Areas
www.recreation.gov
Offers information on biking, climbing, historic/cultural sites, fishing, hiking, horseback riding, museum/visitor centers, and wildlife viewing in Federal Recreation Areas across the country.

Sierra Club
www.sierraclub.com
"The Club" is America's oldest, largest, and most influential grassroots environmental organization.

CAMPING RESERVATION SERVICES

KOA
www.koakampgrounds.com
With over 500 locations, KOA is handy for last-minute campsites.

National Park Service
www.nps.gov/parks.html
Select a National Park, search campgrounds by interests, and make reservations.

Reserve USA
www.reserveusa.com
The largest outdoor reservation service in the country, operated by the National Recreation Reservation Service.

GEAR

L.L. Bean
www.llbean.com
Offers affordable, quality outdoor gear and apparel.

REI
www.rei.com
Renowned supplier of specialty outdoor gear, currently serving more than 2 million active members.

Title 9 Sports
www.title9sports.com
Inspired by, created for, and run by women, Title 9 Sports offers women's athletic apparel.

55

TRACE YOUR ROOTS

★ genealogy ★

To forget one's ancestors is to be a brook without a source, a tree without a root.

—Chinese proverb

So, what's your motivation?
Take a moment.
Dream a little, think big,
and then complete this sentence:
I see myself . . .

Imagine This . . . Even after you knew all about the birds and the bees, you sometimes still wondered, "Where did I come from?" So you made like a detective, researching, interviewing, and piecing together clues to reveal hidden branches of your family tree. The folks in all those fading black-and-white family photos on your great aunt's wall now feel like old friends, the family history section on medical questionnaires no longer flummoxes you, and best of all, you now know whom to thank for your dimpled chin. So c'mon super sleuth, make it easy on your biographers and the next generation. You can do it!

The Payoffs

- **Connections.** Most of us no longer live upstairs or down the block from our relatives. And because we may only see family elders once a year around a sleep-inducing turkey dinner, we may not talk much about family legends. Tracing your roots can help make up for the lost time.
- **Perspective.** Genealogical research marks your place in a family line that extends into the past, rolls through the present, and reaches into the future.
- **Surprise!** You'll likely find one or two. Happily, the secrets, skeletons, and even health issues hidden by previous generations tend to be much less scary with the benefit of historical perspective.
- **Make history**. Correct, amplify, and illuminate your history, and you have something to leave the next generation: a solid foundation they can treasure and build upon.

Meet Your Mentor

KATHLEEN W. HINCKLEY

What She Does: A genealogist and private investigator, Kathy owns and operates Family Detective (www.familydetective.com), which specializes in locating living persons nationwide. Kathy is the author of genealogy books including *Locating Lost Family Members & Friends* and *Your Guide to the Federal Census,* and served as an expert on the PBS series *Ancestors.* Among her many distinguished professional associations, she is executive director of the Association of Professional Genealogists.

Why She Does It: "I married at age eighteen and moved from South Dakota to North Carolina. I was very homesick, so I began writing letters to my mother asking questions about my ancestors. I didn't know the word 'genealogy'—I just wanted to bridge the distance. When my husband and I adopted two Korean-born children, I put digging around in my ancestry aside because it seemed to contradict our desire to parent children of another race. It took me a while to realize that I could love my adopted children, bring their culture into our lives, and still care deeply about my own ancestry. When I volunteered to start helping other people do family research through my local genealogical society, I found that it was just as exciting for me to find an answer for someone else as it had been to unearth my own history. Eventually I turned my hobby into my business. People are motivated by all kinds of things—a family secret that no one will discuss, family members who feel hollow, because they don't even know if they're German, Irish, or Italian. It's human to want to know as much as we can about who we are."

Learning more about my ancestors gave me an appreciation for history, an understanding of past and present family relationships, and a connection to my Scandinavian heritage.

—Kathy Hinckley

Word from the Wise: "Alex Haley's *Roots* and the American Bicentennial got more people interested, and now with the Internet, genealogy has really taken off. In an uncertain world, what could be more comforting than knowing where you came from?"

BADGE STEPS

1. Interview suspects, er, relatives.

Start by talking to your mother and father or nearest living relatives, and ask for stories and details, not just dates and facts. Don't put this off—Kathy says the number-one regret she hears from amateur and professional genealogists alike is that they wish they'd started sooner, when so-and-so was alive. After all, how else are you going to get the colorful details of your grandmother's experiences building ships in WWII?

Unless you take shorthand, record or videotape your interviews. These will become priceless heirlooms to future generations. Even a tight-lipped or forgetful relative might open up when you open a family photo album. Other relatives do best playing off of one another—"No, no, that's not the way it happened!" or "Of course you remember, it was a dark and stormy night . . . " A family gathering or holiday might be a good time to encourage a gregarious family member to tell family stories, but some relatives might reveal the most one-on-one. ***Get your relatives talking.***

2. Follow your family's paper trail.

Now assemble all the documents, papers, and photos you have. In some families, one person is the *de facto* family historian. Is there someone hanging on to big chunks of family memorabilia in your family? Ask to scour their attic, and enlist their help to find as many family documents as possible. Think beyond the obvious family albums, and seek out military records, land deeds, wills, and the family Bible as repositories of information on family names, dates, and milestones.

Kathy says, "Since memories fade and tend to get modified or embellished as they are passed down, I knew I needed birth, marriage, and death certificates to get started, and my mother provided those. She also had a family scrapbook in which she kept newspaper clippings, and that also gave me clues."

The next thing Kathy suggests is filling in your gaps with census data. Taken every ten years in the U.S., census records are invaluable because you can often find the names and ages of every person in a household, when they emigrated, where they were born, and where their parents were born. Many Web sites offer access to these records, including www.ancestry.com. ***Collect family records.***

HEALTH ISSUES

Tracing your roots can make you healthier . . .

As medical science evolves, knowing your genetic history is becoming more and more important. Kathy once compiled a family history that documented three generations of family members scattered throughout the U.S., Ireland, and England. As she looked at death certificates in the family, she noticed a large number of suicides and many incidents of heart disease, which she then compared to demographic averages to identify whether the family was at risk. This not-so-cheery anecdote shows that poking around your history can reveal a family health condition—knowledge can improve or even save your life. If you discover a health trend or incident that troubles you, talk to your doctor about what you can do.

GET A HEAD START ON HISTORY

. . . with online forms

If you want to create a tidier, more elegant family tree for presentation at a family function, make use of some of the free family tree charts at these Web sites:

www.ancestry.com

wwww.familytreemagazine.com

genealogy.about.com

3. Outline your family tree.

To help you organize the information you're compiling, fill in a family tree chart as you go. In the genealogy trade, different terms are used for these. A Pedigree Chart lists you on the left and branches out to your direct ancestors and their forbears on the right. (Some genealogists think the word "pedigree" is more appropriate to dog breeds than Homo sapiens and prefer the term Ancestor Chart.) Technically, a Family History covers a broader spectrum of relatives, including collateral relatives such as your great-grandfather's brothers and sisters.

Most family tree charts put you at the bottom, then branch upward to your parents, great-grandparents, and so on. The result will look as follows:

Bottom line: you, your siblings, and cousins

Second line: your parents, aunts, and uncles

Third line: your grandparents, great-aunts, and great-uncles

Fourth line: your great-grandparents and their siblings

. . . and so on, as far back as you can trace your history with family documents. Once you've filled in family information that's readily available to you, you'll already have a sketch of a family tree. Impressive, isn't it? ***Plant a tree and watch it grow.***

4. Dig deeper online.

Once you've filled in all the information you can about recent generations using family documents, explore your roots further online. The resources available online are getting better every day, with quick and easy search tools such as those listed in Kathy's Picks, page 451.

Choose which family surname you'll work on first, and as you do, be careful about following false leads. As Kathy says, "A beginner will often take their grandfather's name, and run with it once they've found it in records for the right state and county. They need to realize that there are usually several people of the same age and in the same place with any given name, even uncommon names. Sort this out from the get-go."

As you start to fill in the blanks at the roots of your family tree, you'll discover the thrill of finding clues to your ancestry. To stay on track for great discoveries, be sure that you:

- Start thinking like a slightly neurotic, detail-obsessed record-keeper, and note every lead you follow.

INTERVIEW DOS AND DON'TS

You have ways of making them talk . . .

DO review your research and prepare your questions in advance. You might even want to give your questions to the interviewees beforehand, so they can give them some thought.

DO make careful note of interview dates, times, and places—you're a historian now.

DO get the ball rolling by inviting interviewees to tell (or retell) a favorite or familiar story.

DO use photos or other mementos to jog memories and elicit stories.

DO show your appreciation, and consider sharing a written transcript or copy of any tapes as a thank-you.

DON'T push too hard. Your relatives may have reasons for not wanting to "go there," so be ready to move on if they clam up.

DON'T stick to your agenda like glue. Let relatives go off on tangents, and you may learn more than you ever imagined.

DON'T ask yes or no questions!

I DID IT!

"I'd long wanted to talk to my eighty-something father about his life and times—the Depression, WWII, growing up with immigrant parents. But he's very forward-thinking and always claims he doesn't remember much. It took me eight hours on a transatlantic flight and two glasses of wine to get my mother to talk about her younger days! Then my teen-age daughter got an assignment in class: Interview a parent or grandparent about a significant historical event they lived through. My father wanted to help her, and the stories just flowed out of him. She got an A—and we got an audiotape we'll always treasure."

—Sylvia

FAMILY FEUD

"I saw an ad in the back of a magazine selling surname searches. The price was right and I got a nice, official-looking document that detailed the origins of my family name. But when my sister got interested in genealogy and devoted some time to solid research, we found that what I'd gotten was vague, generic, and just not applicable to us at all. I hate it when my sister is right!"

—Tracie

- Take photos of any documents you find, and make copies if possible.
- Cite your sources and capture their contact information, in case you need to follow up later.
- Identify, caption, and date everything. Don't assume you couldn't possibly forget key clues—write them down!

Uncover your family's roots online.

KATHY'S EXPERT TIPS

HIRING A GUMSHOE

If you don't want to do it yourself . . .

- Read "Why Hire a Professional Genealogist?," a brochure from the Association of Professional Genealogists (APG) that can be found online at www.apgen.org/articles/hire.html, and check out their membership directory to locate a genealogist near you.
- Check for credentials. Consider hiring a professional certified through the Board for Certification of Genealogists (BCG) or a genealogist accredited by the International Commission for the Accreditation of Professional Genealogists (ICAPGen). If you hire someone certified or accredited, you know their skills have been tested and that if there's a problem with their research, you can go to their certifying organization and seek redress.
- Consider the source. One reason to work with a professional is to benefit from their ability to "consider the source" of family information; they know what sources are reliable. If you do work with a professional, insist that they provide you with detailed citations of the sources they used.

5. Check out FamilySearch.

The Church of Jesus Christ of Latter-Day Saints (also known as the Mormons) operates a database of genealogy records that are the most extensive in the world and a boon to amateur and professional genealogists alike. Their records are relevant to all of us—not just church members—holding family and personal histories from over 150 countries going back, in some cases, to the 16th century. Why the interest in genealogy? A basic tenet of this Church is that deceased ancestors can be eternally united with their families, so Church members are encouraged to create family trees.

The database is free online at www.familysearch.org. This site features a library catalog to millions of rolls of microfilm online and access to records that hold over 35 million names (including tens of millions of non-Mormons) organized into families and pedigrees, as well as over 600 million names extracted from international databases, United States census records from 1880 on, the U.S. Social Security death database, and links to thousands of other family history resources. If you prefer hands-on research, look in the Yellow Pages for the nearest Church of Jesus Christ of Latter-Day Saints, and ask about their local Family History Center. ***Search and find long-lost family on FamilySearch.***

6. Preserve and present your findings.

By now you've created a family tree and accumulated a wealth of information and documentation. What will you do with it all? A few options:

- Protect your treasured documents (and photos) from decay by storing them in acid-free boxes and envelopes. You might also consider making copies of some of the most important family documents and putting them in a lovely scrapbook as a gift for your relatives.
- Reproduce and label your audio- and videotapes, and add the originals to your archive.
- Create a beautiful, oversized, handwritten Family Tree Chart (with or without photos and annotations). Once you've finished your creation, take it to a good copy shop, and have it scanned at high resolution and printed on beautiful paper. Frame one of the charts for yourself, and give the rest as gifts to family members (along with copies of your tapes, if you like).

Show off and share your research.

CONGRATULATIONS!

What a lovely tree. You've really branched out! You did it!

I DID IT!

Name: ______________________

Date: ______________________

PICTURE THE PAST

Bring those misty, water-colored memories into the 21st century

- Transfer videos, old films, and even slides and prints to CDs or DVDs. Retailers like Target and Walgreens offer the YesVideo service to help you do this, and your local copy or camera shop should also be able to help. You can even set them to favorite family tunes! (See Kathy's Picks for more.)
- Scan and print copies of your family photographs. The sunlight will damage the originals, so keep them safely tucked away in acid-free boxes or archival albums.
- Frame and display your copies of vintage photos in your home. Bright white matting can make yellowish photos look even dingier, so choose a pale color instead. Creative groupings could include several generations of baby photos, juxtaposing images that highlight family resemblances or historical parallels—that snapshot of your grandfather with the brand-new Packard would look great next to the one of your son with the same now-antique car.

BEYOND THE BADGE

If you love it as much as you thought you would, dream on . . .

- **Write a family history.** If an ancestor died in a cholera epidemic, migrated during the Depression, or crossed the prairie on a wagon train, do a little research and provide a narrative about these larger cultural and historical events. Genealogists call this "putting meat on the bones," and it means adding social history to the usual "so and so begat whosit, who begat what's-her-name . . . " timeline. And if you've got a family memoir in you, turn to Be an Author, page 96.
- **Create a Family History home page.** Or add a link to one on your personal Web site (for more, see Go World Wide, page 124). Check out *Planting Your Family Tree Online* by Cyndi Howells, and make use of the genealogy tools at Web sites such as those in Kathy's Picks.
- **Travel.** Many people who are researching their ancestry plan their family vacations around visiting the spot where an ancestor was married or the house where predecessors were raised. A friend of Kathy's, a woman of Irish descent whose family had been in America for three or four generations, reports that she felt "an indescribable feeling of being at home" while in Ireland on vacation. Pursuing family history leads overseas can be a terrific course of action, especially if you have foreign language skills. Kathy's research into her family "went overseas" quickly. "My family were late immigrants from the Scandinavian countries, and I soon ran out of domestic research to pursue." Kathy's Scandinavian roots were easily excavated because church records there have been saved and microfilmed.
- **Hang up a shingle.** As Kathy notes, most professional genealogists run one-person businesses out of their homes. If you've enjoyed doing your own family excavation, want to use your detective skills, and have a desire to help other people find out more about their own families, review Kathy's Expert Tips and explore certification, accreditation, and professional memberships.

TIME-TRAVELING

Research the past

Explore points of entry. The National Archives and Records Administration has records of immigrants who arrived at points of entry around the U.S.—see www.archives.gov/facilities/index to locate your nearest records center. The ancestors of many Asian Pacific Americans who arrived in the U.S. before 1945 were detained at Angel Island, where detainees carved poems into the walls that are now being restored (see www.aiisf.org for details). Many Europeans immigrated through Ellis Island, and you can make a visit to the museum there or search for your family name on passenger lists for free on the official Web site of the Ellis Island Foundation (www.ellisisland.org).

Expect a few dead ends. Kathy says that if your family has roots in the American South, you should prepare for dead ends when you run into the Civil War period; many records were destroyed in fires during the war. New England roots are much easier to trace, with excellent records going back 200 years. African Americans may have the hardest time tracing their roots to their countries of origin, because during the slavery era many Africans were assigned new names by plantation owners upon arrival, and their surnames were often lost. This is why African-American research requires researching slave owners in conjunction with ancestors.

KATHY'S PICKS

BOOKS

The Complete Idiot's Guide to Genealogy by Christine Rose and Kay Germain Ingalls
An excellent introduction to the adventure and challenge of family histories and genealogy.

Locating Lost Family Members and Friends: Modern Genealogical Research Techniques for Locating the People of Your Past and Present by Kathleen Hinckley
Case studies and research resources show you how to access a wealth of public information on long-lost relatives and find out what happened to them.

Scrapbooking Your Family History by Maureen Taylor
Shows you how to uncover your ancestry, then record and display it in an attractive, well-organized heritage album packed with important family memorabilia.

Your Guide to the Federal Census: For Genealogists, Researchers, and Family Historians by Kathleen Hinckley
Learn how to use the federal census to document families, communities, and social histories with confidence.

WEB SITES

www.ancestry.com
This Web site offers the largest collection of family history info on the Web, with family tree software, a learning center, and message boards. Subscription required.

www.cyndislist.com
An authoritative, regularly updated spot that is a key point of departure for genealogy on the Internet, with more than 220,000 links!

www.digitalmemoirs.biz
Digital Memoirs produces personal documentaries in VHS and DVD formats, capturing personal histories so that future generations can know and appreciate the family legacy.

www.genealogy.com
Easy-to-use tools to start your family tree, run searches, and share your findings with your family.

genealogy.about.com
Top-notch tools and tips, and tons of links.

MAGAZINES

Family Tree
www.familytreemagazine.com
All about discovering, preserving, and celebrating your family history. The Web site offers a search tool kit, an articles archive, and much more.

Heritage Quest
www.heritagequestmagazine.com
Tips for family researchers to make the best use of the Internet and research trips abroad, plan reunions and family organizations, create family scrapbooks, and more.

ASSOCIATIONS

Association of Professional Genealogists
www.apgen.org
Supports high standards in the field and offers an online membership directory to locate qualified genealogists.

Board for Certification of Genealogists
www.bcgcertification.org
Check out their "Skillbuilding" section for dozens of helpful articles on researching family history and their online directory to find certified genealogists.

Federation of Genealogical Societies
www.fgs.org
Supports records preservation efforts nationwide. Members receive a newsletter with tips and updates on the latest developments in genealogy.

International Commission for the Accreditation of Professional Genealogists
www.icapgen.org
Provides hints on hiring an internationally accredited genealogist and tips on how to qualify for certification yourself.

National Genealogical Society
www.ngsgenealogy.org
An indispensable resource for budding family historians, with extensive searchable archives that cover 19th-century newspapers and even family Bibles, online tips and genealogy courses, and a service to help digitize family documents.

56

CONNECT WITH YOUR TRIBE

★ family rituals ★

If you have only one smile in you, give it to the people you love.

—Maya Angelou

So, what's your motivation?
Take a moment.
Dream a little, think big,
and then complete this sentence:
I see myself . . .

Imagine This . . . You are grounded in relationships that provide comfort, identity, and real joy, and your days are enriched by simple traditions—a good morning song with your preschooler, dates with a wise elder in your profession, a New Year's Day hike with your honey—that honor and cement those relationships. When you realized you didn't know enough about your best long-distance friend's daily life, your niece's teenage aspirations and dilemmas, or your mom's dreams, you decided it was time to reenergize your most cherished connections. Rituals to the rescue! With a little upfront investment of time, thought, and team spirit, you've created regular rituals and annual occasions that keep you in touch—with your people and your priorities. *You can do it!*

The Payoffs

- **Depth.** Taking the time and making the effort to connect says we value other people. Making it regular and personal with rituals deepens that connection and your relationships.
- **Security.** Who and what can you count on? For a kid, knowing that mom will check under the bed for monsters makes lights-out easier. For you, knowing that Friday night is stitch-n-bitch time with the girls probably makes end-of-the-week deadlines less scary.
- **Transition team.** Life is change—wanted and unwanted, controllable and uncontrollable. Traditions and rituals provide constancy.
- **Identity.** "Family faces are magic mirrors. Looking at people who belong to us, we see the past, present, and future." (Gail Lumet Buckley)

Meet Your Mentor

MEG COX

What She Does: The author of *The Heart of a Family: Searching America for New Traditions that Fulfill Us* and *The Book of New Family Traditions: How to Create Great Rituals for Holidays and Everyday,* Meg has written wide-ranging articles on these subjects for publications including *Working Mother, Parents, Family Fun, Good Housekeeping, Worth, Cooking Light,* and *Child.* She writes a newsletter on ritual each month, has been a regular columnist for Moms Online at AOL, and has served as a "traditions expert" for companies such as Hallmark and Pillsbury.

Why She Does It: "As a kid, I certainly didn't dream about being a traditions expert when I grew up! I knew I wanted to be a writer and did spend seventeen years at the *Wall Street Journal.* When I finally met the right guy and decided I wanted to have children, I was terrified of not being any good at it. I literally woke up one morning and thought that learning about family rituals—the bonding routines that some families make look effortless—would solve my problem. Being a journalist, I decided to interview people who were good at it, research the subject, and write a book. Right on schedule, as I was deciding to do this, I got pregnant. I did three years of serious, exhaustive research for that first book and got to apply what I was learning at home with my newborn."

Word from the Wise: "I'm very interested in simple, heartfelt rituals that work for the way people actually live right here, right now—not in some parallel Utopian universe where we have tons of time, oodles of creativity, and money is no object. Rituals are really just the things we do that make us feel like family, whether we have blood ties or not, and make disparate individuals feel like they're on the same team."

We need rituals so that the things and people that really matter to us don't fall between the cracks.

—Meg Cox

BADGE STEPS

1. Who do you love?

Wouldn't it be nice to have red-letter dates on your calendar when you know you'll connect with your gal pals, scattered clan, or career kindred spirits? This way, when your schedule (or theirs) leaves you feeling out of the loop, you know you'll be back in touch soon. This badge will help you create the kind of annual gatherings and routine get-togethers that connect you with loved ones and reinforce those connections with rituals that give them their due. Why bother? Meg puts it well: "Given the pace of life in the 21st century, rituals give our need for connection a place and a priority on our jam-packed to-do lists."

First, let's define our terms. Your "tribe" may include your nuclear or extended family, the friends who might as well be family, dear ones you see regularly and all too infrequently, or some combination thereof. To define your tribe, give some thought to who matters most to you. Look in your address books for those folks with whom you wish you had more regular ways of connecting. Make two lists: one of people with whom it's practical to hook up once a year and another of a group you'd like to round up more regularly (say, once a week or once a month). To get your connection momentum going, go ahead and dial the phone number or type out an e-mail to one of the "it's been way too long" names in your address book. ***Define your tribe.***

2. Gather 'round an annual event.

Your tribe all belongs to the same global village, but you probably don't all live in the same neighborhood. Why not plan an annual event to bring everyone together? Check the first list you made in Step 1. Are you yearning for an extended family reunion, a meeting of far-flung college friends, or a summit of mothers and daughters with your sisters and nieces? Chances are, they are too. Consider the following advice as you gather the troops for your first annual get-together:

Start early. Begin planning well in advance; it can be tricky to coordinate dates and travel schedules the first year.

Think about the tribe's needs. Grown-up girlfriends might need a slumber party with lots of time to gab, paint each other's nails, and try out facial recipes. Harried homemakers may want room service and spa treatments. Families with children might prefer the great outdoors. An

THE POWER OF RITUAL

Making every day a special event

Meg stresses that rituals can include everything from a simple grace before a meal to an elaborate wedding. No matter how simple the action, the keys are:

- A beginning, middle, and end that mark this as a special time. (For a mealtime grace this might go: bowing of heads, words of thanks, the word "Amen.")
- It has a purpose—honoring a milestone event, stressing the importance of education to a child, acknowledging a shared belief, or simply celebrating a friendship. One group of women who met while working at the same office decided lunch hours just weren't enough, and started a tradition of yearly spring retreats to talk to their hearts' content. Fifteen years, many job changes, and a few children later, their tradition is still going strong!
- It's personal and reflects your values. Plenty of us participate in family or religious traditions that we didn't invent and maybe don't particularly like. The way to change that is to inject personal meaning and relevance.

extended family may want to celebrate birthdays, honor a relative who has passed, or welcome newborns. Piggy-backing a reunion onto a previously scheduled event such as a wedding or graduation could jump-start the process.

Create a team. Get help—and input—from other participants so that you won't be overburdened. Delegate tasks and assign duties. In successive years, rotate responsibilities.

Minimize hardship. To keep costs down, host the reunion at home or rent a vacation house instead of hotel rooms, cook meals in instead of going out, and plan to rotate locations so the travel burden is shared evenly. If an elderly family member can't travel far, hold the reunion someplace near her home.

Make it special. Signify that this is more than just a casual gathering. To make it a truly historic event, mark the occasion with photos, T-shirts, scrapbooks, a cookbook, etc.

Keep up the momentum. Shoot for a date, or at least month, that will work as an annual gathering time, and set a date for next year's event before this year's event ends.

Pick up the phone and make that annual reunion happen.

3. Set up a standing date.

Now turn to the second list you made in Step 1 of people who are near and dear enough to see weekly or monthly. If you spend more time exchanging calls and e-mails about when you might, maybe, hopefully be able to hook up than you do actually getting together, it's time to carve out some carved-in-stone rituals.

As above, consider the needs and interests of the group. And with the principles of ritual in mind (this special time can be recreated regularly) consider these ideas:

Sit down to Sunday dinners. A great finale to the weekend, Sunday dinner isn't just for nuclear families any more. Whether you head to a restaurant, opt for home cooking, or order in, the point is for everyone to simply sit down together for a few leisurely hours. The gang of annual-getaway girlfriends in The Power of Ritual also meet the first Friday of every month for dinner at an inexpensive restaurant they all love. One added bonus of their long commitment to this ritual is red carpet treatment from the restaurant!

FAMILY TIES

Reunions can strengthen them

Maybe Thanksgiving is your family's *de facto* annual reunion. How's that working for you? Why not create a new or additional event that doesn't occur on the busiest travel day of the year? Reunions can be elaborate affairs, featuring hundreds of descendants, professional photographers, and live entertainment. Restaurants, hotels, and resorts are anxious (no surprise) to help you pull off an elaborate event, but Meg stresses the value of low-stress affairs, too. If your gang isn't the dress up/fine wine/dinner-and-dancing crowd, keep it simple. For tips on organizing a family event that is memorable and manageable, check out Meg's Picks, page 459.

I DID IT!

"My three best girlfriends and I realized that we weren't seeing each other as consistently as we had before husbands, children, and career pressures got in the way. We decided to make a weekly commitment to get together at one friend's home (who had a hard time getting out because of kids) to have dinner, drink wine, knit, and be together. It was important to make it a ritual—no more 'When are you free?' 'Well, MAYBE next week . . . ' kind of thing. And we realize that seeing begets seeing. Now when we see each other on Wednesdays, things come up like, 'We're doing such and such on Friday, want to go?' Most of all, being in each other's lives every week *really* means being in each other's lives. No more catch-up dates."
—Deborah

WHOSE TRADITION ANYWAY?

"Our Christmas Eve routine had turned into a rut—too much work for the hosts, nothing for my young kids to do during the long sit-down dinner. But I couldn't think of a way to bow out. This year, since the usual hostess had been ill, I suggested we gather at my home instead. And since I had neither the time nor the inclination to cook, I ordered take-out Chinese, set up a buffet, and we ate in the living room while listening to holiday music and enjoying a fire in the fireplace. It was such a success that I wondered why I hadn't done it years ago. I think the usual hostess was actually glad to be relieved of the burden. Moral? Change can be good—even with traditions!"
—Chrissie

Take the book club concept and run with it. Whatever you do—knit, watch foreign films, swap clothes, get crafty, or bring in experts to talk to you about the stock market or modern art—give it a regular date on the calendar. Once or twice a month works for many.

Do some barn-raising. This means getting through whatever you have to do anyway (workouts, garage sales, or gardening) with a little help from family or friends. Make a group commitment to meet once every week or month to help one another do what needs to be done. One teacher got tired of saying she didn't have time for coffee with friends on weekends because she had too many papers to grade—so she picked a cozy café and started telling girlfriends they could find her there. Friends bring their own paperwork to do or reading to catch up on, and everyone's surprised by how much they can get done while still checking in with one another.

Start a weekly or monthly ritual that brings you together.

MEG'S EXPERT TIPS

MAKING SPECIAL OCCASIONS MORE MEANINGFUL

Holidays. Ditch traditions that have stopped working (if half the guests have young children, why even attempt long, sit-down meals?), and try new ones. Honor an elder or work on Trace Your Roots, page 444, by drawing them into reminiscences; highlight different cultures by inviting guests to bring and talk about traditional foods; play games. One family plays bingo every year after Christmas dinner, even though no one remembers exactly why. Prizes are quirky and fun, and every generation can participate.

Birthdays. Use those numbers and share your feelings. On sixteen consecutive days, send the niece turning sixteen postcards with messages describing something that makes her special or a wish you have for her life. And Meg has written about a woman who wrote down eighty fond memories she has of her grandmother for, you guessed it, the grandmother's eightieth birthday.

Anniversaries. On her tenth wedding anniversary, Meg made her husband a "book" of top ten lists (Ten Reasons I Love You, Ten Places I'd Love to Visit with You, and so on). Scrapbooks that celebrate a shared history are fantastic. One person created such a book filled with mementos from twenty years of going to rock concerts together, including ticket stubs, photos, song lyrics, etc.

4. Take it day by day.

Our days are already filled with ritualized routines. Maybe your workday wouldn't be complete without an afternoon coffee break with a certain coworker during which you compare notes, vent, and then return to your desk reenergized. But if Annie Dillard is right that how we spend our days is how we spend our lives, couldn't we all stand a bit more meaning and connection, day in and day out? To get your minimum daily connection requirements:

- Create an at-the-ready toolbox. Maybe it's a bottle of champagne you keep chilled in the fridge, a tea service you keep in your office for a quick afternoon klatch, or a stack of stamped postcards you keep at your desk so that when you think of someone, you can drop them a line pronto.
- Look for spontaneous opportunities to bring the benefits of connection and ritual into more places in your life. Meg reminds us that rituals are great ways of solving problems and easing transitions. Some of these opportunities are obvious: a graduation calls for pomp and circumstance, and bedtime is an ideal time for parents to soothe and comfort their children. But there are other opportunities to be found, too. When a loved one achieves a goal, such as running a marathon or quitting smoking, this can be cause for celebration. When a friend suffers a setback like a job loss or breakup, ritual and connection can ease the loss. Consider ways you could gather the tribe around a member who deserves a high-five—or a hug. If you're stuck, think about what you would want most in a similar circumstance.

Connect daily.

CONGRATULATIONS!

Group hug, anyone? You did it!

I DID IT!

Name: ______________________________

Date: ______________________________

GO LOW-TECH

And still get high results

Even in the days of e-mail, a regular old telephone call can become a ritual that two (or more) people look forward to and even rely upon. Such a routine can be especially helpful with ailing or aging relatives. For years, Meg had a weekly long-distance phone call with her ill mother. They developed a ritual of working a crossword puzzle together during this call, not because they had nothing to say to each other but in order to avoid the "How are you?/How was your week?" rut—and because it was a favorite activity of Meg's mom! No matter what you do with your time on the phone, "If you make it a regular event," says Meg, "you'll soon find yourself anticipating that call during the week, saving up anecdotes, actresses' outfits to dish, etc. Though you may only speak a few minutes a week, the person you call will become a bigger part of your emotional life throughout the week—and vice versa."

BEYOND THE BADGE

If you love it as much as you thought you would, dream on . . .

- **Connect through service.** A family or group of friends can commit to do volunteer work or another service project together. Examples: cooking and serving in a soup kitchen once a week or on Thanksgiving before your own meal; jointly pledging one Saturday a month to twelve different organizations over the course of a year (see Give a Little Bit, page 476); creating your own grassroots effort (see Champion a Cause, page 46); or even traveling once a year to perform several days of service through an organization like Global Volunteers (www.globalvolunteers.com).
- **Connect—and earn badges.** You can do it with more fun if you earn *You Can Do It!* badges together. Why not make your weekly get-together a time to check in and support a group of friends doing the activities in this book? Create a badge-awarding ceremony or a scrapbook of your group's efforts and successes.
- **Connect through computers.** Remember what our Tech Support expert, Denise Shortt, had to say about computers jumpstarting "communication, connection, collaboration, and community." See Weave a Web of Relationships.

WEAVE A WEB OF RELATIONSHIPS

On the World Wide Web

Create a family or friend Web site. See Go World Wide, page 124, to get started, and turn your Web site into a communal affair by linking to friends' sites; posting reunion, kid, and travel photos; and posting monthly or seasonal updates on what everyone's been up to. Meg knows a family who publishes a monthly family newspaper this way. Family members rotate responsibility, and emphasize different types of content—genealogy, recipes, etc. A good resource is www.geocities.com.

Start a chat group. You can create one just for your family through hosts like Yahoo! and AOL.

Send e-mail. Get creative with this everyday workhorse. Develop a schedule and approach that works well for the participants. Two writers might send each other 250 words of whatever they are working on each day as a way to warm up. People supporting one another in a shared effort to deal with grief, exercise more, or deepen their spiritual life might send each other short, daily, inspirational quotes.

MEG'S PICKS

BOOKS

The Book of New Family Traditions: How to Create Great Rituals for Holidays and Everyday by Meg Cox
Fun, simple everyday rituals for bedtime, dinnertime, even day-care drop-off, plus tons of celebration ideas for birthdays, holidays, and all manner of milestones.

Family Reunion: Everything You Need to Know to Plan Unforgettable Get-Togethers by Jennifer Crichton
Advice about many sizes and types of reunions, with sidebars on everything from genealogy software to grilling for a crowd.

A Grateful Heart: Daily Blessings for the Evening Meal from Buddha to the Beatles by M. J. Ryan (editor)
The title says it all: most are short and sweet.

How to Bury a Goldfish . . . and 113 Other Family Rituals for Everyday Life by Virginia E. Lang and Louise Nayer
Like Meg, these women favor simple rituals that deepen the bonds of family and friends.

The Joy of Family Rituals: Recipes for Everyday Living by Barbara Biziou
Fun ideas for assembling a ritual toolkit.

Lights of Passage: Rituals and Rites of Passage for the Problems and Pleasures of Modern Life by Kathleen Wall, PhD, and Gary Ferguson
Less for families and more for creating rituals throughout life; includes rituals for marking divorce, new beginnings, and entering midlife.

The Thundering Years: Rituals and Sacred Wisdom for Teens by Julie Tallard Johnson
Both wise and practical, this would be a terrific gift for a teenager planning his or her own rite of passage.

Your Family Reunion: How to Plan It, Organize It, and Enjoy It by George G. Morgan
This author writes a genealogy column; especially good for first-timers.

MAGAZINES

Family Fun
www.familyfun.com
The best of the parenting mags for good ideas about traditions and rituals.

Meg Cox's Ritual Newsletter
It's free, practical, wise, and fun! To subscribe, write to Meg at FamilyRituals@aol.com.

Reunions Magazine
www.reunionsmag.com
Six issues a year full of ideas from other family and class reunions; the Web site has tons of info on good reunion locations, vendors for souvenirs, and more.

WEB SITES

www.family-reunion.com
Offers an amazingly thorough planning and resource guide.

www.ritualwell.org
Billed as a resource on "ceremonies for Jewish living," its content is actually broader and contains great ideas for women's rites of passage.

57

PLAY THE FIELD

★ dating ★

Every pot will find its lid.

—Yiddish proverb

So, what's your motivation?
Take a moment.
Dream a little, think big,
and then complete this sentence:
I see myself . . .

Imagine This . . . Whether you're looking for one true love or a few fantastic people to share your fabulous life with, your dance card is full and fulfilling. You no longer think of a first date as a cross between a root canal and a nerve-wracking public speaking engagement, and your last breakup has stopped flashing before your eyes. You don't spend hours on the phone saying "all the good ones are taken," and "it's a jungle out there," because you've busted the myth that you can't change or control the number or quality of your dates. Turns out all you need to do is define your interests, get out and about, and make your wishes known to the right people and in the right places. Ready for a hot date? *You can do it!*

The Payoffs

- **Fun.** You might not think the words "fun" and "dating" go together—but with the right attitude and approach, dating can feel more like play than work.
- **Choice.** When you date the way our expert describes, you're not waiting for the phone to ring or Cupid to give you a nod. Instead, you're increasing your choices about how you spend your time and who you spend it with.
- **Self-knowledge.** While you're getting to know others, you'll learn a thing or two about yourself—who you are, what you want and need, and how you can evolve.
- **Love.** There are no guarantees, but unless your next love happens to wear a UPS uniform and rings your doorbell, dating increases your odds of finding each other.

Meet Your Mentor
NINA ATWOOD

What She Does: Nina is a licensed therapist and the author of *Be Your Own Dating Service: A Step-by-Step Guide to Finding and Maintaining Healthy Relationships* and *Soul Talk: Powerful, Positive Communication for a Loving Relationship*. Nina regularly dispenses advice about love and dating for national media, including *Cosmopolitan, Men's Health,* and *Health*.

Why She Does It: "While I was completing my master's, I started a 'dating coach' practice. I did this because I'm one of those people who did not develop relationship wisdom easily or automatically. I'm twice divorced, so I don't come at this from a high and mighty position—it's more like low and learning! I've learned much the hard way, and when I was learning my lessons, I found there weren't many good tools out there for people like me. There was advice about how to flirt, but not much that really looked at the dynamics of attraction and attachment. So I started doing my own research on dating. One of the first things that I found was that when we feel like we don't have a lot of choices, we tend to make poor choices. But when we have a sense of abundance, that there are lots of good people out there, we tend to make much better choices."

© Debra O'Brien

Word from the Wise: "It's wise to look at dating as practice. It's not that you are guaranteed to meet the love of your life and/or that all your problems will be solved. It's more about moving out of dissatisfying patterns or paralysis. When I begin working with single people, many of them say they have to find someone because they are so miserable. At the end of our work together, they may still be single, but they are also happier and know more about living full, rich, wonderful lives—single, dating, and in relationships."

Single life is the perfect time to step back, take a look at how we're playing the dating game, and learn about life and love.

—Nina Atwood

BADGE STEPS

1. Conquer your fears.

Three dates, with three different people, in three months. Nutty? Not at all, once you face your fears and recognize any relationship ruts you tend to fall into. "Fear sets in after relationship or dating experiences that are disappointing or painful, and to avoid future pain, we construct emotional barriers around our hearts," explains Nina. "But in being guarded from pain, we are also blocked from love because love calls for an open heart and the willingness to take risk." How do we get there from where we are now? Nina offers the following advice:

Map out your past few relationships. List your recent partners' traits, how you felt with them, and how things ended. Notice any common themes or patterns? Is there a type you are attracted to or certain red flags you tend to ignore?

Chalk it up to experience. As you look at your map of prior relationships, commit to learning from the past and to making more conscious choices about your future.

Take your sweet time. Don't go rushing into your next relationship to escape the past (see Why Date?). "Progress slowly, and take the time to really get to know someone," says Nina. "For most women, becoming sexually intimate radically ramps up their emotional risk, so putting off sex helps create more emotional safety."

Learn from your past relationships, and prepare for your future!

2. Define your ideal date.

Whether we're looking for happy dates or happily ever after, it helps to daydream and define. So visualize yourself with your ideal companion, and write about what you see. Be as specific as you can, and try to get past boilerplate ideas like funny (what does that mean to you?) and kind (please elaborate!):

- What kind of activities do you share? (Hiking, camping, or enjoying the great outdoors? Sitting by a fireplace and talking? Going out dancing or to sporting events?)
- What are the qualities of the relationship that you share together? (Comfort and companionship, passion, spiritual connection, etc.)

WHY DATE?

Good answers

Nina says there are three stages of relationships. Stage one is the grief, loss, and recovery that follow the end of a relationship, and stage three is being in an exclusive relationship. Stage two, dating around, often gets short shrift because we want to zoom out of stage one and into stage three. But our expert says that if we spend some time in stage two assessing our needs, meeting lots of new people, and sorting through them to find a partner who isn't just there but is actually good for us, we stand to gain:

- An expanded sense of possibility and greater sense of confidence.
- The sense that we are in control of our love lives, that they are not merely subject to luck and chance.
- A more fulfilling life as a single and increased chances of being part of a happy couple.

- What are the character traits of the person that you see yourself with? (Open and warm, passionate about politics, knows how to play, etc.)

Also define your "nonnegotiables"—the traits and behaviors that you can't live with and the ones you can't live without. If you know, like Nina, that you could not be happy with someone who thought therapy was silly, write it down. Ditto if you know you want someone who wants children and believes in sharing home and child care responsibilities. Nina would rather see us "being a little too selective," instead of "settling for someone who doesn't share our most basic values in life." ***Describe your dream date with a dreamboat.***

3. Describe yourself.

Now turn the attention on yourself. Write down a description of yourself, answering the following:

- What do I love to do? (Play tennis, go to the theater, garden?)
- What do I do well? (Your work, entertaining friends, listening?)
- What do I wish I did more of? (Travel, exercise, reading, writing?)
- How do I spend my money? (Food, music, charity, films?)

Pretend that you are introducing yourself to a stranger . . . or better yet, that a good friend is introducing you. What would they say? Find out by asking one or two to write up a short description of you. You'll learn how good you look on paper, plus you might find an area or two where you'd like to see some growth or change. If you choose to investigate Internet dating, this could be your online profile. ***Write one to three pages about yourself, and ask a close friend to describe you in writing.***

4. Meet your match.

To meet the person you described in Step 2, you'll need to broaden your social network. Nina advises you to be "bold and varied in your methods of meeting new people," and suggests that you:

Spread the word. Tell your friends and anyone else in your social circle (including people like your hairdresser, yoga teacher, and librarian if you like and trust them) that you are interested in meeting any friends and acquaintances of theirs who might be suitable.

Get busy with groups and activities. Do what you want to do anyway (volunteering, a class, a new sport), and you'll enrich your life—whether

PERSONAL GROWTH

The common denominator in all your relationships is you, so

- Understand that perfect people don't exist. Like everyone else, you have quirks, flaws, an imperfect relationship history, and emotional baggage.
- Be realistic in your expectations of people, starting with yourself. Work on accepting yourself as you are and as an evolving person.
- Work on that evolution. Improve your communication skills: Practice asking for what you want and talking about your feelings.
- Become someone you'd enjoy spending time with. Take an inventory of your character traits, and work on the ones you'd like to alter. Do you have the traits you are looking for in a partner?
- Cultivate your own sources of happiness and fulfillment. Strive to bring these into your relationships, rather than expecting your relationships to provide them.

I DID IT!

"I was nearing forty and had made a number of really positive changes in my life. I was in a 'good place,' and wanted someone to share it with. After trying everything I could think of that might help me meet a special someone—church, volunteering, online dating, going to parties I didn't want to go to—I finally took the last step: maxing out my credit card to join Great Expectations video dating service. I told myself that I had gone into debt for far sillier things than finding a husband! I was fortunate in that I met my future husband within a month, and we both knew quickly that we were a match. We were engaged nine months later, and now I feel I have married my best friend. He was worth every penny!"

—Rochelle

MATCHMAKING MISFIRES

"I've met the love of my life. We've been together for ten years and want everyone to be as happy as we are. We have a lot of single friends, so my partner and I started talking about making some matches. It was pretty fun to think of the people we knew who didn't know each other but who we thought might click. But the chess pieces just wouldn't move as we instructed! We've learned, the hard way, to make introductions and then let people do what they will. We can't make them call each other or go on their dates for them—even if we know they'd be perfect together."

—Katrina

you find new friends and dating partners or not. Nina likes church singles groups and arts-related events.

Go online. "Internet matchmaking has evolved into one of the best and easiest ways to make new connections with really great people," says our expert. Check out Nina's Expert Tips, and see Nina's Picks, page 467, for Web sites.

Speed date. It can be rough to get to the end of the evening and find out that no one has requested to meet with you later—much more awkward than not having someone respond to an e-mail. That said, this can be a fun way to make new connections quickly.

Expand your dating pool.

NINA'S EXPERT TIPS

ONLINE DATING

DO be honest in your profile and use a current photo.

DO ask more questions than you might when meeting someone your best friend has known for years. Never ignore a gut feeling that your date has something to hide.

DO get to know your date's background before you become overly invested. Once you're clicking, suggest outings that involve your date's friends, coworkers, or even family members.

DO keep your own safety in mind. Arrange to meet at their work place or a public place, and keep your wits about you—watch the drinking.

DON'T assume that everything you read in someone else's profile is for real. Ask questions about what you read, probe for further details, and consider evasiveness a red flag.

DON'T spend too much time "courting" by e-mail. Talk on the phone when you are interested in someone—and be wary of resistance to this. Arrange a face-to-face early on to ward off disappointment later. You want to make sure that the person you are getting to know is as appealing offline as they are online.

5. Go on a date.

Chances are good that you have now at least eyed—and possibly talked to, e-mailed, or casually met—some new people. If you have not been approached, it's time to take a deep breath and approach someone yourself. You can simply introduce yourself and make it clear that you'd like to see the person again by saying so and offering your phone number, or you can take the plunge and ask for a date yourself. Remember, there are lots of fish in the sea, so the risk is slight, and few people (even if they aren't available or interested) will feel anything but flattered by your attention! When going out with someone you did not meet through a very good friend, follow Nina's "first three dates safety rules":

First date. Coffee or lunch; meet at a café or restaurant; keep it short (one to two hours).

Second date. Lunch, brunch, or after work hours meeting at a restaurant or bar; keep it short again (less than three hours).

Third date. Brunch, after work hours, or dinner; still in a public place; and still keeping it fairly short (three hours or under).

Leave two or three days between dates so that you have time to reflect and make notes about your impressions, particularly if you feel an immediate connection. How many times have we all looked back during a breakup, slapped our foreheads, and wondered why we didn't pay attention to those early red flags—something the other person said or did that we chose not to hear or see at the time but that became a problem down the line? And the converse is true as well: Unless there was less-than-zero chemistry or an obvious lack of common ground, don't be too quick to write off a date.

Nina thinks it's helpful to have a plan for the first few dates to avoid "skyrocket" relationships (that fly and fizzle fast) and to gain "dating around" practice. On a first date, you are finding out if there's enough connection for a second date. On that second date, you are learning if you still click. By that third date, you'll be sharing, listening, and monitoring your feelings to decide whether to keep going. (See Getting to Know You for details.) ***Go on a date—or two, or three—with someone who interests you.***

6. Keep dating.

Now that you've gone out on a couple of dates with someone you've met, check your response. If you feel you're already well on your way to the Healthy Love described on page 466, congratulations! But if you're not quite sure just yet, go out on a date with one or two other people. Nina says that keeping your options open "gives you a sense of abundance and removes the desperation factor. You make better choices because you have more choices." True, dating around can get a little confusing—but not if you keep these tips in mind:

GETTING TO KNOW YOU

To keep the conversation rolling and real communication happening

- Establish rapport by talking about the shared interest or mutual friend that brought you together.
- Pay attention to your body language and your date's, too. People interested in communicating will make eye contact, turn their bodies toward yours, and respond to conversation overtures with enthusiasm.
- Focus on getting to know your date rather than on what the two of you are doing, how you (or your date!) look, or the impression that you are making. Remember the thinking you have done about the kind of person and relationship you are seeking, and bring up subjects and ask questions that elicit this kind of information.
- Probe for details. How do they feel about their work? What do they like to do on weekends? How do they relate to their family? How did their last relationship end, and how long ago did this happen? Ask questions that begin with what or how to avoid getting yes or no answers.

- Make your intentions clear. Be up front about the fact that you are casually dating one (or two) other people at this point and honest (and firm) when you don't want to accept a next date.
- Keep the first few dates nonsexual so you don't get overly attached before you really get a chance to know the person you're dating.
- Beware of controlling personalities. Nina stresses that we should never keep dating someone who exhibits excessive possessiveness, jealousy, or the need to control our time together.
- Make sure your time is respected. Don't wait around for someone who is unreliable or noncommittal about dates and times.
- If your date abuses alcohol or drugs, call it a night—and drive yourself home.
- Break it off after date three if it's not working out. Nina doesn't advise dating more than one person at the same time beyond the three- or four-date point, because someone is likely to become attached and get hurt.
- Pause and reflect as you date. This will help you determine if you want to continue seeing a particular date, but it will also help you date smarter, learn a great deal about yourself, and expand your sense of choice and possibility.

Play the field—be safe, and have fun!

CONGRATULATIONS!

It was so nice to meet you. You did it!

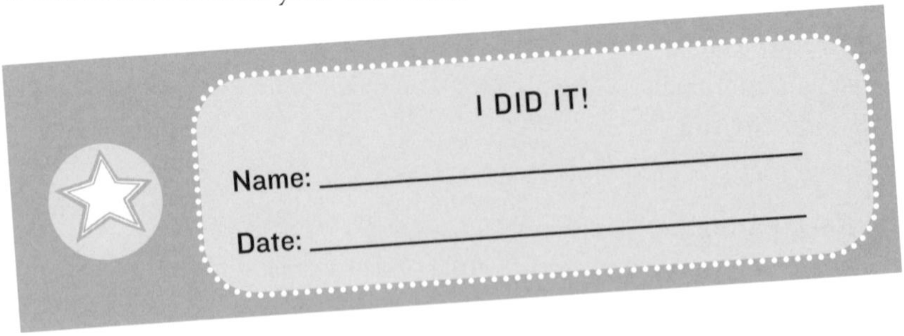

HEALTHY LOVE

Nina's five factors

- Shared values. Fundamental. This means we are basically seeking the same things in life (making a home, raising a family, spiritual growth, career support, etc.). A great couple needn't have mirror-image values, but their core values can't clash either.
- Equal desire for the relationship. Also fundamental, this is when two people emotionally and intellectually choose to be together, to place their relationship as a high priority, and to work on maintaining their connection. (This is *not* one person wanting the relationship and the other person "going along.")
- Intellectual, emotional, and sexual connections. Otherwise known as "chemistry," these factors usually lead us to fall in love. We need more than these components for a happy, long-term relationship, but shouldn't overlook them either. "Falling in love," writes Nina, "is the glue that binds two people together" and can provide incentive for working things out when problems occur.

NINA'S PICKS

BOOKS

Be Your Own Dating Service: A Step-by-Step Guide to Finding and Maintaining Healthy Relationships by Nina Atwood
Everything you always wanted to know about dating but your parents didn't know how to teach you! Emphasis is on creating the foundation for healthy, lasting love.

Getting the Love You Want by Harville Hendrix
Essential for understanding why we choose the people we do, so we can make better choices and accept the choices we have already made.

Simple Abundance: A Daybook of Comfort and Joy by Sarah Ban Breathnach
A wonderful way to start the day (or your date!) with a feeling of abundance, which, coupled with the willingness to take risks, gives us tremendous personal power.

Soul Talk: Powerful, Positive Communication for a Loving Partnership by Nina Atwood
The essential guide to "soul partnering," the new model for man/woman relationships, and the powerful tools for making it work. Vital for dating couples to establish loving behaviors early that lead to lasting connection.

The Truth about Love: The Highes, the Lows, and How You Can Make It Last Forever by Patricia Love, EdD
Wisdom about the biochemistry of love that helps us understand the highs and lows and how to navigate them.

MAGAZINES

In addition to the magazines in which Nina is regularly quoted, including Cosmopolitan *and* Health *magazine, her top picks are:*

Body and Soul
www.bodyandsoulmag.com
For those interested in bringing together the best aspects of personal growth and physical health, this is an excellent resource.

O
www.oprah.com/omagazine
"Nobody provides better life skills resources than Oprah," says Nina. Chock-full of personal growth, insight, and inspiration.

WEB SITES

www.eharmony.com
Uses a matching system based on years of relationship research and provides a structured process for getting to know other members; for those seeking a serious relationship.

www.friendfinder.com
Not just for those looking for dates or romance.

www.match.com
A quick, easy way to get lots of visibility on the Internet to a variety of singles. One caution: You have to do a lot of "weeding" to get to the quality possibilities.

www.soulpartnercoach.com
This is Nina's site, featuring a collection of articles with detailed advice for singles and couples.

58

MAKE LOVE LAST

★ strengthening your relationship ★

It requires infinitely greater genius to make love than to make war.

—Ninon de Lenclos

So, what's your motivation?
Take a moment.
Dream a little, think big,
and then complete this sentence:
I see myself . . .

Imagine This . . . Who's that woman with the grin out to there, walking down the sidewalk like it's cloud nine? Must be a woman in love . . . hey, that's you! You've got a hot date lined up this Friday, and the next one, and the one after that, with a real dreamboat: your partner. That's right—after all this time you've still got the hots for each other. You've also discovered shared passions, deep understanding, and enough inspiration to last a lifetime. Sure it takes considerable time and care, but so do all the wonders of this world—and true love is the greatest of them all. Love is in the air. *You can do it!*

The Payoffs

- **Joy.** When you find the love of a lifetime, you'll know what makes singers sing and dancers dance and dreamers dream . . . and you might even want to join in!
- **Inspiration.** Great love is the key to all greatness. You'll unlock the door to new possibilities and leave it open for generations to come.
- **Vision.** Love takes off blinders we never realized were there. Suddenly you'll notice beauty in familiar places and hope where you thought there was none to be found.
- **Love.** You've heard it said before, but this time you'll know how true it is: Love is its own reward.

Meet Your Mentor

DR. PAT LOVE

What She Does: A licensed relationship and family therapist, Dr. Love has counseled hundreds of couples, authored renowned books on sustaining long-term relationships, including *The Truth about Love: The Highs, the Lows, and How You Can Make It Last Forever* and *Hot Monogamy,* and has been consulted as a relationship expert on most major talk shows, including *The Oprah Winfrey Show* and *The Today Show.*

Why She Does It: "I first got involved in relationship counseling after I went through a divorce that I just didn't see coming. I was determined to find out how it happened and what we might have done as a couple to prevent it. Once I started studying relationships, I realized this was a truly endless topic. I'm constantly learning from my practice and lectures—as an educator, that's part of my job. As the child of divorced parents and having been through a divorce myself, I want to do everything I can to spare others that pain. I think not having the perfect history myself has helped me be more compassionate towards others. I find that 99 percent of the time when I'm counseling a couple, sometime in that session I'm moved to tears by the sheer joy of being able to help them discover a connection that got lost somewhere along the way. It's a sacred moment when people who are at odds finally connect. I try to keep my calm, but inside I'm shouting, 'Yes!'"

Word from the Wise: "In this culture, we're very good at autonomy, but it's rare to see people who are good at cooperation—when you do, it's a real joy and inspiration. Great relationships have a triple bottom line: They help both partners grow and realize their potential, and they help our culture evolve."

While a good relationship makes both people happy, a great relationship makes everybody who comes into contact with that couple happy.

—Dr. Pat Love

BADGE STEPS

1. Dream up your ideal relationship.

Back when you were single, you probably spent some time daydreaming about your perfect relationship: poetry in the park, cozy evenings cooking at home, spur-of-the-moment road trips, winks at each other across a crowded room. But since you've been in your relationship, you may have fallen out of practice. Who can be bothered with wild fantasies when there are schedules to coordinate and an extended family that needs attention?

Daydreams might not seem like the most productive way to spend your time, but Dr. Love says they're key to your happiness. "The first step to a truly great relationship is to imagine what that might look like to you," she says. "Be specific, and set a tangible goal." ***Define your dream relationship.***

2. Make time to make it great.

"Once you know your goals, you need to think realistically about what kind of time it would take to make that fantasy a reality," says Dr. Love. "Most couples do not spend enough time together to create the relationship they say they want." To find time for love in a busy schedule, Dr. Love offers these suggestions:

Prioritize. "Differentiate the things you can do anytime, and the things you can only do once," she says. A friend's wedding shower may take priority, but you probably could sacrifice the occasional happy hour with coworkers.

Schedule it in ink. Set aside a chunk of time every day with your loved one, instead of just hoping to squeeze in a few minutes together between obligations. "Quality time is usually found within quantity time," says our expert.

Make it a habit. Instead of killing time surfing the Web or speed-dialing that friend you've talked to twice today, e-mail or call to ask your partner how the day's going. "Being a happy couple means hundreds of kindnesses per day," says Dr. Love.

Linger a little. "Hold that gaze two seconds longer, and make it a real kiss instead of a quick peck," the doctor recommends. "It doesn't take much more time to convey active interest."

Spend quality time with your loved one.

THE MYTH OF MULTITASKING

What ever happened to undivided attention?

Doing two things at once may impress the folks at the office, but it has the opposite effect on your loved ones. "You may think you're just being efficient, but when you multitask with relationships, it sends a very mixed message," cautions Dr. Love. "When you're pouring your heart out to someone who is emptying the dishwasher, it's discounting and unkind. Sure, I can brush my teeth and pinch my husband's butt at the same time, but emotional situations mean it's time to pull up a chair and listen." Busy parents may feel they should devote their limited time to their kids above all else, but Dr. Love emphasizes that "partnering is a primary part of parenting. Research has shown that your relationship to your partner is your kids' top concern, and they are far more likely to act out when they sense the relationship is unstable." So give yourself and your family a break, already, and have that heart-to-heart chat with your partner—the dishes can wait!

3. Make a move.

We've all said it before: "I would be so happy if my partner would only . . . " But according to Dr. Love, that's not how the pursuit of happiness works: "You can't change someone else; you can only change your own actions. If you take ownership of your role in the relationship, you can set the changes you want in motion." Our expert suggests that great relationships begin with PMS. "By PMS, I mean Positive, Measurable, and Specific actions. For example, you might decide that this week you're going to make a conscious effort to let your partner finish all of her or his own sentences, or clip out five newspaper articles that you think will interest your partner." ***Take the initiative in your relationship.***

4. Start dating again.

Who says you have to give up hot and heavy dating just because you're not single anymore? Get out there and show those singles how it's done:

Set a standing date. Schedule "Date Night" with your partner once a week for the next couple of months—and make it your top priority to be there.

Take turns planning dates. That way, no one has to feel burdened with logistics.

Don't make your date all work and no play. Having your boss and her partner over for dinner isn't exactly a double date, and an evening of shop talk is hardly romantic.

Plan a "gateway" activity. "This is an activity that always makes you and your partner feel closer together after you've done it," explains Dr. Love. If Mozart makes you two into moony-eyed romantics or flying kites makes you giddy, plan accordingly.

Go for variety. "Don't fall back into the same old dinner-and-a-movie routine," says Dr. Love. "Try something new!"

Build the anticipation. Make your date destination a surprise and drop hints, and express excitement about dates your partner has planned, too.

Expect the occasional off night. If a date lapses into complaints, uncomfortable silences, or nonstop interruptions, do the merciful thing and call it a night—then address underlying problems in the morning.

Show your appreciation. If you're having a good time, say so—and if the spirit moves you, smooch away! (See Isn't It Romantic?)

Go on hot dates every week for two months.

ISN'T IT ROMANTIC?

Beyond champagne and chocolate

The most romantic gestures aren't fancy or formal—just follow Dr. Love's advice:

Go out of your way. "When your significant other gets up at five in the morning just to see you off at the airport, that's love!"

Make it personal. "The more you know someone, the more specific and personal a romantic gesture needs to be to show that you care. If you've told your partner a hundred times that you love stargazer lillies, you definitely don't want to get roses instead."

Get creative. "My husband did something wonderful for me the year my father passed away. He went through boxes of old pictures, found the last picture of me with my dad, and framed it for me. That's the best present I've ever gotten."

DR. LOVE'S EXPERT TIPS

ASKING FOR CHANGE IN YOUR RELATIONSHIP

Ask questions. If you're not sure how to handle it, just ask: "If I have a touchy subject to raise, what's the best way to bring it up?"

Skip the lecture. "Because collaboration is a basic human survival strategy, we actually block out distancing criticism." To ensure your partner doesn't retreat into fight-or-flight mode, keep it short and stay calm and constructive.

Don't talk yourself hoarse. "Excessive talking makes many problems worse. Often what really bugs us is seeing in someone else what we don't like in ourselves—and that can only be solved by self-acceptance, not discussion."

Realize no couple is perfect. "Happy, stable couples have the same number of problems as unhappy, unstable couples. The main difference is that they don't escalate the situation and can laugh about it or ignore it."

5. Share your passions.

Opposites may attract, but sooner or later they have to find something they actually enjoy doing together. "Happy, stable couples support one another's passions," says Dr. Love. Most of us find at least one of our partner's favorite pursuits hard to understand—but as our expert says, it's worth making the effort to acquire a taste for it. "It's a red flag for individuals in a couple to persistently pursue a passion without their partner, because you'll end up feeling left out of that special bond between your partner and others who share that interest."

So if your partner truly adores opera, go for a matinee sometime, even if you'd rather be fishing. Choose a shorter opera that seems more your speed, and notice what you actually enjoy about the experience: people-watching, the characters, the costumes. You may feel out of your element at first, but your opera date could end on a high note—and next week, take your partner fishing! ***Bond over your favorite pastimes.***

6. Get better acquainted.

Partners don't come equipped with volume knobs, yet still we find ways to tune them out and anticipate what they're going to say. But if we take time to listen and ask questions over the course of a month, says Dr. Love, we might find out there's more to love about our loved ones than we even knew. There's probably a story in your partner's repertoire you've heard at least a hundred times . . . if your eyes are rolling, you know the one! You may know that your partner once ate five peanut

I DID IT!

"My husband and I are partners in life and in business, and my girlfriends are always saying, 'I don't know how you can handle that . . . it would drive me crazy.' It's true that running a business together means we spend a lot more time together than most couples do, but that doesn't have to be a bad thing! Over the years, we've learned that we each need alone time every day, and every week we need a hot date together. We like to surprise each other with the dates, whether it's a cheese tasting, a salsa dance lesson, or a punk rock show where we're the oldest people there by a decade. We've come to know and admire one another on so many different levels that I find his presence a real joy."
—Jill

DATE CRASHERS

"My partner and I hadn't been out alone together in months, because we had so many social commitments individually and as a couple. Finally we made time for dinner and a movie by ourselves, and we were just settling into the cozy corner booth I'd reserved when wouldn't you know it . . . some friends spotted us across the restaurant and insisted we join them for dinner. There was just no way around it, and of course they meant well—but now we know that on date nights, we definitely need to go somewhere less popular with our crowd!"
—Gennifer

butter and baloney sandwiches, but do you know where and why? Was it after a long day of work on Grandma's farm or on a dare at summer camp? Ask for details and you might learn something new about your partner. ***Get to know your loved one all over again.***

7. Keep the love coming.

Once you're dating again and sharing your innermost passions and ideas, you'll want to keep it coming. Dr. Love suggests that to do that, every day you should play FAIR:

Flirt. Flirting lets your partner know you're interested, which in turn keeps your partner attentive and affectionate. "An energized lover who is interested in you is a turn-on nobody can resist," says Dr. Love. "Besides, if you don't flirt with your partner, someone else might!"

Appreciate. Positive reinforcement is all-important. "If you only point out the one thing your partner did wrong and not the ten things that they got right, where's the incentive for your partner to even try?"

Intimacy. Give your partner your full attention as you share the best parts of your day. "We often share our most exciting moments with a coworker or friend, but letting our partners in could draw us closer together," says Dr. Love.

Risk. "Our brains wake up to novelty, which is why relationships are so exciting when they're new," says Dr. Love. Try venturing beyond familiar favorites in restaurants, on Sunday afternoons, and on vacations. "The shared sense of discovery and adventure can give you the thrill of dating someone new."

Let love become a way of life.

CONGRATULATIONS!

You finally found the love you were looking for—and discovered it was right in front of you all along. You did it!

I DID IT!

Name: ______________________________

Date: ______________________________

THE PLEASURE PRINCIPLE

How passion changes you

According to Dr. Love, that surge of affection you feel when you connect with your partner isn't imaginary. Here are a few more telltale physical signs that your passion is still going strong:

- Your toes tingle when you look into each other's eyes. "It actually releases endorphins."
- You feel ten feet tall. "Since collaboration is our main strategy as humans, intimacy really is a survival skill for us. So when we find joy with our partner, we feel more alive, more self-assured, more powerful."
- Your heart goes pitter-pat. "At a distance of ten feet or so, your heartbeat actually registers in another person's brain."
- It's written all over your face. "The face has more nerve endings than any other part of the body, so others can perceive your feelings even when you don't think you're letting them show."

BEYOND THE BADGE

If you love it as much as you thought you would, dream on . . .

- **Collaborate.** "A good relationship is so energizing, you'll find you have motivation to spare," says Dr. Love. "Chores like housework and cooking can bring a wonderful shared sense of accomplishment when you do them together, and exercise gets a whole lot more appealing when it's a walk in the park with a loved one instead of a solo stint on the treadmill." Now that you're more involved in one another's lifelong passions, you might decide to embark on some joint projects, too. If you notice your partner's weekly jam sessions are sounding better all the time, maybe you could help your partner's band land a gig, and make some great flyers for their first big show. And if one of your goals in life is to bring comfort and hope to people living with HIV/AIDS, maybe you two could spend an hour together every Saturday delivering meals to AIDS patients. "Collaboration brings you closer together and creates great new memories," notes our expert.
- **Communicate.** When tempers flare, as they do for every couple, communication can break down quickly. When you feel yourself or your partner reaching the point where you're just not listening, Dr. Love recommends trying this basic communication drill:
  - Get out a timer, and set it for two minutes.
  - One person gets to talk until the time is up, and then it's the other person's turn to talk—no overtime allowed. "My husband and I need a timer that actually beeps when time has run out because otherwise we know we'll keep going!" laughs Dr. Love.
  - Repeat as necessary. "When you're forced to talk for just two minutes at a time, it forces you to be succinct and get to your point. Plus even when you're really mad, you know you can tolerate whatever your partner has to say for two minutes." You may be pleased to find that even at your most hotheaded, you'll only need to go few rounds before you've both said your piece and made your peace.
- **Celebrate.** Why wait for an anniversary to celebrate your lasting affection? Create a collage of your best moments together over the years, surprise your loved one with a touching toast at your next dinner party, or plan a special trip for just the two of you.

INFORMATION, PLEASE

Relationship counseling 101

As a relationship counselor, Dr. Love sees many couples who are worried they've fallen out of love—but often they've misdiagnosed the problem. "People confuse infatuation with love all the time," says our expert. "Falling in love is easy, but staying in love takes information, skill, and knowledge." Specifically, Dr. Love says couples need:

- Information about what says "I love you" to your partner, and what your own needs are. A good rule of thumb: When in doubt, find out!
- Skill to communicate your needs to your partner (see Dr. Love's Expert Tips, page 472).
- Knowledge about what true love looks like to you both. You got this covered in Step 1; now encourage your partner to do likewise, and compare notes. If you find your partner's concept of love to be markedly different from yours, you might consider a session with a counselor or couple's therapist to explore and reconcile your ideas.

DR. LOVE'S PICKS

BOOKS

Handbook for the Soul by Richard Carlson and Benjamin Shield (editors)
An inspiring book that teaches you why relationships are the essence of life.

Hot Monogamy by Dr. Pat Love
Want to keep the passion alive? This book gives you the formula and a step-by-step process.

The Intimate Couple by Jon Carlson PsyD, EdD, and Len Sperry, MD, PhD (editors)
A comprehensive, hands-on book full of information and relationship savvy.

Not "Just Friends" by Shirley P. Glass, PhD
A take-no-prisoners approach to guarding your relationship from infidelity and recovering from betrayal.

The Truth about Love: The Highs, the Lows, and How You Can Make It Last Forever by Dr. Pat Love
This book is Love 101—tells you what you need to know to create the love you long for. Practical, research-based, very readable, and heartwarming.

WEB SITES

www.divorcemag.com
The Web site for *Divorce Magazine*. Advice on avoiding divorce, strengthening marriage, and supporting remarriage.

www.patlove.com
A valuable resource for understanding and improving relationships.

www.smartmarriages.com
An invaluable site for marriage education resources.

FILMS

Great for cozy date nights:

The African Queen

Amelie

Annie Hall

The Apartment

Casablanca

Chungking Express

Down with Love

Edward Scissorhands

Emma

Eternal Sunshine of the Spotless Mind

Il Postino

I've Heard the Mermaids Singing

Moonstruck

Moulin Rouge

O Brother, Where Art Thou?

On Golden Pond

The Philadelphia Story

Pride and Prejudice

The Princess Bride

Roman Holiday

A Room with a View

Shirley Valentine

Singin' in the Rain

Sliding Doors

Some Like It Hot

Something's Gotta Give

The Story of Us

Strictly Ballroom

When Harry Met Sally

59

GIVE A LITTLE BIT

★ volunteering ★

What do we live for
if it is not to make life
LESS DIFFICULT
for each other?

—George Eliot

So, what's your motivation?
Take a moment.
Dream a little, think big,
and then complete this sentence:
I see myself . . .

Imagine This . . . After pounding some nails for Habitat for Humanity you feel good and tired—with an emphasis on the *good* part. When you clean out your closets and deliver your boxes and bags to your local women's shelter, you feel unburdened—and uplifted. Raising several hundred dollars by walking an AIDS marathon can work wonders for your body and spirit. Yes, there is so much to do, and so little time—but every little bit does count, and this badge makes doing your bit simple. You'll find the best way for you to give, a worthy outlet for your efforts, and a whole new outlook on life. Give a little and everyone gains a lot. *You can do it!*

The Payoffs

- **Meaning.** At the end of the day, many of us are left wondering what it's all about. When you volunteer, you know.
- **Power.** Maybe you can't change the entire world, but volunteering shows you that you can make a difference. For those you help, that's more than enough.
- **Adventure.** You never know where volunteering may lead. You're bound to discover new people, new experiences, and new insights when you risk a glimpse at the world beyond your doorstep.
- **Learning.** Whether you've volunteered to do event planning, political organizing, or basic construction, you can make a real impact on your world and pick up new skills (and resume-friendly experience) in the process.

Meet Your Mentor

CLAUDIA FRERE

What She Does: Oversees the client services department for VolunteerMatch.org, the Web's largest database of volunteer opportunities. VolunteerMatch provides would-be volunteers with an easy way to be matched with local organizations in need of their talents. Claudia has volunteered with many organizations, including tutoring and mentoring commitments with the YWCA and Little Brothers–Friends of the Elderly.

Why She Does It: "Like so many people, I always knew that I wanted to find a way to give, to make things better and have an impact on the things that go wrong in society. I studied International Politics in college, and wanted to 'act locally' while thinking globally. I wanted a commitment that was real but not too deep. So initially I signed on for practical tutoring. This led to a mentoring relationship with my student. I wasn't ready for that kind of commitment at the outset, but I grew into it. The real catalyst for my taking action in my late twenties was a serious health scare, a bout with cancer. This woke me up. I realized my life might be shorter than I'd thought and that I shouldn't put things off until tomorrow. And I realized that I wanted to make my career congruent with my deepest goals, so I was fortunate enough to have found VolunteerMatch."

Volunteering brings out the HERO in us all.

—Claudia Frere

Word from the Wise: "People are surprised by how much fun they have. I advise people to view a volunteering gig as something new to try. That's it, no big deal. This minimizes the fear factor. Instead of going to a movie, why not spend those few hours raising money in a bike-a-thon, addressing envelopes for a fundraising mailing, or helping out at a food bank? You'll meet people, have a new experience, and probably have a really good time."

BADGE STEPS

1. Decide what you have to give.

Think about the amount of time and/or money you can reliably offer. Independent Sector's Give Five Campaign encourages people to give five hours a week and 5 percent of their income to their favorite causes and charities, while many religious groups advocate setting aside as much as 10 percent of household income for charitable donations. But even if you don't have that much time or resources to spare, you may be able to spare a couple hours a month or an all-day event twice a year. Whatever it is, you must be prepared to take that commitment seriously. People will depend on it.

Once you know how much time you can offer, decide how you want to spend that time. What suits your personality and fills your own needs? You may prefer one-on-one relationships to group activity or the other way around. You may yearn to mentor a young person or keep an older one company. Think about what really moves you and what situations bring out the best you have to offer.

Also consider your talents, skills, or hobbies. Can you cook for a charity that provides meals, design a Web site for a fledgling nonprofit, train search-and-rescue dogs? Are you a doctor who can give a morning to a clinic or shelter, a law student who could do legal research for an advocacy organization, a dancer who could teach tap at an after-school or senior center program? You can do the world a favor just by doing what you do best. ***Choose how—and how much—you want to contribute.***

2. Find a cause you can get behind.

Now that you know what you have to offer, who will you offer it to? Look for a charity that shares your concerns. What issues do you feel strongly about? Have you or a loved one been affected by breast cancer or domestic violence? Are you passionate about the environment or world hunger?

Check out your options:

Online. VolunteerMatch.org can help match you with volunteer opportunities according to your interests, location, and schedule. You input your zip code, then narrow the focus based on your personal requirements. When you find an organization, you can read up on them. If you like what you see, click "I like this opportunity" and fill out some infor-

SIMPLE GIFTS

Small acts with big impact

Trade in on your talent. Professionals are asked to share their expertise all the time. One way to make such generous efforts even more meaningful is to say, "Sure, I'll write that press release/provide floral arrangements/share my mailing list—in exchange for your writing a check to my favorite charity."

Have computer, will contribute. You don't even need to leave your desk to make a difference—your contribution may be as simple as forwarding an e-mail about a fundraising event to your e-mail circle, or visiting the Web site of your favorite charity and making an online donation through a secure credit card transaction.

Make it a family affair. Enterprises like VolunteerMatch list thousands of opportunities that are great for kids and teens. Their "Great for Groups" listings can also be ideal for groups of friends or coworkers. www.volunteermatch.org.

mation. An e-mail is automatically sent to the organization, and the organization then contacts you about their program. See Claudia's Picks, page 482, for additional Web resources.

At your place of worship. They can tell you about community services they provide.

At your workplace. Your human resources or community relations department may support specific volunteering programs, and many responsible businesses have giving programs that match employee donations to registered nonprofits.

Through your friends and neighbors. School principals, librarians, and newspaper editors are all good resources for finding good work to be done in your community.

Make five phone calls to explore the options in your area. Ask about their volunteer needs and see if they match yours. Choose one organization, and attend their volunteer orientation or ask to come in and speak with their volunteer coordinator beforehand if the orientation is time-intensive. Don't make a time and/or financial commitment you aren't comfortable with; better to start small and build. If the fit is good, make your service commitment. ***Follow your conscience to the nonprofit of your choice.***

CLAUDIA'S EXPERT TIPS

VOLUNTEER WITH NO FEAR

- Learn as much as you can about what you'll be doing. Ask questions. Going in prepared guarantees a better experience for all involved.
- Don't feel pressured. Some organizations may try to rope you into more than you are comfortable with. Set your limits.
- Give yourself time for reflection, especially if you are working one-on-one in a tutor, mentor, or Big Sister role. Keep in touch with how you're feeling about the experience.

3. Honor your commitment.

Whether your commitment is one hour or one year, follow-through is key. If you travel for work or have small children at home, a weekly appointment to teach reading skills at a set time may not work out for you—no matter how good your intentions are. But you might find it surprisingly easy to integrate volunteering into your everyday life. Your

LIGHTEN UP, ALREADY!

Lighten your load—and brighten someone's day

Dig through your attic. Charities usually welcome donations of clothes and household items, as long as they're in resale condition.

Kick that crappy car to the curb. Charities often sell old cars at auctions—and the real beaters are sold for spare parts.

Make a wish come true. Many women's shelters and other nonprofits have wish lists that can help you give them what's most needed.

THE TAX MAN COMETH

Good thing you have all these tax deductions . . .

Checks and cash gifts. Itemize these and keep clear records for tax purposes. For donations of $250 or more, be sure you get a receipt or official thank-you note on the charity's letterhead.

Payroll deductions. Keep payroll stubs, a W-2 form verifying the amount, and a receipt or official acknowledgment from the nonprofit.

In-kind donations. You can deduct the fair market value of any items you donate—including artwork. Just note the date, location, and items donated, and get a receipt for donations totaling more than $250.

Expenses. You can deduct expenses you incur while volunteering, such as mileage, parking fees, and tolls, so keep records and receipts.

kids can ride along as you make meals-on-wheels deliveries. When you walk your dog, you can make a stop at the neighborhood nursing home and share some puppy love. If you've decided to make a substantial monetary contribution, you could arrange to have a set amount automatically withdrawn from your payroll or bank every month. ***Do your part from the heart.***

4. Make sure it feels good when you do good.

After completing your commitment, check to see what it did for you. How did your expectations mesh with reality? Was it fun, rewarding, draining, dull? Why? Can you give more time, or do you need to do less? Don't let yourself feel trapped or obligated, advises Claudia: "Volunteering shouldn't feel burdensome. If your initial experience wasn't ideal, try to pinpoint why—and then plan accordingly."

Consider what you liked and disliked. Do you want to do more of the same, or try something new? Would you like to work with a different organization, with the same organization in a different capacity, or bring other skills or interests into play? Jot down your thoughts, and have a conversation with your volunteer coordinator. ***Recommit or reconsider.***

5. Pass it on.

As you've earned the badges in *You Can Do It!*, you've gained insight from expert mentors and broadened your horizons. Now it's your turn to pass the favor along and share your newfound expertise with another person or organization. Find a local community venue where you can teach or share one of the skills you've learned by earning a badge. ***Give the world the benefit of your experience.***

CONGRATULATIONS!

You've gained a wealth of experience, and now you know how to pass it on. It's a great feeling, no? You did it!

I DID IT!

Name: ______________________

Date: ______________________

I DID IT!

"Between tutoring and mentoring, I worked with one girl from age twelve to fifteen. She continues to have some challenges, and is currently in an out-of-state program. I may not have contact with her again for years, but she will always be in my life. I recently got a very sweet letter from her letting me know what I had meant to her. We will always be part of each other's life journey. That's forever."

—Claudia

JUST SAY NO

"It's important to set boundaries, particularly when working one-on-one in an unstructured setting. I mentored a young woman for more than a year. About six months into it, she started canceling plans at the last minute and eventually stopped showing up at all. I made myself crazy for another six months trying to come up with things to entice her, meeting with her family, the program facilitator, etc. I finally realized that I was more invested in feeling good about helping her than she was interested in being helped."

—Lisa

BEYOND THE BADGE

If you love it as much as you thought you would, dream on . . .

- **Make a career of it.** Claudia found a way to put her business skills and talents to work for the common good, and your volunteer work could lead to a career in the nonprofit world, too. Grant writing, advertising, public relations, marketing, fund-raising, and accounting skills are all in demand, and could well lead to a position on the board or as an employee.
- **Grow your own grassroots effort.** Washington, D.C., doctor Amy Kossoff routinely found herself writing small personal checks to help her patients in homeless shelters and public clinics. She regularly hosted potluck dinners with a group of female friends, and one of these friends suggested asking guests to bring a donation as well as a dish. With each of the regular potluck group inviting ten friends, diners could grow to over one hundred people. Checks were deposited into a fee-free checking account that one of their members negotiated with a local bank, and Amy doled out the dough—small checks to cover a delinquent utility bill, pay for a prescription, or make a security deposit. (If you have no Amy in your midst, you can simply donate each potluck's take to a worthy local outfit.) They dubbed their grassroots organization "Womenade" because (as one of the friends told *Real Simple* magazine) "if you have lemons, make lemonade. If you have women, make Womenade."
- **Travel—for good.** Some nonprofits provide opportunities to volunteer abroad—we've all heard of the Peace Corps, and Doctors without Borders is an international medical relief organization that sends trained medical personnel abroad. But not all nonprofits require two-year commitments or specialized training. You might be able to serve as a volunteer ambassador from your organization to a sister organization in another country—Claudia knows people who have participated in service missions all over the place, from grassroots groups in Guatemala to a microfinancing effort in India. (In the future, Claudia would like to pursue a commitment that reaches her homeland, the Philippines.) Or you might put your vacation time to good use by taking a "reality tour" with Global Exchange, a nonprofit that takes volunteers on eye-opening trips in Latin America for a nominal fee. (See Claudia's Picks, page 482, for more.)

DONOR SAVVY

Know what your dollars will do

Check out nonprofit portal sites. These post nonprofit tax returns and rate nonprofits according to how well they allocate their resources (see Claudia's Picks, page 482, for details). But take this information with a grain of salt: Some very worthy organizations simply have a broader mission and higher overhead than others, and thus may not look great on paper. So check out the results, not just their expenditures.

Consider the average donation. Some organizations prefer not to rely on corporate sponsorship or a handful of major donors, and instead have a large membership that makes small donations. There is a cost associated with processing such a large number of small donations that may be reflected in online ratings—but your small donation can mean a lot to these organizations.

Join a giving circle. Giving circles evaluate charities, and each member contributes. Search "giving circle" online, or see Claudia's Picks for a starter kit.

See Give Your Money Away, page 378.

CLAUDIA'S PICKS

BOOKS

The Courage to Give: Inspiring Stories of People Who Triumphed over Tragedy to Make a Difference in the World by Jackie Waldman
An inspiring anthology of personal stories.

The Giving Tree by Shel Silverstein
The kid's classic that never fails to inspire.

Voices from the Heart: In Celebration of America's Volunteers by Brian O'Connell
Volunteers speak about how and why they volunteer.

WEB SITES

:: *On volunteering:*

Points of Light Foundation
www.pointsoflight.org
A national clearinghouse for information on volunteering.

President's Volunteer Service Awards
www.presidentialserviceawards.org
You may already be a winner! Track your volunteer hours and qualify for this distinction.

VolunteerMatch
www.volunteermatch.org
A nonprofit online service that matches volunteers with local nonprofit and public sector organizations.

:: *On charitable contributions:*

The Better Business Bureau Wise Giving Alliance
www.give.org
Publishes *Wise Giving Guide* and charity reports on many nonprofits to help donors make informed giving decisions.

Independent Sector
www.independentsector.org
A national leadership forum that coordinates the Give Five Campaign, encouraging people to give five hours a week and 5 percent of their income to causes they support.

Leave a Legacy
www.leavealegacy.org
Information on how to make charitable gifts in your will or estate plan, brought to you by the U.S. Government's National Committee on Planned Giving.

:: *On in-kind donations:*

Goodwill Industries
www.goodwill.org
Find a drop-off location near you. Proceeds provide job training to disabled and disadvantaged individuals.

It's Deductible
www.itsdeductible.com
Sells a software program that explains how to deduct volunteer-related expenses and lists the value of thousands of donated items.

Salvation Army
www.salvationarmyusa.org
To find out how much your tax-deductible donation is worth, use the Valuation Guide provided here.

GRANTS

Computer Recycling Center
www.crc.org/info
Apply for a free recycled, rebuilt computer for your local public school or nonprofit organization.

The Council on Foundations
www.cof.org
Tracks trends and success stories in philanthropy. A terrific resource on grants.

The Foundation Center
www.fdncenter.org
Help hook up your favorite charity with a dream-come-true grant, or find funding for your own fledgling nonprofit.

CAREER RESOURCES

Careers in Non-Profits and Government Agencies, WetFeet Guides
An informative booklet to help you find your nonprofit niche and chart your career path accordingly.

NonProfit Times
www.nptimes.com
Twice-monthly publication with news, reports, and insights on the nonprofit sector. Also lists job opportunities.

OpportunityKnocks
www.opportunityknocks.org
Lists hundreds of nonprofit job opportunities every week, covering thirty-three U.S. states.

dream

It is *never too late* to be what you might have been.

—George Eliot

Learn CPR

Coach little league

Make your own furniture

Write a song

Understand the Federal Reserve

Breed dogs

Become a palm reader

Spend quality time with an elder

Herd goats like Heidi

Earn a black belt

Write a children's book

Join a hockey team

Ride the Trans-Siberian Railway

Start a newsletter

Throw a vase on a potter's wheel

What's Your Fancy?

Call a square dance

Go on an African photography safari

Invent a board game

Be a fiery redhead for a month

Start a greeting card company

Move to New York City

Take a vow of silence for a week

Design a pair of shoes

Build a tree house

Step into the boxing ring

Bake an amazing apple pie

Pitch a no-hitter

Be a foster mom

Canoe through the Grand Canyon

Swing on a trapeze

Spin records at a dance club

Open a bed & breakfast

decorate your own badge

(you'll find blank badges at the end of the book)

60

DREAM ON

★ make your own badge ★

We do not know who we are
until we see
what we can do.

—Martha Grimes

Imagine This . . . You've earned your *You Can Do It!* badges, and now you're thinking you'd like to tackle a dream that isn't captured in these pages. Bravo! Now's your chance to apply what you've learned about how to do it to whatever your heart desires. (And please, e-mail us your ideas at youcandoit@herterstudio.com, and maybe your badge will show up in our next edition!) Since you're one sharp cookie, by now you've probably figured out that while the particular goal and specific steps may vary, the fundamental game plan remains the same. It may not be "scientifically formulated," "patent pending," or "award-winning" (at least not yet!), but the step-by-step process does work. Turn the page to use our tried-and-true method for turning your dream into a reality—and a badge. *You can do it!*

What Do You *Really* Want to Do?

Browse the suggestions on the previous page, and if nothing there fires up your imagination, revisit badge number 1, Dare to Dream, page 2. That should remind you that the sky's the limit and that your possibilities are infinite. Maybe you're a little tired from earning the last fifty-nine badges? Okay, you're entitled to a little nap! But don't let your dream machine get rusty—or go the way of the buried-in-boxes exercycle in your basement. Remember how good it feels to smile at a new goal; to feel the gears of your mind, body, and spirit engage with it; to learn, laugh, and cross the "You Did It!" finish line. And the next time you hear yourself say, "I'd love to . . . but I have no idea where to begin," come back here. We'll remind you. ***Dream up your own badge!***

BADGE STEPS

My favorite thing is to go where I've never been.

—Diane Arbus

1. Envision it.

So you know what you want to do—now imagine yourself doing it. Complete this sentence: "I see myself . . . " ***Close your eyes and see yourself doing your thing with panache.***

2. Why do it?

We listed four of the benefits/rewards/payoffs for doing each of the previous fifty-nine badges. Go one better and come up with five for your badge. ***Write down the payoffs.***

3. Get help.

We found our mentors in the headlines, on bookshelves, down the street, online, at events, and in our phone books. Think about people you already know who have the skills you want, experts you admire from afar, and friends you can ask to put you in touch with an expert on the subject. (When we asked nicely, we found that amazingly accomplished women truly loved the idea of mentoring other motivated women!) ***Find your mentor.***

4. Interview your mentor.

Once you have an expert lined up, ask if you can interview them on the subject and tap their expertise. To get your expert talking, here are ten questions you might ask:

1. How did you get started?
2. What do you find most rewarding about this activity?
3. What do you think people fear most about this activity, and how did you overcome it?
4. What fun starter project would you recommend to beginners, and what are the steps involved in completing this project?
5. What are some common challenges or obstacles beginners face?
6. When you come up against challenges, what's your motivation to keep going?
7. What top three tips do you wish you'd had when you were just starting out?

8. What can beginners look forward to if they invest the time to advance to the next level in this field?

9. Where do you meet other people who share your passion for this activity?

10. What books/magazines/films/Web sites would you recommend I read for support/information/advice?

Conduct an interview.

5. Do your homework.

Now take that list of resources recommended by your mentor and dive in. Go in depth, get some background, and fill in any remaining gaps. ***Research your badge.***

6. Plan your steps.

Now that you've talked to your mentor and researched your badge, formulate a chronological, doable, and *fun* series of steps that will lead you where you want to go. Break the activity into steps and supporting actions as follows:

- Describe the goal of each step in a few words.
- Describe the specific actions you need to take to reach the goal.
- Articulate what the end result of the action should be.
- Set a realistic due date for yourself

Now repeat this process for the five-to-seven steps it will take you to earn your badge. ***Create your badge.***

CONGRATULATIONS!

Some assembly was required, but it was worth it, no? You did it!
Now Do It!

Go confidently in the direction of your dreams. *Live the life you have imagined.*

—Henry David Thoreau

mentor contacts

Heather Ash Amara
Toltec Center of Creative Intent
P.O. Box 12216
Berkeley, CA 94712
510-649-0352
info@tolteccenter.org
www.tolteccenter.org

Nina Atwood
5930-E Royal Ln. #143
Dallas, TX 75230
214-739-2728
nina@ninaatwood.com
www.soulpartnercoach.com
www.ninaatwood.com

Karen Berger
c/o Herter Studio
432 Elizabeth St.
San Francisco, CA 94114
415-282-8143
books@herterstudio.com

Jennifer Berne
University of Illinois at Chicago
jberne@uic.edu

Alison Bing
2152 Union St.
San Francisco, CA 94123
thecontentmaven@hotmail.com

Arlene Blum
arlene@arleneblum.com
www.arleneblum.com

Janet Bodnar
Kiplinger's Personal Finance Magazine
1729 H Street NW
Washington, DC 20006
jbodnar@kiplinger.com
www.kiplinger.com

Brenda Bonhomme
300 Monte Vista Ave.
Oakland, CA 94611
510-655-0238
bbonhomme@earthlink.net

Susan Carvalho
Middlebury College
University of Kentucky
www.middlebury.edu/ls/spanish

Meg Cox
familyrituals@aol.com

Patti Critchfield
Patti's Auto Care
2285 San Pablo Ave.
Berkeley, CA 94702
510-981-9007
pattilb@pacbell.net

Susan Dory
9518 Dayton Ave. N
Seattle, WA 98103
206-781-6061
susandory@hotmail.com

Joann Eckstut
The Roomworks
177 Duane St.
New York, NY 10013
212-625-0400
je@theroomworks.com
www.theroomworks.com

Janet E. Esposito, MSW
In the Spotlight, LLC
P.O. Box 494
Bridgewater, CT 06752
877-814-7705
jesposito@performanceanxiety.com
www.performanceanxiety.com

Stephanie Finch
www.stephaniefinch.com
www.chuckprophet.com

Arin Hart Fishkin
O2 Design Collective
3521 19th St.
San Francisco, CA 94110
arin@o2sf.com
www.o2sf.com

Jona Frank
c/o Herter Studio
432 Elizabeth St.
San Francisco, CA 94114
415-282-8143
books@herterstudio.com

Claudia Frere
VolunteerMatch
claudia@volunteermatch.org
www.volunteermatch.org

Conner Gorry
6015 Spencer Ave.
Bronx, NY 10471
connergo@ekit.com

Lauren Greenfield
Lauren Greenfield Photography
studio@laurengreenfield.com
www.laurengreenfield.com
www.girlculture.com

The Reverend Beth Hansen
Episcopal Church of St. Mary the Virgin
2325 Union St.
San Francisco, CA 94123
415-921-3665 x 314
beth@smvsf.org

Sheila Heen
Triad Consulting
9 Waterhouse St.
Cambridge, MA 02138
617-492-2698
heen@post.harvard.edu
www.triadcgi.com

Laurie Henry
2824 Werk Rd.
Cincinnati, OH 45211
henrylj@email.uc.edu

Laurie Henzel and Tracie Egan
BUST Magazine
P.O. Box 1016
Cooper Station
New York, NY 10276
www.bust.com

Anna Herrera-Shawver
Apple Canyon Co.
P.O. Box 16494
Albuquerque, NM 87191-6494
505-332-2000
anna@applecanyon.com
www.applecanyon.com

Kathleen W. Hinckley
Family Detective
P.O. Box 350877
Westminster, CO 80035
303-422-9371
kathleen@familydetective.com
www.familydetective.com

Georgia Hughes
Georgia@nwlib.com

Nora Isaacs
nora@noraisaacs.com
www.noraisaacs.com

E. Faith Ivery
Educational Advisory Services
DrIvery@e-a-s.com
www.e-a-s.com

Rozann Kraus
The Dance Complex
c/o Herter Studio
432 Elizabeth St.
San Francisco, CA 94114
415-282-8143
books@herterstudio.com

Cathy Langer
Tattered Cover Book Store
1628 16th St.
Denver, CO 80202
303-322-1695 x 2702
cathyl@tatteredcover.com
www.tatteredcover.com

Erika Lenkert
erika@lastminutepartygirl.com
www.lastminutepartygirl.com

Lisa Lewis
www.lisalewis.net

Pat Love, EdD
6705 Highway 290 W
Suite 502, PMB 291
Austin, TX 78735
512-891-0610
www.patlove.com

Cailyn McCauley
707-495-1797
cailynq@mac.com

Terri McGraw (a.k.a. Mrs. Fixit)
McGraw Media Enterprises
www.mrsfixit.com

Ella Jean Morgan
College of Oceaneering
272 S. Fries Ave.
Wilmington, CA 90744
310-834-2501
emorgan@coo.edu
www.coo.edu

Erin O'Neill
P.O. Box 3367
Idyllwild, CA 92549
erin@greencafe.com

Our Bodies, Ourselves
34 Plympton St.
Boston, MA 02118
617-451-3666
office@bwhbc.org
www.ourbodiesourselves.org

Melanie Paykos
3457 S. La Cienega Blvd.
Studio B
Los Angeles, CA 90016
310-287-3420
melanie@mpaykos.com
www.mpaykos.com

Cherry Pedrick, RN
4405 Fenton Ln.
N. Las Vegas, NV 89032
702-656-0603
cherlene@aol.com
www.cherrypedrick.com

Kris Percival
c/o Herter Studio
432 Elizabeth St.
San Francisco, CA 94114
415-282-8143
books@herterstudio.com

Nancy Reinisch
Glenwood Medical Associates
1830 Blake St., 1st Floor
Glenwood Springs, CO 81601
970-945-8503
nrein@rof.net

Carol Ann Rinzler
Harold Ober Associates
425 Madison Ave.
New York, NY 10017
212-759-8600

Linda Rubio
Miwok Livery Stables
701 Tennessee Valley Rd.
Mill Valley, CA 94941
415-383-8048
rubyeo@aol.com
www.miwokstables.com

Jill Salo
P.O. Box 6591
Breckenridge, CO 80424
jill_salo@hotmail.com

Sally Sampson
sally@sampsonsnuts.com
www.sampsonsnuts.com

Julie Shah
Third Wave Foundation
jshahtwf@aol.com
www.thirdwavefoundation.org

Sara Bowen Shea
c/o Herter Studio
432 Elizabeth St.
San Francisco, CA 94114
415-282-8143
books@herterstudio.com

Renee Shepherd
Renee's Garden Seeds
7389 W. Zayante Rd.
Felton, CA 95018
831-335-7228
renee@reneesgarden.com
www.reneesgarden.com

Denise Shortt
denise.shortt@sympatico.ca
www.technologywithcurves.com

Stephanie Sloan
Whistler Blackcomb
sloan@whooshnet.com

Meryl Starr
Let's Get Organized
P.O. Box 71
LaGrangerville, NY 12540
845-485-1818
merylstarr@msn.com
www.merylstarr.com

Shari Stauch
Pool & Billiard Magazine
115 S. Main St.
Summerville, SC 29483
888-POOLMAG (766-5624)
843-875-5115
poolmag@poolmag.com
www.poolmag.com

Francesca Sterlacci
Chair of Fashion Design Dept.
Fashion Institute of Technology
c/o Herter Studio
432 Elizabeth St.
San Francisco, CA 94114
415-282-8143
books@herterstudio.com

Deanna Strand
Strand Flying School
817 Falcon Way
Grand Junction, CO 81506
970-243-4359
ifly@strandflying.com
www.strandflying.com

Isabelle "Izzy" Tihanyi
2160 Avenida de la Playa
La Jolla, CA 92037
858-454-8273
askadiva@surfdiva.com
www.surfdiva.com

we did it! acknowledgments

This book has been a labor of love, all around. It was created as a family, and a family we've become. With humility and thanks to:

Lauren, for inspiring a partnership and a vision that matters; to her family, for asking us to carry on and entrusting us—with courage, grace, and unwavering support—to see that vision through; and to Dean Burrell and Beth Hansen, without whom I never would have had the privilege of knowing Lauren and working on this book.

Our experts, inspiring and extraordinarily accomplished women all, who so generously donated their valuable time and sage advice on Lauren's behalf.

Our team. We searched far and wide for someone to give voice to Lauren's vision, and the brilliant and thoughtful Yvette Bozzini did just that. With imagination, grace, and literary finesse—through pressure-filled months of interviewing and writing and responding to the endless comments of a much-too-big team, Yvette wrote a book that is better, and truer to Lauren's spirit and intent, than any of us could ever have imagined. Julia Breckenreid's beautiful illustrations resulted in sixty badges that are worthy of the accomplishments they reflect (and are cool enough to wear in public!). Alison Bing brought fresh perspective and left-brain order to relentless batches of text, and held sixty pairs of expert hands through final approval. Gena Frassinello, Bessie Weiss, Amanda Scotese, Carolyn Keating, Nara Wood, and Nicole Solis provided invaluable proofing, fact-checking, researching, and indexing assistance, and Debbie Berne, the project's managing editorial linchpin and designer extraordinaire, stands as living proof that raw talent, teachability, patience, guts, empathy, and a firm-but-respectful hand can accomplish great things in terms of both process and result.

Our friends and advisors. Chris Tomasino, Mary Shapiro, Ani Chamichian, Leslie Crawford, Betsy Foster, Diana Kapp, Leslie Berriman, Holly Lee, Carole Bidnick, Laura Lovett, Kathy Huck, Tracey Behar, Steve Childs, and Jeff Campbell—for honest feedback and terrific referrals along the way.

And our publisher. We never would have accomplished any of this, or had the opportunity, without the extraordinary support of Chronicle Books: Mikyla Bruder (who as far as we are concerned is the best editor who ever lived), Azi Rad and Vivien Sung (without whom we would have blown a design gasket long ago), Christine Carswell, Lisa Campbell, Kendra Kallan, Leslie Jonath, Shona Bayley, Tera Killip, Chris Navratil, Deirdre Merrill, Andrea Burnett, Michelle Fuller, and the many others who, by the time the book comes out, will have lent a much-appreciated hand to its publication.

Caroline Herter

★ ★ ★

Yvette Bozzini/writer. Yvette writes all kinds of things: books (like *I Love Parking in San Francisco* and *Secrets from an Inventor's Notebook*—shush, she ghostwrote that one); essays that have appeared in publications including the *San Francisco Chronicle* and *Ben Is Dead;* cranky letters to the editor; and lots of dreamy to-do lists, which, thanks to *You Can Do It!* she finally knows how to tackle.

Julia Breckenreid/illustrator. Julia's graphic illustration, sensitive and whimsical yet always alive, has spanned magazines, books, advertising, packaging, beauty, corporate identity, posters, and newspapers. In addition to being an illustrator since 2001, she is an instructor in the Illustration program at Sheridan College, as well as at the Royal Ontario Museum. Julia lives and works in Toronto.

index

you did it!

dare to dream

bust a move

roam where you want to

take the stage

walk on fire

speak up

champion a cause

rock out!

be your own boss

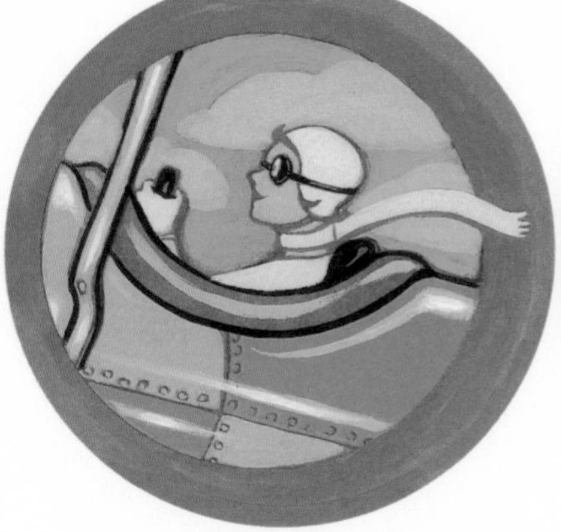

fly solo

sing your heart out

paint a picture

be an author

roll 'em

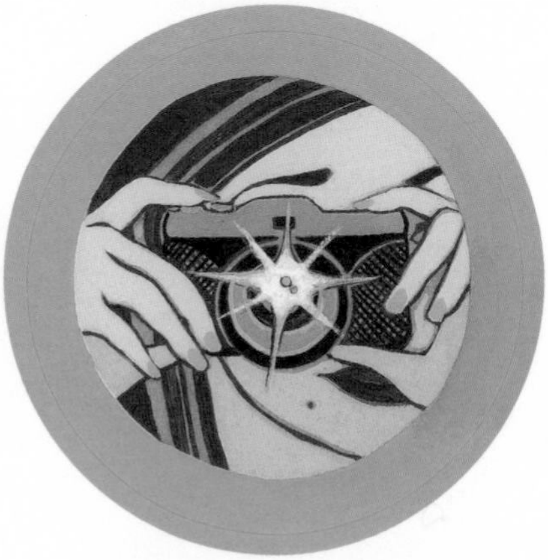

take a (really good) picture

go world wide

dig this

redo a room

bead it

sew fabulous

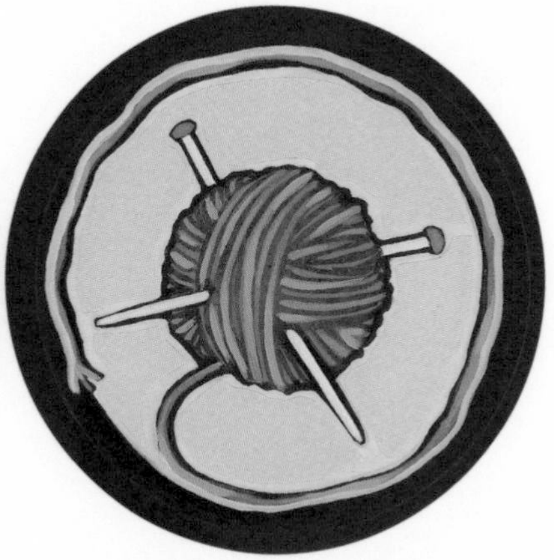

get down to the knitty-gritty

get your way

learn the lingo

go back to school

play a tune (in tune)

be a renaissance gal

get well-read

dine in

know your best cellars

party on!

exercise your options

stretch yourself

hang ten

head for the hills

jump!

go for the gold

dive right in

hit the slopes

beat the boys at pool

take the reins

eat it

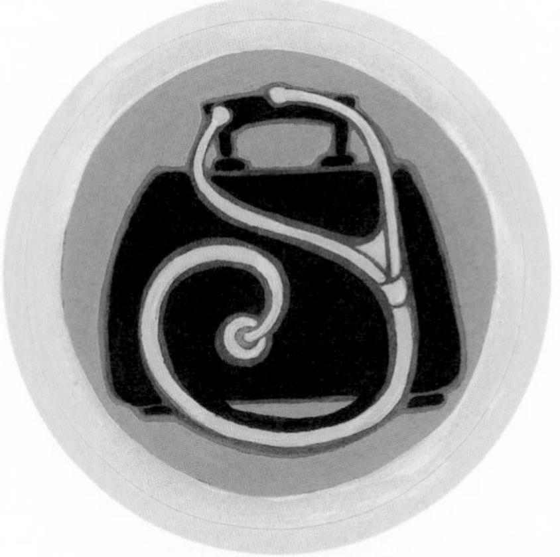

care for your health

quit it

look sharp

find your money

grow your money

give your money away

pop the hood

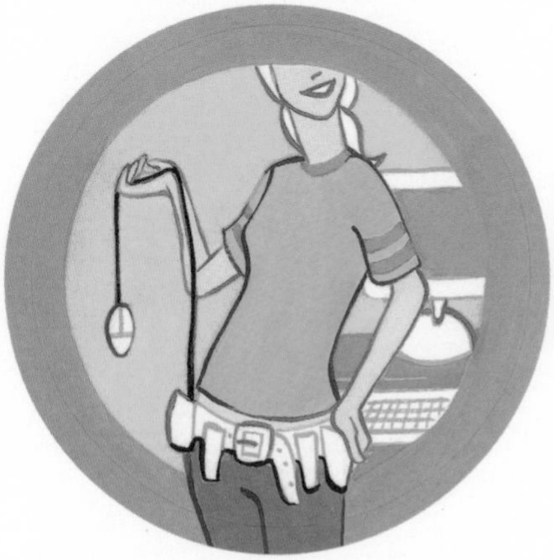

speak geek

make yourself handy

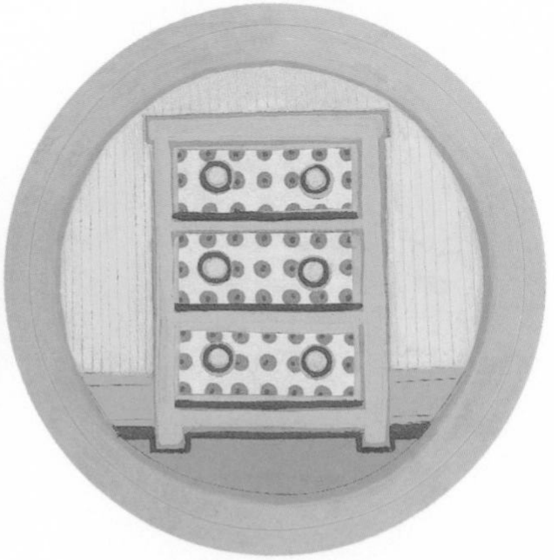

organize it

get an inner life

share what you know

commune with nature

trace your roots

connect with your tribe

play the field

make love last

give a little bit

you can do it!

make your own badge

make your own badge

make your own badge